D1708029

THE COMING OF THE AGE OF IRON

CONTRIBUTORS

James A. Charles, Reader in Process Metallurgy, Department of Metallurgy and Materials Science, Cambridge University

Dennis Heskel, Instructor, Department of Anthropology, The University of Utah

Carl Clifford Lamberg-Karlovsky, Director, Peabody Museum of Archaeology and Ethnology, Harvard University,

Heather Lechtman, Associate Professor of Archaeology and Ancient Technology, Department of Humanities and Department of Materials Science and Engineering, The Massachusetts Institute of Technology

Robert Maddin, University Professor, Department of Materials Science and Engineering, The University of Pennsylvania

Nikolaas J. van der Merwe, Professor, Department of Archaeology, The University of Cape Town

James D. Muhly, Professor, Department of Oriental Studies, The University of Pennsylvania

Joseph Needham, Director, East Asian History of Science Library, Sometime Master of Gonville and Caius College, Cambridge University

Vincent C. Pigott, Research Specialist, Department of Anthropology and MASCA—Ancient Metals Group, University Museum, The University of Pennsylvania

Radomír Pleiner, Research Associate Professor, Ceskoslovenská Akademie Věd, Archeologický Ustav, Prague, Czechoslovakia

Denise Schmandt-Besserat, Assistant Professor, The Center for Middle Eastern Studies, The University of Texas at Austin

Anthony M. Snodgrass, Professor of Classical Archaeology, Cambridge University

Ronald F. Tylecote, Professor of Archaeometallurgy, Institute of Archaeology, University of London

Jane C. Waldbaum, Associate Professor, Department of Art History, The University of Wisconsin at Milwaukee

Theodore A. Wertime, Research Associate, Department of Anthropology, The Smithsonian Institution

Tamara S. Wheeler, Research Assistant Professor, Department of Materials Science and Engineering and MASCA—Ancient Metals Group, The University of Pennsylvania

For Cyril Stanley Smith

Contents

Preface

For a man whose lifetime so nearly coincides with the twentieth century, Cyril Stanley Smith uniquely stands for nineteenth century breadth of vision. Scarcely any aspect of the peculiarly new discipline of materials science and engineering has escaped his searching scrutiny. How new it is only those can attest who have watched this sometime unbelievable century of ours march from x-ray crystallography past the electron microscope to the alchemical marvels of the eras of the atom and space.

"But there's but one in all doth hold his place," says Shakespeare's Julius Caesar. Through masterly translations of the classics in metallury Smith has taken us by the hand to walk backward in time toward man's first intervention in and exposure to the fire-shaped elements of this earth. What a revelation for us all! Through a passion for seeing artifacts as they really are—craftsmanship wed to art—he has illuminated the world of materials with a rare light. All the contributors to this book have been suffused by its glow and by its reflection within his personality.

To honor one who has so educated us all into the mysteries and beauties of human artifice—Cyril would not call it "science"—the editors of and contributors to this book have chosen a novel course. We have agreed to explore the earliest history of iron, in Cyril's view the noblest and most bountiful of metals. We have done so not by volunteered essays but by each fashioning a branch of the common tree. Let this study in depth of *The Coming of the Age of Iron* be a fitting tribute to a most uncommon man named Smith, as both he and his adopted twentieth century enter their evening decades.

The Coming of
the Age of Iron

Edited by
THEODORE A. WERTIME and
JAMES D. MUHLY

NEW HAVEN AND LONDON
YALE UNIVERSITY PRESS
1980

Designed by Sally Harris
and set in Monophoto Bembo type by
Asco Trade Typesetting Ltd., Hong Kong.
Printed in the United States of America by
The Murray Printing Co., Westford, Mass.

Published in Great Britain, Europe, Africa, and
Asia (except Japan) by Yale University Press,
Ltd., London. Distributed in Australia and
New Zealand by Book & Film Services, Artarmon,
N.S.W., Australia; and in Japan by Harper & Row,
Publishers, Tokyo Office.

Library of Congress Cataloging in Publication Data

Main entry under title:

The coming of the age of iron.

Includes index.
1. Iron age—Addresses, essays, lectures.   2. Metallurgy
—History—Addresses, essays, lectures.   I. Wertime,
Theodore A.   II. Muhly, James David.
GN779.C65   930'.1'6   79-26420
ISBN 0-300-02425-8

10 9 8 7 6 5 4 3 2 1

Acknowledgments

We thank Martha Goodway, metallurgist of the Smithsonian Institution, Conservation Analytic Laboratory, for her technical editing of this book; Dean George F. Rapp of the University of Minnesota at Duluth for his many suggestions for improvement; and the hardworking editors of Yale University Press, Alexander Metro and Lawrence Kenney, for their laborious and invaluable contribution to the book's clarity and cohesion. To Bernice S. Wertime, for her willingness to step into endless breaches, we offer fervent and heartfelt appreciation.

Introduction

The main purpose of this book is to give an explicit metallurgical and pyrotechnological content to the term *Iron Age*. In 1819 Christian Thomsen first proposed the three-age system of Stone Age, Bronze Age, and Iron Age. But in the twentieth century the term *Iron Age* has become more and more associated with pottery types and related artifactual aspects of civilization. It accordingly has becomes less and less associated with the metal iron. We do *not* intend this book to reassert or redebate the validity of the Thomsen three-age system as a mode of measuring the movement of civilization. We *do* wish to put into proper technical and social perspective the enormous revolution in material culture that after 1100 B.C. made iron the most pervasive and versatile producers' good of human society.

Indeed from a review of the evidence available to the scholar today on material culture it could be said that iron was only one, focal, end product of the fire-using industries launched in plasters, clays, metals, and glazes toward 9000 B.C. in the ancient Near East—industries preceded by long Stone Age experience in firesetting stones for quarrying and in heating cherts, jaspers, and chalcedonies. Toward 3000 B.C. in the ancient Mediterranean and Near East, men moved from the preeminent use of muscle power for shaping bone, stone, and wood to the preeminent use of fire for shaping wood, stone, clay, plaster, and metal. We note in passing that this revolution in materials affected China slightly less than the Near East, and affected the New World substantially less than either.

Chapter 1, below, strongly emphasizes the interconnected character of the pyrotechnologic arts that in the ancient Near East yielded iron, terra-cottas, cements, and glass as major materials for building, war, agriculture, and esthetic purposes toward the end of the second millennium B.C. At the same time, chapter 7, by Ronald F. Tylecote, cautions that metallurgical furnaces differ from those for the other major fire-shaped materials by requiring that metallic ores must be in direct contact with charcoal or coal to be reduced from their oxide, carbonate, or sulfide states and to be separated from their silicious gangues. This at once gave a different character to metallurgy, especially the metallurgy of iron. To be won from their ores, metals went through a major chemical as well as physical metamorphosis, demanding as fuel charcoal rather than dung or straw.

There is a vast new body of evidence today on the discovery of iron as the inevitable end product of the Age of Bronze (and Silver). Chapter 1 documents scholarship of the early 1960s that led to the first revelations of the accidental production of iron in the copper or lead furnace. In chapter 6 James Charles makes that discovery a near certainty for Bronze Age smiths in the Mediterranean–Middle East as they moved down into the geologic zones of copper ore searching for ever more sophisticated forms of copper and alloying elements. One sees a technical progression from the working of native copper to the melting of copper, smelting of ores (including those of lead and silver), and, finally penetration of the polymetallic zones of the iron and copper gossan, leading to the discovery of the arsenic-bearing and tin-bearing ores that give rise to the material bronze.

This ever more sophisticated search for ores whose color and smell on smelting gave some clue to the alloy to be yielded has been described by Denise Schmandt-Besserat in chapter 5 on the 300,000-year prehistory of ocher. The end product is the harvest of bronze, silver, gold, and base metals that ornaments the literary texts examined by James Muhly in chapter 2, on the Bronze Age. Along with archaeological data, the first written record gives some inkling of the richness and diversity of metals of the Bronze Age setting into which iron was finally launched as a fully utilitarian metal at the end of the second millennium B.C. Indeed northern Anatolia in the era of the Assyrian merchants nearly 4000 years ago was the center of an international culture of metals and trade which embraced three continents and gave rise to the modern instruments of banking and credit.

Chapter 3, by Jane Waldbaum, leaves little doubt that smelted iron was known very early in the Bronze Age and was in fact seeking a milieu as the basic material of war-making, householding, and agriculture (taking over from stone as well as bronze). Men were discovering the contrasting and complementary functions and properties of metals, as pictured by Tamara Wheeler and Robert Maddin in chapter 4. Behind this discovery lay not only the polymetallic, "interfluxing" aspects of metallurgy in the Middle East but also the experience in identifying the metals themselves by their widely varying reactions to fire, corrosion, and working, or by their value as revealed in color, luster, and resistance to oxidation.

Implicit in the transition from gold and bronze to iron is a diminished richness of function identified by the Greek poet Hesiod when he lamented the lost Age of Gold. A technologic metamorphosis is implicit as well. With the advent of iron, garlicky and lethal arsenic was already in use, along with brittle antimony and elusive zinc and even the highly lustrous and non-oxidizing platinum-iridium inclusions found in gold. But the strangest alloying element of all was a common yet mysterious substance called charcoal, which toward 1100 B.C. acted as the chief agent in reducing metals and in adding the quality to iron that made it identifiably steel. The culminating art of quenching steel Homer records for us in one of the most onomatopoeic moments in his *Odyssey*, noted below. The sources of the properties of steel would not be known for another twenty-nine centuries, however; and there is a serious doubt expressed in chapter 12, by Vincent Pigott, as to whether early smiths were deliberately carburizing iron for steel or making best use of the unequally carburized iron they had in hand.

If the opening seven chapters suggest a determinant technical inevitability to the progression from the discovery of copper to the application of iron by an ever more sophisticated Near Eastern smith, chapters 8 and 9 ask us to stop a moment and reconsider the varying cultural ambiences in which metallurgy came to fruition. In chapter 8, Dennis Heskel and Clifford Lamberg-Karlovsky take us to Tepe Yahya, a site in Kerman province in Iran on the Persian Gulf. Yahya occupied an important position between Mesopotamia and the Indus Valley and it or its environs have yielded trade artifacts of chlorite or steatite stone, proto-Elamite tablets, and copper and bronze metallurgy from the fifth millennium B.C. onward. In a similar way, in chapter 9, Heather Lechtman focuses on the Central Andean area of the New World. The authors of both chapters find cultural preference and social organization setting the stage for metallurgy, modifying sharply, or even abrogating, the technical stages set forth in chapter 6 for the Near East. If in Iran early copper metallurgy was influenced by the trend toward natural arsenic additives such as algodonite and domeykite, in the New World copper metallurgy of any kind, including that of the arsenic compounds, was affected by the priority of the discovery

and popular preference for gold. Two different Bronze Ages prevailed
in the New World.

But there is more. The New World avoided smelted iron entirely
(as it did the wheel, rotary motion, glass and cement). All of the Old
World joined the Iron Age, as we shall see in chapters 10 to 14. It did so
with regional idiosyncracies differing as much as do those of China and
Africa. China moved to cast iron and steel through a rich Bronze Age,
whereas Africa was largely content with wrought iron and steel as its
first metals, having largely bypassed the Age of Copper and Bronze. But
the gold-oriented New World did not accept iron at all, however widely
meteoritic iron was worked as a stone. Although the Andean region knew
complex smelting and accordingly knew reject iron, its predilections
foreclosed the use of iron in much the manner that they precluded the
wheel.

In asking why, the respective authors of chapters 8 and 9 give us a
rather detailed material stratigraphy of their areas, suggesting that complex
metallurgy must be supported by an equally complex organization of
society and trade in order to thrive. Although a question might be raised
with respect to Africa, the discussion of iron metallurgy is rightly drawn
into the orbit of contemporary theories of civilization, and questions are
asked as to the rigidity of the technical avenues by which men may have
come to metals. In recent years technology as a perceived agent of change
in human societies has come to take a decidedly second place to population
growth and political organization. Today archaeology sees civilization
as the accompaniment of forces tending toward settled life, crowding,
hierarchical governance, monumental architecture, and systems of written
record. Indeed some authors today call technologic invention merely a
"holding action" in history.

This book does not select among these theories or try to rectify differences of outlook which have moved various authors. The contents
of the book do yield the following thoughts about iron as both the instrument and end product of one of the most profound revolutions in human
history:

1. How free men were to make choices of materials on the basis of
pure idiosyncracy will remain a subject of debate until we know substantially more about the technical tracks by which various ores lent
themselves to exploitation. Did the Incas make a political decision to
exploit the tin bronze of the southern Andes as against the arsenic bronze of

the northern Andes? Or was there an as yet undiscovered technical unknown determining their answer?

2. However many times metalworking artisans encountered smelted iron, the acceptance of the metal as a utilitarian product—a "working" metal—occurred only in such societies and cultures as (a) were predisposed by existing metallurgical tradition as well as by major technical and social change toward developing a new mass metal for common uses and (b) had the organizational facility to produce the metal. Although in the ancient Near East northern Turkey seems to have been a major locale for the discovery of iron, for the reasons just given Cyprus was a focal point in the beginning of the Iron Age, as illustrated in chapter 10, by Anthony M. Snodgrass. One must inevitably compare the lusty polymetallism of smelting on Cyprus with the delicate flower of choice that grew in the rich metallurgical setting of the Andes.

3. In the end, European society was shaped by iron, as Radomir Pleiner reminds us in chapter 11. The same shaping occurred in Africa and China, and each society that adopted iron necessarily came to it almost independently, moved by a process that we shall call negative cultural choice. By this we mean that innovation came about through the overturning of inertial forces and negative outlooks that made iron or any new material an unwanted product, an overturning that came about often through gradual slippage under economic necessity or acceptance of iron in its exotic forms. But total rejection of smelted iron did occur in the New World, as it did in the case of *tumbaga*, an alloy of copper and gold, in the Old World. Diffusive stimuli—which came in the end to push iron, glass, and cement outward from the eastern Mediterranean matrix of pyrotechnology toward the peripheries of the Old World—had the result in each instance of launching a unique adaptation of the metal, as evidenced by the steel of the Near East and the cast iron and steel of China or the wrought iron and steel of Africa. The progression was from the complex to the simple, as each society separated the forms of ores and their associated metals.

4. The gap in every instance between the first appearance of iron, glass, or cement and its adaptation to a social milieu was a long and large one, anticipating the fate of nearly all major inventions in Western civilization. Different authors speculate on the reasons that iron made the final explosive eruption into human affairs that it did. Chapters 10–14 are regional surveys: Snodgrass on the Mediterranean and Pleiner on

Europe, as mentioned; Vincent Pigott on Iran, Nikolaas J. van der Merwe on Africa, and Joseph Needham on China. In the ancient Near East, at least, a combination of circumstances—the interruption of previous population growth; the disruption of trade in copper and tin; the accidental appearance of steel; the shift to new modes of fighting wars, cultivating crops, and carrying on household functions; the first impingements of wood shortages; and the growing influence of mass demands for metals— all made the period 1100 to 500 B.C. a major threshold in history.

5. As is ever the case with the advent of new eras, mankind was backing into an unknown technical future, one that by the time of Greco-Roman civilization would weave iron and its allied pyrotechnologic products (such as window glass) into all aspects of life.

6. With Muhly in chapter 2, we begin to see the emergence of the supercivilizations of Mesopotamia–Egypt and China as impelled in some part by their complex immersions into the metallurgies of war, building, agriculture, and money. Trade, writing, and credit all were given major impetus by the coming of metals, affording these civilizations strong diffusive influences. One must wonder if their influences stopped at the boundaries of the Old World.

We close with a thought about iron in human history, especially as that history has been rewritten by the contemporary ascendancy of Western civilization. In 1970, world production of iron and steel exceeded 1 billion metric tons for the first time. This amounted to a tripling of world output from 1953. By weight it was equivalent to 100 times world annual production of aluminum. Since 1000 B.C., when iron first seriously challenged bronze as the ascendant metal, world consumption of iron has grown exponentially, except for periods of Dark Ages. The world produced perhaps 150,000 tons a year in the age of Augustus, 300,000 tons a year in 1700, and 500,000 tons in 1800 (when the Industrial Revolution was beginning).

Clearly, in view of the foreseeable exhaustion of the world's fossil fuels, man's engineering uses of iron have probably peaked. We cannot predict the ultimate eclipse of iron as man's premier metal, but we can predict the ultimate replacement of metals for some of the dominant uses today (and not by carbon compounds). We shall remain for some centuries in the Age of Iron, until the combustive uses of fire itself are called into question by a future generation impelled to stop the pollution of the earth's atmosphere. As an agent of biological engineering—those biogeochemical processes by which the earth's atmosphere and crust were shaped and carbon dioxide was incorporated into the earth's limestones—iron will continue to be the most important metal in nature. This necessary apposition of biologic engineering to human engineering lies at the heart of the story of iron in this book.

The Pyrotechnologic Background

THEODORE A. WERTIME

The appreciation of iron as the *res substantiae* of civilization is as old as the Greek poet Hesiod, who lived in the 8th or 7th century B.C.[1] From him derives the first thought of an Age of Iron. Coming as it did after the Ages of Gold, Silver, and Bronze, the new era of black metal seemed to Hesiod a much less happy and more somber one, clouded by ever more work and violence (although to Hesiod the Bronze Age had been the real era of war). Indeed Hesiod lamented:

> And I wish that I were not any part of the fifth generation of men, but had died before it came, or been born afterward. For here now is the age of iron.

In reading the archaeological and literary evidence in this volume as to the events of Hesiod's day (and that of Homer, who in the chapter to follow gives us a startling description of the quenching of steel), one can appreciate that the adoption of the often ugly and exacting iron was as much a matter of exigency as it was of free choice; and even then the issue was in doubt. Iron's fate had hung in the balance for several thousand years after Paphlagonian tribesmen had evidently learned to smelt it consistently from its ores. The acceptance of the new metal was thus a matter of opportunity costs vis-à-vis both bronze-age and stone-age materials, determined by a combination of social, economic, technologic, and ecologic circumstances.

Men were being forced toward the new metal by the disruption of the trade in copper and tin in a moment of social chaos in the Eastern Mediterranean. In chapter 4 Wheeler and Maddin see the discovery of the deliberate carburization of iron as giving a large additional positive stimulus to the metal vis-à-vis bronze. Another thesis of this chapter is that not only iron but possibly a tetrad of new and largely untested pyrotechnologic materials—iron (including steel), glass, terra-cotta, and cement—was knocking at the door of civilization for admission. The use of all four materials by Mediterranean cultures contributed mightily to the metropolitan character of later Greco-Roman society and the European society that came in time to be built on its ruins. But, until men and technologies found themselves in a new productive matrix, there was no inevitability that either the technologies or the emergent materials of civilization would necessarily come to flower.

The appearance of such drastically new and disruptive technologies thus can be seen as the concomitant of a critical stage involving not just the carburization of iron to make steel but the shifting fortunes of agriculture and human populations in the Eastern Mediterranean; the interruption of trade in copper and other metals; the movement of iron-carrying tribes from the Black Sea north, south, east, and west; and possibly the first effects of a declining supply of charcoal and other fuels in the area.[2] The intersection of similar curves of deterioration and appreciation brought to bear the power of the Vitruvian waterwheel in Italy and Europe between A.D. 300 and 900, as Europe sank into the Middle Ages.[3] Similar countervailing curves will reconfigure our own technology and civilization in the wake of the exhaustion of fossil fuels and the growing pressures of populations of men and machines on materials ca. A.D. 2000.

Everywhere iron first became known to men in a very low carbon form. This was true because smelted iron was first accidentally discovered in the guise of high-iron slags or bears or salamanders of iron occasionally produced in furnaces for lead or copper. It was true also because the first smelting of iron qua iron took place at temperatures lower than the melting point of iron. The first iron known to 3d millennium B.C. bronze-silver workers in Anatolia was, doubtless, low-carbon iron. As low-carbon iron (and occasionally steel) the metal was forged into the jewelry and ornaments of the 2d millennium B.C. As low-carbon iron it made its appearance in the knife of the housewife at Lachish in Palestine.[4]

The evidence cited by Needham (see chap. 14) suggests that in China wrought iron rather than cast iron may first have tentatively replaced stone, bone, and shell in common tools (which the elitist bronze had left largely unaffected everywhere). As noted by Chêng Tê-K'un, iron rather than bronze terminated the Stone Age.

> From the point of view of tools and implements Western Chou Culture was no higher than that of a neolithic survival. With the

exception of a few bronze *ch'ou* spades, *fu* axes and *pên* adzes, all the agricultural implements and working tools were made of stone, bone, or shell. Bronze was an expensive material, probably far beyond the reach of the common people. The neolithic types of tools and implements could be replaced only after a cheaper metal was produced. The answer was found with the introduction of iron. The metal was known in Western Chou but it was not widely used until Chan-Kuo. Recent excavations have brought to light literally hundreds of iron artifacts from practically all provinces of Chou China.[5]

The further penetration of iron into the social and economic fabric of civilization became a matter of much greater technical complexity than even the issue of bronze versus iron. As Needham attests, early in the history of the Chinese Iron Age, and well before the Han dynasty, cast iron necessarily rich in carbon became the dominant form of iron in China for all but the most highly stressed cutting or thrusting tools, such as axes and swords. By the early Han a conventional baby blast furnace was in use for the production of such cast iron.[6] The tradition of the bronze caster asserted itself sufficiently in the development of a cast iron, also high in silicon and phosphorus, that in time the moldboards of ploughs were cast of iron, along with stoves, kettles, bells, lamps, chisels, and so on. Even Chinese steel was made by the carburization of a bar of wrought (low carbon) iron in a bath of cast (high carbon) iron.

The virtual absence of cast iron in the Mediterranean (except for such reported archaeological traces as a late 2d millennium B.C. furnace at Vardaroftsa in Thracian Greece)[7] bespeaks a conscious avoidance of such iron owing to both cultural and technical factors. The evidence suggests that the advent of iron was prepared by the closing Bronze Age experience in metallizing tools and weapons previously made exclusively of stone, and by the first production of steel out of unequally carburized iron. The inventories of tools and weapons at the end of the eastern Mediterranean Bronze Age are described by Deshayes, Catling, Bass, and Petrie.[8] One finds growing numbers of swords and daggers for war, chisels and saws for construction, and knives for households. The most striking change in this period of decline of the Old Bronze Age civilizations (Mycenaean, New Kingdom, and Hittite), however, was the appearance of a whole new class of bronze agricultural tools, such as scythes, sickles, hoes, shovels, and even ploughs, representing a curve of population growth that would rise until about 1100 B.C., then abruptly drop, not to be restored for several centuries. In such places as Cyprus, the demand for bronze must have been undergoing great expansion, prompting attention to the production of iron and steel well before the disasters of the Sea Peoples swept over the Eastern Mediterranean.

These two experiences, that of China and that of the Mediterranean, give us the parameters of choice represented by the first explorations into the use of iron. While wrought or bloomery iron remained the only attainable metal for the great mass of human beings in Europe until about 1860 A.D. (when mass-produced steel came on the scene), steel and cast iron were the exotic forms that set the limits of experimentation with carbon and in the case of China approached being a mass-produced art. Africa mixed these two metals in a unique way, as demonstrated by Van der Merwe in chapter 13 describing the unusual forms of iron making developed by the Bantu peoples, who brought agriculture and iron to Africa.

Cast iron was not a truly competitive product in Western civilization until the two-phased blast furnace and refinery first appeared, toward 1400 A.D. And then it soon was isolated to naval cannon and frying pans and the like.[9] But steel in time came to be known in a variety of derivations: carburized or case-hardened iron; natural steel from high manganese spathic ores, as in Austrian Carinthia (Noricum) during the Hallstatt period; pattern-welded steel; steel derived from iron sand processes common to the Black Sea and Macedonia; steel gained in the Chinese and Brescian manner by putting bars of wrought iron into molten cast iron; and steel achieved by the controlled fining of cast iron.[10]

Although the higher forms of pattern welding came and went several times, steel imposed upon European and African civilizations a control of manufacturing processes not much less exacting than that practiced by the Chinese in the painstakingly supervised casting of objects. It was never fully understood.

JUDGMENTS OF THE CHARACTER AND UTILITY OF IRON

The modes of introduction of iron as an everyday working metal into both the Mediterranean and China and the attendant difficulties of fabricating it seem to have given both civilizations an ambivalent appreciation of the metal. This came to be after an initial phase in which meteoritic

iron in Chou China and the meteoritic-cum terrestrial iron of adornment
in the Eastern Mediterranean of the 2d millennium B.C. were enormously
expensive and treasured vis-à-vis other metals.

Gaius Pliny the Elder in the eulogy of iron in his *Natural History* called
iron "the best and worst part of the apparatus of life."[11] It was par excellence the stuff of violence and war. The metal had the mysterious quality
of becoming steel. At the same time the elemental stuff of iron seemed
to be a common one, associated with the black of charcoal and the repeated
forging necessary for tools. It might by excessive heat in the furnace
take on the dubious qualities of cast iron (less pretty and more brittle
than cast bronze). Hesiod first recorded the black or gray color of iron
in comparison to gold, silver, and bronze; and he probably knew of the
trifurcated character of the alloy without ever suspecting that it no less
than bronze was composed of a metal and another element.[12]

Aristotle mistakenly described steel as a purified form of iron.[13] This
seemed logical to anyone observing the long immersion of a bar of iron
in a carburizing fire. Aristotle called "water" and "heat" the basic constituents of metals. In both European and Asian alchemical traditions these
were transmuted to "mercury" and "sulfur," representing, respectively,
the smooth-running pure liquid and the combustible drossy earth in iron.
Until charcoal was first identified in A.D. 1781 and 1786 as the light friable
alloying impurity that gave steel its character, steel continued to be thought
of as the clean member of the family and wrought iron, and especially
cast iron, as the dirty members, derived from combustible "sulfur."
Monardes summed up the age-old view in A.D. 1574 in calling iron "foule,
blacke, and darke."[14]

The confusion about the forms of iron and their often unexpected
appearance continued long after the Swedish chemists Rinman and
Bergman in 1781 and the French chemists Monge, Vandermonde, and
Berthollet in 1786 identified their causes with the element carbon.[15] In
the technical handbooks of the 18th and 19th centuries, coming to a head
in Percy's *Metallurgy*, iron still was designated as capricious and hard to
achieve.[16] This was true, even though Fourcroy in the Enlightenment
eulogized its versatility with the thought that the "prosperity of nations,
perfection of human reason, and the multiple arts which are concerned
with iron"[17] were all in a one-to-one correspondence.

In Western civilization, then, the sense of capriciousness carried forward
from the beginning of the Iron Age and was enhanced rather than reduced

when ca. 1400 A.D. the two-stage process of blast furnace and refinery forge turned men to modes of mass production of cast iron and wrought iron, modes that had existed in China from the late Chou dynasty, as noted.

Men faced the need to produce steel on a mass basis and did not know how. They had no adequate definition of steel or cast iron. They confronted the contradictory effects of such elements as phosphorus, silicon, and manganese. (Phosphorus, for example, improves cast iron but is most deleterious to steel.)

Aristotle and Pliny thus each represented an initial contradictory appraisal of iron, one based on impurities in iron, the other on the uses of iron. Fourcroy offered a modification consistent with the growing scientific understanding in the 18th century concerning the versatility of iron and its causes. But the evidence is never all in, and the scientific revolution of this century has altered enormously the old appreciation of iron. Today, based on new understanding of the role of iron in the biogeochemical shaping of the earth's crust and atmosphere, we can say that iron has had two uniquely interacting engineering functions. One lies in biological engineering, the other in human engineering. Iron played a central role in the evolving carbon molecule by giving rise to the poryphorins and to life.[18] Iron in turn absorbs carbon in a manner unique to the metals, making it extraordinarily valuable for man's purposes.

In the points that follow, iron remains not much less mysterious than it was 3000 years ago, even if now, at 1 billion metric tons output per year and requiring 5 percent of the world's energy, it is man's fundamental engineering metal.[19]

We today discern six qualities in iron.

1. The first quality of iron is sheer abundance. In the universe iron is the most common transition element owing to fusion processes taking place in both the birth and death of stars. It was aggregated in the inner planets, particularly Mercury, Venus, and Earth, during the formation of the solar system. By an "iron catastrophe" it probably melted and sank to the core of the Earth early in the history of this planet, becoming the planet's dominant element.

2. The second is the ferromagnetism, which it shares with nickel and cobalt.

3. The third is its high energy as a transition metal, owing to the quantum levels of its atom. This it also shares with cobalt and nickel.

4. The fourth quality is the ability of iron to shift from the ferrous to ferric form and back under differing states of oxidation and reduction, giving it a special role in life processes and in the shaping of the crust and atmosphere of the earth (mainly through iron bacteria).

5. Iron has the capacity on heating to change crystalline form from a body-centered cubic to a face-centered cubic lattice, a capability of great importance in its ability—when carbon is present—to quench into a hard steel, endowing it with special structural and esthetic qualities.

6. Its sixth capability, rare among the engineering metals, is that of accepting carbon and other materials into interstitial solution. In the space age a variety of new steels has emerged, including steel without carbon. Cast iron and wrought iron remain basic products of iron.

THE MODES OF DISCOVERY OF IRON

The Greek writers Aeschylus and Strabo located the birthplace of iron among the Paphlagonian tribes of the Black Sea coast[20] of present-day Turkey, between Samsun and Trabzon, where magnetic high-iron sands are common. Not coincidentally Muhly, in the chapter that follows on the Bronze Age, concludes that the Assyrian colony in Kaneš Cappadocia in the 19th century B.C. already knew smelted iron as *amūtum*, presumably derived in some part from the land of the Hatti abutting on the Black Sea.[21] It was a local product, exceedingly valuable in relationship to other metals and so scarce as to be interdicted for export.

There is a remarkable similarity between the ancient Greco-Roman story of man's discovery of iron and that of his discovery of glass. Pliny, like Strabo, believed that traders in sodium carbonate, stopping for natron on the beaches of modern Lebanon and Israel, learned from their campfires to fuse sand and soda (natron) to make glass.[22] Other stories named the natron of the coast of Egypt. In fact cored glass colored with lead-antimony appeared simultaneously in Egypt and Mesopotamia ca. 1400 B.C.[23] Although glass had antecedents in ancient Middle Eastern glazes and Egyptian blue, the story of Levantine natron can be credited with having an element of truth. The crowning glory of the world of glass was not the sumptuous tableware of Rome but the window glass that protected Roman houses as far north as the frontier post of Vindolanda on Hadrian's wall in Great Britain.[24]

If iron and glass were the premier pyrotechnologic products of the ancient Mediterranean world, one cannot overlook the contemporary history of cement. Since possibly Minoan times, the volcanic tuff of Santorini reportedly had been exported in the Aegean as a component, with lime and slag, of a natural cement.[25] The Laurion silver and lead mines contain still, in their dams and ore-washing sites, an aquarium cement that appears indestructible after 2500 years. It was made with litharge.[26]

Later the pozzolana, or natural cement, of Mt. Vesuvius in Naples came to play for Rome the same role, exemplified by the mortar of the Colosseum. Lime plasters, we now know from the work of Gourdin and Kingery, were on the scene at Cayönü Tepesi in the ninth millennium and at Jericho, Ur, and Egypt at later times.[27] The shift to natural calcium silicates for plasters and stuccos was an easy one. The Mediterranean world was flexing its muscles in the direction of a new urban material culture and paying the price in deforestation and erosion.[28]

Iron, glass, and cement trace their origins to the development of a common furnace-kilning technology in the ancient Mediterranean–Middle East, described by Tylecote in chapter 7. Such a technology was not entirely duplicated anywhere else. It never arrived as such or evolved as such in much of Africa or the New World. Certain iron ores were the chief fluxing agents for removing the silica gangue in copper and lead smelting and left a fayalite or iron-silica slag. However, in time, as we shall see, calcium in the form of limestone or oyster shell asserted its fluxing capabilities in both ceramic and metallurgical operations. Artisans simply kilned pottery and lime in the same kiln or threw oyster shells into a metallurgical bath. In such a juxtaposition pots then became fused and slags acquired a runny character.

The three materials—iron, silica, and calcium carbonate (along with soda)—thus were closely interconnected in furnace operations at temperatures that stayed consistently above the melting point of copper (ca. 1100° C). Although the kilns or furnaces may have come from widely separated sources (the pottery kiln from the cooking hearth and the lime kiln from the fire setting of stone, for example), what emerged during the Bronze Age were four major interwoven pyrotechnologic products. They were terra-cottas, iron, glass, and cement. Bricks and mortar were the basic building materials of the Roman Colosseum, terra-cottas and window glass of the Roman houses in Europe as far north as Britain. Iron was often the least effective building material. As the reinforcement in marble columns, it tended to break them apart (through its oxidation).

Fire was seen to oxidize or reduce metallic ores, consolidate the crystals of stone or clay, fuse glass, and dissociate the grains of gypsum, limestone, and slaggy silicates. The effects were so complex that operations of heating in some different sequence (say the forging of an iron sponge) could have quite different consequences from the initial smelting. Metals were reduced by charcoal; glass was fused by heat. Pliny tells us how this looked to the ancients in his famous disquisition on fire as an agent for modifying nature.

And now that we have described everything that depends upon Man's talent for making Art reproduce Nature, we cannot help marvelling that there is almost nothing that is not brought to a finished state by means of fire. Fire takes this or that sand, and melts it, according to the locality, into glass, silver, cinnabar, lead of one kind or another, pigments or drugs. It is fire that smelts ore into copper, fire that produces iron and also tempers it, fire that purifies gold, fire that burns the stone [cement] which causes the blocks in buildings to cohere. There are other substances that may be profitably burnt several times; and the same substance can produce something different after a first, a second or a third firing. Even charcoal itself begins to acquire its special property only after it has been fired and quenched: when we presume it to be dead it is growing in vitality. Fire is a vast, unruly element, and one which causes us to doubt whether it is more a destructive or a creative force.[29]

The consequences of an interactive furnace-kilning pyrotechnology for civilization were enormous. Schmandt-Besserat has recently shown that the first baked clay geometric forms from sites throughout the old Middle East may have been the initial step on the road of the Mediterranean to joint systems of numeration and writing.[30] These were perhaps ceramics' unique contribution to human civilization. What stands out in this story of the complexities of the advent of iron amid a maze of other fire-using industries were the interconnectedness and massiveness of the thrust toward a literate, trading and communicating, road-building and seafaring, urban, pyrotechnologic civilization emerging in the Fertile Crescent and Eastern Mediterranean.

The experience detailed here culminating in the adoption of iron (and glass and cement) was not duplicated in the Vinča culture on the Danube or in Thailand, China, or the New World. Hopewell culture never even attained the furnace or kiln.

By the same token, early Western civilization was overtaken by problems of environment and energy rivaled only in Han dynasty China and thereafter.

In this context the case for the diffusion of iron worldwide from an Eastern Mediterranean source becomes almost overwhelming. Glass we know to have spread both east and west from the Levant.[31] The pyrotechnologic precedence of the ancient Near East seems beyond doubt.

UBIQUITY AND CHARACTER OF IRON ORES

The facts about the prevalence of iron in the earth's crust (along with silicon, aluminum, and calcium) are well known. The exclusion of the even more abundant aluminum from Western pyrotechnology until the late nineteenth century, except in compounds—clay, mordants (alum), and cements—was a matter of its resistance to reduction by charcoal.

But iron manifested itself early in the Stone Age in the suggestible form of pigments for human ornamentation and cave art (as ocher) as described in chapter 5 by Schmandt-Besserat. It offered further identification in the sometimes slight reddening color of cherts, flints, and jaspers when they were heated to improve flaking. In clay pots it achieved maximum coloring effect at about 900° C, showing red under oxidizing conditions and black under reducing conditions. In early glazes and glass, ferrous ions colored the glass blue and ferric ions yellow (together giving the optical effect of green). The relating of these phenomena was the great technical accomplishment of Bronze Age artisans.

Other characteristics of iron added to the apparent ubiquity of its ores and the metal itself, without, however, getting men through the difficult transition of actually smelting its ores to metal and thus learning the complex relationship of metal to ore. These characteristics were the penchant of the metal to fall from the sky in meteorites and the versatile qualities possessed by its ores (including the qualities of magnetism and the ability to cure ills).

The archaeological and literary evidence of meteoritic iron in the Middle East is presented in chapter 3 by Jane C. Waldbaum. Possibly because of the long and vast experience of the ancient Middle East with the smelting of metals after the 6th millennium B.C., terrestrial iron seems to have been no less used in early artifacts than was meteoritic (although the latter may have seemed to possess more magical virtues than the former). The Stone Age cultures whose appetites seemed to have been most whetted to the use of meteoritic or native iron were those which entered the native metal stage and never got beyond it.[32] These were the Tlingit, Déné, and Eskimos of Canada, Alaska, and the Greenland area, and the Old Copper culture and Hopewell civilizations of the United States. The Hopewell Indians made many objects of meteoritic iron, probably from the Brenham pallasite of Kiowa County, Kansas.

For such peoples meteoritic or native iron was very difficult to fashion (although Hopewell culture understood the annealing of both stone and native copper). But they were often the only such metals available. Native iron, we hasten to add, is a nearly pure iron containing small amounts of nickel, cobalt, copper, and carbon. It is found mainly on Disco Island, Greenland. Some believe that this "telluric" iron was extruded as volcanic magma from deep in the earth. It must be distinguished from both meteoritic iron and iron smelted by man.

Similarly, men availed themselves of iron ores as stones, amulets, and medicinals. In early dynastic Egypt, magnetite was in almost constant use as an amulet.[33] The Old Babylonian dynasty of Mesopotamia employed hematite almost exclusively for cylinder seals.[34] Hematite was similarly employed in the seals of Susian Elam and in Middle Minoan and Late Minoan Crete.

Pliny sums up the medicinal uses of the iron ores, which presumably were ancient.[35] Pyrites were the ores of Cyprus that one roasted with honey in order to produce poultices. Hematite, said Pliny, was good for bloodshot eyes and also cured bladder trouble, piles, and snakebite.

One can be sure that well before the Greeks assigned the modern names to the majority of the iron ores, many of their modern scientific characteristics were already well known.

Magnetite   a black magnetic stone of Mohs hardness of 5.5 to 6.5 and specific gravity of 5.4, containing 72.4 percent iron when pure and generally appearing in massive granular form. Its formula is Fe_3O_4. Pliny said that it possessed "senses and hands."[36]

Hematite   a generally red to black sesquioxide of iron, generally occurring in massive form but also as flakes and scales, and affording about 70 percent metal when pure. Its specific gravity is about 5, its Mohs hardness 5 to 5.5. Its formula is Fe_2O_3.

Limonite   a brown hydrated iron oxide of hardness of 4 to 5.5 and specific gravity of 2.7 to 4.3. Limonite is the general term for hydrous ferric iron oxides.

Goethite   has the formula $HFeO_2$, occurs in lateritic soils, and has a specific gravity of 3.3 to 4.3.

Siderite or *chalybite*   is the carbonate $FeCO_3$ and often appears crystalline and contaminated with calcium, manganese (ankerite), etc. It affords only 48.3 percent iron when pure but can be calcined or sintered.

Pyrite FeS_2 generally affords only 46.5 percent iron and is mainly worked for its sulfur (as sulfuric acid), with iron a by-product.

Laterite   a hydrated mixture of oxides of aluminum and iron but worked in such places as Cuba, where the iron exceeds 50 percent.

Gossan   the multimineraled red iron cap on an exposed sulfide deposit whose chalcopyrite ($CuFeS_2$) has oxidized, with iron leaching at the surface as goethite, and copper migrating to the enriched zones as chalcocite (Cu_2S) or covellite (CuS).

Until recently, the ubiquity of the iron ores and the evidence of their ancient use tempted scholars to conclude that such use (along with that of meteoritic iron) led readily to the accidental smelting of ores. The assumption was that a piece of ore would have worked itself into a campfire or pottery kiln and produced a piece of serendipitous iron. On this basis Coghlan systematically tried reducing various ores in a campfire.[37] In no case did he ever get more than a roasted ore or a cinder. The lesson from all this was that the ubiquity of iron ores alone did not teach men how to achieve the metal. But pyrotechnologic uses of iron—even the early heating of ochers for paints—did enable it to reach a point where its three talents were revealed.

FROM COPPER AND LEAD TO IRON: THE STORY OF FLUXES

As a preliminary to these final sections on man's path to iron, we should remind ourselves again that wrought iron, steel, and cast iron are the three major forms of the metal iron yielded by the seven or so iron ores in a smelting furnace or crucible. If one differentiates steel into its various manifestations ranging from mild steel to hard steel, and cast iron into gray and white iron, the forms of the metal mount to five or six.

In rare cases the type of ore predisposed to a certain type of iron (high manganese spathic ores to the natural steel of Noricum, for example). For the most part, the three major forms of iron mentioned above owed themselves to the absorption of carbon in different amounts in the hearth or furnace (with the possibility that forging could also divest iron of its carbon). As John Percy noted, all iron comes out of the furnace as a poly-crystalline or columnar aggregate.[38] Only forging by man can give it a fibrous character, and only quenching its hard steely character.

For the nonspecialist reader, wrought iron may be defined as a soft, ductile, and fibrous product contaminated by small amounts of slag and largely free of carbon. A mild steel begins at about 0.08 percent carbon. At 0.2 to 0.7 percent carbon (depending upon annealing or quenching) one is fully in the domain of the steely forms of iron. But at roughly 2 percent carbon and up to 4 percent carbon one also enters the domain of cast iron, which has traditionally been described as having a brittle nature.

The absorption of carbon lowers the melting temperature of the iron and predisposes it to be tapped in liquid form as a pig iron. This was the dominant initial smelted product when the blast furnace came into vogue ca. 1400 A.D. A second, fining, process was then required.

For most of the Iron Age before 1400 A.D., except in China and Africa, artisans dealt with smelting conditions that led them toward a spongy iron low in carbon and much interspersed with slag. This was in part because they rarely could or would attain the melting point of the iron, which at 1540° C is substantially above the melting point of the slag. Much heating and forging were thus necessary to extract a workable metal. Steel was an exotic product generally achieved by a deliberate working of carburized wrought iron as described by Wheeler and Maddin in chapter 4, or deliberate decarburization of cast iron as described by Needham in chapter 14. But it also came about in Africa through the preheating of the forced air to the furnace, as described by van der Merwe in chapter 13.

The question at issue in this section is merely How did early metal workers come upon this complex metal, iron, at all, with its attendant diversity of ores and products? The answer is that the working of iron was an inevitable technical by-product of copper and lead smelting anti-cipated by the pyrotechnologic uses of iron enumerated above. Iron was directly involved as a flux in the development of consistent techniques of smelting silicious ores of lead and iron. The trail to the discovery of iron in the lead or copper furnace was one taken by the author in the company of Cyril Stanley Smith.

In September and October of 1962 the two of us examined a traditional lead smelter at Anjileh, near Yazd in Iran, run by a traditional miner-metallurgist named Saidi.[39] At the site was a charcoal-fueled furnace of clay and straw about 8 ft in height, square in section, with a tapering shaft narrowing to an opening of 2 ft 6 in. We found 150 g of hematite being used as a flux for every 6 kg of cerussite ore (still in the twentieth century the prevailing ore in most traditional furnaces in Iran). Later, German engineers had modernized the establishment into a small modern blast furnace with mechanical blowers. To our surprise, a "bear," or salamander of iron, lay near the modern smelter. It was this 3000-lb ball of metal that launched the modern odyssey of the discovery of iron as a by-product of the smelting of lead and copper.

Analyses conducted separately by Smith, Tylecote, and Pleiner indicated that the iron was malleable but could be broken off, leaving a crystalline fracture. It contained no carbon. The percentage composition of a similar bear found at Nakhlak was discovered by Pleiner to be as follows:[40]

SiO_2	Fe	MnO	CaO + MgO	PbO
1.35	76.65+	1.00	2.46	27.03

The metallic iron contained traces of lead, copper, nickel, and manganese. Tylecote observed in a letter of July 1970:

> The pieces are magnetic and were found to be mainly iron (ferrite) with slag and a once-liquid grain boundary phase, which is probably lead. The hardness of the iron is about 200 HV which is high for pure ferrite and is probably due to the fine precipitate that is just visible at a magnification of 400 times. The origin of this material is probably the same as that of the ferruginous furnace bottom from the copper smelter at Talmessi, i.e., reduced ferruginous gangue or flux.

Smith's notes on the expedition of 1962 offer the following footnote:[41]

> T.A.W. has made the important suggestion that, since lead smelting preceded iron by many centuries, the smelting of iron could accidentally have been discovered in a lead smelting furnace and later developed for its own sake. This is the most convincing hypothesis regarding the origins of iron yet advanced—far more likely than the suggestion that iron came out of the smelting of gold sands containing iron, for iron is soluble in gold to the extent of about 50 percent at a normal melting temperature of 1100° C. It is also possible that iron may have originated in copper smelting, for copper smelting furnaces also produce bears under certain conditions [Percy, *Metallurgy* (1861): 423, 431].

In 1966, at the site of Joseph Caldwell's dig at Tal-i-Iblis, Smith, Pleiner, and I tried to put these speculations to a concrete test. With Saidi's help we built a small shaft furnace of clay, operated with a goatskin bellows. To the normal burden of cerussite ore we added excess Fe_2O_3 and charcoal. We achieved a temperature of $1170°$–$1200°$ C but failed in the experiment, mainly because of the relatively high zinc content of our ores (which gave us adventitious *cadmia* or *calamine* on the lip of our furnace). Pleiner, however, found white cast iron in the matrix of lead. He concluded: "It is possible under good conditions ... to reduce not only lead but small samples of metallic iron."[42]

The subsequent study of gossans on Cyprus and at Rio Tinto in Spain has opened the vastly more portentious subject of iron yielded in copper smelting, first discussed by Cyril Smith in 1963:

> I continue to be impressed with the technical plausibility of your ideas on the origin of iron and have puzzled over means of establishing that it actually occurred this way. I take back what I said about the impossibility of getting iron out of copper by a similar mechanism, but the iron which would come out would have a great deal of copper in it and would be quite difficult to forge. To support your view is Woolley's 1939 report on the Alalakh dig in 1939 of "several lumps of mixed copper and iron melted together and yet retaining the form of the vessels in which they have been melted." This level was destroyed by fire in the fifteenth century B.C.[43]

During the pyrotechnological expedition of 1968, our team examined ingots at Anarak covered with a layer of iron, which Tylecote identified as ferruginous furnace bottoms from the traditional copper smelters, not unlike the iron bear at the lead smelter of Anjileh. It may be that the ingots of iron seen at Timna are of the same character. Chemical analysis of Messkani slags showed 2.4 percent metallic iron, a by-product of the use of hematite or gossan fluxes with a roasted chalcocite ore. Of larger import, however, is the fact that the so-called Phoenician slags of Cyprus sometimes contained an identifiable iron, which could be freed of its matrix by hammering and turned into useful objects of iron.[44] Such slags were sold by the Ottomans for resmelting into iron.

A variety of analytic and experimental data adds every day to the picture of iron in copper smelting. Smelting experiments in 1977 carried out by Maddin and Muhly with chalcopyrite ores at the Campia Mining Company near Nicosia in Cyprus yielded a slag interlaced with copper veins and inclusions of iron.[45] The experimenters used no flux. Their fuel was wood, which set up originally an oxidizing or roasting atmosphere, later a reducing one. To such data may also be added the substantial information on iron exsolved into early bronzes first substantially exposed by Cooke and Aschenbrenner in their tests for magnetism in bronze on several hundred Mediterranean objects. One Sardinian bronze yielded more than 20 percent iron. Iron clearly intruded into all phases of the first working of lead and copper.

Although smelting could in cases have been a self-fluxing operation, in general deliberate fluxing was at the heart of metallurgy as well as of all of pyrotechnology, as summarized below. Indeed the earliest smelting must be seen not as the conscious selection of a pure ore but as the experimental employment of an ore mix which could alternatively yield lead, copper, or iron, or a mixture of all three. We shall forgo discussion of the complex questions of the melting points of SiO_2, FeO, CaO, and Al_2O_3 and the narrow zone of melting points of the various metals except iron.

Let us briefly summarize the fluxes employed in copper and lead smelting.

The most common flux was hematite (Fe_2O_3), the almost certain agency of the first reduction of both copper and lead, still in use in traditional practice in the Middle East until 40 years ago. Its first archaeological demonstration is at Timna.[46]

Now that it appears probable that the making of lime on a large scale began in the late Neolithic, often as a concomitant of the quarrying of limestone, one must date the use of CaO or $CaCO_3$ or oyster shell to very early times. Again the first demonstrated use is at Timna.

Manganese oxide (MnO) is a proved flux on Cyprus and at Timna, probably adventitious.[47]

In the context of such gossans as one finds on Cyprus or Rio Tinto, many of the elements in the gossan were automatic fluxing agents at one point or another: goethite ($HFeO_2$), jarosite ($KFe_3(SO_4)_2(OH)_6$), natrojarosite ($NaFe_3(SO_4)_2(OH)_6$), and plumbojarosite ($PbFe_6(SO_4)_4(OH)_{12}$). These varied as men moved from the malachites ($Cu_2CO_3(OH)_2$) and azurites ($Cu_3(CO_3)_2(OH)_2$) to chalcocite (Cu_2S), covellite (CuS), or delafossite ($CuFeO_2$) in the enriched zone. Our example is Cyprus as analyzed by Steinberg and Koucky.[48]

Sources of silica such as cherts and jaspers enabled the so-called Phoenician smelters on Cyprus to recover a surprisingly large proportion of the copper by allowing the molten copper to sink through the slag without forming a matte.[49]

LOCALE OF THE FIRST SYSTEMATIC MAKING OF IRON AND STEEL

We shall be so bold as to suggest that the first systematic pursuit of iron and steel technologies, thus derived, occurred precisely where the Greek authors said that it occurred, namely, the northern reaches of Anatolia and Paphlagonia in modern Turkey. This was one metal-supplying region for the Assyrian colony at Kaneš and the area in which the later Hittite empire emerged. A variety of evidence fortifies this hypothesis, even as it suggests that the actual beginning of the Iron Age—namely, the application of iron as a working metal (according the definition in chap. 10 by Anthony Snodgrass)—probably took place in Cyprus, Palestine, and Greece, if not parts of the Urartian and Assyrian empires. If early copper and lead-silver inevitably brought men to a knowledge of iron, it was by no means inevitable that the metal was accepted or adopted as a working one. The New World is proof of this.

The natural technical progression of the Bronze Age to the first tentative but deliberately smelted iron seems to have been prepared where bronze had reached the abundance and perfection manifested in the vicinity of such sites as Alaca Hüyük, Mahmutlar, and Horoztepe. Northern Anatolia or Turkey along the Black Sea offers copper, lead, and iron ores in an identifiable abundance and format that could only be ideal for taking the first steps to experiment with iron in a variety of forms. One would call this a uniquely polymetallic platform for the discovery of iron, even as one would regard gossan-rich Cyprus as a uniquely polymetallic setting in metallurgical economics for the adoption of iron as a working metal.

The main fact is that the Black Sea of Turkey is lined with a self-fluxing iron sand up to 80 percent pure magnetite, which demonstrably invited experimentation in iron and steel.

Once the technologies seem to have been workable in any way they would in time have found a natural threshold in the Eastern Mediterranean, where the advent of new implements of bronze around 1200 B.C. made possible the very complex technology of Cypriot, southern Turkish, or Iranian gossans. We say this mindful or our earlier admonition that the development of iron came about through technical and economic circumstances that made it the replacement not just for bronze but for stone, bone, and wood.

In book 12 of Strabo's geography, the Greek author launched into a description of tribal people called Chaldaei or Chalybs, also known to Aeschylus and Xenophon. These coastal people lived in much the same way as the modern descendant tribal Laz of Black Sea Turkey.[50] Having come from this region of Anatolia, Strabo knew them well, as well as the narrow and mountainous seaboard of mines and forests from which they gained their livelihood. These were the same Halizoni who in Homer's catalogue of ships were identified with the birthplace of silver.

The region is not far from the Colchis, where Jason and the Argonauts are described by Strabo as having found real fleeces or sheepskins into which gold was sluiced. The Halys River flowing by Samsun was supposed to have been rich in gold, as was the Pactolus Valley near Sardis. Recent excavations by Tahsin Özguc at Masat on the Yesilirmak River, have turned up Mycenaean pottery dated to Late Helladic III-B.[51] We thus have Greek mythology speaking knowingly of gold (for golden fleeces *were* a common phenomenon), Homer of silver, and the later writers, from Strabo to the A.D. nineteenth century British and French travelers, of iron.

The author's almost yearly metallurgical reconnaissances of this region from 1968 to 1976 support this picture of a polymetallic setting, exploited heavily from pre-Hittite through Roman and Turkish times. At Kozlu, near Horotepe, on the Yesilirmak, or Halys River (as the Greeks knew it), copper mining has been dated by radiocarbon to 2800 B.C., and a bloom of raw copper discovered in a village near the mines is undergoing analysis.[52]

But the more convincing evidence of an integral historic metallurgy flowering into the legendary ferrous figure of Tubal Cain is the black iron sands lining the whole southern shore of the Black Sea and extending into Macedonia. These were exploited by the Ottomans under Suleiman the Great, rediscovered by the author's expedition of 1968, and are once again being mined by the contemporary Turkish government for iron manufacture.[53]

Reconstructing the history of the emergence of ferrous metallurgy in this area is a delicate task. One fact seems indubitable, however. The smelting of the iron sands was known to Theophrastus, if not much earlier. According to the pseudo-Aristotelian *De Mirabilibus Auscultationibus*,

attributed mainly to Theophrastus, the sands were smelted in a furnace
with a fireproof stone to produce, not iron, but a silvery steel. Here,
apparently, the process differed from that by which the famous tatara iron
of Japan was traditionally produced.

> It is said that the production of Chalybian and Amisenian iron is very
> peculiar; for it grows together, as they assert, from the sand that is
> carried down by the river. Some say that they simply wash this and
> smelt it in a furnace; but others, that after frequently washing the
> deposit left by the first washing they burn it and insert what is called
> the fire-proof stone which is abundant in this country. This iron is
> far more beautiful than the other kinds; for if it were not burned
> in the furnace it would not differ at all, it appears, from silver. Now
> they say that it alone is not liable to rust; but that it is not plentiful.[54]

H. C. Richardson, after reading this quotation, tried his hand with the
black sands of Arizona but was foiled in eliminating the silicate gangue
as well as in keeping the fine grains of magnetite from blowing in the open
furnace.[55] However, the experiments carried on by Ronald Tylecote
with Black Sea sands gathered in 1968 led us to believe they could be
used in a bloomery process, as in Africa.

> An attempt to concentrate the magnetite by panning was unsuccessful,
> probably because the magnetic character of the olivine and pyroxene
> is due to magnetite inclusions in the silicate crystals which raise the
> specific gravity. For this reason all reduction tests were done on magne-
> tically concentrated material, i.e., 26 percent of the total sample taken
> from the beach.[56]

> Reduction of the total magnetic fraction in hydrogen at 900° C. for
> 24 hours produced little obvious change but microscopical exami-
> nation showed clearly that the magnetite grains and the magnetite
> in the silicate grains was well reduced and now porous. In fact there
> seemed to be less than 20 percent non-reducible particles. The main
> problem was to agglomerate this material, and this was attempted
> by adding charcoal to the charge and raising the temperature to
> 1200° C. to get carburized iron. After this only 20 percent of the
> particles were still metallic and there was little sign of slagging. These
> reduced particles showed a Widmanstätten structure of a strongly
> metallic phase in a less (pearlitic) metallic phase, and they had a con-

tinuous metallic rim. Some looked as though they had been molten, so it would seem that a degree of carburization but no agglomeration had taken place. It would be expected that a small amount of additional low melting point slag phase would help the agglomeration process.[56]

It seems, given the analysis of the texts of the Assyrian colony in Cappodocia, that possibly rare examples of Black Sea iron or steel were already in circulation during the 19th century B.C. In chapter 2 Muhly tentatively accepts amūtum as a smelted bloom of iron. A great deal of discussion has ensued since the time that aši'um was first identified as a possible ore and amūtum, because of its value well beyond that of tin, as meteoritic iron.[57]

Aši'um certainly could not have been common hematite ore. It was searched for generally over metal hearing terrains of the kārum, came in one instance from Hittite country, and was interdicted for sale. If a raw material, it was more likely black sands. If not a raw material but a semi-finished product, then it could have been a small bear or salamander of iron found adventitiously at smelting sites. Amūtum was so precious that it in turn could have been a fortuitous steel not unlike that described by Theophrastus. If it was not, then perhaps artisàns had learned to turn by-product iron into a finished product equal to meteoritic iron in worth.

The most interesting speculation to date about the stainless quality of Chalybian and Amisenian steel derives from very recent studies of Jerzy Piaskowski of Cracow, Poland.[58] Noting that a number of iron artifacts in eastern and central Europe from Hallstatt times on were high in nickel, and with cobalt and arsenic inclusions, Piaskowski ran tests to determine if these artifacts were of meteoritic or terrestrial origin. Two Hallstatt bracelets, for example, showed the silica slag formations characteristic of bloomery iron. This meant that they were from ores smelted by human hands. In trying to reconstruct the so-called fireproof stone (pyrimachos) Piaskowski concluded that the Chalybians were making a high nickel steel by adding the nickel arsenide, chloanthite, consisting of iron, nickel, cobalt, arsenic, and sulfur, to the smelt. It is certain that Turkish chrome could not have been thus employed, because it could not be reduced in a bloomery.

The mystery deepens and hopefully will be resolved by further smelting experiments using the high magnetite sands gathered on the expedition of 1968. The long experience of early metal workers with the arsenides that led to the discovery of arsenical coppers and stannite, as well as the jarosites in gossans, encourages one to believe that chloanthite was not beyond the experience of the first Phaphlogonian makers of fine steel. If high nickel steels of smelted sands thus resulted we shall have to reappraise all so-called meteoritic iron for its actual origins, as analyzed in chapter 3 by Jane C. Waldbaum. For the time being existing analyses must be taken as final.

In any event, one finds in the area of Anatolia–Paphlagonia–Cappodocia a metallurgy sufficiently advanced in copper–silver–gold–bronze–iron to have attracted an Assyrian colony in the 19th century B.C. and Mycenaean searchers for gold in the mid-2d millennium B.C. The long-distance trade in cloth and metals (including tin) forms the substance of the much debated Assyrian tablets. But gold could have been a trading item even at the time of the ascendancy of Ur in the mid-3d millennium. The subsequent Hittite trade in iron will be the subject of later chapters. Anatolia was not without its own splendor in innovative metallurgy judging from the smelted iron dagger of Alaca Hüyük set in a bronze handle.

If the earlier precious, semiprecious, and common metals each played a unique role in metallizing aspects of life (such as exchange and war) and setting them into a new nexus of communications, it was iron toward 1000 B.C. (and in another locale) that transformed human civilization in the Mediterranean into an entity fully dependent upon metal. That is the story to come.

NOTES

1. Hesiod, *The Works and Days*, trans. Richmond Lattimore (Ann Arbor: University of Michigan, 1959), pp. 35–39.

2. For general background on population and ecological change in this era see Colin Renfrew, *The Emergence of Civilisation: The Cyclades and The Aegean in the Third Millenium* B.C. (London: Methuen, 1972), p. 233; W. A. McDonald and G. Rapp, *The Minnesota-Messenia Expedition: Reconstructing a Bronze Age Environment* (Minneapolis: University of Minnesota Press, 1972), p. 142; J. Donald Hughes, *Ecology of Ancient Civilizations* (Albuquerque: University of New Mexico Press, 1975), esp. pp. 68 ff; R. Evans and T. Wertime *Deforestation, Erosion, and Ecology in the Ancient Mediterranean and Middle East*, forthcoming.

3. Marc Bloch, "Avenement et Conquêtes du Moulin à Eau," *Annales d'Histoire Économique et Sociale* 7 (1935): 538–63.

4. Olga Tufnell, *Lachish III: The Iron Age* (London: Oxford, 1953), pp. 388–89.

5. Chêng Tê K'un, *The Archeology of China*, 3 vols. (Cambridge, England: W. Heffer & Sons, 1963), vol. 3, *Chou China*, p. 246.

6. Theodore A. Wertime, *The Coming of The Age of Steel* (Chicago: University of Chicago Press, 1962), pp. 47 ff. See also chap. 14 by Joseph Needham below.

7. H. L. Lorimer, *Homer and The Monuments* (London: MacMillan, 1950), p. 114.

8. Jean Deshayes, *Les Outils de Bronze de l'Indus au Danube (Ive au IIe millénaire)*, 2 vols. (Paris: Paul Geuthner, 1960), vol. 1, 392 ff; Héctor Catling, *Cypriot Bronzework in the Mycenaean World* (Oxford: Clarendon Press, 1964), pp. 78 ff; George Bass, *Cape Gelidonya: A Bronze Age Shipwreck*, Transactions of the American Philosophical Society, New Series, vol. 57, pt. 8, 1967, pp. 84 ff; and Flinders Petrie, *Gerar* (London: British School of Archaeology in Egypt, 1928), pp. 13 ff.

9. Wertime, *Steel*, pp. 164 ff.

10. Ibid., pp. 192 ff.

11. Gaius Plinius Secundus, *Natural History*, trans. D. E. Eichholz, 10 vols. (Cambridge: Harvard University Press, 1962), bk. 34, vol. 9, p. 229.

12. Wertime, *Steel*, pp. 192 ff.

13. Aristotle, *Meteorologica*, transl. H. D. P. Lee (London: Heinemann, 1952), pp. 287–89.

14. Nicolas Monardes, *Dialogo del Hierro*, transl. John Frampton (London: Allde, 1596), p. 114.

15. Alexander Vandermonde, Claude-Louis Berthollet, and Gaspard Monge, "Mémoire sur le Fer," *Mémoires de l'Académie Royale des Sciences*, 1786, pp. 132–200, sums up both Swedish and French researches leading to the discovery of carbon.

16. John Percy, *Metallurgy: Iron and Steel* (London: Murray, 1864), pp. 873 ff. Percy believed that iron was so much more easily produced than bronze that the Iron Age should have preceded the Bronze Age, but his text reflects the contemporary view of iron as a difficult and unpredictable metal.

17. Antoine François, Comte de Fourcroy, "Fer," *Chimie et Metallurgie*, vol. 4, *Encyclopédie Méthodique*, 71, p. 348.

18. A number of recent books have examined the role of iron in the evolution of life and of the biogeochemistry of the earth. See especially J. B. Neilands, *Microbial Iron Metabolism* (New York: Academic Press, 1974), pp. 6 ff. The appreciation of iron as a medicinal was as prominent among such writers as Pliny as was the appreciation of iron as a producer's good.

19. On contemporary iron and steel production and its energy requirements see *Statistical Yearbook* of the United Nations for 1954, pp. 241–3, and 1973, pp. 296–98. Compare with Conference Board, *Energy Consumption in Manufacturing* (Cambridge, Mass.: Ballinger, 1974), pp. 415 ff.

20. The Greek poet Aeschylus (525–456 B.C.) gives us a powerful statement of the Chalybian tradition in *Seven Against Thebes*, transl. Anthony Hecht and Helen Bacon (New York: Oxford University Press, 1973), p. 53. See also *Prometheus Bound* for a description of the tribe (trans. Philip Vellacott [Baltimore: Penguin 1961], p. 41). But as we shall learn, Strabo affords us the most complete description of the Black Sea tribes, along with a discussion of literary references to them in antiquity. He lacks only a reference to the black sands. See H. L. Jones, trans., *The Geography of Strabo*, 8 vols. (Cambridge: Harvard University Press, 1961), vol. 5, pp. 401 ff.

21. See also Paul Garelli, *Les Assyriens en Cappodoce* (Paris: Maisonneuve, 1963), pp. 112 ff., 187, 273 ff., and R. Maxwell-Hyslop, "The Metals *Amūtu* and *Aši'u* in the Kültepe Texts," *Anatolian Studies* 22 (1972): 159–62.

22. Pliny 36. 10. 149 ff.

23. For the early history of glass, see A. Leo Oppenheim et al., *Glass and Glass Making in Ancient Mesopotamia* (Corning Museum of Glass: Corning, New York, 1971), pp. 4 ff., 76 ff., 105 ff., 181 ff.

24. For window glass in Britain see Robin Birley, "A Frontier Post in Roman Britain," *Scientific American* 236 (1977): 38–58. On window glass in Rome, generally, see Alexander Nesbitt, *Glass* (New York: Scribner and Welford, 1879), p. 18.

25. F. M. Lea and C. H. Desch, *The Chemistry of Cement and Concrete* (London: Edward Arnold, 1937), pp. 1 ff.

26. For the composition of Laurion cements, see Constantine Conophagos, "The Water Cisterns of Ore Washers in Laurion and Their Special Hydraulic Mortar" (in Greek), *Annales Géologiques des Pays Helléniques* (special publication, 1975). Conophagos believes that the artisans at Laurion added slags and litharge to the hydraulic cement.

27. See John S. Kopper and Guillermo Rosello-Bordoy, "Megalithic Quarrying Techniques and Limestone Technology in Eastern Spain," *Journal of Field Archeology* 1 (1974): 161–70, and W. H. Gourdin and W. D. Kingery, "The Beginnings of Pyrotechnology; Neolithic and Egyptian Lime Plaster," *Journal of Field Archeology* 2 (1975): 132–50.

28. For the author's studies of the pyrotechnologic background of this material culture see R. Evans and T. A. Wertime, *Deforestation, Erosion, and Ecology in the Ancient Mediterranean and Middle East*, forthcoming; "Pyrotechnology: Man's Fire Using Crafts," University of Texas Symposium on Ancient Technology, forthcoming; "Pyrotechnology: Man's First Industrial Uses of Fire," *American Scientist* 61 (1973): 670–82; "The Beginnings of Metallurgy: A New Look," *Science* 182 (1973): 875–87; "How Metallurgy Began: A Study in Diffusion and Multiple Innovation," *Actes du VIIIᵉ Congres International des Sciences Préhistoriques et Protohistoriques* (Belgrade, 1973), vol. 2, pp. 481–91; "A Metallurgical Expedition Through the Persian Desert," *Science* 159 (1968): 927–35; and "Man's First Encounters With Metallurgy," *Science* 146 (1964): 1257–67.

29. Pliny 36. 10. 157–58.

30. Denise Schmandt-Besserat, "An Archaic Recording System and the Origin of Writing," *Syro-Mesopotamian Studies* 1, pt. 2 (1977): 2–32.

31. Anita Engle, *Readings in Glass History, Nos. 6 and 7* (Jerusalem: Phoenix Publications, 1976), pp. 60 ff.

32. A. P. McCartney and D. J. Mack, "Iron Utilization by Thule Eskimos of Central Canada," *American Antiquity* 38 (1973): 328–39, and J. T. Wasson and S. P. Sedwick, "Possible Sources of Meteoritic Material From Hopewell Indian Mounds," *Nature* 222 (1969): 22–24.

33. A. Lucas and J. R. Harris, *Ancient Egyptian Materials and Industries* (London: Arnold, 1962), pp. 235, 237, 347 ff.

34. Edith Porada and Briggs Buchanan, *The Corpus of Ancient Near Eastern Seals in North American Collections: The Collection of the Pierpont Morgan Library* (Washington, D.C.: Bollingen Foundation, 1948), vol. 2, pp. 39 ff.

35. Pliny, 36. 9. 239 ff.

36. Ibid., 10. 10 ff.

37. H. H. Coghlan, *Notes on Prehistoric and Early Iron in the Old World* (Oxford: Oxford University Press, 1956), p. 45.

38. Percy, *Metallurgy: Iron and Steel*, p. 8.

39. Cyril S. Smith, "Notes on a Metallurgical Journey in Iran, September and October, 1962," unpublished.

40. Reported by Radomir Pleiner in Joseph Caldwell, *Investigations at Tal-i-Iblis* (Springfield, Ill.: Illinois State Museum Society, 1967), p. 398.

41. Smith "Notes," p. 10.

42. Caldwell, *Tal-i-Iblis*, p. 400.

43. A personal letter of Smith dated Feb. 19, 1963. See also Percy, *Metallurgy: Iron and Steel*, p. 153.

44. Arthur Steinberg and Frank Koucky, "Preliminary Metallurgical Research in the Ancient Cypriot Copper Industry," in L. E. Stager and G. E. Wright, eds., *American Expedition to Idalion, Cyprus* (Cambridge: American Schools of Oriental Research, 1974), pp. 158 ff.

45. For the smelting experiments, see Muhly, personal communication. For iron exsolved into ancient bronzes see Strathmore R. B. Cooke and Stanley Aschenbrenner, "The Occurrence of Metallic Iron in Ancient Copper," *Journal of Field Archeology* 2 (1975): 251–66.

46. R. F. Tylecote, A. Lupu, and B. Rothenberg, "A Study of Early Copper Smelting and Working Sites in Israel," *Journal of the Institute of Metals* 95 (1966): 235–43.

47. D. L. Giles and E. P. Kuijpers, "Stratiform Copper Deposit, Northern Anatolia, Turkey: Evidence for Early Bronze I (2800 B.C.) Mining Activity," *Science* 186 (1974): 823–25.

48. No deliberate flux, however, was used in the Maddin–Muhly experiments of 1977.

49. Steinberg and Koucky, "Preliminary Metallurgical Research," pp. 170 ff.

50. See n. 28.

51. Tahsin Özguc, personal communication.

52. Giles and Kuijpers, "Stratiform Copper Deposit."

·53. T. A. Wertime, "National Geographic Society—Smithsonian Pyrotechnological Reconnaissance of Afghanistan, Iran, and Turkey, 1968," *National Geographic Society Research Reports*, pp. 483–92.

54. Launcelot D. Dowdall, trans. and ed., *De Mirabilibus Ausculationibus* (Oxford: Clarendon Press, 1909), col. 833b. For the comparative smelting of iron sands by the Japanese, see William Gowland, "The Early Metallurgy of Copper, Tin, and Iron in Europe," *Archaeologia: London* 56 (1899): 267–322.

55. H. D. Richardson, "Iron, Prehistoric and Ancient," *American Journal of Archaeology* 38 (1934): 555–83.

56. Ronald Tylecote, personal communication. The highest magnetite content of these sands is about 75% although Tylecote was working with about 45% sands.

57. Garelli, *Assyriens*, pp. 112, 114, 116, 187, 202, 219, 273 ff.

58. Jerzy Piaskowski, "On The Manufacture of High-Nickel Iron Chalibean Steel in Antiquity," in Theodore A. Wertime, *Early Pyrotechnology* (Washington, D.C.: Smithsonian Institution Press), to be published.

2

The Bronze Age Setting

JAMES D. MUHLY

The Early Bronze Age of the 3d millennium B.C. saw the first development of a truly international age of metallurgy. There had been isolated examples of spectacular regional developments in the past—Varna and Nahal Mishmar being two excellent examples—but here was an international development spread all the way from the western Mediterranean to the Indus Valley.

Moreover the Early Bronze Age marked the development of a polymetallic metallurgical technology. With few exceptions, Varna being the most notable, the metallurgy before 3000 B.C. was a copper metallurgy with an occasional piece of lead or silver and even a rare bead of gold. In the 3d millennium B.C., all the metals known to ancient man were present and in great variety and combination. Gold, virtually absent before 3000 B.C. save at Varna, now appeared in a series of so-called treasures (really hoards) from Greece to southern Mesopotamia. Silver, and also lead, appeared in a variety of forms, with silver being used chiefly for vessels (also known in gold) while lead was even used for making model boats in the Cyclades. Silver and lead seem to have been most common in the Cyclades, but new discoveries, such as the hoard of jewelry from Mochlos buried in a silver vessel,[1] show that they were used on Crete as well. The material from the Royal Cemetery at Ur included many objects of gold and of silver, even a gold saw from the grave of Puabi, as well as objects of electrum, a naturally occurring alloy of gold and silver in use already in the Varna cemetery.

The great advance in copper metallurgy was the widespread use of copper alloys, in both arsenic and tin. The distribution was complicated, with some areas (e.g., Crete) favoring arsenical bronze while others, such as the Troad, were partial to tin bronze,[2] and still others, notably central Anatolia, made equal use of both at the same time.[3] The situation in Egypt is rather unusual in that tin bronze was virtually unknown while elaborate use was made of additive arsenic. Taking advantage of arsenic's tendency to segregate at the surface and form a silvery outer layer that could be polished, the Egyptians produced a series of mirrors with a "silvered" reflecting surface.[4] This silvery surface was also known in Anatolia and can be seen on several copper bulls from the site of Horoztepe, as shown by the work of Cyril Smith.[5] The Egyptians apparently even used this technique, or that of vapor plating as on the bulls, to plate a spouted copper ewer, if that is the correct interpretation of an object in the Metropolitan Museum described in the literature as being plated with antimony.[6] Nor is plating the correct descriptive term for what was actually an enrichment by surface segregation.

All of this indicates an extraordinary development in metallurgical technology during the course of the 3d millennium B.C. The rate of technological change is quite astounding. The common belief is that, before the 20th century A.D., technological development took place at a snail-like pace with long periods of utter stagnation. Yet consider the example of goldworking in the 3d millennium B.C. Before 3000 B.C. there was virtually no goldwork in the ancient Near East (tomb 109 from Tepe Gawra providing almost all the known examples), yet by 2600 B.C. the jewelry and other metalwork from the Royal Cemetery at Ur were so sophisticated that, as Cyril Smith has stated, the work "reveals knowledge of virtually every type of metallurgical phenomenon except the hardening of steel that was exploited by technologists in the entire period up to the end of the 19th century A.D."[7]

The question is, of course, why all this took place in the 3d millennium B.C. Were metallurgical developments along with the growth of trade, especially trade by sea, the causes of the creation of a proto-urban world, as Renfrew argues, or were they only the effects of that creation? It seems to me that any attempt to explain why things suddenly took off about 3000 B.C. has to explain the most important development, the birth of the art of writing. The invention of writing has not been given proper attention by prehistorians because most of the scholars who have dealt with the third millennium B.C. in recent years have been specialists either in European or in Aegean prehistory. Their worlds are illiterate (or preliterate to be more polite) and they are not accustomed to dealing with written texts or in thinking about the significance of such texts.

Yet in Egypt, Mesopotamia, Syria, to a lesser extent the Indus Valley, and perhaps even China we are dealing with literate record-keeping

civilizations. The ability to write is the most significant intellectual achievement of ancient Egypt and Sumer. Recent attempts to see the birth of
civilization in Europe, or even in the British Isles, based upon a revised
chronology derived from calibrated radiocarbon dates, flounder on this
point.[8] In spite of much recent literature to the contrary there is still a
good case to be made for the primacy of the ancient Near East. It was here
that the important technological and artistic discoveries were made,
culminating in the invention of writing and the emergence of the proto-
urban world in the late 4th millennium B.C. A place such as Malta may
have developed an impressive style of monumental stone architecture
at an early period. Perhaps the earliest such architecture in the world is
to be seen at such Maltese sites as Ġgantija, Taxien, and Hagar Qim,[9]
but what does it lead to? What is the role of Malta in the history of Western civilization?

We must emphasize not the isolated achievement but the full course of
development. The role of Iran in the development of the art of writing is
an instructive example. Recent finds of so-called proto-Elamite tablets
from late 4th millennium contexts at Susa, Godin Tepe, Tepe Yahya,
and Shahr-i-Sokhta indicate that a form of written notation was developing
in Iran at least as early as in Iraq.[10] Yet in Iran that development came to
a dead end while in Iraq ancient Sumer created a remarkable written
language that went from simple account texts and lexical lists to the
Vulture Stele inscription of Eannatum within the course of several hundred
years. The current Italian excavations at the Syrian site of Tell Mardikh,
ancient Ebla, are now making clear just how pervasive and powerful
these Mesopotamian developments really were.[11]

I believe that the extraordinary development of metallurgy during the
course of the 3d millennium B.C. must be seen in these terms, as a response
to developments within the area of Greater Mesopotamia. Here material
from sites such as Tell Asmar in the Diyala, from Tepe Gawra in the north,
beginning with the remarkable electrum wolf's head in Gawra X (Jemdat
Nasr period) and culminating in the rich collection of objects from Gawra
VI, and from Kish and the Royal Cemetery at Ur provide the background
for developments throughout Syria, Anatolia, and the Eastern Mediterranean.

I do not maintain that Aegean metallurgy was a direct import from
Mesopotamia. I would like to suggest that the stimulus ultimately came
from Mesopotamia, through Syria, Cyprus, and Anatolia, and that the

international world that developed in the 3d millennium was a response to the stimulus provided by the expansion of Mesopotamian civilization in the Early Dynastic and Presargonic periods. The factors that produced developments within Mesopotamia itself are beyond the scope of this chapter but recent studies on urbanism and the formation of states have tended to emphasize increases in population as one of the key factors.[12]

As for the concept of a Bronze Age one of the most significant events in the 3d millennium was the development of true tin-bronze alongside an arsenical alloy of copper. Exactly how these alloys were made is still the subject of much debate. Recent research has suggested that the loss of arsenic during smelting had been overestimated, that in fact the recovery rate is quite high and that arsenical alloys, with 1–4 percent arsenic, can be obtained through the smelting of complex arsenides such as domeykite and algodonite (see chap. 8 by Heskel and Lamberg-Karlovsky). Everyone seems to agree that arsenic was not used as a native metal in the Bronze Age and was probably not even recognized as a separate element. Rather, like the carburization of iron, the ancient metalsmith knew how to achieve the desired result but had no idea what actually produced that result.

More controversial is the master alloy theory, involving the addition of a pre-prepared high arsenic content material to molten copper. That such ingots would be silvery in color and were therefore known as *annaku* in Akkadian and *ḏ'm* in Egyptian[13] is extremely unlikely because the former means "tin" and the latter "electrum." The master-alloy theory itself, apart from the attempted philological underpinning, has much to commend it and such ingots are actually known from a later context in Europe.[14]

Not much can be said regarding sources of arsenical ores, because it is still not clear just what we should be looking for, but the evidence suggests that this was a regional development making use of local ore sources. Some copper deposits around the world are famous sources of arsenical copper, such as the Frisian island of Heligoland (Helgoland in German),[15] but there is no need to imagine that such a source supplied copper to a wide area.[16] The fact that different areas used arsenical alloys at the same time says nothing about the origin of that metallurgy. Again this seems to have been an idea that found acceptance over much of the ancient world, probably because it met a common demand. So too did the characteristic style of Early Bronze Age fortification wall, employing a series of horseshoe-shaped bastions or towers, known from Spain (Los Millares) to Palestine (Arad).[17]

Many theories have been presented to account for the spread of metallurgy in the 3d millennium B.C., through Beaker Folk in the west, torque-bearers in Europe and the Eastern Mediterranean, and Khirbet-Kerak people in the Near East,[18] as well as Cycladic colonists in Iberia and Trojan prospectors in eastern Europe.[19] Such theories involve large-scale migration of peoples over vast distances, migrations often identified with one ethnic group such as Indo-Europeans or Hurrians. It is probably best to reject all such theories, along with the elaborate archaeological reconstructions that have accompanied them. There is no evidence to support the existence of any specialized group of metalworkers in the Early Bronze Age, and it has not been possible to substantiate any theory of migration or colonization at this time. Even the famous Indo-European migration into Greece and Anatolia is in need of a complete reinvestigation. It is a complex period but a recent study of the Italian Copper Age sums up the current consensus very well:

> Nothing is to be gained by inventing immediate solutions, either invading Indo-Europeans in south-east Europe, or Levantine or Aegean colonists and traders in Italy. Any theory needs at least a few supporting facts.[20]

The situation in Italy is a classic example of the problem under discussion, for it had become standard practice to derive all features of the Italian Copper Age from the east, with the origins of the Remedello culture (in the Po Valley) and the Rinaldone culture (in central Italy or Tuscany) being seen as imports from the Aegean and the Gaudo culture (in the south, the bay of Naples) being traced to Troy. This was especially true in metallurgy because objects of copper and silver have provided most of the evidence for origins and for trade. Again we are dealing with an arsenical alloy of copper since virtually no true tin-bronze is known from the western Mediterranean in the 3d millennium B.C., but the use of arsenic in itself tells us nothing about the origin of that metallurgy.[21] Nor has it really been possible to identify true Aegean or Near Eastern imports in an Italian context or vice versa. Even the famous silver daggers from Early Minoan Koumasa, long considered to be Italian imports, now appear to be of local Cretan manufacture.[22] This is not to say that no contact existed but only that we should think in terms of the transmission of ideas, not of people or groups of objects. Ethel Eaton sums up the situation as follows: ". . . what impresses us most in our incomplete knowledge of this period is the speed of the spread and practice of metallurgy. . . . The idea of metal working may have been brought to Italy from outside. . . . nevertheless, the manner of its adoption was very much a local affair."[23]

This arsenical copper metallurgy also spread to Iberia, to southern Spain and Portugal, in the 3d millennium B.C. Again it has been traditional to see this as being brought to the area by Aegean colonists and from there spread by the migrations of the Beaker Folk. Recent studies have tended to be very critical of the migration hypothesis, to stress the pre-Beaker background of Iberian metallurgy, and to question the connection between Beaker-type pottery and the expansion of metallurgy in the western Mediterranean and western Europe.[24]

It cannot be denied that all this is part of a basic pattern within scholarship over the past ten years. Everywhere the emphasis is upon local origins and independent development. Much of this is a healthy reaction to the basic methodology of past years, when every new style and every new technique was seen as brought in from the outside by a specific group of people. Now everyone, from the British Isles to India and China, emphasizes the local origins of technology developed by indigenous cultures. Surely the pendulum has swung in the opposite direction and we are seeing the extreme reaction to an equally extreme past position. The truth must lie somewhere in the middle ground. Much present-day antidiffusionist scholarship seems to imply that nobody ever went anywhere during the Bronze Age. The speed and the extent of the spread of arsenical copper metallurgy during the 3d millennium B.C., I would argue, cannot be explained in terms of a series of isolated, independent developments. To accept this is not to believe in colonists from the Cycladic island of Syros living at Los Millares in Spain.[25]

ENIGMA OF THE TIN TRADE AND EARLY IRON IN ANATOLIA

In fact the spread of tin-bronze, the other major development in copper metallurgy in this period, implies the existence of some type of long-distance trade. As there are no known sources of tin anywhere in the Aegean, the Eastern Mediterranean (apart from Egypt), or the Near East, the appearance of tin-bronze in such widely separated areas as north-western Anatolia (Troy), Cyprus (Vounous), and southern Mesopotamia (Ur and Kish) requires a network of trade routes covering a considerable area.

We still have no definite evidence regarding the source or sources of this tin. Tin is a fairly rare element in the earth's crust, and alluvial tin, or cassiterite, is known in only a few areas, from Cornwall to Thailand and Malaysia, all seemingly too remote to be posited as sources for the bronze metallurgy being discussed here. The one exception in Egypt, where three separate sources of alluvial cassiterite have been identified in the Eastern Desert.[26] The presence of Egyptian rock-carved hieroglyphic inscriptions at one of the tin sites (El Mueilha), all from the middle of the long reign of Pepi II, indicates Egyptian presence in the area at the end of the Old Kingdom.[27] The nearby gold mines at Baramiyah were also being worked at this time.[28] Yet the Mueilha inscriptions say nothing about the exploitation of cassiterite. Like the related inscriptions from the Wādi Hammāmāt to the north they refer to expeditions sent in search of stone.[29] Nor do the Sinai inscriptions refer to the exploitation of copper but only of turquoise, and yet we know that Old Kingdom Egypt was mining and smelting some copper in the Sinai. Perhaps, as Hestrin and Tadmor have suggested, the Egyptians did not consider the acquisition of copper (and, I would add, tin) something worth writing down.[30] They recorded only the expeditions in search of costly materials such as gold, turquoise, and amythest.

There is, however, another objection to seeing Old Kingdom Egypt as a source of tin because the Egyptians themselves apparently used only pure copper or arsenical copper before 2000 B.C. Very few analyzed Old Kingdom artifacts are of tin-bronze but there are several, and perhaps further analyses would increase the number. It is unlikely that the Eastern Desert, with sources of alluvial cassiterite so easily accessible to an ancient prospector since nuggets of cassiterite need only be collected from the dry wadi bed, would not have been exploited during the Bronze Age.

The other possibility now being suggested as a source of Bronze Age tin is Thailand. Although the general area has long been the world's major source of alluvial cassiterite, it has never been considered as a possible source of tin for the Bronze Age of southwest Asia or the Eastern Mediterranean, except by Benno Landsberger.[31] The reasons are obvious: distance and obscurity. The distance remains the same, but it is no longer correct to maintain that Thailand is an archaeological and historical unknown before the first reference to the people in Chinese sources in the 6th century B.C. Excavations at Non Nok Tha and Ban Chiang have shown that the use of tin-bronze goes back perhaps into the 4th millennium B.C.[32] However, these excavations have also revealed a regional, seemingly indigenous culture, using only local materials with little or no evidence for contact with the outside world.[33] Thus, although both the pottery and metallurgy are very intesting in their own right, there is, at present, little reason to believe that developments in Thailand had any influence on the rest of the world. The early inhabitants of Thailand knew how to make tin-bronze, but it cannot be demonstrated that they shared either their technology or their materials with anyone else. And the actual date of the first tin-bronze in Thailand is still the subject of much debate. (See discussion by Needham in chap. 14.)

There really is no evidence for sources of or trade in tin before ca. 2000 B.C. The extensive use of tin in early levels at Troy (Troy II, perhaps even Troy I), Thermi, and sites across Anatolia and the Eastern Mediterranean to the Levant (except for Palestine) and Greater Mesopotamia is still a great mystery. The sources of tin being used in the 3d millennium B.C. remain the great enigma of Early Bronze Age archaeology. The truly surprising fact is that, after many years of effort, we still seem to be no closer to a solution. This has suggested to some that we are looking either for the wrong thing or in the wrong places. Tin existed, and it was even being used to fashion artifacts—witness the tin bracelet from Thermi—but the sources of that tin still escape us.[34]

It is not until the early 2d millennium B.C. that we get substantial evidence on the sources of copper and tin. This information comes entirely from contemporary written documents, for scientific analysis has as yet produced no evidence for the Bronze Age sources of copper and tin. With neutron activation analysis and the proper statistical treatment of the data, it should be possible to say something about the provenience of native copper[35] and even of copper smelted from simple oxide and carbonate ores. Thus provenience studies are possibile in the regional worlds of Neolithic and Chalcolithic metallurgy. By the 3d millennium B.C., however, the complexity and extent of the technology involving the smelting of a variety of ores under different conditions with or without the use of fluxes, the introduction of deliberate alloys, the use of scrap metal from many different sources, with the remelting of broken or worn artifacts, thus combining coppers of varying origin and elemental composition—all this makes provenience study through elemental analysis a hopeless task.[36]

Composition analysis and metallographic examination can tell us much about the types of alloys in use, about the ores of copper being smelted and the type of smelting process in use, and about the methods of casting and re-working,[37] but they are not going to tell us anything about the sources of copper and tin being utilized—at least not with the techiques now in use. For provenience and trade the surviving written record provides our only body of evidence, and it is not very satisfactory, being vaguest at the very points where we would hope for most detail.

Our first main body of evidence relating to trade in tin is an excellent example of the problem confronting us. The Old Assyrian letters from the Anatolian merchant colony (or *kārum*) at Kültepe, ancient Kaneš, covering the period known as kārum II, 1950–1850 B.C., provide extremely detailed information on shipment of loads of tin (Old Assyrian *annukum*) from the capital city of Assur to the members of the private business-houses residing at Kaneš.[38] We are told the weight of a load of tin (ca. 65 kg), how the load was placed on the backs of the donkeys, how the caravan was organized, the duties and taxes paid to the local Anatolian princes, and something about the hazards and difficulties of overland trade. We are told about everything except the origin of the tin.

All that we know is that the tin was brought to Assur, presumably from points to the east, and from Assur shipped overland by annual donkey caravans to central Anatolia.[39] We also know that the textiles, representing the other half of the trade goods sent to Anatolia, came from Babylonia to the south.[40] The extent of the tin trade has recently been calculated by Mogens Larsen: "The amount of tin recorded on the available texts is about 13,500 kgs, i.e. some 200 donkey-loads sent from Assur to Kanesh. Again as a conservative estimate, I suggest an export from Assur over a period of fifty years of about eighty tons."[41] Using a copper/tin ratio of 9 : 1 this 80 tons of tin would have been combined with 720 tons of copper to produce 800 tons of bronze. These figures are only estimates, based upon insufficiently published data, but they give some idea of the probable extent of the trade.

Many questions remained unanswered, even beyond the major one regarding the source of the tin. Did the tin come into Assur in the form of cassiterite, there to be smelted to produce metallic tin? Or did the reduction take place elsewhere, with metallic tin being sold to Assur? Or were the Assyrians even shipping cassiterite to Anatolia? No ancient language, to my knowledge, distinguishes between the oxide and the metal. In fact the name cassiterite comes from *kassiteros*, the ancient Greek word for "tin." There are occasional references to something called "white tin" (Sumerian AN·NA BABBAR, Akkadian *annaku pesû*), which could be taken as distinguishing the metal, but this would mean that all references to only *annakum* would have to represent the oxide, which is unlikely.[42]

We do know that the supply of tin was irregular, with tin sometimes being in short supply, and that the price of tin fluctuated accordingly. That is, we are dealing with a free economy based upon supply and demand, without government control. This is in keeping with the current interpretation of Old Assyrian trade as being conducted by private families dominated by the profit motive.[43] The Assyrian merchants went to Anatolia to make money by buying tin as cheaply as possible in Assur and selling it for as much as possible or, in short, by buying cheap and selling dear. In general the Assyrian merchants were able to sell at a markup of about 100 percent,[44] with shipping expenses calculated at about 10 percent the value of the merchandise.[45]

The value of tin is calculated against that of silver. Letters went out from Assur instructing the partners at Kaneš to sell tin at a price no less than six shekels of silver per mina of tin, that being a silver/tin ratio of 1 : 10.[46] If tin was in short supply it was possible to get as much as sixteen shekels of silver for a mina of tin, a ratio of just under 1 : 4.[47] At least one text states that a talent of tin should fetch at least a mina of gold, giving a gold/tin ratio of 1 : 60.[48] All this means that tin was important enough to sell for what the market would bear but hardly expensive enough to justify importing it from Thailand.

The Old Assyrian trade raises many questions that cannot be answered. The greatest puzzle, apart from the source of the tin itself, is why the Anatolian princes had to rely upon foreign Assyrian merchants to supply them with all their tin—this in a country with an old and distinguished history of copper and bronze metallurgy. What about the tin being used in the mid-3d millennium B.C., at sites such as Alaca Hüyük, Ahlatlibel, Mahmutlar, and Horoztepe? What is even stranger is that Anatolia in the Old Assyrian period was a leading center of metallurgical development, as indicated by the material excavated at ancient Kaneš.[49] Anatolia even seems to have developed the world's first iron technology, according to current interpretations of the Old Assyrian texts.

One of the earliest examples of the use of iron for something more than pins and beads is the famous iron sword from tomb K at Alaca Hüyük.[50] Clearly a ceremonial weapon, the blade seems to have been made of smelted iron.[51] This tradition of early ironworking was continued in the

Old Assyrian period, the texts of which use two words, *amūtum* and *aši'um*, both identified as some sort of iron.[52] It has now been suggested that *aši'um* represents iron ore, probably hematite, while *amūtum* is the bloom iron smelted from the ore.[53] *Amūtum* is the metal, with objects always being described as made of *amūtum*, never of *aši'um*. *Amūtum* could also be refined (*ṣarāpu*), presumably a reference to heating and forging in order to hammer out the slag (according to at least one text the metal suffers loss of weight in the process).[54]

Amūtum metal was expensive, the texts giving ratios of 1 : 35 and 1 : 40 with silver.[55] This would mean that iron was 400 times more expensive than tin, even though the iron was local while the tin had to be imported by foreign merchants. Iron was so precious that its circulation was controlled and there was an interdiction against its leaving the country.[56] Small pieces of *amūtum* were collected over a period of time, presumably to be forged into one lump.

The translation of *amūtum* as a bloom of iron smelted from some type of iron ore is very convincing. The texts refer to the refining of the bloom, recording the loss of weight resulting from the removal of the entrapped slag. The Assyrians themselves, naturally, were interested only in wrought iron, not the unforged bloom, and one writer from Assur tells his colleague in Kaneš:

> If the *amūtum* is pure, do me a favor, buy the *amūtum* for me since the price of the *amūtum* is (very) low, whenever you write I will send the silver, if the *amūtum* is not refined, if it is not pure, do not send any.[57]

The translation of *aši'um* as hematite is less convincing for a number of reasons. *Aši'um* is among the materials offered to a local Anatolian ruler as a present (bribe?)[58] and it is a little difficult to believe in the offer of a lump of hematite. Also the interdiction against export really seems to apply to *aši'um*, one text stating that *aši'um* was not to go beyond Luhusaddia (Hittite Lawasantiya), that is, not across the Taurus Mountains into Syria.[59] One famous merchant, Pūšu-kēn, was even thrown into jail (Old Assyrian *kišeršum*) in Kaneš because one of his caravans was caught smuggling *aši'um*.[60] Again, it is difficult to believe that the Anatolian princes were concerned about the export of hematite.

Finally the Old Assyrian language has another word, *šadwānum*, usually translated as "hematite".[61] This word appears in a very interesting text that refers to two different types of copper: fine copper from Taritar(a)

and copper which does not contain hematite (*šadwānum*).[62] This text
seems to indicate that fine or good quality copper (Sumerian SIG_5) contained hematite as a natural fluxing agent and that the Assyrians recognized
the role of hematite as a fluxing agent in the smelting of copper ore.
Although the Old Assyrian texts have many references to copper, recording
single shipments as large as 35 tons, the *kārum* at Kaneš itself was not
involved in the copper trade, which perhaps went directly from the area
of Ergani to Assur.[63]

All this is very speculative, but it gives some idea of the wealth of
material, regarding all aspects of ancient metallurgy, contained in the Old
Assyrian texts. The texts are difficult to translate and the meaning of many
words is still uncertain. *Aši'um* does seem to be some type of metal, perhaps
a form of iron, but it is curious that *aši'um* is the material that could not
be exported while value is always recorded as a ratio between *amūtum* and
silver or gold. Some texts even seem to interchange the two words, as if
they were synonyms.[64] (See also discussion by Wertime in chap. 1.)

This emphasis upon the Old Assyrian texts, in a general chapter on the
Bronze Age is, I believe, justified because these texts give us our first
glimpse into what we might call the economics of the ancient metal
industry. They provide us with some indication of the role of metals in
society, of the effort involved in obtaining copper and tin, of the relative
value of the different metals in use, and our first glimpse into the coming of
the Age of Iron. Indeed, one of the main reasons for translating *amūtum*
as iron is the high cost of the material, for $86\frac{2}{3}$ shekels of silver is given as the
price of $2\frac{1}{6}$ shekels of *amūtum*, giving an iron/silver ratio of 1 : 40, meaning,
it is worth repeating, that iron was 400 times more expensive than tin.

We are accustomed to thinking of tin as the expensive metal, one trans-
ported over great distances at great effort and cost. Yet iron, present in
almost every country of the ancient world and of no practical use in the 2d
millennium B.C., was considered much more valuable than tin. This can
be explained only in terms of supply and demand. Iron was a very rare
metal, one whose methods of production were not really understood but
one which was occasionally produced in ways described by other authors
in this volume. These values supplied by the Old Assyrian texts help to
explain the use of iron as a precious material throughout the 2d millennium.
In the Late Bronze Age, we still find iron being overlaid or decorated with
gold (as in objects from Dendra and Vapheio in Greece),[65] and, from a
tomb at Kition on the island of Cyprus, we find a gold ring wound with

iron wire.[66] At his burial the Egyptian pharaoh Tutankhamun was provided with two ceremonial daggers having elaborately worked hilts and ornate golden sheaths, one dagger having an iron blade, the other a blade of hardened gold.[67] It is interesting that all the touring exhibits of the Treasures of Tutankhamun have included only the gold dagger. The iron dagger has remained in Cairo, being regarded as too precious to ship around the world.

Level II at the *kārum* Kaneš was destroyed in a conflagration very difficult to explain in historical terms[68] but an event that put an end to the tin trade between Assyria and Anatolia. The following period, known as the Age of Hammurapi, or the Old Babylonian Period (ca. 1850–1600 B.C.) saw a shift in the tin trade route from north to west, probably as part of the economic policy of Šamši-Adad I, king of Assyria (1813–1781 B.C.).[69] Much of our evidence for this period comes from the French excavations at the site of Mari, located on the upper Euphrates midway between Aleppo and Baghdad.[70] So important is the material from Mari that the first part of the Old Babylonian period is often known as the Mari Age.

What is of interest here are the references in the Mari texts to metallurgy and the trade in copper and tin. With disturbances in the north, especially in the Zagros mountains, cutting off the trade in tin with Anatolia, Šamši-Adad shifted his interests westward and Mari became an entrepôt on a trade route that brought tin up the Euphrates to Mari. There it was stored and transshipped to places in Syria and Palestine and even beyond the sea.[71] Again the texts are vague as to the ultimate source of this tin, but it seems to be coming from Iran by a southern route through Susa. There is also some indication that Elamites were involved in the trade.

Trade with Iran had for a long time brought many materials into Mesopotamia including steatite, carnelian, turquoise, and lapis lazuli.[72] Because some of these materials, especially lapis lazuli, are known not to have come from Iran, but only through Iran,[73] the association of Iran with tin, tenuous as it is, does not of itself mean that the tin came from Iran.

The tin was shipped to Mari in the form of ingots (Akkadian *lē'u*) and there stored in various parts of the palace known as the *abūsum* (storeroom), the *bīt kunukki* (seal-house), and the *kisallu* (courtyard).[74] From Mari the tin was sent to a number of well-known Syro-Palestinian sites, from Carchemish in the north to Hazor in the south, and to the great international emporium of Ugarit on the coast.[75] From there, according to a balanced account text known as the Mari Tin Inventory,[76] it was shipped to Caphtor

(Akkadian Kaptaru), the island of Crete. Such was the international world of the Old Babylonian metals trade. At the same time Mari itself was importing copper from Alashiya, the 2d millennium B.C. name for the island of Cyprus.[77] Copper from Alashiya was also being shipped as far east as Babylon according to a text from the fifth year of Samsuiluna, king of Babylon (1750–1712 B.C.)[78]

More evidence on the copper trade comes from Old Babylonian Ur, where the excavator, Sir Leonard Woolley, uncovered the house of Ea-nāṣir, a merchant who specialized in the trade in copper, located at what Woolley called No. 1 Old Street.[79] A number of texts found in the area and dating to the reign of Rim-Sin, king of Larsa (1822–1763 B.C.), record Ea-nāṣir's activities in the copper trade, which consisted of importing what is called Tilmun copper, that is, copper from the Kerman district of Iran (and therefore called Magan copper in earlier periods), which was shipped to Mesopotamia up the Persian Gulf to the island of Bahrein (ancient Tilmun).[80] A merchant trading with Tilmun was known as an *Ālik Tilmun*. The most interesting of all these texts is a letter to Ea-nāṣir from someone named Nanni. Ea-nāṣir is accused of not keeping his word, of delivering poor-quality copper ingots and of treating people with contempt in a fashion not befitting a gentleman. All this because Nanni owed him one mina of silver. Nanni closes his letter with the following words:

> Take note that (from now on) I will not accept here any copper from you that is not of good quality. I shall select and take possession of the ingots individually in my courtyard, and I shall exercise against you my right of rejection because you have treated me with contempt.[81]

Ea-nāṣir had his problems; he seems to have had difficulty delivering goods on consignment. Ili-idinnam, in another letter,[82] complained that the copper he paid for a year ago still had not been delivered. Ea-nāṣir himself seems to have gone to Tilmun to obtain the copper for which he had previous orders to buy. Unfortunately these texts give no indication what determined the quality of the copper.

This world of international trade, as recorded in the texts, is supported, at least in part, by contemporary archaeological evidence. Middle Minoan Crete, the world of the first palaces and of Kamares ware,[83] was in contact with the Levantine coast, Cyprus, and Egypt,[84] so it is not surprising that references to Minoan Crete appear in the Mari texts. There may even be archaeological evidence for the "weapon of Caphtorite-workmanship" mentioned in an inventory text from Mari.[85] However, the shipment of tin all the way from Iran to southern Mesopotamia and up the Euphrates to Ugarit and beyond to Crete represents a trade route of epic scope. Yet the price of tin seems to have remained much as it was during the Old Assyrian period, with the tin/silver ratio running from 10 : 1 to 14 : 1.[86] In a famous Mari letter Išhi-Addu, king of Qatna, wrote in protest to Išme-Dagan, son of Šamši-Adad I, regarding the insulting price of 20 minas of tin that he had been paid for two horses. He claims that in Qatna two horses cost 600 shekels of silver.[87] At a tin/silver ratio of 14 : 1 he should have been paid 140 minas of tin and therefore had good reason to complain. There is no indication in the letter that Išhi-Addu thought it at all unusual for someone to make payment for horses in tin.

There seem to have been two different trade routes bringing copper into the Near East during the Old Babylonian period, one from the north bringing copper from Alashiya down the Euphrates and one from the south bringing the copper from Kerman up the Persian Gulf. The ratio between copper and silver is given as 180 : 1 and 240 : 1, although the price equivalences established by Sin-kāšid, ruler of Uruk and contemporary of Hammurapi, give a copper/silver ratio of 600 : 1 (one shekel of silver bought ten minas of copper). However, this is but one of a number of texts giving utopian prices for purposes of propaganda.[88] A similar passage at the beginning of the Laws of Eshnunna is of special interest because it distinguishes between copper (at 180 : 1) and worked or wrought copper at (120 : 1).[89] The question is what is meant by worked copper (erû epšum)? Does it refer to work-hardened copper or to copper fashioned in some form?

With the ratios given here tin was about 18 times more expensive than copper. In the Old Assyrian period the copper/silver ratio ranged from 46 : 1 to 180 : 1,[90] which means that, while the price of tin remained fairly constant, copper became less expensive in the Old Babylonian period. There are a few references to objects of iron in Old Babylonian texts, now using the word *parzillum*, containing the basic Semitic root seen also in Hebrew *barzel* and Arabic *firzil*,[91] and even one text that gives an silver/iron ratio of 12 : 1 ($16\frac{1}{6}$ shekels of silver being equal to $1\frac{1}{3}$ shekels of iron).[92] This would mean that iron was about 140 times more expensive than tin, but this is only on the basis of one text and such evidence is very difficult to evaluate. There is also a Mari text giving a lead/silver ratio of 1800 : 1.[93]

The end of the Old Babylonian period, symbolized by the fall of the city of Babylon to the Hittites ca. 1600 B.C.,[94] is followed by one of the most obscure periods in Near Eastern history, the so-called Dark Age lasting from ca. 1600 to ca. 1400 B.C. A period little known in the Near East, but one of great importance there, as in the rest of the ancient world, for it saw the establishment of the Hurrian kingdom of Mitanni, with its Indo-Aryan background,[95] the expulsion of the Hyksos from Egypt with the founding of the Eighteenth Dynasty under Ahmose,[96] and the establishment of the Mycenaean period in Greece, a truly golden age heralded by the splendid opulence of the Shaft Graves at Mycenae.[97]

The 16th century B.C. also saw the establishment of the first real contact between Europe and the Aegean, with Baltic amber (and perhaps even Cornish tin) finding their way to the Aegean, probably through a series of middlemen.[98] Cornwall was certainly the major source of tin in the west and the extent of its resources is often underestimated. Tin is still the only nonferrous metal mined in any quantity in the United Kingdom and even in 1972 A.D., after millennia of exploitation, the tin fields of southwest England produced 3327 tons of tin-in-concentrate with another 5000 tons of refined tin being recovered from waste and scrap.[99] It is possible that the tin for the great Aegean Late Bronze Age came from Cornwall.[100] No other reasonable source has as yet been suggested.

CYPRUS AND THE LATE BRONZE AGE METALS TRADE

The end of the Dark Age of Near Eastern history was marked by the fall of the civilization of Minoan Crete with the final destruction of the palace at Knossos, the predominance of the Mycenaeans in the Eastern Mediterranean, and the rebirth of written historical records with archives from Hittite Anatolia, Ugarit, and the short-lived new Egyptian captital at El-Amarna, ancient Akhetaten. The fall of Minoan Crete, in the early 14th century B.C., seems to have marked the demise of the Aegean bronze industry. The closing years, around 1400 B.C., saw a spectacular degree of bronze production including objects buried in a series of tombs all to be dated around 1400 B.C., the most notable being chamber tomb 12 at Dendra with its lobster corslet, the best preserved example of Bronze Age armor.[101]

After 1400 there is very little surviving bronze from the Aegean, the most notable exception being the unpublished bronzes excavated at Thebes, a site that has also produced a well-preserved jeweller's workshop.[102] In the 14th century B.C. the focus of the bronze industry in the Eastern Mediterranean seems to shift to Cyprus, which has yielded a notable series of bronzes for 1400–1100 B.C.[103] Cyprus was, of course, one of the great sources of copper in the ancient world. It should be pointed out, however, that the name Cyprus does not mean "copper" and Cyprus is not, by etymology, the "Copper Island."

It is true that English copper and German Kupfer come from Latin cuprum, but the latter was not originally a word for copper. The Latin word for copper is aes, but, since Cyprus was such an important source of copper, there developed in the 1st century A.D. the expression aes cyprium, "Cyprian copper." From this emerged, by ellipsis, the forms cyprium and eventually cuprum, whence came English copper.[104] But the name Cyprus does not owe its origin to any word for copper. The Greek word for copper is chalkós, which also designates bronze. Greek, like most of the ancient Indo-European languages, did not distinguish between copper and bronze. Only Hittite had separate words, with ku(wa)nnan meaning copper and harašu bronze.[105] None of these words has anything to do with the name Cyprus or with the name Alashiya, the Bronze Age designation of the island.

Cyprus was, however, one of the major sources of copper in the eastern Mediterranean during the Late Bronze Age (1600–1100 B.C.). The famous references in the Amarna letters to the ruler of Alashiya sending large amounts of copper to Egypt indicate that Cyprus was a major source of copper, at least in the mid-14th century B.C.[106] The most famous letter in this series of texts contains the following passage:

My brother should not take it to heart that I am sending herewith only five hundred pounds of copper—I am sending this solely as a present for my brother—because, my brother, it is so little. I swear that pestilence, the disease of my lord Nergal, was in the land, and has killed all the people of my land, so there was nobody to produce copper. So my brother should not take it to heart (that it is so little copper). Send back quickly your messenger together with my messenger, then I will send you, my brother, all the copper which my brother wants.[107]

This translation, by A. Leo Oppenheim, nicely gives the flavor of the repetition and awkward style characteristic of Amarna Akkadian. It is curious that this letter, with its emphasis upon troubles in Cyprus and the dearth of copper, actually refers to the largest amount of copper mentioned in the Amarna correspondence (the actual amount is 500 talents, or 33,000 pounds).

The reference to pestilence and the god Nergal has attracted a great deal of attention. On the basis of this passage, Nergal and his West Semitic counterpart Reshef have come to be identified as patron deities of the copper industry on Cyprus, and much has been written about the worship of Nergal/Reshef on Cyprus and about the general connection between religion and the Cypriot copper industry. In particular, a remarkable bronze statuette excavated in 1963 by the French at ancient Enkomi and showing a horned god standing on a copper ingot has been identified as Nergal, the protective god of the copper workers.[108]

What the text actually refers to is the "hand of Nergal," a phrase which, in Akkadian, designates some sort of plague or pestilence. Other diseases are designated by such expressions as the "hand of Šamaš," the "hand of Ištar," and even the "hand of a ghost." As the "hand of Nergal" (*qāti Nergal*) is disease, so the "rule of Nergal" (*palē Nergal*) represents annihilation.[109] But such a reference says nothing about the worship of Nergal on Cyprus or anywhere else.

Nor is it clear that the famous statuette is even standing on a copper ingot. The ingot-shaped object may be nothing more than a four-cornered base for the figure. In short, this statuette presents no convincing evidence for a connection between religion and copper metallurgy on Cyprus. But the statuette does raise the problem of the relationship between Cyprus and the well-known "ox-hide" ingots of copper. Such ingots provide our best evidence for a trade in copper during the Late Bronze Age, as they are spread over a wide area from Sicily to Palestine (and even beyond), and they have long been identified with a trade in Cypriot copper.[110]

Yet few such ingots have been found in Cyprus itself. Apart from several miniature ingots with Cypro-Minoan inscriptions,[111] the only such ingots known to come from Cyprus are one now in the British Museum and found at Enkomi (part of the Enkomi Foundry Hoard excavated in 1897) and fragments of an ingot found with the Mathiati Hoard and now in the Cyprus Museum.[112] Other ingots, said to come from Enkomi, actually come from dealers in antiquities. As O. Davies pointed out back in 1930, most of the known examples of these ingots come from Crete, from Haghia Triada, Tylissos, Mochlos, and now Kato Zakro.[113] At least one intact specimen, and perhaps several fragments as well, come from Mycenae on the mainland.[114]

Furthermore all the Cretan examples can be dated to the 15th century B.C. (L.M. [Late Minoan] IB), for which there is very little evidence for Minoan contact with Cyprus or for copperworking on Cyprus itself. Yet this is the period (time of Hatshepsut and Tuthmosis III: 1504–1450 B.C.) when such ingots appear in a number of Egyptian tomb paintings, but there they are carried by men depicted as Minoans and identified in the hieroglyphic inscriptions as being from Keftiu, or Crete.[115]

This strange situation admits of no easy solution, but it does raise some serious questions about Cyprus as *the* source for Late Bronze Age copper. The evidence for foreign trade in this period provides no encouragement. It is now generally accepted that the great quantity of Mycenaean pottery found in Cyprus from 1400 to 1200 B.C. is to be explained in terms of trade, not colonization. The Mycenaeans brought pottery to Cyprus to exchange for Cypriot copper.[116] Thus pottery went east, copper west, and the famous Cape Gelidonya shipwreck, with its load of copper ingots, is usually seen as a ship making its way west with a load of Cypriot copper.[117] The most elaborate version of this also tries to explain why it is that, in the Levant, although Mycenaean and Cypriot pottery are found together, there is always more Cypriot ware:

> The explanation for this seems to be that the best and the bulk of the Mycenaean exports went to Cyprus. The empty cargo space was then loaded with Cypriote goods for onward trading. When these were sold the ship turned with a small cargo for the Aegean and a large cargo for Cyprus. This in turn was off-loaded in Cyprus and a full cargo of copper taken to Greece.[118]

This is very ingenious, but certain questions must be answered. If the Mycenaeans were importing large amounts of copper from Cyprus then what happened to all that copper? As pointed out above there is really not that much surviving bronze from 14th and 13th century Greece. And where did the copper come from before 1400, when there is little evidence for contact with Cyprus? It is true that the Linear B tablets from Knossos, contemporary with the bronze-rich burials mentioned above, do contain references to copper and even have drawings showing the characteristic ox-hide-shaped ingot. Such an ingot came in a basic weight of about 29 kg, that unit of weight being known as a talent (Greek *tálanta*). In Greek the word *talent* also means "pair of scales" and, on the Knossos tablets, the ideogram for the unit of weight of 29 kg is a pair of scales. A gypsum weight from Magazine 15 at Knossos was also found to weigh 29,000 g.[119] As the copper ox-hide ingots from Haghia Triada also average about 29 kg apiece, it is reasonable to assume that they represent a standard unit for shipping copper so that to purchase one ingot would be to purchase a known amount of copper. All very interesting, but it need have nothing to do with Cyprus. Nothing from Crete suggests Cyprus as a source of the *ka-ko* (*chalkós*) recorded in the tablets. The implication is that the copper came from Crete, and that is just what has been suggested by several scholars,[120] but survey has shown that Crete has no real deposits of copper.[121] Cyprus does have major copper deposits, but almost all the evidence for copper smelting in Cyprus comes from after 1400 B.C.

When we turn to the other major Linear B archive, that from Mycenaean Pylos, the situation is even more disturbing. Unlike the Knossos archive, which comes from the first half of the 14th century B.C., the Pylos archive comes from the end of the 13th century, a time when Mycenaean connections with Cyprus were very extensive. Indeed the Pylos archive comes about the time of the Mycenaean colonization of Cyprus and of the Cape Gelidonya shipwreck. Yet one of the outstanding features of the economic situation recorded in the Pylos tablets is the shortage of copper (or bronze). There are plenty of bronzesmiths (*ka-ke-we chalkeús*), perhaps as many as 400 within the boundaries of the kingdom of Pylos, but very little copper to distribute to them.[122] So desperate was the situation that, facing a critical need for weapons to withstand foreign invasion, the officials at Pylos ordered the melting-down of religious dedications made of bronze. This is the "temple-bronze" (*ka-ko-na-wi-jo*) mentioned in the texts.[123] A sample passage reads: "Thus the mayors and superintendants, and vice-mayors and key-bearers and supervisors of figs and hulls, will contribute temple-bronze as points for darts and spears."[124]

This situation certainly reflects the disturbed conditions at the end of the Late Bronze Age and is part of present theories on the transition from bronze to iron to be discussed below. Cyprus was one area with which the Mycenaeans maintained contact and even colonized. Why then was there a shortage of copper at Pylos? We know from excavations on Cyprus, especially at Enkomi and Kition, that the Cypriot copper industry con-

tinued right into the 12th century B.C.[125] Indeed Paul Åström, in his survey
of Late Bronze Age Cyprus, states that the "copper industry was less active
at Enkomi in Late Cypriote IIB than before, but more important in Late
Cypriote IIC at many sites in Cyprus."[126] In Åström's chronology LCIIC
covers the period ca. 1220–1190 B.C., and the Cape Gelidonya shipwreck
comes in the latter part of this period, followed by the destruction of
Pylos. But this does not explain why Pylos should have been so short of
copper in the late 13th century B.C.

This problem is now compounded by recent work on the nature of the
copper deposits on Cyprus itself. It is commonly assumed that copper
metallurgy underwent a technological development through regular
stages, from the use of native copper to melted copper to smelted oxide
and carbonate ores and ultimately to the use of various sulfide ores. (However, see the discussion by Lechtman in chap. 9.) It is also believed that
the exploitation of sulfides did not take place until the Late Bronze Age
so that before that time the copper in use came either from native copper
or from various oxide and carbonate ores. It is now suggested that, because
of the nature of their geological formation, the copper deposits of Cyprus
have always consisted of low grade sulfide ores, such as chalcopyrite,
having no more than 4 percent Cu. As stated by Constantinou and Govett:
"It is clear that the Cyprus deposits are characterized by the overwhelming
presence of copper as a sulphide and the comparative absence of oxides
and the total absence of native copper due to the unique type of weathering
and the reduced degree of secondary enrichment."[127]

Recent work on excavated material relating to copper smelting from
two Cypriot sites, Athienou and Kition, tends to support these geological
observations. What was developed at both sites was a technique, using
the roasting and smelting of first nodules and later lumps of chalcopyrite
ore, to permit the extraction of small prills of metallic copper. But present
evidence indicates that this technology developed only during the course
of the Late Bronze Age.[128] What about references to copper from Alashiya
in texts from the 18th century B.C.? Only further research holds the possibility of an answer to that and to other questions about Cypriot copper.

The evidence does indicate that we should start to think in terms of
Mediterranean sources of copper apart from Cyprus. It is instructive that
Egypt, while obtaining copper from Alashiya, was also conducting its
own copper mining operations at Timna, along the Wadi Arabah in the
Negev. Recent excavations there have uncovered evidence for the ex-

tensive shaft mining of copper during the Nineteenth Dynasty (1308–1194 B.C.). These are the mines once identified as belonging to the time of King Solomon.[129]

The Egyptian evidence relating to copper and copper ingots also raises a question about the manufacture of bronze. It is sometimes argued that the alloy was created by floating charcoal and cassiterite on top of molten copper. The artistic and textual evidence from the Near East, on the other hand, can be explained only in terms of a process that added metallic tin to copper. The Tomb of the Two Sculptors at Thebes shows a metal-working scene with two ingots depicted, a copper ox-hide ingot painted red and a rectangular bluish-gray tin ingot.[130] As G. A. Wainwright points out:

> Two ingots are figured with the scene, which clearly show that the operation was one of making bronze by fusing together metallic copper and metallic tin, and not by smelting a mixture of the ores of these metals.[131]

A similar scene is shown in the tomb of Rekhmire.[132]

This process is supported by the recipes for making bronze contained in many Bronze Age cuneiform texts. The following text from Mari is a good example:[133]

1. $\frac{1}{3}$ MA·NA AN·NA	$\frac{1}{3}$ mina of tin to $2\frac{5}{6}$ minas
2. *a-na* $2\frac{5}{6}$ MA·NA URUDU·LUḪ·ḪA	of washed copper from
3. *te-ma-yu*	Tema(?) has been alloyed
4. *i-na* 8 GÍN·TA·ÀM ba-l[i-e]l	at the ratio of 8 : 1
5. ŠU·NIGÍN 3 MA·NA 10 GÍN ZABAR	Total: 3 minas, 10 shekels
6. *a-na nam-za-qí-im*	of bronze for a key.

Here the proportions are quite exact: 20 shekels of tin is added to 170 shekels of copper (almost 1 : 8) to make exactly 190 shekels of bronze.

This means that there was a fair amount of metallic tin in use during the Late Bronze Age. By ca. 1400 B.C. tin was being used in Greece to cover clay vases destined for the grave, in order to make them look like silver, and to line ivory cosmetic boxes to keep the ivory from being stained by the rouge or ointment placed inside.[134] This extensive use of metallic tin coincides with the extensive production of bronze just before the final destruction of the palace at Knossos.

Transition from Bronze to Iron

This discussion has centered on the Eastern Mediterranean because it is clear that this area holds the key to understanding the transition from the Bronze Age to the Iron Age and the first real use of iron, as a utilitarian metal, what Snodgrass calls stage 3, when iron became the predominant "working" metal.

According to present theories, as elaborated by Snodgrass,[135] it was a shortage of copper and tin, caused by the disruption of the international trade routes at the end of the Late Bronze Age, that made it impossible to go on producing bronze, thus forcing ancient man to find an alternate material. Just as modern man is faced with an energy crisis and must develop alternate sources of energy, so ancient man, in the 12th century B.C., faced a materials crisis that had to be solved. Ancient man met his challenge, as shown by the following chapters of this volume. It remains to be seen if modern man is going to be able to do as well.

The shortage in copper has already been discussed; however it is to be explained it does seem to have taken place. It remains only to take a look at the evidence for the use of tin and iron in the Late Bronze Age. There is very little that can be said about sources of and trade in tin during the Late Bronze Age, for we have no evidence to discuss. Tin was certainly in use, for an enormous amount of tin-bronze exists from this period, and surviving examples must represent a mere fraction of actual production. Tin was also in use as a separate metal and, like copper, was shipped and used in ingot form. But we can only speculate about the sources of that tin.

It is reasonable to assume that the great bronze industry of central Europe, the Únětice Bronze Age, developed through the exploitation of local sources of tin,[136] but there is no real evidence to prove this. The whole question of Bohemian tin, the nature of the deposits and how and when they were exploited, demands future investigation. For the Aegean world, that of Minoan Crete and Mycenaean Greece, the situation is much worse because there are no local tin deposits. I have suggested Cornwall as a possible source of Aegean tin, more out of desperation than conviction; others have suggested Iberia, Italy, or even Troad. It is even possible that tin was coming from the east through Ugarit.[137]

What is surprising is the number of references to tin in Middle Assyrian

texts from Assur and Nuzi. Tin was lent at interest, court fines were paid
in tin, and the value of goods was even given in terms of tin.[138] There
is no indication as to the source of this tin, but it must be realized that this
is a tradition that goes back to the very beginning of Assyrian history
because in the middle of the 20th century B.C., King Erishum I proclaimed

> a remission of debts payable in silver, gold, copper, tin, barley, wool,
> down to chaff[139]

More colorful is the passage in the Middle Assyrian law code describing
the fate of the man unable to prove his accusation of adultery:

> They shall beat him forty times with rods, he shall do a full month
> of forced labor for the king, they shall cut off his beard, (and) he shall
> pay one talent of tin.[140]

According to ratios given in the texts tin was very cheap, as high as
240 : 1 and 180 : 1 in a tin/silver ratio. What is curious is that bronze was
twice as expensive as tin, for a text says of a payment that

> if (paid) in tin (it should be) at the ratio of four minas (of tin) per
> (shekel of silver), if in bronze at the rate of two minas.[141]

This seems to indicate a great increase in the amount of tin in circulation
during the period 1500–1300 B.C. It would be interesting if this could be
connected to the great increase in the amount of Aegean bronze in the
late 15th century B.C. Tin was actually used to make bronze, apart from
its role in the courts and the marketplace. One text even refers to an alloy
(Akkadian *billatu*) composed of 1 mina of copper and 8½ shekels of tin,
giving a ratio of 7 : 1.[142] In the Old Assyrian period one text gives a ratio
of 8 : 1 (4 minas of copper, ½ mina of tin, the metal being destined for the
smith, Akkadian *nappāḫum*).[143]

An Egyptian text from the Late New Kingdom refers to ingots of
copper and bars of tin being brought as presents to the pharaoh "on the
neck of the children of Alashiya," again showing that the metals themselves were being shipped.[144] Now Cyprus certainly has no tin, so this
reference can only mean that tin came to Egypt through Cyprus. Such
a possibility is of great interest in light of the discovery of two ingots of
pure tin, bearing incised signs in the Cypro-Minoan syllabary, from the
harbor of Haifa, Israel.[145] These ingots could represent part of the cargo
of a ship sailing south from Cyprus. The tin, for some reason, passed
through Cyprus and there it was marked with Cypro-Minoan signs. This

suggests that Cyprus was a shipping point on the tin route and perhaps served a similar function with copper as well, and gives us some idea of the international trade routes interrupted at the end of the Late Bronze Age.

Such was the world of the copper and tin trade and the development of a bronze metallurgy during the course of the second millennium B.C. The evidence indicates a far-flung network of trade routes, with considerable fluctuation in supply and therefore in the price of copper and tin. The other metals were also in use, especially silver and gold, as well as lead and even an occasional piece of iron. This is not the place to discuss the surviving iron objects from the Bronze Age for that is done in chapter 3 by Jane Waldbaum.

The important thing to realize is what those objects represent in terms of Bronze Age history and technology. The Homeric poems, although probably first written down in the 8th century B.C.,[146] indicate that what is for us the Age of Bronze was so regarded by the ancient Greeks as well. The Heroic Age, the time of the Trojan War and before, was a world of bronze, and iron had no place in it. Iron was a gray metal, expensive and difficult to work. As such it was deemed fit to be awarded as a prize in athletic competitions, along with tripods, cauldrons, gold, and women.[147] So Homer describes the competition organized by Achilleus at the funeral games in honor of his dead friend Patroklos:

> Now the son of Peleus set in place a lump of pig-iron,
> which had once been the throwing-weight of Eëtion
>   in his great strength:
> but now swift-footed brilliant Achilleus had
>   slain him and taken
> the weight away in the ships along with the other
>   possessions.
> He stood upright and spoke his word out
>   among the Argives:
> "Rise up, you who would endeavor to win this prize also.
> For although the rich demesnes of him who wins it lie far off
> indeed, yet for the succession of five years he will not
>   have to go in
> to the city for it, nor his ploughman either.
>   This will supply them."[148]

This was the Age of Bronze, when weapons and armor were properly made of bronze and tin itself was used to decorate chariots and armor, described as overlaid with gold and tin.[149] Iron must have been used at least for ploughshares, as Homer indicates.

Homer is quite consistent in his use of bronze and iron. There can be no doubt that iron, like Dorians and Ionians, was not considered to belong in the Bronze Age. Only in his similes, generally thought to reflect the world of Homer's own time, the world of the Early Iron Age, does Homer refer to the use of iron in a practical way. Whereas the narrative of Homer mentions bronze, the imagery of Homer reflects the world of iron. The images come from scenes that the poet himself had seen, not from the formulaic tradition of oral poetry.

All contemporary evidence from the Bronze Age itself supports this interpretation of the role of iron. As a metal iron had been around for a long time, as shown by several authors in this volume, but it served no useful purpose, no utilitarian role. Iron was a curiosity and there was no incentive to make it anything else. The surviving artifacts of iron to be dated before 1200 B.C. support this conclusion, as do the textual references to iron. Texts from Susa,[150] Mari,[151] Alalakh,[152] Qatna,[153] and El-Amarna[154] all refer to the use of iron, but only for rings, pieces of jewelry, and ceremonial weapons decorated with precious metals and semiprecious stones.[155] A curious exception is a text from Nuzi that refers to a coat of scale armor for a horse with scales made of iron.[156]

There are many references to iron in Hittite texts but again as a semi-precious metal confined to ceremonial and ritual use. Thus a text records a collection of one type of object (identity unknown) made of different materials: iron, lapis lazuli, carnelian, and rock crystal.[157] It is important to realize that, although there are many references to iron in Hittite texts, there is no evidence that the Hittites had a monopoly on the production of iron. This common misconception is really based upon one Hittite text, the famous "Iron Letter", which states only that the Hittites were smelting iron in Cilicia and that the Assyrian king wished to receive some iron as a present.[158] Yet the number of references to iron in Hittite texts must indicate a significant predominance in the use of iron in 2 millennium B.C. Anatolia.

It follows that, as the Hittites had no monopoly on the production of iron, they did not pass it on to the Philistines. Again we are dealing with a theory based upon one text, for the idea of a Philistine iron monopoly is based upon the reference, in 1 Samuel 13 : 19–21, to there being no smith in the land of the Israelites. This along with the archaeological evidence, does indicate some degree of control in the actual working of iron.[159]

On the basis of the present evidence it does seem that iron technology developed in the Near East, perhaps even in the Levant, and spread from there across Cyprus to the Aegean. The magnificent ax from Ugarit,[160] with its blade of iron set in a mounting of bronze decorated with gold, is an example of Levantine work in iron and an actual example of the sort of object described in the inventory texts from Qatna and the Amarna letters that record the gifts sent to Pharaoh by Tušratta, king of Mitanni. Recent work on early iron objects from Palestine shows how this technology developed after 1200 B.C.[161] From Cyprus comes one of the earliest examples of quench-hardened steel, showing that by 1000 B.C. it was possible to produce a steel blade superior to anything that could be done with tin-bronze.[162]

From Cyprus, ironworking seems to have spread to the Aegean, where finds from the Kerameikos and Agora of Athens show how iron technology developed, again after 1200. The areas of the Aegean world that have produced early objects of iron, such as Attica, Crete, Naxos, and Rhodes, are areas that maintained contact with the Levant and the Near East following the general collapse of Mycenaean civilization around 1200 B.C. The development of iron technology in the Aegean is well documented by Anthony Snodgrass in chapter 10. I would like only to emphasize how much his work has changed our evaluation of the role of the Aegean in the general development of iron metallurgy.[163] Before his work everyone accepted the explanation that iron was introduced into the Aegean from the north, being brought by European (Dorian, Nordic, or Aryan) invaders at the end of the Late Bronze Age. Snodgrass has shown that, in fact, Europe lagged behind the Aegean and that the Hallstatt Iron Age was several hundred years behind comparable developments in Greece.

There is much to be learned about ancient crafts and craftsmen from the surviving literature. The famous simile on the quenching of iron in the ninth book of the *Odyssey* was certainly written by someone who had watched the process and understood what it was all about. The description comes in the narration of the blinding of the cyclops Polyphemos as Odysseus and his men, after getting the giant drunk on wine, plunge a glowing stake of olive wood into the socket of his single eye:

The blast and scorch of the burning ball
    singed all his eyebrows
and eyelids, and the fire made the roots
    of his eye crackle.
As when a man who works as a blacksmith
    plunges a screaming
great ax blade or adze into cold water,
    treating it
for temper, since this is the way steel
    is made strong, even
so Cyclops' eye sizzled about the beam
    of the olive.[164]

There are two important phrases in this passage, both difficult to translate, that show well the state of technology current when it was written.

The words "treating it for temper" represent an attempt to translate the word *pharmassōn*, used only here in all of Homer. Related to English words like pharmacy it seems to imply that the iron was being treated in some magical way, by means of drugs. Also, a literal translation of line 393 would be "for it [the quenching], contrary to expectation, makes the strength of iron, at least."[165] Homer here seems to be puzzled by the discovery that, while most things turn soft in water or even dissolve, iron seems to harden. All this indicates that the *Odyssey* passage comes from a period when the quench-hardening of steel was just being introduced into Greece and the whole process was still quite new and very mysterious.

It is essential to point out the fact, obvious to every metallurgist, that quenching in cold water hardens only carburized iron or steel. Quenching would have no effect on wrought iron. Because Homer specifies that this was done in order to harden the iron, he can be talking only about carburized iron or steel. This is not to say that Homer, or anyone else in antiquity, understood the role of carbon in the formation of steel. The true role of carbon was not discovered until 1786. It took a long time even to recognize that steel was an alloy, as Cyril Smith has pointed out: "The fact that steel was also an alloy was not so clear; indeed, it was not definitely accepted until the very end of the eighteenth century A.D., 3000 years after the practical discovery."[166] This places the discovery of carburization around 1200 B.C., a date supported by present archaeological and metallurgical evidence. The ancient blacksmith must have come to realize that holding a piece of iron in the fire in contact with charcoal over a prolonged period of time produced a superior metal, even though he thought only that the fire somehow "purified" the iron.

Once ancient man had been forced to develop the technology necessary to making iron a utilitarian metal and, in terms of hardness and durability, one even superior to bronze, the production and use of iron spread very quickly. Because almost every country had local deposits of iron ore, the metal could be produced everywhere and at a cost greatly reduced from that of bronze.[167] By the 7th century the Greek world was actually making use of an iron currency, as spits of iron, each weighing about 2 kg, were in circulation as a form of currency in southern Greece. Six iron spits equaled one drachma, and *drachma* became, and still is, the word for the basic unit of currency in Greece. When silver coinage was introduced, at the end of the 7th century B.C., a drachma coin contained 6 g of silver. Thus 12 kg of iron equaled 6 g of silver, giving an iron/silver ratio of 2000 : 1.[168] In the 19th century B.C. the iron/silver ratio was 1 : 40. The change represents *The Coming of the Age of Iron*.

Notes

The following abbreviations are used for the most frequently cited publications.

AAA	*Athens Annals of Archaeology*
AASOR	*Annual of the American Schools of Oriental Research*
AJA	*American Journal of Archaeology*
Anat. St.	*Anatolian Studies*
ARMT	*Archives royales de Mari. Transcriptions et traductions.*
Ar. Or.	*Archiv Orientální*
BA	*The Biblical Archaeologist*
BIN	*Babylonian Inscriptions in the Collection of J. B. Nies*, Yale University.
BSA	*Annual of the British School of Archaeology in Athens*
CAD	*Chicago Assyrian Dictionary*
CCT	*Cuneiform Texts from Cappadocian Tablets in the British Museum*
CRAI	*Comptes Rendus de l'Académie des Inscriptions et Belles Lettres*
EA	Number of Amarna letter in edition by J. A. Knudtzon, *Die El-Amarna Tafeln*, 2 vols., Leipzig, 1915.
HSS	Harvard Semitic Studies
ICK	*Inscriptions cunéiformes du Kültépé*
IEJ	*Israel Exploration Journal*
JAOS	*Journal of the American Oriental Society*

JCS   *Journal of Cuneiform Studies*
JESHO   *Journal of the Economic and Social History of the Orient*
JFA   *Journal of Field Archaeology*
JHS   *Journal of Hellenic Studies*
JNES   *Journal of Near Eastern Studies*
KBo   *Keilschrifttexte aus Boghazköi*
RA   *Revue d'Assyriologie et d'Archéologie orientale*
RDAC   *Report of the Department of Antiquities of Cyprus*
SAM   *Studien zu den Anfängen der Metallurgie*
SCE   *Swedish Cyprus Expedition*
SIMA   *Studies in Mediterranean Archaeology*
TCL   *Textes cunéiformes du Louvre*
TCS   *Texts from Cuneiform Sources*
UET   *Ur Excavation Texts*

1. C. Davaras, "Early Minoan Jewellery from Mochlos," *BSA* 70 (1975): 101–14, p. 107 f. In general see P. Faure, "Le problème du minerai d'argent dans la Crète antique," *Acta of the Third International Congress of Cretological Studies*, vol. 1, Athens, 1973, 70–83; K. Branigan, "Silver and Lead in Prepalatial Crete," *AJA* 72 (1968): 219–22. For lead see also H. G. Buchholz, "Das Blei in der mykenischen Kultur und in der Bronzezeitlichen Metallurgie Zyperns," *Jahrbuch des deutschen archäologischen. Instituts* 87 (1972): 1–59. For evidence of lead smelting, with finds of litharge, in Middle Helladic Thorikos see H. Mussche, "Recent Excavations in Thorikos," *Acta Classica* 13 (1970): 125–36 (and D. G. Mitten, *AJA* 77 [1973]: 95).

2. K. Branigan, *Aegean Metalwork of the Early and Middle Bronze Age* (Oxford: Oxford University Press, 1974), pp. 71–76.

3. See the analytical tables in H. Z. Koşay and M. Akok, *Ausgrabungen von Alaca Höyük. Vorbericht über die Forschungen und Entdeckungen von 1940–1948*, Ankara, 1966. For Horoztepe see T. Özgüç, "New Finds from Horoztepe," *Anatolia* 8 (1964): 1–25 (with table of 30 spectrographic analyses).

4. E. R. Eaton and H. McKerrell, "Near Eastern Alloying and Some Textual Evidence for the Early Use of Arsenical Copper," *World Archaeology* 8 (1976): 169–91, p. 183 f.

5. C. S. Smith, "An examination of the Arsenic-rich Coating on a Bronze Bull from Horoztepe," in *Application of Science in the Examination of Works of Art.* ed. W. J. Young (Boston: Fine Arts Museum, 1973), pp. 96–102.

6. Ewer illustrated and described as being plated with antimony in *Encyclopaedia Britannica*, vol. 15, s.v. "Metalwork, Decorative," p. 246 and plate I. Colin G. Fink and Arthur H. Kupp, "Ancient Egyptian Antimony Plating on Copper Objects: A Rediscovered Ancient Egyption Craft," *Metropolitan Museum Studies* 4, Pt. 2 (March 1933): 163–67.

7. C. S. Smith, "Art, Technology, and Science: Notes on their Historical Interaction," *Technology and Culture* 11 (1970): 493–549, p. 499.

8. This is based upon the assumption that Europe remained without any written history or native system of writing until contact with the Greco-Roman world. Some believe in an Old European Linear Script, in existence in the 6th millennium B.C. (cf. M.

Gimbutas, *The Gods and Goddesses of Old Europe, 7000–3500 B.C.* [Berkeley: University of California Press, 1974], pp. 85–88). I do not believe that the identified signs represent any real system of writing and, again, they certainly led nowhere. This is not the place to discuss the problems raised by the Tartaria tablets; the date of that material is still much in question.

9. For Malta see C. Renfrew, *Before Civilization* (London: J. Cape, 1973), pp. 147–66, and "Malta and the Calibrated Radiocarbon Chronology," *Antiquity* 46 (1972): 141–45. For the monuments see J. D. Evans, *Prehistoric Antiquities of the Maltese Islands* (London: Athlone, 1971), and D. H. Trump, *Malta: An Archaeological Guide* (London: Faber, 1972).

10. For recent finds see H. Weiss and T. Cuyler Young, Jr., "The Merchants of Susa: Godin V and Plateau-Lowland Relations in the Late Fourth Millennium B.C.," *Iran* 13 (1975): 1–17; W. Sumner, "Excavations at Tall-i Malyan (Anshan)," *Iran* 14 (1976): 103–15; and C. C. Lamberg-Karlovsky, "Urban Interaction on the Iranian Plateau: Excavations at Tepe Yahya, 1967–1973," *Proceedings of the British, Academy* 54 (1973): 1–43 (pagination of separate reprint).

11. There is already a considerable bibliography on the finds at Tell Mardikh, with its archive of more than 15,000 tablets. For the present see P. Matthiae, "Ebla in the Late Early Syrian Period: The Royal Palace and the State Archives," *BA* 39 (1976): 94–113; "Ébla à l'époque d'Akkad: archéologie et histoire," *CRAI* (1976): 190–215; "Le palais royal et les archives d'etat d'Ébla protosyrienne," *Akkadica* 2 (1977): 2–19; and "Le palais royal protosyrien d'Ébla," *CRAI* (1977): 148–72.

12. G. A. Johnson, *Local Exchange and Early State Development in Southwestern Iran* (Ann Arbor: University of Michigan, 1973), Museum of Anthropology, Paper no. 51, and H. T. Wright and G. A. Johnson, "Population, Exchange, and Early State Formation in Southwestern Iran," *American Anthropologist* 77 (1975): 267–89. Also the papers published in B. Spooner, ed., *Population Growth: Anthropological Implications* (Cambridge, Mass.: MIT Press, 1972), and E. R. Service, *Origins of the State and Civilization: The Process of Cultural Evolution* (New York: Norton, 1975).

13. E. R. Eaton and H. McKerrell, *World Archaeology* 8 (1976): 179 f.

14. H. Otto and W. Witter, *Handbuch der ältesten vorgeschichtlichen Metallurgie in Mitteleuropa* (Leipzig: J. A. Barth 1952), p. 44, and H. McKerrell, "The Use of Tin-Bronze in Britain and the Comparative Relationship with the Near East," in *The Search for Ancient Tin* (Washington D.C.: Smithsonian Institution Press, 1978), pp. 7–24, p. 19 (but I cannot accept the Near Eastern example from Gordion cited by McKerrell as it represents something entirely different.)

15. Cf. W. Lorenzen, *Helgoland und das früheste kupfer des Nordens* (Ottendorf: Niederelbe-Verlag 1965), pp. 16–28.

16. Contra E. Sangmeister, "Aufkommen der arsenbronze in SO-Europa," in *Actes du VIIIe Congrèss internationale des sciences préhistoriques et protohistoriques* (Belgrade, 1971), vol. 1, 109–129. For a balanced view see H. H. Coghlan, "Some Reflections on the Prehistoric Working of Copper and Bronze," *Archaeologia Austriaca* 52 (1972): 93–104; I. R. Selimkhanov, *Enträtselte Geheimnisse der alten Bronzen* (Berlin, 1974), p. 47 f.; J. A. Charles, "Early Arsenical Bronzes—A Metallurgical View," *AJA* 71 (1967): 21–26; and idem, "Arsenic and Old Bronze: Excursions into the Metallurgy of Prehistory," *Chemistry and Industry*, June 15, 1974, pp. 470–74.

17. See discussion in J. D. Muhly, *Copper and Tin* (Hamden, Conn.: Archon, 1973) (Transactions of Connecticut Academy of Arts and Sciences, vol. 43), p. 284 f. (with notes).

18. For the Beaker Folk see H. N. Savory, *Spain and Portugal: The Prehistory of the Iberian Peninsula* (London: Thames & Hudson, 1968), pp. 183–89. The classic discussion of the torque bearers is by C. F. A. Schaeffer, in *Ugaritica II* (Paris: Geuthner, 1949), pp. 49–120. See also M. Gimbutas, *Bronze Age Cultures in Central and Eastern Europe* (The Hague: Mouton, 1965), p. 32 f. In general see S. Piggott, *Ancient Europe* (Chicago: Aldine, 1965), pp. 77 f., 102 f. The most extreme example of this point of view is by P.W. Lapp, *The Dhahr Mirzbáneh Tombs: Three Intermediate Bronze Age Cemeteries in Jordan* (Jerusalem, 1966), pp. 86–116 (see review by M. J. Mellink, *Journal of Biblical Literature* 86 [1967]: 337–38). For the assumed connection between Khirbet Kerak pottery and metallurgy see J. B. Hennessy, *The Foreign Relations of Palestine during the Early Bronze Age* (London: Quaritch, 1967), pp. 75, 88, 116 n. 22.

19. B. Blance, *Die Anfänge der Metallurgie auf der Iberischen Halbinsel* (Berlin: Gebr. Mann, 1971) (SAM 4), pp. 89–102, 156 f., and L. Aitchison, *A History of Metals*, 2 vols. (New York: Interscience, 1960), vol. 1 pp. 49–75 ("Traders from Troy").

20. C. Renfrew and R. Whitehouse, "The Copper Age of Peninsular Italy and the Aegean," *BSA* 69 (1974): 343–90, p. 381.

21. Cf. G. Barker, "The First Metallurgy in Italy in the Light of the Metal Analyses from the Pigorini Museum," *Bollettino de Paletnologia Italiana* 80 (1971): 183–212 (with metallurgical appendix by E. Slater). For early metal finds in the western Mediterranean see P. Phillips, *Early Farmers of West Mediterranean Europe* (London: Hutchinson, 1975), pp. 114, 120, 125 f., 145, and J. Guilaine, *Premiers bergers et paysans de l'Occident méditerranéen* (The Hague: Mouton, 1976) (Civilisations et Sociétés, 58), pp. 177–80, 197, 206 f.

22. C. Renfrew and R. Whitehouse, *BSA* 69 (1974): p. 168 f., The theory of Cretan connections is defended by K. Branigan, "The Round Graves of Levkas Reconsidered," *BSA* 70 (1975): 37–49.

23. E. R. Eaton, "Eneolithic Blades from Buccino (Salerno)," *Bollettino del Centro Camuno di Studi Preistorici* 10 (1973): 89–100, p. 98. See also H. McKerrell and E. R. Eaton, in "Buccino: The Early Bronze Age Village of Tufariello," ed. R. Ross Holloway et al., *JFA* 2 (1975): 11–81, p. 77 f. (true tin-bronze ca. 2000 B.C.).

24. R. J. Harrison, "A Reconsideration of the Iberian Background to Beaker Metallurgy," *Paleohistoria* 16 (1974): 63–105. For the Beaker problem itself see R. J. Harrison, "Origins of the Bell Beaker Cultures: Some Speculations," *Antiquity* 48 (1974): 99–109, and R. Harrison, S. Quero, and C. Priego, "Beaker Metallurgy in Spain," *Antiquity* 49 (1975): 273–78. See also R. J. Harrison, *The Bell Beaker Cultures of Spain and Portugal*, to be published as a Bulletin of the American School of Prehistoric Research.

25. For a critical evaluation of the "Colony" theory see A. Gilman, "Bronze Age Dynamics in Southeast Spain," *Dialectical Anthropology* 1 (1976): 307–19. The current reaction against the "Colony" hypothesis began with C. Renfrew, "Colonialism and Megalithismus," *Antiquity* 41 (1967): 276–88. It should be pointed out that there still are those who accept the hypothesis (cf. J. Yakar, "Hittite Involvement in Western Anatolia," *Anat. St.* 26 [1976]: 117–28, p. 123) and who even believe that specific identifications can be made. Thus Beatrice Blance believes that the settlers at Mesas de Asta (Roman Asta Regia) came from Tigani on the island of Samos, on the basis of parallels in the

pattern-burnished were found at both sites (*SAM* 4, pp. 65 f., 100 f.). The Trojan connections of the Gaudo culture in southern Italy are discussed by R. Ross Holloway, "Gaudo and the East," *JFA* 3 (1976): 143–58.

26. See J. D. Muhly, *Supplement to Copper and Tin* (Hamden, Conn.: Archon, 1976) (Trans. Conn. Acad. of Arts and Sciences, vol. 46), p. 102 f, and *JNES* 36 (1977): 156. A report on the 1976 expedition to the Eastern Desert to examine these deposits, by El-Ramly, Muhly, Rapp, and Wertime, will appear in a forthcoming number of *Expedition*.

27. Pepi II reigned for a total of 94 years, covering most of the 23d century B.C. The inscriptions from El Mueilha are to be published by Dr. Lanny Bell of the University Museum, University of Pennsylvania. A preliminary report will appear as part of the publication mentioned in n. 69. Cf. T. A. Wertime, "Tin and the Egyptian Bronze Age," in *Immortal Egypt*, ed. D. Schmandt-Besserat (Malibu, Calif.: Undena, 1978), pp. 37–42.

28. For the gold mines at Baramiyah see W, F. Hume, *Geology of Egypt* (Cairo: Government Press, 1937), vol. 2, pt. 3, p. 736 f. For ancient references to the mines see A. Eggebrecht, "Baramije," in *Lexikon der Agyptologie*, ed. W. Helck and E. Otto (Wiesbaden: Harrassowitz, 1973), p. 627. The area was known to the ancient Egyptians as $\underline{d}$ *w* $\underline{db}$3, "mountain of Edfu."

29. For the Hammāmāt inscriptions see G. Goyon, *Nouvelles inscriptions rupestres du Wadi Hammamat* (Paris: Adrien Maisonneuve, 1957) (and reviews by W. Helck, *Orientalistische Literaturzeitung* 54 [1959]: 17–21, and W. K. Simpson, *JNES* 18 [1959]: 20–37). For a survey of work on Old Kingdom inscriptions see H. Goedicke, "Hieroglyphic Inscriptions of the Old Kingdom," in *Textes et Langages de l'Égypte pharaonique (Hommage a Jean-François Champollion)*, Cairo, n.d. (Institut français d'archéologie orientale du Caire, Bibliothèque d'Étude, LXIV/2), vol. 64, pt. 2, pp. 15–24.

30. R. Hestrin and M. Tadmor, *IEJ* 13 (1963): 287 n. 60.

31. B. Landsberger, "Tin and Lead: The Adventures of Two Vocables," *JNES* 24 (1965): 285–96, p. 293. For tin in southeast Asia see K. F. G. Hosking, "The Primary Tin Deposits of South East Asia," *Minerals Science and Engineering*, Oct. 1970, pp. 24–50.

32. T. S. Wheeler and R. Maddin, "The Techniques of the Early Thai Metalsmith," *Expedition* 18, no. 4 (1976): 38–47, esp. 38, and D. T. Bayard, "Early Thai Bronze Analysis and New Data," *Science* 176 (1972): 1411–12.

33. C. Gorman and P. Charoenwongsa, "Ban Chiang: A Mosaic of Impressions from the First Two Years," *Expedition* 18, no. 4 (1976): 14–26; D. T. Bayard, "Excavation at Non Nok Tha, Northeastern Thailand, 1968," *Asian Perspectives* 13 (1970, publ. 1972): 109–43. On the question of early plant domestication see C. F. Gorman, "Modèles a priori et préhistoire de la Thailande. A propos des débuts de l'agriculture en Asie du Sud-Est," *Études Rurales* 53–56 (1974): 41–71, and R. D. Hill, "On the Origins of Domesticated Rice," *Journal of Oriental Studies* (Hong Kong) 14 (1976): 35–44.

34. For a summary of recent work see R. Maddin, T. S. Wheeler, and J. D. Muhly, "Tin in the Ancient Near East: Old Questions and New Finds," *Expedition* 19, no. 2 (1977): 35–47. See also J. Maréchal, "Le problème de l'étain dans l'Antiquité," *Archéologia* 52 (1972): 62–66, and H. E. Crawford, "The Problem of Tin in Mesopotamian Bronzes," *World Archaeology* 6 (1974): 242–47; J. D. Muhly, "New Evidence for Sources of and Trade in Bronze Age Tin," in *The Search for Ancient Tin* (Washington, D.C.: Smithsonian Institution Press, 1978), pp. 43–48.

58   JAMES D. MUHLY

35. This is being done in a program at the University of Minnesota conducted by George Rapp.

36. For the Stuttgart program of metallurgical analysis see J. D. Muhly, "The Copper Ox-hide Ingots and the Bronze Age Metals Trade," *Iraq* 39 (1977): 73–82. Also H. W. Catling, *Cypriot Bronzework in the Mycenaean World* (Oxford: Oxford University Press, 1964, p. 12 f. For the lack of reliability in analyses see W. T. Chase, "Comparative Analysis of Archaeological Bronzes," in *Archaeological Chemistry* (Washington, D.C.: American Chemical Society, 1974), pp. 148–85. For attempts to identify the type of ore used through analysis of artifacts see R. Bowman et al., "A Statistical Study of the Impurity Occurrences in Copper Ores and Their Relationship to Ore Types," *Archaeometry* 17 (1975): 157–63. In general see R. F. Tylecote, "The Composition of Metal Artifacts: a Guide to Provenance?" *Antiquity* 44 (1970): 19–25; H. Härke, "Probleme der optischen Emissionsspektralanalyse in der Urgeschichtsforschung," *Prähistorische Zeitschrift* 53 (1978): 165–276.

37. See C. S. Smith, "The Interpretation of Microstructures of Metallic Artifacts," in *Application of Science in Examination of Works of Art* (Boston: Fine Arts museum, 1965), pp. 20–52.

38. Recent summaries by P. Garelli, *Les Assyriens en Cappadoce* (Paris: Adrien Maisonneuve, 1963), and K. R. Veenhof, *Aspects of Old Assyrian Trade and its Terminology* (Leiden: Brill, 1972).

39. M. T. Larsen, *Old Assyrian Caravan Procedures* (Istanbul: Nederlands Historisch-Archaeologisch Instituut in het Nabije Oosten, 1967).

40. See text (Tablets in the Collections of the Staatliche Museen, Berlin [*VAT* 9249]) quoted by M. T. Larsen, *The Old Assyrian City-State and its Colonies* (Copenhagen: Akademisk Forlag, 1976), p. 87 f, n. 8. See also Veenhof, *Aspects of Old Assyrian Trade*, pp. 98–103. This text records the "Akkadians" (i.e., the Babylonians) coming to the "City" (i.e., Assur) to sell their garments (see also *CAD*, s.v. *Akkadû*, 273a). In a number of texts (such as *CCT* IV 29b, *BIN* IV 4, *CCT* IV 11a, and *TCL* XIX 26) garments are described as being *ša Akkedê*, "after the fashion of the Akkadians" (see texts cited in *CAD*, s.v. *abarniu*, 35b; *Akkadû*, 273a).

41. Larsen, *Old Assyrian City-State*, p. 90.

42. Muhly, *Copper and Tin*, p. 246, 411 n. 78. See also the Middle Assyrian text *Keilschrifttexte aus Assur juridischen Inhahlts* 274 (cited in *CAD*, s.v. *gurru*, 140b).

43. A. Leo Oppenheim, *Trade in the Ancient Near East* (Moscow, 1970) Fifth International Congress of Economic History), p. 17, and Veenhof, *Aspects of Old Assyrian Trade*, p. 399 f. See also R. Mc. Adams, "Anthropological Perspectives on Ancient Trade," *Current Anthropology* 15 (1974): 239–58.

44. See figures recording purchase and sale prices compiled by Garelli, *Assyriens*, p. 280.

45. See text *TCL* XIX 24 (quoted by *CAD*, s.v. *awû*, 524a).

46. As in *BIN* IV 19 and *TCL* IV 26 (both cited in *CAD*, s.v. *batāqu*, 163b).

47. See the text *TCL* IV 29 (quoted in *CAD*, s.v. *bašû*, 146b, *batqu*, 166b).

48. As in text *TCL* IV 17 (quoted in *CAD*, s.v. *batāqu*, 162b).

49. See T. Özgüç, "Die Grabungen von 1953 in Kültepe," *Belleten* 18 (1954): 373–90, p. 388 f., and "Report on a Work-Shop Belonging to the Late Phase of the Colony Period (Ib)," *Belleten* 19 (1955): 77–80.

50. H. Z. Koşay, *Les fouilles d'Alaca Höyük* (Ankara, 1951) (*Türk Tarih Kurumu Yayinlarindan*, V/5), p. 167 and plate 182, and "A Great Discovery," *Illustrated London News*, July 21, 1945, pp. 78–81, 78 f.

51. T. A. Wertime, *Science* 182 (1973): 885. To the list of EBA iron objects from Anatolia given by J. Waldbaum (*From Bronze to Iron* [Göteborg: Paul Åströms Förlag, 1978] [SIMA LIV] p. 19 f.) add the iron dagger from tomb C (D. Stronach, "The Development and Diffusion of Metal Types in Early Bronze Age Anatolia," *Anat. St.* 7 [1957]: 89–125, p. 102).

52. B. Landsberger, "Kommt Ḫattum 'Hettiterland' und Ḫattī'um 'Hettiter' in den Kültepe-Tafeln vor?" *Ar. Or.* 18, no. 1 (1950): 329–50, p. 331 f., and Garelli, *Assyriens*, p. 274 f.

53. R. Maxwell-Hyslop, "The Metals *Amūtu* and *Aši'u* in the Kültepe Texts," *Anat. St.* 22 (1972): 159–62.

54. Text is *CCT* IV 4a, discussed in ibid., and *CAD*, s.v. *amūtu*, 97b–98a. See also J. K. Bjorkman, *Meteors and Meteorites in the Ancient Near East* (Tempe, Ariz.: 1973) (Center for Meteorite Studies, Publ. no. 12), p. 112.

55. *BIN* VI 28 (35:1); J. Lewy, *Die altassyrischen Texte vom Kültepe bei Kaisarije* (Constantinople, 1926), 39a (40:1). According to the texts a ring of *amūtum* was worth 10 shekels of silver, another 15 shekels (see references cited in *CAD*, s.v. *annuqu*, 142).

56. All such references seem to be to *aši'um*. For this problem see below. There are also references to searching the country for *aši'um* and also requests from Assur to write if any *aši'um* becomes available (as in *BIN* IV 45).

57. Text is *ICK* I 55 (quoted in *CAD*, s.v. *amūtu*, 98a).

58. Text is *TCL* IV 39 (quoted in *CAD*, s.v. *irbu*, 175a).

59. Text is *CCT* II 43 (quoted in *CAD*, s.v. *aši'u*, 441b; *ebar*, 1b).

60. Text is B. Kienast, *Die altassyrischen Texte des Orientalischen Seminars der Universität Heidelberg und der Sammlung Erlenmeyer* (Berlin, 1960), 62 (discussed by Larsen, *Old Assyrian City-State*, p. 198 and n. 29). See also K. K. Riemschneider, "Prison and Punishment in Early Anatolia," *JESHO* 20 (1977): 114–26, p. 115; Veenhof, *Aspects of Old Assyrian Trade*, p. 307 f.; and M. T. Larsen, "The Old Assyrian Colonies in Anatolia," *JAOS* 94 (1974): 468–75, p. 474 f.

61. Larsen, *Old Assyrian City-State*, p. 199 n. 35.

62. Text is *ICK* II 54 (quoted in ibid., p. 91 f.).

63. Ibid., p. 92.

64. As, for example, the text *BIN* IV 45 (quoted in *CAD*, s.v. *aši'u*, 441b). For general discussion see H. Limet, "Les origines du travail du fer en Mesopotamie ancienne," *Présences* 92 (1976): 3–16, esp. p. 7 f.

65. See lists of early iron objects in H. G. Buchholz and V. Karageorghis, *Prehistoric Greece and Cyprus* (London: Phaidon, 1973), p. 27 f.; Waldbaum, *From Bronze to Iron*, pp. 18–19.

66. V. Karageorghis, *Excavations at Kition*, I. *The Tombs*, 2 vols. (Nicosia: Department of Antiquities, 1974), p. 62 f.

67. I. E. S. Edwards, *The Treasures of Tutankhamun* (New York: Metropolitan Museum of Art, 1972), no. 36., and H. Carter, *The Tomb of Tutankhamen* (New York, 1972), p. 154 f.

68. T. Özgüç, "Early Anatolian Archaeology in the Light of Recent Research,"

Anatolia 7 (1963): 1–21; L. L. Orlin, *Assyrian Colonies in Cappadocia* (The Hague: Mouton, 199–247); and J. G. Macqueen, *The Hittites and their Contemporaries in Asia Minor* (London: Thames & Hudson, 1975), p. 29 f.

69. M. T. Larsen, "The City and its King: on the Assyrian Notion of Kingship," in *Le palais et la royauté (archéologie et civilisation)* (Paris: Geuthner, 1974) (XIXe Rencontre Assyriologique Internationale), pp. 285–300, esp. p. 286 f.

70. For a survey of work at Mari see A. Malamat, "Mari," *BA* 34 (1971): 2–22, and J.-R. Kupper, *La civilisation de Mari* (Paris: Les Belles Lettres, 1967) (XVe Rencontre Assyriologique Internationale).

71. J. M. Sasson, "A Sketch of North Syrian Economic Relations in the Middle Bronze Age," *JESHO* 9 (1966): 161–81, p. 164 f.; A. Malamat, "Northern Canaan and the Mari Texts," in *Near Eastern Archaeology in the Twentieth Century: Festschrift Nelson Glueck* (New York: Doubleday, 1970), 164–77, p. 164 f.

72. Cf. M. Tosi, "The Problem of Turquoise in Protohistoric Trade on the Iranian Plateau," *Memorie dell'Istituto Italiano di Paleontologia Umana* 2 (1974): 147–62. The classic description of relations between Mesopotamia and Iran is the Sumerian epic poem *Enmerkar and the Lord of Aratta*. For this and other references in Sumerian texts see G. Pettinato, "Il commercio con l'estero della Mesopotamia meridionale nel III millennio a C. alla luce delle fonti letterarie e lessicali sumeriche," *Mesopotamia* 7 (1972): 43–166.

73. Lapis lazuli is known to come from the Badaḫšān area of northern Afghanistan. See H. Kulhe, "Die Lapislazuli-Lagerstätte Sare Sang (Badakhshan): Geologie, Entstehung, Kulturgeschichte und Bergbau," *Afghanistan Journal* 3 no. 2 (1976): 43–56; L. W. Adamec, *Badakhshan Province and Northeastern Afghanistan*, (Graz, 1972) (Historical and Political Gazetteer of Afghanistan, vol. 1), p. 152 f. Reports of ancient tin sources recently discovered in Afghanistan raise new possibilities regarding tin in the ancient Near East.

74. Most of the Mari texts relating to the tin trade are published (in transcription and translation) in J. Bottéro, *Textes economiques et administratifs* (Paris: Imprimerie Nationale, 1957) (*ARMT* VII).

75. A. Malamat, "Syro-Palestinian Destinations in a Mari Tin Inventory," *IEJ* 21 (1971): 31–38; J. D. Muhly, in *The Search for Ancient Tin*, pp. 44–45.

76. G. Dossin, "La route de l'étain en Mésopotamie au temps de Zimri-Lim," *RA* 64 (1970): 97–106 (and see J. M. Sasson *RA* 65 [1971]: 172).

77. J. D. Muhly, "The Land of Alashiya: References to Alashiya in the Texts of the Second Millennium B.C. and the History of Cyprus in the Late Bronze Age," in *Proceedings of the First International Congress of Cypriot Studies*, vol. 1 (Nicosia: Society for Cypriot Studies, 1972), pp. 201–19, esp. p. 204. For new references to copper from Alashiya see C. F. A. Schaeffer, "Les peuples de la mer et leurs sanctuaires à Enkomi-Alasia aux XIIe– XIe S. av. N.E.," in *Alasia*, I (Paris: Klincksieck, 1971), pp. 505–66, esp. p. 547 f.

78. A. R. Millard, "Cypriot Copper in Babylonia, c. 1745 B.C.," *JCS* 25 (1973): 211–14.

79. Sir Leonard Woolley and Sir Max Mallowan, *Ur Excavations*, vol. VII, *The Old Babylonian Period*, ed. T. C. Mitchell (London: British Museum and The University Museum, 1976), p. 123 f. The texts from this period were published by H. H. Figulla and W. J. Martin, *Letters and Documents of the Old Babylonian Period* (London: British

Museum and The University Museum, 1953) (*UET* V). See W. F. Leemans, *Foreign Trade in the Old Babylonian Period* (Leiden: Brill, 1960), pp. 38–55.

80. A. Leo Oppenheim, "The Seafaring Merchants of Ur," *JAOS* 74 (1954): 6–17, and Muhly, *Copper and Tin*, p. 221 f.

81. Text is *UET* V 81. Translation after A. Leo Oppenheim, *Letters from Mesopotamia* (Chicago: University of Chicago Press, 1967), p. 82 f., no. 12. See also W. F. Leemans, *Foreign* Trade, p. 40, no. 17.

82. Text is *UET* V 20. See Leemans, *Foreign Trade*, p. 45, no. 26.

83. G. Walberg, *Kamares, A Study of the Character of Palatial Middle Minoan Pottery* (Uppsala: Almqvist and Wiksell, 1976) (*Boreas*, vol. 8), and G. Cadogan, *Palaces of Minoan Crete* (London: Barrie and Jenkins, 1976), pp. 29–36. Also K. Branigan, "Crete, the Levant and Egypt in the Early Second Millennium B.C.," in *Proceedings of the Third International Cretological Congress* (Athens, 1973), vol. 1, pp. 22–27.

84. W. A. Ward, *Egypt and the East Mediterranean World, 2200–1900 B.C.* (Beirut: American University of Beirut, 1971), pp. 71–125; F. Schachermeyr, *Ägäis und Orient* (Vienna: Böhlau, 1967); W. S. Smith, *Interconnections in the Ancient Near East: A Study of the Relationships between the Arts of Egypt, the Aegean and Western Asia* (New Haven: Yale University Press, 1965); S. Dietz, "Aegean and Near-Eastern Metal Daggers in Early and Middle Bronze Age Greece: The Dating of the Byblite Bronze Hoards and Aegean Imports," *Acta Archaeologica* 42 (1971, publ. 1972): 1–22; S. Hood, *The Arts in Prehistoric Greece* (New York: Penguin, 1978), pp. 140, 153–55, 233–38.

85. K. R. Maxwell-Hyslop, "An Illustration to a Mari Inventory?" *Iraq* 32 (1970): 165–66.

86. *ARMT* VII 88 (10:1); 233 (14:1). Cf. J. Bottéro, *ARMT* VII, p. 294.

87. Text is *ARMT* V 20. Cf. J. M. Sasson, *JESHO* 9 (1966): 164 f.

88. For these texts see A. K. Grayson, *Assyrian Royal Inscriptions* (Wiesbaden: Harrassowitz, 1972), vol. 1, p. 20 f. and n. 64. See also the chart, giving the prices from all these texts, in E. Sollberger, *Ur Royal Inscriptions*, pt. 2 (London: British Museum and The University Museum, 1965) (*UET* VIII), p. 16 (although only the Sin-Kāšid text and the Eshnunna Laws mention copper). The "Chronicle of Market Prices" (cf. A. K. Grayson, *Assyrian and Babylonian Chronicles* [Locust Valley, N.Y.: Augustin, 1975] [*TCS*, V], pp. 60 f., 178 f.,: Chronicle no. 23) is too poorly preserved to be of any use.

89. A. Goetze, *The Laws of Eshnunna* (New Haven, 1956) (*AASOR*, 31), p. 28 f. Goetze, however, read the signs as *erum ma-sum₆*, "refined or washed copper."

90. Garelli, *Assyriens*, p. 294 f.

91. P. Artzi, "On the Cuneiform Background of the Northwest-Semitic Form of the Word *brd̲l*, *b(a)rz(e)l*," *JNES* 28 (1969): 268–70; E. von Schuler, "Beziehungen zwischen Syrien und Anatolien in der späten Bronzezeit," in *La Siria nel tardo Bronzo* (Rome: Centro per le Antichità e la Storia dell' Arte del vicino Oriente, 1969), pp. 97–116, esp. p. 99. The word for iron almost always appears in Old Babylonian as the Sumerian logogram AN·BAR, but *Yale Oriental Series* II 82 (= E. Ebeling, *Mitteilungen der altorientalischen Gesellschaft* 16, 1/2 [1943]: 46 f.) preserves the accusative form *pa-ar-zi-la-am* (in line 26). The word even appears once in Old Assyrian as *pár-zi-lam* (Landsberger, *Ar. Or.* 18, no. 1, p. 332). At Mari there is *pár-zi-lum* (*ARMT* 19, 337:2).

92. Text is *Cuneiform Texts from Babylonian Tablets etc. in the British Museum* VI 25a,

62 JAMES D. MUHLY

line 8 (J. Kohler and A. Ungnad, *Hammurabi's Gesetz*, (Leipzig: Eduard Pfeiffer, 1911), vol. 5, p. 48 f., no. 1221).

93. Text is *ARMT* XIII 3 (G. Dossin et al., *Textes divers, offerts à A. Parrot à l'occasion du XXXe anniversaire de la decouverte de Mari* (Paris: Geuthner, 1964). See Landsberger, *JNES* 24 (1965): 287 f., who gives the ratio as 1500:1 but the text says that 10 talents of lead cost ⅓ mina of silver.

94. For background see J. D. Muhly, "Near Eastern Chronology and the Date of the Late Cypriot I Period," in *The Archaeology of Cyprus: Recent Developments* (Park Ridge, N.J.: Noyes Press, 1975), pp. 76–89, and B. Mazar, "The Middle Bronze Age in Palestine," *IEJ* 18 (1968): 65–97.

95. O. Szemerényi, "Structuralism and substratum—Indo-Europeans and Semites in the Ancient Near East," *Lingua* 13 (1964): 1–29; A. Kammenhuber, *Die Arier im Vorderen Orient* (Heidelberg: C. Winter, 1968); and T. Burrow, "The Proto-Indoaryans," *Journal of the Royal Asiatic Society* (1973): 123–40.

96. T. G. H. James, "Egypt: from the Expulsion of the Hyksos to Amenophis I," in *Cambridge Ancient History*, 3d ed. (Cambridge, 1973), vol. 2, pt. 1, 289–312. Note that, according to the Kamose Stela, Egypt was importing gold, silver, lapis lazuli, turquoise, and bronze from the Levant. See H. S. Smith and A. Smith, "A Reconsideration of the Kamose Texts," *Zeitschrift für ägyptische Sprache und Altertumskunde* 103 (1976): 48–76, p. 60.

97. O. T. P. K. Dickinson, *The Origins of Mycenaean Civilisation* (Göteborg: Paul Åströms Förlag, 1977) (SIMA, XLIX), and E. T. Vermeule, *The Art of the Shaft Graves of Mycenae* University of Cincinnati, 1975 (Lectures in Memory of Louise Taft Semple, 3d ser.).

98. There is no evidence that the Mycenaeans themselves ever reached the Baltic area. Likewise, to suggest the presence of Cornish tin in the Aegean is not to believe that the Mycenaeans built Stonehenge.

99. D. Slater, *Tin* (London, 1974) (Mineral Resources Consultative Committee, Report no. 9).

100. J. D. Muhly, "Tin Trade Routes of the Bronze Age," *American Scientist* 61 (1973): 404–13, and Maddin, Wheeler, and Muhly, *Expedition* 19, no. 2 (1977): 42.

101. For a list of the tombs see E. A. Catling and H. W. Catling, in M. Popham et al., "Sellopoulo Tombs 3 and 4, Two Late Minoan Graves near Knossos," *BSA* 69 (1974): 195–257, p. 253 f. For the Dendra find see N. M. Verdelis, "Neue Funde von Dendra," *Mitteilungen des deutschen archäologischen Instituts, Athenische Abteilung* 82 (1967): 1–53, and A. M. Snodgrass, "The First European Body-armour," in *The European Community in Later Prehistory: Studies in Honour of C. F. C. Hawkes* (London: Routledge and Kegan Paul, 1971), pp. 33–50.

102. E. Demacopoulou, "Excavations in Thebes 1973," *Teiresias* 4, no. 1 (1974): 8–10, and "Mycenaean Jewellery Workshop in Thebes," *AAA* 7 (1974): 162–73 (in Modern Greek with English summary).

103. H. W. Catling, *Cypriot Bronzework in the Mycenaean World* (Oxford: Oxford University Press, 1964). For some recent finds see V. Karageorghis, "A Late Cypriote Hoard of Bronzes from Sinda," *RDAC*, 1973, pp. 72–82, and "Kypriaka I(a): A Late Bronze Age Bronze Cauldron," *RDAC*, 1974, pp. 60–64. Also the large hoard of bronze

vessels from the upper burial in tomb 9 at Kition (V. Karageorghis, *Excavations at Kition*, I. *The Tombs* (Nicosia: Department of Antiquities, 1974), p. 62 f.).

104. Muhly, *Copper and Tin*, p. 174 f.

105. Ibid. All the languages written in cuneiform seem to have separate words for copper and bronze, with Sumerian URUDU and ZABAR, Akkadian *erû* and *siparru*. So does Egyptian, with *ḥm·tj* and *ḥsmn*.

106. See J. D. Muhly, in *Proceedings of the First International Congress of Cypriot Studies*, vol. 1, p. 209 f.; Y. Lynn Holmes, "The Foreign Trade of Cyprus during the Late Bronze Age," in *The Archaeology of Cyprus: Recent Developments* (Park Ridge, N. J.: Noyes Press, 1975), pp. 90–110, esp. p. 90 f.; and P. Åström, *The Cypriote Late Bronze Age: Relative and Absolute Chronology, Foreign Relations, Historical Conclusions* (Lund: Swedish Cyprus Expedition, 1972) (*SCE*, IV/1D), 773 f.

107. Text is *EA* 35. Translation by Oppenheim, *Letters from Mesopotamia* (Chicago: University of Chicago Press, 1967), p. 120 f., no. 66.

108. For the Horned God identified as Nergal/Reshef see C. F. A. Schaeffer, in *Alasia* (1971), vol. 1, p. 509 f. For the find itself see J.-C. Courtois, "Le sanctuaire du dieu au lingot d'Enkomi-Alasia," in *Alasia*, vol. 1, 151–362. For another interpretation of the find see H. W. Catling, "A Cypriot Bronze Statuette in the Bomford Collection," in *Alasia*, vol. 1 15–32. For religion and copper metallurgy see J. D. Muhly, *Supplement to Copper and Tin*, p. 91 f.

109. For Nergal and his attributes see E. von Weiher, *Der babylonische Gott Nergal* (Neukirchen: Neukirchener Verlag, 1971) (Alter Orient und Altes Testament, 11).

110. Basic bibliography in T. S. Wheeler, R. Maddin, and J. D. Muhly, "Ingots and the Bronze Age Copper Trade in the Mediterranean: A Progress Report," *Expedition* 17, no. 4 (1975): 31–39. Add R. F. Tylecote, "Properties of Copper Ingots of Late Bronze Age Type," in *Festschrift für Richard Pittioni* (Vienna: Deuticke, Horn, Berger, 1976), vol. 2, 157–72.

111. P. Dikaios, *Enkomi, Excavations 1948–1958*, 3 vols. (Mainz am Rhein: P. von Zabern, 1969 [1, 3], 1971 [2]), vol. 1, p. 294, and vol. 2, p. 691 (Inv. 1995); vol. 1, p. 301 and vol. 2, p. 764 (Inv. 774); vol. 2, pp. 729, 885 (Inv. 885). For illustrations of the ingots see vol. 3a, plate 138. See also C. F. A. Schaeffer, in *Alasia*, vol. 1, p. 553, fig. 18.

112. See catalogue in H. W. Catling, *Cypriot Bronzework in the Mycenaean World*, p. 267 f. For the Mathiati ingot see also J. L. Bruce, "Antiquities in the Mines of Cyprus," in *SCE* (Stockholm, 1937), vol. 3, pp. 639–71, esp. p. 641 and fig. 328.

113. O. Davies, "The Copper Mines of Cyprus," *BSA* 30 (1928–30) (1932): 74–85, esp. 79.

114. G. F. Bass, in G. F. Bass et al., *Cape Gelidonya: A Bronze Age Shipwreck* (Philadelphia: American Philosophical Society, 1967) (*Transactions of the American Philosophical Society*, 57/8), p. 61. Not all the pieces listed there are actually from ingots. See Muhly, *Supplement to Copper and Tin*, p. 93.

115. For these scenes see Bass, *Cape Gelidonya*, pp. 62–67.

116. S. A. Immerwahr, "Mycenaean Trade and Colonization," *Archaeology* 13 (1960): 4–13, esp. 12. See also H. W. Catling, "The Cypriote Copper Industry," *Archaeologia Viva* 1, no. 3 (1969): 81–88 (and in the same volume P. Åström, "The Economy of Cyprus and its Development in the IInd millennium," pp. 73–80).

117. Basic publication is Bass et al., *Cape Gelidonya* (and see review by G. Cadogan, *JHS* 89 [1969]: 187–89). The interpretation of this shipwreck has become very controversial. Bass answers his critics in "Cape Gelidonya and Bronze Age Maritime Trade," in *Orient and Occident: Festschrift Cyrus H. Gordon* (Neukirchen: Neukircher Verlag, 1973) (Alter Orient und Altes Testament, 22), pp. 29–38. See also C. F. A. Schaeffer, in *Alasia*, vol. 1, pp. 554–58; D. L. Clarke, "The Economic Context of Trade and Industry in Barbarian Europe till Roman Times, in *Analytical Archaeologist: Collected Papers of David Clarke* (London and New York: Academic Press, 1979), pp. 263–331, pp. 300–02.

118. V. Hankey, "Mycenaean trade with the South-eastern Mediterranean," in *Mélanges de l'Université Saint-Joseph* 46 (1970–71): 11–30, p. 20 f.

119. A. J. Evans, "Minoan Weights and Mediums of Currency, from Crete, Mycenae and Cyprus," in *Corrola Numismatica: Numismatic Essays in honour of Barclay H. Head* (London, 1906), pp. 336–67, and M. Ventris and J. Chadwick, *Documents in Mycenaean Greek*, 2d ed., ed. J. Chadwick (Cambridge: Cambridge University, 1973), p. 57.

120. Notably by P. Faure, "Les minerais de la Crète antique," *Revue Archéologique* N.S., 1 (1966): 45–78, and "Le problème du cuivre dans la Crète antique," in *Proceedings of the IInd International Congress of Cretan Studies* (Athens, 1968), vol. 2, pp. 174–93.

121. T. S. Wheeler, R. Maddin, and J. D. Muhly, *Expedition* 17, no. 4 (1975): 32 f.

122. For the bronzesmiths see M. Lejeune, "Les forgerons de Pylos," *Historia* 10 (1961): 409–34. For the shortage of bronze see J. Chadwick, *The Mycenaean World* (Cambridge: Cambridge University Press, 1976), p. 141 f.

123. M. Ventris and J. Chadwick, *Documents in Mycenaean Greek*, pp. 352 f., 509 f., esp. p. 513 (by J. Chadwick): "The shortage of metal attested by the whole of the *Jn* series of tablets will explain the need for these desperate measures; imports of raw material have been cut off precisely at the time when there is an overwhelming need for weapons."

124. *Ibid.*, p. 512 f. (text is Jn 09 + 829: Ventris and Chadwick no. 257).

125. Summary in V. Karageorghis, *Kition: Mycenaean and Phoenician Discoveries in Cyprus* (London: Thames & Hudson, 1976), pp. 26, 72 f., 169 f. See also J. Lagarce, "La cachette de fondeur aux épées (Enkomi, 1967) et l'atelier voisin," in *Alasia*, vol. 1, pp. 381–432, esp. 432. Catling even argues (in *Alasia*, vol. 1, p. 29) that "during the twelfth century B.C. copper production came under the especial care and protection of gods worshipped in the sanctuaries of the Cypriot manufacturing cities,"

126. P. Åström, in *SCE*, IV/1D (Lund, 1972), p. 769.

127. G. Constantinou and G. J. S. Govett, "Genesis of sulphide deposits, ochre and umber of Cyprus," *Transactions of the Institution of Mining and Metallurgy* 81B (1972): 34–46. For general works on the copper deposits of Cyprus see L. M. Bear, *The Mineral Resources and Mining Industry of Cyprus* (Nicosia, 1963) (Cypriot Ministry of Commerce and Industry, Geological Survey Dept., Bulletin no. 1).

128. Earliest evidence comes from Kalopsidha. See P. Åström, *Excavations at Kalopsidha and Ayios Iakovos in Cyprus* (Lund: Paul Åströms Förlag, 1966) (*SIMA*, II), pp. 74, 113–15 (metallurgical report by T. Watkins). Work on the material from Athienou, by Maddin, Muhly, and Wheeler, will appear as part of the final report by the excavators, T. Dothan and A. Ben-Tor, to be published in *Qedem*. Also Muhly, Maddin, and Wheeler, *RDAC*, forthcoming.

129. G. Weisgerber, "Altägyptischer Bergbau auf der Sinaihalbinsel," in *Die Technik-*

geschichte als Vorbild Moderner Technik (Essen, 1976) (Schriften der Georg-Agricola-Gesellschaft, no. 2), pp. 27–43; A. Lupu and B. Rothenberg, "The Extractive Metallurgy of the Early Iron Age Copper Industry in the 'Arabah, Israel," *Archaeologia Austriaca* 47 (1970): 91–130. Popular account by B. Rothenberg, *Timna, Valley of the Biblical Copper Mines* (London: Thames & Hudson, 1972).

130. The color is certainly designed to represent the specific metals involved and to distinguish between copper and tin.

131. G. A. Wainwright, "Egyptian Bronze-Making," *Antiquity* 17 (1943): 96–98, p. 97.

132. Ibid., "Egyptian Bronze-Making Again," *Antiquity*, vol. 18 (1944): 100–02. Also G. A. Wainwright, "Rekhmirê's Metal-workers," *Man* 44 (1944): 94–98 (no. 75), p. 98: "Though we have many scenes of metal-working in ancient Egypt, there is no single instance of *smelting* the metal from its ore. The scenes are always of *melting* the ready-made metal."

133. Text is G. Dossin, "Archives de Sûmu-Iamam, roi de Mari," *RA* 64 (1970): 17–44, esp. 25, text n. 6. The specification *te-ma-yu*, which appears in several texts from this archive, is really of unknown meaning.

134. Maddin, Wheeler, and Muhly, *Expedition* 19, no. 2 (1977): 42 f., and S. A. Immerwahr, "The Use of Tin on Mycenaean Vases," *Hesperia* 35 (1966): 381–96, J. D. Muhly in *The Search for Ancient Tin*, pp. 46–47.

135. A. M. Snodgrass, *The Dark Age of Greece* (Edinburgh: Edinburgh University Press, 1971), p. 237 f. It should be pointed out that 13th century texts at Ugarit give no indication of a shortage of copper and put the copper/silver ratio at 200 : 1 (*PRU* V 101 : 6–8). Cf. M. Heltzer, "The Metal Trade at Ugarit," *Iraq* 39 (1977): 203–11, p. 204.

136. For this material see Gimbutas, *Bronze Age Cultures in Central and Eastern Europe*, and Piggott, *Ancient Europe*, p. 123 f.

137. The tin ingots with Cypro-Minoan signs (see below, n. 145) could have come through Ugarit as the Cypro-Minoan script was used there, although it was more common on Cyprus.

138. The texts in question come from Assur, Nuzi, and Tell Billa, as well as new texts from Tell al-Rimah. See Muhly, *Copper and Tin*, p. 302 f. A Nuzi text gives 36 minas of tin as the price of an ox, 24 minas of tin for an ass. See E. A. Speiser, *New Kirkuk Documents relating to Family Laws* (New Haven, 1930) (*AASOR*, 10), p. 57 f. (text no. 25 [H 79]). See also the texts given by B. L. Eichler, *Indenture at Nuzi. The Personal Tidennutu Contract and its Mesopotamian Analogues* (New Haven: Yale University Press, 1973), p. 110 f.

139. For text see A. K. Grayson, *Assyrian Royal Inscriptions*, 1: 10, #62. Translation quoted is that of *CAD*, s.v. *andurāru*, 117a.

140. Text is Assyrian Law Code, #18 (as quoted in *CAD*, s.v. *gadāmu*, 8b).

141. Text is *HSS* XIV 37 (as quoted in *CAD*, s.v. *annaku*, 129a).

142. Text is *Keilschrifttexte aus Assur verschiedenen Inhalts* 205 (quoted in *CAD*, s.v. *billatu*, 226a).

143. Text is *CCT* I 37b (quoted in *CAD*, s.v. *annaku*, 128a).

144. Text is *Papyrus Anastasi* IV. 17. 7–8. English translation in R. A. Caminos, *Late Egyptian Miscellanies* (Oxford: Oxford University Press, 1954), p. 71. See also Muhly, *Copper and Tin*, p. 245 (with notes).

145. Wheeler, Maddin, and Muhly, *Expedition* 19, no. 2 (1977): 44 f.

146. For a basic introduction to modern Homeric studies see G. S. Kirk, *The Songs of Homer* (Cambridge: Cambridge University Press, 1962), and *Homer and the Oral Tradition* (Cambridge: Cambridge University Press, 1976).

147. Basic collection of passages in D. H. F. Gray, "Metal Working in Homer," *JHS* 74 (1954): 1–15.

148. *Iliad* 23. 826–35. Translation by R. Lattimore (Chicago: University of Chicago Press, 1951), p. 472. The translation "pig iron" is an attempt to render what is, in the original Greek, a difficult phrase. *Solos autochoōnos* seems to mean a "massive lump," with the connotation of something smelted or cast.

149. *Iliad* 23. 503 (chariot), 560–62 (armor). The classic passage for the use of tin in inlay decoration is the description of the Shield of Achilleus (*Iliad* 18. 468–612), a passage often compared with the techniques used in the production of the inlaid daggers from the Shaft Graves of Mycenae.

150. *Mémoires de la Délégation en Perse*, XXII, p. 153, no. 141 (= V. Scheil, *RA* 25 (1928): 42 (quoted in *CAD*, s.v. ḫullu, 230a).

151. *ARMT* V 5; *ARMT* VII 244 and 247 (cf. J. Bottéro, in *ARMT* VII, p. 301 f.); *ARMT* XIX 337.

152. Tablet 410 (D. J. Wiseman, *The Alalakh Tablets* (London: British Institute of Archaeology at Ankara, 1953), p. 107. For cuneiform text see D. J. Wiseman, *JCS* 8 (1954): 29).

153. J. Bottéro, "Les inventaires de Qatna," *RA* 43 (1949): 1–40; 137–215. Texts mentioning iron include 165 (p. 154), 176 (p. 156), 245 (p. 162), and 310.

154. Major text is *EA* 22 (inventory of wedding gifts sent by Tušratta when his daughter Taduhepa married Amenophis III). Also *EA* 25 (Tušratta to Akhenaten).

155. I do not accept the 3d millennium references to iron daggers discussed by E. Sollberger, *The Business and Administrative Correspondence under the Kings of Ur* (Locust Valley, N.Y.: Augustin, 1966) (*TCS* I), p. 99 f. (and Glossary, no. 54). A·NA in these texts is the Akkadian preposition, not an early word for iron.

156. Text is *HSS* XV 145 (as quoted in *CAD*, s.v. binâtu, 237b).

157. Text is *KBo* XV 24 (a building ritual). The object in question is called an *enzu*, a word of unknown meaning (hardly the Akkadian word for "goat" in this context!).

158. Text is *KBo* I 14. Cf. C. Zaccagnini, "KBo I 14 e il "monopolio" hittita del ferro," *Rivista degli Studi Orientali* 45 (1970): 1–10. The letter, though from the Hittite King, is written in Akkadian.

159. Which is not to deny the use of iron, only the monopoly over the production of iron. For a catalogue of iron objects in relevant contexts see W. Kimmig, "Seevölkerbewegung und Urnfelderkultur. Ein archäologisch-historischer Versuch," in *Studien aus Alteuropa*, vol. I, 1964, (Beihefte der Bonner Jahrbücher, 10/1), 220–83. The most interesting passage is the description of the armor of Goliath (I Samuel 17: 5–7) with his spearhead weighing 600 shekels of iron. See K. Galling, "Goliath und seine Rustung," in *Volume du Congrès, Genève, 1965* (Leiden: Brill, 1966) (suppl. to *Vetus Testamentum*, XV), 150–69. Also Waldbaum, *From Bronze to Iron*, pp. 17–37, 67–73.

160. Color illustration of ax from Ugarit in E. Strommenger and M. Hirmer, *5000 years of Mesopotamian Art* (New York: Abrams, 1964), plate XXXIV and p. 428. See also

C. F. A. Schaeffer, in *Ugaritica*, I (Paris: Geuthner, 1939), p. 107 f., figs. 100–03 and plate XXII. The ax dates to ca. 1400 B.C. and the iron blade, with 3.25 percent Ni, is probably of meteoritic iron. It was not a serviceable weapon. See H. C. Richardson, "A Mitannian Battle Axe from Ras Shamra," *Berytus* 8 (1943): 72.

161. See chap. by Maddin and Wheeler. See also K. R. Maxwell-Hyslop, et al., "An Iron Dagger from Tomb 240 at Tell Fara South," *Levant* 10 (1978): 112–15.

162. E. Tholander, "Evidence of the Use of Carburized Steel and Quench Hardening in Late Bronze Age Cyprus," *Opuscula Atheniensia* 10 (1971): 15–22.

163. Beginning with "Barbarian Europe and Early Iron Age Greece," *Proceedings of the Prehistoric Society* 31 (1965): 229–40.

164. *Odyssey* 9. 389–94. Translation by R. Lattimore (New York: Harper and Row, 1965), p. 147. For modern discussion of this passage see D. L. Page, *The Homeric Odyssey* (Oxford: Oxford University Press, 1955).

165. Cf. W. B. Stanford, *The Odyssey of Homer* (New York: Macmillan, 1965), vol. 1, p. 361, and R. Maddin, J. D. Muhly, and T. S. Wheeler, "How the Iron Age Began," *Scientific American* 273, no. 4 (1977): 122–31, p. 129 f. The operation described by Homer is quenching, not tempering as often stated. Quenching and tempering are distinct metallurgical operations that have been hopelessly confused by modern translators of ancient Greek literature.

166. C. S. Smith, "The Discovery of Carbon in Steel," *Technology and Culture* 5 (1964): 149–75, esp. 150. See also T. A. Wertime, "The Discovery of the Element Carbon," *Osiris* 11 (1954): 211–20.

167. This is not to imply that iron was "cheap," only that it was less expensive than bronze. In antiquity all metal was expensive and seldom wasted. A Middle Babylonian letter states:

Should he (the slave) escape (in his copper chains weighing six minas), he (his custodian) will be investigated, and twelve minas of copper will be collected from him (as quoted in *CAD*, s.v. *eṣēru*, 334a).

The authorities seem more concerned about the loss of the copper than of the slave!

168. As worked out by P. Courbin, "Dans la Grèce archaïque: valeur comparée du fer et de l'argent lors de l'introduction du monnayage," *Annales* 14 (1959): 209–33, esp. 226. The basic study of these spits is by Zofia Gansiniec, "The Iron Money of the Spartans and the Origins of the Obolos Currency," *Archeologia* 8 (1956): 367–413 (in Polish, with summaries in Russian and English). See also M. Caramessini-Oeconomides, "Iron Spits," *AAA* 2 (1969): 436–45 (modern Greek with English summary).

3

The First Archaeological
Appearance of Iron and the
Transition to the Iron Age

JANE C. WALDBAUM

The known finds of iron from prehistoric and Bronze Age contexts have often been listed or summarized.[1] These published lists vary somewhat, depending on the size of the area being covered and the time of the study. The exact number of such pieces changes constantly. Not only are new examples steadily being added with new excavation, but also frequently cited examples sometimes turn out on investigation to be spurious in date, context, or even attribution as iron.[2] Nevertheless, it is possible to amass enough verifiably authentic examples to enable us, when we add the evidence in contemporary literary documents, to draw a picture of the earliest stages in the use and manufacture of iron.

An interesting question concerning the earliest stages of iron manufacture is the extent to which iron extracted from terrestrial ores by smelting was utilized in relation to iron obtained directly from metallic meteorites. Since meteoritic iron is rich in nickel and smelted iron usually is not, the two varieties are often distinguished by testing for nickel. Where such tests have been made they are noted in the text.

PREHISTORIC IRON, BEFORE CA. 3000 B.C.

To date, fourteen iron objects have been recorded at only four sites dating before ca. 3000 B.C. (table 3.1). The objects are a four-sided instrument from grave A at Samarra in northern Iraq, dated ca. 5000 B.C., with a preserved length of ca. 4.30 cm; three small, nearly spherical balls from a period II habitation level at Tepe Sialk in northern Iran, ca. 4600–4100 B.C.; nine beads from predynastic graves 67 and 133 at El Gerzeh, and a con-

69

Table 3.1. Meteoritic and Smelted Iron before ca. 3000 B.C. from the
Near East and Eastern Mediterranean

	Meteoritic	Smelted	Not analyzed	Total
Iran	3 ("balls")	—	—	3
Mesopotamia	—	1 (tool?)	—	1
Egypt	1 (bead)	—	9	10
Total	4	1	9	14

temporary ring from grave 1494 at Armant in Egypt, all ca. 3500–3100
B.C. The Sialk balls were described as "very hard and heavy" and were
apparently used as polishers. The Samarra piece, the Sialk balls, and one
of the Gerzeh beads were analyzed for nickel. The Samarra piece was
smelted; the others were meteoritic (the bead had a nickel content of
7.50%; the ball showed a characteristic Widmanstätten structure).[3]

EARLY BRONZE AGE, CA. 3000–2000 B.C.

In the 3d millennium finds of excavated iron increase. They are known
from several sites in each of three main regions: Mesopotamia, Anatolia,
and Egypt. They come in a variety of forms, some quite splendid, others
mere lumps or bits of rust.

a. Mesopotamia: a fragment from Uruk-Warka, found between
temples D and E of the Anu Ziggurat, Early Protoliterate period, ca.
3100–2800 B.C.; a lump from Khafajah, Early Dynastic (ED) II, ca. 2800–
2600; three "button-like" pieces of inlay, Kish, palace A, floor of room
61, ED II or III, ca. 2800–2340; fragments of a dagger blade with copper
handle, found among a hoard of copper objects, Tell Asmar, ED III, ca.
2450–2340; fragments of a flat tool blade, Ur, Royal Cemetery, tomb
PG/580, ED III; fragment, Tell Chagar Bazar, level 5, grave G 67, ED
III; two fragments, Tell Chagar Bazar, level 3, ED III; fragments, Mari,
near the pre-Sargonic Temple of Ishtar, ED III.

The pieces from Uruk, Tell Asmar, Ur, and Chagar Bazar level 5
were analyzed: those from Uruk and Ur proved to be meteoritic (Ur,
10.9% Ni; Uruk, % Ni unstated); those from Tell Asmar and Chagar
Bazar contained no nickel and are therefore smelted.[4]

b. Anatolia: macehead or finial, treasure L, Troy, EB II, ca. 2600–
2400 B.C.; dagger blade with gold handle, tomb K; two pins with gold
heads, tomb MA; pendant, tomb MA'; crescent-shaped plaque, tomb

MC; fragments of a knife "which seems to be iron," tomb T.M., all from Alaca Hüyük, all Early Bronze (EB) III, ca. 2400–2100 B.C.; corroded lump, Tarsus, small treasure, room 74, EB III, ca. 2100 B.C.; sword with obsidian hilt carved in the form of two leopards and inlaid with gold and amber spots, Dorak "royal tomb" clandestinely excavated and since disappeared, tentatively dated EB III, ca. 2400–2300, by a cartouche of Fifth Dynasty pharaoh Sahure, said to have been found with the treasure.

The dagger, one of the pins, and the plaque from Alaca and the macehead from Troy were analyzed. The dagger contained no nickel, the pin 5.08 percent Ni (3.44% NiO); the plaque 4.30 percent Ni (3.06% NiO); two samples of the macehead showed two different readings: 3.02 percent Ni (2.44% NiO), and 6.34 percent Ni (3.91% NiO).[5]

c. Egypt: deposit of rust adhering to a flint wand, Giza, Valley Temple of Mycerinus, Dynasty IV, ca. 2565–2440 B.C.; rusted tool, Giza, in joint of outer stones of Pyramid of Cheops, Dynasty IV (if authentic, but possibly any time up to 19th century A.D.); mass of rust corroded to group of copper tools, Abydos, Dynasty VI, ca. 2345–2181; blade of *pesesh-kef* amulet with silver sphinx's head, Deir el-Bahari, Tomb of Princess Aa Shait, Dynasty XI, ca. 2133–1991.

All four pieces were analyzed and only the amulet from Deir el-Bahari is meteoritic (10% Ni); the rest showed no nickel and are terrestrial in origin.[6]

Of some ten or more examples of iron found in Mesopotamia, six are unidentifiable lumps or fragments; the rest, though not well preserved, are more interesting: the tools (?) from Samarra and Ur, the dagger blade from Tell Asmar, inlay pieces from Kish. Most of these examples, including the fragments, were found in contexts that indicate some special, precious, or ritual status for the iron within them—the dagger was found in a sealed hoard, deliberately buried, the tool from Ur was in a rich grave, the fragments from Mari and Uruk were in or near temples, the inlay from Kish was on a palace floor, the Samarra and Chagar Bazar level 5 pieces were in graves (though not so rich as that from Ur), and the Khafajah piece was in a hoard of beads.

Anatolia produced nine or ten objects of some significance, most from the single site of Alaca Hüyük, and most of recognizable function. In the category of weapons and tools there are the Dorak sword, the dagger and knife from Alaca, and perhaps the Troy macehead; the rest are jewelry or decorative objects: two pins, the pendant, and plaque from Alaca. Of uncertain function is the lump from Tarsus. As in Mesopotamia, the contexts of all objects found in this era were special: the Alaca and Dorak pieces came from "royal" graves, the Troy piece was in a treasure, and the Tarsus piece in a small hoard or treasure.

Egypt produced about fourteen objects down to the end of the 3d millennium. Of these, ten are prehistoric and rather small (the nine Gerzeh beads and the Armant ring), two are unrecognizable rusty deposits (from Giza and Abydos), one is an amulet (Deir el-Bahari), and one is the questionable tool from Giza. Once again, the contexts seem to speak for some kind of revered status: the objects from Gerzeh, Armant, and Deir el-Bahari were from tombs, the "rust" from Giza was in a funerary temple, the tool from Giza, if authentic, from a pyramid (though probably not deliberately placed in such a position).

Summing up the evidence to the end of the 3d millennium we find that iron was used sporadically and treated as a precious material in almost every instance. This is attested by contexts—graves, treasure hoards, temples—and by the nature of the objects themselves. Weapons and tools are clearly ceremonial in function, combined with gold and other precious materials as at Alaca and Dorak, and not intended for daily use; jewelry is also treated in this way, for example, the Gerzeh beads strung with gold, carnelian, and agate beads and the gold and iron pins from Alaca.

Geographically the iron is so far limited in distribution to eight rather scattered sites in Mesopotamia from as far south as Ur to as far north as Chagar Bazar, four sites in Anatolia, and six in Egypt. The single example from 5th millennium Iran is perhaps anomalous.

Chronologically, most of the material falls in the second half of the 3d millennium—the Early Dynastic III period in Mesopotamia, the Early Bronze III period in Anatolia, and Fourth Dynasty or later in Egypt. Exceptions are the somewhat earlier pieces from Uruk and Khafajah and the prehistoric pieces. At the present time the chronology of the late 3d millennium pieces cannot be much more closely defined, so it is impossible to tell just how closely contemporaneous these examples from the three great cultural centers of the Early Bronze Age might actually be. It is tempting to see here some clustering or pattern, but more than the bare suggestion of it would be premature.

According to analyses, both meteoritic and smelted iron were in use simultaneously during this time (table 3.2). Of five analyzed pieces in

Table 3.2. Meteoritic and Smelted Iron in the Early Bronze Age from the
Near East and Eastern Mediterranean

	Meteoritic	*Smelted*	*Not analyzed*	*Total*
Mesopotamia	2 (fragment, tool?)	2 (dagger blade, fragment)	5	9
Egypt	1 (amulet)	3 (tool? rust)	—	4
Anatolia	3 (pin, plaque, macehead)	1 (dagger)	5	9
Total	6	6	10	22

Mesopotamia two are meteoritic (Ur, Uruk), three are smelted (Samarra, Tell Asmar, Chagar Bazar level 5); of four analyzed examples in Anatolia three are meteoritic (two from Alaca, one from Troy);[7] one is smelted (Alaca); of five from Egypt two are meteoritic (Gerzeh, Deir el-Bahari), three are smelted (two from Giza, one from Abydos). The Sialk balls are also meteoritic. From present evidence one cannot determine whether smelted or meteoritic iron deserves precedence. The earliest piece of all, the Samarra implement, is smelted, while the 5th millennium Sialk pellets and the 4th millennium Gerzeh bead are meteoritic. All these examples, however, are so widely scattered in time and space as to indicate caution in drawing conclusions. The one distinction to be made seems to be that the Samarra implement and the Gerzeh beads were worked—the metal of the beads was flattened and then bent into tubular shape—while the Sialk balls apparently resulted from a chance discovery of a few small pieces of meteorite, collected for their weight and hardness, used unworked, and probably not recognized as metallic.[8]

Within the 3d millennium both meteoritic and smelted iron were in use together in at least one site: Alaca. Some fairly elaborate objects were made of either kind of iron, for example, the smelted Tell Asmar and Alaca dagger blades vis-à-vis the meteoritic Ur tool and Troy macehead. On the other hand, all the analyzed jewelry—the pin and crescent from Alaca and the amulet from Deir el-Bahari—turned out to be meteoritic.

Beyond the tests for nickel, no other types of analyses seem to have been done on this earliest iron, probably because most was so badly corroded. Thus, although we know that smelted iron was already occasionally made use of, we cannot assess whether the individual pieces result from accidental or deliberate smelting or how well worked any of them is. Whether all were of soft wrought iron or whether any had been sub-

Table 3.3. Meteoritic and Smelted Iron in the Middle Bronze Age from the
Near East and Eastern Mediterranean

	Meteoritic	Smelted	Not analyzed	Total
Egypt	—	1 (spearhead)	—	1
Anatolia	—	—	4	4
Cyprus	—	1 (lump)	1	2
Crete	—	—	1	1
Total	0	2	6	8

jected to carburizing or heat treatment remains unknown. We know that
iron was rare and valuable in this period, but we do not know if it was
desired for its usefulness or practicality. Judging from the finds in hand,
however, one would say not.

MIDDLE BRONZE AGE, CA. 2000–1600 B.C.

In contrast to the second half of the 3d millennium B.C., the first half of
the 2d millennium is poor in reported finds of iron (table 3.3). In the three
regions where iron was first found no example is known from Mesopotamia, only four are known from Anatolia, and one is from Egypt (and
that suspect). Yet two new locales, Crete and Cyprus, appear with one
and two examples, respectively. Whether the general dearth is due to the
arbitrary nature of excavation or whether it reflects a genuine temporary
decline in iron usage remains to be seen.

a. Anatolia: small piece of decorative inlay set in the bronze head of
a pin, small pieces of "wire" used to fasten an arrowhead to its shaft,
and unidentified fragments all come from Alishar Hüyük, stratum II,
ca. 1900–1700 B.C.; a fragment was found at Kusura, period C, ca. 1800–
1600 B.C. None was analyzed.[9]

b. Egypt: spearhead with flat, leaf-shaped blade and cylindrical socket
(presumably hammered), 30.50 cm in length, from Buhen, Nubia, grave
K 32, Dynasty XII, ca. 1991–1786 B.C., smelted iron, authenticity questioned.[10]

c. Cyprus: one lump each, Lapithos tomb 313 C–D, Middle Cypriot
I, ca. 1800–1750 B.C., and tomb 322 A, Early Cypriot III B; ca. 1875–
1800 B.C. The piece from tomb 313 was analyzed and found to be smelted.[11]

d. Crete: "cube" from Mavrospelio, tomb XVII pit, Middle Minoan
II, ca. 1800–1700 B.C., not analyzed.[12]

With the exception of the Buhen spearhead all Middle Bronze iron finds seem rather nondescript. In context, however, they still seem valued or "special." The Buhen spearhead and the finds from Crete and Cyprus were all from graves—that from Lapithos tomb 322 in association with gold and silver—though none was so rich as the most elaborate of the 3d millennium contexts.

Only two pieces were analyzed—the Buhen spearhead and Lapithos tomb 313—and both of these are smelted, so it is not known how or where meteoritic iron continued to be used in this era.

While material evidence for the use of iron in the early part of the 2d millennium is undeniably sparse, a certain amount of information is now available in contemporary literary documents. A number of terms, all interpreted as iron of one sort or another, are known in the "Cappadocian" texts of the Old Assyrian trading colony of Kültepe in central Anatolia, dated ca. 1900–1800 B.C. At least one of these terms, Akkadian *amūtu*, refers to a very expensive commodity, worth more than eight times the value of gold, and traded only in very small quantities suitable for decorative or luxury items (see discussions by Wertime and Muhly in chaps. 1 and 2).[13]

Around the same time as the Kültepe texts or slightly later, iron makes its first appearance in the documents of the Old Hittite Kingdom. In the well-known Anitta text, iron, in the Sumerian form of AN·BAR, is used for a throne and a scepter (?);[14] and an iron throne is also referred to in an Old Kingdom ritual text of roughly the same age.[15] Since no such objects have been found, the true function of the iron in such "thrones" —how big the thrones were and whether they were made entirely of iron or only inlaid or decorated with iron, as Maxwell-Hyslop implies[16]— can only be guessed at.

Outside Anatolia iron also figures in significant texts of the early 2d millennium. An Alalakh text dating to the 18th century B.C. refers to 400 ŠUKUR-weapons (spears?) of iron (AN·BAR),[17] an impressive number for a utilitarian purpose that cannot be equaled in the excavated material. More modest, and more in keeping with the finds, is the text from Mari, ca. 1700 B.C., mentioning an iron bracelet sent to Mari by the king of Carchemish.[18] Here we have a single item of jewelry worthy of being sent as a royal gift from one king to another, together with other rich and costly objects.

The combined textual and material evidence in the early 2d millennium attests that iron is still used as a precious and rare material, associated with royalty or the temple, or buried with other valuables in tombs. For the first time there emerges a picture of iron as a commodity or trade item. Here too, whether the terms used refer to meteoritic or smelted iron or both, it is on the market as a luxury good, more costly even than gold, much sought after, and not readily available. Only once, at Alalakh, are we confronted with documentation for a large number of iron weapons, though nowhere can we find physical evidence for such usage either in actual warfare or in storage of weapons.[19]

LATE BRONZE AGE, CA. 1600–1200 B.C.

Excavated evidence for use of iron increases considerably in the Late Bronze Age over that for the Early and Middle Bronze Ages. Not only do iron objects increase in number during these centuries, but they are also distributed over a wider geographic area. This area stretches from Mesopotamia to mainland Greece and includes most of the regions of the Levant (Syria-Palestine, Anatolia, Egypt) as well as Greece and the islands of the Eastern Mediterranean (Cyprus, Rhodes, Lesbos, Crete).

a. Mesopotamia: a dagger with a copper blade and hilt made of two iron plates fastened to the blade with an iron rivet, and a small, spherical bead came from Nuzi, stratum II (the bead from the floor of temple A), Hurrian period, ca. 15th century B.C. Neither was analyzed.[20]

b. Syria-Palestine: battle-ax with cast-on copper socket decorated with gold, Ugarit (Ras Shamra), votive offering in a sanctuary, stratum I.2, ca. 1450–1350 B.C.; rings (number unspecified), Minet el-Beida, tomb 3, 13th century B.C.; lumps mixed with lumps of copper, Alalakh level IV, room 8 of Niqmepa palace, ca. 1450–1370 B.C.; two arrowheads, Alalakh levels II and II–I, ca. 1350–1273 and 1350–1185 B.C.; spatula, Alalakh level I, ca. 1270–1185 B.C.; ring, Megiddo tomb 912 B, LB II, ca. 1400–1200 B.C.; two arrowheads and a handle, Tell es-Zuweyid, level N 204–209, LB II, ca. 1400–1230/1170 B.C.[21] Only the Ugarit ax-blade has been analyzed; it is apparently meteoritic, containing 3.25 percent nickel. It also contains 0.41 percent carbon, bringing it into the range of mild steel.[22]

c. Anatolia: fragment (of an armor scale?) and circular plaque, Alaca Hüyük, stratum IIIa, ca. 1500–1300 B.C.; a stamp seal, two nails, a needle, an arrowhead, a dagger, a bracelet, a plaque, a fragment, a long, conical, socketed handle (spearbutt?) with remains of a wooden shaft, and an "ax-like" object are all Alaca Hüyük, strata IV–II, ca. 1800–1200 B.C.[23] The following are all from Boğazköy: fragment, lower city level 2–1b, ca. 1450–1300 B.C.; fragment, Büyükkale, levels IVb–III, ca. 1450–1200; chisel, lower city level 2, ca. 1450–1350; lugged ax-blade, Büyükkale, level III, ca. 1300–1200; lugged ax-blade, lower city level 1b, ca. 1350–1300; conical spearbutt, Büyükkale, level IIIa, ca. 1300–1200; conical spearbutt, lower city level 1 in temple I in Hittite debris, ca. 1300–1200. None was analyzed.[24]

d. Egypt: arrowhead, Thebes, middle palace of Amenhotep III, Dynasty XVIII, ca. 1417–1379 B.C.; two masses of rust found under a bronze ax-head, Tell el-Amarna, Dynasty XVIII, ca. 1379–1362; small pin used as box fastening, Abydos, Dynasty XVIII, ca. 1567–1320; from the Tomb of Tutankhamun, Thebes, Dynasty XVIII, ca. 1350 B.C.: *Urs*-headrest, found under mummy's mask; "eye-of-Horus" amulet on gold *uzat* bracelet, found near lower part of thorax of mummy; dagger blade with gold and jewel encrusted haft and sheath (length of gold sheath ca. $8\frac{1}{4}''$, width ca. $1\frac{3}{4}''$); sixteen miniature chisel blades set in wooden handles found together in a box, six different blade shapes (total weight of blades ca. 4 g). The headrest, dagger, and chisels have been analyzed, and all are apparently meteoritic (nickel content unstated).[25]

e. Cyprus: lumps, Ayios Iakovos, sanctuary, Late Cypriot II, ca. 1300–1200 B.C.; small pin found in a jar, Hala Sultan Tekke, mid-13th century B.C.; traces of iron in socket of agate scepter, Kourion, unstated context, unreliable excavation, now Cesnola Collection, Metropolitan Museum, New York. None was analyzed.[26]

f. Mainland Greece: ring, Vaphio, tholos tomb, Late Helladic (LH) I–II, ca. 1550–1400 B.C.; ring with bezel and part of hoop in iron, the whole overlaid in gold, Kakovatos, tholos A, LH II, ca. 1450–1400; small square plaque, Volo, tholos tomb, LH II, ca. 1450–1400; fragments of a ring, Asine, chamber tomb I, LH II (late) or LH III, ca. 1450–1200 B.C.; three rings with large oval bezels once engraved though the designs are now obscured by corrosion, laminated (from the outside) of iron, copper, lead, and silver, Dendra, tholos tomb, LH III a, ca. 1400–1300; pendant with gold mountings and granulations at either end, Dendra, chamber tomb II, LH III b, ca. 1300–1200; traces of iron on a lead clamp used to attach door jambs to wall (function of iron not certain), Gla, palace, LH III a–b, ca. 1400–1200; tool (drill point?), Thebes, Kadmeia, jeweler's

workshop, LH III b, ca. 1300–1200; two rings, Mycenae, chamber
tombs 10 and 28, "Late Mycenaean," ca. 1550–1200; ring, Melathria
near Skoura, chamber tomb, LH III a–b, ca. 1400–1200. None was
analyzed.[27]

g. Crete: decorative nail with flat head ornamented with gold rosette,
Knossos, Late Minoan (LM) I–II, ca. 1600–1400 B.C.; two rings, one
plain, one with large bezel engraved with figure-eight shields and running
spirals and laminated of gold, bronze, iron, Phaistos, tomb, LM, ca. 1600–
1200 B.C. (?); chunk of meteorite, length ca. 29 cm, width ca. 21 cm,
thickness, 10 cm, weight ca. 20 lb; traces of saw marks on surface, found
in Hagia Triada Palace but not in situ, presumably LM I, ca. 1600–1500
B.C. None of these pieces, including the presumed meteorite, has been
analyzed.[28]

h. Aegean Islands other than Crete: fragments, Rhodes, Ialysos,
Moschou Vounara Cemetery, tomb 69, LH III b (?), ca. 1300–1200 B.C.;
tanged knife, Lesbos, Thermi, Late Bronze (?), ca. 1400–1200 B.C. (date
uncertain).[29]

Coupled with the more widespread appearance of iron in the later
2d millennium is a greater variety of object types and functions. Not only
do we have as before small items of jewelry, ceremonial weapons, and
the like, but also we begin to have evidence for at least occasional utilitarian
applications of iron—a few tools and weapons from Hittite levels at
Boğazköy and Alaca, a single tool from Mycenaean Thebes, a few odd
arrowheads from Egyptian Thebes, Alalakh, and Tell es-Zuweyid. These
utilitarian finds, however, are still few; at no site, including the Hittite
capital of Boğazköy, do they begin to approach in number their counterparts in bronze. Furthermore, the majority of iron finds continue to be
precious objects and curiosities, often combined with other luxury materials—jewelry with added gold, ceremonial daggers and battle-axes with
elaborate handles, amulets, and funerary apparatus. They are, as before,
usually found in such contexts as royal or wealthy tombs, as in Egypt
or Mycenaean Greece, or in palaces, sanctuaries, and temples.

Meteoritic iron continued to be used, as the analyzed pieces from the
Tomb of Tutankhamun and Ugarit show, and although these are few
in number relative to the total found (most of which were *not* analyzed),
they show that reliance on smelted metal as a source was not yet absolute.
The Hagia Triada meteorite—if authentic—provides evidence for working
of meteoritic iron in the Aegean. The traces of saw marks indicate that
the piece was being cut up for manufacture of some small objects; but

Table 3.4. Meteoritic and Smelted Iron in the Late Bronze Age from the
Near East and Eastern Mediterranean

	Meteoritic	Smelted	Not analyzed	Total
Mesopotamia	—	—	2	2
Egypt	16 (headrest, chisels, dagger blade)	—	4	20
Anatolia	—	—	20	20
Syria-Palestine	1 (ax-head)	—	9	10
Cyprus	—	—	3	3
Greece	—	—	13	13
Crete	1 ? (piece of meteorite, not analyzed)	—	4*	4
Aegean Islands	—	—	2	2
Total	18 ?	0	57*	74

*Includes possible piece of meteorite from col. 2.

given the poor context in which it was found and the lack of analysis, both date and attribution should be treated with caution for the present. It is not known, of course, whether this is a piece of a meteorite that fell nearby or whether it is imported.

We have no evidence for determining the location and distribution of iron meteorites in any part of the Bronze Age; whether several meteorites were known and utilized in more than one region or whether only one or two major ones were known and worked and their products shipped as precious gifts is unknown. It has been suggested that the Tutankhamun iron was imported to Egypt;[30] but the meteoritic headrest and chisels from this tomb are of types peculiar to Egypt and were thus manufactured there, wherever the raw material originated. (The equally Egyptian amulet does not appear to have been analyzed.)

Meteoritic iron does seem to have been recognized as such in antiquity. Bjorkman has collected a number of ancient Near Eastern texts dealing with meteors and meteorites; some seem to show both observation of meteorite falls and understanding of the relationship between iron derived from meteorites and its cosmic origin.[31] The Hittite term "black iron of heaven" (AN·BAR GE$_6$ nepišaš) and the Egyptian term "iron of heaven" (bia' n pet) also seem to reflect this association, although the latter did not come into use until the Nineteenth Dynasty and was then used to refer to all iron, without distinction as to origin.[32]

We have little or no evidence for production of smelted iron in the Late Bronze Age. Further analyses of the excavated pieces would doubtless reveal at least some smelted objects, but to date this has not been done. Other chapters raise the possibility of the accidental production of small amounts of iron or iron slag as a by-product of copper smelting, either through the use of iron-rich copper ores or through the use of iron oxides as fluxes.[33] The difficulty for the ancient metalworker, of course, would lie in his being able to recognize as such the iron recovered in this way and to produce useful metallic iron from the bits of spongy bloom that would have resulted from accidental smelting. Copper smelting could surely not have been a regular or reliable source of iron but might account for some of the occasional small lumps and pieces of smelted iron known since the beginning of the Bronze Age.

Evidence for deliberate smelting is even scarcer. Reports of "iron works at Kizlarkaya" in the vicinity of Boğazköy have since been refuted,[34] and no other archaeological remains are known. Only one text seems to refer to manufacture of iron. The much discussed letter of Hattusilis III, king of the Hittites ca. 1250 B.C., probably to Shalmaneser I of Assyria, attempts to put off the latter's request (or demand) for a shipment of iron of unspecified size and to appease him with a gift of an iron dagger blade.[35] The text declares that it is a bad time for producing iron, that iron will be produced but is not yet finished, and that there is no stored iron available in the king's seal-house in Kizzuwatna (probably Cilicia). Smelting, if this is what is implied here, does not seem from this text to be a booming industry. Rather, it is a seasonal affair, slow and unreliable; and a gift of a single iron dagger blade is still considered worthy of royal exchange (see discussion by Muhly in chap. 2).

There are more texts dealing with use of and trade in iron in the Late Bronze Age than with its manufacture. Most such documents are Hittite, but literary sources referring to iron are also known from Assyria, North Syria (Mitanni, Qatna, Ugarit), and Egypt, indicating either the exchange of small objects of iron among monarchs or use and storage of iron ritual and ceremonial objects in palaces or temples. Iron blades, arrowheads, and rings covered with gold are among the royal presents sent from Tušratta of Mitanni to Pharaohs Amenhotep III and Akhnaten of Egypt.[36] Iron occurs among the temple inventories of Qatna;[37] iron is buried with other precious materials as foundation deposits in Middle Assyrian temples and in Hittite palaces,[38] and it appears frequently in Hittite inventories and rituals in primarily cultic contexts.[39] Iron often occurs in these Hittite ritual texts in lists with other metals—gold, silver, copper (or bronze), lead, tin—possibly indicating that the participants wanted to use or invoke something of every such material known to them.

Composite objects constructed of several metals are also referred to; for example, an iron kettle with a lead lid in which to trap evil spirits and a statue with a frame of tin (?) and a head of iron.[40] No actual objects of these descriptions have been found, so questions of size, quantities of metal, and processes of manufacture cannot be answered completely. Such objects need not have been very big to fulfill a ritual function, however. In one text, lists of deposits of metal and stone placed under the foundations of a new house include iron objects described as two pairs of oxen, a hearth, props (?), and a door, each of which has a prescribed weight of one shekel (about half an ounce).[41] Whatever the case, the ceremonial or symbolic, rather than the utilitarian nature of iron is strongly reinforced by these texts.

Owing largely to the Hattusilis letter, the Hittites have often been credited with holding a "monopoly" over the "secret" of producing iron and/or the distribution of finished products. This view has long been questioned and cannot be upheld in light of the textual evidence and the local nature of many of the finds from regions other than Anatolia (e.g., the typically Aegean rings from Dendra and Phaistos, the peculiarly Egyptian headrest and amulet from the Tomb of Tutankhamun).[42] If the Hittite king could send an iron dagger as a gift, so could the king of Mitanni.

The Hattusilis letter may indicate a certain degree of Hittite control over the production of smelted iron, which was then shipped out as raw material to the correspondent (presumably the king of Assyria), but it says nothing of similar relations in other directions and it does not account for the contemporary usage of meteoritic iron in Egypt, Ugarit, and possibly Crete. Use of iron in Hittite Anatolia, though somewhat better documented than elsewhere, does not differ markedly in kind from that known in other regions during the Bronze Age. There is no evidence in either texts or finds that the Hittites made substantial military or agricultural applications of iron or that their iron technology was significantly advanced over that of their neighbors. If the Hittites had any such "secret," they did not yet see fit to apply the results on a major scale.

Attempts to account for the virtual disappearance of iron implements

from Hittite sites by attributing it to plundering[43] will have to consider
the relatively large numbers of contemporary bronze artifacts that were
left untouched at a time when bronze tools and weapons were desirable
and still the rule. Likewise, it is not possible to hypothesize the complete
disintegration of large amounts of iron by corrosion; some traces would
almost always remain for the careful excavator. Furthermore, the survival of quantities of iron objects in recognizable shapes despite corrosion—objects from only a few hundred years later than the time we are
speaking of—helps to invalidate this argument.

THE TRANSITION TO THE IRON AGE

The "Iron Age" per se began when iron ceased to be considered precious and was finally accepted as the predominant material for making
tools and weapons (see the discussion by Snodgrass in chap. 10). This
era first reached fruition in about the 10th century B.C. in the large region stretching from Greece to the Levantine coast, around the 9th century B.C. in Mesopotamia, and somewhat later in Europe and regions
farther to the east. By this time iron had become commonplace in everyday life, its acceptance attested not only by abundant archaeological
finds at many sites but also by literary sources. The matter-of-fact listing
of large numbers of iron weapons, the taking of great quantities of unworked iron as tribute or booty, and the metaphorical expression of
the army's might in putting its enemies "to the iron dagger" all begin
to appear in Assyrian records of the 9th and 8th centuries B.C. and continue thereafter.[44] The late 8th century Greek poet Hesiod may have
been the first to refer to the men of his own era as a "race of iron"
(*Works and Days* 174–78) and to use this phrase to symbolize the decline in moral and ethical values from the original "golden age" of hap-
piness and innocence to the dreary and mundane present. Hesiod's attitude
shows that iron had been demoted in status from precious to ordinary by
the time he wrote.

Before this stage was reached, however, the utilitarian potentialities
of iron went through a period of development that is usually termed
the "Early Iron Age," beginning around 1200 B.C. in the Eastern Mediterranean. This phase is identified in the archaeological record by the
partial conversion of tool and weapon manufacture from bronze to iron
to a point at which implements of iron equal or surpass in numbers

their counterparts in bronze. The reasons for the conversion appear to be as much historical as technological. At this time a related sequence of events led almost simultaneously to the collapse of most of the important Bronze Age civilizations—the Hittite Empire, Mycenaean Greece, New Kingdom Egypt, the North Syrian kingdoms of Ugarit and Alalakh; the resultant shifts of populations caused the influx of new peoples into Cyprus, Palestine, Anatolia, and parts of Greece.[45]

Although the widespread adoption of iron is often credited to the fall of the Hittite Empire and the breakup of its presumed monopoly and the dissemination of the "secret" of iron production to other areas of the Near East, no resultant revolution in technology or rapid increase in use of iron can be detected to suggest that this was the case. Instead, events around 1200 B.C., of which the demise of the Hittites is but one, signal the beginning of a transitional period of 200–300 years throughout the Eastern Mediterranean. During this period bronze continued to be preferred for utilitarian purposes, but iron began to be viewed as an acceptable substitute (see discussion by Wertime in chap. 1). The aftermath of historical destruction—redistribution of power, disruption of old trading patterns, and general decline in the level of material culture—likely contributed to the need to develop new resources over a fairly wide area. Lack of tin or decreased access to it as a raw material for making bronze also has been suggested as a possible reason for the intensive development of iron.[46] The development of latex and other synthetics by nations cut off from natural rubber supplies in World War II provides a modern analogy.

Since the number of iron objects increases so sharply from the 12th century onward and since I have presented the archaeological evidence for this increase in detail elsewhere,[47] the following discussion will focus on the growing usage of weapons and tools in general rather than on the enumeration of individual objects.

Weapons

Iron military weapons appear in the 12th century, primarily in tombs in Syria, Palestine, Cyprus, the island of Naxos, and possibly Greece proper (see the discussion by Snodgrass in chap. 10). The finds are few and scattered; the number of forms is limited to daggers, arrowheads, and a single long sword of a type known at the same time in bronze from a period I tomb at Hama in Syria. There is no concentration of

finds in any one area. Iron weapons were everywhere outnumbered
by bronze weapons occurring in a greater variety of types. On the
other hand, although most of these weapons were found in tombs,
they do not seem to have the strictly ceremonial character we have
observed in iron weapons of the Bronze Age.

Some of the daggers are combined not with gold but with bronze
—a dagger from Tell el-Far'ah South in Palestine has a cast bronze
hilt; another example from Kouklia in Cyprus has three bronze rivets
in the hilt. Furthermore, some sites yielded multiple examples of iron.
Several examples of iron were sometimes grouped in the same tomb
—the sword from Hama in Syria was buried with three iron arrowheads; the Tell el-Far'ah dagger was found with several iron bracelets;
the Kouklia dagger was from a group of cemeteries in which at least
six contemporary tombs contained one or more pieces of iron.[48] This
evidence suggests that iron was somewhat more freely available than
before but still not in common or ordinary use.

The trend toward conversion from bronze to iron continued in the
11th century. Iron weapons are more widely distributed than before,
occurring at a greater number of sites in each region and appearing in
a greater variety of types, though still not approaching bronze weapons in number or percentage of examples found. Most of the types
produced in each area are represented in iron as well as bronze; not
only swords, daggers, and arrowheads but also spearheads and spear
butts, lanceheads, pikes, and armor scales are known. For the first time
a type not previously known in bronze appears in iron. The iron pike
from Lapithos, T. 417 in Cyprus, dated Cypro-Geometric I A (probably late 11th century), is the earliest example of a type which became
characteristic of Cyprus in both iron and bronze and was later exported
to Crete.[49]

In no area, however, do iron weapons appear in significantly greater
concentration than in any other; nor can one detect any situation in which
one group of people held the lead in its development over any other.
The common assumption that the Philistines in 11th century Palestine
held a monopoly on iron weapons to the detriment of their enemies
the Israelites is based on a biblical text (1 Samuel 13 : 19–22) in which
the kind of metal controled by the Philistines is not specified (see discussion by Muhly in chap. 2). Examination of the physical remains
at sites associated historically with the Philistines shows some iron in use,

but here as elsewhere bronze weapons appear in greater proportions than iron ones. A military advantage owing to possession of iron weapons cannot be demonstrated by the finds and is not a necessary assumption in explaining the dominance of the Philistines over the Israelites, as the latter were at this time poorer in material culture and in technological tradition.[50] The full military potential of iron was not yet being exploited in the 11th century B.C.

In the 10th century iron weapons appear for the first time in greater proportions than bronze. In Palestine, Cyprus, Greece, and Crete excavated iron weapons outnumber but do not replace bronze, while at Hama in Syria, iron weapons reach about 40 percent of the total in period III tombs (10th/9th centuries)—approaching, though not surpassing those of bronze. No strikingly new types of weapons are noted; but there are some indications that certain types of weapons were now being made mostly, if not exclusively, in iron—for example, spearheads in Palestine, swords at Hama, pikes and swords in Cyprus, swords and possibly daggers and arrowheads in Greece.[51] Very few bronze weapons of any type are found on Crete or the other islands of the Aegean. Again, we cannot speak of dominance in any one area.

From the Levantine coast to the western shores of the Aegean iron weaponry has become the rule rather than the exception, though use of bronze for this purpose is not completely supplanted.

Tools

Because ordinary tools are not commonly placed in graves, evidence for the development of agricultural, industrial, and domestic implements is much spottier than for weapons, and there are few areas where a continuous development of any tool type may be traced in either bronze or iron. An exception is the one-edged knife, which actually may serve dual functions as both cutting tool and personal weapon, and is often buried with the dead. The knife is, in fact, the most frequently occurring iron tool type in the transitional period. In the 12th century B.C. knives are almost the only iron tools found anywhere in the Eastern Mediterranean. A number of them which have bronze rivets in their hafts for the attachment of wooden or ivory handles or hilt plates may possibly be linked typologically, though they differ somewhat from each other in overall form. These occur at Tell Qasile in Palestine, Hama, Naxos, Lefkandi in Euboea (one example each), Kouklia in Cyprus (three examples), and

Perati in Greece (two examples).[52] This practice of bimetallism is echoed occasionally in contemporary weapons (see above) and continues for a time in most of the areas named.[53] Whether bimetallism was practiced primarily for decorative or for technological reasons, or both, is a matter for further study.

While iron knives appear with some regularity in 12th century B.C. contexts, no iron implements with strictly agricultural function are known at this time. This may be due in part to the lack of properly stratified material in many regions, such as Greece and Syria, where most excavated material is funerary in nature. Where 12th century material from habitation sites exists, however, as in Palestine and Cyprus, large numbers of bronze implements have been found—including ploughshares, axes, adzes, hoes, and other equipment, most of which are forms not duplicated in iron.[54]

In 11th century contexts agricultural use of iron appears for the first time. Though most tool types continue to be made exclusively in bronze, such objects as a ploughshare from Gibeah, a sickle from Beth Shemesh, and a hafted ax-head from Tell el-Far'ah South—all from occupation levels—testify to the advent of iron for practical use in Palestine, though it is still far less commonly used than bronze.[55]

At Hama in Syria and in Greece and Cyprus, where most 11th century material is from tombs, the commonest iron tool type remains the one-edged knife. It may be significant, however, that in both Syria and Cyprus these knives now outnumber their counterparts in bronze, while in Greece they are about equal to them in number (though very few of either material were found).[56] In Crete, the Subminoan site of Karphi provides the only nonfunerary material, and here a variety of bronze tools was found with no parallels in iron.[57]

In the 10th century, finds of iron agricultural implements increase significantly in Palestine, where iron tools now outnumber, though do not replace, those of bronze. Iron axes, adzes, hoes, ploughshares, sickles, and chisels can all be found in 10th century contexts at Tell Jemmeh (Petrie's Gerar); one or more of these types also occurs at Tell Abu Huwam level III, Tell Beit Mirsim B3, Beth Shemesh level II, Megiddo level VA–IVB, Tell el-Far'ah North niveau III, and Ta-'anach.[58] Unfortunately, in no other area do we have a sufficient number of finds of this era to draw any significant conclusions. Few tools of any description have been published from 10th century Syria,

Cyprus, Greece, Crete, and the Aegean Islands, and these few are almost all knives found in burials. Perhaps it is significant, however, that iron knives in every area seem to have completely replaced those of bronze (though one would want much more evidence before stating this as fact). One or two agricultural implements have been found in an early stratum at Sardis in western Anatolia that seems to date from this time; but excavation at this level was confined to a limited sounding, so we have no idea of the actual extent of agricultural uses of iron at this site.[59]

Despite the paucity of information in many areas it seems possible to reach the tentative conclusion that iron was approaching something like common use throughout the Eastern Mediterranean for both weapons and agricultural tools by the end of the 10th century B.C. and never really lost this position thereafter. Certainly this was true of weapons, where the line of development is clearer. With tools we have clear-cut evidence in only one area—Palestine—but an analogous development elsewhere seems likely, especially as widespread acceptance of iron and knowledge of ironworking can be demonstrated by the adoption of iron for weapons. It may be possible to suggest here, as Pleiner and Bjorkman did for Assyria, that military applications of the new material somewhat preceded other uses;[60] but judging from the situation in Palestine at least this cannot have been by much.

At the same time, however, iron did not entirely lose its status as a metal suitable for jewelry and decorative objects. In fact, at a number of sites in the Eastern Mediterranean a considerable increase in iron jewelry from the 12th to 10th centuries can be demonstrated, showing that it still had a certain value for that purpose.[61] Bronze did not disappear from use, however. The manufacture of bronze tools and weapons continued for a long time in antiquity. Snodgrass has shown a resurgence of bronze usage for vessels, jewelry, and some weapon types in Greece after ca. 900 B.C.;[62] this may indicate a rejuvenation of the tin trade, which enabled greater degrees of specialization and choice between bronze and iron to take place.

Technological difficulties in the production of iron may account for the slowness with which it was adopted for practical use. Iron ores are widely available and accessible to most areas of the Eastern Mediterranean;[63] but efficient methods of manufacture for wrought iron were not easily developed by smiths accustomed to the casting of bronze objects, and techniques for improving the hardness and strength of wrought iron by the addition of carbon, quenching, and proper heat treatment would be needed for the development of more advanced applications of iron. The inherently different techniques used in working bronze and iron and the greater difficulty of iron working would inhibit mass production of iron implements until the training of blacksmiths had become sufficiently specialized as to develop its own traditions and methods of working.

Unfortunately, we know very little about the technology of early iron manufacture in the Bronze Age or the transitional period, as we have neither the blacksmith shops themselves nor very many scientific analyses of the finished products to tell us the level of competence they had reached. We know that smelted iron existed as early as the 3d millennium (and possibly before), though whether it was accidentally or deliberately produced is not known. We know nothing of the quality of these objects. Their scarcity and expense, and the fact that meteoritic iron continued to be used side by side with smelted iron down to at least the 14th century B.C. show that deliberate production was not a frequent activity.

Certain techniques, such as carburization, could have been accomplished more or less accidentally by heating iron in a charcoal fire. Two late 12th/early 11th century B.C. knives from Idalion in Cyprus were found on analysis to have been carburized. One of these knives had also been quenched, making it the earliest iron implement known to have undergone this treatment.[64] This occurrence did not herald the start of universal adoption of this technique, however. Analysis of other objects from a number of different sites in the Near East and Europe (most of them quite a bit later in date than the Idalion knife) show that while the addition of varying amounts of carbon came to be a fairly regular thing, the techniques of quenching and subsequent heat treatment were only occasionally applied.[65]

Little is known about the production of iron or the general organization of the blacksmith craft in most places, either in the Bronze Age or in the Early Iron Age. Archaeological resources are of very little help in these periods. Not only is there no evidence for blacksmith shops or tools in the Bronze Age (see above), but the dearth of information continues for several centuries thereafter. What little archaeological evidence there is for the smelting and forging of iron is scattered from western Italy to Palestine and does not precede the turn of the 1st millennium by much.

A number of transitional period establishments for the smelting of copper and the working of bronze are known in Cyprus and Palestine.[66] At some of these, iron-rich copper ores were the primary raw material, or iron oxides were utilized as fluxes;[67] but so far there is no recognizable trace of contemporary ironworking at the same sites, either in direct association with the copper works or separately. At Metsamor, in Soviet Armenia, finds provisionally interpreted as relating to large-scale copper and bronze production extended from the 3d millennium to the 8th century B.C. and may have been joined by iron production around 1000/900 B.C., though this is doubtful.[68] Iron slags have been identified at Vardaroftsa in Macedonia dated to the 12th century B.C., but their association with a full-fledged iron industry at this date has been questioned.[69] Perhaps somewhat later, though the date is in question, is a hearth that "may have been used as a forge," found together with lumps of iron ore at the site of Malthi in southwest Greece.[70]

The so-called iron smelting furnaces of Gerar (Tell Jemmeh) have long been in the literature but are poorly understood.[71] Petrie gave no description of the contents of the furnaces or of any associated finds such as slags. Forbes asserts that "no piece of ore was ever smelted in these 'smelting furnaces'" and believes instead that they may have been military forges.[72] Although Tell Jemmeh is being reexcavated, these installations have not yet been scientifically published; and the type of metallurgical activities engaged in there is not established.

The earliest clear-cut evidence for forging in Greek lands comes in the late 8th century B.C. metalworking site at Mezzavia on Pithekoussai (modern Ischia), a Greek colony off the Italian west coast. Various structures uncovered in excavations contained large amounts of bloom-iron, slags, a smith's forge with stone anvils, fragments of finished iron, and whetstones. The complex seems also to have been involved in the working of other metals, as the finds included fragments of bronze ingots, unfinished miscast bronzes, bits of bronze sheet and wire, and lumps of lead. Iron does not appear to have been smelted on the site but to have been imported, perhaps from central Italy, in the form of bloom-iron.[73] While the information to be gained on early metallurgy from this site is very promising, it dates to the full Iron Age and does not provide us with knowledge of the earliest industrial production of iron.

Despite the relatively late date, however, at Ischia the crafts of blacksmithing and bronzesmithing were not yet strictly separated, a fact which is also suggested by analysis of certain iron artifacts from elsewhere. A number of scholars have noted that analyses of iron swords and daggers from 9th to 7th century Luristan often reveal techniques of manufacture more appropriate to the bronzesmith than the blacksmith.[74] Pleiner's analysis of a few 8th century implements from Khorsabad also shows use of techniques not completely consistent with skilled ironworking,[75] yet another indication of the lack of complete control over the special techniques for producing high-quality iron.

The earliest literary references to blacksmiths add very little to our knowledge of early iron technology and the organization of its craft. A 12th century Assyrian text mentions one blacksmith as a craftsman attached to the staff of the royal palace, a status that was still common in Assyria in the 8th and 7th centuries. Although ironsmiths are distinguished from coppersmiths in the terminology of Assyrian texts, their functions often overlapped; both texts and finds attest to blacksmiths who worked in copper and coppersmiths who worked in iron[76] —still more confirmation of the lack of strict specialization that persisted into the Iron Age. Kinnier Wilson equates the *šelap(p)ājû*, a group of foreign metalsmiths working in Assyria, with the Chalybes, a people living in the Pontic region whom later Greek tradition associated with early mastery of iron, and views them as highly specialized traveling craftsmen.[77] Yet even if this theory is correct, it tells us little or nothing about the kind of technology practiced by either or both groups.

Given the uncertain technical capabilities of the early smiths and the unreliable nature of many of their products, we can begin to understand the reasons for the rather halting adoption of iron, and the continued production of bronze utilitarian implements begins to fall into place. Early experiments with smelted iron as a precious metal and the widespread availability of iron ores naturally led metalworkers to turn to iron when, as seems likely, decreased trade and shortages in supplies of tin drove the price of bronze too high. A transitional period of more intense development of iron resulted in the production of greater numbers of implements that, though variable in quality, began to approach bronze in cost and efficiency. By the end of the 10th century B.C. in the Eastern Mediterranean the full Iron Age was reached. Iron had become fully accepted as a material appropriate for many of the daily needs of life, the blacksmith's craft was established (though not always distinct from that of the bronzesmith), and it remained only to improve the techniques of working iron and to widen its applications to even more types of useful equipment—a process which has continued down to our own time.

ACKNOWLEDGMENTS

I am delighted to dedicate this article to Cyril Stanley Smith, who has done so much to advance the study of early iron metallurgy, and who has generously given me the benefit of his expertise on several occasions. I would also like to thank Lawrence E. Stager for reading the manuscript and making a number of helpful suggestions, and John Cullinan and Sarah and Max Cohn for their help in preparing the manuscript.

NOTES

1. E. g., Stefan Przeworski, *Die Metallindustrie Anatoliens in der Zeit von 1500–700 vor Chr.*, Internationales Archiv für Ethnologie, vol. 36, suppl. (Leiden, 1939), pp. 138–55; Gerald A. Wainwright, "The Coming of Iron," *Antiquity* 10 (1936): 5–24, esp. 7–18; Herbert H. Coghlan, *Notes on Prehistoric and Early Iron in the Old World*, Pitt Rivers Museum—Occasional Papers on Technology (Oxford, 1956), pp. 32–34, 61–67; Robert J. Forbes, *Studies in Ancient Technology*, 2d ed. rev., 9 vols. (Leiden: E. J. Brill, 1964–72), 9: 236–75; Hans-Günter Buchholz and Vassos Karageorghis, *Prehistoric Greece and Cyprus*, Trans. F. Garvie (New York: Phaidon, 1973), pp. 27–29; Jane C. Waldbaum, *From Bronze to Iron: The Transition from the Bronze Age to the Iron Age in the Eastern Mediterranean*, Studies in Mediterranean Archaeology, vol. 54 (Göteborg: Paul Åströms Forlag, 1978), chap. 2.

2. For discussion and evaluation of many of these see Waldbaum, *Bronze to Iron*, chap. 2.

3. Ernst Herzfeld, *Die vorgeschichtlichen Töpfereien von Samarra*, Die Ausgrabungen von Samarra (Berlin: D. Reimer, 1930), 5: 1, 5, fig. f, pl. 47; L. Halm in Roman Ghirshman, *Fouilles de Sialk* (Paris: Geuthner, 1939), 2: 206; Wainwright in William M. F. Petrie, Gerald A. Wainwright, and Ernest MacKay, *The Labyrinth, Gerzeh and Mazguneh* (London: British School of Archaeology in Egypt, 1912), pp. 15–19, pl. 4.1, 2, 5; C. H. Desch, "Sumerian Copper," British Association for the Advancement of Science (hereafter BAAS), *Report of the 96th Meeting . . . 1928* (London, 1929), 437–41, esp. 440–41; Alfred Lucas, *Ancient Egyptian Materials and Industries*, 4th ed., rev. by J. R. Harris (London: E. Arnold, 1962), p. 237; Sir Robert Mond and Oliver H. Myers, *Cemeteries of Armant* (London: Egypt Exploration Society, 1937), 1: 117, 120, pls. 43.1, 46.5.

4. Uruk: Ernst Heinrich in Arnold Nöldeke, Arndt von Haller, Heinz Lenzen, and

Ernst Heinrich, *Achter vorläufiger Bericht über die von der deutschen Forschungsgemeinschaft in Uruk-Warka unternommenen Ausgrabungen*, Abhandlungen der preussischen Akademie der Wissenschaften 1936, Phil.-Hist. Klasse no. 13 (Berlin, 1937), p. 53; Khafajah: Cornelius Hillen, "The Early Development of Metal-working in the Ancient Near East" (Ph.D. diss., University of Chicago, 1955), p. 120; Kish: Ernest MacKay, *A Sumerian Palace and the "A" Cemetery at Kish, Mesopotamia, Part II*, Field Museum of Natural History Anthropology Memoirs, vol. 1.2 (Chicago, 1929), pp. 97, 123–24, pl. 36.2; for date: *Cambridge Ancient History*, 3d ed. rev. (Cambridge: Cambridge University Press, 1971), 1.2: 241, 274–75 (hereafter *CAH*³); Tell Asmar: Henri Frankfort, *Iraq Excavations of the Oriental Institute 1932/33*, Oriental Institute Communications, no. 17 (Chicago: University of Chicago Press, 1934), pp. 59–61; idem, "Early Iron in Iraq," *Man* 50 (1950): 100; Desch, "Sumerian Copper," BAAS, *Report of the Annual Meeting, 1933* (London, 1933), p. 303; Ur: Charles Leonard Woolley, *Ur Excavations* (London and Philadelphia: Trustees of the British Museum and of the Museum of the University of Pennsylvania, 1934), 2: 49, 293 (confused with Al-'Ubaid), 542; Desch, "Sumerian Copper," BAAS, *Report of the 96th Meeting*, pp. 440–41; Chagar Bazar: Max E. L. Mallowan, "The Excavations at Tall Chagar Bazar, and an Archaeological Survey of the Ḫabur Region, 1934–5," *Iraq* 3 (1936): 1–86, esp. 11, 26–27, 58; idem, *Iraq* 4 (1937): 93–185, esp. 98; Mari: André Parrot, review of Mallowan, "Excavations at Tall Chagar Bazar . . . 1934–5," in *Archiv für Orientforschung* 12 (1937–1939): 151–52.

5. Alaca, tomb K: Hâmit Z. Koşay, *Les fouilles d'Alaca Höyük*, Türk Tarih Kurumu Yayinlarindan (hereafter TTKY), ser. 5, no. 5 (Ankara, 1951), p. 167, pl. 182.4; Theodore A. Wertime, "The Beginnings of Metallurgy: A New Look," *Science* 182 (30 Nov. 1973): 875–87, esp. 885; idem, "Pyrotechnology: Man's First Industrial Uses of Fire," *American Scientist* 61 (1973): 670–82, esp. 682 n. 17; tombs MA, MA', MC: Koşay, *Ausgrabungen von Alaca Höyük*, TTKY, ser. 5, no. 2a (Ankara, 1944), pp. 107, 119, 129, 187 ff.; pls. 87, 95, 100; tomb T.M.: Remzi O. Arik, *Les fouilles d'Alaca Höyük*, TTKY, ser. 5, no. 1 (Ankara, 1937), p. 95, fig. 129D; Troy: Wilhelm Dörpfeld, *Troja und Ilion* (Athens: Beck and Barth, 1902), 1: 385, fig. 356, p. 423, table II; Hubert Schmidt, *Heinrich Schliemann's Sammlung trojanischer Altertümer* (Berlin: G. Reimer, 1902), p. 244, no. 6116a, b; Keith Branigan, *Aegean Metalwork of the Early and Middle Bronze Age* (Oxford: Clarendon Press, 1974), p. 56 (mistaking two samples of the same object for two different objects); for date cf. Carl W. Blegen, John L. Caskey, Marion Rawson, and Jerome Sperling, *Troy* (Princeton: Princeton University Press, 1950), 1: 208–13; Tarsus: Hetty Goldman, *Excavations at Gözlü Kule, Tarsus* (Princeton: Princeton University Press, 1956), 2: 33; Dorak: James Mellaart, "The Royal Treasure of Dorak . . .," *Illustrated London News* (28 Nov. 1959): 754, figs. 20, 21; idem, *CAH*³ 1.2: 391 (mistakenly refers to two iron weapons instead of one).

6. Giza, Mycerinus Temple: George A. Reisner, *Mycerinus: The Temples of the Third Pyramid at Giza* (Cambridge, Mass.: Harvard University Press, 1931), p. 36; Dows Dunham and William J. Young, "An Occurrence of Iron in the Fourth Dynasty," *Journal of Egyptian Archaeology* (hereafter *JEA*) 28 (1942): 57–58; Cheops pyramid: Col. Howard Vyse, *Operations Carried on at the Pyramids of Gizeh in 1837* (London, 1840), pp. 275–77; Abydos: William F. Petrie, *Abydos Part II. 1903* (London: Egyptian Exploration Fund, 1903), p. 33; Deir el-Bahari: G. Brunton, "'Pesesh-kef' Amulets," *Annales du Service des*

Antiquités de l'Égypte 35 (1935): 213–17, esp. 214, fig. 4; Desch, "Sumerian Copper," BAAS, *Report of the Annual Meeting, 1936* (London, 1936), p. 310. For discussion of several of the above cf. Lucas, *Egyptian Materials*, pp. 237–38; Christofer Hawkes, "Early Iron in Egypt," *Antiquity* 10 (1936): 355–57.

7. Because of their relatively low nickel content the meteoritic nature of these pieces has been questioned. Coghlan, *Early Iron*, pp. 33–34, suggests that they are derived from low-nickel meteoritic iron. According to Brian H. Mason, *Meteorites* (New York and London: Wiley, 1962), p. 131, "No iron meteorite contains less than 4% nickel—actually most modern analyses . . . show at least 5% nickel, and some of the analyses with lower nickel contents are probably erroneous." Both Mason, *Meteorites*, and John D. Buddhue, *The Oxidation and Weathering of Meteorites* (Albuquerque: University of New Mexico Press, 1957), pp. 129 ff., point out that older analyses of meteoritic iron tended to yield too low a nickel content. Buddhue also notes the possibility of loss of nickel content through weathering. Either or both of these possibilities would be enough to account for the relatively low percentages of nickel in the Troy and Alaca specimens as well as in the Ras Shamra ax (below, n. 21).

8. L. Halm in Ghirshman, *Fouilles de Sialk*, 2: 206; cf. Coghlan, *Early Iron*, pp. 29–32, on problems of working meteoritic iron.

9. Alishar: Hans H. von der Osten, *The Alishar Hüyük, Seasons of 1930–32, Part II* (Chicago: University of Chicago Press, 1939), pp. 253, 264, 273, figs. 284, 290; date: Seton Lloyd, *Early Anatolia* (Harmondsworth: Penguin Books, 1956), pp. 33–34; Kusura: Winifred Lamb, "Excavations at Kusura Near Afyon Karahisar," *Archaeologia* 86 (1936): 1–64, esp. 39; date: idem, *Archaeologia* 87 (1937): 217–73, esp. 217.

10. David Randall-MacIver and Charles L. Woolley, *Buhen* (Philadelphia: The University Museum, 1911), pp. 193, 211, pl. 88; Randall-MacIver, "The Iron Spear of Buhen," *Antiquity* 9 (1935): 348–50; Wainwright, "Coming of Iron," pp. 9–11.

11. Einar Gjerstad, John Lindros, Erik Sjoqvist, and Alfred Westholm, *The Swedish Cyprus Expedition* (hereafter *SCE*) (Stockholm, 1934), 1: 97, no. 44, 148, no. 32; Paul Åström, *The Middle Cypriote Bronze Age* (Lund: H. Ohlssons, 1957), pp. 135, 200, 240–41. Åström includes the lump from T. 313 C–D with MC material, although Gjerstad assigns it to EC III.

12. E. J. Forsdyke, "The Mavro Spelio Cemetery at Knossos," British School at Athens, *Annual* (hereafter *BSA*) 28 (1926–27): 243–96, esp. 279, 296, fig. 1.

13. Benno Landsberger, "Tin and Lead: The Adventures of Two Vocables," *Journal of Near Eastern Studies* 24 (1965): 285–96, esp. 290–91 n. 25; idem, "Kommt Ḫattum 'Hettiterland' und Ḫattī'um 'Hettiter' in den Kültepe-Tafeln vor," *Archiv Orientální* 18.1–2 (1950): 329–50, esp. 331 n. 14; Paul Garelli, *Les Assyriens en Cappadoce* (Paris: A. Maisonneuve, 1963), pp. 112–13, 187, 202, 219, 272–76, 284. For other possible terms meaning iron in these texts cf. K. R. Maxwell-Hyslop, "The Metals Amūtu and Aši'u in the Kültepe Texts," *Anatolian Studies* 22 (1972): 159–62; Judith K. Bjorkman, "Meteors and Meteorites in the Ancient Near East," *Meteoritics* 8 (1973): 91–130, esp. 110–13.

14. KBo III 22 vs 75: Bedrich Hrozný, "L'Invasion des Indo-Europeeans en Asie Mineure vers 2000 av. J.-C.," *Archiv Orientální* 1 (1929): 273–99, esp. 280–81; Hans G. Güterbock, review of Przeworski, *Metallindustrie*, in *Orientalia* 12 (1943): 146–51, esp. 150–51.

15. KBo XVII 88 iii 11, 25: Erich Neu, "Ein althethitisches Gewitterritual," *Studien zu den Boğazköy-Texten*, vol. 12 (Wiesbaden: O. Harrassowitz, 1970), p. 36.

16. Maxwell-Hyslop, "*Amūtu* and *Aši'u*," p. 161.

17. Donald J. Wiseman, *The Alalakh Tablets*, Occasional Publications of the British Institute of Archaeology at Ankara, no. 2 (London, 1953), p. 107, no. 410.

18. Georges Dossin, *Archives royales de Mari*, vol. 5 (Paris: Geuthner, 1952), p. 21, no. 5, line 9.

19. Aharon Kempinski and Silvin Košak, "Hittite Metal 'Inventories' (CTH 242) and their Economic Implications," *Tel Aviv* 4 (1977): 87–93, esp. 87, suggest that the paucity of metal finds in ancient sites may be explained by the standard practice of enemy looting of metal implements during invasion or raid. They cite KUB XXVI 69 vi 7 ff., "The *Araunna*-people have looted the bronze implements of the town as customary," in support.

20. Richard F. S. Starr, *Nuzi*, 2 vols. (Cambridge, Mass.: Harvard University Press, 1939), 1: 94, 470, 475; 2: pl. 125 KK (dagger).

21. Ugarit: Claude F. A. Schaeffer, *Ugaritica* (Paris: Geuthner, 1939), 1: 107 ff.; Harry C. Richardson, "A Mitannian Battle Axe from Ras Shamra," *Berytus* 8 (1943): 72; Wilhelm Witter, "Über die Herkunft des Eisens," *Zeitschrift für deutsche Vorgeschichte*, Heft 1–2 (Leipzig, 1942), p. 55; Coghlan, *Early Iron*, pp. 34, 63; Minet el-Beida: Schaeffer, "Les fouilles de Minet-el-Beida et de Ras Shamra," *Syria* 10 (1929): 285–97, esp. 292; Alalakh: Charles L. Woolley, *Alalakh* (Oxford: Oxford University Press, 1955), pp. 120, 282, 279; Megiddo: Philip L. O. Guy and Robert M. Engberg, *Megiddo Tombs* (Chicago: University of Chicago Press, 1938), p. 162; pl. 128.19, fig. 176.7; Tell es-Zuweyid: William F. Petrie, *Anthedon, Sinai* (London: British School of Archaeology in Egypt, 1937), pl. 25.93, 97, 100. Some doubt may attach to the dating of some of these pieces.

22. Because of the low nickel content, L. Brun, who made the analysis (Schaeffer, *Ugaritica* 1: 110 n. 2), denied that the iron was meteoritic and considered it to be smelted from pyrrhotite ore (ferrous sulfide), which has a nickel content of 2–5%. Witter, "Herkunft des Eisens," p. 55, and Richardson, "Mitannian Battle Axe," p. 72, prefer the meteoritic attribution, stating that pyrrhotite ore would have been too difficult to smelt by available methods. Pending reexamination it is probably safest to consider the blade meteoritic with perhaps too low a reading for nickel (see above, n. 7).

23. All these objects are rather loosely attributed to the Hittite period, which encompasses all of strata IV–II, ca. 1800–1200 B.C. (Hâmit Z. Koşay and Mahmut Akok, *Ausgrabungen von Alaca Höyük*, TTKY, ser. 5, no. 6 [Ankara, 1966], p. 118); thus some may fall in the earlier part of the 2d millennium, or Middle Bronze Age. Since the findspots and levels are not given in the catalogue of metal objects in the publication (pp. 183 ff.), it is impossible to assess the contexts in which they were found.

24. Alaca: Koşay, *Fouilles*, 1951, pl. 85.3, p. 140; Koşay and Akok, *Alaca Höyük Excavations*, TTKY, ser. 5, no. 28 (Ankara, 1973), p. 98; Koşay and Akok, *Ausgrabungen*, 1966, pp. 184, 191, 195, 197, 198, 227–28, pls. 41–43, 46; Boğazköy: Rainer M. Boehmer, *Die Kleinfunde von Boğazköy aus den Grabungskampagnen 1931–1939 und 1952–1969*, Wissenschaftliche Veröffentlichung der deutschen Orient-Gesellschaft (hereafter WVDOG), vol. 87 (Berlin, 1972), pp. 137, 138, 144, 145, pls. 43–46; stratigraphy and dating: W. Schirmer, *Die Bebauung am unteren Büyükkale-Nordwesthang in Boğazköy:*

Ergebnisse der Untersuchungen der Grabungscampagnen 1960–1963, WVDOG, vol. 81 (Berlin, 1969), p. 39, fig. 17. I have omitted Boehmer, *Kleinfunde*, pp. 147, 149, 151, 158, nos. 1300, 1368–71, 1513, 1628–30, because although they were found in level 1 of the Hittite era, Boehmer feels they might be intrusive from later Phrygian levels.

25. Thebes: William C. Hayes, *The Scepter of Egypt*, 2 vols. (Cambridge, Mass.: Harvard University Press, 1959), 2: 255; Amarna: F. L. Griffith, "Excavations at El-'Amarnah, 1923–24," *JEA* 10 (1924): 299–305, esp. 303; Abydos: John Garstang, *El Arábah* (London: B. Quatrich, 1901), p. 30; Tomb of Tutankhamun: Howard Carter, *The Tomb of Tut-Ankh-Amen*, 3 vols. (London: Cassell and Co., 1927, 1933), 2: 109, 122, 135, pls. 77b, 82a, 87b; 3: 89 ff., pl. 27a, c, e, g, j, m; Lucas, *Egyptian Materials*, p. 239; Wainwright, "Iron in Egypt," *JEA* 18 (1932): 3–15, esp. 7; Bjorkman, "Meteors," pp. 124, 125.

26. Ayios Iakovos: Gjerstad et al., *SCE* 1: 317, no. 17: L. Åström, *Studies on the Arts and Crafts of the Late Cypriote Bronze Age* (Lund: Berlingska Boktryckeriet, 1967), pp. 2, 87; Hala Sultan Tekke: Paul Åström, personal communication, April 1973; Kourion: John L. Myres, *Handbook of the Cesnola Collection of Antiquities from Cyprus* (New York: Metropolitan Museum of Art, 1914), p. 374, no. 3001.

27. Vaphio: Chrestos Tsountas, "Ereunai en tai Lakonikei kai o Taphos tou Vapheiou," *Archaiologike Ephemeris* (hereafter *ArchEph*) (1889): 129–72, esp. 147: Kakovatos: Kurt Müller, "Alt-Pylos II. Die Funde aus den Kuppelgräbern von Kakovatos," *Mitteilungen des deutschen archäologischen Instituts, Athenische Abteilung* 34 (1909): 269–328, esp. 275, pl. 13.35; Volo: K. Kourouniotis, "Anaskaphe Tholotou Taphou en Volo," *ArchEph* (1906): 211–40, esp. 236–37; Spyridon Iakovides, "The Appearance of Iron in Greece," *Athens Annals of Archaeology* 3 (1970): 293–96, esp. 295; Asine: Otto Frödin and Axel W. Persson, *Asine* (Stockholm: Generalstabens litografiska anstalts förlag, 1938), p. 373; Dendra: Persson, *The Royal Tombs at Dendra Near Midea* (Lund: C. W. K. Gleerup, 1931), pp. 33, 56, figs. 35, 79, 102, pl. 33; Gla: A. de Ridder, "Fouilles de Gha," *Bulletin de correspondance hellénique* 18 (1894): 271–310, esp. 293–94; Chrestos Tsountas and J. Irving Manatt, *The Mycenaean Age* (London, 1897), p. 381; Thebes: Buchholz and Karageorghis, *Prehistoric Greece*, p. 27, no. 20; Sarantis Symeonoglou, *Kadmeia*, vol. 1, *Mycenaean Finds from Thebes, Greece. Excavation at 14 Oedipus St.*, Studies in Mediterranean Archaeology, vol. 35 (Göteberg: Paul Åströms Förlag, 1973), pp. 15, 70, fig. 274.8; Mycenae: Tsountas, "Anaskaphai Taphon en Mykenais," *ArchEph* (1888): 119–79, esp. 135, 141, 147; Melathria: A. Dimacopoulou, "Mycenaean Chamber Tombs Near Skoura in Lakonia," *Athens Annals of Archaeology* 1 (1968): 40–41.

28. Knossos: Arthur J. Evans, "Knossos. Summary Report of the Excavations in 1900. I. The Palace," *BSA* 6 (1899–1900): 3–93, esp. 66; Phaistos: L. Savignoni, "Scavi e scoperte nella necropoli di Phaestos," *Monumenti Antichi* 14 (1904): 501–666, esp. 593–94, figs. 55, 56; Müller, "Alt-Pylos," p. 275 n. 1 (thinks that plain ring is silver, not iron); Hagia Triada: Spyridon Marinatos, "Two Interplanetary Phenomena of 468 B.C.," Akademia Athenon, *Pragmateiai* 24, fasc. 4 (1963): 24–45, esp. 43, pl. 1; Iakovides, "Iron in Greece," p. 294, fig. 1. Marinatos, "Two Interplanetary Phenomena," p. 44, also alludes to the interesting practice of calling certain Minoan seals "... when the stone has a deep chestnut or black colour, sometimes 'haematite' and sometimes 'meteorite.' Anyhow, whenever the seal is heavy as if it were metallic, it is certainly a matter of mete-

orite." One would certainly want analyses of any such objects before making such an assumption.

29. Rhodes: Giulio Jacopi, "Nuovi scavi nella necropoli micenea di Jalisso," *Annuario della R. Scuola Archeologica di Atene* 13–14 (1930–31): 253–345, esp. 284, fig. 26; Lesbos: Winifred Lamb, *Excavations at Thermi in Lesbos* (Cambridge: Cambridge University Press, 1936), p. 207, pl. 25.

30. Carter, *Tut-Ankh-Amen*, 2: 135.

31. Bjorkman, "Meteors," pp. 91–124, esp. 110–18.

32. Ibid., p. 114.

33. On this see, e.g., Arthur R. Steinberg and Frank L. Koucky, "Preliminary Metallurgical Research on the Ancient Cypriot Copper Industry," in *American Expedition to Idalion, Cyprus: First Preliminary Report, Seasons of 1971 and 1972*, eds. Lawrence E. Stager, Anita Walker, and G. Ernest Wright, Bulletin of the American Schools of Oriental Research Supplement, no. 18 (Cambridge, Mass., 1974), p. 152; Wertime, "Man's First Encounters with Metallurgy," *Science* 146 (4 Dec. 1964): 1257–67, esp. 1262; idem, "A Metallurgical Expedition through the Persian Desert," *Science* 159 (1 Mar. 1968): 927–35, esp. 935; and Strathmore R. B. Cooke and Stanley Aschenbrenner, "The Occurrence of Metallic Iron in Ancient Copper," *Journal of Field Archaeology* 2 (1975): 251–66, esp. 252–53.

34. Machteld J. Mellink, "Archaeology in Asia Minor," *American Journal of Archaeology* 66 (1962): 71–85, esp. 74; Schirmer, *Bebauung am unteren Büyükkale*, p. 35.

35. KBo I 14: 20–27: Albrecht Goetze, *Kizzuwatna and the Problem of Hittite Geography* (New Haven: Yale University Press, 1940), pp. 29–39.

36. Jörgen Knudtzon, *Die el Amarna Tafeln* (Leipzig: J. C. Hinrichs, 1915), 1: 159, 163, 173, 201.

37. Charles Virolleaud, "Les tablettes cunéiformes de Mishrifé-Ḳaṭna," *Syria* 9 (1928): 90–96, esp. 92; idem, *Syria* 11 (1930): 311–42.

38. K. R. Maxwell-Hyslop, "Assyrian Sources of Iron. A Preliminary Survey of the Historical and Geographical Evidence," *Iraq* 36 (1974): 139–54, esp. 140; Radomir Pleiner and Judith K. Bjorkman, "The Assyrian Iron Age: The History of Iron in the Assyrian Civilization," *Proceedings of the American Philosophical Society* 118 (1974): 283–313, esp. 286; James B. Pritchard, ed. *Ancient Near Eastern Texts Relating to the Old Testament*, 2d ed. (Princeton: Princeton University Press, 1955), pp. 356–57 (KBo IV 1 i passim).

39. E.g., Hrozný, "Bericht über *Tešup*-Tempel," *Hethitische Keilschrifttexte aus Boghazköi* (Leipzig: J. C. Hinrichs, 1919), 1–27 (KBo II 1 passim); Pritchard, *Texts*, pp. 357–58 (KUB XXIX 1 i 49, ii 52); see also Emmanuel Laroche, "Études de vocabulaire VI," *Revue hittite et asianique* 60 (1957): 9–15. I owe these and other references to Prof. Harry A. Hoffner, Jr.

40. Kettle: KUB XXXIII 8 iii 7 f.; statue: KUB XXIX 1 ii 52. Hoffner's contention that tin and iron are used here to symbolize strength seems unlikely (cf. "A Hittite Text in Epic Style About Merchants," *Journal of Cuneiform Studies* 22 [1968]: 34–45, esp. 43). Neither tin nor unsteeled iron could be considered especially strong. The association does make sense, however, as a symbol of value; though necessary for making bronze, tin, like iron, was a scarce commodity in the Bronze Age.

41. KBo IV 1 i passim.

42. Cf. Waldbaum, *Bronze to Iron*, pp. 19, 22–23.

43. Above, n. 19.

44. Pleiner and Biorkman, "Assyrian Iron Age," pp. 286–96.

45. Cf. Nancy K. Sandars, *The Sea Peoples: Warriors of the Ancient Mediterranean* (London: Thames and Hudson, 1978), for a recent study of these events.

46. Waldbaum, *Bronze to Iron*, pp. 66, 72–73; Anthony M. Snodgrass, *The Dark Age of Greece* (Edinburgh: Edinburgh University Press, 1971), pp. 231, 238, 239. For the Bronze Age tin trade cf. James D. Muhly, *Copper and Tin: The Distribution of Mineral Resources and the Nature of the Metals Trade in the Bronze Age*, Transactions of the Connecticut Academy of Arts and Sciences, vol. 43 (New Haven, 1973), pp. 155–535.

47. Waldbaum, *Bronze to Iron*, chaps. 3, 4.

48. Hama sword, tomb G IV 315: Poul J. Riis, *Hama, fouilles et recherches de la fondation Carlsberg 1931–1938*, vol. 2, pt. 3 (Copenhagen: Nationalmuseets Skrifter, 1948), pp. 121, 217; Tell el-Far'ah (S): Petrie, *Beth Pelet I: (Tell Fara)* (London: British School of Archaeology in Egypt, 1930), p. 7, pls. 21.90, 25.17; Kouklia: Hector W. Catling, personal communication, June 1967, from the joint St. Andrews University–Liverpool Museum expedition to Cyprus conducted by T. B. Mitford and the late J. H. Iliffe.

49. Pike: Gjerstad et al., *SCE* 1: 228 no. 12a, pl. 51.1; in Crete: James K. Brock, *Fortetsa: Early Greek Tombs Near Knossos* (Cambridge: Cambridge University Press, 1957), pp. 201, 202; discussion, Gjerstad, *SCE* 4.2: 130, 212, 374, fig. 19.7; Snodgrass, *Dark Age of Greece*, p. 251.

50. Waldbaum, *Bronze to Iron*, p. 42.

51. Ibid., tables IV.2, 4, 6, 8.

52. Tell Qasile: A. Mazar, "Excavations at Tell Qasile, 1973–1974, (Preliminary Report)," *Israel Exploration Journal* 25 (1975): 77–88, esp. 78, pl. 7B; Hama: Riis, *Hama* 2/3: 124, 237; Kouklia: Catling, personal communication, 1967; Perati: Spyridon Iakovides, *Perati. To Nekrotapheion*, 3 vols., Bibliotheke tesen Anthenais Archaiologikes Hetaireias, 67 (Athens, 1969), 2: 98, fig. 10; 344, fig. 149; 459; Lefkandi: Mervyn R. Popham and L. H. Sackett, *Excavations at Lefkandi, Euboea, 1964–66* (London: British School of Archaeology at Athens, 1968), p. 14, fig. 22.

53. Cf. Waldbaum, *Bronze to Iron*, chap. 3; idem, "A Bronze and Iron Iranian Axe in the Fogg Art Museum," in *Studies Presented to George M. A. Hanfmann*, ed. David G. Mitten, John G. Pedley, and Jane A. Scott (Mainz: Phillipp von Zabern, 1971), pp. 198–99.

54. Waldbaum, *Bronze to Iron*, tables IV.2, 6. Cf. Hector W. Catling, *Cypriot Bronzework in the Mycenaean World* (Oxford: Clarendon Press, 1964) and L. Åström, *Arts and Crafts*, pp. 8–13, for Cypriot tool types in bronze, especially from foundry hoards.

55. Gibeah: William F. Albright, "Excavations and Results at Tell el-Fûl (Gibeah of Saul)," *Annual of the American Schools of Oriental Research* 4 (1922–23): 17; Beth Shemesh: Elihu Grant and G. Ernest Wright, *Ain Shems Excavations (Palestine)*, pt. 5. (text), Haverford College Biblical and Kindred Studies no. 8 (Haverford, 1939), p. 153; Tell el-Far'ah (S): John L. Starkey and G. Lankester Harding, "Beth Pelet Cemetery," *Beth Pelet II* (London: British School of Archaeology in Egypt, 1932), pl. 62.17.

56. Waldbaum, *Bronze to Iron*, chap. 3 and tables IV.3–8.

57. Ibid., chap. 3 and tables IV.9, 10. A few odd examples of iron were found at Karphi but do not add much to our knowledge of iron usage in Crete; cf. British School of Archaeology in Athens, Students, "Excavations in the Plain of Lasithi. III. Karphi," *BSA* 38 (1937–38): 57–145, esp. 91, 92, 102, 106, 121–22, pl. 28.1, 3.

58. Waldbaum, *Bronze to Iron*, chap. 3, tables IV.1, 2; cf. G. Ernest Wright, "Iron: The Date of its Introduction into Common Use in Palestine," *American Journal of Archaeology* 43 (1939): 458–63. Some of the levels at the sites mentioned may continue into the 9th century.

59. Waldbaum, *Bronze to Iron*, p. 35.

60. Pleiner and Bjorkman, "Assyrian Iron Age," p. 296.

61. Waldbaum, *Bronze to Iron*, figs. IV.2, 4, 6, 8, 10, 12.

62. Snodgrass, *Dark Age of Greece*, pp. 228, 237–38.

63. Waldbaum, *Bronze to Iron*, chap. 5.

64. Erik Tholander, "Evidence of the Use of Carburized Steel and Quench Hardening in Late Bronze Age Cyprus," *Opuscula Atheniensia* 10 (1971): 15–22.

65. H. C. H. Carpenter and J. M. Robertson, "The Metallography of Some Ancient Egyptian Implements," *Journal of the Iron and Steel Institute* 121 (1930): 417–54; Pleiner, *The Beginnings of the Iron Age in Ancient Persia*, Annals of the Náprstek Museum 6 (Prague, 1967), pp. 30–34; A. France-Lanord, "Le fer en Iran au premier millénaire avant Jésus-Christ," *Revue d'histoire des mines et de la metallurgie* 1 (1969): 86–119; Maxwell-Hyslop and Henry W. M. Hodges, "Three Iron Swords from Luristan," *Iraq* 28 (1966): 164–76, esp. 169, 175–76; Vera Bird and Henry Hodges, "A Metallurgical Examination of Two Early Iron Swords from Luristan," *Studies in Conservation* 13 (1968): 215–22; Cyril S. Smith, "The Interpretation of Microstructures of Metallic Artifacts," in Boston Museum of Fine Arts Research Laboratory, *Application of Science in Examination of Works of Art*, Proceedings of the Seminar: September 7–16, 1965 (Boston, 1967), pp. 20–52, esp. 42; Coghlan, *Early Iron*, pp. 180–92.

66. Waldbaum, *Bronze to Iron*, pp. 59–62.

67. Above, n. 33.

68. Walter Sullivan, *New York Times* (31 Oct. 1971), p. 96; Robert Maddin, "Early Iron Metallurgy in the Near East," *Transactions of the Iron and Steel Institute of Japan* 15 (1975): 64–68, but cf. note on p. 64 expressing doubt on the nature of the site. Lack of adequate publication at the present time precludes further discussion here.

69. Snodgrass, *Dark Age of Greece*, p. 255.

70. Mattias N. Valmin, *The Swedish Messenia Expedition* (Lund: C. W. K. Gleerup, 1938), pp. 103, 412–13; date: Vincent R. d'A. Desborough, *The Last Mycenaeans and their Successors* (Oxford: Clarendon Press, 1964), p. 94; idem, *The Greek Dark Ages* (London: Benn, 1972), pp. 84, 251.

71. Petrie, *Gerar* (London: British School of Archaeology in Egypt, 1928), p. 14, pls. 6, 7, 25; for more reliable dating: Wright, "Iron," pp. 460–61.

72. Forbes, *Studies in Ancient Technology* 8 (1971): 121; 9 (1972): 245.

73. Jeffery Klein, "A Greek Metalworking Quarter: Eighth Century Excavations on Ischia," *Expedition* 14: 2 (1972): 34–39.

74. Maxwell-Hyslop and Hodges, "Three Iron Swords," p. 169; Bird and Hodges, "Metallurgical Examination," p. 222; France-Lanord, "Fer en Iran," p. 106.

75. Pleiner and Bjorkman, "Assyrian Iron Age," p. 307.

76. Ibid., pp. 286–87, 303.

77. J. V. Kinnier Wilson, *The Nimrud Wine Lists* (London: British School of Archaeology in Iraq, 1972), pp. 98–100; M. Mallowan, in the foreword to Kinnier Wilson, p. xii, is skeptical of this identification.

4

Metallurgy and Ancient Man

TAMARA S. WHEELER and ROBERT MADDIN

Metals first became familiar to man as rocks in the area where he lived, an environment with which he was intimately involved for survival and for expression of his social and religious ideas. Certain properties of metal-bearing rocks, such as color, luster, and weight, made them attractive for collection and use in the natural state. Man realized that heat made some lithic materials, such as flints and cherts, easier to work, and when he applied this technological knowledge to metallic rocks he discovered that some rocks, like native copper, could be formed into serviceable tools through a sequence of hammering and heating. Continued experimentation in heating rocks eventually revealed that certain blue and green stones (azurite and malachite) could yield liquid metal when the stones were heated sufficiently with charcoal and that the liquid metal could be cast into shape; thus man gained greater flexibility in the fabrication of tools, weapons, ornaments, and statuary, among other items.

As with other materials, the properties of metals which were important to ancient man were those that he could perceive with his senses. These properties were the ones which made metals valuable and which could be consciously utilized. Of the approximately 70 metallic elements, only 8 (iron, copper, arsenic, tin, silver, gold, lead, and mercury) were recognized and used as metallic before the 18th century A.D. The properties of these eight metals that were significant to ancient metallurgists were the following:

1. The color of metals largely determined their value. The alteration of color through combinations of metals and through surface patination must also have been an intriguing property.
2. The luster of metals, from rapidly darkening iron to ever-lustrous gold, was at some points in the past a determining factor in value.

99

After the means of effective ironworking were learned, iron lost most of the *cachet* inspired by difficulty of production, but the shiny metals like the stable gold and silver have retained their value, no doubt because of the combination of pleasing color and luster.

3. The ability of bronze to reflect light was an attribute exploited in the production of Greek and Etruscan polished bronze mirrors.

4. The acoustic properties of metals were utilized in the production of copper gongs and brass and silver bells.

5. The ease with which molten metal can be cast into a variety of intricate forms was appealing.

6. In the technical sphere, the hardness, although not as great as that of flint and obsidian, and therefore potential sharpness of some metals made them interesting to ancient smiths.

7. The strength and malleability of some metals permitted them to be used effectively in the manufacture of certain tools and weapons.

8. The ease with which some metals could be used for welding and soldering gave them value.

9. The ability of metals to be recycled through remelting and refabrication gave them a stable value because even broken metal objects still had a use in primitive economies.

Individually these properties do not set metals apart from all other materials used by ancient man, but taken as a group they suggest the unique role which metals assumed. Although the metals of antiquity have varying combinations of properties, a distinction between metals and other materials, such as stone, bone, and wood, must have been made. In order for the metals used in greatest quantity (copper and iron) to achieve maximum value, even in ancient terms, they must be extracted from minerals by thermal means. The need for thermal conversion indicates the value that metals must have quickly assumed in some ancient economies, because of the time and energy required to achieve the proper environment for melting and smelting. Charcoal production, for example, meant that wood, brush, or dung had to be collected and prepared. The melting or smelting process required that ore be mined or picked up; obviously useless materials had to be removed; furnaces or crucibles had to be built. Even on a small scale the production of metal demanded greater effort than flint knapping or bone cutting.

Therefore, both the beauty and utility of metals attracted man to them. Cyril Smith has emphasized the initial decorative use of metals in ancient societies and the role of individual craftsmen as innovators.[1] Beyond ornamentation and ceremonial embellishment sometimes came a practical stage, in which pioneering achievements, particularly in the production of copper and iron and their alloys, became the bases of extended systems of production. Iron, for example, prized for its rarity in the Bronze Age, was first used for jewelry (see Waldbaum, chap. 3). The following discussion, based in Smith's work,[2] looks inside metals in an attempt to discover why they became an important material to ancient man.

PURE NONFERROUS METALS

Modern metallurgical studies, through which the achievements of ancient smiths can be recognized, are based on standard principles and techniques. Most of the metals used in antiquity preserve evidence of their thermal and mechanical history in the microstructures. The microstructures are studied under the optical microscope after metallographic preparation, which involves polishing to obtain a smooth, scratchless surface and etching with a chemical agent to emphasize the grain structure.

Metals are crystalline. Each grain of a metal is a crystal which forms as the metal solidifies from the molten state. In "pure" metals, a term which indicates that alloying elements were not deliberately added (all metals contain certain amounts of naturally occurring impurities), grains are visible because different crystals solidify from different starting orientations, thus causing the reflected light from one grain to be directed to the observer differently from that of another.

The size and shape of the grains can indicate the cooling conditions and the type of mold into which the metal was cast. If copper is cast into a poorly insulated mold, heat loss and thus solidification are rapid, giving the grains little time to grow and therefore resulting in a structure of small grains. In a well-insulated mold, slower cooling results in a large grain structure with the grains more or less regular in configuration (equiaxed) (fig. 4.1). A third type of grain structure—columnar —occurs when heat is extracted directionally, as in a mold which is partially insulated, so that the grains are elongated in the direction of the most rapid heat loss. A fine grain size makes the copper somewhat

Fig. 4.1 Polished section of a copper Middle Bronze Age bar ingot from Har Yeruham, Israel.
The section is in a 1-in. mount. The large equiaxed grains, because of variations in shading, are
clearly visible. × 4, etched with ammonium peroxide.

harder than does a large grain size; in some cases, the ancient smith might
have perceived that copper cast into a thin or open mold was harder to
work than copper slowly cooled in a well or partially insulated mold.

The effectiveness of pure cast copper for weapons and tools was limited because of the softness of the material, but the disadvantages could
have been outweighed by the ease with which copper can be cast. Pure
coppers can be hardened by working and the increased strength imparted by hammering was no doubt recognized in attempts to shape the
object further or sharpen the edge after casting. In some cases, working
was necessary only for final shaping or edge sharpening so the object
was left in an unannealed, worked condition (see fig. 4.3). Working by
hammering or grinding cannot proceed indefinitely because working
produces concentrations of defects in the crystal (dislocations) which
greatly reduce ductility, so that the metal cracks. Heating of the object
at a temperature above about 300°C (at least in the cases of copper, gold,
and silver) but below the melting point alters the distribution and reduces
the density of dislocations, thus restoring the ductility and allowing

Fig. 4.2. Section of a piece of copper scrap or a needle blank from Gournia, Crete. Most likely Late Minoan I in date. Annealing twins (parallel bands within grains) are visible. ×4, etched with ammonium peroxide.

further working. The sequence of working and annealing can be repeated indefinitely until the desired shape is attained. Some metals and alloys, the atoms of which crystallize in a geometric arrangement called face centered cubic, can form "annealing twins," which appear in the optical microscope as parallel bands within a single grain (fig. 4.2). Annealing twins in face centered cubic metals, except aluminum, occur upon heating or annealing after working. The object is hammered to a certain degree at a temperature below a critical temperature, called the recrystallization temperature, which varies in each pure metal and alloy and which is affected by impurities within the metals. After working, the object is held at a temperature above the recrystallization temperature. The presence of annealing twins testified to the sequence of working and heating. A final working may be the smith's last step so that the scars of working, as well as the annealing twins, are visible (fig. 4.3).

Other pure metals used in ancient times include, most notably, the

Fig. 4.3. Mace head from Lahav, Israel. Perhaps chalcolithic in date. Annealing twins and strain markings are visible, indicating that the object was hammered and annealed and given a final shaping not followed by annealing. × 500, etched with ammonium peroxide and sodium dichromate.

precious metals and metals for alloying copper. Not all the alloying materials may have been isolated before being added to copper; they will be considered individually in an attempt to clarify the issue.

Gold is appealing to ancient and modern people for its color, luster, and resistance to corrosion. Since gold often occurs as a native metal, it was easy to recover and must have attracted man early. Gold is easy to work since it is soft and ductile; it may be hammered into sheets of less than 0.0025 mm thickness without annealing. Gold also occurs in combined form, thus requiring that some ingenuity be used in isolating it. In placer deposits, gold often forms a natural alloy with varying amounts of silver. As an ore, gold occurs in quartz veins in combination with lead, copper, and sometimes zinc. There are several processes by which gold can be separated from its impurities. One is by amalgamation with liquid mercury, a substance which can be boiled away easily, leaving relatively pure gold behind. Where gold and silver occur as a natural alloy, electrum, separation of the silver may not have always been desirable, since gold requires some alloying materials to increase its strength and to help maintain its shape; the silver could, however, have been removed through cupellation.

Silver occurs as a native metal, mostly with native copper, but sometimes in alluvial deposits as electrum. A common source of silver is in lead ores such as galena and cerussite, and thus it must be separated from the lead. This is usually accomplished by cupellation, in which the lead is oxidized, leaving silver behind. Ancient silver cupellation techniques did not permit a high level of silver recovery, as the constant reworking of the Laurion slags in antiquity proves. Silverworking is relatively easy, although silver is not as malleable as gold.

Lead is also easily recoverable, through the roasting of galena (PbS) to remove the sulfides or through heating of cerussite ($PbCO_3$) with charcoal to remove the oxygen so that it passes off as a gas. It is easy to work and, because of its weight, was used for making anchors and weights. Tin is not found as a native metal but usually occurs as cassiterite (tin oxide, tin stone, black tin) in alluvial deposits or in granite or quartz veins. Cassiterite can be converted relatively easily to pure tin through smelting, since tin stone contains almost 80 percent tin. As a pure metal, tin is not very useful because it must be worked slowly to avoid cracking and in casting has a directional solidification which makes a finished object prone to breakage. These limitations may partially explain why so few ancient tin objects are known, even though tin was widely used in alloying copper. Rarity and expense were also important factors in the pattern of tin usage. The greatest effectiveness of tin in ancient times was as an alloying material for copper; in this role tin became one of the most expensive and sought after materials in the Eastern Mediterranean and Near East.

Arsenic and zinc may be considered together since, in the study of ancient metallurgy, they have several common characteristics. They were not produced as metals until late, although there is some evidence for the Hellenistic use of metallic zinc.[3] As alloying elements of copper, they may have occurred with copper ores and, with smelting under reducing conditions, formed natural alloys, the effectiveness of which was noticed and exploited by the ancient smith.

NONFERROUS ALLOYS

The discovery that the addition of a second metal to copper improved some of its properties probably took place about the mid-4th millennium B.C. in Southwest Asia (and perhaps around the same time in Southeast Asia). Alloying was originally dependent on the availability of materials to mix. Initial exploitation of alloys may be attributed to the color and texture changes visible with the unaided eye, but it would have taken little time to realize that the combination of minerals produced stronger, harder objects with lower melting points and that objects made of alloys were easier to cast because of increased fluidity. The hoard found at Nahal Mishmar in the Judean Desert is a spectacular example of the use of a mixed ore which yielded increased fluidity of the metal for casting and for cosmetic effect; the variation in arsenic contents (less than 2–12% in the analyzed pieces)[4] suggests the use of ores containing both copper and arsenic because arsenic has a low vapor point and is released into the atmosphere if not smelted under reducing conditions. The variation in arsenic content shows that either the amount of arsenic was not known, as in a combination ore, or that the amount added and the smelting conditions varied from smelt to smelt. The former suggestion is more likely (see discussion by Charles in chap. 6).

When the advantages of naturally occurring alloys were perceived, smiths may have made an effort to collect minerals which were similar in color to the natural impurities in the mixed ores and added these ores to pure copper. Experiments with different alloying materials and contact with other smiths and metal traders would have isolated the most useful alloying elements. Since tin occurs rarely in the Old World, the knowledge of its effectiveness as an alloying agent and the material itself can only have come from a limited number of areas. Therefore, tin was not the first alloying component of copper in many areas, as has been clearly demonstrated by the work of Eaton and McKerrell,[5] but it was a metal which eventually became the dominant alloying element for copper and was sought and prized for this reason.

The basic information for the scientific study of alloys is contained in phase diagrams. These diagrams relate temperature and alloy composition, thus indicating the solubility of the metals in one another, melting points of various alloys, and any solid state transformations in the system. The most important phase diagram for the study of ancient

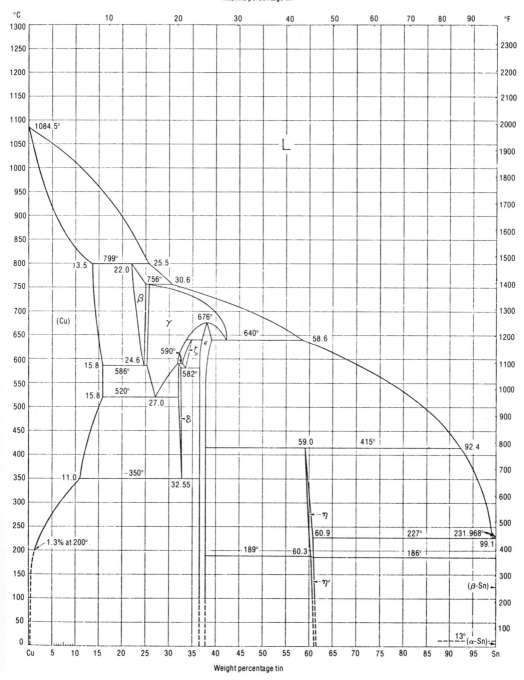

Atomic percentage tin

Fig. 4.4. The copper–tin phase diagram (American Society for Metals Source Handbook).

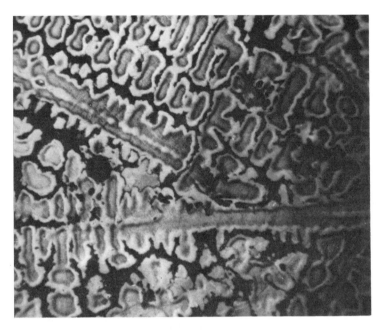

Fig. 4.5. Bracelet from Non Nok Tha, Thailand, burial 31, layer 17, ca. 1100 B.C. Within some corrosion (black areas) are seen cored dendrites, treelike structures with slight gradations of shading in the branches reflecting differences in chemical composition. × 200, etched with ferric chloride.

nonferrous metallurgy is the copper–tin system (fig. 4.4). Temperature is indicated on the ordinate and copper and tin on the abscissa, with pure copper at the left origin of the coordinates, pure tin on the right end, and linear gradations of alloy composition between the two.

Phase diagrams were developed in the laboratory under near equilibrium conditions and therefore indicate conditions which may not exist in less controlled situations. If the cooling of the alloy from the liquid state is infinitely slow, the solid and the liquid will have time to adjust, thus making a homogeneous alloy. In casting, however, there is insufficient time for the compositions to equilibrate, so the alloy will have differences in chemical composition apparent in the optical microscope. In the copper–tin system, the first particles to solidify in a molten bronze are richer in copper than in tin; thus, as solidification occurs, the tin content of the remaining liquid increases. Continuation of the solidification process results in a structure with gradually increasing amounts of tin. The structure is called cored; it forms by the growth of dendrites, so-called because of their treelike shape, and the gradually

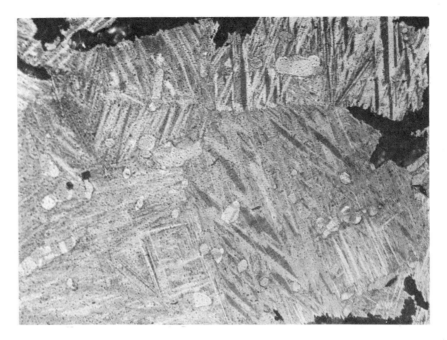

Fig. 4.6. Necklace from Ban Chiang, Thailand, ca. 500–0 B.C. The structure is typical of a hot-worked and quenched bronze containing 22 to 25 percent tin which has undergone a solid state or martensitic transformation. × 500, etched with ammonium persulfate.

differing amounts of copper and tin in the arms of the dendrites are designated as coring. A cored dendritic structure is clear evidence that an object was cast (fig. 4.5). The gradual variations of composition in dendrites may sometimes be detected in color changes visible in the optical microscope, but working tends to obscure the dendritic structure. Worked alloys must be examined with more sensitive techniques, such as X-ray diffraction, scanning electron microscopy, and electron beam probe, to determine compositional differences.

The copper–tin phase diagram contains information pertinent to the study of ancient metals. According to the phase diagram, a 10 percent tin bronze is composed of two phases. In practice, however, there is seldom any phase change below 500°C in this diagram: a 10 percent tin bronze is a single-phase structure. Secondly, a bronze containing 22–28 percent tin, usually the maximum amount of tin used in bronze in ancient times, must be hotworked and quenched from a temperature above 586°C if the suppression of several phases which impart brittleness to the material is to be effective (fig. 4.6).

The strength of the bronze is partly a function of the tin content. Almost any concentration of tin in the range of 2–15 percent will harden copper, but the optimum strength will be imparted by about 10 percent tin. According to the analyses of Eaton and McKerrell, in the early part of the Middle Bronze Age in Southwest Asia tin content varied widely;[6] this variance suggests that smiths were experimenting to determine the proportions which would produce the best bronze. The majority of bronzes produced in this period contain 5–10 percent tin.

The copper–zinc system should also be mentioned because although most ancient brasses are thought to have resulted from combined copper–zinc ores, the smith nonetheless exploited the special properties of this natural alloy. Unlike the situation presented on the copper–tin phase diagram, the solubility of zinc in copper decreases only slightly with decreasing temperature; in reality, the copper–zinc and copper–tin systems are similar in this respect. If the amount of zinc in the brass exceeds about 45 percent the resulting alloy is too brittle for use. The copper–arsenic system is similar to the copper–zinc system, but the solubility of arsenic in copper is not as great as that of zinc in copper.

The dendritic pattern formed by the solidification of an alloy of copper is altered through working. As in "pure" metals, the working process leaves scars known as strain markings. If the object is heated to a temperature below the melting point but above a critical temperature, the atoms rearrange themselves to relieve that strain caused by working and form annealing twins. All alloys of copper can be appreciably hardened through working, although the alloying elements reduce the amount of working necessary and in fact make prolonged working without frequent annealing difficult.

SMELTING OF NONFERROUS METALS

As the discussion of phase diagrams indicates, metals vary in their ability to dissolve other metals and nonmetallic substances as well. Insoluble particles present in the metallic matrix provide clues to smelting procedures and types of ores used. A reliable identification of the composition of the insoluble particles is done with the energy dispersive X-ray spectrometer associated with the scanning electron microscope, although slight differences in color may also be used to detect compositional differences.

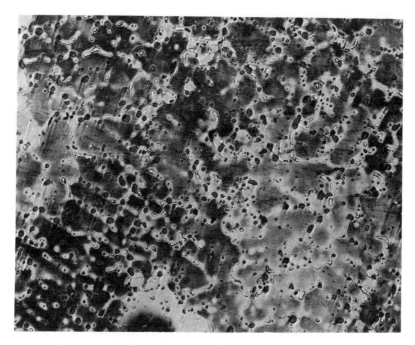

Fig. 4.7. Copper oxhide ingot from Enkomi, Cyprus, now in a private collection in Los Angeles. Copper sulfide particles (gray spheres) are arranged among dendritic arms. × 50, etched with ammonium peroxide.

Some discussion is necessary about the formation and types of copper ores. An important ore contains the mineral chalcopyrite, a compound of copper, iron, and sulfur. If after formation chalcopyrite is exposed to weathering through contact with air and most significantly with water the chalcopyrite compound breaks down and may form several secondary copper ores. Certain conditions cause removal of the iron, so that most secondary ores do not contain iron. Chalcocite, for example, is a sulfide ore which does not contain iron. The presence of iron in the finished product could result from the use of an iron ore flux or chalcopyrite.

Weathering also causes oxidation and conversion of the sulfides, thus giving rise to the carbonate ores azurite and malachite, the silicate chrysocolla, and the oxide cuprite, all of which can be easily smelted, unlike chalcopyrite, which should be roasted to oxidize the sulfides before smelting.

Fig. 4.8. Piece of bronze scrap from Athienou, Cyprus, 14th/13th centuries B.C. Copper iron sulfide particles have been deformed into longitudinal stringers through working of the object. Note the presence of annealing twins. × 200, etched with ammonium peroxide and sodium dichromate.

The weathering process is never complete, so that small amounts of sulfur remain in the carbonate or oxide ore. The amount of sulfide is is not great enough to retard the smelting process, but the insoluble sulfide particles will be visible in the optical and scanning electron microscopes. The presence of copper sulfide particles containing no iron suggests therefore that the object being studied was made from an ore such as malachite or azurite that had not been competely weathered. Copper sulfide particles are present in most of the Bronze Age copper oxhide ingots analyzed to date, indicating that they were made from fairly well-weathered ores (fig. 4.7.).

Copper-iron sulfide particles in the finished object are considered to result from the use of a chalcopyrite ore, which had to be roasted in order to be smelted successfully (fig. 4.8). The use of chalcopyrite ores suggests that, in some areas, weathered ores either had been exhausted or had never existed in exploitable quantity. It had been maintained that roasting and therefore the use of chalcopyrite did not start until

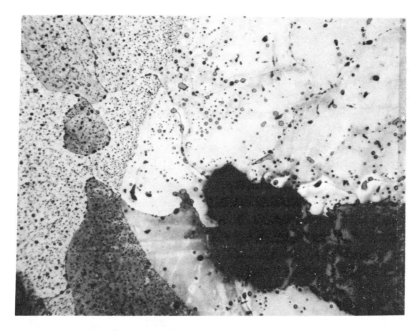

Fig. 4.9. Copper oxhide ingot fragment from Gournia, Crete, Late Bronze Age. The ingot shows a distribution of copper sulfide (gray spheres) and copper oxide (small black dots) particles, indicating that the ingot was made from partially weathered ores and cast in contact with air. Black areas are corrosion pits. × 200, etched with sodium dichromate.

Roman times, but recent study of smelting products from Kition and Athienou on Cyprus suggests that copper was being produced from sulfide ores by the 14th/13th centuries B.C.

In copper which has not been alloyed with tin or zinc or a specific deoxidizer, copper oxide particles are usually seen. They indicate that casting occurred in a situation in which the molten copper was in contact with air. Although the copper oxide is often distributed as a eutectic in a fine mixture of copper oxide and copper, slow cooling or annealing will allow the copper oxide to coalesce into globules (fig. 4.9).

ANCIENT FERROUS METALLURGY

Ancient working of nonferrous metals provided few techniques which could be applied to the production of strong and effective iron objects but did acquaint smiths with properties similar to those of iron. The search for different kinds of copper ores probably also revealed iron

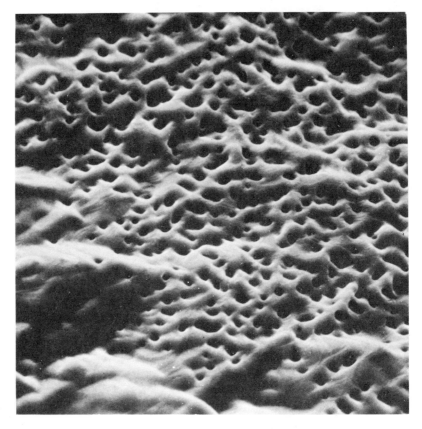

Fig. 4.10. Electron micrograph of modern sponge iron. The specimen was reduced at 767° C ($P_{CO} = 0.4911$ atm, $P_{CO2} = 0.0556$ atm, $P_{he} = 0.4533$ atm). × 2400 (Prof. Y. K. Rao, University of Washington).

ores, which were used in copper smelting as fluxes to combine with and remove the gangue from the ore. Secondly, the smith observed that the iron never became molten but was spongy at the temperatures attained in the copper smelting furnace (maximum of 1300°–1400°C). Because temperatures sufficient to melt iron could not be reached, iron could not be cast like copper or its alloys. Finally, the working techniques of the smith could be applied to iron, with hammering necessary to form objects. Heating when working was no longer possible was necessary in both copper and iron manufacture; in the case of iron, the hammering had to be done at temperatures above 800°C.

Fig. 4.11. Iron fragment from Murlo, Italy, late 7th–6th centuries B.C. Slag is strung out vertically, in the direction of forging. × 50, etched with 2% Nital (nitric acid in ethyl alcohol).

The production of iron from its ores has been described in several places, including chapter 7 in this volume by R. F. Tylecote, so here we shall anticipate only briefly. In the ancient Near East and Eastern Mediterranean, iron was smelted as a direct process in which sponge iron was produced in a single operation. Charcoal was layered in a furnace with chunks of iron ore, usually magnetite or hematite, until the furnace was filled. A tuyere, or clay pipe, was inserted into the bottom of the furnace. Fire was introduced either through a flue or the tuyere and a blast of air forced into the furnace, at first gently to remove the water of hydration and then strongly to increase the heat. The charcoal oxidized, forming carbon monoxide, which rose through the ore and reduced it. Reduction took place at about 1200°C and, since iron melts at 1528°C, the metal was not liquid but a spongy mass (fig. 4.10).

Caught up in the mass was slag, formed from the worthless components of the ore, or gangue. The gangue was mostly silica, which combined with part of the ferrous oxide to form a fusable silicate, the greater part of which was fayalite. After a period of experimentation, a flux was added to remove the gangue, but some of the flux was also sometimes trapped as slag. Since slag in the form of pure fayalite is viscous at around 1170°C and brittle below that point, it had to be squeezed out of the sponge iron by hammering at or above that temperature—a process known as forging. Forging produced a continuous network of iron grains, sometimes interrupted by stringers of remaining slag elongated in the direction of the deformation of the iron bloom (fig. 4.11). When the sponge iron had been compacted and much of the slag removed, the iron bloom could be shaped into the objects desired by further hammering.

Bronze Age smiths knew the location of iron ores and something about solid state iron smelting, as well as how to fashion iron objects through hammering and to soften them through heating to permit further working. The crucial process in effective iron production—carburization, in which iron is converted to steel—may have been developed in the two centuries following 1200 B.C. in one of the coastal areas of the Eastern Mediterranean. To carburize an iron object, it is heated in intimate contact with charcoal for a prolonged period of time. The discovery that prolonged heating in a charcoal fire greatly hardened iron must have been accidental; it may have been made during the normal limited iron production schedule which prevailed in the Bronze Age or whether some other factor forced increased experimentation with iron. Uncarburized iron is not an acceptable substitute for bronze because it is not as strong, so the desire for extensive production of iron for domestic and agricultural purposes may have resulted in part from a significant technological change, although social, political, and economic factors can be no means be discounted.

The ancient smith did not realize that it was the absorption of carbon from the fuel which transformed iron into a product superior to bronze for some purposes; he thought that the fire purified or altered the metal in some other way. Reference to the iron–carbon phase diagram (fig. 4.12) makes clear the reasons for the ancient smith's success in developing efficient tools and implements through case carburization. The solubility of carbon in iron is very small at room temperature, but it increases greatly above 910°C, temperatures which could be achieved with good charcoal and bellows, as proved by successful Bronze Age copper smelting. A copper or bronze object does not absorb carbon, so, although the technical means for carburization were known, the

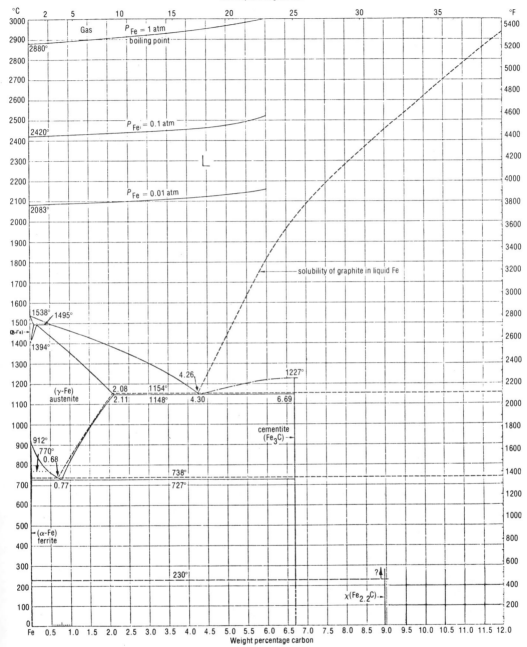

Fig. 4.12. The iron–carbon phase diagram (*The Making, Shaping and Treating of Steel*, U.S. Steel Corp., 1971). Key: ——·——, cementite (Fe₃C) liquidus (calculated); ———, iron-χ-carbide (Fe₂.₂C) transformation (calculated); ———, iron-cementite (Fe₃C) equilibrium diagram (experimental); ———, iron-graphite equilibrium diagram (experimental), except where coincident with iron-cementite (Fe₃C) diagram; ——··——, uncertain region of cementite (Fe₃C); ·····, Curie temperature of ferrite.

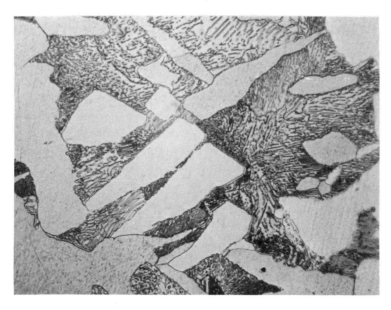

Fig. 4.13. Iron ingot from Khorsabad, Iraq (Oriental Institute A12461), 8th century B.C. Pearlite, composed of dark cementite and light ferrite, among ferrite grains. × 1250, etched with 2% Nital.

technique itself could not have been transferred from the production of nonferrous metals. The amount of carbon absorbed into the iron depends on the length of time the object is left in the fire, as well as the temperature of the fire.

Iron with absorbed carbon is arranged in a two phase structure called pearlite, which consists of alternate layers of iron (ferrite) and iron carbide (cementite) (fig. 4.13). Ferrite is soft and ductile and cementite is hard and brittle, so the variation in the thickness of the layers affects the hardness of the carburized iron. The metal is soft if ferrite is the dominant, continuous phase and hard if cementite is the major component. The strength of the object thus depends in part on the amount of carbon which has been absorbed into the surface layers or, in the ancient smith's view, the length of time he has left the object in the fire.

Carbon can be introduced into an iron object by means other than carburization of the finished product. The interstices of an iron bloom sometimes trap carbon, which is forged out into stringers in the metal, thus becoming part of the finished object. Secondly, additional carbu-

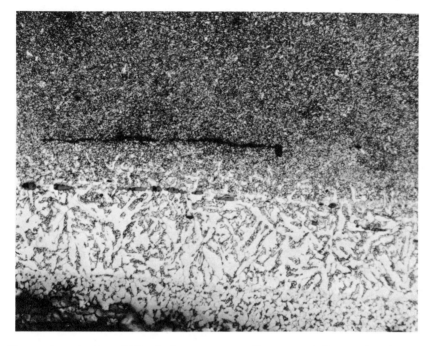

Fig. 4.14. Iron adze from Al Mina, Turkey, 430–375 B.C. The micrograph illustrates the technique of laminating iron sheets with different carbon content. The upper, high carbon layer (dark) gave the working edge of the adze hardness. × 100, etched with 3% Nital.

rization can occur during forging, when a fairly high temperature is maintained by repeatedly placing the object in a charcoal fire for re-heating. Decarburization can occur during heating if there is an inadequate charcoal cover.

The situations which produce accidental carburization may be detect-able by the modern researcher. The carbon caught up in an iron bloom would appear as uneven streaks in polished metallographic sections and the surface of an object made from a carbon-containing bloom can show decarburization during forging. On the other hand, carburization which occurred during forging is more difficult to detect microscopically, but one would predict that the carbon content would be low and the con-centration uneven; any forging after the final heating would also have the effect of decarburizing the surface. Therefore, careful observation of a large sample of iron objects should permit determining if ancient smiths "carburized" intentionally. Incontrovertible proof of deliberate

Fig. 4.15. Scanning electron photomicrograph illustrating a replication technique for the detection of relic carbides in corroded irons. The light lamellae are iron carbide. × 1250. —40° tilt of replica.

carburization can be derived from objects made by laminating layers of iron of varying carbon content, for there would have been no reason to make such a structure unless the different properties of the layers were understood. The earliest known laminated object is a knife from the Ramesseum which probably dates to 900–800 B.C.[7] A continuous series of Near Eastern, Egyptian, and Classical laminated objects follows this Egyptian knife;[8] an adze from Al Mina demonstrates the technique (fig. 4.14).

The metallurgical study of ancient irons is made difficult because so many irons are in a badly corroded condition. There are, however, several techniques which permit the identification of pearlite in a totally corroded iron object. One involves careful study of a polished surface with the optical microscope at magnifications above × 1000;[9] since the layers of pearlite have different chemical compositions, these differences can be sometimes distinguished even in iron oxide. A second technique is based on the study of gold-enhanced thin-film replicas of a polished surface which are examined in the scanning electron microscope, Areas of different chemical composition do not show up in the scanner, but the specimen is tilted to accentuate the geometrically different levels of the constituents. Since the cementite layers are harder than the ferrite plates even in a corroded iron, the cementite layers stand out clearly (fig. 4.15).

On the basis of our research and that of others, it is apparent that smiths were carburizing intentionally on a fairly large scale by at least 1000 B.C. in the Eastern Mediterranean area. Tholander has examined a 12th century knife from Idalion which is carburized and perhaps quenched (infra).[10] An iron pick, found in association with 11th–10th century pottery at a site on Mount Adir in northern Israel, must also have been carburized. Because the pick is in an astounding state of good preservation, with only a veneer of corrosion, metallurgical analysis through the removal of samples was deemed unsuitable because it would harm the aesthetic value of the object. Hardness readings on the tip, however, average Rockwell C 38, characteristic of a hardened steel. This is equivalent to a Diamond Pyramid Hardness of 370 kg/mm^2 and to a tensile strength of about 175,000 psi. Since few contemporary iron objects have been studied, the extent to which carburization was used cannot now be precisely determined. Evidence for carburization is found in 11th century Palestine—at Taanach (fig. 4.16) and Hazorea (fig. 4.17)—and in the 10th century at Tell el-Fa'rah South (fig. 4.18). The corpus of carburized early irons grows almost daily, with case for deliberate carburization becoming concurrently stronger.

The second process significant in making iron a metal in some ways superior to bronze is fast cooling, or quenching, a process which had no effect on the strength of bronze. Quenching also has no effect on iron if it has no carbon. There are degrees of rapid cooling which affect the strength of iron once it has been carburized. A carburized iron left to cool in the air exhibits coarse pearlite, while a steel which is waved in the air at the finish of shaping will have a finer pearlite. The pearlite reaction can be suppressed by even more rapid cooling through the quenching of the hot object into water or some other cold medium. The product which results from quenching is called martensite, which is significantly harder than pearlite but also more brittle (fig. 4.19).

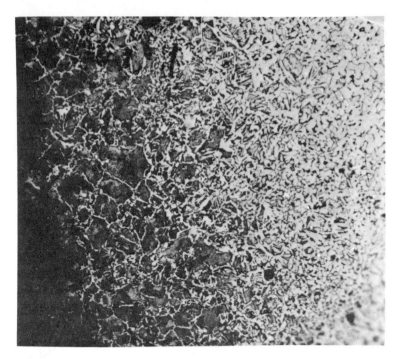

Fig. 4.16. Rough iron tool from Taanach, Israel, probably 11th century B.C. Dark carburized areas near the edge of the specimen (left) illustrate the nature of carbon distribution in a case carburized object. × 50, etched with 3% Nital.

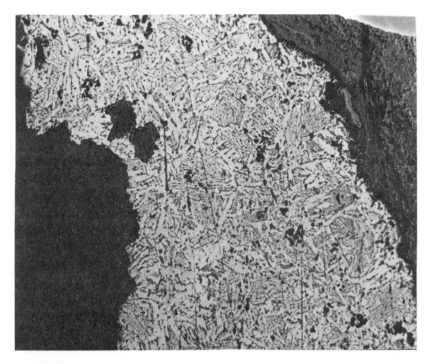

Fig. 4.17. Core of metallic iron surviving in an ax from Hazorea, Israel, 11th century B.C. The darker carbides illustrate that the ax must have been heavily carburized in order for carbon to have penetrated to the center of the object. Carbon content measured metallographically as 0.38%. × 50, etched with 3% Nital.

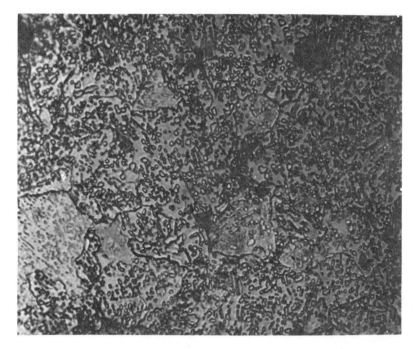

Fig. 4.18. Iron knife from Tell el-Fa'rah South, Israel, tomb 240, probably 10th century B.C. The carbides are present here in the form of dispersed pearlite, broken up by hammering at a high temperature. Carbon content measured metallographically as 0.40%. × 1000, etched with 3% Nital.

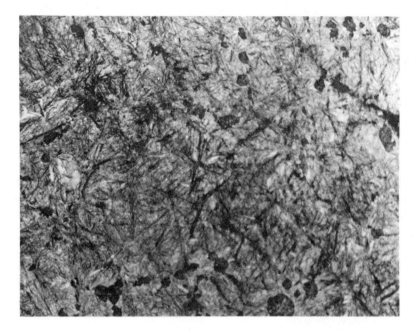

Fig. 4.19. Iron chisel from Al Mina, Turkey, 430–375 B.C. The needlelike structure is martensite, a product of quenching into water or other cold liquid. × 200, etched with 2% Nital.

It is more difficult to obtain clear evidence of deliberate quenching than of carburization. First, the outer layers of a case carburized object are those in which martensite would be formed because the rapidity of cooling slows relative to the thickness of the object, so heat loss is naturally quicker on the surface. In a corroded iron, the most heavily corroded area is almost always the surface, so much so that it is usually difficult even to identify carburized areas. Secondly, quenching into water could have been done simply to cool the object quickly, for immediate use and to eliminate the danger of having hot objects about in the shop. It is, of course, possible that quenching eventually was recognized as having the effect of hardening steel, but it is impossible for the modern researcher to determine when this occurred. Homer's comment in *Odyssey* 9. 391–94 is the clearest indication that the blacksmith realized that quenching improved some of the properties of steel, since the verb used indicates some magical effect and iron is specifically referred to as the material being improved (see discussion by Muhly in chap. 2). Of uncertain date, although possibly contemporary with the reference in Homer, are four steel tools from Egyptian Thebes which show combined bainitic–martensitic structures indicative of quenching.[11] Clear analytical evidence for deliberate quenching is in a chisel from Al Mina level III (430–375 B.C.), in which an insulating material seems to have been placed on the tip of the tool to inhibit the surface brittleness caused by quenching.

CONCLUSIONS

Iron became a medium superior to bronze for tools and implements only when it was carburized. Carburization is not a process which affects copper or copper alloys, so a direct transfer of technology from the working of one metal to the other cannot have taken place. Because the process of carburization cannot be detected by looking at the iron, realization of its effectiveness must have been made by a smith who spent a significant portion of his time at the forge working with iron. Customer response and the smith's awareness that some of the tools he made were better than other iron and bronze implements must have encouraged continued experimentation. It seems unlikely that the accidental carburization of iron jewelry and amulets would have been apparent, although it is possible that some iron fibulae wore better than bronze counterparts. In sum, the true Iron Age in the Eastern Mediterranean was based partly on the discovery that iron became harder when it was carburized, a discovery which probably took place when sufficient demand for iron tools allowed smiths to experiment extensively with iron.

The coming of the age of iron in the Eastern Mediterranean was the culmination of six millennia of experimentation: from the manipulation of rocks to the production of steel. We can read the record of these years of experimentation in the microscope and can sometimes envision the triumphs and frustrations of the many miners, smelters, and smiths who created a technological transformation in society. The study of the scientific background to the development of metallurgy adds an objective dimension to the reconstruction of ancient systems—a tangible reflection of human desires and ways of life.

ACKNOWLEDGMENTS

The research on which this paper is based was generously supported by the National Science Foundation through the divisions of anthropology, history, and philosophy of science and metallurgy. The material from Israel was collected during a visit supported by the exchange program of the University of Pennsylvania and the institutions of higher learning in Israel. We wish to thank the Applied Science Department of the Hebrew University for its hospitality and the Department of Antiquities of the State of Israel which, through the director Avraham Eitan, encouraged and facilitated our research. We are also indebted to the Laboratory for Research on the Structure of Matter of the University of Pennsylvania for access to its facilities and personnel, especially Alexander Vaskelis, scientific photographer, Jacqueline White, deputy supervisor of the analytical chemical facility, and Robert White and Nancy Yang, electron microscopists.

Special thanks are due the following colleagues who generously allowed us to study their material and publish the information: David Alon, excavator of Lahav; Amnon Ben-Tor, excavator at Hazorea; Amnon Ben-Tor and Trude Dothan, directors of the Athienou excavations; Philip Betancourt for the Gournia material; J. A. Brinkman of the Oriental Institute for the Khorsabad ingots; Albert Glock, director of the Taanach excavations; Chester Gorman, director of the Ban Chiang excavations; K. R. Maxwell-Hyslop for the Fara objects in the Institute of Archaeology, University of London; P. R. S. Moorey for the Al Mina chisel and adze in the Ashmolean Museum; Henry Mudd of the Cyprus Mines Corporation for the Enkomi ingot in Los Angeles; Y. K. Rao for access to his study on iron domains; Wilhelm G. Solheim II, director of the Non Nok Tha excavations; Miriam Tadmor, curator in the Israel Museum, for the Middle Bronze Age bar ingots; Floyd Tuler of the Applied Science Department of the Hebrew University who made the hardness readings on the Mount Adir pick; and P. G. Warden of the Murlo excavations.

The pick was found in excavations carried out in the early Iron Age site of Har Adir by David Davis on behalf of the Israel Department of Antiquities and Museums. We wish to thank Mr. A. Eitan, the director of the department, for his permission to publish the pick.

We are greatly indebted to Martha Goodway and Theodore Wertime for their careful and thoughtful editorial assistance.

NOTES

1. For example, see C. S. Smith, "Matter versus Materials: A Historical View," *Science* 162 (1968): 637–44.

2. C. S. Smith, "The Interpretation of Microstructures of Metallic Artifacts," in *The Application of Science in the Examinations of Works of Art*, ed. C. S. Smith (Boston, 1965), pp. 20–52.

3. M. Farnsworth, C. S. Smith, and J. Rodda, "Metallographic Examination of a Sample of Metallic Zinc from Ancient Athens," *Hesperia* (suppl.) 8: 126–29.

4. C. A. Key, "Ancient Copper and Copper Arsenic Alloy Artifacts: Composition and Metallurgical Implications," *Science* 146 (1964): 1578–80.

5. E. R. Eaton and H. McKerrell, "Near Eastern Alloying and Some Textual Evidence for the Early Use of Arsenical Copper," *World Archaeology* 8 (1976): 169–91.

6. Ibid., p. 173, table 4.

7. H. C. H. Carpenter and J. M. Robertson, "The Metallography of Some Ancient Egyptian Implements," *Journal of the Iron and Steel Institute* 121 (1930): 423, 428–30.

8. J. D. Muhly, T. S. Wheeler, and R. Maddin, "An Iron Adze of the Fifth-Fourth Centuries B.C. from Al Mina," *Levant* 9 (1977): 159–61.

9. R. Knox, "Detection of Iron Carbide Structure in the Oxide Remains of Ancient Steel," *Archaeometry* 5 (1963): 44–45.

10. E. Tholander, "Evidence of the Use of Carburized Steel and Quench Hardening in Late Bronze Age Cyprus," *Opuscula Atheniensia* 10 (1971): 15–22.

11. A. R. Williams and K. R. Maxwell-Hyslop, "Ancient Steel from Egypt," *Journal of Archaeological Science* 3 (1976): 294–301.

5

Ocher in Prehistory: 300,000 Years of the Use of Iron Ores as Pigments

DENISE SCHMANDT-BESSERAT

Cyril S. Smith has pointed out that, in the history of technology, many materials have first captured human attention through their esthetic appeal and were used for artistic/magical/religious purposes long before their functional properties were discovered.[1] Nothing illustrates this idea better than the fact that hematite, limonite, and goethite, the chief iron ores, were used intensively as red, brown, and yellow pigments (commonly called ochers) 300,000 years before their metallurgic properties were discovered. The purpose of this paper is to review chronologically the evolution of the use of ocher from the first evidence available in Lower Paleolithic to the Neolithic period.

First Evidences of the Use of Ocher

The present state of our knowledge suggests that the story of ocher began 300,000 years ago at Terra Amata, near Nice, France.[2] Several pieces of ocher were found at that site within an Abbevillian/Acheulean context, usually associated with *Homo erectus*. The ocher was probably identified and collected along the daily hunting trails and brought back to the settlement. Marks of wear on the ends of the pieces evidence their use. It seems likely that ocher was assuming a specific function in the encampment, but so far we do not know what that function was. A common assumption among archaeologists is that body paint may have played an important role in the social life of early man. It is also theorized that the red color of ocher—the color of blood and life—may have conferred a special value on it.

The pieces of ocher do not constitute unique evidence of an esthetic/ magical/religious concern by *Homo erectus*. At Lazaret, France, the skull of a wolf left by departing hunters at the entrance to their hut seems to have had some ritual meaning.[3] The selection of colorful stones as raw materials for some hand axes, especially at the site of Colombo Falls,[4] evidences an esthetic concern. Beyond these, one can only speculate as to motives.

MOUSTERIAN (CA. 70,000–40,000 B.C.)

The Mousterian culture is characterized by the appearance of burial customs, probably derived from a belief in life after death. We may get a glimpse of the significance of ocher for Neanderthal man when we consider the burial customs evidenced at la Chapelle aux Saints, France. Here, a man about 50 years of age was laid in a grave provided with funerary gifts which we presume represented the most important items for his survival in this or another world. The gifts included food (a leg of bison), tools (a few pieces of flint), and several lumps of ocher;[5] however, ocher is by no means found generally in graves. Sepultures at La Ferrassie, Shanidar, and Gafzeh, for example,[6] which evidence a complicated paraphernalia, do not seem to include it.

Pech de l'Aze (level I, 4), France,[7] is an example of Mousterian habitats where ocher has been found. Francois Bordes discovered in the cave a quantity of mineral pigments, including 3 fragments of red ocher, traces of yellow ocher, and 103 blocks of manganese. Manganese dioxide produces a black mineral pigment which is often found associated with ocher in ancient remains. The much greater proportion of manganese does not necessarily imply a predilection of Neanderthal man for black rather than red but rather that manganese is abundant around Pech de l'Aze while ocher is not. The proof of their use as coloring material is evidenced by the fact that several blocks bear traces of having been scratched with flint tools to produce a black powder which could be smeared with the fingers, while others were either rounded smooth by wear or had been shaped into rectangular or pointed "crayons." Ocher appears also at Arcy-sur-Cure at La Grotte de l'Hyène (level XV),[8] as well as at La Grotte du Renne (level XIV).[9] It is reported in sites in Eastern Europe such as Vorograd,[10] which yielded a number of lumps of red ocher. Excavations at the cave of Gafzeh in Israel produced numerous ocher fragments in all Mousterian levels.[11]

CHATELPERONIAN (CA. 40,000–29,000 B.C.)

In the Chatelperonian, the earliest phase of Upper Paleolithic, ocher began to be used in considerable quantities in human settlements.[12] The best documented site of the period is Arcy-sur-Cure, near Paris, France, dated $31,500 \pm 400$ B.C. by C-14. The human remains of the site present an ethnological problem because they belong to an archaic type which preserves certain characteristics of Neanderthal, and it is difficult to decide whether they are evolved Neanderthaloids or primitive *Homo sapiens*.[13] In this context, Leroi-Gourhan excavated what seems to be the floor of a hut, 3–4 m in diameter.[14] It was marked by packed earth heavily strewn with ocher in such a fashion that the cultural layers were stained purple, contrasting with the preceding yellow layers of the post-Mousterian.[15] Was the ocher strewn intentionally on the living floor for esthetic/magical/ religious reasons or was it simply the result of its intensive preparation for use in the hut? Indeed, the site yielded ample evidence for the preparation of the pigment, as there were numerous grinding stones and pestles bearing traces of ocher.[16] The ground stone industry, in particular mortars and pestles, which are usually associated with the appearance of sedentary farming communities and with the preparation of agricultural products such as grains, may in fact have developed for the purpose of preparing pigments in the earliest phase of the Upper Paleolithic.

The most remarkable finding—indeed most crucial for the topic of this volume on the coming of the age of iron—is the fact that at this time hematite was manipulated in connection with fire. At Arcy-sur-Cure, ocher was found within several hearths, and the great varieties of hues of ocher found on the site suggest that calcination of ocher was practiced to increase the available range of colors.[17] The Chatelperonians were already aware that the roasting of natural ochers intensifies their color and transforms yellow ochers into red and red ochers into deeper hues. The physical process set up by calcination is the loss of water of the iron hydroxides and their conversion into iron oxides: $2Fe_2O_3 \cdot 3H_2O \rightarrow 3H_2O + 2Fe_2O_3$. The degree of temperature required is about 260–80° C; the process is irreversible. The resultant hues are dependent on the mineral composition of the samples and also on the temperature during roasting. The variety of shades achieved by calcination range from orange-red and bright red to deep red-brown, including light red, Brun rouge, Pardo rojo, Burnt Ocher, and Burnt Roman ocher.[18]

Since such practices of ocher calcination are evidenced throughout the following periods of the Paleolithic era, we believe that it was an intentional process related to the preparation of better pigments. It is a futile game to hypothesize that *if* campfires could have produced a higher degree of temperature Chatelperonian man would have witnessed the smelting of iron in his hearth and mankind could have been ushered into the age of metal ca. 40,000 B.C. Campfires, however, do not reach temperatures higher than 700° C, and the smelting temperature of iron is 1100–1500° C. Thousands of years were necessary for the development of pyrotechnology to reach these ranges of temperatures in kilns and enable man to discover the presence of metal in the red stones. In the meantime it could only be used for its striking red color, which probably was given a magical significance by early man. The achievement of special hues must have been important, as evidenced by hematite plaques showing marks of having been used with the double aim of source of pigment and for mixing color. Flat limestone slabs were also used as palettes to mix different ocher pigments and achieve a desired color.[19] Also puzzling at Arcy-sur-Cure was the presence of several balls of ocher the size of a fist. One contained a large flint blade, a second a fragment of the bone of a reindeer. The others were heavily mixed with flint chips.[20]

AURIGNACIAN (29,000–22,000 B.C.)

In the Aurignacian period appeared the first positive indication of at least one use of the ocher pigments. The evidence consists of paintings on limestone blocks, representing the very beginning of human figurative art—the first striving of man "to express himself in ways other than the spoken word or chanted language."[21] Aurignacian is also the period in which the presence of *Homo sapiens* is fully attested, and indeed these works of art are fully recognized as his achievement. The art monuments of the period are rare and consist mostly of small decorated limestone slabs, blocks, or bone fragments. Painting is present, but the favorite technique of the period is deep incision, characterized by a broad groove performed with a flint point. Whatever meaning the decoration had, it was the depiction rather than the color which was important. The motif repertory is limited to animal figures and schematic sexual human representations such as female pubic triangles.[22] The style is rudimentary and crude.

Paintings appeare at the sites of La Ferrassie and Abri Castanet. At La

Ferrassie D. Peyrony recovered the palette of the painter: a 28 cm × 29 cm squarish limestone plaque whose colors were mixed in three prepared areas.[23] The palette immediately shows the color predilection: two areas are black and a single one red. What may have been the reason for this choice? Was it the availability of the pigments? Personal taste or the prescription of a ritual? Or was it simply the chance of preservation?

At both La Ferrassie[24] and Abri Castanet, all the paintings are animal representations and they are mostly painted black, which contradicts Breuil's theory that man's first painting cycle began with red outline.[25] In La Ferrassie, however, a particularly well preserved example shows a block bearing the outline of a cervid (deer or reindeer) galloping with upraised tail and outstretched neck. The animal is painted in black, but red ocher was used to emphasize certain parts of the body and in particular the inner side of the hind leg. On another part of the same block, an area had been smeared with red and used as a background for further black animal figures. At Castanet two blocks out of four, possibly fallen from the ceiling, bear red spots or parallel lines superimposed on black designs of animals.[26]

GRAVETTIAN (CA. 22,000–18,000 B.C.)

The Gravettian period initiates the first representations of the human figure. The favorite models are female. They are executed either in bas-relief on limestone blocks, such as the Venuses of Laussel, or in the round, such as the famous Venus of Willendorf. The figures are shown frontally and devote a specially careful treatment for the representation of the central part of the body, in particular the large pendulous breasts, wide hips and thighs with fat rolls, protruding stomach, and pubic triangle. In contrast, the featureless faces, filiform arms, and pointed legs are neglected. These new developments in art are of interest to our present study because the examples mentioned above—the Venus with the horn at Laussel,[27] and the Venus of Willendorf[28] as well as a figurine at Dolni Vestonice[29] —still bear the traces of having had their nude bodies rubbed with red ocher. We wonder if there is any possible connection with a new burial ritual which is evidenced during the Upper Paleolithic period and consists of spreading ocher over the bodies of the dead.[3]

At least 27 Upper Paleolithic burials with ocher have been reported in an area extending from England to Russia.[31] The famous skeleton of

Cro-Magnon was ochered. The custom is also evidenced in Italy, where
a youth about 18 years of age was found buried with yellow ocher under
the chin and red ocher profusely sprinkled over his body and the entire
grave.[32] At Markina-Gora in Russia a grave had been lined with ocher to
receive the tightly flexed body of an adult male.[33] At Soungir, near
Moscow, the burial custom consisted of laying the cadaver over a layer
of burning charcoal covered with a thick stratum of bright ocher and
then oversprinkling it with ocher.[34] At Malta, Siberia, a young child had
been sprinkled with ocher before being buried with small funerary gifts
including a necklace, bird figurines, and weapons.[35]

Both male and female skeletons have been found treated with ocher;
in the case of the Grimaldi burial, however, only the male skeleton bears
traces of ocher, possibly demonstrating a distinction from the adjacent
female.[36] In some instances, and in particular in Moravia, the head alone
of the cadavers was colored. Was ocher in short supply or were there
specific beliefs concerning the skull?[37] In the Cavillon grave at Grimaldi,
a groove 18 cm long had been traced on the floor of the grave departing
from the nose–mouth area of the skull and filled with ocher toward the
outside so as to suggest the breath of life.[38]

Parallel to these new developments, the ancient Mousterian tradition of
providing the dead with pieces of ocher is still evidenced; for instance, at
the site of Gorodtsovskaya a 5 or 6-year-old child had a pile of yellow
clay and bits of red ocher among his funerary gifts.[39]

The Gravettian marks the beginning of the decorated cave sanctuaries.
During this period, wall paintings and engravings hardly reach the dark
areas of the caves but rather are limited to their entrance, where the light
still penetrates.[40] This factor had, of course, disastrous consequences for
the preservation of the representations, which deteriorated easily not only
from the effects of light but also through human vandalism. The cave of
Oulen, France, is one of the few early sanctuaries still preserved. Four
panels occupy a wall leading to a cul-de-sac. The composition displays
a total of four mammoths, two ibexes shown in red outline, and a series of
signs including triangles, "brackets," groups of short strokes, and a spot.
The predominant pigment at Oulen is red ocher. The special meaning
attributed to color in these representations is suggested for instance in a
group of four strokes where three are painted black and the fourth red.[41]

At l'Abri Labatut[42] and Gargas, two other early sanctuaries, appears
the stenciled hand motif which was to persist all through the Upper

Paleolithic period. The 150 hands of Gargas are displayed in impressive compositions including as many as 40 hands. The majority are painted black, but 48 examples are red,[43] and rare examples are yellow and white. The hand paintings involve a particular technique of applying the pigment by blowing the finely ground powder through a tube made of a bird bone or a hollow reed over the hand laid on the cave wall. The outline of the palm and spread-out fingers therefore appears in negative on a colored area. A further use of ocher at Gargas was the smearing of the interior of a small natural niche in the cave wall.[44]

Ocher continues to be present in the Upper Paleolithic settlement remains and especially at Laugerie-Haute.[45] The cultural layers deriving from the long occupancy of the site of Kostienki are in parts heavily stained with ocher,[46] and once again lumps of ocher are recurrently found in connection with the hearths of the site.[47] The painters of Kostienki were storing their ocher supply in pits or caches[48] and were making use of short ribs of mammoth for palette. The broad spatulate end of the rib was conveniently used to triturate the ocher and the narrow end served as a handle.[49]

In the Perigordian VI layer of Laugerie-Haute (Peyrony Perigordian III), ca. 20,000 B.C., I found a unique example of a piece of hematite bearing an engraved decoration, probably an animal.[50] Ocher seems thus to have been valued by Paleolithic man as a raw material for the manufacture of pigment, but not as a precious material in itself worth of bearing decoration. Later on, on the contrary, the Egyptian civilization was attracted by and made great use of the metallic shine of hematite for the carving of personal ornaments and small figurines.

SOLUTREAN (18,000–15,000 B.C.)

The Solutrean culture is puzzling in the uniqueness of its assemblage, compared to the remaining cultures of the Upper Paleolithic. There is a conspicuous absence of burials, for example. The use of ocher during the Solutrean period is equally disconcerting. Pigment is still present in cultural layers such as Laugerie-Haute, Le Trilobite, Le Pré-Aubert, Le Fourneau du Diable; and "crayons" were found at Pech de la Boissiere, Le Placard, and at Badegoule.[51] But except for the suggestion of Peyrony that the cave of Laugerie-Haute was once decorated at this level, deduced from the several red-colored fragments he found fallen from the roof,[52] the cave sanctuaries

seem to have been discontinued. There are very few art monuments of the
Solutrean period and most of them are engraved rather than painted.
One exception in France is a large limestone slab at Le Roc that bears a
natural fossilized pattern and evidences diffuse traces of ocher.[53]

In Spain, at the site of Parpallo, near Valencia, was found a series of small
limestone slabs as large as the palm of the hand and painted red or black.
The representations include animals such as ibexes associated with geometric signs such as strokes and series of dots. The novelty here is that for
the first time the animals are not shown merely in outline but with a flat
wash covering the surface of the body. This seems to be a first attempt at
modeling, and it is notably successful in a particular example where only
the upper part of the body was filled, using the natural color of the stone
to indicate the lighter part of the coat of the animal under the belly.[54]

MAGDALENIAN (15,000–10,000 B.C.)

The climax of the mastery of the use of pigment by Paleolithic man was
reached in the polychrome paintings of the caves at Lascaux and Altamira
in the Magdalenian period. The friezes are monumental in scale and produce
a dramatic effect. The Great Hall of the Bulls at Lascaux (ca. 15,000 B.C.)
measures 17 m × 10 m and presents a frantic stampede of colorful cattle
and horses in disarray.[55] At Altamira, the great ceiling covers an area of
18 m × 8 m and includes, among other animals, 15 red and black bisons in
various postures. The palette of the Lascaux painter includes blacks,
bisters, yellows, yellow-browns, chestnut browns, niger browns, bright
and deep reds. All these colors are remarkably near one another on the
prismatic band and excite only a limited range of the color sensation.
In our own modern conception of harmony a color is to be matched to its
complementary, that is, the color farthest away on the chromatic scale.
In the case of ocher, the ideal match is green, which by contrast intensifies
and strengthens the value of red. Green pigments may be provided by
copper ores such as malachite, but this mineral is not common in Europe
and it was the prerogative of the Neolithic cultures of the Middle East to
introduce them.

The light background of the limestone caves was taken advantage of to
enhance the qualities of the colors. The animals placed as dark (solid or
contour) appeared deeper, purer, and more dramatic, especially against the
dazzling white of the calcite deposits of Lascaux.

The compositions are executed in various monochrome or polychrome arrangements. The frieze of the dead man is painted with a black outline; the herd of reindeer crossing a stream is rendered with a red outline. Flat red, black, or brown wash fills the figures of various animals, horses and cattle in particular. Several effects seem to be sought in polychromy: first a bold red/black contrast, as illustrated in the red cow with a striking black head and neck or the bright red area introduced in the black coat of a bison, possibly to indicate the shedding of his hair. In both cases the colors are bluntly juxtaposed. The same is true in the checkerboard signs, where each space is filled with black, red, or bister.

A more subtle use of polychromy is achieved in the series of galloping horses. Here the outline, as well as the mane, fetlocks, and hooves, is intense black. The upper part is filled in with black; the rump and chest are in bister or brown. The pure white of the background is used as a third color to emphasize the lighter part of the coat under the belly. The colors merge softly in a natural fashion. On some of the horses, a light black mottling is added over the brown of the rump to create an impression of modeling and suggest the hairy quality of the wild horse coat. A large jumping cow harmoniously combines a black forepart, a red body, and a brown rump. Here again all colors are harmoniously blended and the noncomplementary hues create a simultaneous tone contrast in which each color makes its neighbor look softer and more subtle.

At Altamira the bisons are sketched in black and the bodies filled with red.[56] Black areas are added to emphasize the hump, parts of the neck, and the limbs. The colors are washed and scraped away in certain parts to create effects of light and dark and delineate the fleshy parts of the body and the limbs. This successfully creates an effect of modeling. An illusion of movement is also conferred on the animals by subtle juxtaposition of values. At Altamira, the head of a bison seems to project from the rock surface because of its darker color in contrast to the body. The relative position of the legs, one in front of the other, is also suggested by different shades. At Lascaux, in a group of two bisons pictured galloping in opposite directions, the dark mass of the heads, contrasting with the textured treatment of the bodies, adds a marked diagonal thrust to the leaping motion of the animals.[57] Details such as the eyes, muzzle, and leg joints are added with fine incisions. At Angles sur l'Anglin polychromy is the final touch on high relief. The profile of a man which is presented with the usual Paleolithic upturned nose has rosy cheeks and black hair and beard.

The pupil of the eye was also given some expression by the addition of black paint.[58]

At all sites the chromatic composition is so esthetically pleasing that it is a temptation to believe that, whatever the meaning of these paintings, the techniques used to achieve them were directed by a keen esthetic drive. A compact group of five small deer at Lascaux, for instance, each of different shades—one black, one bister, and three reddish in different combinations—seems to evidence a mere joy for color effects. However, the two ibexes, one black and one red, confronting each other on either side of a large quadrangular sign, may well have convered a special message through their colors.

The Paleolithic painters developed a number of techniques to apply the pigments. The simplest method, represented at Baume Latrone[59] and Bedeilhac,[60] consisted of dipping the hand in ocherous clay and tracing the outlines of animals with the fingers along the cave wall. Such designs show the parallel furrows left by two or more fingers. At Lascaux[61] and Covalonas, Spain, ibexes and does have a punctate outline, probably achieved with a pad of moss or other fibrous vegetal or organic material.[62] Broad and fine outlines required brushes of different sizes. They were possibly made of tufts of animal hair such as horsehair or the shredded end of a reed. Fine brush strokes are clearly visible on the bisons' beards and manes at Altamira. At Font de Gaume[63] and Abri Blanchard[64] ocher pieces shaped like crayons could have been used directly to draw fine sketches on the wall. The fluffy effect of the horses' manes and the frieze of black galloping ponies at Lascaux must have been achieved by blowing the finely powdered pigment through a tube, such as was done in the painting of the negative hands at Gargas.

The quantity of ocher found in the cave of Font de Gaume was estimated by Capitan to be 10 kg.[65] It was found in the shape of red or yellow pieces together with black manganese.[66] Most fragments showed traces of striations and had obviously been scraped with a flint tool. The process was repeated on different faces of the lump, thus creating a trihedral form with sharp edges. The powder achieved in this manner must have been further ground in mortars such as those found at the site, which were made of granite pebbles and have a central shallow cavity.[67] Because a granular product would not adhere to the wall (nor could it be transformed into a fluid form), the pigment had to be made extremely fine. Since the ocher in Dordogne seems to be soft and clayey, fineness was probably easy to achieve; however, in areas where ocher is found in specular form, reaching a hardness of 6.5, this processing certainly was time consuming and arduous. The pestles were usually pebbles such as those found in Pair-Non-Pair, Les Roches de Pouligny, Le Mas d'Azil, and La Salpetrière. Horncores also served this purpose, as evidenced by the two bison horncores stored at the museum of Macon which bear traces of pigments on their extremity and show wear by friction in a concave mortar.[68]

The product was mixed with the fingers on large stone slabs such as the specimen found by Breuil at L'Abris des Roches de Pouligny or on bone scapulae of large bovids such as those excavated by Daleau at Pair-Non-Pair. These examples bear traces where the painters wiped their fingers on the scapulum at the end of the process.[69]

The ocher of Font de Gaume seems to have been collected by the hunters in the nearby Vallon de la Gaubère, where natural pits of red, yellow, and black-brown ocher are still known today.[70] As mentioned above, some particularly soft pieces of colorful ocher were shaped in the form of short sticks with one or both ends pointed. Some pieces of ocher were found perforated, as though prepared for use as pendants.[71]

There is no indication that Paleolithic man practiced the levigation of clayey ochers in order to separate the granulous sand particles inadequate for painting from the red substance. The levigation process of ocher—the reverse of that for gold sifting—suspends the desired product in water while the sand remains. Levigation would, therefore, have involved a device for the collection of the ocherous liquid clay and its deposition.[72]

We do not know what binder was used to transform the pigment into a fluid. Urine, animal blood, fat, and marrow have all been suggested. Empirical tests suggest that water gives on the whole a brighter color and a better glow than any of these substances and is by far the easiest to apply, considering the large areas covered.[73] The porous surface of the limestone walls would allow the color to penetrate deeply; this would explain the long preservation of the paintings.

The prepared colors were stored in "tubes" of animal bones. At the cave of Les Cottés the tubes were made in the metatarsian of a reindeer, cut above the epiphyse, and heavily decorated with geometric motifs; at Spy such tubes were made in a thin bird bone, and at Les Chaffaux in a cervid antler. All were found filled with prepared pigment.[74] At Font de Gaume, bivalve shells were used for the same purpose.[75] They are the remote antecedents of the gold unguent box in the shape of a shell found in the royal cemetery of Ur among the belongings of Queen Puabi.[76]

We wonder if the elegant spatulae of Rey made in the ribs of reindeer and often decorated with a fish or fish tail were involved in the collection or preparation of ocher. An early undecorated specimen of the Laugerie-Haute couche B[77] was found with traces of ocher on the rounded end.[78]

The site of Pincevent near Fontainebleau, France, so carefully excavated by Leroi-Gourhan, is shedding new light on the presence of ocher in open-air Magdalenian encampments. Ocher was present in all huts/tents excavated. By carefully mapping the locations of ocher particles Leroi-Gourhan pointed out that it was concentrated in selected areas. It was absent around the bedding areas, was present in small quantity in circulation zones, and was heavily strewn around the hearths, radiating from there in asymmetrical fashion in the direction of the zone of circulation; thus it was probably carried with the feet. There was also a striking difference between the main hearths directly outside the entrance of the habitat, where most activity such as flint chipping and cooking was taking place and where ocher was found in large quantity, and the shallow secondary hearths inside the habitat, where only faint traces of ocher were found.

Furthermore, the quantity of ocher was in proportion with the number of flint tools. For example, hearths with an accumulation of 300–500 flint tools showed an impressive quantity of ocher, while hearths with 38 tools bore only traces. The greater concentration seems, therefore, to have been related to the length of occupation of the site. This suggested to Leroi-Gourhan that the presence of ocher, so often attested in Paleolithic habitats, was probably not the result of a ritual or esthetic decoration but the result of the preparation of ocher for an unknown function which was performed around the hearth.[79] In the case of La Salpetrière, Gard, France, the floor of a Paleolithic tent built under the shelter of the entrance of a cave was covered with two colors. The oval shape which marked the habitat had been precisely divided into a red zone to the east and a black zone to the west. Both merged in a striking contrast according to what seemed to be a well-defined line. This, being contrary to the example of Pincevent, suggested to the excavator, Escalon de Fontan, the possibility that a consecration rite was performed in the habitat.[80]

There is no direct evidence at Pincevent of the purpose for which ocher was used. The Magdalenian IV–V period (ca. 11,000 B.C.) represented the climax of Paleolithic mobiliary art. Objects such as spearthrowers and perforated staffs, discs, daggers, and bones are profusely decorated with naturalistic and geometric motifs. Some bear traces of having been treated with ocher. For instance, two decorated bones from La Madeleine, one

engraved with the representation of a wounded reindeer[81] and the second
with a human carrying a long stick,[82] still had traces of red pigment. The
same observation is true for a bone of Gorge d'Enfer[83] covered with nota-
tions, a dagger from Pekarna,[84] and the "bull roarer" at La Roche.[85]
It is of course difficult to decide if they were treated intentionally or if,
as Semenov suggests, the coloring happened accidentally when the objects
contacted the ocher scattered in the habitat.[86] Among the rare examples
of figurines of this period, the shameless Venus of Laugerie-Basse is
certainly painted intentionally with a large band of ocher above the
waist.[87]

MESOLITHIC IN WESTERN EUROPE (12,000–8000 B.C.)

The collapse of the European Paleolithic cultures was followed by an
era of impoverished cultures. The cave sanctuaries were forever abandoned
and the only traces of the use of ocher in art are the modest painted pebbles
of the Azilian culture. They bear red painted geometric motifs involving
strokes and dots in patterns sometimes very reminiscent of our alphabet.
Piette's idea that they represented an early system of recording[88] was
immediately discarded. Painted pebbles are found at several sites of the
period, particularly Mas d'Azil[89] and Laugerie-Haute.[90] They occur at
Beldibi in Turkey[91] at approximately the same time and later in Palestine
in the Chalcolithic culture of Beersheba.[92] They are also part of the assemblage of the archaic culture of the American Southwest, and in modern
times the Australian aborigines use almost identical ones in their rituals.
There the pebbles are carried by the elders in a belt around the waist and
are carefully unwrapped for ceremonial occasions. They are never to be
seen by women.

Ocher continued to be part of the Mesolithic burial paraphernalia, in
particular in the Azilo-Tardenoisian cultures. At the cave of Ofnet, near
Nordlingen in Bavaria, a series of 6 to 27 male and female skulls was found
buried together in a number of pits. In all instances they were surrounded
by pieces of red ocher. Some skulls were painted red; other decorated
objects included shell and bone ornaments and deer teeth.[93] The same
custom is evidenced at the Hohlenstein cave in Württemberg, where one
cranial pit at the entrance to the cave yielded three skulls surrounded by red
ocher. The skulls belonged to a man, a woman, and a child.[94] At Quiberon,
in Brittany, France, ocher was applied to the beads which decorated the
skeletons of a communal burial.[95]

Mesolithic in the Near East (10,000–8000 b.c.)

While Europe fell in to a dormant state, great novelties were introduced by cultures of the Near East such as the Natufian. Increased sedentariness encouraged life in small villages of about 50 houses such as Ain Mallaha. The activities of the fishing/gathering society still included the use of ocher. More than 20 pestles and grinders, some with traces of ocher, were found in one of the circular Natufian houses.[96] Found here also were flat discs of limestone or basalt presumed to be palettes.[97]

The Natufians left few artistic remains. At Hayonim they are only represented by grooved fragments of limestone painted with red ocher.[98] At Ain Mallaha, one of a series of carved pebbles which have been interpreted as the representations of schematized human faces was smeared with ocher,[99] as was a small headless figurine.[100] The famous reclining gazelle found by René Neuville at the cave of ez-Zuetina in the Judean hills also bears traces of ocher.[101]

Many kinds of burial customs were evidenced in the Natufian settlements. Some of them involved ocher. A collective burial at Ain Mallaha contained 5 to 9 skulls with a few fragmentary bones. Each of the pits contained pieces of red ocher and one skull had clear evidence of paint.[102] This custom is identical to that from the European Mesolithic described above. Red ocher is recurrently found around the Natufian skeletons buried in pits and laid in contracted position.[103] One of the most impressive burials at Ain Mallaha seems to have been performed in the house of the dead individual. The skull had been laid near the hearth on the plaster floor previously painted red.[104]

Nearly all Mesolithic cultures of the Near East employed ocher, although in different fashions. At Zawi-Chemi (Iraq) a few pieces of red ocher have been found in the cultural layers,[105] as well as one stone partly covered with red.[106] At Karim Shahir (Iraq) a little clay figurine was standing near the center of a circular pit of red ocher.[107] At Beldibi small spheres of ocher were found that were very similar to the tokens usually made of clay.[108]

Neolithic (8000–6000 b.c.)

The Neolithic period brought a considerable impetus to the use of pigments. Ocher was still the most common and popular coloring matter. At sites such as Jarmo[109] and Belt Cave[110] it occurs in quantity at all levels.

However, at Catal Hüyük the craftsman greatly increased the range of his palette by adopting a series of new mineral pigments such as green malachite, blue azurite (both of which are copper ores), and gray galena.[111] Even red ocher was in some instances replaced by cinnabar or mercury sulfide for the preparation of a deep red.

The preparation of the pigments seems at this period to have been performed in specialized workshops. At Beidha (Jordan), such a workshop produced a quantity of red ocher and green malachite stored in the shape of cakelike lumps.[112] At Ali Kosh (Iran) one room of the Ali Kosh phase produced many grinding implements including grinding slabs, handstones, and heavy stone tools, many of which were coated with red ocher or asphalt.[113]

The wall paintings at Catal Hüyük are among the first examples of paintings on man-made brick and plaster walls, but more important, they are the first compositions to associate (even if it is on rare occasions) the cold and warm colors of the prism and to introduce harmony by complementary colors. The gray, blue, and green appear next to the usual red, brown, buff, yellow, pink, orange, purple, white, and black. The repertory of motifs includes geometric, symbolic, and naturalistic motifs, including hunting scenes and representations of funerary rites. Mellaart has interpreted the heavily decorated ensembles as shrines. The function of the paintings seems to have been ritualistic since after they had served their purpose they were obliterated with a white wash.[114]

In the shrines the decorations did not consist only of paintings but also of high or bas-reliefs such as bull heads also enhanced with color.[115] In prepottery Jericho, in what seems to have been an early shrine, John Garstang discovered three almost life-sized plaster figures portraying a trinity: a bearded male, a female, and a child.[116] The figures were meant to be seen frontally and are flat. The front is modeled into fine features, and the decoration of the child included ocher paint in long slashes on the forehead, possibly a representation of the hair, and around the mouth to indicate a beard or a tattoo.

The normal Neolithic houses throughout the Near East often involved red paintings. At Catal Hüyük wall panels, posts, niches, and sometimes doorways were painted red.[117] At Beidha the highly burnished plastered floors and walls included a red, purple, or brown painted area about 1 m wide running parallel to the base of the walls and continuing up them as a dado. A similar red band outlined the hearths as well as other important architectural features.[118] A similar arrangement may have been used at Asikli Hüyük (Turkey).[119] At Tepe Guran (Iran)[120] and Cayönü Tepesi (Turkey)[121] the floors were built in a terrazzo technique with small pieces of red-colored stone chips imbedded in white plaster.

The two Neolithic industries par excellence, weaving and pottery, both made use of red ocher. For the use of color in weaving we rely literally on a shred of evidence, a tiny piece of fiber colored in red found between the beads of a necklace at Catal Hüyük.[122] A clay figurine painted with a red pattern suggesting a printed garment provides a second-ary evidence.[123] A series of clay stamp seals also from Catal Hüyük is often interpreted as a device for printing such textile patterns.[124] Geo-metric motifs reproduced on the wall paintings seem also to be copied from the kilim, or woven carpet, industry.[125]

Around 6300 B.C. an innovation in the domain of pottery was the application of a red slip or wash on the outer surface of vessels such as are evidenced at Tepe Guran and Ali Kosh. Burnishing added a special shine to the reddish surface. Furthermore, motifs were painted with red ocher on a number of bowls. The most ancient patterns recorded so far are from Tepe Guran and seem to imitate basket weave or network. Somewhat later a close pattern of diagonal blobbed lines is usual at Tepe Guran, Jarmo, Tepe Sarab; geometric motifs such as zigzags, chevrons, and open triangles occur at Tepe Guran, Ali Kosh, Tepe Sarab, and Hajji Firuz.[126]

In Jericho, prepottery Neolithic B, a funerary rite involved the plastering of the lower part of human skulls. The features were indicated with fine modeling of the mouth, the nose, ears, and eyelids. The eyes were inlaid with shells. The top of the skull was uncovered and in one instance was painted with broad bands of dark ocher, perhaps to represent a headdress.[127] The same custom is evidenced at Palestine and at Tell Ramad, level II (Syria) where 6 skulls showed a large red area on the forehead.[128] Plaster balls, also painted red, were associated with them.[129] A more typical communal burial was excavated at Ali Kosh in the Bus Mordeh phase, in which a mass of human limbs was spread with ocher.[130] Among the 400 skeletons excavated at Catal Hüyük, 11 were ocher burials. Most of them seem to have been females and to have belonged to shrines. A crippled girl of about 17 years of age who had suffered from a broken femur was treated with ocher over her body and cinnabar (mercury oxide) on the skull. The funerary gifts of the ocher burials were usually poor. A mother buried with her child had some freshwater mussels filled with red ocher and another had shells and red painted pebbles.[131]

Ocher was featured in the cosmetic sets of many women's graves, including shells filled with red ocher, baskets with rouge (red ocher mixed with fat), a small spoon, fork and palette, ointment sticks, and an obsidian mirror.[132]

THE USE OF OCHER FROM THE CHALCOLITHIC TO THE PRESENT TIME

In the transition between Neolithic and Chalcolithic, green/blue burials appeared at Catal Hüyük (levels VII–VI, 6050–5950 B.C.). Malachite and azurite were applied to the skeletons in various fashions, covering either the long bones or parts of the skulls such as the eyebrows or the occipital regions. Blue or green apatite or turquoise beads also appear among the funerary gifts.[133] This seems to indicate a shift in the Near East from red to blue/green as the color considered most beneficial to the dead,[134] underlining the great importance of lapis lazuli and turquoise in the Bronze Age, especially in Sumer and Egypt. The extent of the trade in lapis lazuli ca. 2500 B.C., with all the difficulties involved in reaching the remote mines in Badakshan, may well be explained by an urgent belief in its necessity for the well-being of the dead in the next life. Possibly the same explanation applies to the turquoise mines in the Sinai peninsula and in Iran, though the current theory is that *lapis* and turquoise were desired for decoration. At that time the beads of carnelian, calcinated to a blood-red color and imported from India, are the only witness of the age-old tradition of red funerary offering.

Through the ages ocher continued to be the predominant pigment for mural paintings and pottery decoration. The Sumerians, Elamites, Egyptians, Minoans, Mycenaeans, and Etruscans had their elaborate tomb, temple, or palace paintings principally based on mineral pigments and ochers in particular. The same is true of classical and medieval frescoes. Today ocher is still present in the palette of the artist, either as a natural product (raw sienna, burnt sienna) or as a synthetic. Known as Mars colors, the synthetic ocher is made by precipitating a mixture of soluble iron salt and alum with an alkali like lime or potash.[135]

CONCLUSION

Ocher appears to have been associated with human industries in the time of *Homo erectus*, ca. 300,000 B.C. From the Mousterian period on, ca. 70,000 B.C., it recurrently appeared among the remains of human habitats. From 30,000 to 11,000 B.C., a great increase in the number of caches of ocher, mortars and grinders for its preparation, and accumulation of processing debris around the campfires indicates that ocher was playing a predominant role in human society during the Upper Paleolithic period. The naturalistic and geometric paintings on cave walls, blocks, pebbles, and bones cannot account for the great amount of coloring matter processed by Paleolithic man. We do not know what the main uses of ocher were at the time. We have to postulate that they involved manifestations that did not survive to our age and may have included body paint, tanning and coloring of skins and furs for the superstructure of the tents and the beddings and garments, and the decoration of objects in perishable materials such as bark, wood, wickerwork, and vegetal fibers.

We sense that the bright colors of ocher (yellow-red) must have had symbolic meaning for early man through the ages. This sense is given credence during the Mousterian (ca. 60,000), when ocher became part of funerary rituals and was included as lumps among the objects thought to be propitious for the dead in the next life. We lack any insight into the prophylactic or beneficent qualities it conferred, and the reason for instance that red pigment seems to have been preferred in the Paleolithic paintings of the Pyrenees, while black predominated in the Dordogne. In Neolithic times ocher penetrated the potter's workshop. Red decoration on pottery is almost as old as pottery itself, being used for overall slips or designs on parts of the vessels. Under both oxidizing and reducing atmosphere, the pigment alternately turns red, brown, or black.

In the Chalcolithic period, again for unknown reasons, blue/green seems to have gained popularity at the expense of red. Today blue is still considered a desired protection against the evil eye all over the Near East. It is a tantalizing thought that the esthetic appeal of the bright colors of the iron ores may have led to the recognition of their metallic properties, upon which our own civilization relies. One cannot doubt that the search for pigments did familiarize man with the various appearances of the main iron ores and the location of their sources and helped him to develop the habit of collecting and storing them. The goal of achieving better and brighter colors by calcination may well have led toward the process of smelting.

In the case of the copper and lead ores there is little relation between the preparation of pigments and the search for metal: there is evidence of native copper annealing and lead smelting after level IX (ca. 6400 B.C.) at Catal Hüyük, preceding the use of copper pigments.

Man's natural attraction for color sensations led to important steps in the evolution of technology. The use of pigments may be considered as the lengthy and necessary preliminary stage leading to metallurgy.

APPENDIX: OCHERS

Hematite, or red ocher, derives its name from the Greek *haimatite*, "blood-like". In fact its natural appearance is black, but finely ground hematite produces a bright to deep red powder. It is a mineral iron oxide and the most valuable of all iron ores. Its chemical composition, Fe_2O_3, corresponds to 70 parts of iron for 30 of oxygen.

The crystals of hematite are mostly tabular and their habit is usually rhombohedral. These crystals are black, glistening, and opaque except when reduced to minute splinters by natural or mechanical action, when they become red, transparent, or translucent. The color varies with the degree of hydration and the presence of impurities such as silica, clay, and calcium carbonate.

Hematite is produced by sublimation, sedimentation, or by metasomatic process. It is commonly found in nature and is associated with bedrocks of all ages. It is a common deposit at the bottom of marshy ponds.

The mineral appears in various forms, including an earthy red variety mixed with clay; a columnar or fibrous form; and a botryoidal or specular form, in which the aggregate consists of black grains with a metallic luster.

The hardness of crystallized hematite is 5.5 to 6.5 on the Moh scale and its density is about 5.2.

Goethite, or yellow ocher ($Fe_2O_3 \cdot H_2O$), is an iron hydroxide and consists of 62.9 percent iron, 27 percent oxygen, and 10.1 percent water. It is usually associated with other iron ores, found especially in the upper portion of the deposits, where it is produced by weathering. It is found in radiated, globular, or botryoidal masses as well as in earthy substances.

The crystals of this mineral are prismatic. Their color is yellowish, reddish, or blackish brown with a metallic luster. Once reduced to thin splinters, the crystals become translucent, of a yellow, brown, or blood-red color with a refractive index of about 2.5.

The hardness of goethite is 5 and its density 4.4.

Limonite, or brown ocher ($2Fe_4O_3 \cdot 3H_2O$), is also an iron hydroxide. It appears as a black lustrous mass, but the fracture is brown and its streak is yellow-brown. Limonite is the usual result of the decomposition of other iron-bearing minerals. It appears in several varieties, including a compact nodular form and an earthy variety composed of clay, sand, phosphates, silica, manganese, and organic matter.

Its hardness is a little over 5 and its density about 3.7.

ACKNOWLEDGMENTS

Research assistance by Mary Irby and Ellen Simmons is gratefully acknowledged.

NOTES

1. Cyril S. Smith, "Cyril Stanley Smith, On Art, Invention and Technology,' *Technology Review* 78 (1976): 40.

2. Henry de Lumley, "A Paleolithic Camp at Nice," *Scientific American* 220 (May 1969): 42–50.

3. Henry de Lumley, "Une Cabane Acheuléenne dans la Grotte du Lazaret," *Memoires de la Société Préhistorique Francaise* 7 (1969): 217.

4. François Bordes, *The Old Stone Age* (New York: World University Library, 1968), fig. 21.

5. A. Bouyssonie, J. Bouyssonie, and L. Bardon, "Découverte d'un Squelette Humain Moustérien à la Bouffia de la Chapelle aux Sains (Corrèze), *l'Anthropologie* 19 (1908): 517.

6. B. Vandermeersch, "Ce que revèlent les sépultures Mousteriennes de Qafzeh en Israel," *Archaeologia* 45 (Mar.–Ap. 1972): 12.

7. François Bordes, *A Tale of Two Caves* (New York, 1972), p. 93.

8. André Leroi-Gourhan, "Les Fouilles d'Arcy-sur-Cure," *Gallia Préhistoire* 4 (1961): 5.

9. Ibid., p. 15.

10. Richard G. Klein, *The Mousterian of Upper Russia* (Ph.D. diss., University of Chicago, 1966), p. 187.

11. Vandermeersch, "Les sépultures Mousteriennes," p. 11.

12. Hallam L. Movius, Jr., "The Chatelperronien in French Archaeology: The Evidence of Arcy-sur-Cure," *Antiquity* 43 (1969): 119.

13. André Leroi-Gourhan, "Etudes des restes humains fossiles provenant des grottes d'Arcy-sur-Cure," *Annales de Paleontologie* 44 (Paris, 1958).

14. Movius, "The Chatelperronien," p. 118.

15. André Leroi-Gourhan, "Le Chatelperronien: Problème Ethnologique," *Miscelanea en Homenaje al Abate Henri Breuil* 2 (Barcelona, 1965), p. 79.

16. Movius, "The Chatelperronien," p. 79.

17. Leroi-Gourhan, "Les Fouilles," p. 10.

18. Frederick W. Weber, *Artists' Pigments* (New York, 1923), p. 95.

19. Movius, "The Chatelperronien," p. 79.

20. André Leroi-Gourhan, "Chronologie des Grottes d'Arcy-sur-Cure," *Gallia Préhistoire* 7 (1964): 46; *Les Religions de la Préhistoire* (Paris, 1971), p. 74.

21. Philip van Dören Stern, *Prehistoric Europe* (Toronto, 1969), p. 119.

22. André Leroi-Gourhan, *Préhistoire de l'Art Occidental* (Paris, 1971), p. 242.

23. D. Peyrony, "La Ferrassie," *Préhistoire* 3 (1934): 68, fig. 70.

24. H. Breuil, "L'Art Parietal Franco-Cantabrique," in Hans-Georg Bandi, *L'Age de Pierre* (Paris, 1960), p. 15.

25. D. Peyrony, "La Ferrassie," pp. 70–71 and figs. 71–72.

26. D. Peyrony, "Le Gisement Castenet, Vallon de Castelmerle, commune de Sergeac (Dordogne)," *Bulletin de la Société Préhistorique Francaise* 32m (1935): 440–42.

27. J. G. Lalanne and Chanoine J. Bouyssonie, "The Gisement paléolithique de Laussel," *l'Athropologie* 50 (1947): 131.

28. M. Szombathy, "Die Aurignacienschichten im Loss von Willendorf," *Korrespondenzblatt für Anthropologie, Ethnologie und Urgeschichte* 40, no. 9/12 (1909).

29. Alexander Marshack, *The Roots of Civilization* (New York, 1972), pp. 302–03.

30. This idea was suggested to me by Ellen Simmons.

31. Leroi-Gourhan, *Les Religions de la Préhistoire*, p. 61.

32. Luigi Cardini, "Nuovo Documenti sull'Antichita dell' Uomo en Italia: Reperto Umano del Paleolitico Superiore nella i Grotta delle Arene Candide," *Razza e Civilita* A Anno III, 23 (Mar.–June 1942): 5–25.

33. Richard G. Klein, *Man and Culture in the Late Pleistocene* (San Francisco, 1969), p. 90.

34. Otto Bader, "Nouvelles Sépultures Paléolithiques en URSS," *Archeologia* 4 (May–June 1965): 62.

35. A. L. Mongait, *Archaeology in the USSR* (Hardsmondsworth, 1961), p. 97.

36. Leroi-Gourhan, "Chronologie," p. 68.

37. Ibid., p. 61, 68.

38. Ibid.

39. Klein, *Man and Culture*, p. 96.

40. Leroi-Gourhan, "Chronologie," p. 149.

41. Ibid., pp. 325–26.

42. Ibid., p. 151.

43. G. Malvesin-Fabre, L. R. Nougier, and R. Robert, *Gargas*, edition Edouard Privat (Toulouse, 1954), p. 11.

44. Leroi-Gourhan, "Chronologie," p. 249.

45. Denis Peyrony and Elie Peyrony, "Laugerie-Haute près des Eyzies," Archives de l'Institut de Paleontologie Humaine, *Mémoire No. 19* (Paris, 1938), p. 28.

46. Klein, *Man and Culture*, p. 196.

47. Ibid., p. 198.

48. Ibid., p. 171.

49. Klein, *The Mousterian*, pp. 170–71.

50. Peyrony and Peyrony, "Laugerie-Haute," p. 19.

51. P. E. L. Smith, "Le Solutréen en France," Bordeaux, *Mémoire No. 5* (1966), 383.

52. Peyrony and Peyrony, "Laugerie-Haute," p. 39.

53. Henri Martin, *Le Solutréen de la vallée du Roc (Charente)* (Angoulème, 1928), p. 48.

54. L. Pericot-Garcia, *La Cueva del Parpallo, Gandía,* (Madrid, 1942), figs. 628, 631.

55. Annette Laming, *Lascaux* (Harmondsworth: Penguīn Books, 1959), p. 64.

56. E. Cartailhac and H. Breuil, *La Caverne d'Altamira à Santillane* (Monaco, 1906), p. 96 ff.

57. Sylvia Bialko, "Paleolithic Cave Painting: A Modern Critical Analysis," Unpublished paper, Dec. 1972.

58. Dorothy Garrod, "Finding the Earliest Realistic Portrait in the History of Man," *The Illustrated London News*, July 16, 1949, p. 91 ff. Also, Leroi-Gourhan, "Chronologie," p. 249.

59. H. Bégouen, "La Grotte de la Baume-Latrone à Russan (Sainte Anastasie)," *Mémoires de la Société Archéologique du Midi de la France* 20 (1941): 101–30.

60. H. Bégouen, "Les peintures et dessins de la grotte de Bedeilhac," *IPEK* (1929): 1–5.

61. Laming, *Lascaux*, p. 107.

62. Leroi-Gourhan, "Chronologie," pl. 108.

63. L. Capitan, H. Breuil, and D. Peyrony, *La Caverne de Font de Gaume aux Eyzies (Dordogne)* (Monaco, 1910), pp. 50–51 and fig. 27.

64. Paolo Graziosi, *Paleolithic Art* (New York, 1960), pl. 113c.

65. Capitan et al., *La Caverne de Font de Gaume*, p. 48.

66. Pigments, including ocher, were found in the following Upper Paleolithic sites: Les Cottes (Vienne), Les Roches de Pouligny (Indre), Chatelperron (Allier), Arcy (Le Trilobite) (Yonne), Spy (Belgium), La Ferrassie, Cro-Magnon, Sergeac (Dordogne), Douhet (Charente Inferieure), Pair-non-Pair (Gironde), Le Bouitou (Corrèze), Isturitz (Basses-Pyrenées), Badegoule (Dordogne), Solutré (Saône-et-Loire), Monthaud (Indre), Noailles (Corrèze), Oullins (Gard), Altamira (Spain); Puy-de-Lacan (Corrèze), La Madeleine, Laugerie, Raymonden, Teyjat, Les Eyzies (Dordogne), Bruniquel (Tarn-et-Garonne), Montgaudier, Vilhonneur (Charente), Saint-Marcel (Indre), Le Chaffaux, Lussac (Vienne), Sordes, Aurensan (I), Marsoulas, Mas d'Azil, Montfort (Pyrenées), and Thayngen (Switzerland).

67. Mortars were found in numerous sites, including Arcy-sur-Cure, La Madeleine, Laugerie-Basse, Le Souci, Gorge d'Enfer (Dordogne), Oullins (Gard), La Grotte du Gros Roc, au Douhet (Charente Inferieure), Les Roches de Pouligny, Saint-Marcel (Indre), Marsoulas (Haute-Garonne), La Salpetrière, Oullins, Marsoulas.
The earliest mortars with traces of pigment found in the Middle East are in the Upper Paleolithic level of Qafzeh (Israel).

68. Cartailhac and Breuil, *La Caverne d'Altamira*, p. 117.

69. Peyrony and Peyrony, "Laugerie-Haute," pp. 118–19.

70. Capitan et al., *La Caverne de Font de Gaume*, p. 52.

71. Ibid., p. 50 and fig. 28.

72. F. Pupil, "l'Industrie de l'Ocre," *Bulletin de la Société Préhistorique Francaise* 39 (1942): 229–30.

73. Charlotte Rogers, "Paleolithic Mineral Pigments" (Term paper, Spring 1974); Bonnie Froman, "Pigments and their Use by Paleolithic Man" (Term paper, Fall 1974).

74. Cartailhac and Breuil, *La Caverne d'Altamira*, p. 118.

75. Ibid., p. 48. Other sites including shells filled with ocher are Bruniquel, La Salpetrière (Gard), Les Eyzies, and Le Mas d'Azil.

76. C. L. Woolley, *Ur Excavations*, vol. 2, *The Royal Cemetry* (London, 1934), pl. 165, U.10932.

77. André Leroi-Gourhan, "La Spatule aux Poissons de la grotte du Coucoulu à Calviac (Dordogne)," *Gallia Préhistoire* 14 (1971): 258, fig. 5. Other spatulae were found at the following sites: Coucoulu, Laugerie-Basse, La Madeleine, Isturitz, Bisqueytan, Brassempouy, El Pendo, Saint-Marcel, Gourdan, La Vache, l'Abri du Poisson, and Castlemerle.

78. Peyrony and Peyrony, "Laugerie-Haute," p. 24 and fig. 13:6.

79. André Leroi-Gourhan and Michel Brézillon, "Fouilles de Pincevent," (la section 36), *VIIe Supplément à Gallia Préhistoire*, Centre Nationale de la Recherche Scientifique, 1972, pp. 89–93.

80. M. Escalon de Fontan, "Un Campement de chasseurs de rennes prés du Pont du Gard," *Archeologia* 4 (May-June 1965): 20–21.

81. Marshack, *Roots of Civilization*, pp. 269–70.

82. Ibid., p. 209.

83. Ibid., p. 55.

84. Ibid., p. 260

85. Johannes Maringer, *The Gods of Prehistoric Man* (New York, 1960), p. 88.

86. S. A. Semenov, *Prehistoric Technology* (Bath, 1964), pp. 4–5.

87. Leroi-Gourhan, "Chronologie," pl. 53.

88. Edouard Piette, "Les Galets Coloriés du Mas d'Azil," *l'Anthropologie* 7 (1896): 385–427.

90. Peyrony and Peyrony, "Laugerie-Haute," p. 74, fig. 55.

91. Enver Bostanci, "Beldibi ve Magracikta Yapilan 1967 yas Mevisimi Kazilari ve Yeni Buluntular," *Türk Arkeoloji Dergisi* 16-1 (1967): fig. 2.

92. Jean Perrot, "The Excavations at Tell Abu Matar near Beersheba," *Israel Exploration Journal* 5 (1955): fig. 19.

93. W. Scheidt, *Die Eiszeitlichen Schadelfunde aus der grossen Ofnet-Höhle und von Kaufeetsberg bei Nordlingen* (Munich, 1923).

94. Emmanuel Anati, *Palestine before the Hebrews* (Knopf, 1963), p. 176.

95. Marshack, *Roots of Civilization*, p. 347.

96. Jean Perrot, "Excavations at Eynan (Ain Mallaha) Israel," *Yearbook of the American Philosophical Society* 10 (1960): 545.

97. Jean Perrot, "Le Gisement Natoufien de Mallaha (Eynan), Israel," *l'Anthropologie* 70 (1966): fig. 18.

98. O. Bar-Yosef and E. Tchernov, "Archaeological Finds and the Fossil Faunas of the Natufian and Microlithic Industries at Hayonim Cave (Western Galilee, Israel)," *Israel Journal of Zoology* 15 (1966): 117.

99. Perrot, "Eynan," p. 545.

100. Perrot, "Mallaha," p. 474.

101. René Neuville, "Le Paléolithique et le Mésolithique du Désert de Judée," *Archives IPH* 24 (1951): pls. 14, 15.

102. Anati, *Palestine before the Hebrews*, p. 174.

103. Ibid., pp. 170–71.

104. Perrot, "Mallaha," p. 445.

105. Rose L. Solecki, "Zawi Chemi Shanidar: A Post-Pleistocene Village Site in Northern Iraq," *Report of the VIth International Congress on Quaternary* (Warsaw, 1961), p. 407.

106. Ibid., p. 409.

107. R. J. Braidwood and B. Howe, *Prehistoric Investigations in Iraqi Kurdistan*, The Oriental Institute of the University of Chicago, Studies in Ancient Civilizations, no. 31 (1960), p. 53.

108. Bostanci, "Beldibi," fig. 3.

109. Braidwood and Howe, *Prehistoric Investigations*, p. 45.

110. Carleton S. Coon, *Cave Explorations in Iran, 1949*, Museum Monographs (University Museum, University of Pennsylvania: Philadelphia, 1951), pp. 75–76.

111. James Mellaart, *Catal Hüyük: A Neolithic Town in Anatolia* (New York, 1967), p. 131.

112. Diana Kirkbride, "Beidha: Early Neolithic Village Life South of the Dead Sea," *Antiquity* 42 (1968): 268.

113. Frank Hole, Kent V. Flannery, and James A. Neely, *Prehistory and Human Ecology of the Deh Luran Plain*, Memoirs of the Museum of Anthropology of the University of Michigan, Ann Arbor, No. 1 (1969), p. 44.

114. Mellaart, *Catal Hüyük*, p. 132.

115. Mellaart, *Catal Hüyük*, fig. 36.

116. John Garstang, "Jericho: City and Necropolis (fifth report)," *Annals of Archaeology and Anthropology* (University of Liverpool) 22 (1935): pl. LIII.

117. Mellaart, *Catal Hüyük*, p. 149.

118. Kirkbride, "Beidha," p. 270.

119. Ian A. Todd, "Asikli Hüyük: A Protoneolithic Site in Central Anatolia," *Anatolian Studies* 16 (1966): 139.

120. Peder Mortensen, "Excavations at Tepe Guran, Luristan. II. Early Village Farming Occupation," *Acta Archaeologia* 36, (1964): 110–21.

121. Robert J. Braidwood, Halet Cambel, Charles L. Redman, Patty Jo Watson, "Beginnings of Village Farming Communities in Southeastern Turkey," *Proceedings of the National Academy of Sciences* (U.S.A.) 69 (June 1971): 1236.

122. Mellaart, *Catal Hüyük*, p. 150.

123. Ibid., fig. 50.

124. Ibid., pl. 121.

125. Ibid., p. 150.

126. Denise Schmandt-Besserat, "The Use of Clay before Pottery in the Zagros," *Expedition* 16 (1974): 15–16.

127. Kathleen Kenyon, *Archaeology in the Holy Land* (London, 1960), p. 52.

128. Henri de Contenson, "Troisième Campagne à Tell Ramad, 1966," *Annales Archéologiques Arabes Syriennes* 17 (1967): 20.

129. Henri de Contenson and Wilhelm J. van Liere, "Sondages à Tell Ramad en 1963," *Annales Archéologiques de Syrie* 14 (1964): 111.

130. Hole, *Deh Luran*, p. 36.

131. Mellaart, *Catal Hüyük*, pp. 207–08.

132. Ibid., p. 209.

133. Ibid., p. 208.

134. Sara Otto-Diniz, "Prehistoric Gemstones in the Near East: A Medium of Expression" (unpublished paper, 1974).

135. Rutherford J. Gettens and George L. Stout, *Painting Materials: A Short Encyclopedia* (New York, 1966), p. 129.

6

The Coming of Copper and Copper-Base Alloys and Iron: A Metallurgical Sequence

JAMES A. CHARLES

A historical study of man's use of metals can be made with knowledge of the archaeological evidence and the dating that can be achieved by carbonaceous and ceramic associations. It is not the intention here, however, to discuss in detail the varying views as to the areas where metal usage began or how it developed, but rather to consider the scientific and technical aspects of copper and bronze development within a general archaeological framework and to assess the significance of this achievement in relation to the discovery and use of iron.

The most abundant element in the Earth's crust is, of course, oxygen, since the great bulk of everything is present as oxide. The metallic elements fall in order of percentage by weight as follows:

Si	Al	Fe	Ca	Na	K	Mg	Ti	Mn
28	8	5	3.6	2.8	2.6	2	0.4	0.1

Remarkably, seven metallic elements and oxygen compose over 98 percent of the Earth's crust, and only three of the industrially important metals, Al, Fe, and Mg, are present in amounts above 2 percent. Most other useful metals occur in amounts below 0.1 percent and copper is present in less than 0.5 part in 10,000 at 0.0045 percent.

Quite obviously, if the minerals containing these small quantities had been uniformly distributed, their original historical isolation and large-scale recovery and use would not have been possible, and civilization would not have developed as it has. Fortunately, during the formation and subsequent deterioration of the Earth's crust, various natural agencies have led to local concentrations of specific minerals as deposits. For example, during the extremely slow cooling of molten rocks, or magmas, marked segregation occurred during crystallization. Heavy crystallites settled and solute-enriched liquids were rejected to last-freezing regions. In other ways also gross heterogeneity developed. Subsequently, erosion and transport, solution and reprecipitation have also resulted in high local concentrations of some metal compounds.

These local concentrations of minerals are usually readily recognizable by their color, morphology, and texture. In subsequent history more sophisticated techniques of detection at lower concentration in country rock have been employed, but there can be little doubt that in prehistory the initial collection and subsequent recognition for use were by color and form; concentration in primitive mining would have been to release by breaking and hand-picking. The origins and development of metallurgy lie in man's recognition of the differences in color and texture and his collection of materials on this basis. The unchanging luster of gold, the color of native copper, their malleability, and a growing awareness of association with other materials would have stimulated the activity.

The significance of color cannot be overemphasized, as Denise Schmandt-Besserat reminds us in chapter 5. The association of oxidic materials such as the basic carbonates green malachite ($CuCO_3 \cdot Cu(OH)_2$) and blue azurite ($2CuCO_3 \cdot Cu(OH)_2$) and the dull red cuprite Cu_2O with the native copper would have been evident, and in the heating and perhaps melting of native copper with charcoal their reduction noticed. This would promote a purposeful search for these colored minerals even when they were not in association with native copper, once the local source of the metal itself had been depleted. The color of minerals may also have led smiths to experiment with visually similar materials. As will be discussed later, the transition from arsenical copper to tin bronze may have been made through the similarity of appearance of the arsenical copper minerals or arsenopyrite as sources of the arsenical addition and stannite, from which tin additions may be made to copper.

As other chapters note, minerals were collected in Neolithic times for use as pigments, which again stresses the importance of color and texture.

STABILITY OF METAL COMPOUNDS

The existence of native metals and the ease with which metal compounds can be reduced to metal—and thus the order in which they have been used in history—are related to the comparative stability of the compounds. In an extracting or smelting stage the aim is to reduce all the metal compound of the value being sought, with as little reduction of other compounds present as possible, so that a slag containing all the unwanted earthy material can be discarded. In developed practice this would then be followed by a refining stage during which impurity levels unavoidable from the first strongly reducing stage are lowered by oxidation; during refining some value will be oxidized and lost to the refining slag, but this may then be recycled to the smelting stage. The selection of extraction and refining operations would depend on the stability of the metal compounds involved under the particular reduction/oxidation conditions produced in relation to their components and to other metals present.

How can this relative stability be assessed? It is not the intention here to present more than the bare physicochemical bones of assessment, so that real processes can be considered in a satisfactory way in the subsequent discussion.

The heat of formation (ΔH) has sometimes been used as a measure of the affinity of a compound's constituent elements for one another, and the comparison of one compound's heat of formation with that of another as an indication of which would be formed preferentially—the heat of formation being defined as the change in heat content, or enthalpy (H), which occurs when the molecular weight of a compound is found from its elements ($\Delta H = \Sigma H$ products $- \Sigma H$) reactants, taking into account the temperature and specific heat of the components. The existence of spontaneous reactions, which take place with a lowering of the heat content—that is, spontaneous endothermic heat-adsorbing processes which ought not to occur considering the heat of formation alone—and the fact that the total heat or energy content of a system H is made up of two terms, a free energy G that is available to do useful work in terms of energy transfer and a bound energy TS (where T is the absolute temperature and S is known as the entropy) that cannot do useful work and that is concerned with the state of the atoms in the system, have led to a much more useful concept:

$$H = G + TS$$
$$\text{or} \quad G = H - TS \qquad \text{Gibbs free energy function.}$$

The bound energy, TS, is associated with the state of the reactants in a system—their randomness or order in terms of the position and motion of the atoms or molecules of which they are made up. Thus we have the concept of zero entropy of a perfect crystalline solid at absolute zero temperature, that is, $S_0 = O$, and the idea that there is a major increase in randomness or entropy (the bound energy of the system) when we go from crystalline solid to liquid equal to the latent heat of fusion divided by the absolute temperature at which the change takes place, ΔS of melting $= \Delta H_L/T$. Conversely, a decrease in entropy would imply that as the consequence of phase change or a reaction, a system ends up in a more restricted, less random state.

The total entropy of a system is the sum of the entropies of all the components, so that if a reaction increases the gas volume, for example, $2C + O_2 \rightarrow 2CO$, there is a big increase in entropy because there is more randomness overall.

We can define the energy available to do work as the change in total heat content associated with a reaction less the change in bound energy associated with the state of all the reactants and products:

$$\Delta G = \Delta H - \Delta TS \qquad \text{Gibbs free energy change}$$

For any natural process that tends to occur spontaneously there must be a fall in free energy in the system available to do work, and the extent of the decrease in ΔG measures the thermodynamic tendency for a reaction to occur. It is the only valid way of describing the stability of a system. ΔG must be negative for a reaction to occur, but no such prediction can be made from either ΔH or ΔS alone.

Thus, thermodynamically, whether a reaction can proceed depends on the state and temperatures of the reactants reflecting their entropy as well as on whether there is a change in the heat content of the system.

The free energy of differing reactions, once they have been derived or measured, can be compared with one another as a function of temperature in graphical form on what is known as an Ellingham diagram, named after its originator.[1] Ellingham diagrams have been considerably improved and extended over the years, notably by Richardson and Jeffes.[2] On one diagram are plotted the ΔG^0 values against temperature for reactions involving 1 mol of a common reactant, for example, oxygen (fig. 6.1), with all the phases being present as pure substances—the suffix signifies this standard state, with no liquid or solid solutions involved and with gases at 1 atm pressure.

There are several important points to notice about the form of the diagram in figure 6.1. The similarity in the upward slopes of all the lines

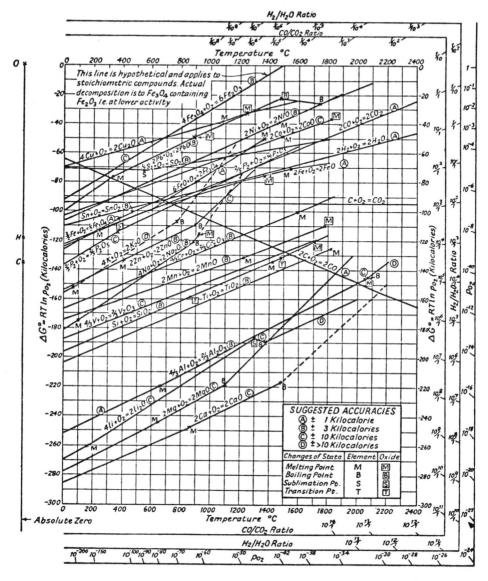

Fig. 6.1. Free energy–temperature chart for oxide formation (from David R. Gaskell, *Introduction to Metallurgical Thermodynamics* [New York: McGraw-Hill, 1973], p. 269, fig. 10.13).

for the formation of oxides from oxygen and solid or liquid metal reflects the similarity of the entropy change $d\Delta G^0/dT = -\Delta S^0$, most of which arises from the disappearance of 1 gram mol of gaseous oxygen. The system is becoming more ordered as the reaction occurs. Changes of slope on a given line are similarly the result of entropy changes accompanying a change of state of the metal or its compound, for example, in melting or boiling.

Figure 6.1 also indicates an increasing stability of oxides to lower positions on the graph. That is, oxides with higher negative values of ΔG^0 are more difficult to reduce. Reduction is easier to effect for metallic oxides at higher temperatures, the less negative ΔG^0 reflecting decreased oxide stability. Metals appearing lower on the diagram reduce the compounds of those above. Thus in "thermit" processes aluminum metal can be used to reduce a wide range of oxides.

The positions of the lines representing the reactions for the oxidation of carbon are most significant. They have a common point of intersection at 710° C, where $\Delta G = O$ for reaction

$$2CO \rightleftharpoons C + CO_2$$

Solid carbon will be in equilibrium with a mixture of carbon monoxide and carbon dioxide. Below this temperature carbon dioxide will predominate, but with carbon monoxide becoming the more stable component of the gas at high temperatures. The unique position of the curve representing the oxidation of carbon to carbon monoxide ($2C + O_2 = 2CO$), the stable oxide at high temperatures, with the free energy of reaction becoming increasingly negative, is due to the large increase in entropy which occurs with the formation of 2 vol of gas from the reaction. Thus the fact that carbon is an effective reducing agent for most metal oxides given suitable temperature conditions. The metal oxides become less stable with increasing temperature and carbon monoxide more so.

It is a fact, however, that reactions between solids are relatively insignificant in practice since solid state diffusion processes are generally slow. In most processes carbon monoxide acts as an intermediary reactant, but at high temperatures the presence of solid carbon keeps the partial pressure of carbon dioxide low by

$$C + CO_2 \rightarrow 2CO$$

The overall thermodynamics of the process, therefore, correspond to reduction by carbon, but the rate processes involved are concerned with the faster gas–solid reactions.

The Ellingham diagram indicates that below 700° C carbon monoxide is a· stronger reducing reagent than carbon itself, and it is this primary reduction by carbon monoxide which is of major importance in the formation of, say, sponge iron in the cooler zones of a furnace.

As we have already pointed out, diagrams can be prepared for any range of compounds involving 1 mol of a common reactant. In the case of sulfides carbon does not act as a common reductant. There is no carbon monosulfide counterpart of carbon monoxide, and carbon disulfide itself is notoriously unstable. Thus the practice for sulfide ores came to consist of initial oxidation or roasting, followed by carbon reduction in the furnace.

Those metals occurring naturally in metallic form are high on the graph in figure 6.1 since they are formed most easily during natural breakdown processes and they themselves are also less liable to undergo subsequent corrosion. The history of the extraction of metals by man follows a similar order to their position on the diagram. Thus gold oxide is unstable, having a positive value of free energy of formation. Metallic gold is stable under oxidizing conditions. Silver oxide and copper oxide have relatively low negative values of free energy for oxide formation and so may more readily be formed by special crustal formation conditions and subsequently less easily reoxidized to a compound. At the other end of the free energy and time scales, such metals as aluminum, magnesium, and calcium have high negative free energies of oxide formation, and their oxides are thus very stable and more difficult to reduce. Only recently, by advanced techniques such as electrolysis from molten salts, have we been able to isolate these metals.

In contrast, the ease of refining a metal by oxidation of any other given element is reflected by how much farther down the graph the curve for that impurity element lies; the interval between the curves for the two elements, the matrix and the impurity, indicating the negative free energy change for the refining under standard state conditions (in practice, of course, solutions would exist and conditions would not be standard state). For example, when refining lead, antimony and tin oxidize away relatively easily, but silver and copper cannot be removed in this way; different techniques have to be applied. To a degree, therefore, the contents of impurities in metals will indicate what refining technique was employed, if any, and thus, in some cases, give an idea as to the date or provenance of the material.

For example, the silver content of primary lead is an important indicator to the degree and sophistication of the refining techniques adopted. It is also impossible to separate precious metals by simple refining techniques. The age of silver may be related to variations in prime sources in terms of other noble metals and in particular, to the incidence of electrolytic techniques in the 19th century.

This then is the thermodynamic background to the likely form of occurrence of the raw materials for metal production and the relative ease with which the metals would have been obtained and refined from the raw materials.

THE BEGINNING—NATIVE COPPER

As noted elsewhere, when man is living close to nature his particular intelligence develops an awareness of natural materials, recognizable by color, texture, and weight. It is also common that within a given framework of conditions man will separately arrive at similar deductions. There is nothing to suggest that an awareness of mineral forms and acting on that awareness would have been a localized phenomenon; it would have occurred wherever the evidence of mineralization was clear. As noted below, this evidence was strong where arid climates had overtaken humid ones, as in the Middle East. Variations in social conditions and social practices would, however, have produced different levels of attainment stemming from the basic recognition and collection of minerals and even in developments from the initial crude smelting.

The metallurgical story begins with the collection and use of native metals, copper and gold. In this chapter we are particularly concerned with copper. Pieces of native copper would be found and collected, together with the oxidized copper minerals closely associated with the metallic material. From the thermodynamic argument previously employed it is clear that copper is a fairly stable material and is also relatively easily reduced from its compounds, which have low stability.

Geological Origin of Native Copper

Various crustal reduction processes have been suggested to explain the origin of native copper. The largest North American deposits are ascribed to magmatic origins with precipitation from a sulfur-deficient lava or from the reduction of copper sulfide by hydrothermal solutions. The most interesting and the most significant explanation in archaeological terms, since it may relate to most Central Asian and European historical deposits, is that copper was formed by the weathering and breakdown of originally sulfidic materials, as explained by J. W. Barnes.[3] In any sulfide ore body part will lie between the ground surface and the water table, the upper regions being essentially oxidizing in character and those below the water table being of a reducing nature since they are without oxygen access.

In simplest terms, a chalcopyrite ($CuFeS_2$)/pyrite (FeS_2) mineralization would have oxidized initially in the upper zone in relation to the iron through bacteria of the type *Thiobacillus ferroxidans*, where the pyrite is converted to ferrous sulfate and sulfuric acid and then by further oxidation to ferric sulfate. The acid solution which then existed, would have then oxidized the chalcopyrite to copper sulfate.

One product in the oxidation to the ferric state was limonite, $2Fe_2O_3 \cdot 3H_2O$, which separated from the cyclic reaction and accumulated to form a hard cellular iron oxide capping at the surface known as a gossan, or "iron hat." The highly soluble copper sulfate produced in the surface regions passed downward with percolating water and precipitated at lower levels. High carbon dioxide availability then precipitated the green and blue basic carbonates malachite ($CuCO_3 \cdot Cu(OH)_2$) and azurite ($2CuCO_3 \cdot Cu(OH)_2$). Siliceous conditions would have produced chrysocolla ($CuSiO_3 \cdot 2H_2O$).

When the copper leach solutions passed into the unoxidized copper mineralization below the water table, the copper salt was displaced by iron to form precipitated copper sulfides. This occurs in what is known as the zone of secondary sulfide enrichment, characterized by chalcocite (Cu_2S), covellite (CuS), or an enriched mixed copper pyrite known as bornite (Cu_5FeS_4).

The situation could now be changed by a significant alteration in the level of the water table, as produced by an advance of glaciation, yielding arid deserts elsewhere. Essentially, iron-free copper sulfide zones formed by secondary enrichment were now exposed to dry, oxidizing conditions, and the sulfides oxidized to cuprite (CuO) and native copper. Subsequently, an increase in humidity may have given rise to carbonates in association. Thermodynamically the process is governed by the higher stability of iron compounds and their use in reducing copper compounds and is controlled by variations of water and oxygen access. Natural processes were preparing the way for those of man.

The view expressed by Barnes is that, with the rapid onset of an arid period, ideal conditions would have obtained for the oxidation of secondary enrichment areas low in iron to copper and to cuprite. It is, as he points out, important in relation to the definition of areas where metallurgy would have developed first. A zone several hundred kilometers wide was formed in front of the last (Würm) glaciation. In this zone the warm and humid interglacial climate changed rapidly to one that was cold and arid. Extension of the zone from the normally accepted limits of overall glaciation down to the pertinent areas would have been by the development of alpine glaciers in the mountain ranges of the Balkans, Pontics, Taurus, Caucasus, Alborz, and Zagros. These reached much farther south, producing the arid conditions that were conducive to the formation of copper. It was in these mountains that Neolithic man first used metals when the ice sheets finally retreated.

Presumably erosion of the copper deposit would reveal the native copper locally at the surface and in streams close to the deposit. With its attractively colored mineral associations it would be collected and its associations would be recognized for surface mining. However, native copper is not common and the deposits formed in this way were probably fairly small. The use of the native metal appears to have occurred over a very long part of the Neolithic period—from ca. 8000 B.C.—although such early finds are relatively rare.

The purity of native copper would depend, of course, on the association of other elements in the original sulfidic deposit from which it was formed and the degree to which the free energies of formation of the compounds of these are similar to copper or to iron. Native coppers are, in fact, generally very pure, and the chief impurities are usually silver, silicon, and iron, the last two being present mainly as nonmetallic oxidic inclusions in the copper matrix rather than in solution in the copper itself.

Studies attempting to characterize native coppers by trace element analysis and by particular attention to the composition of nonmetallic inclusions are presently in hand at several laboratories.

Fabrication and Annealing

Although extensive forming of native copper can be achieved by cold hammering, the metal will work-harden and tend to crack if deformation is taken too far. Judging by the amount of working evident even in Neolithic pieces and by the evidence of metallurgical structure, it is clear that annealing was employed from an early stage.

There appears to be a natural, inquisitive impulse in man to investigate the effects of fire. Children with no knowledge of technology will put objects in bonfires to see what happens! Presumably the heating and annealing of native copper occurred as a result of this curiosity. Perhaps fire-setting was used initially to disintegrate the lumps of metal and associated cuprite and country rock for easier separation, and the softness of the original metal would become associated with the heating process. At some stage, therefore, it was found that native copper could be shaped more readily if it was periodically annealed in a fire by relatively mild heating. That this was so is readily discernible metallographically by the directionality developed by nonmetallic phases in the copper and by the presence of annealing twins in recrystallized copper grains.

The work-hardening characteristic was also clearly recognized in that the required edge sharpness on tools and the overall strength were obtained by a final cold hammering.

The recrystallization temperatures of pure metals are about 0.3 of the melting point and of impure metals and alloys about 0.5 of the melting point. Native copper, therefore, recrystallizes at temperatures in excess of about 330° C depending on purity. Heating beyond recrystallization does not significantly reduce the hardness of the material in the subsequently cooled condition (although grain growth will have some minor effect). There is, however, an advantage in using a higher temperature environment to reach the fully recrystallized, annealed condition more rapidly. Also, in terms of hot formability, the higher the temperature achieved, the lower would be the hot hardness and the longer the forging time available at maximized softness—that is, forging above the recrystallization temperature does not introduce work-hardening. There would thus have been an advantage in increasing the temperature of the fire in which the objects were being heated to assist forming by hammering.

Expertise gained earlier in the designing of hearths and kilns for the firing of clay and the baking of stones for flaking would have been transferred to the treatment of the native metal at higher temperatures. The necessity of draft for the rapid kindling of fire and the generation of intense heat would have been known from experience of wind and blowing, and this knowledge would have led to the use of shaped bowls or trenches strategically placed in relation to wind directions and to the use of bellows and tuyeres for both kilns and furnaces.

Since cuprite and other oxidized minerals are usually closely associated with native copper, it seems likely that the first reduction process achieved would not have been in the form of smelting to a liquid product, but in the solid state reduction of copper oxide by CO:

$$CuO + CO \rightarrow Cu + CO_2$$

when annealing native copper with which it was associated. Such granular, directly reduced copper could be hammer-welded into larger pieces.

Introduction of Melting for Native Copper, Leading to Smelting

Eventually, with higher temperatures achieved, possibly by connection with a ceramic tradition in which the firing of pots in kilns had developed a pyrotechnology including drafting, the native copper could be melted. The fact that it took the shape of a containing hearth or crucible when solid could then have led to the casting method as a means both of attaining a required shape without extensive and tedious forging and of consolidating smaller pieces of native or directly reduced copper, which up to that point would have been useful only for such items as beads and pins. The production of Danubian shaft hole ax forms in copper by cored casting in the hearth of the furnace followed by forging has been described elsewhere.[4] Clearly, the production of such large components required a method involving the consolidation of material in the liquid state regardless of whether its origins were in native copper or smelted ore. The copper was usually melted or smelted into shapes or ingots within the furnace hearth itself. To have run the metal from the furnace would have required substantially still higher temperatures and represents a pyrotechnical development of greater proportions.

Given sufficiently reducing conditions, achieving the temperature at which native copper can be melted would also have made possible the reduction of many copper minerals, as previously intimated. There seems little reason, therefore, to consider the step from the melting of native copper to the smelting of ores as an abrupt event, or even as a separate stage at all. If the native copper were to be consolidated by melting and casting there would be less reason to physically separate it initially from associated oxidic minerals, so achieving economy of effort. As the native copper became more scarce and finely disseminated and the associated minerals proportionally more extensive in the material used, but without there being failure to produce the required melted copper, attention would have switched to the suitable heating of the strongly colored "stones" for the production of the metal.

There is a problem in deciding precisely which artifacts were produced from melted native copper and which from smelted oxidic minerals. In unmelted native copper the presence of iron oxide and siliceous inclusions rather than cuprous oxide should be definitive, since in the fully melted condition separation of nonmetallics is achieved and any oxygen in solution in the copper (as likely to arise on melting and casting) would form the copper–cuprous oxide eutectic. The mere presence of cuprous oxide, however, cannot be taken as proof of melting or smelting since it has apparently been shown to occur in some "unmelted" native coppers, perhaps because of a magmatic origin or the incorporation of associated surface oxide during the welding of separate pieces.

The uncertainty remaining in this area needs to be investigated with modern metallographic techniques. A matrix analysis for impurities would be unlikely to reveal any systematic difference. In the first place the impurity content in any given zone of mineralization varies considerably; that is, it is not possible to type a given ore body by a specific level of impurity, although the presence of an impurity at significant levels or its absence may be characteristic. Secondly, native copper associated with an ore body may carry impurities associated with the rest of the body at variable levels. Thirdly, in a crude melting or smelting process the other elements present will be reduced or oxidized to variable degrees from operation to operation. In addition there are the problems of segregation within a casting, which may be extensive for some solutes and which make accurate sampling of a historic object difficult.[5]

With continued mining and mineral collection, the proximity of the sulfide ores (chalcocite, covellite, or bornite) in the secondary enrichment zone to the native copper and oxidized minerals would have been recognized. Experiments would have been conducted to investigate their reaction to varying conditions of fire, since all the other specifically colored materials from the deposit giving a green color to the flame from the furnace had given metallic copper when so treated.

We do not know whether the initial practice involved the separation of a molten copper–iron sufide phase (matte), which was then oxidized to copper, or whether the sulfides were first roasted on the outside of the fire, furnace, or kiln in the solid state to oxide, which was then treated as oxidic ore. The latter is probably the most likely, a part of the practice associated with and perhaps controlled by the recognition of the pungent sulfur dioxide fume.

It is my view that, again, it is not possible to treat the smelting of sulfide ores as a distinctly separate phase of development. The smelting of oxidized ores near the surface would have come first, but within the secondary enrichment zone of a deposit considerable mixing occurs. Preliminary heating with access to air may have become an early practice. Frequently, copper artifacts are ascribed to a sulfide smelting process because the material contains residual sulfide particles. These could have come not only from sulfates in the reduction of highly oxidized ores but also from mixed charges where insufficient care had been taken to oxidize all the sulfide by roasting and where the main component was oxidic. The presence of sulfide particles in tin bronze could be attributed even to the use of a stannite surface addition, as described later.

Eventually the smelting practice would have been extended to the primary sulfide minerals of the deposit, chalcopyrite, so clearly distinguishable by its metallic, goldlike appearance. Each development stage from native metal to oxidic ore to sulfide represented an increase in the available material and the possible metallurgical activity.

Introduction of Flux

An important difference introduced with the change from the mere melting of coarse native copper to the reduction of ore, albeit in a handpicked, concentrated form, was that separation of the molten reduced copper from the ore involved liquid–solid separation on a very small scale from associated nonreduced earthy gangue minerals in the ore particles—silica, lime, alumino-silicate, etc. The mixture of fine droplets of copper and solid oxide particles could not easily be separated from one another, nor would collection on the hearth be efficient. Lumps of copper-rich material recovered from the fire when cold would contain the entrained gangue. In order to achieve good separation it was necessary to reduce the melting point of the gangue mixture with a flux so that a single slag could be produced which would give a liquid–liquid separation within the furnace through droplet coalescence and growth. The melting point of the slag would still be considerably higher than that of the copper, so that after initial coalescence and separation the copper would continue to move down through cooler regions below the main draft, whereas the slag would tend to freeze out above; some slag might move down onto the hearth, separating above the denser copper.

The most readily available and useful fluxes would be found in the iron oxides, particularly limonite, which was available from the gossans associated with a copper deposit. These gossans, although enriched in iron by substantial separation of the copper, as described earlier, contain some copper salts and could have been included initially for this reason. Copper salts can be clearly seen from published photographs of Cornish gossans from the Woodwardian collection.[6] The material looks like limonitic iron, is earthy in texture, and has shades of brown; sometimes it has streaks or zones of colored copper minerals or even a substantial amount of sulfidic remnant as chalcopyrite. Here again the natural association of materials could have led to the selective use of gossans as fluxes since they contained some of the colored minerals initially sought and when added gave a better result. Ultimately this developed into the use of limonite alone, by comparison again of color and texture with the bulk of the gossan.

Thus the incorporation of iron oxide as a flux for the gangue would have developed to give fusible slags, with melting points usually below the temperatures attained in the furnaces, ca. 1400° C. The temperature levels developed in the process can be estimated from the mineral constitution of solidified slag and the separation of iron in associated copper droplets, as elegantly shown by Milton et al. on Timna material.[7]

First Production of Iron

The use of iron oxide as a flux is particularly important since it constituted a new type of development—the incorporation of a constituent for an effect rather than for a product. It demonstrates a growing understanding of the behavior of materials in fire and how their behavior might be controlled. More than this, however, it can clearly indicate an origin of the production of metallic iron. In certain cases reduction to metallic iron would have occurred where the gangue content of the ore used was low or where there was no juxtaposition with other gangue material, so that the iron oxide was not reduced in activity by combination with silica, etc.

The presence of some form of iron in the raked-out fire, similarly ductile as copper when forged hot under the hammer, even if of different color when cold, would have been quickly noted. Also, under conditions where the activity of iron is high, that is, conditions likely to lead to metallic iron formation, some iron solution in the liquid copper produced would have occurred, to be rejected in copper solidification.

Where the initially produced copper was remelted in a crucible, because the original form was too dispersed (droplets, sponge, etc.), this iron would separate as a rim of distinct material. Experiments in this area have been described by Tylecote[8] (see also the discussion by Wertime in chap. 1). Another possibility for the discovery of iron in connection with copper smelting exists in the similar appearance of cuprite (CuO) and red iron oxide, hematite (Fe_2O_3). The latter might have been used by mistake (though this is perhaps unlikely, given the long history of fluxing in copper smelting with various forms of iron oxide).

The occurrence of *occasional* iron artifacts (other than from meteoritic material) in the earliest periods of the Bronze Age fits with these theories —either the chance development of metallic iron through the erroneous selection of similar minerals or the use of iron oxide base fluxes that were themselves sometimes reduced; in the latter case the iron developed as separate pieces of sponge or was rejected from copper on the remelting and resolidification of extracted material (see the discussion by Waldbaum in chap. 3). The stability of copper and iron oxides in terms of temperature or the reducing strength of a system can be judged from the Ellingham diagram.

The incidence of iron in the cinders of the furnace would increase with improved furnace operation: higher temperatures and maintained high CO/CO_2 ratios. In this connection it should be pointed out that the greatest heat release from the combustion of C to CO to CO_2 occurs in the CO to CO_2 stage. Thus it is easier to achieve high temperatures in shallow fires, where complete combustion is achieved by the air admitted and conditions are oxidizing. To obtain higher temperatures and maintain overall reducing conditions requires a good localized bottom draft with a rapid feed of fuel and always plenty of excess fuel around the combustion zone. Together with lagging of the furnace itself this ensures not only that less heat is lost to the surroundings but also that the heat spreads into unburnt charcoal, where above 700° C CO is produced by the Bondouard reaction

$$CO_2 + C \rightarrow 2CO$$

The extent of the oxidizing zone in the bed is thus minimized; in the rest of the bed reduction reactions can proceed to relatively low temperatures with the higher oxides converted to lower and then iron oxide (FeO) itself converted to iron. Some separation from associated gangue materials, which were usually self-fluxing with the iron oxide, would occur to a degree depending on the temperature achieved. At a temperature of ca. 1200° C these typically fayalite slags would be free-running. The iron produced would, of course, be solid and remain above the hearth. Should a piece of iron enter the oxidizing, combustion zone it would tend to be reoxidized, although some protection is afforded by the solution of carbon itself into the reduced iron once produced elsewhere in the bed, and this carbon would tend to oxidize preferentially.

It seems likely, therefore, that as the Bronze Age developed, the effort to obtain better copper smelting led to improved furnace operation. More efficient use of fluxes and greater control of combustion and heat conservation meant there was an increased incidence of metallic iron occurring in the spent charge material and associated with the solidified copper. Eventually there developed an upsurge of interest in iron for its own sake. Such an interest would be associated with the level of development reflected in the change from copper to copper-base alloys, and their purposeful selection for specific properties.

Usefulness of Native Copper

What was the usefulness of native copper or smelted copper? Copper's value has been frequently understimated in the context of implements and weapons in the Chalcolithic era. Frequently authors give the erroneous impression that because an artifact was made of copper it would have been of relatively little practical use.

The hardness of the copper that would have been collected or made would have been of the order of 50 DPH (diamond pyramid hardness, or Vickers hardness in kilograms of square millimeter of indentation produced) in the as-cast or fully annealed condition. Cold-working by hammering can raise this hardness to 115 DPH or even more without cracking, harder in fact than annealed pure iron or low carbon steel (90 DPH, 110 DPH). It has been shown that some of the cast Balkan copper axes had been subsequently substantially cold-worked to shape, annealed, and then cold-worked again, with most final hardening restricted to the surface and cutting edges only, presumably by relatively light hammering. Thus a component was produced with a reasonably sharp edge and a tough core; it was capable of being repaired by cold reforging or annealing and cold reforging or by grinding. Certainly as a weapon for killing animals, human or otherwise, the hammered copper ax would have been perfectly practicable; for many agricultural uses it would have been tougher and more suitable than stone.

THE DEVELOPMENT OF COPPER-BASE ALLOYS

It is now generally accepted that a distinct phase of metallurgical development occurred at the beginning of the Bronze Age with the introduction of arsenical materials into the charge to produce copper-arsenic alloys.

Copper–Arsenic Alloys

Copper-arsenic alloys have many advantages over pure copper both in terms of fabrication by casting and working and in the resultant mechanical properties. The alloys were similar to the tin bronzes which followed in terms of performance in use, as has been described by the author elsewhere.[9]

The arsenic contents which were obtained indicate that there was either deliberate use of high arsenic content copper minerals or the addition of arsenic-rich materials to an otherwise normal copper smelt or melt. The alloy must have been discovered accidentally, perhaps through the use of enargite (Cu_3AsS_4) or tennantite (Cu_3AsS_3), where there may be replacement of As by Sb in antimonial isomorphs. Enargite and tennantite are metallic gray in appearance and are sufficiently alike in texture (although not of similar color to the secondary copper sulfides with which they occur) to encourage smiths to experiment with them. Barnes has pointed out that additionally the oxidation of the copper arsenides produces an astonishingly wide range of green basic copper arsenates of general formula $Cu_3As_2O_8 \cdot nCu(OH)_2xH_2O$, many of which, conichalcite for example, closely resemble malachite.[10] Arsenopyrite, another possible sulfidic arsenic addition of strong metallic luster, oxidizes to green minerals also, either the pale green scorodite ($FeAsO_4 \cdot 2H_2O$), or to the more malachite-like pharmacosiderite ($6FeAsO_4 \cdot 2Fe(OH)_3 \cdot 12H_2O$). As Barnes comments, these could easily be confused with the more usual oxidized copper ores and produce a superior copper.

Barnes prefers the use of the arsenate-containing materials rather than of the primary sulfarsenides as marking the discovery of selected copper minerals to produce alloys of improved properties. As he points out, the oxidized ores lie closer to the surface and would be mined first and most easily. The very marked similarity between the basic copper arsenates and the carbonate malachite presents problems, however, in explaining the apparent selection of specifically high arsenic content materials to give up to 8 percent arsenic in the final alloy. If the material was so easily confused with malachite this would be difficult to achieve.

On the other hand, bearing in mind that by this time mining of sulfide deposits had already occurred, enargite, tennantite, or even arsenopyrite would have been more easily distinguished as required materials for the improved copper, occurring in dense form without oxidation, leaching, or dispersion by weathering. Further, the metallic gray copper arsenides, nickel arsenides, and arsenopyrite give off a characteristic garlic smell when bruised by hammering or when heated. This smell may have been used as a means of identification of arsenic-rich materials. It is even possible that native arsenic or the strongly colored arsenic minerals such as orpiment or realgar, which would have been known as pigments, could have been employed. Needham produces textual evidence that in early Chinese practice arsenic additions based on sulfide were employed to turn copper into artificial gold and silver (arsenic decolorizes the copper).[11]

Although the smelting of mixed ores may have occurred in early stages, in due time the separated effects of smelting, say, roasted chalcopyrite or malachite on its own to give copper and the effect of mixing enargite and chalcopyrite or the green arsenates with malachite would have been noted. The separate existence of unalloyed smelted copper and the use of copper for specific purposes such as rivets are proof of this.

If arsenic-rich additions were made at some stage—rather than the deliberate use of arsenical copper ores, which could have been a ·first stage—how were they made? To add the material generally to a furnace charge would be inefficient and wasteful of a valuable material, particularly if preparing the alloy from smelting a mixed arsenide–sulfide charge where a proportion of the arsenic would be oxidized. From the beginning all collected minerals for smelting would have been deliberately placed in a central position in the furnace to maximize heating and collection as metal below. The remelting of scrap or stock ingot would have been handled in the same way.

Hand in hand with the ceramic tradition, however, clay crucibles had
been used from an early stage for melting copper and perhaps for smelting
small quantities of pure oxidized copper ores where slag separation was
not a problem. The most deliberate way of making an addition with
maximum control would have been to remelt copper in contact with a
given quantity of the addition in a crucible under charcoal—a method
later used widely. Such crucible additions could simply have been a
separately prepared high arsenic-copper master alloy. In work carried out
by both Eaton and McKerrell[12] and by Stickland,[13] however, it has been
shown to be practically possible for a wide range of arsenic and tin minerals
including sulfides to be used directly as surface additions under charcoal
to give arsenical copper and bronze, respectively. The important physicochemical aspects of such surface additions are dealt with again below in
the discussion of tin bronze.

Copper–Antimony Alloys

Antimonial copper sulfides are isomorphic with arsenic materials. In
a purely random situation using enargite/tennantite (Fahlerz), antimony
could be expected to occur. As Forbes remarks, many antimony-contain-
ing coppers have been found among the oldest copper alloys,[14] but in
most cases the percentage of antimony is so low that it can be ascribed
to the natural impurities of the copper ore used rather than to any addition of a specific antimonial material during the smelting of the copper.
There were, however, a few centers where the addition of antimony was
apparently a standard practice, giving levels as high as 15–20 percent Sb.
Such a center was Velen St. Viel in Hungary, an important metallurgical
site in the Middle Danube basin in the Late Bronze Age, where local
sources of antimony gave both the metal itself and the high antimony
copper which was used for specific purposes and traded quite widely as
a substitute for tin bronze.[15]

PROPERTIES OF COPPER–ARSENIC AND COPPER–ANTIMONY ALLOYS

Arsenic as an addition to copper functions as a deoxidant, improving
the quality of castings and greatly increasing the work-hardening capability of the material. The rough cast shape produced by the smith could
be hammered to a given high strength and hardness more readily than
pure copper and was capable of cold-working to a much harder material

without cracking. In terms of mechanical properties, in the work-hardened condition a high arsenic material can be classed with tin bronze. But it is not considered to have such good mechanical properties in the as-cast state. Copper–arsenic alloys are liable to segregation, particularly inverse segregation, when arsenic-rich liquid may even exude at the surface of the casting to give a silvery coating. This is a possible reason for its use in some specific ritual or decorative applications. The level and form of the segregation in copper–arsenic alloys are not usually sufficient to cause brittleness, and the material can be readily worked.

Copper–antimony alloys, on the other hand, are increasingly hard and brittle in the range 3–7 percent Sb, as normally encounted, giving hardness values of from 75 to 125 kg/mm^2.[16] The alloy produces very high degrees of segregation and is so brittle in as-cast states (because of the intergranular phases produced) that it cracks readily on working. Prolonged heating of the alloy at 650° C in homogenization experiments produced more uniform microstructures and reduced hardness somewhat. The intergranular phase producing the brittleness of the material in cold work and also making it hot short in hot forging was deduced from metallography and electron microprobe analysis to have arisen from coring in the original α dendrites, followed by the remaining liquid solidifying at 31 wt percent antimony as the eutectic $\alpha + \beta$ structure at 645° C. This was then followed by the decomposition of the β component of the eutectic, eventually to the ϵ phase (Cu_3Sb). Both these intermetallic compounds are brittle at normal temperatures.

Not a great deal of information is available from the metallurgical literature on the characteristics of high antimony alloys; most work relates only to its effect as an impurity in copper and copper alloys. Corson discussed the possibility of replacing tin in bronzes with antimony within the context of the World War II shortage of tin.[17] This motive for using antimony could well have been significant even in Bronze Age times in Europe. In his opinion a 7 percent Sb bronze has some uses if properly cast and annealed. He states it has low elongation, high hardness, and a strength about equal to that of "red brass." Roast, writing at about the same time, described and tabulated the composition and properties of four antimony "bronzes," three with 8 percent Sb and one with 16 percent Sb, with and without other minor alloying additions.[18] He considered the 8 percent Sb alloys to be suitable for gear wheels and similar purposes, being somewhat in the class of cast irons, at least as far as lack of toughness is concerned. He says "it will be noted from these results that 10 percent Sb gives a very brittle alloy which could not be recommended."

Taken as a whole the literature confirms the findings of my own practical investigation that copper–antimony alloys are hard and brittle in the as-cast state and give great difficulty in working, relieved to some extent by homogenizing by prolonged heating. Thus, while they might have been occasionally used as a substitute for tin bronze, arising as they do mainly in Middle to Late Bronze Age periods, their use was restricted and not successful.

Advent of Tin Bronze

The period in which copper–arsenic alloys were used was, as stated, short in comparison with the long period during which tin bronze was produced in very large quantities and was the material which both dominated the cultural pattern and typifies this Age of Man. Although the period during which copper–arsenic was used exclusively was relatively short, it should be noted that subsequently for about 500 years both materials occurred together in the same cultures in widely scattered metallurgical centers. An examination of lists of analyses from indivdual excavations will show that when the arsenic levels are high, the tin is low and vice versa, the only satisfactory explanation for which is that arsenic or tin, but very seldom both, were purposely added to a common copper base. That additions were separately made is also suggested by the occurrence of bronze artifacts and scrap together with pure copper ingots in the same hoards.

If the use of both copper–arsenic and copper–tin alloys was concurrent for a time, with the former eventually dying out, was the introduction of tin a purely accidental event or did it stem from some association with previous copper–arsenic practice or from an aspect of smelting for base copper? There are several significant points in relation to this question.

Tin occurs, rather rarely, in association with chalcopyrite and pyrite as the sulfide stannite ($Cu_2SFeS.SnS_2$). Stannite resembles the arsenical copper ores in its semimetallic appearance and, in fact, may be isomorphous with them. This is indicated by the fact that a sample of Cornish stannite recently purchased by the author from suppliers for work by Eaton contained approximately five times as much arsenic as tin and produced a button of arsenical bronze on smelting.[19] The color of the stannite may be silvery to bronze and could be confused not only with an arsenical copper sulfide such as enargite but also with arsenopyrite. Similarly, in the oxidized material from a deposit originally containing stannite, cassiterite (SnO_2), produced as finely divided needle-tin or as more massive "wood tin," would be mixed with the oxidized copper ores such as the carbonate malachite and the arsenates. Now, however, it would be distinguishable as having very different characteristics, being dark brown, hard, and of high density.

In this category of mixed oxidized material would come the gossan, or iron cap, of the deposit, the use of which as a flux which might or might not be copper-bearing has already been mentioned. Insoluble cassiterite would remain concentrated in this iron oxide-rich material of the gossan after the copper had been largely leached out, whether the tin was initially there as the oxide or as stannite.

Thus there are two main alternatives in the development of tin bronze:

1. The introduction of tin to the copper followed successful use of a material (stannite) that looked like primary high arsenic copper ores or a separate high arsenic source such as arsenopyrite but that on careful inspection would be distinguishable from them. The increased density as compared to the other materials mentioned might have been added to subtleties of color and texture as points of identification.

2. The use of gossan from some deposits in fluxing for smelting to copper might introduce some relatively low level of tin, say 3 percent, but with attendant marked differences in properties to the copper normally produced. The difference between one gossan and another might then have been quickly narrowed to the presence of the dense brown/black cassiterite in an otherwise rather earthy, textured material. Once identified as a desirable constituent it would be sought more widely, and where else but in the places associated with deposits produced by weathering and natural concentration, with which man was already familiar through the metallurgy of gold?

Having established that cassiterite was a desirable alternative to arsenic addition for previously smelted copper, early man would have used it independently but concurrently with arsenic, depending on local conditions; perhaps developed applications took particular advantage, say, of the inverse segregation characteristic of arsenic to achieve silvery surface colorations.

In my view theory 2 has the most to commend it, although both may have obtained. It correlates better with the separate use of arsenic and tin in that cassiterite is so markedly different from the copper and arsenic minerals employed. Where the use of an alternative is based on similarity in appearance and occurrence a mixed alloy is more likely to result with less control. The relatively rare occurrence of low levels of tin in some arsenical copper could have resulted from the incorporation of stannite but could equally well have resulted from the remelting of mixed scrap, which would not be so easily distinguished as being of one alloy or the other.

Tin can be readily added to copper by a simple process of putting cassiterite and flux (presumably in this case gossan) on the surface of molten copper under charcoal. Similarly, tin oxide is fairly readily reduced to tin by admixture with charcoal and suitable flux in a heated crucible. The interesting point emerges that although metallic tin has been recovered from the Bronze Age, the quantities involved are small. Founders' hoards usually consist of high purity copper ingots, bronze artifacts, and scrap but with no recovery of metallic tin, which they were able to make and which might have been used for alloying. The inference is, of course, that tin was traded and used normally as cassiterite and, as discussed elsewhere,[20] may not have been recognized in earlier digs in which bronze hoards were revealed.

There are two possible ways additions were made in the production of bronze: by the use of metallic tin as an ingot material or by cementation-type processes in which stannite (tin pyrites), $Cu_2S \cdot FeSSnS_2$, or cassiterite (stannic oxide SnO_2) or stannic oxide produced by roasting stannite were added to the surface of molten copper via a slag under charcoal in a furnace, with the metal being reduced into the melt. Interestingly, the recovery of tin to the melt in this latter way can be extremely easy and efficient, and the thermodynamic reason is not hard to find. The driving force for a chemical reaction in terms of the free energy change is influenced by the effective chemical concentration, known as the "activity" of both reactants and product. For a reaction

$$A + B = C + D$$

$-\Delta G = -\Delta G^0 + RT \, lnK$, where $K = \frac{a_C \cdot a_D}{a_A \cdot a_B}$ for a given temperature

(a = activity).
In the reaction

$$SnO_2 + C \rightarrow Sn + CO_2$$

which is highly endothermic (heat absorbing), requiring a furnace temperature of $1250°C$, the activity of the products can be substantially lowered by dissolving the tin formed in copper, assisting the reaction in the rightward direction. In practical terms this will mean that the temperature of operation can be lowered somewhat, although not of course to a level below the liquidus of the alloy produced (about $1050°C$), and that the recovery of tin will be more efficient since the activity of tin and thus the tin content in the final slag will be in equilibrium with the activity of tin in the product (i.e., tin dissolved in copper) rather than with pure tin at an activity of 1. In modern tin extraction practice, which produces the pure metal, the slag has to be separately treated for recovery of the 20–40 percent Sn it will contain. While tin metal could be produced, it seems likely, therefore, that Bronze Age smiths recognized that the best overall recovery from a valuable raw material was obtained by employing cassiterite directly as an addition.

The possible use of stannite under charcoal as a surface addition, rather than as a source of a tin oxide–iron oxide–copper oxide mixture, is interesting. There is no doubt that it will work, as practically demonstrated by P. Stickland in cooperation with the author. Without much practice or experience we produced a bronze. The solution of tin at low activity in the copper may enable the reduction of SnS_2 by copper. The Cu_2S formed would be soluble to the extent of about 1 percent, to be rejected on solidification as sulfide inclusions in the bronze. Another possibility is the reaction between copper oxide in the slag phase and the stannite, with the tin released dissolving in the copper at low activity. Arsenic additions may be made in a similar way since the activity coefficient of arsenic in copper is very low.

That cassiterite quickly became the main raw material in its own right must be assumed from the relative scarcity of mixed deposits, stannite, or tin-rich gossans, and from the need for high tin sources that would give ease of addition and a consistently high tin content in the bronze, perhaps even with elementary forms of mineral dressing to achieve this. In prehistoric times the discovery of concentrated surface deposits, particularly placers, would have been relatively easy. The occurrence of near-surface materials in large and generally rich mineral concentrations obviously would have been much more widespread. The extent to which this is true can be gauged by the recorded history of mineral exploitation in recent centuries. Early man scavenged the surface of material useful to him that had been built up over previous millennia; the condition cannot be repeated and is scarcely represented today. It is not at all un-likely that coarse, readily recognizable surface placer deposits of cassiterite would have been available. In view of the significance of mineral forms to the history of metallurgical development it is vitally important that archaeologists involved in excavations should be familiar with them. The article quoted illustrates these forms and tells how they may be identified in the field.[21]

Eclipse of Copper–Arsenic Alloys

Eventually the use of copper–arsenic alloys died out altogether and the Bronze Age developed and flourished on the tin bronze which gave it its name in history. Why was the use of the earlier alloy abandoned? One view is that the tin bronze was considered to give superior properties, although except for castings left as such—where the superiority is even then arguable—there is no evidence that this is so. In any case, the use of copper–arsenic alloys for forged components and for silvery-surfaced components could have continued. In my view there were several reasons for the change, which may have been additive.

1. As Professor U. Franklin pointed out at the 1977 Archaeometry Conference in Philadelphia, the smelting of a copper sulfide–arsenide mixture must lead to substantial arsenic loss since an oxidizing stage, either prior roasting or "converting" of the separated copper iron sulfide, is necessary and As_2O_3 formed in such a process will sublime. Tylecote, submitting a paper at the same meeting, had indicated the low arsenic recovery in his smelting experiments when treating a sulfide ore. It is possible, therefore, that the earlier copper–arsenic alloys were based on the reduction of naturally oxidized ores such as malachite with arsenates, and that the move to sulfidic copper ores necessarily eliminated arsenic and made another addition necessary. This argument precludes, of course, the separate addition of arsenic to previously smelted copper by way of a master alloy or by a surface addition of a high arsenic mineral under reducing conditions.

2. There is no doubt that the preparation of arsenical material, by whatever means, was not easily controlled. The ores which would have been distinguished as arsenic-bearing would have been of variable com-position. Further, the sensitivity of the arsenic content to oxidation to As_2O_3 sublimate would mean that variable losses would occur, especially during crucible handling and casting in air, even assuming that fully

reducing conditions could be maintained at all earlier states of the alloy preparation. It is interesting to note that, in fact, the arsenic contents of copper–arsenic alloy artifacts vary much more widely than those of tin bronze.

Tin additions from cassiterite, on the other hand, guaranteed a consistent alloy. The mineral is almost always of very high purity as SnO_2, and losses during the subsequent handling of the molten alloy are low.

3. Even assuming that arsenic additions were made under reducing conditions, either using oxidized minerals containing arsenic or by a surface addition of an arseno-sulfide to previously smelted copper, the availability of recognizable arsenic-rich minerals would have been limited, with no evident topographical lead as to how to find more. Once it was known, presumably from association with the role of the phases in a gossan, that cassiterite could be used as an addition in the production of tin or directly as a surface addition to molten copper under reducing conditions, there would have been a clear topographical lead to the occurrence of further supplies. Cassiterite's high stability and density and man's previous experience with materials associated with placer deposits of gold are two factors that would clearly have indicated where more of the material could be found.

4. The garlic smell of the heated minerals may have facilitated their recognition and use, but may also have contributed to their eclipse. The handling and treatment of high arsenic minerals and the presence of arsenious oxide fume in the exhaust from furnaces and from the surface of molten metal in crucibles and molds would be bound to be reflected in a low standard of health and short life expectancy among the smiths. Toxic smoke bombs, or "holy smokes," in early Chinese alchemy are noted by Needham[22] to have contained arsenic sulfide and sulfur as the inorganic part. Even though the long-term unpleasant effects of arsenic were well known by this time it was used in small doses for its purported aphrodisiac properties. The medical view given by Needham is that arsenic compounds produce a mild vasodilation in the initial stages but that this is only the first sign of its potent action on the capillaries. Degenerative changes occur in due course as the element builds up and the chronic stage of poisoning is reached, with local effusions, edema, loss of appetite, nausea, polyneuritis, muscular atrophy, etc.

Of the Greek gods on Mount Olympus only the metalworker Hephaestus is described by Homer as being physically imperfect—he was lame and thus the butt of jokes. Both muscular atrophy and polyneuritis in limbs would cause lameness. In my view Hephaestus (and his Roman counterpart, Vulcan) reflects the traditional view of the unhealthiness of the smith's craft, stemming mainly from the use of the early arsenical materials. With the introduction of tin bronze, a perfectly safe material, conditions could be favorable for more vigorous operation and an increase in the number of craftsmen with long-established skill—an example of evolution in technology, where the use of the new material would flourish even if it was not immediately recognized that there were personal advantages to a smith in making the switch. Even today experimentation with high-arsenic alloys is considerably dangerous. Proper care and precaution—sealed equipment, fume disposal, and modern hygiene—have to be taken.

RELATIONSHIP OF THE SMITH TO SOCIETY

To what extent would these developments leading to the full technology of the Bronze Age have affected or been affected by the social structure of the local population? Although no great specialization would have been necessary within a community for the utilization of small pieces of native copper, it is clear that with the increasing complexity of operations and the skill and judgment required, the production of bronze artifacts would have become a field for metallurgical specialists, divorced from the production of food, textiles, carpentry, and pots, which could be carried on in the home as part of the household chores.

Specialists became craftsmen skilled in recognizing minerals and their association and in releasing minerals by excavation, mining, and breaking. Furnace craft, or pyrotechnology, developed concomitantly. It is interesting, if not amusing, to learn of the problems encountered by present-day experimenters in reproducing primitive smelting operations where the production of a sizable bun ingot from the hearth, rather than porous lumps from the furnace charge, presents a major difficulty. Even with relatively modern solid fuel furnace equipment, close and protracted use of a particular furnace may be necessary to achieve enough skill to produce satisfactory results, as experienced by the author when setting up a small cupola unit for the production of cast iron some years ago.

Having produced the molten metal, the craftsman smith, for so he must now be designated, would feed it to a mold, perhaps a simple one or possibly a cored ax mold of complex design or even a mold produced by investing a wax pattern in clay and then melting out the wax. In addition to practicing these "main line" activities related to the production of bronze, the metallurgical specialist of the day would have been familiar with the production of lead, eventually using it as a purposeful addition to improve the fluidity of bronze for casting. He would have had, from earliest times, immense skill in the fashioning and joining of gold and the use of silver, even to the point of being able to produce diffusion-bonded silver coatings on copper.[23] In all these areas, detailed study shows how significant and purposeful was the technology that was employed.

The high degree of skill associated with specialization would cause one to expect that workers in metal occupied a special, high status in the society, even among craftsmen whose skills were more suited to the home than to the deposits in mountains and the open sites for furnaces. Because of the nature of his work, the availability of the raw materials, and the special value of his products, it is likely that in some societies the early smith became itinerant, obtaining primary raw materials and scrap, smelting and bartering his products. Such behavior would explain the not infrequent occurrence of smelters' hoards not directly linked with other evidence of occupation. Later, however, demand outpaced what this type of operation could supply, and metals had to be procured in bulk and continuously, often from great distances and even from other countries. Ownership of mines meant wealth and power and the desire for raw material could lead to war. Once a society came to depend on metals, the acquisition of metals and the formation of a more settled and controlled group of smiths, either to use locally obtained raw materials or to work imported semifinished products such as ingot copper, would become vital to power and growth. Thus developed the centuries-long copper trade known from tablet inscriptions found in Egypt, Mesopotamia, and Assyria.

No evidence from the earliest records, such as Homer, suggests, however, that by then the smith did in fact have a high status among craftsmen, whatever his position may have been earlier. By this time many crafts had become centralized and all seem to have become identified with a degree of the magic stemming from increased complexity and subtlety.[24] The prestige of the smith seems, therefore, to have become eventually submerged in the society. In Greek practice the slave-craftsmen worked side by side with their masters, the free artisans, presumably bringing a degree of know-how from other societies. By the time of Plato and

Plutarch the skills of the craftsmen ranked with the lowest levels of human values in relation to the beauty of art and philosophy not motivated by necessity. In their view it did not necessarily follow that because an artifact was useful or beautiful its craftsman should be held in higher esteem.

Perhaps the greatest flowering of technique and skills had occurred before this situation had developed, when smiths may have held a strong position and been widely encouraged—perhaps as in the time of the Minoan and Mycenaean civilizations, when great strides seem to have been made. What is undoubtedly true is that esteem and patronage for the craftsman and technologist have been the mark of commercially healthy, developing societies, both in history and in contemporary comparisons.

Summary

Thus, at the end of the Bronze Age the scene is set for the coming of iron. There existed a highly skilled class of men, able to perform intricate metal production and fabrication processes and adept in pyrotechnology. Their knowledge enabled them to recognize that the occasional iron lumps occurring in copper smelts operating at higher temperatures could be formed into useful components; and further, that by charging iron ores of similar color and texture to the gossans or other iron oxide fluxes used in copper smelting, iron could be made independently in larger quantities, from readily available raw materials.

Notes

1. H. J. T. Ellingham, "The Physical Chemistry of Process Metallurgy," *Journal of the Society of Chemistry and Industry* 63 (1944): 125.

2. F. D. Richardson and J. H. E. Jeffes, "The Thermodynamics of Substances of interest in Iron and Steel Making from 0° C to 2400° C," *Journal of the Iron and Steel Institute* 160 (1948): 261.

3. J. W. Barnes, personal communication, and "Some Problems of Bronze Age Geology in the Middle East," Univ. of Wales Inter. Collegiate Colloquium, Mineral Exploitation Dept., Univ. College, Cardiff, 16–17 May 1974.

4. J. A. Charles, "Metallurgical Examination of South-East European Copper Axes," *Proceedings of the Prehistoric Society* 35 (1969): 40–42.

5. J. A. Charles, "Heterogeneity in Metals," *Archaeometry* 15 (1973): 105–14.

6. J. A. Charles, "Where Is the Tin?" *Antiquity* 49 (1975): 19–24.

7. C. Milton, E. J. Dwornik, R. F. Finkleman, and P. Toulmin, "Slag from an Ancient Copper Smelter at Timna, Israel," *Historical Metallurgy* 10 (1976): 25–35.

8. R. F. Tylecote, "Can Copper be Smelted in a Crucible?" *Historical Metallurgy* 8 (1974): 54.

9. J. A. Charles, "Early Arsenical Bronzes—A Metallurgical View," *American Journal of Archaeology* 71 (1967): 21–26.

10. Barnes, "Some Problems of Bronze Age Geology."

11. J. Needham, *Science and Civilization in China*, vol. 5, pt. 2 (Cambridge: Cambridge University Press, 1974), p. 256.

12. E. R. Eaton and H. McKerrell, personal communication.

13. P. Stickland and J. A. Charles, undergraduate research project, Dept. of Metallurgy, Univ. of Cambridge, 1975.

14. R. J. Forbes, *Metallurgy in Antiquity* (Leiden: E. J. Brill, 1950), p. 263.

15. O. Davies, "Antimony Bronze in Central Europe," *Man* 35 (1935): 86–89.

16. S. J. Chick and J. A. Charles, undergraduate research project, Dept. of Metallurgy, Univ. of Cambridge, 1973.

17. M. G. Corson, "Silicon Bronzes for Sand Castings," *Iron Age* 149 (1942): 46.

18. H. J. Roast, "Antimony Bronze—Physical Properties of Certain Alloys," *Metal Industry* 63 (1943): 105.

19. Eaton and McKerrell, personal communication.

20. Charles "Where Is the Tin?" pp. 23–24.

21. Ibid.

22. Needham, *Science and Civilization in China*, p. 256.

23. J. A. Charles, "The First Sheffield Plate," *Antiquity* 42 (1968): 278–85.

24. M. I. Finley, "Metals in the Ancient World," *Journal of the Royal Society of Arts* (Sept. 1970): 4.

7

Furnaces, Crucibles, and Slags

RONALD F. TYLECOTE

METALLURGICAL FURNACES AND THE SMELTING OF COPPER

Metallurgy requires at least two types of furnaces: those for the extraction of metals from suitable minerals and those for the remelting or forging of the metal produced in order to form it into artifacts.

Because extraction metallurgy evolved after the production of pottery we can reasonably suppose that it owes something to this prior pyro-technology. But it would be wrong to suppose that they have much in common. The chemical transformation of an ore to a metal is quite different from the physical hardening by fire of pottery in a kiln. A pottery kiln would not be a suitable furnace for smelting, the first part of the metal-lurgical process, although it would be possible to remelt smelted metal in such a furnace. In order to obtain the reducing conditions necessary to divorce a metal from the oxygen with which it is combined in a simple oxide mineral, it is necessary to have close and intimate contact between the ore and the reductant, charcoal. This is rarely the case in a pottery kiln and can be brought about only with some difficulty. In any event it is much simpler to design a furnace for the job. This need be only a clay bowl or a hole in the ground into which, once it is hot enough, the right proportions of ore and charcoal are introduced. The temperature in such a furnace would have to be maintained with the aid of a blast from a pair of bellows. But, since only 100 liters of air/min are required, this can be obtained easily from the most primitive skin or pot bellows.

We have an example of such a furnace for copper smelting from the Chalcolithic period (4th millennium) at Timna.[1] Although near the top of a hill it can have been worked only with the aid of a blast of air from a pair of bellows. All around it are small pieces of slag of the normal ferrous silicate type. The existence of such a slag at such an early date shows that one of the problems of smelting had to be overcome rather earlier than

Table 7.1. Composition of Copper Smelting Slags (In percent)

| | Chalcolithic Timna site 39* | Late Bronze Age | | Roman Apliki, Cyprus† | Modern† |
		Ras Shamra Syria†	Apliki, Cyprus†		
FeO	34.9	65.78	65.54	43.1	46.5
MnO	0.8	tr	tr	11.0	—
SiO$_2$	36.8	18.50	21.30	28.8	33.0
CaO	12.1	2.4	1.14	4.24	6.75
MgO	1.42	tr	tr	3.53	—
Al$_2$O$_3$	0.98	5.1	7.80	3.95	8.10
Cu	2.64	1.9	0.91	0.70	0.35
K$_2$O	4.04	—	—	—	—
Na$_2$O	1.36	—	—	—	—
S	—	0.26	1.14	1.28	0.45
P$_2$O$_5$	—	0.27	—	—	—

* A. Lupu, *Bulletin of the Historical Metallurgy Group* 4, no. 1 (1970): 21–23.
† J. Du Plat Taylor, *Antiquaries Journal* (London) 32 (1952): 133–67.

expected. If we take an absolutely pure copper oxide mineral such as cuprite (Cu$_2$O), tenorite (CuO), or even malachite (CuCO$_3$ · Cu(OH)$_2$), we can recover the copper merely by heating the finely ground mineral with charcoal in a crucible.[2] We shall get fine particles of pure copper, or globules if the temperature is high enough ($>1100°$C). But these particles may be scattered among a great deal of excess charcoal which must be burned away or later winnowed or washed away before we can get the copper globules to cohere and form a larger mass.

The early introduction of smelting, with the production of ferruginous slags, shows that these pure ores were not very plentiful. As noted in chapter 1 either iron-containing ores were used, in which case the iron was removed as a slag with the aid of additions of silica, or the ores contained silica, which was removed with additions of iron oxides. Either method would result in the production of ferrous silicate slags (table 7.1).

These slags have two most important properties: their free-running temperature (the temperature at which they behave as a liquid with low viscosity) is relatively low, i.e., about 1150–1250° C, and also copper has very low solubility in them, so that little copper is lost within the slag; what is lost is merely due to physical entrapment. This may be recovered by grinding up the slag to release the fine copper globules (prills) trapped within. This explains why so much early slag has been broken up into very small pieces.

The property affecting the physical separation of slag and copper is density. During smelting, slag and metal form simultaneously, and separation occurs low down in the furnace since the slag has a specific gravity of about 3.5 to 4.0, while the metal has a specific gravity of about 8.9. However, this separation takes time; if the primitive smelter was willing to hold the mixture of slag molten at the bottom of the furnace for some time after smelting, complete separation would theoretically occur. But this is difficult and it is likely that in the Chalcolithic period, at any rate, he would settle for a mixture of slag and metal. Many smelting sites, whether of copper or iron, have yielded mortars or hollows in nearby rocks; some of these have been used for grinding ores. But in many cases there is little doubt that they have been used for breaking slags.[3]

While many of the early artifacts are made of pure copper, a good many are of arsenical copper containing from 1 to 7 percent of arsenic (table 7.2). In some cases this metal was the result of smelting and not alloying with high arsenic minerals.

Arsenic is a relatively volatile substance and arsenical oxide (As_2O_3) even more so. If arsenical copper oxide minerals are smelted—and smelting such minerals can occur only under reducing conditions—one would expect the product to retain some of the arsenic. In fact, calculation shows that most of the arsenic present below 7 percent will be retained, whereas in the case of ores containing over 7 percent As, a good deal will be lost, resulting in a final product of this order. If, after smelting, the arsenical copper is held under oxidizing conditions, in a crucible for example, the arsenic will be progressively lost as the more volatile arsenical oxide, or white arsenic, As_2O_3. The existence of artifacts with high As content shows therefore that little refining in a crucible was carried out and that the artifacts were cast as soon as possible after the metal was melted under charcoal. Lorenzen has shown that the recovery of As from a 1–2 percent arsenical oxide ore from Helgoland is about 100 percent.[4]

Some Caucasian copper beads contain 14–24 percent As and are therefore silvery in color.[5] There is no doubt that these were made by the addition of high arsenic minerals to the crucible. It has been found that arsenical copper containing as much as 10 percent As may be held under reducing conditions for a very long time without loss of arsenic, and it is very likely that additions of arsenical minerals were responsible for

Table 7.2. Some Examples of Early Smelted Copper Artifacts

Object	Provenance	Date (B.C.)	Composition (%)				Wt (kg)
			As	Sb	Pb	Ni	
1. Flat ax	Egypt	3500	0.49	nd	0.17	1.28	1.56
2. Reamer	Syria (Amuq)	3400	1.35	nd	0.003	0.93	
3. Reamer	Syria (Amuq)	3400	0.04	nd	0.01	0.16	
4. Spatula	Iran (Yahya)	3800	1.7	<0.1	0.05	<0.01	0.065
5. Chisel	Iran (Yahya)	3800	3.7	<0.1	0.05	<0.01	0.095
6. Awl	Iran (Yahya)	3800	0.3	<0.1	0.05	<0.01	0.029
7. Hammer-ax	Prague		0.77	0.77	0	0.022	
8. Hammer-ax	USSR (Tibava)	3000	1.15	0	0	0.01	
9. Hammer-ax	USSR (Tibava)	3000	3.10	—	—	—	
10. Ax-adze	Romania (Tirgu-Ocna)		0.8	0	0	0.01	
11. Staff-head	Israel, Beersheba	3800	12.0	0.72	tr	0.05	
12. Ornament	Israel, Mishmar	3300	3.5	0.18	0.034	0.17	
13. Ornament	Israel, Mishmar	3300	11.9	0.61	0.039	1.22	
14. Tool	Israel, Mishmar	3300	1.92	tr	—	1.90	
15. Tool	Israel, Mishmar	3300	—	—	—	—	
16. Ax	Israel, Kfar Monash	3300	1.15	—	0.06	0.71	
17. Ax	Israel, Kfar Monash	3300	4.07	—	—	1.25	
18. Ax	Israel, Kfar Monash	3300	—	—	—	1.01	
19. Chisel	Israel, Kfar Monash	3300	3.55	—	—	—	
20. Saw	Israel, Kfar Monash	3300	—	—	—	0.49	
21. Spearhead	Israel, Kfar Monash	3300	2.20	—	—	0.70	
22. Not identified	Alisar Hüyük	2800	2.43	—	—	—	

Table 7.2. (cont'd)

Object	Provenance	Date (B.C.)	Composition (%)				Wt (kg)
			As	Sb	Pb	Ni	
23. Vessel	Ur	2900	0.65			tr	
24. Pin	Tell Asmar	2500	2.08			0.9	
25. Beads	Caucasus, Stanitsa, and Constantinovka	2000–3000	24.2	0.03	o	0.004	

Sources: 1. H. C. H. Carpenter, *Nature* 130 (1932): 625–56.

2–3. R. J. Braidwood, T. E. Burke, and N. H. Nachtrieb, *Journal of Chemical Education* 28 (1951): 88–91.

4–6. R. F. Tylecote and H. McKerrell, *Bulletin of the Historical Metallurgy Group* 5, no. 1 (1971): 37–38.

7–10. S. Junghans, E. Sangmeister, and M. Schröder, *Kupfer und Bronze in der frühen Metallzeit Europas*, vol. 2 (Berlin, 1968).

11–15. C. A. Key, *Israel Exploration Journal* 13 (1963): 289–90.

16–21. C. A. Key, *Science* 146 (1964): 1578–80.

22–24. C. H. Desch, *Report to the British Association* (1936), pp. 1–3.

25. I. R. Selimkanov, *Soviet Archaeology*, no. 1 (1962), pp. 57–65.

Table 7.3. Composition of Ferruginous and Manganiferous Fluxes from Copper
Smelting and Other Sites (in percent)

	Timna*		Rio Tinto gossan[†]	Manganese ore; Hotezel	Hematite ore; Cumbria
	Iron	Manganese			
Fe_2O_3	60–85	—	73.0	15.1	73.7
MnO_2	—	30–80	—	81.00	—
SiO_2	5–15	5–15	11.9	5.67	16.6
CaO	—	—		—	1.53
Al_2O_3	—	—	—	—	1.30
Cu	—	—	0.05	1.01	0.04
Pb	—	—	1.20	—	0.005
S	—	—	1.20	—	0.17
Sn	—	—	0.20	—	—
As	—	—	0.77	(12.5 ppm)	(100 ppm)
Sb	—	—	0.02	—	—

* A. Lupu and B. Rothenberg, *Archaeologica Austriaca* 47 (1970): 91–130.
[†] See n. 47 (a).

some of the lower arsenic contents. But severe loss of arsenic can take
place when the metal is worked under oxidizing conditions in the solid
state.[6]

In the case of the sulfide minerals of copper, an oxidation stage is
necessary during smelting and one can assume that a much higher loss of
arsenic would take place.

Fluxes

Complex ores have to be smelted with the aid of siliceous or ferruginous
fluxes (see table 7.3). The fluxes themselves may contain elements such
as As, Pb, Sb, Co, and so on, which can contribute such elements to the
metals produced. For example, an attempt was recently made by the
author to smelt low-grade copper oxide mineral with a ferruginous
gossan containing 0.7 percent As. I found that the resulting metal, which
was mostly iron, contained 0.4 percent As. In the same way it is possible
to incorporate elements from the fuel and the furnace lining. As far as
the fuel is concerned, about 40 kg of charcoal is needed to smelt 1 kg of
copper sulfide ore. If the ash content of this charcoal is about 3 percent,
which is an average amount, it contributes 1.2 kg to the slag and metal.
Most of the ash will be lime and alkalis which will help the free-running

temperature of the ferrous silicate slag, but the less oxidizable heavy metals such as Ag, Pb, As, Sb, Ni, and Co are likely to partition, not necessarily equally, between slag and metal. Such elements reflect the soils in which the trees are grown.

It is not surprising that for these and other reasons, as shown in a recent paper, there is no correlation between the trace element content of the ores and metals, but there does seem to be a correlation between the *type* of ore (i.e., whether it is native metal, sulfide, or carbonate) and the trace elements in the metal.[7]

The result of the smelt mentioned above shows how easy it would be to reduce iron out of the fluxes during reduction smelting of iron-fluxed copper oxide ores. Normally all operations would be reducing and, unless there is very careful control, iron would be dissolved by the molten copper. Many of the early analyses do not show substantial amounts of iron, probably because this element had not been sought, or else the metal was the product of sulfide ores. Recent work has shown that a good deal of early copper is strongly magnetic[8] and, where the cause of this has been sought, it has often been found to have been due to the presence of dendrites of a high-iron solid solution in the copper. At room temperature, this alpha-iron is strongly magnetic. Iron dissolves only slightly in copper and when its solubility is exceeded (less than 1% under average conditions of cooling), it is rejected as a magnetic iron-rich phase.

The Late Bronze Age

Although the evidence for the extractive metallurgy of copper in the Chalcolithic period is reasonably sound, we have no really satisfactory evidence for the Early and Middle Bronze Ages. But the Late Bronze Age (LBA) is noted for the vast increase in the output of copper that took place. Evidence for this lies in the storerooms of most of the museums of the world.

As far as smelting technique is concerned, we have a few more examples of copper smelting furnaces than in the earlier periods. It appears that the copper itself was produced mainly near the mines in small units. The oxhide ingots weighing 30–38 kg are an exception to this, and one might assume that China was producing ingots of comparable size. Britain and other European countries seem to have been producing plano-convex ingots weighing only 2–4 kg from small furnaces. It was not until the Roman period that the ingot size reached 20 kg.

For details of furnace technology we must again rely on Israeli work in the Negev.[9] In this area, which is now known to have Egyptian connections, the furnaces excavated date to the 14–12th centuries B.C. and it is reasonable to assume that this type of furnace is typical of those used for oxide ores during the LBA in the more developed areas of Asia Minor.

The Negev furnaces have been dug into the sandy soil of the desert and are of roughly cylindrical shape, about 60 cm in diameter and the same in height (fig. 7.1). The edges have a stone kerb and the bowls are lined with a limy cement. The ground in front of the furnace had been cut away to give access for tapping slag and the furnaces were blown through tuyeres of complicated form (fig. 7.2). Near the furnaces are the remains of large discs of slag with a central hole, weighing about 30 kg. Many ends of tuyeres with holes of about 2 cm diameter were also found. It is clear from these remains that the slag was tapped at the end of the smelt to leave a plano-convex ingot in the hemispherical bottom of the furnace. Taking into consideration the quality of the ore, the weight of the slag discs, and the size of the furnace, one may calculate that the weight of the ingot would be about 3–4 kg, which is fairly typical for LBA ingots. It is a fair assumption that these ingots supplied the Egyptian markets although on the tomb paintings only oxhide-shaped copper ingots are depicted.[10]

An LBA settlement at Apliki in Cyprus showed evidence of metalworking[11] and there is no doubt that smelting had been carried out in the vicinity where copper ore was being mined in the late 1930s. The sulfide ore was heap-roasted and silica was used as a flux for the ferruginous ores (table 7.4). The slag heaps contained many pieces of discarded furnaces; some of the tuyeres were D-shaped, and one tuyere had a right-angled bend. The slag analyses are given in table 7.1.

The copper sulfide deposits in the Austrian Alps have been worked since at least 1200 B.C.,[12] and the remains of furnaces and slag heaps have been found on many sites. The area of the smelting sites averages 100–150 m^2 and the size of the dumps about 30 m^3. The two furnaces found on a site at Kitzbühel suggest an above-ground cylindrical furnace of about 50 cm internal diameter with a slag-tapping pit in front.[13] This may be one of the earliest sites known to have processed sulfide ores. Two types of slag were found.[14] One slag occurred in the form of a flat cake about 30 cm in diameter, was extremely inhomogeneous, and contained some of the original charge. This slag seems to have been tapped in a very viscous

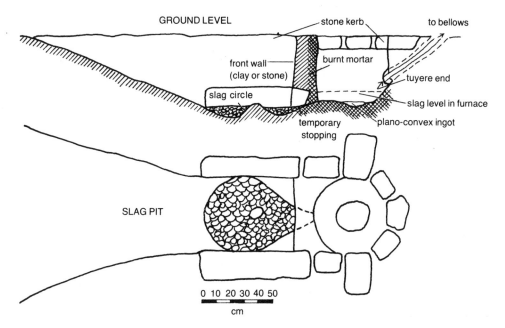

GROUND LEVEL

to bellows

stone kerb

front wall
(clay or stone)

burnt mortar

tuyere end

slag circle

slag level in furnace

plano-convex ingot

temporary
stopping

SLAG PIT

0 10 20 30 40 50
cm

Fig. 7.1. Reconstruction of copper smelting furnace from Timna, Palestine, dated about the 12th century B.C. (see n. 9).

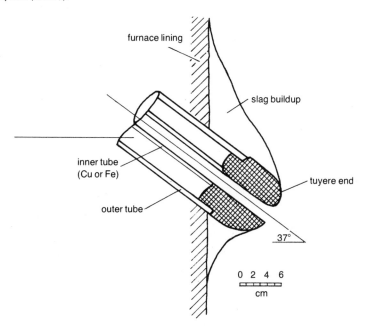

furnace lining

slag buildup

inner tube
(Cu or Fe)

tuyere end

outer tube

37°

0 2 4 6
cm

Fig. 7.2. Reconstruction of tuyeres found on site 2 at Timna (after Tylecote et al.[9]).

RONALD F. TYLECOTE

Table 7.4. Composition of Some Examples of Copper Ores (in percent)

	Oxide (Parazuelos, Spain)*	Oxide (Burgas Bulgaria)[†]	Sulfide (Harz, Germany)[‡]	Sulfide (Mitsero, Cyprus)[§]	Sulfide (Bocheggiono, Italy)[∥]	Sulfide (Velem St Veit, Hungary)[‡]
Cu	20.5	9.0	26.0	2.3	11.2	17.35
Ag	tr	nil	1.86	nil	0.81	—
Pb	0.5	24.0	tr	nil	0.03	29.9
As	1.21	nil	0.23	nil	0.06	6.04
Sb	0.5	nil	24.11	tr	tr	16.64
Zn	—	nil	4.16	0.46	0.33	—
Fe	27.8	8.4	9.32	36.51	27.01	1.4
S	tr	—	36.64	6.29	30.45	28.60
Sn	0.1	nil	—	—	—	—
Bi	—	nil	—	—	0.24	—
Co	—	nil	—	—	—	—
Ni	0.3	nil	—	—	—	—

* See n. 38.
[†] O. Davies, *Man* 36 (1936): 119.
[‡] See n. 25.
[§] O. Davies, *Annual of the British School at Athens* 30 (1928–30): 74–85.
[∥] A. Mosso, *The Dawn of Mediterranean Civilisation* (London, 1910).

state and contains drops of matte (mixed sulfides of copper and iron) about 5 mm in diameter.

It appears that this "badly settled rich slag" had been crushed to release the matte, as shown by dumps of slag fines. It must be remembered that matte does not separate as easily as metallic copper from slag, because the specific gravity of the matte (4.6) is much closer to that of slag (3.5). Two grades of matte were found, one containing 35–40 percent Cu and the other 60–65 percent Cu. A few discs were found of rich matte 3–5 mm thick, but this was rare.

The matte must have been dead-roasted to oxide. The final smelting of the oxidized matte, to which silica must have been added, resulted in a very homogeneous slag in the form of thin discs about 3–6 mm thick and 20 cm in diameter. This was probably achieved in the same type of furnace and tapping pit as used for matte smelting. The result was an impure plano-convex ingot of "blister" copper containing about 98 percent copper and weighing about 6 kg.

Experiments have been undertaken by Neuninger and his colleagues to show how readily sulfide ores may be smelted. The technique used

Table 7.5. Composition of Products Resulting from the Experimental Smelting of a Copper Sulfide Ore (in percent)

	Matte	Raw copper
Cu	45.71	90.87
S	20.67	trace
Fe	2.02	some
Sb	13.00	3.81
As	1.48	0.18
Ba	7.40	—
Total	90.28	94.86+

Source: See n. 15.

was based on a comparatively recent but primitive process used on the Philippine island of Luzon.[15] The sulfide (Fahlerz) ore which contained barytes was put into a clay crucible and covered with silica sand. The crucible and its contents were then heated in an electric furnace for 30 min at 1300° C. This produced a lower layer of matte and an upper layer of slag.

The matte which separated during this operation was broken up and placed in a porcelain basin and partly roasted with the aid of a propane burner. It was then placed in a large crucible with charcoal above and below. A tuyere led air from a pump into the lower charcoal layer and the crucible was heated externally to 1200° C. This seems to have oxidized most of the matte to copper but the contents were re-roasted in the porcelain basin and then put into a graphite crucible and heated to 1200° C. The molten copper was "poled" with green twigs to reduce the oxygen content. The analyses are given in table 7.5 and show the expected loss of arsenic but a much smaller loss of antimony.

Pittioni estimates that about 20,000 tons of raw copper has been produced in this area over a period of a thousand years up to the end of the Urnfield period (600 B.C.).[16] Slag from the early smelting sites was used to grog potter's clay in settlements far removed from the mining centers.

We have now a carbon-14 date for an Irish mine producing low grade sulfide ores with stone tools in about 1270 ± 90 B.C. in the Irish Middle Bronze Age (MBA).[17]

Ingot Types

As I have mentioned, we have some doubt about the type of ingot made (if any) in the Copper Age but no doubt about those made in the Late

Bronze Age. These are of two types: the plano-convex ingots, relatively flat on top and hemispherical on the bottom, which would be a natural shape to make in a bowl furnace, and the oxhide-shaped ingots, which are quite different.

The plano-convex ingots form in the bottom of the smelting furnace as a result of the liquation of the smelted copper from the superincumbent slag. Metallic copper has more than twice the density of this slag and, in due course, falls through the slag to form the ingot. When the smelting of the ore charge is complete it can be allowed to solidify, and the brittle slag can be broken away, revealing the copper ingot. The more convenient process, however, is to drain off the slag in the liquid state at the end of the smelt and then to withdraw the ingot of raw copper after it has solidified. The melting point of the slag would be about 1150° C and that of the copper below 1084° C.

Analyses of plano-convex ingots show them to be of copper.[18] Metallographic examination of a copper ingot from Cornwall shows it to have solidified in the furnace and not run into a mold near the furnace. This agrees with Timna (Israel) practice in the Early Iron Age (EIA) (ca. 1100 B.C.).

The plano-convex ingots, being furnace material, have not been refined in any way, but due to primitive smelting conditions they are relatively pure by some modern standards. As we see from the Cornish LBA example, they contain considerable amounts of sulfur and oxygen, as would be expected.

The other type of ingot is of oxhide or double-ax shape, current in the Eastern Mediterranean during Minoan and Mycenaean times.[19] There is no doubt that these were traded over a wide area. They are depicted on Egyptian tomb paintings (ca. 1450 B.C.).

Examination of some of the 19 oxhide ingots from Haghia Triada in Crete, which might have been imported from Cyprus and which were found to be of almost pure copper,[20] shows that they were not formed in the furnace but must have been cast from a spout or launder. The ingots weigh about 30–40 kg with a thickness of about 4 cm. They show the typical gassy appearance of blister copper. The top surface is roughened by the blisters while the bottom surface, although smoother, shows cavities due to gas evolution from the metal or from the moisture in clay. The sides are smoothest of all. The corners tend to be thicker than the rest of the ingot and the edges show a "rim," resulting from the initial rapid solidification against a cold mold wall.

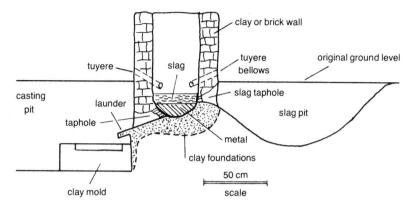

Fig. 7.3. Possible furnace for the smelting of copper and the casting of oxhide ingots.

Surprisingly, there is no sign of a runner connecting the ingot with the furnace. The ingots are far too big to have been cast from separate crucibles and the organization involved in separate crucible melts would be almost impossible. There is no doubt that these ingots have been made by tapping a whole furnace containing 30–40 kg of molten copper through an extended taphole having some sort of launder system as shown in figure 7.3. The slag/metal volume ratio is such that the furnace would be of considerable size, certainly larger than those excavated at Timna (Israel). There is no question of allowing the furnace to fill up with metal as in the modern converter because it is impossible to keep a layer of metal molten in these furnaces when its thickness exceeds a few inches. The slag, however, would probably be tapped at intervals to minimize the distance between the tuyeres (the source of heat) and the molten copper.

Circumstantial evidence for highly developed extractive techniques can be seen in China in the Shang period. After about 1300 B.C. we have quite large artifacts that required a substantial extractive industry. By the time of the western Chou dynasty (770 B.C.) the artifacts are not only large but there is a greater number of them, as indeed we find in LBA Europe. A bronze caldron was found at Anyang in 1946; it weighed 1400 kg and was about 1 m across. Of course, these may have been the product of good organization rather than large capacity smelting and melting. It is only during the Ming period (A.D. 1368–1644) that we have details of the traditional melting furnaces that may have been used for the caldrons of earlier periods. We have, unfortunately, no details of the smelting furnaces.[21]

For the early periods in the Middle East we have no satisfactory evidence of copper ingot shape. In the LBA, oxhide-shaped ingots were used in the Aegean and small plano-convex (bun-shaped) ingots were used elsewhere. In the Roman period we find plano-convex ingots weighing as much as 20 kg.[22]

If arsenical coppers were the direct product of smelting and not of alloying we should expect to find ingots of such material. Although plano-convex ingots of arsenical copper are known, they are a comparative rarity and are not necessarily restricted to early periods. Most archaeologists think that the ingot torcs or "Osenhalsringe" described as "cast neckrings with recoiled ends" represents the earliest ingot material known.[23] These bars or rings are admittedly for the most part arsenical,[24] but it does not seem reasonable to expect an early smelter to have formed his product into a long narrow bar, 28 cm long, in the bottom of his smelting furnace or to have tapped it into such a long narrow mold. Although these rings are often referred to as cast, the one from Leiten in Austria (now at Linz) has been wrought[25] and one would expect them to have been worked from more compact pieces of ingot. The shape might be compared with the iron "currency bars" of later date which were made as intermediate products suitable for swords and general smithing. Because copper, however, is not so easily welded by smithing, the long narrow bars and neckrings would not have been of much use for making axes or halberds but only for the pins, and the wire coils used as armrings, which the hoards often contain. We seem to have no evidence for an ingot form that could have been used as a starting point for the neckrings and for the production of more massive objects. Perhaps the Chalcolithic and Copper Age smelting furnaces never produced massive bun ingots but merely scraps of metal among the slag, which was broken up to release these pieces of metal. These might then have been melted in crucibles and cast into a short bar ingot that could then be forged into a long bar or neckring. These bars could be easily broken up by the melter, put into a crucible, and cast into more massive objects such as axheads and halberds. Some of the early stone molds show bar-like cavities which would have served this purpose.

Crucible Furnaces

For the purpose of melting scraps of metal in crucibles, a ring of stones, a pile of hot charcoal, and a clay tuyere connected to bellows are all that

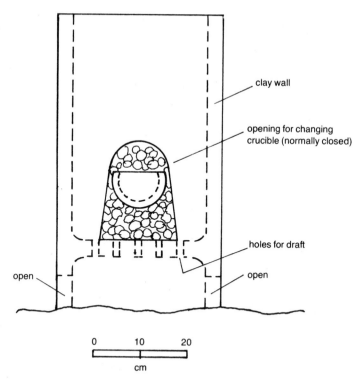

clay wall

opening for changing
crucible (normally closed)

holes for draft

open

open

0   10   20

cm

Fig. 7.4. Brazier-type melting furnace based on finds from Abu Matar.

would have been required. Nothing would have remained of this arrangement except, perhaps, the clay tuyere. It is possible to obtain sufficiently
high temperatures for melting bronze (950° C) with a cylindrical furnace
with a grate like a brazier. The air would have entered underneath the
furnace assisted by the chimney effect of the cylindrical portion (fig. 7.4).
Usually there would have been a side hole through which the crucible
could have been placed in the hottest part of the fire a short distance above
the grate. The grate would of course be of clay, pierced with holes like a
pottery kiln.

The earliest known crucible furnace is perhaps that from Abu Matar,[26]
the Late Chalcolithic site near Beersheba (3300–3000 B.C.), where the
remains were found of circular furnaces 30–40 cm in diameter with
3-cm-thick vertical walls, at least 12–15 cm high. The inside surfaces had
become well vitrified owing to the presence of wood ash and metal. The

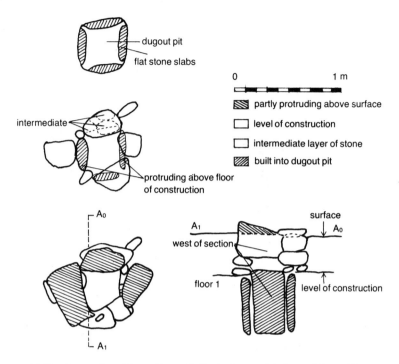

Fig. 7.5. Melting furnace from Timna. *Source*: B. Rothenberg and A. Lupu, *Museum Haaretz Bulletin*, no. 9 (June 1967) pl. x.

crucibles were oval with rounded bottoms 11 × 8 cm outside and 7 cm deep internally. They were made of gray clay that had been mixed with chopped straw. No molds or tuyeres were found, but a copper flat-ax, awls, and mace heads were recovered from this and other nearby sites. Apart from this site, we have no further evidence of crucible furnaces until we come to the finds in the Timna area of Israel of the LBA–EIA transition period.[27] The crucible furnaces at Timna consisted of square stone boxes, that is, four stone slabs had been set into the ground on edge with a kerb of small stones on top (fig. 7.5). This kerb may have been a later heightening of the furnace due to buildup of material around it. The box was full of wood ash, and unless assisted by a blast from a tuyere, little draft would have reached the crucible in the furnace as found. One must assume that the fire was cleaned out frequently when in use and that there was an opening into the bottom of the furnace as in the Roman period forge furnaces.

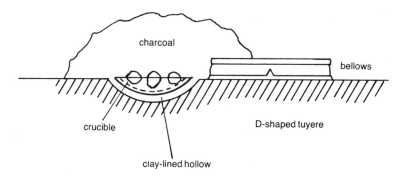

Fig. 7.6. Method of use of D-shaped tuyere from Ambelikou, Cyprus, for crucible melting.

Smithing and Founding

The tuyere, being made of hard-burned clay, is another artifact that has a good survival rate. The simplest of these is a conical piece of clay with a cylindrical hole. More complicated ones have a hole which is large at one end to take the bellows nozzle and small at the end which enters the furnace. This end is often vitrified and slagged.

Copper and Bronze Age tuyeres seem to be no different from those of any other period and perhaps the best examples are found in the Early Timber Grave culture burials at Kalinovka,[28] which are dated to about 2000–1800 B.C. These crucible hearth tuyeres show the features just described in a very clear manner. It is interesting that they belonged to a bronze-founder and were buried with him in his grave, showing that the smith had an important social position. Evidence of this type is lacking elsewhere and does not appear again until Viking times.

This grave is one of the most interesting metallurgical deposits yet found but here we will confine ourselves to the tuyeres. The end which takes the bellows nozzle is about 20 mm diameter but the hearth-end seems to be extremely narrow (5.00 mm) compared with the 20-mm-diameter tuyeres from smelting sites such as those at Timna and in Sinai. Most of the tuyeres from the barrow at Kalinovka show some decoration. One also sees this on tuyeres from Timna and other sites and this may aid bonding into the furnace linings. Here it is probably incidental and just one of those little things craftsmen cannot help doing. Similar narrow-ended tuyeres were found in another barrow but they were not decorated.

Some tuyeres are D shaped in section and have a flat side. This is, presumably, so that they could be laid on the ground, as shown in figure 7.6.

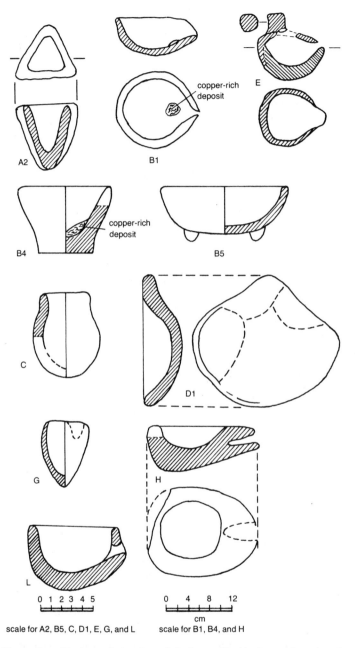

A2

B1

copper-rich
deposit

E

B4

copper-rich
deposit

B5

C

D1

G

H

L

0 1 2 3 4 5

0   4   8   12

cm

scale for A2, B5, C, D1, E, G, and L   scale for B1, B4, and H

Fig. 7.7. Types of crucibles in use during the periods discussed in this chapter. A2: triangular crucible from Mikulčice, Moravia, 8th century A.D.; B1: hemispherical crucible from Tel Zeror, Israel LBA–EIA; B4: flat-bottomed flared crucible from Tel Qasile, Israel (11th cent. B.C.) LBA–EIA (see n. 41); B5: hemispherical crucible with feet from Troy III (2100 B.C.) (dimensions very approximate) (see n. 39); C: necked crucible from Huntsham, U.K. Roman (courtesy N. Bridgewater); D1: crucible with horizontal pinch from Kalinovka, USSR LBA (see n. 28); E: lidded crucible from Dinas Powys, Wales, 7th century A.D. (courtesy L. Alcock); G: pointed bottom (internal rim); Corbridge, U.K. Roman; H: socketed crucible from Meser, Israel (3000 B.C.) (see n. 33); L: crucible from Keos poured through a hole at one end; LBA. (see n. 36).

The crucibles used in such a smithing hearth would have been heated mostly by radiant heat from the fire above and for this reason would have been large and shallow.[29] But they would have needed to be poured very quickly when removed from the fire as loss of heat would have been rapid.

Melting Furnaces

A more sophisticated crucible furnace dated to the Roman period was found at Beer Ora in the Arabah.[30] This was found adjacent to the smelting furnaces, which were essentially of the same type as the LBA–EIA furnaces at Timna. This furnace consisted of an oval bowl 65 cm long × 45 cm wide and 30 cm deep. It was enclosed by a kerb of small flat stones and was lined with clay. When found the bowl was full of charcoal and wood ash.

Roman sites often show signs of flattish, simple hearths[31] that could have been used for many purposes such as crucible smelting and iron smithing. Often they were used for more than one purpose.

Crucibles may be made from clay or stone. The earliest is probably also from Abu Matar[32] and the remains indicate a hemispherical oval crucible about 11 × 8 cm across and 7 cm deep, with a wall thickness of 1 cm and a definite lip for pouring.

Crucibles of the oval type with a handle at the end or side have been found at Meser in Israel, at Thermi on Lesbos, at Lerna, and at Sesklo in Greece.[33] This type was devised as one way of overcoming the problem of pouring in a Chalcolithic or Bronze Age (BA) context. Since the melting point of a pair of copper tongs such as those from Enkomi in LBA Cyprus is at most 1084° C,[34] and copper must be poured with at least 20° C superheat, i.e., 1100° C, there is quite a problem in pouring a crucible containing copper—although this problem is minimized with bronzes. It is probable that the tongs were tipped with clay. The crucibles from Meser (3000 B.C.), Thermi (3000–2500 B.C.), and Lerna V (2750 B.C.), all show one of the ways of overcoming this problem (fig. 7.7).[35] This method used the molding (at the end or side of the crucible) of a boss which contained a hole of about 1-cm diameter into which a clay-covered rod or stick could be inserted so as to rotate or even raise the crucible for pouring.

Another way of overcoming this problem is that shown by the crucibles from Kea (Keos) and Serabit (1550–1200 B.C.), which have a hole at the pouring end and rounded bottoms so that they can be rocked.[36] The crucible from Serabit could have held about 870 cm³ or 7.6 kg of bronze, which would have been poured by rotating the crucible through 40°;

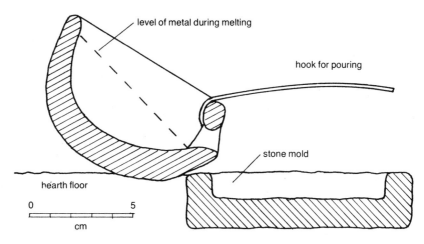

Fig. 7.8. Possible technique for tipping the type of crucible found at Serabit and on Aegean sites.

the mold would have been in sand in front of the crucible and exposed by pushing away the charcoal from in front, as shown in figure 7.8. The crucible would have been rotated either by pushing with a rod or stick or by pulling on the front bar with a hook, as shown.

Some of the Egyptian tomb paintings[37] show the pouring of a thick open-type crucible (such as those from El Argar, Spain[38]) by means of withies. Although the sap in the withies would, for a short time, have prevented loss of ductility through charring, one would not expect them to have lasted long enough to fill the whole row of about 18 molds. Perhaps there is some artistic licence involved here; it is possible that it shows one of several melts.

Occasionally one finds crucibles with feet or a pedestal. One of the earliest examples is from Troy III (2200–2050 B.C.) and if one had not found them on other sites (such as in Early Christian Ireland) one would doubt their use as crucibles.[39] The Trojan crucible had four legs and contained a deposit of gold and copper carbonate. The crucible from Balaubash, Russia (1500–1300 B.C.) had a base and it is doubtful whether this would have been considered a crucible unless it had had a deposit.[40] It must be remembered that "crucibles" can sometimes be sherds or whole pots that might have been intended for water. They may have picked up metallic residues merely by being close to metallurgical operations. The only way to be sure about a crucible is to look for intense vitrification caused by wood ash together with slag contamination. Sometimes ordinary pottery sherds can fall into the ash layers of hearths and be vitrified in this way, but it is unlikely that they will contain slag or metallic residues as well.

The greater proportion of early crucibles found are hemispherical or boat shaped. Some of the circular crucibles have flat bottoms, such as those from Tel Qasile[41] and Timna in Israel. Later ones are very often triangular or like modern crucibles—round and slightly flared with flat bottoms (fig. 7.7).

Crucible Slags

Early crucible slags are formed by the reaction between the clay of the crucible and the ash of the fuel and are therefore more likely to be sodium or potassium aluminum silicates rather than cuprous silicate, which has a high formation temperature and which does not seem to appear in analyses. The latter, if formed at all, tends to be amorphous and thus escapes phase analysis. But most crucible slags contain iron, which could be introduced in three ways: (1) as smelting slag entrapped in the metal, i.e., as the ferrous silicate $2FeO \cdot SiO_2$, (2) as metallic iron, present as a second phase in the original metal, and (3) as iron introduced by the use of unprotected iron stirring rods. The second is more common than was hitherto realized. A piece of copper strip from a 13th century B.C. temple at Timna was found to contain 5–10 percent of iron in metallic form and had a Vickers diamond pyramid hardness of 95 as a result.[42]

The sulfur present in some slags arises, no doubt, from the separation and oxidation of the residual sulfide or matte phase from the smelting process (table 7.6).

Phases detected by X-ray diffraction are iron oxides and double oxides such as the spinel-type phase, $CuFe_2O_4$, or the oxide, delafossite ($CuFeO_2$). It seems that these slags are essentially alkali silicates or alkali–aluminum silicates with some iron and copper. But the main components that give the reddish color to relatively unoxidized examples of these slags are metallic copper and Cu_2O, which are not in solution; these red glassy slags resemble ruby glasses in their composition (i.e., they consist of a dispersion of metallic copper and/or Cu_2O as discrete phases in a glass matrix) with little crystalline material present although, very often, crystalline SiO_2 can be detected as a product of devitrification.

Modern crucible slags are not very different, although they may often contain elements introduced from cover fluxes and other compounds

Table 7.6. Analyses of Crucible Slags (in percent)

Provenance Period	Irish* EC Iron Age			Abu Matar[†] Chalcolithic	Beckford Worcestershire[‡] EIA	Range
SiO_2	45		20	46–60	58	18–60
CaO		4		10–15	7.5	3–15
FeO	7		23	6–25	6	3–30
Al_2O_3				8–10	16	10–20
K_2O				—	5	0–9
Na_2O				—	—	0–9
Cu	23	28	20	8–47	5	5–47
Zn			4.8	<0.1	—	—
S	9.7	5	10	—	—	0–10

*R. J. Moss, *Proceedings of the Royal Irish Academy* (C), 37 (1924–27): 175–93.
† See n. 26.
‡ W. J. Britnell, personal communication. The analyses were made by C. M. Wilson of the Dept. of Ceramics of the University of Sheffield.

added to protect the melt during melting down. Slags so formed by melting a leaded gunmetal (85% Cu, 5% Sn, 5% Zn, and 5% Pb) in a plumbago (graphitic clay) crucible were found to contain major amounts of Zn, Cu, Mn, Fe, Pb, and Sn. Trace amounts of barium were also found. The only crystalline phases were alpha-quartz, cassiterite, and willemite (Zn_2SiO_4). The matrix was an amorphous glass. The barium and the manganese would have been introduced from the cover fluxes. The iron would arise from bad melting practice (i.e., the use of a badly protected iron stirring rod). These results show what can be expected from the use of X-ray fluorescence and X-ray diffraction techniques on such materials.

Fuel Ash

A good many of the products of melting hearths and other smithing hearths are nothing more than vitrified fuel ash with or without some contamination from the earth or the furnace lining. An examination of these products can sometimes give an indication of the fuels used (table 7.7). As already mentioned, the ash is often a reflection of the soils in which the plants grow, although dung (a very common fuel in early times) tends to show a relatively high phosphorus content due to its animal origin.[43] Peat and coal are high in sulfur, unlike wood charcoal, which is low in this element. Coal, however, is usually much higher in alumina than other

Table 7.7. Composition of Fuel Ashes (in percent)

	Charcoal*	Coal*	Peat*	Dung (Kudatini, India)†	Bone (3CaO · P₂O₅)
CO₂ ⎫					
K₂O ⎬	22.0	1.0–2.0	0.6–4.0	8.25	—
Na₂O ⎭					
CaO	25	2–12	24–30	4.4	54
MgO	7.64	0–10	1–7	—	—
Al₂O₃	0.92	20–40	0.3–5 ⎫		
Fe₂O₃	tr	9–26	12–19 ⎬	9.5	—
MnO₂	31.6	0–0.2	— ⎭		
SiO₂	8.0	25–53	3–30	67.4	—
P₂O₅	4.9	0.2–2	0.2–2.5	3.4	46
H₂SO₄	—	0.3–5	10–20		

*See n. 22.

† F. E. Zeuner, *University of London Institute of Archaeology*, bull. no. 11 (1959), pp. 37–44.

fuels, although severe clay contamination of the ash can produce the same result.

LEAD AND SILVER SMELTING FURNACES

Lead is one of the earliest metals to have been smelted and has been found in several Chalcolithic contexts. The earliest dated lead find is probably that found at Catal Hüyük, Anatolia, dated to about 6500 B.C.[44]

Lead occurs in nature both as a carbonate mineral such as cerussite and as the sulfide, galena. The latter is far more common and can be smelted much more easily than the sulfide ores of copper. There is no need to pre-roast it; one merely has to grind it and add it to a wood or charcoal fire when, by the double decomposition reaction,

$$2PbO + PbS \rightarrow 3Pb + SO_2,$$

lead will separate out in liquid form at the bottom of the fire due to its low melting point of 327° C. This implies that some oxidation of the galena occurs in the higher levels of the fire, which is comparatively easy in a brazier or open-type low shaft furnace. The primitive Peruvian furnaces mentioned by Barba seem to have openings at the top for this purpose.[45] Some of the lead is lost in the slags, which are complex alkali–lead silicates (table 7.8). From the medieval period onward the lead lost

Table 7.8. Composition of Lead and Silver Slags, and Litharge (in percent)

	Silver-lead slag (Rio Tinto)[*]	Litharge and cerussite (Nordeifel; 2d cent. A.D.)[†]	Lead (Pentre Ffwnden) (Roman)[‡]	Smelting slags (Laurion) (Greek)[‡]	Nineteenth cent. ore hearth (Alston)[∥]
PbO	1.5	77.34	32.3	10.7	3.0
SiO$_2$	26.2	—	58.2	33.8	28.5
CaO	—	—	8.0	13.8	24.0
FeO	58.6	0.58	0.8	15.2	25.0
Al$_2$O$_3$	—	—	—	3.9	7.0
ZnO	—	—	—	6.7	10.6
Cu	0.03	3.8	—	—	—
Ag	0.00632	—	0.0004	0.06	—
CO$_2$	—	present	—	—	—

[*] See n. 47(a).
[†] H. G. Bachmann, *VI Congreso Internationale Mineraria Hispanica Iberoamerica* (Leon, 1970), vol. 1, pp. 15–29.
[‡] D. Atkinson and M. V. Taylor, *Flintshire Historical Society* 10, no. 1 (1924): 5–23.
[§] See n. 68.
[∥] M. Dufrénoy, *Voyage Métallurgique en Angleterre* (Paris, 1837).

was recovered from the slags by smelting them at higher temperatures with iron and iron oxides to give the usual ferrous silicate slag.

Most lead ores contain some silver and there is little doubt that, from the LBA onward, most of the silver was obtained from ores of this type. It is an interesting fact that primitive lead smelting tends to recover all the silver, although it rejects some of the lead to the slag phase. Recent work using an open brick brazier type of furnace gave the following results:[46]

Silver	(g/ton of lead)
Galena ore	11
Lead from first smelt	24
Lead from second smelt	20

Silver

Although silver does occur in native form, it is comparatively rare. Silver also occurs as the mineral cerargyrite (AgCl), which can be smelted to silver merely by heating to about 800° C when the chloride oxidizes and the oxide dissociates. But it is clear that a good deal of early silver was derived from the cupellation of lead. This process takes advantage of the fact that when silver-containing lead is heated (preferably above the melting point of silver, 960° C), the lead oxidizes and in turn vaporizes, leaving the silver behind. Normally this would be done in shallow clay plates, or cupels. From the Roman period this would be done on cupels of bone ash, which absorb some of the lead oxide (litharge). This and much of the litharge floating on the surface can be recovered and resmelted with charcoal back to lead. The silver is left on the cupel as a sessile drop, or globule.

There are large quantities of prehistoric slags near the copper mines of Rio Tinto[47] and Tharsis[48] in Spain, which contain small amounts of silver but very little copper, and it is now believed that that these represent slags resulting from the smelting of the high-silver layers at the base of the gossan. The silver values have been concentrated by a leaching process into argentojarosites containing 0.20 percent Ag, which are now almost entirely worked out but which were extensively smelted in LBA and, perhaps, Roman times. Exactly how the silver was recovered is not known at present, but the slags are essentially fayalite, like other slags, and contain some lead (1.37%), so it is possible that lead ores were added to the argento-jarosites to collect the silver and the silver metal was recovered from the high-silver lead by cupellation. Litharge has been found at Tharsis and is said to date from the pre-Phoenician period. The lead remaining in the slags from the LBA or EIA silver mines at Rio Tinto contained about 0.06 percent silver, equivalent to 600 g/ton, which indicates that the silver content of the lead produced was at least equal to that of the famous silver mines of Laurion in Greece of later date.[49]

Slag has been found at the 8th century B.C. Phoenician site at Tejada, between Seville and Rio Tinto, in the form of plano-convex lumps looking rather like rotary querns.[50] These lumps are very porous and look as though metal has liquated through them. A possible clue to their origin is given by an 18th century A.D. account of the extraction of antimony from a Scottish mine.[51] Here the prepared antimony sulfide, which prob-ably contained some lead sulfide, was heated in a furnace to about 600° C in a perforated clay vessel in such a way that the Sb_2S_3 could liquate and be collected in a vessel below (fig. 7.9). The solid gangue was left behind and would form a slag in the perforated container and be discarded, as were the lumps at Tejada.

In this way the antimony sulfide was concentrated. It was then heated

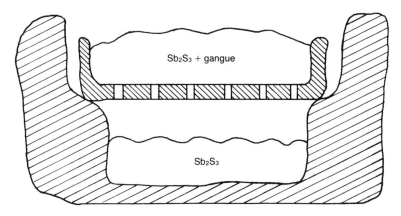

Fig. 7.9. Detail of technique used for antimony sulfide extraction in the 18th century A.D.

in a crucible with metallic scrap iron and an alkali flux. This was placed in a hotter furnace (about 1000° C), whereupon the reaction,

$$3Fe + Sb_2S_3 \rightarrow 3FeS + 2Sb,$$

took place. The iron sulfide, which was partly oxidized and slagged with the alkali flux, was discarded, and the metallic antimony (regulus), which melts at 630° C, was refined by mixing with antimony from a previous smelt and more flux to remove residual iron.

The history of the application of this process is not well known, and antimony was not a very valuable metal in its own right. The only difficulty in the application of this process to silver-containing galena is that pure galena melts at 1100° C. Yet a mixture of Ag_2S and 20 percent PbS melts at 623° C and there are many other low melting point phases in systems containing Ag, Sb, and Pb sulfides which could be produced from the following minerals which are known to exist in Spain and elsewhere:

Pyrargyrite	As_2SbS_3
Proustite	Ag_3AsS_3
Freieslebenite	$(Pb, Ag)_8Sb_5S_{12}$
Stibnite	Sb_2S_3
Jamesonite	$Pb_4FeSb_6S_{14}$.

GOLD AND OTHER PRECIOUS METALS

Gold is another native metal which rarely forms compounds in nature. In antiquity there is no doubt that all the metal was recovered from native gold: nuggets or grains collected by crushing quartz and concentrating the fine gold by washing. No chemical reaction is involved and the particles are normally agglomerated by melting in a crucible. Since the melting point of gold ($1063°$ C) is almost the same as that of copper there would be no difficulty with this operation. But platinum, which melts at $1770°$ C, was a problem and could be agglomerated only by sintering it with the aid of molten gold. The latter would diffuse into the solid grains of platinum and form a solid solution Au–Pt compact which could be worked at normal temperatures ($800–1000°$ C).

Iron

The production of iron can be divided into two sections, smelting and smithing. With iron, smithing implies hot-working and could have been known first and indeed practiced on meteoritic iron. But there is no evidence for this; all the work done on meteoric iron was carried out by cold hammering without annealing.

Pure iron has a melting point of $1540°$ C, a temperature that could not be obtained until the 19th century A.D. Therefore all early wrought iron was produced in the solid state by chemical reduction of iron ore to solid, nearly pure, iron at about $1200°$ C with the aid of charcoal. The reduced iron was removed as a lump, or "bloom," which was a mixture of solid iron, slag, and pieces of unburned charcoal. In some cases this lump was broken up and the small pieces of iron were separated by hammering; they could be distinguished from the rest by the fact that they were ductile and would flatten on hammering. They were then welded into a larger piece by heating in a smith's fire and hammering. In some cases the bloom consisted of coherent iron and could be smithed in one piece. In other cases, the bloom was too large and had to be cut into smaller pieces, which were individually smithed.

If the ratio of fuel to ore was large and the bellows efficient, the iron could be made to absorb so much carbon that it formed an alloy of iron and carbon, or cast iron, which melts at $1150°$ C and would form pools at the bottom of the furnace. When solid, these liquated lumps could be broken up and re-melted in a crucible in a hot smithing fire and cast like bronze. It seems that people early in Asia Minor and Europe occasionally made cast iron by accident, but only the Chinese appreciated the advantages and made it regularly. Even so, it would not fullfil all the applications required of iron; wrought iron had to be made either by conversion of

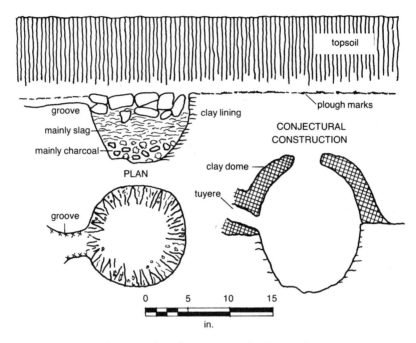

Fig. 7.10. Bowl furnace for iron smelting from West Brandon Co., Durham, U.K. (see n. 52).

cast iron in a smith's fire or in the European manner as a bloom requiring a lower fuel/ore ratio.

The Earliest Iron-Making Furnaces

The most primitive type of furnace for making iron is the bowl furnace, which is no more than a hole in the ground or rock into which air from bellows could be directed through a tuyere and a short, probably dome-shaped superstructure of clay (fig. 7.10).[52] The broken ore and the charcoal would be mixed together or charged in layers onto a hot charcoal fire. The maximum temperature should be at least 1150° C. This type of furnace has no outlet for slag, and the slag runs down to the bottom forming a cake, or "furnace bottom," or in some cases just small prills of slag. The bloom remains above the slag. After the process is completed the clay dome would be broken away, the bloom removed, and the furnace cleaned out.

This type of furnace was superseded in Roman times by the "developed" bowl furnace, which looks very similar to the Timna copper-smelting

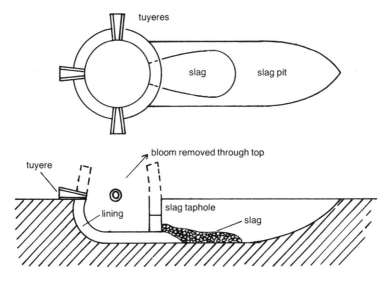

Fig. 7.11. Developed bowl furnace for iron smelting.

furnace (fig. 7.11).[53] This may be taken as evidence that iron smelting
was not invented by advanced copper smelters but by more primitive
copper smelters. Whatever the explanation, the EIA is typified by the
non-slag-tapping bowl furnace, while the art of tapping slag used in the
developed bowl furnace was not introduced into Europe until Roman
times.

The bowl assists the maintenance of reducing conditions, which is even
more important for smelting iron than it is for smelting copper. The
smithing furnace does not need reducing conditions and although a hole
in the ground can be used, it is not necessary, as one can see from primitive
forges still in use in developing countries. All that is needed is a tuyere
held down by a stone long enough to keep the bellows from scorching.
Then a pile of charcoal is ignited with air from the goatskin bellows.
The smith places his piece of iron in the charcoal near the mouth of the
tuyere and a good heat can easily be obtained (1200° C). With wrought
iron, most of the work can be done by cold hammering and annealing
at 700° C, and many primitive smiths work this way today.[54]

The Near East and Europe   There are hardly any remains of early
furnaces known from Asia Minor or Persia. Dorner found the remains
of a bowl furnace in a premedieval context at Asameia near Nymphaios

on the western slopes of Kahtacay near Yenikale in Turkey.[55] Much slag in the form of furnace bottoms was found; Dorner suggests that the furnace measured 0.4 m in diameter, with walls 3–4 cm thick and 1 m high.

Farther east at Sirzi, near Malataya, Bachmann found a large deposit of slag in a valley.[56] He claims that it came from a natural draft furnace because of its similarity to slags from African natural draft furnaces. It was not free flowing at the working temperature of the furnace and yet had a very high iron content, suggesting the use of a rich ore. It his conclusions are correct, it shows that we have at least one other type of furnace at this time (8th century B.C.).

Most of our evidence dates from the classical and Hellenistic periods (after 500 B.C.). From a vase of this period we have a good representation of what is almost certainly an iron-smelting furnace in a smithy.[57] It is a shaft furnace blown with bellows, and a model in the South Kensington Museum resembles closely the Hungarian furnace from Gyalar.[58] In front of it is a smith working a bloom or piece of iron on an anvil.

Austria (not surprisingly considering its connection with Hallstatt) has provided many examples of early furnaces. They may be classified into three types: (1) the bowl furnace, which we seem to have at Hüttenberg, together with a roasting hearth, (2) the shaft furnace, which may or may not have induced draft, and (3) the domed furnace. Only the latter is new and, so far, peculiar to Europe and the British Isles.

When interpreting furnace remains, it is always difficult to be sure that the bowl furnace is a true bowl and not merely the bottom part of a shaft furnace. The shaft furnaces at Lolling and Feisterwiese in the Erzberg were used by Straube as models for the smelting experiments in which he used a forced draft.[60]

But the Lolling furnace had multiple tuyeres and seems to have been blown by induced draft. This type of furnace was found by Gilles in the Siegerland area of Germany[61] and experiments have been made with it. The third type of furnace is the domed furnace from Engsbachtal, also in the Siegerland.[62] This is an unusual type but a similar one was found at Levisham in north Yorkshire which is also dated to the pre-Roman Iron Age (IA).[63] It is almost certain that the induced draft shaft furnaces were not slag tapping and yielded a bloom consisting of pieces of iron which had to be separated from the slag and residual charcoal by hammering. Both the bowl and domed furnaces would be forced draft and the earliest of them would be non-slag-tapping. This seems to be the essential

difference between earlier Iron Age furnaces and the later immediately
pre-Roman and proto-Roman furnaces in Europe.

A unique type of La Tène furnace now being excavated in the Austrian
Burgenland has a domed furnace with many tuyeres and a diameter of
about 1 m.[64] The furnace appears to taper at the top to give a hole or
shaft with a throat diameter of 25 cm. The tuyeres have a bore of 3.5 cm
and it is clear that the blast would not be able to penetrate to the center
of a furnace of this diameter. It seems that each tuyere produced a bloom
below it and that the slag ran down toward the center and could possibly
be tapped from the furnace through a side opening. There would be
a "dead" zone in the center and it is possible that there were charging
"ports" in the dome immediately above each tuyere.

Africa   The iron industry penetrated into sub-Saharan Africa by way
of North Africa to Nigeria and through Egypt to the Sudan. The Early
Iron Age phase has persisted in Africa until the present day but is fast
dying out. Luckily, anthropologists have obtained a great deal of information on African ironworking in the last few years, which has been used to
interpret the evidence from more northerly areas (see discussion by van
der Merwe in chap. 13).

The furnaces used by the Nok culture of Nigeria (400–200 B.C.) were
shaft furnaces of quite large diameter (0.3 to 1 m). They were blown
through short tuyeres by forced draft and do not seem to have produced
true tap slag. But a number of discarded saddle querns had been used for
breaking up the mixtures of metal and slag.[65] The furnaces had thin clay
walls built above slag pits cut into the natural soft rock and had a striking
resemblance to the shaft furnaces of Jutland[66] and North Germany[67]
in use during the first few centuries A.D.

The furnaces in recent use in Africa are of several types, from the small
bowl furnaces of Kordofan[68] and the central Sahara to the 3.5-m-diameter
induced draft furnaces of Togoland.[69] Some of the induced draft furnaces
had more than 100 tuyeres. One type of bellows-blown furnace used by
tribes in the Mandara Hills and the Nigerian plateau uses a long single
tuyere which goes down the center of the shaft like a long proboscis,
terminating just above the hearth.[70] Presumably, an area with an EIA
tradition lasting 2500 years will develop more types of furnaces than an
area with a much shorter tradition.

The metal from the Nok culture shows an extraordinary degree of purity and freedom from slag inclusions, which is what would be expected if the raw bloom had been carefully broken up in the cold state to extract the iron rather than if the whole mass had been forged at a high temperature as was generally done in medieval Europe.[71]

The smithing technique is typical of the EIA, with a large number of artifacts showing spheroidized pearlite due to long periods in the temperature range 600–750° C. In no case had quench hardening been used. Even today a traditional African smith would not quench harden the blade of a socketed ax he had made from a piece of 0.6 percent C rail-steel of European origin. The need for stronger steels was satisfied merely by increasing the carbon content; the blooms of iron produced in about 1910 at Oyo, Nigeria, contained 1.67 percent C.[72]

India In the Indian subcontinent there is plenty of evidence to show that in about A.D. 400 the area had a technological level similar to that of Asia Minor and Europe, but we have no Indian furnaces datable to periods as early as this.

The famous pillars of Delhi and Dhar date from about A.D. 300[73] and, like the columns from the temple at Konarak,[74] are similar in structure to the beams from the bathhouses in the Roman period.[75] At Besnagar there are some wedges that are said to date from 125 B.C. and that are possibly of Greek origin.[76]

More recent Indian bloomery furnaces have been for the most part shaft furnaces with internal heights up to 3 m (all forced draft) and most of them slag tapping.[77] The only natural draft furnace in this region was found in Burma; it had 20 tuyeres and was 3.2 m high.[78] In the Indian central provinces at Tendukera, developed bowl furnaces of the Catalan type were in use in the 1850s.[79]

One interesting development in India is the melting of steel in crucibles. Bloomery steel and charcoal were put into sealed crucibles and heated for 4 hr in a hearth with a forced draft. This is an improvement on the African process of heating pieces of iron in a clay envelope and then forging them. The Indian product was a homogeneous carbon steel of 1 to 1.6 percent C and was known as *wootz* and exported to the West. Perhaps it is synomonous with Damascus steel since this is probably the town through which it entered the West in medieval times.

China China seems to have entered the Iron Age by about 600 B.C. and could therefore have derived it from Asia Minor. But the fact that cast iron appears early suggests that the Chinese Iron Age might have had independent origins, or else the Chinese were quick to appreciate the value of their first accidental piece of cast iron and turn it to good account. As elsewhere, the Iron Age was slow to develop and one of the first uses of iron was cast iron molds for hoes, sickles, and chisels, some of which were undoubtedly cast in bronze (475–221 B.C.).[80] According to literary sources, iron caldrons were being cast in 512 B.C., and the 5th century B.C. saw the beginning of iron weapons.[81] It is difficult to believe that the latter were made of cast iron and one would infer that they either knew how to convert cast iron to wrought iron or that they could also work the direct process when necessary.

The first blast furnace explosion was recorded in 91 B.C. and was followed by many others. This indicates that cast iron was being produced on a large scale, like that of bronze. Bronze was used for caldrons weighing 1400 kg as early as the Late Shang or Chou dynasty (1000 B.C.). We have no archaeological evidence of these blast furnaces before the Han period (200 B.C.). The furnaces were 1.4 m internal diameter at the top and were built of refractory bricks. Thick-walled clay tuyeres were used: 1.4 m long, 0.28 m outer diameter at the furnace end, and 0.6 m at the other. The charge was charcoal and a ferruginous sand which seems to have been a mixture of ground-up hematite and magnetite sand.[82]

So far there is no archaeological evidence for the bloomery (direct) process in China but a long tradition (from Han times) of crucible manufacture of steel, as in India. There is also a reference to the "roasting" of cast iron (A.D. 1334) to make "ripe" iron and wrought iron and the mixing of these to make steel. It appears that the roasting referred to is the malleabilization of cast iron by oxidation. But all the useful references are 17th century or later.[83]

All these processes were assisted by air from piston-blowing machines which were often water-driven. They were all very much more efficient than the bag, pot, and concertina bellows of the rest of the iron-using world and it appears that it is to their mechanical supremacy that the Chinese metallurgists owe their success.

Lu Da gives details of the structure of early Chinese artifacts and we see that the molds of the Warring States period (475–221 B.C.) were made of white cast iron while a coffin nail of the same period consists of wrought iron with ferrite and slag.[84] The discovery of a spade or shovel of the same period, made of blackheart malleable iron, was an early example of the

roasting process and was made by heating white iron. A steel sword of
the Han period had a martensitic structure so we can safely assume that
the production of wrought iron and steel, and the quench hardening of
steel, were well understood by A.D. 24.

Henger has analyzed two white iron castings, which contain 4.19 and
4.32 percent carbon and are low in phosphorus, sulfur, and silicon.[85]
Obviously these are cold blast charcoal irons made with low-phosphorus
ores.

While we know that the Chinese used the blast furnace for cast iron
production, at least from the beginning of our era, there does seem to be
some evidence for the medieval use of crucible smelting for the production
of cast iron with coal—a process well attested to for 19th century China.[86]
Recent finds in Mongolia have revealed cart hubs and caldrons dating
from the 13th century A.D. made from white cast iron with 0.5 to 1.27
percent sulfur and 0.21 to 0.55 percent phosphorus.[87]

The Roman Period

Furnace Types and Technique   As in the earlier period, the furnaces can
be divided into two basic types, shaft and bowl. The former represents
the development of the natural induced blast furnace. The simple bowl
furnace grew in height and diameter until it had to have more than one
tuyere. The indications are that slag tapping was almost universal in the
Roman-occupied regions, although this was by no means so outside it.
(Furnace typology is shown diagrammatically in fig. 7.12.) There is some
doubt as to whether the induced draft shaft furnace was actually used
outside Africa and perhaps India, but there is a type of tall narrow shaft
furnace which was in operation in Lower Saxony[88] in about the 1st
century A.D. and which spread to North Jutland[89] (C-14 date 210 ± 100
A.D.) and then to East England in about the 4th to 5th century A.D.[90]

This type, which can conveniently be called a slag-pit furnace, was about
1.6 m high and 0.3 m diameter and had four tuyeres, which could not
have had bellows attached to them according to Voss and Thomsen,[91]
although Pleiner disagrees with this.[92] The latter were similar to the
Polish furnaces, which seemed to be somewhat shorter and fatter (1 m
high × 0.5 m diameter) and which are thought to have been blown
by bellows.[93]

One feature common to this type was a pit beneath the furnace into
which slag flowed at a critical time in the smelting process, which may

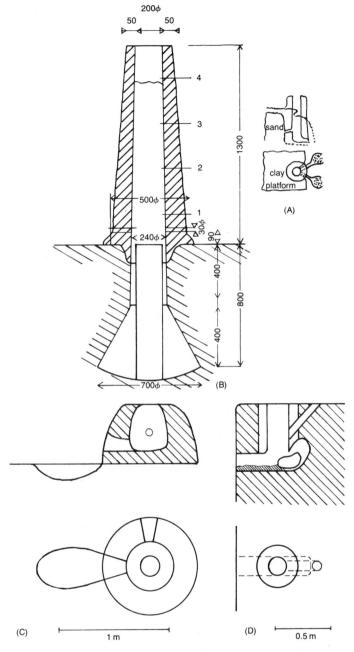

Fig. 7.12. Other types of iron smelting furnaces. (A) Roman shaft furnace (source: n. 97) (scale, ft);
(B) slag-pit furnace (source: n. 66 [b]) (dimensions, mm); (C) domed furnace (source: R. F.
Tylecote, *JISI* 192 [1959]: 26–34) (scale, 1 m); (D) Slav furnace (source: n. 110) (scale, 0.5 m).

have been automatically controlled by the temperature–time regime in the furnace itself or may have been assisted by external stimulation.

The Saxo-Jutish furnaces had thin walls and after one smelt, when the slag-pit was full, the furnace shaft was moved in one piece and positioned over a new and empty pit.[94] The slag lumps (*Schlackenklotz*) were allowed to remain in situ, and as a result whole fields of such furnace bottoms have been excavated in Poland.[95] The Polish furnaces seem to have had thicker walls than the Saxo-Jutish types and it is possible that they were rebuilt each time. In type, they resemble the EIA furnaces of the Nok culture of Nigeria.

On the whole, the idea of moving the furnace was not as good as allowing the slag to run into a pit in front or at one side, from which it could be removed when cold. This technique had long been normal practice in sophisticated copper smelting sites, and the developed bowl furnace, using the same technique, was carried forward into the Roman Iron Age.

Apart from this there was no change in technique. The product was a solid bloom of impure metal extracted through the side of the shaft furnace or the top of the bowl furnace. This situation persisted into medieval times with little change. But there was an improvement in what might be described as the "division of labor." The ores were generally roasted before charging with charcoal into the furnace; the working up of the bloom (5–10 kg) was done outside the smelting furnace in a second—forging—hearth.

We seem to meet more discarded pieces of cast iron in the Roman period—probably because of greater output rather than a higher "accident" rate.[96] Either the significance of this accident was not appreciated or else the demand for malleable iron, rather than castings, put it out of mind—in the Western world at least.

There was no change in the composition of the slag. The addition of lime, which, when it exceeds about 10 percent, raises the free-running temperature, was not normally practiced (see table 7.9). But the quantity and the size of the blocks were far in advance of anything the EIA could produce. Tap-slag blocks from a British 2d century site weighed as much as 18.0 kg,[97] while the furnace bottoms from Jutland[106] weighed as much as 170 kg.[98] To quote a French authority: "The forest of Aillant was able to provide 300,000 tons of ferruginous slag which arose from the production of 75,000 tons of iron, representing the manufacture of 15–20 million objects weighing 3 to 4 kg each."[99]

Table 7.9. Composition of Iron Smelting Slags (in percent)

	Turkey, 6th cent. B.C. [*]	Nigeris, 5th cent. B.C. [†]	U.K., 25–45 A.D. [‡]	Noreia, Austria, 400 B.C. [§]	Yonne, France, Roman [‖]	Ashwicken, U.K., Roman [#]	Meroe, Sudan, 1–500 A.D. [**]	Jutland, 210 ± 100 A.D. [††]	High Bishopley, U.K., 13th cent. A.D. [‡‡]	Harthope Mill, U.K., 13th cent. A.D. [§§]	Zelechovice, Czechoslovakia, Slavic [‖‖]
FeO	55.7	46.7	53.0	55.5	46.0	62.1	42.4	41.2	31.0	39.0	77.6
Fe_2O_3	14.0	10.7	22.9	12.6	4.8	7.7	20.8	3.6	26.4	5.0	16.22
SiO_2	8.6	25.5	16.0	24.5	31.8	21.2	20.7	22.7	20.3	29.4	—
CaO	5.2	1.4	2.8	2.0	2.1	0.4	2.4	1.4	2.7	5.5	—
MnO	7.2	2.4	tr	2.4	2.2	0.5	2.4	16.8	13.1	2.5	—
Al_2O_3	1.9	8.9	1.5	2.5	9.9	3.2	6.7	1.0	2.4	9.7	2.37
MgO	4.9	0.9	0.5	1.4	0.8	1.4	0.9	1.1	1.9	4.9	—
P_2O_5	2.0	1.0	0.4	0.1	0.3	1.7	1.0	2.2	—	0.4	—
K_2O	—	0.6	—	—	0.45	—	0.54	0.05	—	—	—
Na_2O	—	0.05	—	—	0.31	—	0.12	—	—	—	—
S	—	—	—	—	—	—	—	—	—	—	0.18

[*] See n. 56.

[†] See n. 65.

[‡] R. E. M. Wheeler, Maiden Castle, Dorset, Research Report of the Society of Antiquaries, London, no. 12 (1943).

[§] B. Neumann, Die Ältesten Verfahren der Erzeugung Technischen Eisens (Berlin, 1954).

[‖] See n. 99.

[#] See n. 97.

[**] See n. 100.

[††] R. Thomsen, Varde (Denmark), personal communication.

[‡‡] R. F. Tylecote, JISI 192 (1959): 26–34.

[§§] See n. 114(c).

[‖‖] See n. 110.

It is not certain whether the whole of this slag deposit is of Roman date. But even if only part of it is Roman, it shows the scale of operation at this time. Needless to say, dumps of this size, containing 30–50 percent iron, were in great demand for reworking in later periods in many European countries.

The Roman occupation did little to alter the situation in Egypt, but it is possible that the Roman penetration into Nubia was responsible for the improvement of technique in the Meroitic Kingdom farther south.

Here the situation became quite different and there are large slag heaps at Meroe in the Sudan, the surface layers of which date well into the Roman period (A.D. 1–400).[100] But some of the remains are technologically datable to as early as 200 B.C. and might be related to earlier contacts with the north. Alternatively, as Trigger has suggested, the Iron Age may have been introduced to this area via Ethiopia and southern Arabia.[101] Iron is not well represented in the later Meroitic graves, unlike in the Egyptian pyramids, but this may be due to the fact that we are dealing with a later date when iron was plentiful in the area and commonly used for weapons. As in Egypt itself, once the novelty of iron had worn off and it had ceased to be a precious metal, there would be a reversion to the more decorative nonferrous metals.

Production of Iron in the Migration and Medieval Period

In the early stages of the period one can detect little change in the methods of iron production from the Roman or, indeed, pre-Roman Iron Age. This is to be expected since the Migration People were essentially in an EIA phase. There was certainly no immediate increase in the size of the bloom; on the contrary, most of those found have proved to be somewhat smaller than the 8 kg Roman maximum that has been surmised. The Irish blooms weigh 5.2 and 5.4 kg, respectively. In Britain, historical evidence suggests that 14 kg was reached by A.D. 1350 without the use of water power.[102]

It is possible that the limit of bloom size was dictated more by the problems of smithing and working than by those of smelting. Peoples such as the Swedes[103] and the Slavs[104] went on producing slender ax-shaped currency bars which did not exceed 32 cm in length and 116 g in weight. In most countries the blooms were smithed into small pieces which were usually bar shaped.

The furnaces themselves appear to be of two basic types: (1) the horizontally developed bowl furnace of the Roman period with slag tapping facilities (we have many examples of this type from Britain),[105] and (2) the vertically developed bowl furnace. The latter is perhaps shown by the furnace found by Guyan at Bergen-Hofeisen near Schaffhausen.[106] Unfortunately, like many furnaces, it clearly did not survive to its full height and we cannot be certain what this may have been. But Johannsen and others agree that there was a type of early medieval furnace from which the bloom was extracted through the top rather than at the side, as in the shaft and some developed bowl furnaces.[107] This type eventually became the Catalan hearth of the Pyrenees [108] and appears to have been used in northern England in the postmedieval period.[109]

The more primitive Migration Peoples continued to use simple bowl furnaces and there were other types such as the Slav furnaces found by Pleiner at Zelechovice.[110] The most interesting problem is the fate of the shaft furnace found in several Roman locations. The Saxo-Jutish[111] tall slender shaft furnace seems to have made its way across the North Sea to eastern England[112] and then died out. But it probably lingered on in Central Europe finally to blossom as the Styrian high bloomery furnace (*Stückofen*) and the blast furnace.[113] But we lack examples demonstrating the continuity of this type.

The next aspect of interest in ironworking in this period is the application of waterpower. Most of the smaller production units lie near streams, but it is clear that this water was not used as a source of power. For one reason, the power required to produce an air flow of 300 liters/min is not great and could easily be produced by manual means. Secondly, these units were obviously based on very small capital resources and the exploitation of waterpower required substantial capital. Its use in metallurgy therefore had to compete with its use in nonmetallurgical processes such as corn-grinding and cloth fulling; considering that the latter activities consumed more power than blowing, they were given priority in the West. But in China the development of metallurgical blowing engines was one of the reasons for their superiority and the early adoption of a cast iron tradition.

In any event we have no sound evidence for the use of waterpower in Europe until 1408 A.D., when a water-powered bloomery furnace was used in Britain,[114] and 1463, when Filarete's blast furnace appeared in Italy.[115] It is, however, very likely that waterpower was used in Europe during the 14th century.

It seems that, in Europe, monastic or episcopal bodies were the only

ones with sufficient capital to invest in the iron industry and that the large
scale development of this industry depended on the rise of the religious
institutions. Thus in 1408 we find the Bishop of Durham establishing
the first documented water-powered bloomery in Britain, and in spite
of the absence of references to hammers, we feel that the power was made
available for hammers.[116] Once the principle was established, the way
was open for the production of larger blooms, since power hammers,
based on fulling mills, would be available to work them. Later, continuous
operation, made possible by the application of waterpower to bellows,
made the blast furnace possible. Outside China there is certainly no
evidence for a manually blown blast furnace, and on the basis of the
continuity of operation required of such a piece of equipment one would
not expect manually or foot operated blowing apart from temporary
stoppages when treadmilling a waterwheel might just be a possibility.

Once the application of waterpower had been introduced by the early
15th century, the bloom size increased to over 100 kg. The bloom was
cut up and the pieces were reworked in a second hearth, known as a string-
hearth in England. This hearth appears to have been very like the low
bloomery hearth but it worked intermittently. Unfortunately we lack
material evidence of this period and have to extrapolate early and postmedieval data to fill it.

In Europe the ultimate in bloomery hearths was the Catalan hearth of
the 19th century, which has been adequately discussed by Percy and
others.[117] In Britain, as shown by the hearths near Sheffield[118] and in
the Lake District[119] and in Scandinavia as shown by Evenstad's furnace
in Norway (1 m high),[120] the low bloomery hearth in which the bloom
was removed through the top was almost universal. The exceptions appear
to be the Stückofen in Styria, which, being 3–5 m high, had to allow the
bloom to be removed through the side,[121] and the Osmund furnace of
Sweden, which seems just too tall for top removal ($\sim$2.0 m).[122]

Smithing Techniques

The size of the bloom in the Roman period varied from the 5 or 6 kg
spindle-shaped currency bars, still in vogue, to the 10 kg blooms of unknown shape incoorporated into the bathhouse beams from Corbridge[123]
and Catterick[124] in Britain, and Saalburg in Germany.[125] These were
probably smaller blooms, supplied by local tribes to the Roman workshops. This iron would be reworked and welded into structures weighing

up to 500 kg. The four iron bars in the Lake Nemi, Italy, anchors totaled 414 kg,[126] and we have many anvils weighing up to 50 kg that were also made from smaller blooms.

Smithing furnaces for forging and welding were made in various shapes and sizes to suit the work. As we can see from contemporary primitive practice they do not need to be very sophisticated—merely a hole in the ground and a single clay tuyere to protect the bellows. The largest known example is probably the one erected for welding the bathhouse beam found at Corbridge;[127] charcoal can be piled around and a tuyere inserted wherever it was necessary to raise the temperature for forging or welding. Such a method was used in the manufacture of ships' stern frames right into the 20th century.[128]

The blooms were of course no less inhomogeneous than those of the Early Iron Age and the variable carbon content has led many people to talk about intentional carburization.[129] But the fact is that reheating can remove or add carbon, according to the carbon level of the area of the bloom heated or to the precise position of the metal in the hearth, relative to the tuyere.

The average Roman material shows a substantial reduction in the amount of phosphorus compared to the pre-Roman period. This difference may point to better discrimination and the knowledge that low phosphorus metal was better for carburizing. But there are many examples of high phosphorus iron in the Roman period, and most of the metal used was of low carbon content and therefore not carburized.

However, the knowledge of carburizing and quench hardening was now more widely applied than before and we do not lack examples of properly executed carburizing followed by suitable heat treatment.

Slags and Other Residues

The composition of iron smelting slag is generally the same as that from copper smelting, except for the copper content (cf. tables 7.1 and 7.9). This can make its diagnosis difficult, but normally it contains less than 0.5 percent Cu while copper smelting slags, even today, usually contain more than this amount. Some examples of the composition of iron smelting slags are given in table 7.9, and many of these are free running at 1100–1200° C and have been tapped from the furnace in liquid form.

A good deal of slag stays in the furnace and is mixed with charcoal. This is often called "cinder" for want of a better term and is much the

Table 7.10. Composition of Hammer Scales (in percent)

	Benwell	Ashwicken	Chichester
Fe	7.7	—	0.11
Fe_2O_3 Fe_3O_4	74.1	85.8	14.32
Fe_2O_3	8.5	—	48.48
SiO_2	1.45	9.94	22.68
CaO	1.80	1.2	0.31
Al_2O_3	6.47	0.9	3.18
MgO	—	0.3	0.19
P_2O_5	—	0.73	0.36

Source: See n. 96.

same as the tap slag in composition if one ignores the entrapped charcoal.

Hot forging produces hammer scales, which consist of flakes of magnetite and wüstite and which are often found more or less oxidized to hematite by weathering (table 7.10).

When oxidized metal is reheated in the forging hearth, the wüstite (as magnetite scale) often falls off and is combined in the bottom of the hearth with fuel ash and earth to give forging slags or "smithing furnace bottoms."[130] These slags are often found as small well-shaped planoconvex lumps of solidified slag measuring from 8 to 20 cm in diameter. They are often highly magnetic on the top (flat) side due to their magnetite content. On the whole these bottoms are ferrous silicates with some wüstite or magnetite present.

In some cases, the smelting slags of the pre-Roman Iron Age and medieval period formed furnace bottoms of this type but they usually contain far more charcoal and are rarely magnetic. In many cases they resemble the cinder referred to above except for their shape.

NOTES

1. B. Rothenberg, "The Chalcolithic Copper Industry at Timna," *Museum Haaretz Bulletin*, no. 8, June 1966, pp. 86–93.

2. Christopher B. Donnan, "A Pre-Columbian Smelter from Northern Peru," *Archaeology* 26, no. 4 (1973): 289–97.

3. R. F. Tylecote, *Metals and Materials* 4 (July 1970): 285–93.

4. W. Lorenzen, *Helgoland und das früheste Kupfer des Nordens* (Ottendorf-Niederelbe, 1965).

5. I. R. Selimkanov, *Soviet Archaeology*, 1962, no. 1, 57–65.

6. H. McKerrell and R. F. Tylecote, *Proceedings of the Prehistoric Society*, 38 (1972): 209–18.

7. R. Bowman A. K. Friedman, J. Levuer, and J. Ocilstead, *Archaeometry* 17, no. 2 (1975): 157–63.

8. C. Milton, E. J. Dwornik, R. B. Finkelman, and P. Toulmin III, *Journal of the Historical Metallurgy Society*, no. 1, 1976, pp. 24–33.

9. R. F. Tylecote, B. Rothenberg, and A. Lupu, "A Study of Early Copper Smelting and Working from Sites in Israel," *Journal of the Institute of Metals* 95 (1967): 235–43.

10. P. E. Newberry, *The Life of Rekhmara* (London, 1900), pl. XVIII.

11. J. Du Plat Taylor, *Antiquaries Journal* (London) 32 (1952): 133–67.

12. Ernst Preuschen, "Über die früheste Kupfergewinnung in den Öesterreichischen Alpen," in "*Kupfer*," (Hamburg: Nord-deutsche Affinerie, 1966), pp. 32–35.

13. H. Neuninger, E. Preuschen, and R. Pittioni, *Archaeologica Austriaca* 46 (1969): 99–109.

14. R. Pittioni, *Archaeologica Austriaca* 3 (1958): 19–40.

15. H. Neuninger, E. Preuschen, and R. Pittioni, *Archaeologica Austriaca* 47 (1970): 87–90.

16. R. Pittioni, *Man* 48 (1958): 120.

17. J. S. Jackson, *Archaeologica Austriaca* 35, no. 5 (1968): 92–114.

18. R. F. Tylecote, *Cornish Archaeology* 6 (1967): 110–11; in *Festschrift for R. Pittioni* (Vienna: Deutike, 1976).

19. R. Maddin and J. D. Muhly, "Some Notes on the Copper Trade of the Ancient Mid-East," *Journal of Metals* 26, no. 5 (1974): 1–7.

20. T. S. Wheeler, R. Maddin, and J. D. Muhly, *Expedition* 17, no. 4, (1975): 31–39.

21. Noel Barnard, *Bronze Casting and Bronze Allovs in Ancient China* (Canberra: Australian National University and Monumenta Serica, 1961).

22. R. F. Tylecote, *Metallurgy in Archaeology* (London, Ed. Arnold, 1962), p. 33.

23. V. G. Childe, *Dawn of European Civilisation* (London, 1957), pp. 128–29.

24. S. Junghans, E. Sangmeister, and H. Schröder. *Metallanalysen Kupferzeitlicher und Bronzezeitlicher Bodenfunde aus Europa*, vol. 1 (Berlin, 1960).

25. H. Otto and W. Witter, *Handbuch der Ältesten Vorgeschichtlichen Metallurgie in Mitteleuropa* (Leipzig, 1952).

26. J. Perrot, *Israel Exploration Journal* 5 (1955): 17–40, 73–84, 167–89.

27. B. Rothenberg, *Timna; Valley of the Biblical Copper Mines* (London, 1972).

28. M. Gimbutas, *Bronze Age Cultures in Central and Eastern Europe* (London, 1965).

29. R. F. Tylecote, *Report of the Department of Antiquities Cyprus*, 1971, pp. 53–58.

30. See n. 27, p. 219.

31. C. Mahany, Alcester, Warwickshire, personal communication; report forthcoming.

32. See n. 26, p. 80.

33. M. Dothan, *Israel Exploration Journal* 9 (1959): 13–29; W. Lamb, *Excavations at Thermi, Lesbos* (Cambridge, 1936); J. L. Caskey, "Excavations at Lerna: 1954," *Hesperia*

24 (1955): 25–49, pl. XIV f; C. Tsountas, *Dhimini and Sesklo* (Athens, 1908) in modern Greek).

34. H. W. Catling, *Cypriot Bronzework in the Mycenaean World* (Oxford, 1964).

35. See n. 33, pp. 13–29.

36. J. L. Caskey, *Hesperia* 31 (1962): 263–83; F. Petrie, *Researches in Sinai* (London, 1906).

37. See n. 10.

38. H. Siret and L. Siret, *Les Premiers Ages du Métal dans le Sud-Est de l'Espagne* (Anvers, 1887).

39. H. Schliemann, *Ilios, the City and Country of the Trojans* (London, 1880).

40. See n. 28.

41. B. Maisler-Mazar, *Israel Exploration Journal* 1 (1950); 123; 8 (1958): 180; Tylecote et al., "Study of Early Copper Smelting and Working."

42. B. Rothenberg, personal communication; report forthcoming.

43. F. E. Zeuner, *University of London Institute of Archaeology*, bull. no. 11 (1959), pp. 37–44.

44. J. Mellaart, *Catal Hüyük* (London, 1967).

45. Alonso Barba, *El Arte de los Metales*, R. E. Douglas and E. P. Mathewson (London, 1923).

46. R. F. Tylecote, *British Journal of Historical Sciences* 2, no. 1 (1964): 25–43.

47. (a) L. U. Salkield, *VI Congreso Internationale Mineraria Hispanica Iberoamerica* (Leon, 1970), vol. 1, pp. 85–98; (b) J. C. Allan, *Bulletin of the Historical Metallurgy Group* 2, no. 1 (1968): 47–50.

48. S. G. Checkland, *The Mines of Tarshish* (London, 1967).

49. E. Ardaillon, *Les Mines du Laurion dans l'Antiquité* (Paris, 1897).

50. They were observed on the occasion of a visit paid to the site by the kind invitation of Professor A. Blanco-Freijeiro, Director of Antiquities, Madrid.

51. Sir John Sinclair, *The Statistical Account of Scotland* (Edinburgh, 1794), vol. 11 525–28.

52. G. Jobey, *Archaeologia Aeliana: Society of Antiquaries, Newcastle-Upon-Tyne* 11 (1962): 1–34.

53. J. H. Money, *Journal of the Historical Metallurgy Society* 8, no. 1 (1974): 1–16.

54. Author's observation, Kabushiya, Sudan, 1969.

55. F. K. Dorner et al., "Arsamaia am Nymphaios," *Jahrbuch des Deutschen Archaeologischen Institutes: Berlin* 80 (1965): 88–235.

56. H. G. Bachmann, *Archiv für Eisenhüttenwesen, Duesseldorf Verein Deutscher Eisenhüttenleute* 38 (1967): 809–12.

57. H. Blümner, *Technologie und Terminologie der Gewerbe und Künste bei Griechen und Römern* (Leipzig, 1886–87), vol. 4, p. 152.

58. Exhibited in Budapest in 1897. Model in Science Museum, South-Kensington, London.

59. K. Klusemann, *Mitteilungen der Anthropologische Gesellschaft in Wien* 54 (1924): 120.

60. H. Straube, *Archiv für Eisenhüttenwesen: Düsseldorf* 35 (1964): 932–40.

61. J. W. Gilles, *Archiv für Eisenhuttenwesen: Dusseldorf* 28 (1957): 179–85.

62. J. W. Gilles, *Stahl und Eisen* 56 (1936): 252.

63. J. Rutter, personal communication; report forthcoming.

64. A. J. Ohrenberger and K. Bielenin, *Burgenländische Forschungen*, no. 2, 1969, pp. 79–93.

65. R. F. Tylecote, *Journal of the Historical Metallurgy Society* 9, no. 2 (1975): 49–56.

66. (a) O. Voss, *Kuml* (1962), pp. 7–32; (b) R. Thomsen, *Kuml* (Aarhus, Denmark, 1963), pp. 60–74.

67. W. Wegewitz, *Nachricht. Niedersachsens Urgeschichte*, Special Report no. 26 (1957).

68. W. Gowland, *Archaeologia (London)* 56, no. 2 (1899); 267–322, fig. 23.

69. J. Hupfeld, "Die Eisenindustrie in Togo," *Mitteilungen aus den Deutschen Schutzgebieten*, ed. F. von Dankelmans (1899), pp. 175 ff.

70. R. Gardi, *100 A, 1. Lloyd's Registry of Shipping*, no. 4, 1959, p. 32.

71. See n. 65.

72. C. V. Bellamy, *Journal of the Iron and Steel Institute* (hereafter *JISI*) 66, no. 2 (1904): 99–126.

73. Sir Robert Hadfield, *JISI* 85, no. 1 (1912): 134–86.

74. H. G. Graves, *JISI* 85, no. 1 (1912): 187–202.

75. J. H. Wright, *Bulletin of the Historical Metallurgy Group* 6, no. 1 (1972): 24–27.

76. See n. 73.

77. R. F. Tylecote, *JISI* 203 (1965): 340–48.

78. J. W. Gilles, *Archiv für Eisenhüttenwesen* 23 (1952): 407–15.

79. Tylecote, *JISI* 203 (1965): 340–48.

80. Lu Da, *Acta Metallurgia Siniatica, Peking* 9, (1966): 1–3 (transl. in Durrer Festschrift, *Vita pro Ferro*, ed. W. U. Guyan (Schaffhausen, 1965), pp. 65–70.

81. See n. 21.

82. J. Needham, *The Development of Iron and Steel Technology in China* (London: Newcomen Soc., 1958).

83. Ibid.

84. Da, *Acta Metallurgia Siniatica, Peking* 9 (1966): 1–3.

85. J. W. Henger, *Bulletin of the Historical Metallurgy Group* 4, no. 2 (1970): 45–52.

86. See n. 82.

87. N. N. Terekhova, *Soviet Archaeology*, 1974, no. 1, pp. 68–78.

88. See n. 67.

89. See n. 66(a).

90. There is a slag block from Aylsham in the museum at Norwich of the same type as those found in Jutland and Lower Saxony.

91. See nn. 66 and 67.

92. Dr. R. Pleiner, personal communication.

93. K. Bielenin, *Prähistorische Zeitschrift* 42 (1964): 77–96.

94. See nn. 66 and 67.

95. M. Radwan and K. Bielenin, *Revue d'Histoire de la Sidérurgie, Nancy* 3 (1962–63): 163–76.

96. R. F. Tylecote, *Metallurgy in Archaeology* (London, 1962), p. 243.

97. R. F. Tylecote and E. Owles, *Norfolk Archaeology, Norwich* 32 (1960): 142–62.

98. See n. 67.

99. J. Monot, *Revue d'Histoire de la Sidérurgie, Nancy* 5, no. 2 (1964): 273–97.

100. R. F. Tylecote, *Bulletin of the Historical Metallurgy Group* 4, no. 2 (1970): 67–72.

101. B. Trigger, *African Historical Studies* 2, no. 1 (1969): 23–50.

102. R. F. Tylecote, *Organon* (Poland), 1965, no. 2, pp. 157–78.

103. I. Serning, in Durrer Festschrift, pp. 73–90.

104. R. Pleiner, *Slovenska Archaelogice, Bratislava* 9 (1961): 405–50.

105. J. H. Money, *Journal of the Historical Metallurgy Group* 8, no. 1 (1974): 1–20.

106. W. Guyan, in Durrer Festschrift (see n. 80), pp. 163–94.

107. O. Johannsen, *Geschichte des Eisens*, 3d ed. (Düsseldorf, 1953).

108. J. Percy, *Metallurgy: Iron and Steel* (London, 1864), pp. 279–319.

109. D. W. Crossley and D. Ashurst, *Post Medieval Archaeology* 2 (1968): 10–54.

110. R. Pleiner, *Revue d'Histoire de la Sidérurgie, Nancy* 3 (1962–63): 179–95.

111. See nn. 66 and 67.

112. See n. 102, p. 157.

113. See n. 78.

114. (a) G. T. Lapsley, *English History Review* 14 (1899): 509–29; (b) R. A. Mott, *JISI* 198 (1961): 149–61; and (c) R. F. Tylecote, *JISI* 194 (1960): 451–58.

115. J. R. Spencer, *Technology and Culture* 4 (1963): 201–06; C. S. Smith, T. A. Wertime, J. Needham, and L. C. Eichner, *Technology and Culture* 5 (1964): 386–405.

116. See n. 114 (b). I now accept Mott's view.

117. See n. 108, pp. 278–315.

118. See n. 109.

119. R. F. Tylecote and J. Cherry, *Transactions of the Cumberland and Westmorland Avchitectural and Antiquarian Society* 70 (1970): 69–109.

120. Ole Evenstad, *Bulletin of the Historical Metallurgy Group* 2, no. 2 (1968): 61–65.

121. R. Schaur, *Stahl und Eisen* 49 (1929): 489–98.

122. E. Tholander, *Journal of the Historical Metallurgy Society* 9, no. 2 (1975): 68–70. Percy, *Metallurgy*, pp. 279–319.

123. Sir Hugh Bell, *JISI* 85 (1912): 118–28.

124. See n. 75.

125. L. Jacobi, *Das Römerkastell Saalburg* (Homburg v. d. Höhe, 1897).

126. G. Calbiani, *Metallurgia Italiana, Milano*, June 1939, pp. 359–70.

127. See n. 123.

128. R. F. Tylecote, *Solid Phase Welding of Metals* (London, 1968), pp. 12–13.

129. G. Becker and W. Dick, *Archiv für das Eisenhüttenwesen, Duesseldorf* 36 (1965): 537–42.

130. See n. 96, p. 254.

8

An Alternative Sequence for the Development of Metallurgy: Tepe Yahya, Iran

DENNIS HESKEL and CARL CLIFFORD LAMBERG-
KARLOVSKY

Since the discovery of Tepe Yahya in 1967, six seasons of excavation at the site and analytical work on the metallurgy materials have expanded and altered our view on the development of metallurgy on the Iranian plateau. Tepe Yahya is located in the Soghun Valley 225 km south of Kerman in a region of the Zagros Mountains abundant in copper resources.

The sequence of occupation at Tepe Yahya extends from ca. 5000 B.C. through the first centuries A.D.[1] In this paper, the synchronic and diachronic development of metallurgy and related aspects of social development throughout the 4th and 3d millennia B.C. are examined.

In the past thirty years there have been several important attempts to establish a sequence for the development of metallurgy, notably Childe in 1944, Wertime in 1973, and Renfrew in 1972.[2] Unfortunately, none of these studies correlated the theoretical framework with significant data from a single site and/or larger archaeological region.

Childe established a sequence of four modes of production based on the economic utilization of the metal.[3] Mode O includes the use of native copper as a curious stone for manufacturing small ornaments; mode 1, weapons and ornaments made from copper and its alloys and a few tools for industrial use; and mode 2, copper and bronze tools used in handicraft production but not in husbandry. The metal types in mode 2 include knives, saws, specialized axes, adzes, and chisels. Mode 3 is distinguished by the use of metal tools in agriculture and for rough work. Tools in mode 3 include sickles, hoe blades, and hammer heads.

Although these modes proved useful in examining over 4000 years of Egyptian prehistory, this conceptualization remains too generalized to afford an understanding of 4th and 3d millennia metallurgical development in the entire Near East. The development of socio economic-technological stages, however, is a valid addition to previous models of archaeological/metallurgical information.

Wertime has described "the technical and historical phases of early copper metallurgy" as follows: hammering and annealing of native copper; evolution of casting and smelting; and the origins of bronze.[4] He also states that multiple deposits of copper, lead, iron, and other metals, fluxing techniques, and "the discovery of interacting impurities in the course of casting and smelting" led to polymetallism after the introduction of smelting.[5]

The concept of polymetallism is an intriguing one, particularly in the development of iron technology. Its utility in dealing with a copper metallurgical development is not as useful, since the evidence from Iranian sites strongly suggests a variety of developmental schemes at each site and region. It is apparent from our evidence that technological development is greatly dependent on cultural as well as technological factors.

The absence of systemic correlations between the development of metallurgy and the changes in other aspects of the cultural system has been a serious drawback in previous research on metallurgical development. The dicovery of "interacting impurities" is far too hazy a concept to describe the development of polymetallism and/or the use of alloys.

Renfrew has established an evolutionary scheme that includes a degree of geographical diversity.[6] This concept consists of eight basic steps: simple use of native copper, cold hammering of native copper, annealing of native copper, smelting of copper from its ores, casting copper in an open mold, casting-in and the use of two-piece molds, alloying with arsenic or tin, and lost wax casting.

The detailed evidence of metallurgical development on the Iranian plateau strongly indicates that this unilinear scheme is too simplistic to afford an understanding of the complex process. The lack of connection between archaeological context and Renfrew's metallurgical development is extremely limiting.

The study of metal objects and, to a lesser degree, metallurgical production materials has been an intricate part of archaeology on the Iranian plateau. The earliest systematic archaeology of a 4th and 3d millennia site in this area was done in 1908 by Pumpelly at Anau.[7] Gooch used wet chemical analysis on the metal objects from Anau to suggest a change in ore selection and in cultural-trade contacts between Anau I–II and Anau III.[8] Evidence for this change is based on the introduction of copper–tin bronze in the later period. Although it was briefly glossed over, many of the Anau III objects were made of copper–arsenic alloy. Tin and arsenic do not appear together in any object in significant quantities.

During the next forty years a number of important sites were excavated in Iran in which metallurgical analyses, mostly wet chemical, were performed and included in appendixes. Some of these sites include Tepe Hissar, Tepe Sialk, Tepe Giyan, Geoy Tepe, and Shah Tepe.[9] None of these reports made an attempt to correlate the role of metallurgy diachronically or synchronically.

One of the most innovative studies of this time was Coghlan's attempt in 1942 to correlate ceramic kiln advances with changes in metal technology.[10] The data were drawn from Tepe Sialk and Susa but failed to account for the obviously different pyrotechnologies involved in metal and ceramic production. As Wertime correctly states, "There is little comfort in trying to deduce the origins of smelting directly from the pottery kiln or bread oven."[11]

One of the most recent approaches to delineating the development of metallurgy in Iran was the Tal-i-Iblis project of Joseph Caldwell in 1966 and 1967.[12] Tal-i-Iblis in the Kerman Province of southeastern Iran contains some of the earliest evidence of copper production and use. In 1968 detailed survey of metal resources in the Anarak mine region (near Kashan, Iran) by Wertime, Pleiner, and Smith also provided important and useful insights on the occurrence of polymetallic deposits and modern bazaar metalworking practices.

Dr. Smith's work on the native copper, primarily from Tepe Sialk and the Talmessi mine region, has established the early and continued use of native copper with arsenic impurities.[13] It is necessary to add, however, that the Anarak–Talmessi mine region is one of the few in the world (the only one known in Iran) to have a significant amount of domeykite (Cu_3As) and algodonite (Cu_5As) close to the surface and included in copper-bearing gossans.[14]

In any attempt to examine the nature of Iranian metallurgy one must consider the following factors: the presence of copper–arsenic minerals in significant quantities close to the surface; the lack of sulfarsenide deposits in Iran; the early use of copper–arsenic alloy throughout Iran; the low quantity of arsenic in the native metal; the similar weathered appearance of domeykite, algodonite, and native copper; and the total compatability of impurity patterns and metallurgical production in the use of domeykite and algodonite to provide the arsenic in the early alloys.[15]

Spectrographic and metallographic analyses on four objects from Tepe Yahya undertaken by Tylecote and McKerrell indicate that a copper–arsenic alloy was used in the early 4th millennium B.C.[16] and a single copper tin bronze, with 8 percent tin, belonged to the early 3d millennium. Analyses of additional metallurgical materials from Yahya have now been completed and are reported here for the first time.

PERIODS VI–VA (4500–3200 B.C.)

The most interesting major metallurgical innovations discovered at Tepe Yahya occur during periods VI–VA. Only two metal artifacts were found in period VI (4500–4000 B.C.), the earliest occupation of the site. Both are small crude awls circular in cross section, the points of which are deformed and flattened. Analysis of one of the awls indicated it was made of native copper. The period VC (4000–3800) B.C.) metal corpus consists of five pieces: a pin, a bent sheet metal ring, a corroded bead, corroded sheet metal, and a broken knob-headed pin. The knob-headed pin may date to VC–VB and is significant because it represents the earliest piece that has been cast, cold worked, and annealed. The VC corpus shows an expanded repertoire of metal shapes. Both VI and VC contain small utilitarian objects.

Periods VB (3800–3500) and VA (3500–3200) represent a dramatic change in the quantity and quality of metal objects found at Tepe Yahya. Approximately 35 objects have been found in a VB–VA context including simple pins, spatulas, a knob-headed pin, tacks, needles, chisels, decorated pins, blades, a copper ingot, and waste ore pieces. The objects tend to be tools rather than trinkets. The technology used to produce the artifacts includes a full range of the processes used for the succeeding 2000 years: cold working, annealing, flat casting, edge hardening, and copper–arsenic alloying.

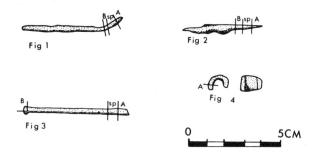

Figs. 8.1–8.4. Fifth and fourth millennia copper objects.

The copper–arsenic alloys found at Tepe Yahya during period VI and in fact throughout the 4th and 3d millennia B.C. probably resulted from the addition of natural copper arsenides to the native metal, based on the impurities found in the metal by spectrographic analyses and the presence of these copper arsenides at Tepe Hissar and Tal-i-Iblis. These copper arsenides are algodonite ($Cu_{5-8}As$, or 80–87% Cu by weight) and domeykite (Cu_3As, or 72% Cu by weight). It is important to note the presence of significant quantities of copper arsenides with copper oxide and copper carbonate ore gossans and with native copper deposits in the Talmessi–Anarak mine region in Iran. This mineral deposit is a rare source, certainly in Iran and probably in the entire Near East. This type of polymetallic deposit, including uranium, cobalt, nickel, zinc, and other elements, is essential to the formation of these arsenides.

Unfortunately there have been few studies of the physical properties of copper–arsenic alloys.[17] Marechal compared the hardness of a range of different copper–arsenic alloys to their copper–tin counterparts.[18] His results conclusively indicate that copper–arsenic alloys are at least as hard as copper–tin bronzes with equal percentages of arsenic and tin. Arsenic also acts as a deoxidant when added to copper. This improves the ease of casting objects by reducing formation of gases that result in blowhole formation in the solid metal. These results should disprove the belief that copper–tin bronzes are metallurgically superior to copper–arsenic alloys and that this supposed superiority was the reason behind the late 3d millennium shift to tin bronze.

The finished form of these objects represents a significant change in the ability of metalsmiths to handle their material more professionally. A sample of metal objects from periods VI–VA were examined by metallographic and semiquantitative emmission spectrographic analysis.

Tepe Yahya XC 3, 1973 (fig. 8.1) is a small period VI copper awl 5.6 cm in length x a maximum 0.3 cm in width. Transverse sections from the point and body area were taken for metallographic analysis.

The point is irregularly circular in cross section and has thin surface malachite–chloride and cuprite layers of corrosion. There is also granular corrosion between the cuprite and the metallic area. The deformation visible in cross section indicates extensive hammering. There are several large and irregular cavities, now filled with cuprous oxide (Cu_2O) throughout the section. The metal contains very few impurities and has no original, evenly distributed, cuprous oxide inclusions.

This section, when etched with potassium dichromate, shows intersecting strain markings with no annealing twins. It is a highly deformed native copper with large grain size. The deformation of the grains is parallel to the cavities in the polished section. There are no visible grain boundaries and no evidence to indicate that the piece was ever heat treated (pl. 8.1a; figs. 8.1, 8.2).[19]

The body section of the awl is roughly circular in cross section. It contains no cuprous oxide inclusions and very few impurities. It has a V-shaped cavity now filled with cuprite. It has the same elongated and highly deformed appearance as the point when etched. The metal has several "white phase" inclusions which may be silver or possibly domeykite. Spectrographic analysis of a similar body section from the same object shows only 0.002 percent silver present as an impurity. A Vickers diamond pyramid hardness (DPH) test of the point indicates little edge hardening and an average hardness of 115 kg/mm².

This copper awl was found in an excellent period VI context in the north step-trench. The awl was found in fill between two floors of a small room. The architectural exposure consisted of several small rooms, not exceeding 2 × 2 m² and a singular circular bin with dog-kennel type entry into three articulating rooms. The ceramics of period VI are uniformly a coarse chaff-tempered ware with occasional burnishing and red paint. The flint industry consists of retouched blades, sickle blades, burins, end scrapers, drills, microlithic geometrics, and denticulated tools of types without ready parallel on the Iranian plateau and differing from the later period V inventory. Fewer than a dozen obsidian blades, 3 turquoise and 1 carnelian bead represent the

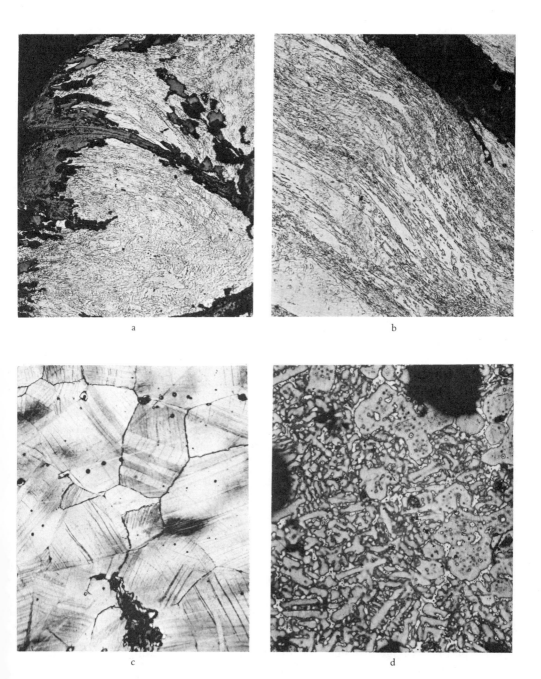

Plate 8.1. (a) Section from a copper awl × 100; etched with K₂CrO₇ + FeCl₃ (alcohol); elongated and deformed grains. (b) Section from a copper pin × 200; etched with K₂CrO₇; elongation of grains. (c) Section from a copper knob-headed pin × 500; etched with K₂CrO₇; twins and equiaxed grains. (d) Section from a piece of dross × 100; etched with K₂CrO₇; cored structure.

sum of imported materials. Numerous tools and decorative elements were manufactured from shell, bone, and clay. By and large period VI has little evidence for far-reaching contact with distant communities. The ceramics conform to what Dyson has referred to as the "soft-ware-horizon" of 5th millennium Iran. The production and consumption of ceramic materials seem locally restricted. There appear to be no specialized activity areas or functional areas on the site. Analysis of economic subsistence patterns suggests that the agricultural base consisted of various cereals and legumes complemented by domesticated sheep, goat, and cattle.

Period V at Yahya is stratigraphically divisible into three continuous phases: VC, 4000–3800 B.C.; VB, 3800–3600 B.C.; and VA, 3600–3400 B.C. Period V appears to be directly continuous from the earlier VI settlement. Changes in ceramic types are quantitative in nature between periods VI and V. Throughout the three phases of period V there are no abrupt changes in architectural or material inventory. Throughout periods VI and V, changes which do occur are cumulative and gradual, quantitative in nature not qualitative.

The architecture of period V incorporates the increasing use of standard size bricks, and the presence of hearths in rooms, buttresses, stone doorsills, and brick benches, within multi room dwellings. The distribution of materials within period V domestic dwellings does not indicate differential distribution of wealth within the community. Also the architecture does not indicate differences in function or status. Throughout period V there is an increasing utilization of rare and imported items, i.e., carnelian, turquoise, alabaster, obsidian, and a single lapis lazuli bead in period VA. The ceramics of period V indicate an increasing contact with other communities. Thus, for the first time in period VB more than 10 percent of the painted black or buff ceramics can be paralleled with Susa and Tal-i-Bakun. In the succeeding period VA a painted black on red is paralleled at Tal-i-Iblis and numerous sites in Kerman Province and Baluchistan. Our settlement surveys indicate that periods VB and VA represent the largest number of settlements (population?) within this area of Iran. Sites are far more numerous in this period (average 2–5 hectares) than at any other time until the Late Iron Age. The increasing use of imported materials within domestic houses, the production of metal artifacts, alabaster, and chlorite bowls, and the greater variety of ceramic types and technological production methods such as higher firing temperatures and an increased variety of pigments for painting, all converge to support the impression of an increasingly complex agricultural society in which surplus production could be utilized to maintain craft specialists. Analysis of paleofaunal materials reveals an increasing efficiency in farming techniques and greater variety of agricultural produce. The analysis of metal artifacts from period V supports the view that throughout this period there is a cumulative development in productive technology combined with an increasing population and cultural complexity.

The three period VC objects analyzed are T. Yahya XC 8b-40, a copper pin; C-7-15, also a pin; and C tt5-3-1, a copper bead fragment.

T. Yahya C-7-15, 1969 (fig. 8.2) is a pin, circular in cross section, with a sharp and slightly deformed point. It is 4.3 cm in length × 0.3 cm in maximum diameter. Two transverse sections were taken: one from the point area and the other from the body section.

The section of the point area is deformed by cold hammering. The hammering of the metal to form the object created a cavity where the metal was not totally joined. The metallic area is very pure with no cuprous oxide inclusions. Spectrographic analysis of a sample from this artifact indicates only 0.002 percent Ag as an impurity while the section has the usual copper corroded surface. The body section of the pin is less deformed than the point. It is also very pure and lacks cuprous oxide inclusions.

Both sections, when etched with potassium dichromate, exhibit the same elongated and deformed copper grain structure as the period VI awl. This object was never heat treated and is made from native copper (pl. 8.1b).

This object was found in fill directly above the floor of a room. It comes from the largest architectural exposure of period VC at Yahya, a house complex of at least 16 rooms of varying size. This pin was found in one of the larger rooms near a corner hearth.[20]

The knob-headed pin, XC 8b-40 (fig. 8.3), indicates a different production technique. The point of this pin is broken off, and the piece is circular in cross section with an extensively worked knob head. Two sections were examined from this piece: a transverse body section and a longitudinal knob-head section.

The body sample of a circular cross section has common copper corrosion products. The metal is pale and there are gray-blue noncuprous oxide inclusions present. Spectrographic analysis indicates that this is a pure copper with only 0.02 percent Ag as an impurity. It has definitely been cast and subsequently worked and heat treated.

The longitudinal knob-head section is roughly pentagonal, with the top and corner areas showing some deformation. The flow lines and strain markings, which appear upon etching, indicate that the knob head was hammered into its present shape almost entirely from the cast rod. The piece was also annealed but not after its last cold working (pl. 8.1c).

The body section has large equiaxed grains with numerous strain markings and twins when etched. It was also worked after the last anneal. Flow lines indicate hammering perpendicular to the long axis of the pin which resulted in the circular cross section. A Vickers hardness test of the knob head indicates some edge hardening and a very high average DPH 185 kg/mm^2.

The object was not found in direct association with any features or architectural exposure. It was found in trash deposits outside houses of period VC in the northern step-trench. The trash deposits were relatively void of cultural materials but rich in paleobotanical materials that provided an excellent corpus for flotation.

T. Yahya C tt5-3 1970 (fig. 8.4) is a copper bead fragment 1.1 cm in width totally corroded with malachite and cuprite layers. It is roughly rectangular in cross section with rounded corners.

This object is slightly earlier than the C-7-15 pin previously discussed. It was found embedded within bricks in a wall directly beneath the C-7-15 architecture and thus represents the earliest phase of period VC. There is no ready explanation as to why the object was found within a typical thumb-impressed brick.

Period VB–VA represents a fluorescence of technological innovations at T. Yahya. Item XCE tt2-3 1973 (fig. 8.5) is a copper pin. 8.1 cm in length × 0.3 cm in width. The light gray resin attached to the upper body on all sides was probably used as hafting material. The pin is rectangular in cross section until 2.8 cm above the point, where the metal has been hammered into a shape with a circular cross-section.

A longitudinal section of the point area, which is narrow and deformed, has corrosion at the surface. There are a number of large spherical cuprous oxide inclusions with no apparent directionality, and the metal has a reddish hue.

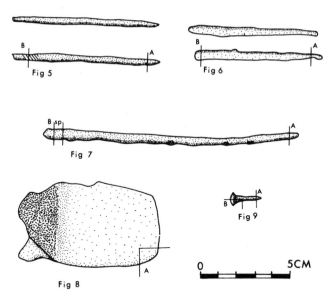

Figs. 8.5–8.9. Fourth millennium copper and copper–arsenic objects.

The section when etched has very small grains, annealing twins, and a few strain markings. Spectrographic analysis reveals only 0.04 percent Ag as an impurity. A Vickers hardness test on the point area indicated no edge hardening and an average VHN of 120.

A transverse section at the opposite end of the pin is rectangular in cross section with rounded corners. There are several small cavities along the surface. The cuprous oxide inclusions are not distorted. The etched section has very small equiaxed grains, strain markings, and twins. This pin was cast into a rod and then hammered and annealed into its final shape.

This pin was found in fill directly beneath period VA architecture. The associated ceramics within the series of lenses and trash levels were all of period VB. No architecture was evident in the 30 cm of trash levels beneath which was a period VB architectural exposure. It appears that the area in which this pin was found is a late VB trash area associated with architecture not evident in the excavated portions of the trench.

A copper pin/stylus, B 18 1971 (fig. 8.6), is also rectangular in cross section except for the point area, which is circular in cross section. The end of the pin is flattened, probably for hafting.

A longitudinal section of the well-rounded point area is mostly corroded. The small remaining metallic areas show extreme elongation and distortion of the cuprous oxide inclusions, indicating working. There are small areas of "white phase" present. The spectrographic analysis of this piece shows 1.5 percent As, 0.03 percent Ag, and 0.96 percent Sb. The antimony is unusual but the percentage of arsenic is similar to that found by Tylecote and McKerrell analyses.[21]

A transverse section from the opposite end of the pin/stylus is rectangular in cross section with slightly distorted corners. It has a corroded surface with a blue layer between the cuprite and the remaining metallic area. There are also numerous, very elongated gray-blue inclusions in the metal that are not cuprous oxide. When etched, the metal contains strain markings, very small equiaxed grains, and twins. The fine grains suggest chill castings. This piece was probably cast into a rock and hammered and annealed into its final shape.

This pin/stylus comes from the latest VA context. It was found in disturbed fill which uniformly underlies the period IVC architectural complex. The associated materials in this fill are exclusively of VA type and do not suggest the mixing of IVC and VA when the IVC building complex was constructed. Rather, they appear to be VA trash levels in which there existed a simple feature: an infant burial laid out in a brick-lined tomb.

C-S-8 1969 (fig. 8.7) is a copper pin (14 cm in length × 0.6 cm in maximum diameter) circular in cross section with a rounded, blunt, and deformed point. The nonpointed end of the pin is rounded.

A transverse section of the point is semicircular and reveals the common surface corrosion products. There are very large undistorted cuprous oxide inclusions, but the piece appears essentially as cast. When etched, the section has twins, small equiaxed grain size, and a few strain markings near the edge. The spectrographic analysis indicates the presence of only 0.008 percent Ag as an impurity.

A transverse section of the end of the pin is circular and shows very large undistorted cuprous oxide inclusions. Etching with potassium dichromate and ferric chloride in alcohol reveals twins and some strain markings around the edges of the section. This pin was cast into a rod and hammered and annealed into its final form.

The pin was found in a layer of stones and sherds directly beneath a wall of the C-7 architecture previously discussed. The rooms of this building complex were constructed over a layer of rubble for foundation support. The pin C-5-8 1969 was located in this rubble.

A flat ax, XC tt1-7 1970 (fig. 8.8), appears to have been cast into a single-piece rod. It is 7.7 cm in length × 3.5 cm in width × 0.1 cm in thickness. The blade edge is wide and has rounded corners.

A transverse section of the rounded, blunt, and undeformed blade edge has the usual corroded surface. The piece was hammered and annealed. The etched section has small equiaxed grains, annealing twins, and a few strain markings. The cuprous oxide inclusions are elongated parallel to the top and bottom of the blade. The edge has not been work hardened. Spectrographic analysis indicates only 0.07 percent Ag as an impurity. This ax was cast and then extensively hammered and annealed.

This flat ax was found resting on a partly preserved plastered surface of a VA architectural exposure. The entire house plan could not be determined within the limited exposure. No extraordinary features or attributes were associated with the house. Beneath an articulating room we excavated one of the three period VA infant burials. The burial appears to have been placed beneath the floor of the house in a flexed east-west position with head facing the south. Two painted VA pots were interred with the infant.

A copper nail, XC tt-2-2-5 1971 (fig. 8.9), is 1.6 cm in length × 0.7 cm in diameter at the head × 0.05 cm in diameter at the point. The point, blunt and deformed from use, has the usual corroded surface. This sample has numerous cuprous oxide inclusions which have been elongated by hammering and which curve in the direction of the point. Etching reveals annealing twins, strain markings, and medium-sized grains.

A longitudinal section of the nail head, whose surface has several small depressions along its edge, shows little distortion and a well-formed shape. It contains numerous, very large cuprous oxide inclusions with no distortion. When etched, the section contains numerous twins, no strain markings, and a large grain size. A hardness test across the nail head section indicates a small amount of edge hardening and an average DPH of 100. This nail, cast into shape and slightly retouched by hammering and annealing, was slowly cooled after the last anneal.

This nail was found in fill directly above a plastered basin of unknown function located outside an architectural complex. All the materials associated were of period VA. There was no evidence of burning around the plastered basin or associated artifacts.

Two ore samples were also examined: XBE 14 1973 and XBE 9a 1973. Both ore pieces were partially shaped by hammering but they were not used for smelting. They are complex sulfide ores containing chalcopyrite, pyrite covellite, iron oxide, and chalcocite based on spectrographic analysis. Their rejection is consistent with an apparent native cuprous oxide–carbonate ore metallurgy as revealed by the objects' impurity patterns. A large copper ingot, XCE tt1-5-1973 (6.2 cm × 5 cm × 4 cm), was also found in VB context. Unlike all other materials discussed, this object was returned to the Iran-Bastan Museum, Tehran, and was not analyzed. It confirms the use of produced metal rather than solely native copper by VB times.

The early 4th millennium sequence at Yahya is extremely important for detailing the development of metallurgy at the site. It is during this period that the shift from hammering native copper to the casting, hammering, and annealing of native copper and the copper arsenides and the production of copper by smelting ores first occurs.

PERIOD IVC (3200–2900 B.C.)

Period IVC is an extremely interesting period in terms of trade. Metallurgically it represents a continuity of period VA + B technology associated with a change in stylistic forms. There have been more than 20 metal objects and production artifacts recovered from the IVC context. The objects include simple pins, elaborately decorated pins, bracelets, decorative items, spatulas, nails, and beads. During this period pins with elaborate headed and decorative pieces dominate the metal corpus, as they do at contemporary Susa. It is also during this period and the succeeding one, IVB, that copper arsenic alloying is fully and most completely utilized.

Period IVC at Yahya is of considerable interest and of great significance. Unlike preceding periods the IVC architectural exposure represents a single large structure which is not domestic in nature. The architecture and associated remains support our contention that the IVC complex is a proto-Elamite administrative center. Settlement surveys show that there is a slight gap in occupation at Yahya between periods VA and IVC. Our survey data also indicate a dramatic shift in population numbers, from 52 period VA sites to 27 Aliabad sites, (the period in which Yahya is uninhabited between periods VA and IVC) and finally only 3 period IVC sites. These data convincingly suggest a population decrease or shift from sedentarism to nomadic subsistence patterns. It is interesting to note that at the time of greatest political centralization evidenced by the IVC administrative complex there is the least evidence for population density. The various hypotheses of cause and explanation of this phenomenon have been dealt with elsewhere.[22]

The period IVC architectural exposure, over 450 m² and extending into the bulk of unexcavated areas, represents a simple building complex with evidence for changes in the architectural plan over time. Period IVC represents the expansion of proto-Elamite control from its center in Khuzistan to the eastern portions of the Iranian plateau around 3000 B.C. This process of proto-Elamite expansion can be further documented at Godin Tepe in northwestern Iran and at Sialk, near Kashan in central Iran. In each instance the proto-Elamites established their colony within an indigenous and distinctive culture. The expansion of the proto-Elamites, we have agreed, was facilitated by their strong centralized political state in Khuzistan and their desire to control foreign resources and trade routes, and was directed toward incorporating the productive economics of foreign culture areas.[23] The materials of period IVC include proto-Elamite tablets, cylinder sealings, cylinder seals, Jamdet-Nesr type ceramics, beveled-rim bowls, bowls of chlorite, alabaster, beads of agate, carmelian, turquoise, and clay and metal implements (decorated pins, knives, chisels). The entirety of this inventory was found on the floors of different rooms of the complex.

A copper pin roughly circular in cross section and 7.7 cm in length × 0.4 cm in maximum width, BW/CW 12–1 1971 (fig. 8.10) has a broken and dull point. A transverse section from the end of the pin is irregular in shape. The metal is pale in color with a number of irregular, very small, gray, elongated inclusions. There are a number of large gray inclusions between the metallic core and the cuprite layer. Spectrographic analysis shows the addition of 1.35 percent As and a 0.16 percent Ag impurity. The longitudinal section of the point shows a flat sharply angled edge. The inclusions are oriented parallel to the sides of the piece and broken up into stringers. The inclusions include both a gray-blue

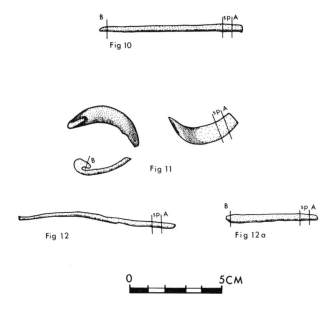

Figs. 8.10–8.12a. Late 4th and 3rd millennia copper, copper–lead, and copper–arsenic objects.

material and cuprous oxide. Etching reveals very small grain size, numerous strain markings, and a few annealing twins. This pin was manufactured by casting a rod and hammering the metal into its final shape and annealing. The piece was worked after the last anneal.

The copper bracelet with a hook, XBE tt1–10 1973 (fig. 8.11) is roughly rectangular in cross section. This fragment, 3.8 cm in length × 0.9 cm in width, has a hammered-over hook at one end. Spectrographic analysis indicates that this object contains 1.04 percent Pb, 0.9 percent Ag, and 0.48 percent Ni as impurities.

A transverse sample, irregular in cross section, made across the bracelet has the usual surface corrosion with a blue layer between the metal and the cuprite. There are numerous elongated gray lead inclusions.

A longitudinal section of the hook also has the blue material between the cuprite and the metallic area. The metal is pale in color and has numerous distorted inclusions. The point is broad and very irregular. The etched section has a large number of annealing twins and very small equiaxed grains; there are no strain markings. A Vickers hardness test of this section indicates no edge hardening and an average DPH of 100. This bracelet was cast into a rectangular bar and extensively hammered and annealed into its final shape.

A fragment of copper wire, C 1 1969 (fig. 8.12), is circular in cross section, 8.6 cm in length × 0.13 cm in diameter. A spectrographic analysis of a sample from this object includes only 0.03 percent Ag as an impurity. A longitudinal section has the usual surface corrosion. It has elongated inclusions and a U-shaped cavity formed when the flat sheet was folded over to form the wire. There are some white inclusions in the cuprite. Etching reveals very small grains, twins, and strain markings; the intergranular corrosion follows the flow lines across the sample.

A copper pin, circular in cross section, B 20 (fig. 8.12a), has a broken point and an elongated blunt end, probably for hafting purposes. It is 5 cm in length × 0.4 cm in maximum diameter. Spectrographic analysis indicates that this is pure copper with 0.3 percent Ag and 0.4 percent Ni as impurities. A longitudinal section shows the point to be rounded, blunt, and with a lot of intergranular corrosion. The cuprous oxide inclusions are very elongated, and there are some large white phase inclusions present. When etched, the section contains strain markings, twins, and very small grains.

A longitudinal section of the elongated blunt end shows elongated distorted stringers. It has the usual surface corrosion and a thin blue inclusion between the cuprite and the metallic areas. The end is well rounded and has some intergranular corrosion. There are some white metallic inclusions present, possibly domeykite. When etched, this piece also has small equiaxed grains, annealing twins, and a few strain markings. The pin was cast and then hammered and annealed into its final shape.

Several ore and slag pieces were recovered from a IVC context. The ore based on X-ray diffraction and X-ray fluorescence analysis tends to be mainly malachite with substantial quantities of iron oxide, which may have acted as a flux. The slag recovered needs further analysis but appears to be a fluid and well-heated slag with fayalite and wüstite formation. The copper left in the slag is in small spherical drops.

This period is notable mostly for the increase in status-like decorative pins and the decrease in tool objects.

PERIOD IBV (2800–2400 B.C.)

Period IVB can be stratigraphically divided into IVB₁ (2600–2400
B.C.) and IVB₂ (2800–2600 B.C.). The distinction is an important one,
for it separates two stratigraphic aspects of this period which are of
fundamental significance. Period IVB₂ consists of an exposure of domestic architecture built *directly* on the wall of earlier period IVC.
The alignment of the building is, however, entirely different. Within
the 350 m² of exposure in the south step-trench we have recovered
a simple two-room house complex, two subsurface kilns, portions of
two other rooms, and three large articulated above-surface ovens.
Two Persian Gulf-type seals and a simple cylinder seal were found
on the floor of the rooms. In addition, a number of chlorite vessels
were found with carved motifs, birds, and geometric motifs.[24] It is
important to realize, however, that the carved chlorite is not of the more
typical "inter-cultural style."[25] On the floor of the structures and in
the above-lying fill were found numerous alabaster and calcite bowl
fragments. In addition to the metal objects discussed below from period IVB₂, we found on the floor of one room a well-preserved, large,
and heavy shaft-hole ax. This ax remains in the Iran-Bastan Museum
and has not been submitted for analysis. It is the heaviest and largest
metal object from the 3d millennium at Tepe Yahya, being approximately the size of a modern day ax-head. The ovens and kilns of period
IVB₂ do not appear to be for industrial production of ceramics or metal
—no slag or associated materials were recovered. If, as we suspect, the
pieces were for cooking, their size would indicate cooking for larger
numbers than occur within a nuclear family.

   Period IVB₁ projects an enigmatic picture. In the north and south
step-trenches we have uncovered a total of over 450 m² of IVB₁ and
a consistent picture emerges. Directly above the IVB₂ architecture is
a series of floors, surfaces, and lenses entirely sealing the lower IVB₂
architecture. The total accumulation of IVB₁ ranges from 0.5 to 1.5
m. In no instance have we recovered an architectural complex within
IVB₁—only rare disarticulated walls, pits, and an occasional hearth.
On the surface and floors we recovered hundreds of carved chlorite
bowl fragments in every stage of production. This evidence, together
with the discovery of four chlorite mining areas within 25 km of
Yahya, supports the contention that Yahya was at this time engaged

in the large scale production of carved chlorite bowls of intercultural style. Additionally, a program of neutron activation analysis indicated that the mines and production of chlorite at Yahya were for a foreign market.[26] The ceramics of IVB_2 indicate direct continuity from IVB_1.

The metal corpus of period IVB contains the highest percentage of copper–arsenic alloyed objects and exhibits a sophisticated technology despite the lack of a comparable aesthetic development in metal objects. There are ca. 65 metal objects and metallurgical production artifacts that date to this period. The objects include pins, needles, blades, spatulas, projectile points, beads, decorated pins, rings, and chisels. The pieces in period IVB_1 especially tend to be more tool oriented than those from period IVC, suggesting their use in chlorite bowl production. The presence of Fe, Ni, and in one sample, Sn, in addition to Ag as impurities raises the question of whether sulfide ores were utilized during this period. It must be noted that the earlier Shahr-i-Sokhta and contemporaneous Susa material have the same impurities. At Shahri-i-Sokhta the use of copper-rich sulfide ores, such as chalcocite and covellite, has been documented by current research.[27]

A copper spatula, B-2-6 1973 (fig. 8.13) (period IVB_2), is roughly rectangular in cross section with rounded edges. The tang is tapered and the corners are rounded, probably for hafting. It is 7.3 cm in length × 1.6 cm in maximum blade width × 0.3 cm in thickness. The spectrographic analysis of a sample from this piece contains 1.4 percent As, 0.001 percent Ag, and 0.05 percent Ni.

A transverse section of the tang end shows an irregular and distorted edge. A large diagonal cavity in the section shows that the spatula was cast in a single-piece mold and the tang section was hammered into shape. There are a large number of cuprous oxide inclusions which are elongated in the same direction as the cavity. The etched section reveals the presence of a highly cored cast structure heavily deformed from working. There are a large number of strain markings and very small grains.

A transverse section of the spatula blade reveals a rounded, blunt, and deformed edge. There is intergranular corrosion present, particularly at the blade edge. The metal is pale in color, probably from the presence of the arsenic in the object. The numerous cuprous oxide inclusions are elongated and broken up, indicating a number of cold working and annealing sequences. Etching shows the extensive deforma-

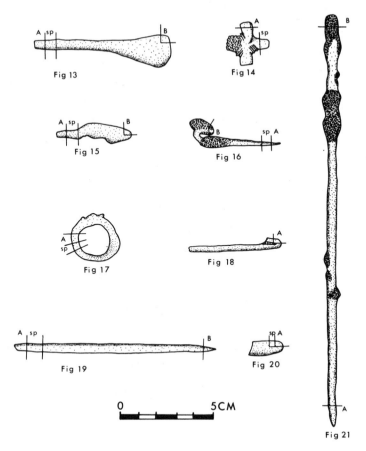

Figs. 8.13–8.21. Third millenium copper, copper–arsenic, and copper–tin objects.

tion of the copper–copper arsenic phases. There are many strain markings and a medium grain size.

The object was found in a IVB$_2$ pit filled with stone rubble, bone, and sherds. The pit was 1.7 m wide and 0.8 m deep. The spatula was found toward the bottom of this trash pit.

A perforated X-shaped bead, XC tt2-2B 1970 (fig. 8.14) (IVB$_1$), is one of the more interesting pieces from this period. It is 2.4 cm in length and width x 0.5 cm in thickness and has a drilled perforation diagonally through the bead. It also has a series of grooves incised into the outer edges. Spectrographic analysis of a sample from the object indicates the presence of 3.4 percent As, 0.002 percent Ag, and 2.4 percent Pb.

This bead is one of the only copper–arsenic–lead alloys from Tepe Yahya, an alloy well suited to use to cast this intricately decorated object. The bead retains its as-cast condition.

A transverse section of one of the appendages of the X is square in cross section with rounded corners. It has extensive intergranular corrosion, but the section retains its original cast dendritic structure. Lead is present as large spherical inclusions.

This object was found on a finely plastered floor outside an architectural complex; the minimal exposure and the presence of a simple well suggest it is within a building complex. It was excavated from the northern step-trench, where the stratigraphic division between IVB_1 and IVB_2 is not as clear as on the south side of the mound. It is, however, not probable that this piece belongs to period IVB_2.

A small (4 cm in length × 0.9 cm in maximum width) projectile point, XB tt2–6 1971 (fig. 8.15), has been cast in a single-piece mold which is rectangular in cross section. A transverse section of the tang has extensive intergranular corrosion as well as the usual surface corrosion. There are numerous elongated cuprous oxide inclusions. There are also several white inclusions visible, which, according to electron microbeam probe analysis, contain a copper-high (ca. 12%) arsenic phase. The etched sample has very small equiaxed grains with some annealing twins and a few strain markings. This projectile point was cast and then fashioned into final shape with a number of cold working and annealing sequences. A longitudinal section of the blade edge was entirely corroded and has the usual surface corrosion. The point is deformed and rounded, although it is thin.

A single spiral-headed pin circular in cross section, XC tt2–2D 1970 (fig. 8.16), has a rounded and blunt point. The head has been hammered from the body of a cast rod and shows some deformation. The pin is 4.7 cm in length × 0.6 cm in maximum diameter. Spectrographic analysis shows that the piece contains 1.6 percent As and 0.002 percent Ag. A longitudinal section of the very deformed point area is totally corroded and contains the usual surface corrosion.

A longitudinal section at the bend in the spiral head has extensive intergranular corrosion which has outlined some equiaxed grains. The metal is pale in color. The numerous cuprous oxide inclusions are slightly elongated. There are some white copper–arsenic inclusions remaining. The etched section contains strain markings, some annealing twins, and medium-sized, roughly equiaxed grains. The spiral head was formed by cold working and annealing the cast rod of the pin.

A pale copper ring circular in cross section, BW tt5-5 1969 (fig. 8.17) (IVB_1), has been manufactured by hammering a straight rod in such a way as to bend it until the ends met. It is 2.5 cm in diameter and made from a rod 0.3 cm in diameter. A transverse section from the ring has the usual surface corrosion, with some intergranular corrosion which has outlined large equiaxed grains. There are a large number of irregularly shaped cuprous oxide inclusions evenly located throughout the section. Etching reveals a large number of annealing twins and a large grain size.

The spectrographic analysis shows the absence of arsenic with 0.003 percent Ag, 0.61 percent Ni, 0.34 percent Fe, and 0.1 percent Sn present as impurities. This is a unique combination of impurities at Yahya and may represent a different technology, possibly from sulfide ore use and/or the trading of a finished metal object from Shahr-i-Sokhta or points east, where metal with this impurity pattern is more common. The presence of tin is notable but not totally surprising in light of Tylecote and McKerrell's report stating the presence of 8 percent tin in an object from a IVB context.[28]

This piece was found in a typical IVB_1 context. In an area over 100 m² a simple good surface was isolated on which we recovered dozens of carved chlorite bowl fragments, a simple hearth, and several small trash pits. On this surface we recovered this copper ring as well as a number of other copper implements.

A copper needle, BW tt5-5 1969 (fig. 8.18) (IVB_1), has the eye formed by hammering over the end of the rod up on itself. The point is broken off. The needle, which is circular in cross section, measures 3.5 cm in length × 0.3 cm in diameter. This is a well-manufactured piece and far less crude than similar types found elsewhere in Iran and assigned to the same period.

A longitudinal section of the bend of the eye is almost totally corroded with the presence of usual copper corrosion products. The curvature is regular and even. The metallic area has slightly elongated cuprous oxide inclusions. Spectrographic analysis of another sample from the same object indicates the presence of 1.2 percent As and 0.008 percent Ag.

A large plain pin, 11 cm in length × 0.5 cm in maximum width, BW tt5 1969 (fig. 8.19), has the remains of a wooden handle as a concretion. There is no evidence of the resin or rope used to haft the wood handle to the pin, the point of which is sharp and narrow. The pin is square in cross section except for the area 3 cm up from the point, which is circular in cross section.

A transverse section of the blunt end has slightly rounded corners. It has the usual surface corrosion as well as three small cavities from hammered folds in the metal. There are a large number of undistorted cuprous oxide inclusions. The metal is pale in color. The etched sample has very small equiaxed grains, and a slightly distorted cored structure. Spectrographic analysis shows that the piece contains 1.4 percent As, 0.068 percent Ag, and 0.54 percent Fe. The presence of iron as an impurity in this period, and in the succeeding period IVA, as well as at 3d millennium levels at Susa and Shahr-i-Sokhta may indicate either the rise and development of a new sulfide-ore-based metal technology, the decrease of technical proficiency in removing iron oxide from the metal, or the increased use of iron as a flux.

A longitudinal section from the point of this piece reveals a blunt flat, actually blade-like pointed end. This may be due to deformation but the edge is not distorted and is quite small. Such a tool would have served well for carving the small details on the chlorite bowls. The metal is pale in color and contains elongated cuprous oxide inclusions. When etched, a distorted cored structure is visible; there are also some strain markings. The pin almost retains its as-cast shape, although it has been slightly cold worked and annealed.

A chisel blade fragment, B-1-4 1970 (fig. 8.20) (IVB$_1$), is rectangular in cross section. It is 1.9 cm in length × 0.7 cm in maximum width × 0.3 cm in maximum thickness and has a distorted flattened blade edge. The blade is thick and dull with rounded corners. A longitudinal section of the piece has the usual surface corrosion. It has numerous very elongated cuprous oxide inclusions which form a lamellar-like structure. There is intergranular corrosion primarily at the rounded and deformed blade edge, which has outlined some small equiaxed grains. The etched section reveals an elongated, deformed cored structure with annealing twins and strain markings. Spectrographic analysis indicates 0.38 percent Ni as the only impurity. A Vickers hardness test does not indicate any edge hardening and an average DPH of 90. The chisel was cast and then extensively cold worked and annealed.

This object was also found on one of the surfaces (beneath the previous surface of the BW tt5-5 object) so characteristic of period IVB_1. No features were found in association with the object.

A large circular copper stylus, reddish in color and measuring 22.5 cm in length, B 13 1970 (fig. 8.21) (IVB_2), is pure copper without any significant impurities. A longitudinal section of the rounded and blunt point area shows the presence of surface corrosion products. The object had numerous elongated cuprous oxide inclusions which re-formed into spheres after annealing. The inclusions are cuprous oxide globules. The etched section contains small elongated grains. annealing twins, and some bent twins.

A transverse section of the blunt end is circular and very corroded. and there are a large number of elongated cuprous oxide inclusions which have formed stringers. When etched the section reveals twins, bent twins, strain markings, and small elongated grains. This stylus has been subjected to a series of cold working and annealing sequences.

Two crucible fragments were discovered in a IVB context. The crucibles are handmade, coarse chaff-tempered ware. They indicate, based on grain size alteration analysis by Dr. W. Kingery and Robert Cava, that the inside surface of the crucibles was heated to a higher temperature than the outside surface.

An irregularly shaped metal piece, BW tt5-4 1969 (pl. Id), is 2.2 cm × 1.8 cm × 1.1 cm in size. The metallic area, with several blowholes, has two phases: a large, reddish, copper-rich phase and a pale white phase, probably algodonite, which has some gray-blue inclusions. The white phase occurs as veinlets around the dendritic, cast copper-rich phase. The piece is in the as-cast condition.

This object also shows that corrosion preferentially attacks the copper-rich phase, which is the reason for white phase inclusions remaining in cuprite areas. The artifact is most probably a spilled/splashed residue from a casting/smelting operation which helps to prove the presence of metal production at Tepe Yahya itself during the IVB period. Electron microbeam probe studies of this sample show that the red phase is copper rich with 1 percent arsenic concentration and the white area is a copper–arsenic phase with 12 percent arsenic.

PERIOD IVA (2400–1800 B.C.)

Period IVA represents perhaps the longest period of direct cultural continuity at Tepe Yahya. To date we have recovered over 300 m² of three superimposed levels of architecture in the south step-trench and 200 m² of four superimposed architectural levels in the north step-trench. Although there is strong evidence to support chronological continuity from IVB to IVA, there are also significant differences between the two major periods in material inventory. Architecture is well preserved and domestic in nature. The houses are often appointed with chimneyed hearths and plastered floors and walls. The rooms are large and the material remains in the rooms suggest a considerable amount of wealth and resources uniformly distributed within the community. Unlike the immediately earlier periods there is little evidence to suggest the large scale manufacture of any commodity for a centralized administrative authority. The settlement is suggestive of an agriculturally productive community without obvious craft or class distinctions. Few objects are indicative of large scale exchange with foreign communication. Chlorite is present but no longer in the intercultural style, ceramics are in the majority unpainted (5 sherds can be identically paralleled in the Kaftari levels at Tepe Malyun in Iran) and without ready parallel in Iran, save for the cemetery at Shah-dad.[29] The cylinder seals found are of a crude, degenerate style without parallel. The materials of period IVA have been reviewed elsewhere.[30]

It is important here to point out (1) the long direct, chronological continuity of period IVA, (2) the imposing domestic architecture and apparent equal distribution of wealth, suggestive of a productive "middle class" agricultural community, (3) the near absence of typological parallels in the ceramics to other sites on the Iranian plateau (save for Shah-dad), (4) the presence of two etched carnelian beads, a stamp-sealing on a sherd of Harappan script, and a Harappan terra-cotta cake with a stamp seal of a dancing cross-legged man. This latter material remains the only evidence on the Iranian plateau which indicates contact and contemporaneity with the Indus civilization.

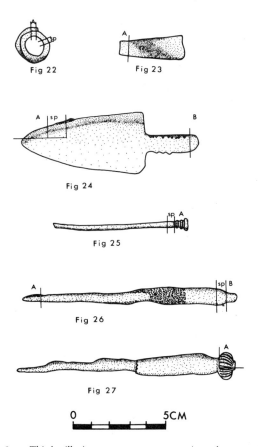

Figs. 8.22–8.27. Third millenium copper, copper–arsenic, and copper–tin objects.

The metal corpus of period IVA is large and impressive, both technologically and stylistically. The frequent use of a copper arsenic alloy
(although decreased in frequency from period IVB), the suspected use
of sulfide ores, and the excellent use of the total range of casting, hammering, and annealing indicate a technological continuity from the
other periods. The 45 objects recovered include pins, hooks, rods,
spatulas, awls, needles, clips, decorated pins, blades, projectile points,
and a crucible fragment.

A reddish copper ring, XBE tt2-2 1973 (fig. 8.22), was found inside
a ceramic storage vessel in the lowest IVA architecture in the northern
step-trench. This ring, 2 cm in diameter, was manufactured by ham-

mering a rectangular rod to form $1\frac{1}{2}$ complete circles. Spectrographic analysis of a sample from this object indicates that the ring is made of pure copper without significant impurities. Two sections were taken for metallographic analysis: section 1 is the outer end of the ring, and section 2 is an inner section which has undergone less working. Both have the usual surface corrosion. Both are rectangular in cross section.

Section 1 has a large number of cuprous oxide inclusions that have been elongated by working and re-formed into spheres. The corners of the section are irregular and slightly rounded. The section, when etched, contains strain markings, medium-sized slightly elongated grains, and distinctive flow lines that run parallel to the long side of the section.

Section 2 has a number of small spherical cuprous oxide inclusions. This section has been reduced less than section 1. Etching reveals a more random flow line pattern, medium sized grains, and some annealing twins. This ring was made by a series of cold working and annealing sequences which bent the rod over on itself.

A knife blade fragment, XBE tt1-2 1973 (fig. 8.23), found directly on the floor of the lower most IVA architecture in the northern step-trench is lenticular in cross section. It measures 4 cm in length × 1.7 cm in maximum width and is heavily corroded. A transverse section through the blade reveals a rounded blade edge. The section has the usual surface corrosion and some intergranular corrosion at the blade edges. It has large, irregularly shaped cuprous oxide inclusions and no copper arsenic corrosion. When etched, elongated grains, bent twins, strain markings, twins and some deformed equiaxed, medium sized grains become visible. The grains appear smaller at both edges. This knife blade, which was cast and then cold worked and annealed, was worked after the final anneal.

A large well-made projectile point, B-BW tt2-12 1970 (fig. 8.24), has a beveled blade edge and incised tang. It comes from the fill of the third, earliest building level of IVA. There is also a slight midrib. The blade is lenticular in cross section; the tang is rectangular. It is 10 cm in length × 3.7 cm in maximum width at the blade–tang junction. It appears that the incised decoration on the tang was cast with a piece and that then grooves were chiseled out.

A transverse section of the blade from the midrib thickening to the edge shows a thin and well-made point. It has a slight bevel 0.5 cm from the blade edge on one side. There is extensive intergranular corrosion.

The grains are elongated and distorted; the inclusions are elongated and gray-green. The section has the usual corrosion. The etched section has small grains, annealing twins, and strain markings. It has been work hardened after a final anneal. A Vickers hardness test indicates the blade edge has a DPH of 150 while the center section has a DPH of 112. Spectrographic analysis indicates that this object is made of copper with 0.43 percent Ni and 0.17 percent Fe as impurities.

A transeverse section of the tang was totally corroded. The sides are slightly rounded. No evidence for the nature of the decoration could be determined.

A circular pin 7.7 cm in length with a series of grooves and ridges on the head, XBE tt2-2-29 and 30 1973 (fig. 8.25) has a broken point. The incised grooves and ridges have been cast with the piece and then finished with a chisel-like tool. A longitudinal section of the decorated head indicates that the object was cast as a single piece and the incised decoration retouched afterward. The lack of deformation around the irregularly shaped, raised ridges shows that the basic shape is as cast. The section has the usual corrosion. The metal is very pale in color with numerous elongated inclusions and intergranular corrosions. The etched section has equiaxed grains and annealing twins. Spectrographic analysis shows 2.2 percent arsenic and no impurities. This pin was cast and then the incised decoration added by cold working and annealing. It was not worked after the final anneal.

This object came from the second architectural level of period IVA in the northern step-trench. It is in this level that the etched carnelian beads and the two Harappan sealings were found. The architecture is substantial and well preserved and materials associated on the floors are among the most valid of period IVA.

A pin, B-2-1 1969 (fig. 8.26), 12.1 cm in length and circular in cross section, has a head which has been elongated and bent over by hammering. A longitudinal section of the point, which is rounded and blunt, is totally corroded. The point, which shows the usual corrosion, is large and seems to have been deliberately flattened and expanded.

A transverse section of the head reveals large and irregularly shaped gray-green inclusions. The head was hammered from the top of the body of the pin, which is circular in cross section. Intergranular corrosion has outlined small equiaxed grains. The etched section reveals twins, bent twins, and small grains. Spectrographic analysis shows that this is a low-tin bronze with ca. 2.4 percent tin, 0.007 percent Ag, and 0.42 percent Fe as impurities. It is compositionally very similar to a IVB piece. This pin was cast and then the head of the pin was elongated by a number of cold working and annealing sequences.

This object was found directly beneath a plastered floor of the latest IVA architecture in the southern step-trench. It represents the last period of IVA occupation of Yahya, which has uncorrected C_{14} dates between 1600 and 1700 B.C.

A large pin with an incised globular bead like head, XBE tt1-1 1973 (fig. 8.27), is an extremely important piece. It resembles 3d millennium pins from Susa, Mesopotamia, and Mehi (Pakistan), although the pins from these locales have lapis beads instead of copper ones. Perhaps this represents provincial stylistic copying. This bead has a flattened raised rod, protruding from the center of its upper surface, that makes the copper sphere appear separate and attached to the pin. In fact, this is a single solid cast piece. The spherical bead has a series of diagonal lines as cast decoration around the outer surface.

A longitudinal section from the head of the very pale pin reveals extensive, blue-gray intergranular corrosion and the usual surface corrosion. No spectrographic analysis was performed. There are a large number of cuprous oxide eutectic-like structures. The etched section reveals as-cast structure with very large equiaxed grains. The inclusions are columnar in pattern. This piece was not worked after casting. The grains near the surface are smaller; and the entire piece was very slowly cooled.

The IVA metal corpus is an impressive one that indicates both technological and stylistic continuity with preceding periods in the use of copper–arsenic and a few low-tin bronze alloys as well as in the use of similar ores and methods of manufacture of the metal and the finished objects.

CONCLUSIONS

It is apparent from the data that none of the evolutionary schemes presented either accounts for the actual technological progression for a single site/region or, more importantly, provides the necessary cultural correlations with the technological developments to be of use archaeologically.

Period VC–VA represents the time when all the metallurgical techniques used for the succeeding 2000 years were introduced at Tepe Yahya. Documentation of the shift from hammered native copper to the use of cast and annealed pure copper and copper–arsenic alloys, the latter formed by the addition of algodonite and domeykite to smelted copper, during a period of cultural continuity cannot be ignored. Whatever the origin of metallurgy, its introduction and rapid development in Iran occur without any major observable cultural discontinuities.

The several evolutionary schemes of metallurgical development thus fail to deal with the problem/solution of the effect of technology on ancient societies. These technological schemes have value and interest but lack use by archaeologists. Only by correlating these developments with other aspects of society can useful questions and solutions about the adoption of technology and its effect on society arise.

The copper–arsenic alloys from period V to the end of period IVA at Tepe Yahya are important. The technological data available throughout the Near East reveal a strong similarity in the introduction, significance, and level of technological competence achieved by the ancient smiths of the copper–arsenic system throughout the 4th millennium. At Tepe Yahya the exploitation of the copper–arsenic minerals, algodonite and domeykite, from the Talmessi mine region of Iran and located ca. 800 km north of Tepe Yahya seems a logical deduction.

There are virtually no copper sulfarsenides in Iran and all the copper–arsenic alloys used in the 4th and 3d millennia apparently derive from the copper arsenides from the unique Talmessi–Messkani mine source. These arsenides are: algodonite ($Cu_{5-8}As$, or 80–87% Cu by weight) and domeykite (Cu_3As, or 72% Cu by weight). These minerals occur with, and have a weathered appearance very similar to that of, native copper.

The copper arsenides can be treated like native copper or smelted metal, although the native Cu–As metal has a lower melting point and must be treated under reducing conditions. Skinner feels that the impurity patterns of early Near Eastern copper–arsenic alloyed objects is consistent with the use of algodonite and domeykite.[31] Selimkhanov has also suggested the use and presence of domeykite in early alloyed objects from Trans-Caucasia.[32]

The Anarak–Talmessi region is the most interesting polymetallic deposit in Iran. The major metallic mineralizations include copper, nickel, cobalt, lead, zinc, iron, and arsenic.[33] Of the many individual mines in this area the major copper deposits are at the Talmessi and Messkani mines. Chalcocite, the primary ore, occurs in veins and impregnations. Nickel arsenides and cobalt arsenides occur as small veinlets. Schurenberg reports that "during the mineralization the content of sulfur diminished while the concentration of arsenic increased so that parts of the copper sulfides were displaced by algodonite and domeykite."[34] These copper arsenides are primarily located near the surface and in the oxidized and secondary enriched zones. This is the area in which native copper is located and these mines have a substantial amount of this material. Smith felt that native copper from the Talmessi mine was used at Tepe Sialk in the earliest periods and continued to be used through the 1st millennium.[35] This native metal contains some copper arsenic phases.

The presence of a polymetallic ore deposit with significant quantities of domeykite and algodonite is unique in Iran and rare in the world.[36] When this easily accessible and relatively plentiful source of arsenic is contrasted with the total lack of enargite and other sulfarsenides in Iran, and in view of the early 4th millennium use of natural copper–arsenic alloys as established in this chapter, this mine region is a prime candidate for the single source of the arsenic used in early Iran.

The similar appearance of weathered native copper and copper–arsenides suggests the use of copper–arsenide minerals along with native copper. Native copper, which had been hammered, is documented in 5th and 4th millennia Iran. The use of copper–arsenic alloys during the first introduction of true metallurgy has also been documented here. The rapid spread of copper–arsenic mineral utilization throughout Iran attests to the success of the alloy, to experimentation and observation by the ancient smiths, and to the communication network of technological ideas/concepts of early 4th millennium Iran. The impurity patterns, ores, and slags examined from Tepe Yahya and elsewhere in Iran suggest an oxide/carbonate ore to metal technology consistent both geologically and metallurgically with the use of algodonite and domeykite minerals as the source of arsenic found in the finished objects. The uniqueness of this deposit adds validity to this conclusion and certainly assuages the doubts associated with most examinations of resource source and utilization.

Recent work by McKerrell and Tylecote demonstrates that toxicity is not a problem to those working with copper–arsenic alloys,[37] although Charles in chapter 6 questions this conclusion. Other studies show that copper–arsenic alloys have properties very similar to copper–tin bronze and as such are suitable for sophisticated metallurgical production of tools and ornaments.

Tin bronze, on the other hand, was present at Tepe Yahya only in 3d millennium contexts and then in very limited quantities. These few tin bronze pieces were probably the result of trade/exchange rather than the beginning of a new technological trend in southeast Iran. Tin bronze was extensively used in the contemporary Indus Valley civilization and in the preceding Nal Cemetery[38] and Mundigak III contexts.[39] The presence in period IVA at Tepe Yahya of an Indus seal impression and two etched carnelian beads is suggestive.

Examination of the technological data in light of stylistic and other archaeological information also provides insights into the cultural history of Tepe Yahya. The periods of maximum technological innovation, periods V and IVB, do not represent the periods of major political and social change. The technology of IVA provides valuable and consistent supporting evidence for the presence of a prosperous town at Yahya during this time. The stylistic elaboration of the period IVC pins gives an indication of possible differentiation in social status and the use of metal objects to support this differentiation. This is during a time that the technological continuity indicates an indigenous cultural continuity coupled with the introduction of foreign elements of material culture and possible foreign political-economic control. The lack of stylistic and functional similarities of the metal objects of periods V–IVC, despite the continuity of technology, reflects both the differing utilization of a metallurgical technology diachronically at Tepe Yahya and the synchronic situation throughout Iran.

Throughout the two millennia examined, the technological continuity and consistent synchronic similarities of this technology within Iran strongly suggest technical communication and exchange among Iranian metalsmiths and the presence of an indigenous population of craftsmen throughout the prehistory of Tepe Yahya. It is important to note that there are few stylistic correlations in the metallurgical inventory of any but a general nature that can be postulated among the different regions of Iran during this time span.

The most difficult aspect of this study is determining the effect of the introduction of metallurgy on Tepe Yahya society. There are no drastic observable cultural changes during this period. The metal objects comprise both tools and ornaments, with tools predominant. It does not appear that pure social–wealth differentiation was the sole motivating factor behind the adoption of this technology; in fact, the archaeological assemblage argues convincingly against such an interpretation. Rather, the introduction of copper and copper–arsenic alloys seems to have satisfied an essential and/or profitable demand in society. The continued consumption of metal coupled with the time and resources necessary for its production suggest that social and economic demand were sufficient to stimulate production. It then becomes essential to consider what group of people in society would accept and promulgate such an innovation and what occurs to this group vi-à-vis the rest of society through time.

A close examination of the ethnographic evidence on the acceptance of technological innovations reveals that acceptance of an innovation in an egalitarian society depends on its acceptance by those more equal members of that society.[40] In essence every society including an egalitarian one contains members more respected because of wealth, age, or wisdom. These members or this group controls the acceptance/rejection of technological innovations into that society. The successful acceptance and continued production of the particular innovation soon result in a wide degree of wealth–social status separation in the society with the more equal group established as the elite.

Accepting this model as a postulate by which to examine the Tepe Yahya example, we must fulfill two major preconditions: (1) the proved introduction of a technological innovation that is accepted and becomes an integrated aspect of that society and (2) a shift from an egalitarian to a social status–wealth-differentiated society must occur within a reasonably short period of time. If both these preconditions can be observed, we can begin to suggest that the more equal group in the earlier period becomes the socioeconomic/political elite in the later period.

Examination of the archaeological evidence of period V–IVC at Tepe Yahya and in fact at other contemporaneous Iranian sites does reveal the presence of both preconditions and thus points to the conclusion. Although recent work by Young and Lamberg-Karlovsky suggests that the IVC structure at Yahya represents a proto-Elamite colony, it seems

conceivable that this colony would make use of and/or find its organizational task facilitated by the presence of the more equal elite.[41] This
colony may in fact partially consist of this indigenous elite group.

Our conclusion indicates that the introduction of technological changes
in metallurgical production does not lead to immediate observable
changes in the social system at Tepe Yahya throughout the 4th millennium. A *major* reorientation in the social system at Tepe Yahya is
observable only during period IVC and results from the acculturative
process of proto-Elamite colonization. The changes in period IVC are
not the effect of new technological innovations but rather the direct
result of the introduction of a new proto-Elamite sociopolitical structure. We suggest that the reason for this rests in the distinction between
part-time and full specialists. That is, major changes in the social system
can be observed in the archaeological record only when full-time
specialists are present. At Yahya, the archaeological evidence suggests
that the productive technology in metallurgy is in the hands of part-
time specialists. In no instance do we have at Yahya evidence for large
scale production of metals within specified areas of the community,
and there are no large scale metallurgical installations, i.e., bowl furnaces,
slag heaps, and so on, indicating specialized activity areas of production.
The absence of the above argues against full-time specialists and production. Local production is further suggested by the different uses of
the basic metal technology on contemporary sites (Hissar, Sialk, and
Shahr-i-Sokhta metal analysis is being undertaken by Dennis Heskel).
The essentially different extractive and production technologies on the
above sites argues against centralized production within a single area
and large scale trade in metal goods. Thus, we would relate the major
developments in extractive and production technologies in the 4th millennium on the Iranian plateau with part-time groups (cottage industries) which changed the social structure little if any. This contrasts with
the later presence of full-time specialists, which by their nature transform economic aspects of production and resource management (political institutions controlling large scale commodity trade).

The implications of this situation clearly differ from the common
assumption, namely, that technological innovations lead to rapid and
major changes in social institutions. At Yahya throughout the 4th
millennium, where almost all known copper–bronze metallurgical
techniques are utilized (except sulfide ore extraction), there are no

major changes observable in the archaeological record which reveal quantitative or qualitative changes in the social institutions. The community throughout the 4th millennium seems the have been based on an entirely self-sufficient agricultural productivity with limited trade and weak lines differentiating social status within the community.[42]

Such a study tends to weaken the materialist (economic determinist) reconstruction of historical processes, for as Durkheim has made plain, it is the social milieu, not the antecdent change in a linear succession, that is the background of the causes of change, or "the first origins of all social processes of any importance should be sought in the internal constitution of the social group."[43]

NOTES

1. Carl Clifford Lamberg-Karlovsky, *Excavations at Tepe Yahya 1967–1969*, Progress Report I, American School of Prehistoric Research, Bull. no. 27, Peabody Museum, Harvard University; "The Proto-Elamite Settlement at Tepe Yahya," *Iran* 9 (1971): 87–88; "Tepe Yahya 1971: Mesopotamia and the Indo-Iranian Borderlands," *Iran* 10 (1972): 89–101; "Urban Interaction on the Iranian Plateau: Excavations at Tepe Yahya 1967–1973," *Proceedings of the British Academy* 59 (1974): 64–103; with Maurizio Tosi, "Shahr-i Sokhta and Tepe Yahya: Tracks on the Earliest History of the Iranian Plateau," *East and West* 23, no. 1–2 (1973): 21–58.

2. Vere Gorden Childe, "Archaeological Ages as Technological Stages," *Journal of the Royal Anthropological Institute of Great Britain and Ireland* 74 (1944): 7–24; Theodore Wertime, "The Beginnings of Metallurgy: A New Look," *Science* 182 (1973): 875–87; Colin Renfrew, *Before Civilization* (New York: Knopf, 1972).

3. Childe, "Archaeological Ages as Technological Stages," pp. 14–21.

4. Wertime, "Beginnings of Metallurgy."

5. Ibid.

6. Renfrew, *Before Civilization*, chap. 9.

7. Raphael Pumpelly, *Explorations in Turkestan 1904* (Washington, D. C.: Carnegie Institute, (1908), pp. 178–204.

8. Ibid.

9. For the reports on Hissar see E. Schmidt, *Excavations at Tepe Hissar, Damghan* (Philadelphia: University of Pennsylvia Press, 1937); for Sialk, R. Ghirshman, *Fouilles de Sialk* (Paris: Geuthner, 1938); for Giyan, G. Contenau and R. Ghirshman, *Fouilles du Tepe Giyan* (Paris: Paul Geuthner, 1935); for Geoy Tepe, T. Burton Brown, *Excavations in Azerbaijan,* (London: John Murray, 1948); and for Shah Tepe T. J. Arne, *Excavations at Shah Tepe, Iran* (Stockholm: Elanders Boktryckeri Aktiedbolas, 1945).

10. Henry H. Coghlan, "Some Fresh Aspects of the Prehistoric Metallurgy of Copper," *Antiquaries Journal* 22 (1942): 22–38.

11. Wertime, "Beginnings of Metallurgy," p. 881.

12. Joseph Caldwell, *Excavations at Tal-i Iblis*, Springfield, Illinois State Museum Preliminary Reports, no. 9 (1967); Joseph Caldwell and Shapour M. Shahmirzadi, *Tal-i Iblis: The Kerman Range and the Beginning of Smelting*, Springfield, Illinois State Museum Preliminary Reports, no. 7 (1966).

13. Cyril S. Smith, "Metallographic Study of Early Artifacts Made from Native Copper," *Actes du XIᵉ Congress International d'Histoires des Sciences* (Paris: Centre National Recherche Scientifique 1965), pp. 237–43.

14. Dr. Ulrich Peterson, Department Geology, Harvard University, personal communication. See also H. Schurenberg, "Ueber Iranische Kupfererzvorkommen mit komplexen Kobalt-Nickelerzen," *Jahrbuch Mineralogische Abhandlung* 99 (1963): 200–30.

15. Brian Skinner and Frederich Luce, "Stabilities and Compositions of Alpha-domeykite and Algodonite" *Economic Geology* 27 (1971): 117–29.

16. H. McKerrell and Ronald F. Tylecote, unpublished manuscript on the analysis of six metal artifacts from Tepe Yahya.

17. Jean R. Maréchal, "Etude sure les propriétés mécaniques des cuivres a l'arsenic," *Metaux: Corrosion-Industries*, 33 (1958): 378–83; H. McKerrell and Ronald F. Tylecote, "The Working of Copper-Arsenic Alloys in the Early Bronze Age and their Effect on the Determination of Provenance," *Proceedings of the Prehistoric Society*, new ser. 38 (1972): 209–18.

18. Maréchal, "Étude sur les propriétés mécaniques des cuivres à l'arsenic," pp. 378–81.

19. Smith, "Metallographic Study of Early Artifacts from Native Copper," p. 241.

20. For an illustration of the architecture and provenance of this object see Clifford C. Lamberg-Karlovsky, *Excavations at Tepe Yahya 1967–1969*, Progress Report I, American School of Prehistoric Research, Bulletin no. 27, Peabody Museum, Harvard University, 1970, p. 106.

21. See n. 16.

22. Carl Clifford Lamberg-Karlovsky, "Foreign Relations in the Third Millennium at Tepe Yahya," *La Plateau Iranien et l'Asie Centrale des Origines a la conquete Islamique leurs Relations a la lumiere des Documents Archeologiques* (Paris, 1977), pp. 32–43.

23. Ibid.

24. Lamberg-Karlovsky and Tosi, "Shahr-i-Sokhta and Tepe Yahya," 38–42.

25. Philip Kohl, "The Balance of Trade in the Third Millennium," *Current Anthropology* (1978), in press.

26. Ibid.

27. D. Heskel, (Ph.D. diss., Harvard University), to be published.

28. See n. 16.

29. Ali Hakemi, *Catalogue-Shahdad*, (Tehran: Iran-Bastan Museum, 1972), pp. 13–64.

30. For full references and documentation see n. 1.

31. Skinner and Luce, "Stabilities and Compositions of Alpha-domeykite and Algonodite."

32. I. R. Selimkhanov, "Spektralanalytische Untersuchungen von Metallfunden," *Archaeologica Austriaca* 16 (1960): 71–79; "Spectral Analyses of Metal Articles from Archaeological Monuments of the Caucasus," *Proceedings of the Prehistoric Society* 28 (1962): 68–79.

33. Geological Survey of Iran, *Copper Ore Deposits in Iran*, Report no. 13 (Tehran, 1969), p. 63; see also n. 14.

34. As reported by Schurenberg in n. 14.

35. As reported in Smith, "Metallographic Study of Early Artifacts Made from Native Copper."

36. Dr. Ulrich Petersen, Department of Geology, Harvard University, Jan. 1976, personal communication.

37. As reported by McKerrell and Tylecote in n. 17.

38. Harold Hargreaves, "Excavations in Baluchistan, 1925," *Memoires of the Archae ological Survey of India* 35 (1929): 1–89; Stuart Piggott, *Ancient India* (Baltimore, 1950).

39. Jean M. Casal, *Fouilles de Mundigak*, Mémoires of the French Archaeological Delegation in Afghanistan, vol. 1 (Paris, 1961), p. 37–48.

40. Pertti J. Palto and W. L. Muller "Snowmobiles: Technological Revolution in the Arctic," in *Technology and Social Change*, ed. H. R. Bernard and Pertti J. Palto (New York, 1972); Harry M. Cleaver, Jr., "The Contradictions of the Green Revolution," *Monthly Review* 24 (1972): 80–111; M. Walsh, "Machine Age Maya," *Memoires of the American Anthropologist* 60, pt. 2, no. 2 (1958); W. Edwards, "The Theory of Decision Making," *Decision Making*, ed. W. Edwards and A. Tversky (Baltimore: Penguin, 1967), pp. 13–64.

41. T. Cuyler Young, Jr. and H. Weiss, "The Merchants of Sura: Godin V and Plateau-Lowland Relations in the Late Fourth Millennium B.C.," *Iran* 13 (1975): 1–8; see also reference in n. 22 for a different interpretation.

42. See n. 24 for full reference.

43. Emile Durkheim, *The Rules of Sociological Method* (Glencoe: Free Press, 1950), p. 71.

9

The Central Andes:
Metallurgy without Iron

HEATHER LECHTMAN

*Because of the inconspicuous ubiquity of materials and
the constancy of their individual properties they serve as
a fine touchstone to reveal man's individual and social characteristics.*
Metallurgy is a fully human experience.

Cyril Stanley Smith
"Metallurgy as a Human Experience"

New World metallurgy means Andean metallurgy, for it is the
Andean area alone that developed complex and sophisticated metallurgical technologies, and it is there that for millennia cultural stimuli
supported a high level of commitment to and investment in metallurgy.
Long-standing traditions of metallurgy were maintained in the Andean
culture area; some of these we recognize as typically Andean metallurgical styles.[1] From the Andes metallurgy moved north, where it flourished among the cultures from present-day Panama to Mexico. Yet
even in Mesoamerica it never lost the imprint of the Andean tradition.

Not surprisingly, a sophisticated set of metallurgical technologies
developed in the Andean world. The Andes mountain chain contains
some of the richest ore deposits in the world. The placer golds of
Colombia and Ecuador, the tin fields (cassiterite ores) of Bolivia, the
rich and complex copper ores of Peru and Chile, the silver deposits from
Peru to Bolivia are well known today and were exploited liberally in
pre-Columbian times.[2] The Andes are a veritable mine, and Andean
peoples were sitting right on that mine. The ores they utilized, the metals
and alloys they made, the "direction" their metallurgy took at any given

267

time and in any region of this vast land mass were governed by a complex set of interactions among technical know-how, concepts of and attitudes about metals—what metals are, how they are to be made, to look, and to be used—and sociopolitical events that either allowed regional isolation or fostered pan-Andean communication. We can come close to a full understanding of Andean metallurgy because, as materials scientists, we have available the laboratory procedures to interpret that metallurgy from the objects, the ores, crucibles, and slags that are part of the archaeological record. But we will never understand the Andean metallurgical *tradition*, the style of Andean metallurgy, or even the specific events in Andean metallurgical technology, unless, as anthropologists, we try to reconstruct that technology within the dynamics of a larger cultural framework.

The Search for Models of Metallurgical Development

How did metallurgy develop in ancient societies? For a considerable time this question has been uppermost for many historians of metallurgy and for archaeologists concerned with pyrotechnologies and their relation to culture change. It has led to the formulation of various models that share many of the following features:

  1. Unilineality: metallurgies develop along a certain course, starting from the simplest of technological features (e.g., hammering of native copper) and continuing on to the most complex (such as the smelting of sulfide ores or the manufacture of iron);
  2. Staging: as metallurgies develop along their unilineal course, they pass through a series of stages in an ordered sequence, the stages relating either to the way in which the metal is manufactured[3] or to the way it is utilized;[4]
  3. Evolution: metallurgical stages develop historically from one another; each stage depends upon the preceding stage; there is a fundamental technical "logic" imbedded in the staged development as technological events evolve in a nonrandom and predictable way.[5]

The problems with these and similar models arise from varied sources. Because they rely so heavily upon data from the Old World, most especially from the Near East (where, according to some, metallurgy was not only invented but was uniquely invented), they are not formulated on the basis of cross-cultural, comparative studies. Although certain aspects of these models may hold up regardless of the cultural context of the data, others do not. It is quite likely, for example, that in those areas of the world where native metals were abundant, the earliest techniques for manipulating them included hammering, abrasion, and polishing, the same kinds of techniques already common for working stone. On the other hand, even the maxim that metallurgical technologies proceeded from the simple to the complex may not always be the case, as the new and startling material from Southeast Asia seems to suggest.[6] In Peru, where metallurgy seems to have first appeared in the Andes, there is no reason to believe, for example, that a "melting stage" preceded a "smelting stage." In fact, experimentation with smelting seems to have begun extremely early, perhaps because such a large variety of ores was available and native copper was rare. Certainly the single course, multistaged, quasi-evolutionary track postulated for the Near East does not account for the dynamics of Andean metallurgy.

In an effort to understand *how* metallurgy developed we have begun to look more and more narrowly at the technical events in isolation from the accompanying real world of social human beings. Some perceive "a complex technical logic in early metallurgy;"[7] yet, if there is a pattern in the technological developments themselves, that pattern can only reflect cultural activities—human choices, decisions, and accidents. The logic of early metallurgy is more likely a logic that we, in trying to understand it, have imposed. It is certainly not a logic inherent in the physical properties of metals and ores and it is not a logic determined by ancient craftspeople. To be sure, complex sulfide ores are harder to smelt than simple oxides, and copper could be won from its oxide ores only by reducing it. Such chemical reactions are immutable, and wherever people have smelted ores they have had to make those reactions occur. But there is no autonomy to metallurgy any more than there is to any technological system. Metallurgy is as much a cultural phenomenon as it is a series of physical and chemical phenomena.

We should be asking not only *how* metallurgy developed but *why* it developed as it did in any given setting and at any given time. We have tended to abandon anthropology for history. The new models of metallurgical development are efforts toward a history of early metallurgy rather than an anthropology of early metallurgy. If we were, instead, to rely more heavily upon the case study method, as exemplified in chapter 8 by Heskel and Lamberg-Karlovsky, we could begin to document systematically not only the kinds of interactions people had with their material world but also the factors that seem to have inform-ed those interactions. The patterns that emerge from such studies might not suggest any inner technical logic, but they will surely reflect the "logic" of a functioning sociocultural system of which the technology is one part.

Metallurgy has assumed international importance in archaeological studies—in the Andes, in Africa, in Southeast Asia, in China, in Europe, in Southwest Asia. For the first time we will be in a position to compare data from all the great traditions of early metallurgy—but they must be anthropological data. By that I mean that they must respond to issues that are anthropological in kind, and they must be taken according to the best methods of field and laboratory anthropology. If there is a commonality to the way in which the great metallurgical traditions developed among peoples all over the world *irrespective of culture*—a commonality fixed by the physical and chemical properties of matter and the energy systems required to manipulate those properties—then we will recognize it and build our models accordingly. Only by study-ing culture process—which in this case means studying technologies in cultural contexts—can we tell if certain technological developments are independent of such process and thereby universal. Examining metal-lurgy by itself will never give us the answer. Those are the studies that should allow us to formulate models, if models we must have, for the growth of metallurgical technologies among early societies.

METALLURGY OF THE CENTRAL ANDES: PERU

The Andean culture area is much too large and diverse both geographically and culturally to permit description of its early metallurgy in a brief article.[8] Our discussion is confined to that portion of the Central Andes that is today Peru, since the evidence presently available points strongly to Peru as the area where metallurgy began in the Andes, where it con-tinued to receive consistent input and cultural support enabling it to develop into an important tradition, and whence it spread both to the north and to the south.

Despite the prominence of Peruvian metallurgy in the Andean area, we have relatively little information about that metallurgy or about developments it stimulated in other significant metallurgical centers such as those of Colombia. That is probably because the Andes have quite mistakenly been considered a backwater metallurgically, both in terms of the sophistication of the technology itself and with regard to the levels of metal production. No one, except perhaps Nordenskiöld, has referred to a "Bronze Age" in the Andes and no one would take such a suggestion seriously.[9] Apart from the early work of scholars such as Boman, Ambrosetti, Latcham, Nordenskiöld, Bergsøe, and Mathewson, and that of Root, Caley, and Easby,[10] who have pioneered modern technical studies of Andean metallurgy, the subject has been largely neglected. As a result, we have neither the carefully planned archaeological-laboratory case study research efforts I urge that we undertake nor the overwhelming number of chemical analyses and statistical data on metal objects and ores that grace—or plague—efforts to comprehend the early metallurgies of the Near East and Europe.

In the Andes, we are at the very beginning of our studies of the prehistoric development of metallurgy, yet even with the relatively sparse data at hand it is clear that the Andean tradition was vital and sophisticated and that its course was quite different from that plotted by the model builders for the Old World. It is much too early to see even a glimmer of a model that would fit the Andean picture, but as that picture emerges it makes plain the fact that Andean metallurgy reflects the Andean cultural framework in which it developed; it was greatly influenced by the extremes of the Andean mountain and coastal landscape both with regard to the location of metallic ores and to the difficulty of communication among the peoples who lived in that landscape; and it was clearly a mechanism through which Andean social, political, and religious values could be expressed and manipulated.

The topography of the Central Andean area greatly affected the course of development of Andean civilization (see fig. 9.1). The Andes mountain range dominates the Pacific coast of South America. In the Peruvian region, the seacoast itself is a narrow desert strip, often no more than 20–50 km wide, that hugs the north–south shoreline. The desert is interrupted by a series of some forty river valleys, running in a prevailing east–west direction and carrying water, primarily during the rainy season in the highlands, from the mountains to the dry coast. The river valleys narrow rapidly as they rise abruptly into the rugged mountains to the east.

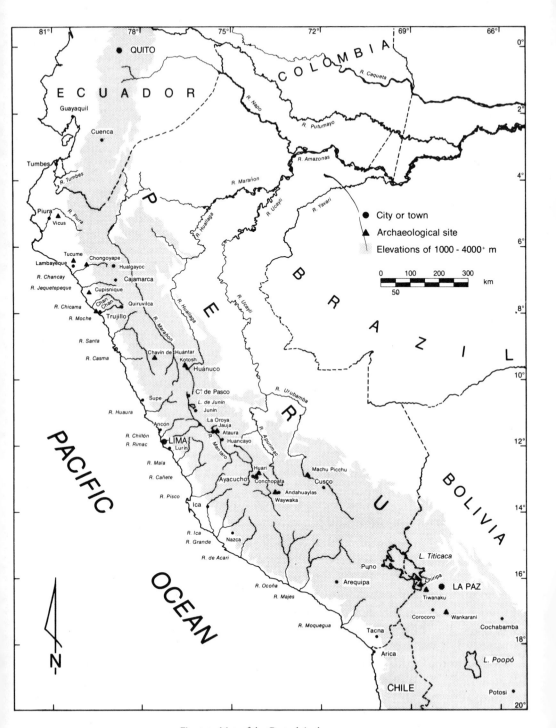

Fig. 9.1. Map of the Central Andean area.

The mountains themselves rise to great heights, are precipitous, extremely difficult to maneuver except on foot, and have always been a
major barrier to easy communication among peoples living in this zone.
Nevertheless, for a considerable period of prehistory, the majority of
Central Andean peoples lived in the highlands, in the fertile intermontane
valleys that occasionally open up in the massive mountain chain (such
as that watered by the Río Urubamba, near Cusco, the capital of the
Inca dynasty), on the high, rolling, and barren *puna* where they grazed
their herds of llamas and alpacas, and on the broad, flat plateau—the
Peru–Bolivia *altiplano*—that rises above 4000 m and lies mainly to the
south and west of Lake Titicaca.

The Andean landscape is a vertical landscape and an isolating one.
People clustered on the desert coast along the river valleys where they
could take advantage of the irrigation potential of river waters at the
same time that they exploited the rich marine life of the Pacific Ocean.
But the desert always remained an obstacle to intervalley communication.
In the sierra, communities lived in pockets, surviving in the harsh environment by utilizing the many ecological zones that change so rapidly
with altitude and exchanging the products of those zones. Movement
was up and down the vertical landscape, rarely north and south along the
backbone of the Andes themselves.

In the main, Central Andean culture history is understandably characterized by regionalism. Whereas the cultures of the south coast of Peru
may have had regular association with peoples of the southern highlands
in a series of kin-based exchange patterns,[11] the political development
of south coast cultures was very different from that of the highlands
and certainly bore little relation to events in the north. Archaeologists
working in Peru delineate north, central, and south coast and north,
central, and south sierra as convenient geographic parcels within which
they conduct research, and those designations correspond roughly to
regional zones of fairly isolated cultural development in pre-Columbian
times.

Nevertheless, as table 9.1 indicates, there were three important periods
of major cultural integration among the widely separated and regionally
diverse groups that occupied the Central Andean area. These periods,
referred to as horizons,[12] are well documented archaeologically and, for
the horizon associated with *Tawantinsuyu* (the Inca empire), ethnohistori-
cally as well. The Late Horizon refers, of course, to the political integration

Table 9.1. Chronology of Peruvian Pre-Hispanic Cultures

Period	Dates
Late Horizon	A.D. 1476–1534
Late Intermediate	A.D. 1000–1476
Middle Horizon	A.D. 600–1000
Early Intermediate	200 B.C.–A.D. 600
Early Horizon	1000–200 B.C.
Initial Period	1800–1000 B.C.
Preceramic Periods	?–1800 B.C.

by Inca military conquest of Andean peoples not only in the Central Andes but from the Río Ancasmayu in southern Colombia to the Río Maule in central Chile, virtually the entire Andean culture area. The Early Horizon, by contrast, appears to have resulted from the spread of a religious cult, associated primarily with a north highland culture whose art style and cult are known as Chavín. The cult diffused to the north and south, and its influence can be traced through Chavinoid pottery, textiles, and carved stone stylistic motifs all along the Peruvian coast from the Lambayeque Valley in the north to the Ica Valley in the south and in extensive areas of the north and north-central sierra.

Any effort to understand the development of metallurgy in the Central Andes must take into account not only the location of metallic ores and the variety of such ores available to indigenous populations, the level of sophistication of pyrotechnologies, and Andean sociocultural institutions but also the overwhelming aspects of the environment. Verticality, isolation, regionalism, waves of pan-Andean communication must all be considered. The remarks that follow neither set out all that we know about the early metallurgy of the Peruvian area nor suggest a structure for its development. There is neither space for the former nor sufficient data for the latter. Instead, I have focused on particular periods, regions, or metallurgical "events" that illuminate problem areas in the current state of our knowledge of the subject or that seem particularly helpful in any effort to interpret early metallurgies from a cross-cultural perspective.

Earliest Evidence of the Use of Metals

Whereas metallurgy in the Old World began with the manipulation of native copper and, thereafter, of native copper arsenides[13] which allowed production of copper-arsenic bronzes, the scant evidence we have for metal use in the Central Andes suggests that there gold was the first metal with which people experimented. Our earliest finds of worked gold are from the middle of the Initial Period.[14] Gold seems to have dominated the Andean scene until the latter part of the Early Horizon,[15] although the number of metal finds from this roughly 1500-year period is extremely small.

At the same time, recent excavations have uncovered examples of copper ores and slags, gilt copper artifacts, solid castings of copper, and one artifact of copper-silver alloy from sites scattered throughout the highlands and coast of the Central Andean area from northern Bolivia to central Peru. The dates of all these finds are not certain, but they seem to cluster about 1000 B.C. Our picture of the earliest metallurgy in the Andes is changing as the data trickle in, but we are far from any clear interpretation of those data. It may well be that in the Central Andes gold was used earlier than any other metal and that its prominence in the archaeological record during the period of spread and influence of the Chavín cult (roughly 800–400 B.C.) reflects a religious and ceremonial bias of the cult for that metal. But what has seemed until recently a gold-dominated metallurgy during the Early Horizon now begins to appear as a gold-oriented metallurgy in those areas most heavily influenced by Chavín (the north coast and sierra and the central and south coasts of present-day Peru) superimposed upon concurrent metallurgical developments of a different kind that involved copper and possibly silver. Because we have so small a corpus of metal and metallurgical materials from the Early Horizon and because the precise dating of much of that material is not possible, we cannot argue strongly about the real effects of the Chavín presence upon metallurgical events. My feeling is that gold may have had special symbolic significance for the cult and that certain religious values or doctrine were expressed through its use. In that sense, the cult was associated with the metal and probably had a lot to do with dissemination either of the metal or of interest in working it. But it seems clear that Andean metallurgy was also developing along certain other lines and that the prevailing socioeconomic situation during the Early Horizon—a stable agricultural economy which fostered the establishment of cohesive villages; the breakdown of regional isolation and restricted trade, which permitted exchange of goods and ideas[16]—enabled those developments. Whether the Chavín cult itself in any way stimulated the technological changes in metallurgy that we can now begin to document or if, instead, it remained wholly absorbed in a goldworking tradition it is still too early to say.

Let us look briefly at the archaeological materials from the early periods.[17] The first documented metal finds in the Central Andes comprise a group of tiny pieces of hammered gold foil excavated by Grossman at the habitation site of Waywaka in the south-central highlands of Peru. His radiocarbon determinations for Muyu Moko phase A pottery with which the gold foil was associated give dates that group around 1500 B.C.,[18] placing the material in the middle of the Initial Period. The excavator also uncovered a goldworker's tool kit consisting of a polished stone anvil (porphyry) and three small stone hammers, each made of a different type of stone. Although we cannot claim the hammering of gold into thin foil as sophisticated or even as true metallurgy, nevertheless the care with which the stone tools were made and stored and the fact that a special set of tools had been fabricated specifically for goldworking indicate local production and considerable skill and attention to the technical aspects of the job. Wherever gold foil was found at Waywaka, it was associated with small, cylindrical beads of lapis lazuli.

We have, thus far, no other evidence for goldsmithing between this unique Initial Period find and other small pieces of worked gold that date to the Early Horizon, at about 1000 B.C. None of the excavators at the well-known central Peruvian coastal site of Ancón[19] reports any metal finds there among the Early Horizon levels. Thomas Patterson found five nugget-shaped beads, apparently of gold, in a burial at the Tank Site at Ancón which he dates slightly before 1000 B.C. The beads, unworked but drilled through the middle for stringing, turned out to be pyrite.[20] Uhle and Willey found two small sheets of beaten gold in the Chavín-related cemeteries excavated at the nearby coastal site of Supe.[21]

Until 1975, no metal finds of any kind were reported by excavators at the type site of Chavín de Huántar itself, in the north-central Peruvian sierra. Luís Lumbreras, who has excavated extensively there, uncovered no metal associated with the Chavín occupation.[22] In 1975, however, Richard Burger found a single, tiny piece of sheet gold at the site. Part of the sheet is folded over onto itself and is either soldered or welded at the seam. The find was made in an excavation approximately 120 m to the southwest of the temple at Chavín de Huántar, in the area currently known as Chakinani or La Florida. The gold object was located in a layer of fill containing ceramic fragments of the Janabarriu phase, that phase when the temple and associated settlement at Chavín reached their greatest extent. The sherds are similar to pottery published by Lumbreras and Amat as Rocas style. Burger suggests that the refuse with which the gold was mixed came from an elite residence and, on the basis of the ceramic materials, estimates a date of about 600 B.C. for the find.[23] At another central highland site, Kotosh, Izumi and Terada report a few finds of worked gold from the phase they call Kotosh–Chavín: two small, folded-over sheets of gold and a gold ring. The radiocarbon dates associated with this period at Kotosh are 1200 ± 150 B.C. and 870 ± 120 B.C.[24]

The most important find of Early Horizon goldwork that comprises more than just occasional small bits of hammered gold was made near the Peruvian north coast town of Chongoyape in the Lambayeque Valley. Lothrop suggested that the objects—which include 3 tall gold crowns, a gold headband, a pair of gold tweezers, 4 undecorated and 7 decorated gold ear spools—came from a single grave.[25] All these objects are made of hammered sheet gold and show superb mastery in the handling of the metal and in repoussé skills. The crowns are decorated in high relief with motifs such as plumed jaguar heads or an anthropomorphized jaguar figure in a style that is pure Chavín. The ear spools are of considerable interest, since each is constructed of a flat, undecorated disc attached to a cylindrical tube that passed through the ear. Lothrop's study of these spools revealed that the joins between the frontal plaques and the tubes were made by welding (not hammer welding, but fusion welding in which the gold was heated along the edges to be joined until it melted and the edges fused). We have no other objects associated with this group of gold artifacts, but they were certainly made during the period of Chavín influence on the Peruvian north coast and probably during the later stages of its manifestation there. Several similar kinds of relief-decorated Chavín-style artifacts of sheet gold have been reported that are related in terms of their iconography and manufacture.[26]

Another group of metal objects of Chavín style found near Chongoyape is definitely late in the Chavín sequence (perhaps ca. 400 B.C.), as indicated by the pottery found with the gold. Lothrop described the contents of the grave, which included pottery, a stone bowl, spoon, and ring, an anthracite mirror, some cinnabar, and various metal objects made of sheet gold including several pottery beads encased in gold foil and one bimetallic pin of gold and silver.[27] Hollow gold beads in this grave lot were made by hammering out two hemispheres of gold and joining them along the equator of the resulting spherical bead. Lothrop was not able to ascertain the method of joining but states that it was probably effected by welding. Two of the decorative pins are interesting because, in each case, the pinheads were fashioned in two pieces, like the gold beads, and then soldered onto the pin shaft. One of the pins has a gold head soldered onto a silver shaft. William Root's analysis of the shaft metal proved it to be 74 percent silver and 26 percent gold, by weight.[28]

A final group of sheet gold objects which Lothrop considered of Chavín style may or may not be Early Horizon pieces.[29] Much more sophisticated than any of the materials mentioned above, they include nose ornaments with gold wire attachments soldered in place, ear spools with soldered joints between frontal plaque and tube, and spoons with handles representing human figures in the round. One of these handles is fashioned to represent a man blowing into a conch shell, made of silver, that he holds between his hands. The figure itself is hollow and made of pieces of preformed sheet gold either soldered or welded together to produce the form.[30] Root analyzed several of these objects,[31] and found they are made of gold with a high silver (14–24%) and a low copper (4–7%) content, which may represent a naturally occurring variety of gold. On the other hand, a sample of one of the nose ornaments showed it to be made of an artificial gold alloy containing 53 percent gold, 40 percent silver, and 7 percent copper. Such an alloy could have been produced intentionally or by inadvertent mixing of metals in the crucible, but it is certainly not a naturally occurring alloy. Root's analyses of the metal of the shaft of the bimetallic pin, mentioned earlier, indicated that it was a silver-gold alloy containing 26 percent gold. It is highly unusual for native silver to contain such high proportions of gold, and the metal from which the pin shaft was fabricated may also represent an alloy made by melting together silver and gold. In any case, if this last group of objects falls within the Early Horizon it must be attributed to the very end of that period.

The various pieces presented here constitute a substantial portion of the total corpus of Early Horizon metal finds, published and unpublished. Their characteristics are straightforward: they are all made of hammered sheet gold, the earlier pieces undoubtedly of native gold, and the objects (as distinct from the small bits of metal sheet) are exquisitely fashioned. They are ceremonial or ornamental in function. By the end of the Early Horizon, soldering and welding were fairly common techniques, and bimetallic objects of gold and silver (or a silver-gold alloy) were occasionally produced. If the last-described group of objects belongs to the end of the Early Horizon, by that time gold and silver were being alloyed, and we have the first appearance of what was to become a lasting tradition in Peruvian metalworking—the manufacture of three-dimensional forms by metallurgically joining pieces of preshaped metal sheet.[32]

Apart from the single Initial Period gold find from Waywaka, all the other material falls within the period when the Chavín cult had spread rapidly throughout large areas of coastal and north highland Peru (roughly 1000–800 B.C.) and during which its influence remained marked (roughly 800–400 B.C.). Whatever cultural unification may have resulted from that spread, it was clearly religious in nature. Thomas Patterson has likened the phenomenon to the early spread of Christianity in the Old World.[33] If Chavín also represents some sort of political domination of the region, we still lack the evidence to describe it.[34]

With this brief and general background to the earliest appearance of metal in the Central Andean area—a picture that has remained virtually unchanged for decades—we can begin to evaluate some newer evidence that, although sketchy and sporadic in nature, nevertheless begins to indicate that other metallurgical developments of a very different sort were also taking place.

In 1970, Carlos Ponce Sanginés published some of the results of his work at Wankarani, Chiripa, and related sites in the Bolivian altiplano not far from the site of Tiwanaku (Tiahuanaco). He reported having found copper smelting slags in the earliest levels at Wankarani and similar kinds of slags at Pukara de Belén, La Joya, and Chiripa. He also claims to have analyzed the slags by emission spectroscopy, but he has still not published those analyses. On the basis of Ponce's radiocarbon determinations, one can surmise a date of roughly 1200–800 B.C. for the levels at which the slags were found at Wankarani.[35] But his reporting of the finds is too succinct, and there has been no supplementary publication relating the slags to other material from the excavations.

On the other hand, David Browman, who has been excavating in the same general area during the past few years, has found remains of copper ores at some of these sites which date to the Early Horizon. Three small samples from Chiripa, associated with levels dating from 900–100 B.C. (uncorrected radiocarbon dates), have all been identified as brochantite [$3Cu(OH)_2 \cdot CuSO_4$] and quartz. Another sample from Santa Lucia, in the Cochabamba Valley about 300 km southeast of Chiripa, has also been identified as a mixture of quartz and brochantite. Finally, a sample from Chullpapata, within 5 km of Santa Lucia, contains quartz, brochantite, and antlerite [$2Cu(OH)_2 \cdot CuSO_4$]. The Santa Lucia and Chullpapata ores also date to the 900–100 B.C. period. Two samples of ore from Tiwanaku are quartz and brochantite, in one case, and quartz, brochantite, and antlerite in the other. Browman has assigned no date within the Tiwanaku sequence (roughly 1000 B.C.–A.D. 1000) to these samples, however.[36] Wendell Bennett, who excavated at Tiwanaku in the 1930s, also reported finding "small pieces of copper sulphate and other copper ores ... throughout the excavations."[37]

Thus, although Ponce's finds are neither clearly nor fully reported, we cannot take them lightly. His work, together with that of Browman, suggests that the smelting of copper ores may have already begun in the Bolivian altiplano by mid-late Early Horizon times in an area uninfluenced by Chavín. All of the ores collected by Browman are copper sulfates, an interesting fact since the Bolivian highlands experience long periods of seasonal rainfall every year producing conditions normally far too humid for the formation and retention of sulfates of copper in any quantity. Such minerals generally form in exceptionally arid environments, such as that of Chuquicamata in Chile, where they are found abundantly. In fact, the presence of copper sulfate ores in the north Bolivian highlands might even suggest their importation there from drier areas to the west, nearer the Chilean coast. In the case of Ponce's slags, we can have no idea of the ores that produced them until his analytical data are available.

A second piece of evidence that departs dramatically from the gold-working tradition associated with Chavín influence takes the form of a small bead of hammered sheet metal found at the site of Malpaso, in the middle Lurín Valley of central Peru. The bead was found by archaeologist Thomas Patterson, who describes it as a surface find and dates it to about 1000 B.C., at the time of the last occupation of the site.[38] The bead is made of a copper-silver alloy (roughly 45% silver, 41% copper, remainder corrosion products) which was once molten and, after solidifying, was hammered into thin sheet from which the bead was then formed.[39] To my knowledge it is the earliest object made of a copper-silver alloy. That alloy type became quite popular on the south coast of Peru in the Late Intermediate Period[40] and was also used by the Mochica in the Early Intermediate Period. Its unique appearance at Malpaso is thus difficult to reconcile, for such an alloy is prepared by melting together copper and silver metal. Thus far we have no evidence for either the use of these two metals in coastal Peru this early in the Early Horizon or for the alloying of these metals. Nevertheless, since there were no later occupations at Malpaso, the bead must be reckoned with. If it was not manufactured locally, it may have been brought from the central sierra. Browman has shown that exchange between the central coast and highlands of Peru was active during this period and, furthermore, that the mining of copper was of considerable importance in the central sierra as early as 1000 B.C.[41]

> In the area of [Ataura–Acllahuasi] . . . we can demonstrate mining for copper as early as 1200–1000 B.C. Ceramics I [Browman] collected from the site [Ataura] were all clearly later Initial Period. Ceramics excavated first by Ramiro Matos, and later by Chahud for the Museo de la Universidad Nacional del Centro, Huancayo, also all date to that period. I date the Initial Period to 1750–1000 B.C., and the Early Horizon to 1000–1 B.C. Since the materials are late Initial Period . . . they could have been no later than 1000 B.C. . . .
>
> As far as I am aware, no copper goods were found [at Ataura]. But there was copper ore. I did not excavate any. But in the two excavations of Matos and Chahud, copper ore was recovered. Also in a couple areas of the site, the copper content was so high that both human bones and regular animal refusee bone were heavily saturated with copper salts.[42]

Copper and silver ores are abundant in the Central Peruvian highlands. Although we do not yet have evidence of silver mining or the use of native silver in the manufacture of artifacts, the mining of copper was well established there by the second half of the Early Horizon. This new evidence for the early mining and production of copper in the central highlands is important for a number of reasons. In the first place, just as the north Bolivian sierra (the Tiwanaku–Wankarani–Chiripa area) was uninfluenced by Chavín, so too was the south-central and southern sierra of present-day Peru largely outside of what has been called "the Chavín interaction sphere."[43] That is not to say that there was no contact between peoples of the central sierra and those of the central coast, where Chavín influence, at least until about 650 B.C., was very strong. Quite the contrary. Such contacts were evidently economically important and frequent. It simply means that the religious aspect of Chavín and the art style through which the religion was expressed are barely manifest in the south-central and southern highlands. In both Bolivia and Peru, highland peoples close to sources of copper and outside of the Chavín orbit were the initiators of copper metallurgy—at least as far as the presently available data allow us to surmise.

Secondly, Browman and his colleagues[44] argue that trade in copper between about 1000 and 650 B.C., was important between central sierra sites such as those near Jauja (Ataura and Acllahuasi) and the lowlands—both the Pacific coast to the west and the Amazonian lowlands to the east. The economic networks along which the copper traveled were, they claim, developed by highland llama caravan trains that brought high altitude products—camelid wool, potatoes, copper—to the low altitude zones, where they were exchanged for products grown at such elevations (e.g., coca and maize). In other words, according to this interpretation, copper was one among many important goods exchanged, vertically, up and down the Andean slopes.

Finally, in direct contrast to the coastal peoples, who by 1000 B.C. were primarily agriculturalists and living in settled communities, the central highlanders—at least in the Jauja–Huancayo area which has been extensively studied—were pastoralists who herded llamas, gathered wild plant foods, and practiced limited wet-season horticulture (root crops such as potatoes, ulluco, and oca and grains like quinoa and cañihua).

> The preference for hunting and herding over agricultural pursuits until the Wari conquest ... produced settlement patterns consisting of non-permanent, perishable dwellings, easily transportable, and with seasonal occupation only of dwelling sites. The typical base camp settlements are small villages, seasonally occupied, and situated near a spring, stream or other dependable water resource to supply sufficient water for llama herds and suitable land for wet-season horticulture. The largest villages during the wet-season may have had a few score semi-subterranean or subterranean, pithouses, with

population sizes generally no larger than 100 persons. Other seasons of the year saw dispersal into smaller herding groups.[45]

These same herders must also have been the miners of copper ores and the producers of copper metal, at least in the area studied by Browman. Perhaps mining and metallurgical activities occupied that part of the year when people were gathered in permanent villages, for during the dry season, roughly half the year, they would disperse to the best pasturelands. In the Central Andes, then, it may have been the llama and alpaca herders, the dwellers of the high puna, who, living close to abundant metal ores, first utilized those ores and exchanged their metal products for other items necessary to survival in a rugged and inhospitable environment. One wonders why, if this is the case, more examples of copper artifacts from this period are not found on the coast. The bead from Malpaso may, in fact, represent one such example. The level of copper production was, presumably, quite low, as was the overall scale of metallurgy during the Early Horizon, whether we refer to gold or to copper.

The last group of materials to be evaluated that bears on the question of the utilization of copper during the Early Horizon also comes from the Lurín Valley, from a coastal necropolis in the zone known as the Tablada de Lurín. The excavator and interpreter of the objects, Gabriela Schwoerbel, has written several reports describing them, the most extensive of which she presented at the Second Peruvian Congress of Andean Man and Culture that met in Trujillo, Peru in 1974.[46] The metal objects are all burial goods, excavated in the cemetery, and are dated by radiocarbon measurements of associated materials to the period between 950 ± 100 B.C. and 450 ± 240 B.C. Schwoerbel sorts the assemblage into three groups according to the function of the objects: adornments, arms, and utilitarian items. Most of the pieces fall into the first category and are made of sheet copper with openwork or repoussé designs. Some of these plaques are quite large and were used as diadems. A few cast pieces occur in the form of pins to secure cloth headdresses.

Among the group of arms figure heavy, solid copper mace heads (some cast, others hammered) and spear-thrower hooks (*ganchos de estólica*). The spear-thrower hooks are described as being of solid copper which has been hammered. One of them, Schwoerbel reports, was associated with remains that date to 950 ± 100 B.C.[47] The remaining copper objects, considered utilitarian in the broadest sense of the term, comprise needles with eyes, depilatory tweezers, and tubes of various kinds used as musical instruments.

Almost all of these copper objects are covered with a thin layer of gold. Schwoerbel describes the gold as having been beaten into very thin sheet and then applied to the surfaces of the copper. She makes a point of stating that the technique of covering copper with gold (*el enchapado*) is already found on objects that correspond to the 950 ± 100 B.C. date but does not specify which gilded objects in particular belong to that early date.[48]

The Tablada de Lurín material is intriguing and controversial. One is tempted to think that the Lurín Valley, between the coast and the mid-valley site of Malpaso, was somehow engaged in the manufacture and/or exchange of copper objects by about 900 B.C. On the other hand, many of the objects Schwoerbel illustrates in her 1974 paper, particularly the star-shaped mace heads (which one supposes are covered with a thin layer of gold), are similar in style to the heavy and often gilt copper mace heads from the Peruvian far north coast site of Vicús. If they are in any way associated with such north coast objects, they would be more accurately dated, at the earliest, to about 200 B.C., that is, toward the end of the Tablada sequence, which corresponds to the beginning of the Early Intermediate Period. Ríos argues, on the basis of some of the pottery associated with the burials—pottery of a new type as yet not well defined but known as "Frijoloide," or kidney-bean-like—that the metal objects cannot be of Early Horizon manufacture since the ceramics in no way resemble coastal Early Horizon pottery. She feels all of Schwoerbel's material is from the first few centuries B.C., between the end of the Early Horizon and the florescence of regional Early Intermediate Period cultures. Karen Stothert has recently excavated at Villa El Salvador, a site in the sandy reaches of the Tablada de Lurín, located approximately 4 km south of the Tablada necropolis. The site dates to the very end of the Early Horizon and the first phases of the Early Intermediate Period. Among her finds were copper points and ingots as well as gilt copper ornaments. The mace heads characteristic of the Tablada necropolis were not encountered at Villa El Salvador, however. Some but not all of the pottery from the necropolis is identical to that found at the Villa, but the necropolis was used as a burial ground for a long period of time, and it seems clear that some of the necropolis burials are earlier than those at the Villa. According to Stothert, the so-called *frijoloide* vessels from the necropolis are unique and, in her opinion, they are probably late Early Horizon in date. She feels they may date to some time between 450 and 50 B.C. but that Schwoerbel's 950 B.C. date is too early. On the other hand she does point out that "the problem of the pottery of the late Early Horizon is that it varies tremendously from region to region, and we don't even know what the Early Horizon styles of the south central coast look like."[49] Somehow we must reconcile the early radiocarbon dates with the artifacts. Schwoerbel, after all, excavated them and reiterates that some of the copper pieces are from the mid–Early Horizon. If that proves to be the case, we may have our first evidence for the casting of copper, for the manufacture of arms of metal, and for gilding, that metallurgical set of processes which perhaps more than any other captured the interest and provoked the inventiveness of Andean metalworkers throughout the prehistoric period.

Comments   It would be foolish to attempt any generalizations or careful evaluations of these beginnings in Andean metallurgy when we see that within the last thirteen years (Thomas Patterson found the Lurín bead in 1966) bits and pieces of information have slowly collected to alter our previous notions of the nature of Early Horizon metallurgy as gold-dominated, concentrated largely in the Pacific coastal zone, and extremely limited in its output. As more systematic excavations are carried out in the central and south sierra we should expect some clarification of the situation. The data are still too scant and unconnected—and too often taken from unexcavated materials, especially in the case of gold objects—to serve as the basis for a well-drawn picture.

But some observations are still worth making. The total production of metals of whatever kind was extremely low in the Early Horizon. Highland pastoralists may have been responsible for some copper manufacture, on a seasonal basis, during the early part of that period. On the other hand, by the close of the Early Horizon, it is clear that on the north coast, where Chavín influence was particularly strong, highly skilled goldsmiths, perhaps full-time specialists, were producing the remarkable kinds of goldwork Lothrop has described. Even so, metal appears not to have been a major medium for the carrying of cultural message, for ideological propaganda, by the Chavín cult. It is nowhere near as important as pottery, and it may not have been as major an artistic vehicle as textiles.

Nevertheless, in certain respects, Chavín had a more lasting effect on the Andean metallurgical tradition than one might suppose. The close association between the Chavín presence and the utilization of gold remains unaltered. Though metal was not used abundantly, when it was used it was gold that was employed. What the valued properties of the metal were we cannot say—its very rarity, its shininess, its color. Whatever they were, those properties continued to be paramount throughout Andean prehistory, the culmination of their value accorded by the Inca dynasty to whom gold was sacred and for whom it served as a visual statement of political power. Such standards of value were already set by the period of Chavín influence.

It should not be thought that this early and long-standing interest in gold, or in goldenness, hindered metallurgical development in the Andes or led to a metallurgical deadend. By the close of the Early Horizon, the simple hammering of gold sheet or foil of the kind we saw at Waywaka had developed into the manufacture of three-dimensional objects made by soldering or fusion welding together many pieces of preshaped gold sheet. The solders used on the latest and finest pieces from the north coast are both gold solders and silver solders; in other words, they are alloys of gold or silver with other metals. Thus the early insistence upon gold, upon gold in the form of sheet, and upon the metallurgical rather than the mechanical joining of pieces of sheet gold to produce three-dimensional forms led to the development of alloys that could be adapted to such requirements. The first alloys in the Andes were solders, alloys used for their melting and bonding properties rather than metals alloyed for hardness or for improved mechanical or casting characteristics. Needless to say, the control of heat, especially heat directed locally to the precise areas of a soldered or welded metal join, was entirely mastered by this time.

Chavín set the stage in other respects as well. As we shall see, one of the most important and deeply rooted of Andean concerns with respect to metals was that they be golden in color—not all metals, but certainly those used for adornment, for status purposes, ceremonially, and for power display. The importance of the color of metallic gold cannot be overemphasized. One of the responses to this concern was the early development of a large metallurgical repertoire of methods for gilding the surfaces of objects made of baser metals, such as copper.[50] If some of Schwoerbel's gilt copper material from Lurín does prove to be of Early Horizon date, it will constitute our first example of what became one of the most inventive routes for the development of Andean metallurgy.

Whether the Chavín interest in gold, or rather its artistic expression through the medium of gold, closed its eyes to other metals and in a sense inhibited their development it is difficult to say. If the Malpaso copper-silver bead and some of the Tablada de Lurín copper objects are indeed Early Horizon central coast phenomena, we cannot argue for parochialism of Chavín metallurgy. Even with our paucity of data, however, it seems clear that copper metallurgy began at least by the middle of the Early Horizon and that the centers of production were outside the areas most heavily influenced by Chavín. What does stand out as extremely interesting about the early copper data is that the evidence points to the smelting of copper ores as probably the first step in the manufacture of copper, perhaps in conjunction with use of the native metal. As Georg Petersen has pointed out, however, native copper rarely occurs at or near the surface anywhere along the Andean cordillera.[51] It is found at considerable depths, but we have no evidence to suggest that the earliest miners were probing those depths. Only in a few sites where prior erosion has caused native copper to outcrop does one find it in the Andes and, even in those locations, it is present in small quantity. For this reason, it is not remarkable that the first copper produced in the Andes may have been from smelted oxide or sulfate ores of the metal. The finds of copper sulfate at Tiwanaku, Wankarani, and Chiripa are remarkable, however, since those sites cluster geographically and, as a group, are not far from Corocoro, a major and well-known Bolivian source of native copper. The sites near Tiwanaku should be a major focus of study to document this early metallurgical technology. We ought to know not only what ores were being smelted and if native copper was utilized but what relationship copperworking in northern Bolivia may have had with developments such as those reported by Browman far to the north of Bolivia. How widespread was the manufacture of copper during this earliest of Andean horizons, and what were the copper objects of exchange carried by the llama caravans in view of the rarity of the metal? Were they, too, primarily ornamental items?

Gold and copper were the first two culturally used metals in the Andes. One was obtained in its native state, the other may have been smelted even in its earliest production. Both continued to be used, and together they remained the major metals upon which all further developments in Andean metallurgy rested.

The First Florescence of Metallurgy—The North Coast of Peru during the Early Intermediate Period

The Mochica culture dominated the north coast of Peru from about A.D. 0 to 750.[52] Judging from Mochica settlements found in the intervening valleys, the kingdom of the Mochica peoples extended from the Lambayeque Valley in the north to the Nepeña Valley in the south. Since the early 1960s, important finds of pottery and metal objects of Mochica style from the sites of Cerro Vicús and Loma Negra in the far north coast Piura Valley have indicated a strong Mochica presence well outside the geographic area normally regarded as having been under Mochica political domination.

Lanning describes the salient features of the Early Intermediate Period succinctly and well.

> The Early Intermediate Period, beginning about 200 B.C., was again a time of revolutionary change. The first really large cities were built at this time, and some of them served as the capitals of fairly large regional states. Most of the valley-wide irrigation systems of the coast were built during the Early Intermediate Period. For the first time, intensive warfare became a factor in the everyday life of the ancient Peruvians. Fortresses and fortified towns and cities sprang up all across ancient Peru. Population, which had been expanding steadily since late preceramic times, now reached its maximum size in many parts of Peru. Art and technology reached their peak on the coast at this time, and some of the finest masterpieces in the history of art date from the Early Intermediate Period.
>
> On the whole, the picture we get of coastal life at this time is one of an intensely specialized and stratified society with well-defined ranks and professions symbolized by details of dress and ornament. There were rulers and ruled, soldiers and civilians, farmers and city people, priests and laymen, craftsmen.[53]

Among the technologies that flourished was metallurgy, and it is fair to say that the most important developments in metallurgy were those accomplished within the Mochica state.

During the first few centuries of the Early Intermediate Period, the use of copper became widespread within the Central Andean area. Whether on the coast or in the highlands, in the north or south, most excavators have found copper among grave goods in the form of objects fashioned from the metal or discs or cakes of "stock copper" in the as-cast condition. Although production levels were not high, copper objects were common, and the north coast was certainly the main center of copper production. Ornaments—whether for state, religious, or personal use—still dominated the repertoire of products, but tools such as chisels, needles, spindle whorls, fishhooks, and occasional celts were frequently made. For the first time, heavy weapons of solid copper, particularly mace heads of various kinds, were available. These are especially prominent among the finds from the site of Cerro Vicús in the Piura Valley,[54] but they also figure among the materials Schwoerbel reported from the necropolis at Tablada de Lurín. Copper metal was prized and may have signified real wealth, for upon burial solid, cast discs of copper were often placed in the mouths or in the hands of the dead.[55]

The best of the few chemical analyses that have been made of Mochica copper have included samples from what are probably ingots, or, as Kroeber has called them, "stock copper."[56] There is no question that the Mochica were smelting some of their copper and probably from ores locally available to them.[57] These ores appear to have been of the oxide varieties, but there is some suggestion that metalworkers may have also been experimenting with sulfide ores, not necessarily of copper but of lead and silver. Larco has reported the presence of "pure lead, perhaps from silver-lead ore, ... in [Mochica] tombs."[58] The lead might have been a by-product of smelting such ores to win metallic silver. During a metallurgical site survey I conducted in the Peruvian Andes in 1974,[59] I uncovered remains of what was clearly a process for winning silver from some form of lead-silver sulfide ore. The "lead cakes" and other scoria were found at the central coast site of Ancón, and the single sherd associated with the materials was typical of Early Intermediate Period pottery from that site. The association between the sherd and the scoria is a tentative one, however.

Finally, among excavated pieces of Mochica copperwork analyzed by Clair Patterson, three objects contained arsenic in the 2 percent concentration range with associated high bismuth and antimony impurities. Patterson has argued that these constituents of the copper might have been introduced "from inadvertent mixtures of azurite or malachite with small quantities of a green copper arsenate mineral such as olivenite."[60] It is also possible, however, that the arsenic originated from the occasional mixing of small amounts of enargite or tennantite ores (copper sulfarsenides) with the purer "stock copper." In any case, our evidence is sketchy, but the problem is worth pursuing. If sulfide smelting was carried out in coastal Peru at this time, it was on a small scale and may have been entirely directed toward the winning of metallic silver from lead-silver ores. Objects made of silver are not infrequent within the corpus of Mochica metal artifacts.

Copper was hammered into sheet from which hollow figures in the round were assembled, in the technical style already developed in the Early Horizon; it was cast both in open molds and by the lost-wax process;[61] it was alloyed with gold, with silver, and with combinations of those two metals; and hammered and cast objects of copper were gilded.

The alloy systems developed during the Early Intermediate Period are extremely important, for they continued to be used in later periods, and some of them dominated the Andean metallurgical scene up to the time of the Spanish invasion. We have already made note of the bead from Malpaso, Lurín Valley, as perhaps the earliest example of a copper-silver alloy. The Mochica material indicates that metalworkers used this alloy over a wide range of silver concentration, from a few percent to over 30 percent, by weight, of silver.[62] The alloy became particularly popular both on the north coast within Chimú territory and on the south coast, where it was used extensively by Chincha metalworkers during the Late Intermediate Period.[63]

Copper-silver alloys have two properties that were important for Andean craftsmen: their toughness when hammered and their development of enriched silver surfaces when hammered and annealed. These alloys were used almost exclusively for the manufacture of objects made of sheet metal. Even with silver concentrations as low as about 5 percent by weight, the metal becomes hard, but not brittle, when hammered into thin sheet. The flexibility and toughness of copper-silver sheet metal allowed it to be shaped easily and, once formed, to retain its shape with far greater strength than pure silver or even sterling silver (7.5% copper). It was thus an excellent material for metalworkers whose forte was the production of items from elaborately hammered and joined pieces of metal sheet.

The surface enrichment properties of copper-silver alloys have been described in some detail.[64] Suffice it to say that, particularly for alloys containing about 10 percent or more of silver by weight, the repeated sequences of hammering, annealing, and removal of the surface copper oxide scale formed upon annealing—sequences necessary to the fabrication of sheet metal from the alloy ingot—produce enriched silver surfaces on the resulting sheet as the surface copper is removed. Thus metal made from such alloys, of mottled copper color when cast, is bright silver in color after having been hammered into sheet. The formation of silvered surfaces on objects hammered from these alloys is an inescapable consequence of annealing and of the attendant loss of surface copper through oxidation. There is, essentially, no way of preventing it.

Copper-silver alloys were used by the Mochica to produce objects of sheet metal because the sheet was hard and tough and because objects made of such sheet looked like silver. In later periods, these alloys continued to be used for the same reasons, and the well-known *vasos retratos*, or effigy beakers, of Chimú and Chincha origin, said to be of silver, are sometimes made of copper-silver alloy.[65] Kroeber also reports objects made of silver sheet with a composition of 74 percent silver, 23 percent copper, 3 percent gold, and a trace of lead.[66] That this makeup represents the composition of native silver is unlikely. It more closely resembles intentional alloys Root found characteristic of south coast metallurgy of later periods.[67]

One is led to speculate upon the genesis of copper-silver alloys in the Central Andes. Copper ores that contain silver are found abundantly in the central highlands. They are sulfide ores. The smelting of copper ores containing argentiferous tetrahedrite (freibergite), for example, a mineral type extremely common to the Peruvian Andes, could easily have resulted in the direct production of alloys of copper and silver. Analyses of samples of such ores being mined in Peru today indicate silver concentrations between about 6 and 18 percent by weight. The ratio of copper to silver in such an ore is about 4:1, and one would expect the smelted alloy to contain these two metals in approximately the same proportion, giving an alloy of roughly 80 percent copper, 20 percent silver by weight. As a sulfide, however, it could not be smelted by reduction techniques without at least some prior roasting. Furthermore, since tetrahedrite contains substantial amounts of antimony, one would expect to find antimony in metal smelted from it. Clair Patterson's analysis of a Mochica copper-silver ornament and Root's analyses of south coast objects made of the alloy indicate the presence of only trace amounts of antimony.[68] A careful comparative study of Early Intermediate Period and Late Intermediate Period objects made from these alloys should indicate if, at any point, argentiferous copper ores were used in their production. For the moment, it appears that the Mochica probably manufactured their copper-silver alloys by melting together metallic copper and metallic silver, either the native metals or, much more likely, metals smelted from the kinds of ores discussed earlier in this section.

By far the most important alloy system developed during the Early Intermediate Period and often used by the Mochica in the manufacture of sheet metal objects was that of copper-gold. Copper and gold when melted together form a complete solid solution series throughout the entire range of possible alloy compositions, and objects varying widely in composition have been encountered. Some silver is also often found in these Andean alloys either because the gold used contained some silver, as placer gold from the Andes often does, or because gold was added to a copper-silver alloy. For example, Clair Patterson analyzed an ingot of Mochica origin excavated by Max Uhle in the Moche Valley. It contains 60 percent copper, 31 percent gold, and 10 percent silver.[69] By contrast, Kroeber reports the compositions of several pieces of Mochica "sheet gold," also excavated by Uhle, as containing, in one case, 68 percent gold, 13 percent copper, 19 percent silver, and in another, 67 percent gold, 11 percent copper, 22 percent silver by weight.[70] Copper-gold alloys such as these are often referred to in the literature of the New World as *tumbaga*, a term more often associated with the metal as it came to be used by the peoples of Colombia in the remarkable lost-wax castings they made from it. The Mochica ingot analyzed by Clair Patterson is a copper-rich tumbaga. The alloys described by Kroeber may be considered gold-rich tumbagas with a high concentration of silver. In fact, such metal is equivalent to 16-karat gold.

Copper-gold alloys, like copper-silver alloys, become hard upon hammering but retain their flexibility. They were, therefore, perfectly suited to the sheet metal tradition already characteristic of north Peruvian metalworking. But these alloys were used and subsequently highly developed primarily for another property—the gold color that they confer upon articles made from them once the surfaces of such objects are suitably treated. The literature on the surface enrichment properties of tumbaga alloys is extensive. Root and Lechtman give good accounts of the technical processes involved in developing gold surface layers on objects made from such alloys.[71] For example, the Mochica ingot analyzed by Clair Patterson, containing 60 percent copper and 31 percent gold, is not golden but distinctly coppery in color in its cast condition. As in the case of the copper-silver alloys, when such an ingot is hammered to produce thin metal sheet, copper is lost from the surfaces of the alloy through oxidation upon annealing. Objects made from copper-rich tumbagas of this type soon develop deep golden surfaces as increasing amounts of surface copper are lost in the hammering and annealing process. When silver is also present, the surfaces of the object may require additional chemical treatment to remove some of the silver as well, thereby enriching the gold. We now know, in fact, that Andean metalworkers were capable of dissolving silver from such enriched gold-silver surface alloys with naturally occurring acid minerals, a highly sophisticated chemical process.[72] Evidently this discovery had already been made by the Mochica though it was most widely adopted by the Chimú, who several centuries later dominated the entire north coast of Peru. It is also clear that the Mochica alloys reported on by Kroeber are, essentially, high-gold tumbagas. They too could have been only pale gold in color when the ingots were initially cast. As the metal was hammered and annealed to form sheet, copper was lost through oxidation and pickling. The surfaces of the resulting sheet were probably even paler in color than the original ingot, because of the presence of substantial amounts of silver in the enriched gold surface layer. Undoubtedly some of this silver was removed chemically to produce a deep golden surface color.

The tumbaga alloys with their inherent gold enrichment properties swept through the Americas from Peru to Mexico and were in common use in that entire region when the Spaniards invaded Central and South America in the 16th century. They constitute the most significant contribution of the New World to the repertoire of alloy systems developed among ancient societies. In the Central Andes, copper-rich tumbagas continued to be used after the Early Intermediate Period primarily to produce gold-colored objects of sheet metal in contrast to their use in Colombia, the Isthmian area, and Mexico, where they were employed primarily in castings. In the Late Intermediate Period the Chimú used them to develop gold surfaces on objects that contained as little as 12 percent of gold by weight.

Copper-rich tumbagas and their attendant surface-enrichment effects
were used by Andean peoples to produce objects that looked like gold.
In effect, such systems may be considered a variety of gilding. Unlike
the more common gilding methods, however, they are distinguished by
incorporating the gold within the body or fabric of the object itself rather
than merely applying the gold to the surface of the object. The new and
extensive finds of metal from the Piura Valley, both at Cerro Vicús and
at Loma Negra, have made it plain that gilding of copper objects by the
external application of gold was also important and extensively practiced
by the Mochica or Mochica-influenced peoples. At least half of the copper
objects from these sites, most of which are sheet copper but many are
solid castings, are gilt. Again, we are concerned mainly with a nontool
assemblage that includes face masks, nose ornaments, ear spools, ceremonial
axes, and so forth. Research into the processes by which these objects
were gilded has been carried on at the Laboratory for Research on
Archaeological Materials at the Massachusetts Institute of Technology for
the past several years. Thus far, only the Loma Negra materials have
been studied, but our results show that gilt copper objects from that
site, all of which display surface layers of gold of incredible thinness—
about 0.5 μm thick—were gold plated by electrochemical deposition of
the gold onto the copper.[73] This astonishing discovery points not only
to the remarkable sophistication of Mochica metallurgy but also to the
emphasis of the culture and of the metallurgy upon the color and quality
of metallic gold.

In exploring the metals and alloys of primary interest to the Mochica
during the Early Intermediate Period, I have not dwelt upon details of
metalworking techniques such as casting, soldering, or welding, of which
they were masters. The sweat-welded joins used in the manufacture of a
set of hollow gold jaguars made of sheet gold are as elegant as any goldsmithing techniques in the ancient or for that matter the modern world.[74]
The Mochica metalsmiths were probably the finest metal craftsmen who
worked in the Central Andean area in the prehistoric period.

Comments Most students of early metallurgies consider "true metallurgy" as involving two important achievements: the winning of metals
from their ores and the alloying of metals. We are used to thinking of
copper as the "first" smelted metal and of copper-arsenic as the "first"
alloy system. Models built upon Old World data generally consider the

simple smelting of copper oxide ores as prior, developmentally, to the production of alloys of copper, although Heskel's work indicates that this classical canon is probably in error and that alloys made of native copper with copper arsenides are as early if not earlier than copper smelted from its oxide ores.[75]

It is entirely possible that "true metallurgy" in both its aspects—smelting (of copper ores) and alloying (in the production of solders)—was achieved in the Andes by the end of the Early Horizon and before the emergence of the Mochica state. But the Mochica put metallurgy on its feet. In terms of the quality of metalwork, their products were never again equaled in the Central Andean area. Copper became the metal upon which all further developments in alloying and in smelting were based. In and of itself, copper was highly valued among the Mochica; most of their tools, arms, and instruments were made of it and it formed the basis of their alloys. But in this latter role copper was in the service of attitudes about metals—metals of adornment, metals of status, metals of power—that influenced the alloys made from it. These were alloys that altered the properties of copper not so much to make it harder or stronger but to confer upon its surfaces a different color—indeed, to transform it so that it actually seemed to be another metal altogether, sometimes metallic silver but primarily metallic gold. The copper–silver and copper–gold alloy systems developed during the Early Intermediate Period, particularly on the north Peruvian coast, had to be malleable, hard, and capable of retaining the shape they assumed upon plastic deformation through hammering. North coast metallurgy was sheet metal oriented, and the alloys it developed had to fulfill the requirements of a sheet metal tradition. Both copper-silver and copper-gold did so admirably. In addition, the Mochica used these alloys to produce metal qualities that were obviously paramount for them, goldenness and silveriness. In this sense, copper, through its alloys, was a vehicle for achieving those desired qualities. It remained a handmaiden to gold and to silver, both of which continued to be used in the manufacture of the finest objects.

The interest in surfaces and in the display of gold as the significant visual aspect conveyed by a metal object led to the development not only of tumbaga alloys but of external systems of gilding copper as complex as electrochemical deposition. The sophistication of Mochica metallurgy— one is tempted to say of Mochica chemistry—is extraordinary. It gives us insight into what "metalness," at least in part, may have meant to the

Mochica, and certainly what resourceful means they used for achieving
such qualities. These attitudes may have been inherited from Chavín.
Ultimately, they became Andean values indoctrinated by the Inca dynasty.

Regionalism vs. A Pan-Andean Tradition[76]

In the course of the development of Andean metallurgy, two regions
emerged as preeminent centers of metallurgical innovation: the northern
Andes, comprising what is today north central and northern Peru and
Ecuador, and the southern Andes, including the Peruvian and Bolivian
altiplano, northwestern Argentina, and northern Chile.[77] In these regions
we can trace a consistent involvement with metal technologies over
long periods of time. The northern metalworkers could rely upon abundant
local resources of copper, silver, and gold ores while their southern counterparts, in addition to these, counted tin from the extremely rich deposits
of cassiterite (SnO_2), extending from the southern shores of Lake Titicaca
to northern Argentina, as part of their mineral wealth. The questions to
be asked are whether the metallurgies that flourished in these two zones
were separate and distinct regional developments; whether they influenced
one another and in what way; and whether at particular points in history
or under certain circumstances they merged to produce a truly pan-Andean
metallurgy.

We do not have the data yet to allow us to answer these questions.
Studies of South Andean metallurgy are particularly scarce,[78] and little
recent research has been undertaken or reported. Even so, certain aspects
of these regional developments suggest where future inquiries might
best be directed to resolve some of the issues just raised. If, in the discussion
that follows, I refer largely to events, as we can reconstruct them, from
the northern portions of Peru, that is both because our most abundant
data are from there and because my own investigations, both in the laboratory and in the field, have focused largely on the Peruvian Andes.

Just at the time that scholars of Near Eastern, European, and Central
Asian metallurgy have become interested in and excited by the phenomenon of arsenic bronze used as an important alloy in the early stages
of the metallurgies of those areas,[79] we find that copper-arsenic bronze
was equally significant in the development of Andean metallurgy. In an
important article, Caley indicated the frequent use of arsenic bronze,
particularly in the northern regions of what is today Peru, during a period
of between five and twelve centuries,[80] but he adds that "not even a

rough time estimate is at present possible for any other region of South America."[81] The presence of arsenic in Andean copper artifacts has been known for some time, but only Caley, Fester, and Kroeber emphasize the significance of these alloys as true bronzes.[82] When was arsenic-bronze first used in the Andes and how long did it persist? How was the alloy made, that is, in what form was the arsenic introduced? What are the implications of the manufacture of arsenic bronze for our reconstruction of the development of Andean metallurgy and for our evaluation of its sophistication?

Considering the data from northern Peru, we are fortunate in having 25 analyses of metal artifacts excavated by Max Uhle at the famous Moche Valley site of the Huaca de la Luna. All the objects, including 15 ingots, 5 implements, and 5 "ornaments" were found by Uhle in Mochica graves dating to Moche levels III–IV, in other words, to the latter half of the Early Intermediate Period (roughly A.D. 300–500). They were analyzed by William Root, Walter Morley, and Clair Patterson;[83] five of the objects were analyzed independently by two investigators with identical results as far as their arsenic content is concerned. The analyses show that of the 15 ingots, 2 contain 0.1 percent arsenic, 13 contain no arsenic; of the 5 implements, 1 contains 0.1 percent arsenic, 4 contain no arsenic; of the 5 "ornaments," 1 contains 2.0 percent arsenic, 2 are described as containing arsenic of about that same concentration level, that is, high arsenic,[84] and 2 contain no arsenic. Clearly the Mochica were not using arsenical copper either in manufacturing their stock metal, the ingots, or in their implements (chisels, for example). A concentration of 0.1 percent arsenic constitutes its presence as a trace element and can in no way be considered a deliberate addition, although it does suggest that copper ores containing some arsenic were close at hand. It would be difficult to argue that the Mochica metalworkers were purposely making their ornaments of high arsenic copper, that is, of arsenic bronze, on the basis of these data. The evidence suggests either that minerals containing arsenic were occasionally added to the stock copper in the case of the three ornaments in question or that a copper ore rich in arsenic was unknowingly smelted to give a high copper-arsenic alloy which was then fashioned into the ornaments. Why such accidental mixing of copper and arsenic should be confined to the ornaments alone is unclear (unless of course the arsenic was considered special and valuable, as were the ornaments, and it was incorporated for that reason!); if its presence is

Table 9.2. Analyses of Copper and Copper-Alloy Objects Excavated in the Moche and
Lambayeque Valleys

Site	Period and approximate date	Object: excavation no. MIT no.	Wet chemical (% by weight)		
			As	Cu	Sn
Cemetery: Huaca del Sol–Huaca de la Luna	Early Intermediate (Moche IV) ca. 400 A.D.	Pin?: H8000B-3=65 MIT 545 Needle/pin: H8000B-3=64 MIT 546 Celt?: H8000B-40=12 MIT 547			
Chan Chan S.I.A.R.	Late Intermediate (Late Chimú) ca. 1400–1450 A.D.	Needle: SF1FS62 MIT 360 Needle: SF1FS65 MIT 361	2.55 3.66	92.8 0.79% Ag 95.5	
El Milagro de San José	Late Intermediate (End Early Chimú–Imperial Chimú) ca. 1200 A.D.	Needle: H160506A-2:2 MIT 438 Needle: H160506A-4:9 MIT 439 Bead or spindle whorl: H160506A-7:5 MIT 450			
Cerro la Virgen	Late Intermediate (Late Chimú) ca. 1300–1450 A.D.	Needle: H7236-2:4 MIT 440 Needle: H3968B-1:17 MIT 441 Needle: H3968B-2:4 MIT 442 Needle: H3968B-2:45 MIT 443 Needle: H3968B-2:337 MIT 444 Needle: H3968C-1:1 MIT 445 Ornament: H3968B-2:53 MIT 451			

						Emission spectrographic* (% by weight)								
Ag	Al	As	Au	Bi	Ca	Fe	Mg	Mn	Ni	Pb	Sb	Si	Sn	Zn
L	—	—	FT	—	—	VFT	VFT	—	FT	FT	—	—	—	—
L	—	—	L-M	—	—	VFT	VFT	—	FT	FT	—	FT	—	—
L	—	—	L	—	—	VFT	VVFT	—	FT	FT	—	—	—	—
	FT	—	FT	0.003	VFT	0.002	T	—	0.026	0.0007	0.001	0.007	—	—
T	FT	—	VFT-FT	0.001	VFT	0.003	T	—	0.021	0.026	0.004	0.006	0.0005	—
0.015	1.0	—	VFT	—	0.01	—	—	—	0.03	0.9	—	0.12	—	—
0.70	1.0	—	—	—	0.01	—	—	—	0.03	0.25	—	0.10	—	—
<0.01	0.03	1.90	—	—	0.003	0.24	0.016	—	—	—	—	0.15	—	—
0.05	0.7	—	—	—	0.01	0.06	—	—	0.03	0.08	—	0.10	—	—
0.03	0.3	0.92	VFT	—	FT	—	—	—	0.02	0.25	—	0.03	—	—
0.08	0.65	1.18	—	—	FT	—	—	—	0.1	0.56	—	0.03	—	—
0.1	1.6	2.65	—	—	FT	—	—	—	0.06	0.8	—	0.04	—	—
0.06	VFT	0.26	—	—	FT	—	—	—	0.04	1.0	—	0.03	—	—
0.01	0.7	1.19	—	—	FT	—	—	—	0.03	1.4	—	0.06	—	—
L	<0.01	—	—	—	0.002	—	0.02	—	—	0.55	—	0.10	—	—

(Continued overleaf)

Table 9.2. (cont'd)

Site	Period and approximate date	Object: excavation no. MIT no.	*Wet chemical* (% by weight)		
			As	Cu	Sn
Medaños La Joyada	Late Horizon– Colonial (Chimú-Inca– Colonial) ca. 1450–16th cent. A.D.	Needle: E1102-3:6 MIT 446 Needle: E1102-5:12 MIT 447 Needle: E1102-5:31 MIT 448 Needle: E1102-7:5 MIT 449 Common pin†: E1102-0 MIT 453 Fragment metal sheet: E1102-0 MIT 457A Spindle whorl: E1102-2:7 MIT 458 Ornament: E1102-5:53 MIT 459 Fishhook: E1102-2:141 MIT 462 Ornament: E1102-3:4 MIT 464		88.2	9.08
Lambayeque One	Late Intermediate (Imperial Chimú) ca. 1150–1300 A.D.	Agricultural tool: A.M.N.H. 41.1/5936 MIT 822			
Túcume One-el Purgatorio	Late Horizon (Chimú-Inca) ca. 1450–1530 A.D.	Chisel?: A.M.N.H. 41.1/606 MIT 820			

* As was determined by quantitative spectrographic analysis in all samples in which it was present; all other elements were analyzed semiquantitatively; samples MIT 545, 546, 547 were analyzed by qualitative methods.

† Similar common pins from Santa Fe, Argentina, are illustrated in Fester (1962: fig. 2).

Legend:—not detected, VVFT <0.0001%, VFT 0.0001–0.001%, FT 0.001–0.01%, T 0.01–0.1%, L 0.1–1.0%, M 1.0–10.0%, H >10.0%.

					Emission spectrographic* (% by weight)									
Ag	Al	As	Au	Bi	Ca	Fe	Mg	Mn	Ni	Pb	Sb	Si	Sn	Zn
0.03	0.8	1.53	—	—	FT	—	—	—	0.02	—	—	0.04	—	—
0.05	0.4	0.87	—	—	0.01	—	—	—	0.03	0.6	—	0.06	—	—
0.09	0.9	1.15	—	—	0.025	—	—	—	0.03	0.3	—	0.055	—	—
0.04	0.8	1.91	—	—	0.03	—	—	—	0.035	0.5	—	0.04	—	—
FT	—	—	—	—	VFT	L	FT	T	L	L	—	VFT	—	H
0.03	0.025	—	—	—	0.006	0.28	T	—	—	0.10	—	T	—	—
0.02	—	—	—	—	<0.001	0.12	0.015	—	—	0.38	—	0.03	—	—
0.10	—	—	—	—	0.005	—	L	—	—	—	—	0.10	—	—
0.015	—	—	—	—	0.002	0.16	0.06	—	—	0.06	—	0.16	—	—
0.09	—	2.27	—	—	0.004	—	<0.01	—	—	0.05	—	0.05	—	—
FT	FT-T	1.43	—	—	FT	FT-T	FT	—	FT-T	VFT	—	T	FT	—
FT	VFT	5.60	—	—	FT	FT	VFT	—	FT	—	—	FT	—	—

purely accidental, we should expect it to appear randomly in all types of object.

Nevertheless, the evidence argues strongly for the occasional and perhaps unintentional use of arsenic bronze in the second half of the Early Intermediate Period in the Moche Valley, which, as we have seen, was one of the most important centers for metallurgical experimentation, growth, and elaboration in the northern Andes. By the Late Intermediate Period (roughly A.D. 1000–1470), however, the situation in that same valley and in the extensive region to the north and south ultimately controlled by the Chimú had reversed. Many implements (chisels, agricultural tools, needles for sewing or weaving) were now made of arsenic bronze whose arsenic content hovered between about 2 and 6 percent by weight. As Caley has shown, there is no question that this alloy was intentional. Although we do not have the numbers to prove it, my guess is that the majority of all copper-based objects made at this time in the north, regardless of use—and exclusive of those made of copper-gold or copper-silver alloys—were of arsenic bronze. Table 9.2 lists the analyses made at MIT between 1969 and 1976 of objects excavated from the cemetery that lies between the Huaca del Sol and the Huaca de la Luna in the Moche Valley (an Early Intermediate Period site); from Chan Chan, the capital of the Kingdom of Chimor, El Milagro de San José, Cerro la Virgen, and Medaños La Joyada, all Late Intermediate Period sites in the Moche Valley; and from the site of El Purgatorio, Túcume as well as a grave site, designated by Wendell Bennett as "Lambayeque One,"[85] located halfway between the small town of San José and Lambayeque, both in the Lambayeque Valley.[86] They illustrate the strong preference for arsenic bronze in the north during the Late Intermediate Period.

The crucial question, however, is what happened in the interval between the Early Intermediate and Late Intermediate Periods, the important interval of the Middle Horizon (roughly A.D. 600–1000)? Here our data are less sure. Caley gives analyses of objects that contain arsenic, all from the collections of the Museo Nacional de Arqueología y Antropología in Lima, which might fall within this period.[87] Since they were not excavated, the intervals he assigns them are either A.D. 4th–8th century or 8th–12th century. Only provenance seems controlled: all 9 objects are from the north, 8 from the coast and 1 from the sierra. Six contain arsenic in the 1–3 percent concentration range, while 3 have between 0.21 and 0.77 percent. The average value of arsenic concentration (1.4%) in the first interval

(4th–8th cent.) is essentially the same as that (1.6%) for the second (8th–12th cent.); minimum and maximum concentrations are 0.2 to 2.9 and 0.5 to 3.1 percent, respectively.

At this point, rather than continue with the discussion of the chronology of arsenic bronze, let us consider the processes by which the bronze may have been made, beginning with the simplest system and proceeding to the most complex. Arsenic is found primarily in two types of mineral. It may be present as the simple sulfide of arsenic in orpiment (As_2S_3) or realgar (AsS); or as one component of various copper-arsenic minerals: metallic-looking copper-arsenic minerals such as domeykite (Cu_3As), semimetallic sulfarsenides of copper such as enargite (Cu_3AsS_4) and tennantite [$(Cu,Fe)_{12}As_4S_{13}$], or the more "earthy" copper arsenates such as olivenite [$Cu_2(AsO_4)$ (OH)] and chenevixite [Cu_2Fe_2 $(AsO_4)_2$ $(OH)_4 \cdot H_2O$]. It also commonly occurs as the arsenical form of pyrite— arsenopyrite or mispickel—(FeAsS). Of these minerals, olivenite and chenevixite, the copper arsenates, are the weathered, oxidized products of copper sulfarsenides such as enargite or tennantite.

The simple addition of either orpiment or realgar to a batch of copper mineral (oxides, chlorides, or carbonates of copper) which is then smelted under conditions to remove sulfur but not arsenic, if possible, would result in an alloy of copper and arsenic. Although both these minerals were used as pigments at such distant sites as Pachacamac and Sacsay- huaman[88] (orpiment is a bright lemon to golden yellow, realgar a strong red to orange-yellow color), their virtual absence from the north coast argues against their metallurgical use there (see n. 94), as does the lack of any obvious relationship between these strongly colored red and yellow minerals and the green or blue minerals that were normally used for copper smelting (e.g., malachite, azurite, atacamite, chrysocolla, chalcanthite, etc.).[89] Domeykite is another mineral which would be easy to use for the manufacture of copper-arsenic bronze since, in its natural state, it is already an "alloy" of those two elements (Cu_3As). Simply melting it with a batch of molten copper would produce the desired result.[90] Caley has argued that, given both the simplicity of this technique and the "fairly common" occurrence of domeykite in the Andes, "this process would have been quite feasible in South America."[91] Clair Patterson also specu- lates about the use of domeykite but argues against it because of the con- siderable difference in color and texture between domeykite (a tin-white to steel-gray colored mineral, metallic in luster which tarnishes to brown and subsequently to iridescence) and the common green minerals such as malachite.[92] In a metallurgical site survey I conducted in the Peruvian Andes during 1974[93] I took particular care to try to locate copper-arsenic minerals in northern Peru, both on the coast and in the sierra, in an effort to establish possible sources of the arsenic we find in the archaeological artifacts. Not only is domeykite absent from the north coast, it is extremely rare in the Andes generally[94] except in special instances, such as its association with the rich native copper deposits at Corocoro in Bolivia.[95] According to Dana it is also found in several localities in Chile, namely at San Antonio near Copiapó in Atacama, at Chañarcillo in Coquimbo, and at Rancagua.[96] It is so uncommon in Peru that the mineralogical museum at the Universidad de Ingeniería in Lima, which houses the finest mineral collection in the country, had not a single specimen from Peru. For northern metallurgists to have found domeykite would have been to find the proverbial needle in a haystack.

We come next to the arsenates, olivenite and chenevixite. The first can assume various shades of olive-green, greenish brown, grayish green, or grayish white and is adamantine to vitreous in luster. It is a secondary mineral found in the oxidized zones of ore deposits, where it is associated with minerals such as malachite, azurite, and limonite ($Fe_2O_3 \times H_2O$). The only South American occurrences listed by Dana are in Chile at Collahuasi and Copiapó and possibly, with chenevixite, at Chuquicamata.[97] Chenevixite, a greenish yellow to olive-green mineral, has been identified at Chuquicamata. According to Georg Petersen, it occurs in the oxidation zone of polymetallic deposits such as enargite and tennantite. It is one of the compounds of arsenic that remains stable in the oxidation zone in arid climates, but in humid climates it is susceptible to leaching from rain waters.[98] The fact that it is found at Chuquicamata is not surprising, for the Atacama desert is one of the most arid regions in the world, and mineral species are found at Chuquicamata that are extremely rare anywhere else. Chuquicamata is, in fact, a particularly rich source of copper arsenates because it is the only porphyry copper deposit in South America which has enargite as one of its main primary ore minerals. The occurrence of chenevixite there ought not to suggest that it might also be found in any quantity in the coastal deserts of northern Peru, however, where rain does fall every few years, where the humidity is high enough to support vegetation in the *lomas* just inland of the desert, and where the copper deposits have no primary arsenic minerals. I found no trace of either olivenite or chenevixite during the course of my survey, but as G. Petersen points out, the latter mineral can be overlooked quite easily because it is close in color to both malachite and arsenopyrite. Nevertheless, if these minerals exist on the coast they are there in very small quantity, and their presence in the highlands in any appreciable concentration is not common because of their relative solubility.[99] Possible but not probable is Clair Patterson's contention that "the gross excesses of arsenic, bismuth, and antimony" in the three Uhle Moche ornaments described above, in which he found a high concentration of arsenic "probab[ly] originated from inadvertent mixtures of azurite or malachite with small quantities of a green copper arsenate mineral such as olivenite."[100] But it should be kept in mind that, as Ing. Edgardo Ponzoni S. of the Ministerio de Minas in Lima put it, the north coast is distinctive for its lack of arsenic minerals,[101] and except for arsenopyrite I found none during the course of my survey.[102] Whereas occasional and unintentional mixing of such minerals with other "staple" copper minerals might possibly account for the data from Moche phases III–IV, it would certainly not explain the source of the arsenic so common to Late Intermediate Period arsenic bronzes.

These bronzes were almost certainly made with sulfarsenide ores of copper that are abundant throughout the Peruvian highlands, particularly in the northern sierra from Quiruvilca to Sinchao (near Hualgayoc). Mines at both these sites impressed me not only with the abundance of minerals such as enargite and tennantite but with their shallowness as well. In Sinchao, samples of pure enargite (identified at MIT by X-ray diffraction analysis) containing 45.7 percent copper and 14.0 percent arsenic were obtained from workings at depths of 1–2 m below the surface.[103] The Quiruvilca enargite contained 45.4 percent copper and 15.1 percent arsenic on wet chemical analysis. Thus discovering and extracting these shiny black ores would have presented no difficulty to early Andean miners. Which of these ores was used—including arsenopyrite, found abundantly nearer the coast in the Jequetepeque Valley, for example, or in the region between Contumaza and Cascas—we are not yet able to say,[104] but careful laboratory study of the artifacts and of samples of all these minerals will undoubtedly distinguish among them. For example, Caley's analyses indicate the presence of antimony in one-third of the objects he examined.[105] The mineral used in these instances may have been tennantite ($Cu_{12}As_4S_{13}$) which, mineralogically, is closely associated with tetrahedrite ($Cu_{12}Sb_4S_{13}$), the two elements arsenic and antimony substituting for one another in various proportions and forming a complete solid solution series from tetrahedrite, containing only antimony, to tennantite, containing only arsenic.

That sulfide ores were smelted in the Andes in pre-Columbian times may come as a surprise to some. Clair Patterson, for example, states categorically: "South American metallurgists did not smelt sulfide ores because there was an abundance of oxidized ores available. There is no evidence of slagging furnaces, slags, deep mines, or cultural factors associated with a sulfide smelting era to indicate sulfide smelting. All chemical compositions of grave-associated Mesoamerican and South American metal artifacts can be understood on the basis of native metals or metals smelted by reduction from oxidized ores."[106] Caley, on the other hand, has pointed out the use of sulfide ores on several occasions,[107] although the presence of sulfur in a metal can arise not only from the smelting of a copper sulfide ore but from contamination of the metal by sulfur arising from the presence of sulfates that may be associated with the oxides or carbonates being smelted. Such salts would be reduced to sulfur during smelting and incorporated to a certain extent into the metallic copper. In his 1973 paper, however, Caley is careful to point out the following: "That sulfide ores were smelted is indicated both directly and indirectly by the analytical data. The presence of small proportions of residual sulfur in four of the samples is a direct indication, and the presence of considerable arsenic in all the samples, along with antimony, bismuth, or both, in most of them is an indirect indication."[108] The two important points to be made are (1) that sulfide ores were in common use in the northern Andes by the Late Intermediate Period and the source of the ores was the highlands, and (2) that Andean metalworkers had developed technologies sufficiently sophisticated to cope with the roasting and reduction regimes necessary to the processing of sulfide ores on a significant scale. We do not know if the copper sulfarsenides (enargite and tennantite) were smelted as such to produce copper-arsenic bronze or if they were added to batches of oxide or carbonate ores, to batches of partly reduced copper sulfide ores, or even directly to molten copper. Whatever the method, the arsenic mineral had to be at least partly roasted initially in order to drive off most of its sulfur as SO_2 gas. Upon the elimination of the sulfur the mineral could then be smelted in a reducing environment normal to the treatment of the simpler oxides and carbonates.

In fact, McKerrell and Tylecote have shown that, whereas arsenic is lost through the formation and volatilization of As_2O_3 during the oxidation roasting of copper arsenic ores, no loss of arsenic occurs during reduction smelting.[109] Furthermore, McKerrell has indicated that, on the basis of his experiments in smelting various mixtures of copper oxides and arsenic sulfides, a preliminary partial roasting to eliminate sulfur can leave as much as 50 percent of the arsenic still in the charge, depending upon the temperature and the vapor pressure of the As_2O_3.[110] Subsequent reduction smelting of such a charge would retain essentially all of the arsenic. It is thus easy to see how Andean metalworkers could have begun with ores such as those at Quiruvilca or Sinchao and, by partially roasting them and subsequently smelting them under reducing conditions, retained high concentrations of arsenic (such as those given in table 9.2) in the arsenic bronze produced. Final working of that bronze by hammering and annealing it under oxidizing conditions to produce the desired artifacts would normally result in further loss of arsenic through oxidation. McKerrell and Tylecote contend that the arsenic levels in worked bronzes were, in fact, controlled by just this mechanism.[111]

The importance of establishing the first appearance of arsenic bronze in the north, the circumstances of its use there during the Middle Horizon, its occurrence or absence as a significant alloy in the south, and the nature of the ores supplying arsenic to the bronzes are now apparent. We are dealing with several phenomena at once: the change from the use of copper to the use of bronze; the change from the simple reduction smelting of copper oxide and carbonate ores to the much more complex roasting–reduction sequences normal to the smelting of the more recalcitrant sulfide ores;[112] and the change from the exploitation of locally available coastal ores of copper to the exploitation of complex sulfide ores in the highlands.[113] What we must ask is whether this remarkable concatenation of technological and social events (for the exploitation of highland ores could have been achieved only through trade, exchange, or through the vertical control of ecological zones extending into the high sierra by an archipelago system such as that outlined by Murra[114]) was the further development of a northern regional metallurgy with firm roots in the rich metallurgical traditions of north coastal Chavín and, later, Mochica technology or whether it arose as a direct result of influence from the spread of Tiahuanacoid culture elements from the southern altiplano. And if we examine the latter argument, what exactly might

the effects of southern influence have been in the north: Did the Tiahuanacoid spread introduce arsenic bronze to the peoples of the north;
did it introduce not the alloy but the technology by which to smelt sulfide
ores; or was the effect one of liberalizing to a certain extent the northern
view of its own local metallurgy, enabling it to open up and to utilize
new sources of ores and to experiment with different processing regimes?
For if the northern metalworkers were capable of smelting copper sulfarsenide ores, they were also capable of smelting other sulfides, sulfides of
copper and argentiferous sulfides of lead, for example. Do we see in
Middle Horizon metallurgy a pan-Andean technology characterized
by the smelting of sulfide ores and the use of bronze, particularly of the
copper-arsenic variety?

To answer these questions we must have much more information than
is presently available about Middle Horizon metallurgy in the north but
particularly about the development of metallurgical technologies in the
south. My own guess is that the consistent, innovative quality of north
Andean metallurgy, its momentum from the Early Horizon through to
the Middle Horizon, the obvious preoccupation of the northern peoples
with metal and the expertness of their craftsmanship all culminated in
important, self-generated technological changes there at or about the
time of the Middle Horizon. The presence in Moche phases III and IV
of high arsenic bronzes, even infrequently, suggests that at that early
date, though the alloy may have been an accidental one, the Mochica
were aware of its properties and may well have tried to reproduce it.
In my view, northern metallurgy was an impressive regional development
with a great deal of internal variation from area to area but essentially
altered very little by outside influences until the establishment of the
Inca hegemony. But the guess will remain just that until substantiated.

At the moment, our data for South Andean metallurgy are scant. To
begin with Argentina, Fester analyzed a group of objects belonging to
the Aguada phase,[115] that is, to the beginning of the ninth century, from
the Valley of Hualfín, near Belén in the Province of Catamarca, northwest
Argentina.[116] All contain high concentrations of arsenic (between 1.17
and 7.11% by weight). Fester comments that the objects are unusual in
that, prior to his study, only one other object from Argentina, reported
by Boman, showed arsenic at this concentration level. This was a fragment
of a plaque from La Paya in the Province of Salta which contained 5.20
percent arsenic and 1.46 percent sulfur.[117] On the other hand, Fester

shows little surprise at the presence of the arsenic in the group he examined, since the mines at Las Capillitas, 50 km from Hualfín, contain enargite, tennantite, and tetrahedrite. Furthermore, of the 33 objects analyzed, 19 contained from 0.18 to 1.22 percent zinc as an impurity. Zinc was apparently a common element in the Las Capillitas primary ore deposit. Thus he was able to establish that the source of the ores used in Belén was Las Capillitas.

This group of objects is curious, however, since many also contain tin in about the same concentration as arsenic (between 0.91 and 2.05%). Caley concludes that the group studied by Fester is rather special and that those objects containing tin were probably smelted from an unusual ore.[118] In any case, Fester's analyses, as atypical as they may be, provide our first evidence for the use of arsenic bronze in a local area of northwest Argentina during the period that most concerns us, that is, the 7th–11th centuries. Fester supposes that the highlanders smelting the ores at Las Capillitas used only the fully oxidized minerals, that is, the copper arsenates, for he assumes that they had not developed a technology that could process the complex sulfide ores. He gives no proof to substantiate this idea, however, which he clearly states is conjectural. The impurity levels in the objects, including substantial amounts of antimony, argue the contrary, that sulfide ores were almost certainly smelted to produce these unusual alloys.

Apart from this study, we have virtually no published information about arsenic bronze for Argentina, Bolivia, or Chile. Thus we cannot presently evaluate whether the material from Hualfín is atypical and can be overlooked in a developmental study because the objects happened to be made from the only ore source available and that source was rich in arsenic. We simply must have analyses, particularly from the Bolivian altiplano,[119] of copper and copper alloy objects from the beginning of the Middle Horizon and, hopefully, earlier. Thus far, the analyses we have indicate that copper was used in the early phases at the site of Tiwanaku itself (e.g., the metal cramps used in setting the stone blocks in some of the buildings there are made of copper[120]), and in the later phases copper-tin bronze seems to appear. As mentioned earlier, Ponce Sanginés reports copper slags having been excavated at Wankarani, Chiripa, Pukara de Belén, and La Joya, indicating that during Tiahuanaco phase I copper ores were already being smelted.[121] The vast majority of reported analyses of Bolivian and Argentinian objects shows them to be made of copper-tin bronze, but as Caley has pointed out, many of the early analyses are incomplete and the analysts may not even have looked for arsenic.[122] And many objects, in fact the majority, are from the Late Horizon.

Should we find that arsenic bronze was a development largely limited to the northern Andes and disseminated from there, we must still raise the question of the possible acquisition by northern metalworkers of sulfide smelting technology from South Andean centers. Again, we are handicapped by lack of data. We do not know whether the southern craftsmen were smelting sulfide ores, although the analyses of the complex alloys from northwest Argentina certainly suggest that they were. Caley also argues that they were, on the basis of the high residual sulfur content found in copper-tin bronzes from Machu Picchu.[123] Mathewson reports inclusions of cuprous sulfide particles in all the bronzes he studied metallographically from that site.[124] Both analysts are dealing, however, with Late Horizon metallurgy. Ambrosetti cites the chief impurities found in the objects from Calchaquí, northwest Argentina, as nickel, iron, cobalt, zinc, lead, arsenic, and, in several, sulfur.[125] Many of these elements, of course, would be common to the normal range of sulfide ores found in Argentina, but this is weak evidence.

Perhaps more significant is the fact that south Andean bronze was overwhelmingly of the copper-tin variety, whether or not it was preceded or accompanied by a copper-arsenic type. The single fact upon which all investigators seem to agree is that the source of the tin was cassiterite (SnO_2), the oxide of that metal which abounds in Bolivia and in northern Argentina both as placer deposits and in veins. I am not aware of a mixed source of copper-tin ores in this region that could have been mined and smelted directly to give tin bronze.[126] The manufacture of copper-tin bronze was, therefore, of an entirely different nature from that of the copper-arsenic variety. Since cassiterite is an oxide of tin, it can be mixed with oxides or carbonates of copper and smelted directly; it can be added to molten copper and subsequently reduced; or it may be smelted to produce metallic tin that is then added to copper metal to form bronze. The latter was probably the method used in the Andes. In any of these processes, nothing more than simple reduction of the tin ore is involved, and if the copper is also in the form of oxides, carbonates, or chlorides the procedure is relatively simple and straightforward. Only if the copper ores are sulfides does the regime necessitate a prior roasting stage followed by reduction smelting of those ores. Thus conceptually as well as technically the manufacture of the two types of bronze is different. One involves the two-stage treatment of a complex ore; the other is a simple addition of one species of mineral or metal to the other, each of which is processed in much the same way.[127]

Thus the late Middle Horizon may have seen the meeting of two separate and distinct regional technologies, each having culminated in the production of a bronze based upon the utilization of ore types common to its own geographic sphere. Neither may have had much effect upon the other—that is the issue I raised at the outset—but further laboratory examination of excavated material should resolve the question. The very fact that by the end of the Middle Horizon both regions had developed "a bronze" is intriguing in and of itself. It suggests that a metallurgical pan-Andeanism preceded *Tawantinsuyu* and rested upon the widespread availability of ideas, techniques, and ways of viewing the material world that manifested themselves locally in diverse forms. In the north certainly metallurgical concepts were shared from Peru to Colombia yet were tailored to meet the requirements of long-standing local habits of working with metals and of thinking about metals.[128]

The Andes, unlike the Near East, saw bronze of both varieties develop quite late in the metallurgical scheme of things, long after smelting had become common practice and alloying was a highly sophisticated art.

Cultural Meanings Of Bronze

Whatever the metallurgical interaction between the north and the south during the Middle Horizon, both regions developed their respective bronzes thereafter almost to the exclusion of copper or of other copper-based alloys until the Inca conquest (although the alloys of copper and silver and copper and gold were always important in the north for the manufacture of certain kinds of objects made of sheet metal, as opposed to castings). The two bronzes developed side by side, as it were, and there was even some use of copper-tin bronze in the north in the latter part of the Late Intermediate Period (see table 9.2).

In the southern Andes, copper-tin bronze was used for every conceivable kind of object—ornaments, implements, weapons—whether cast or forged. In his superb study of the Late Horizon bronzes from Machu Picchu, Mathewson establishes the mastery of the alloy by Inca metalworkers and their appreciation and control of the properties and working characteristics of the metal.[129] High-tin bronzes (generally between about

10 and 13% tin) were used in castings in order to take advantage of the two main qualities of such alloys: strength and superior castability. On the other hand, low-tin bronzes of about 5 percent tin were used for objects that were forged in manufacture, such as axes, chisels, depilatory tweezers, *tumis*, *tupus*, and so forth, since these alloys are ductile and are easily worked cold without becoming brittle. When hardness was required above and beyond that naturally conferred upon the alloy by the addition of these relatively small amounts of tin, the smiths work-hardened the edges of *tumis*, chisels, and other cutting tools to give them added durability and sharpness. One object, a *tumi* with an ornamental llama head, was made of both alloy types—the cast llama head is of high-tin bronze, the forged knife of low-tin bronze. The head was cast onto the shank of the knife! Annealing and hot forging were among the techniques common to the smith.

Thus copper-tin bronze became the all-purpose metal in the southern Andes during the Late Intermediate Period and, of course, remained so during the Late Horizon. It was used for the most utilitarian of objects and for the ceremonial, for objects within the aesthetic locus[130] of high-land cultures as well as for the tools of war. It was, in a sense, the Andean stainless steel—ubiquitous, handsome, capable of being handled in a variety of ways to achieve different aesthetic and utilitarian ends, and, from its wide dispersal throughout the south, it seems to have been available to people at all social levels. This is not surprising, given the rich resources of copper and tin in the Bolivian sierra.

We have scarcely any technical studies of the northern copper-arsenic artifacts. All of the arsenic bronzes I have examined thus far, and the majority of those reported by Caley, are objects that were hammered to shape—spindle whorls, agricultural blades, chisels, needles for sewing or weaving, and so forth. What we lack are studies of castings from this region. I have seen and have commented elsewhere upon the large numbers of massive cast and sometimes partly worked "copper points" (figs. 9.2–9.6) common to at least the area between the Moche and Lambayeque valleys, if not more extensively, in the Late Intermediate Period.[131] These implements comprise agricultural blades, possibly spear points, chisels, and other similar kinds of objects that often were hafted on a wooden pole of some sort. They are commonly found in hoards, sometimes of several hundred, and both the Museo de Arqueología of the Universidad Nacional de Trujillo and the Museo Arqueológico Brüning in Lambayeque house

Fig. 9.2. Implements of copper or a copper alloy (probably copper-arsenic). Chan Chan, Peru. Collection: Museo de Arqueología, Universidad Nacional de Trujillo.

Fig. 9.3. (above) Implements of copper-arsenic bronze, front view. Lambayeque Valley, Peru. Collection: Museo Arqueológico Brüning, Lambayeque.

Fig. 9.4. (left) Rear view of implements shown in fig. 9.3.

Fig. 9.5. Chisel-like tool of copper-arsenic bronze, excavated by Wendell Bennett at Túcume, Lambayeque Valley, Peru. Top view showing socket. Collection: American Museum of Natural History/MIT.

Fig. 9.6. Side view of Túcume "chisel" showing sharp cutting edge.

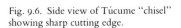

myriad examples. Bennett describes several of these types, particularly the agricultural implements, that he excavated in "Middle Chimú" graves in the Lambayeque Valley.[132] One such implement, a long, pointed tool socketed at one end and measuring 55 cm in length, was found upon quantitative spectrographic analysis to contain 1.43 percent arsenic (see table 9.2), an arsenic concentration high enough for us to consider it an arsenic bronze. Another of these objects, which Bennett called "a hollow copper chisel or tool . . . obviously intended to be hafted," is from a late Chimú grave excavated at the site of El Purgatorio, Túcume, Lambayeque Valley.[133] Quantitative spectrographic analysis of this object, which is illustrated here in figures 9.5 and 9.6, revealed that it is a copper-arsenic bronze containing 5.60 percent arsenic (see table 9.2).[134]

I am virtually certain that the vast majority of the so-called copper points from the "Middle Chimú" and other Late Intermediate Period sites in the north are arsenic bronzes. Many I have seen were obviously never used or intended for use. Some of the presumed agricultural implements are much too heavy to have been functional as tools. Others are cast with relief decorations of serpents or other designs on one side. Still others are miscast or cast almost as ingots, in spite of their hoelike shape, with one pronounced concave surface indicating that the metal was probably cast into a flat, one-piece mold open at the top. The distinctive feature of all these objects, whether they were used or not, is the amount of metal they contain. More than anything else, they appear to be "depositories" or "concentrators" of metal. It seems clear from their weight, their burial in large numbers, the unfinished quality of some, the ingotlike quality of others, that the bronze metal itself was considered of value and was amassed. Perhaps it indicated wealth or status, perhaps it had other associations. The interment of individuals with solid discs of copper in their mouths or in intimate association with their bodies was characteristic of Mochica burials, as was pointed out earlier, and Kroeber argued that the massive chunks used in such fashion must have represented actual wealth.[135] He was describing oval slugs of about 6 cm diameter. Graves of later periods in the north also often contain pieces of metal, usually small thin sheets wrapped round with thread, in the mouths or hands of the deceased. But the Late Intermediate Period artifacts are of a different nature; they are much larger (those described by Bennett average 30 cm in length and 0.8 cm in blade thickness) and can weigh several pounds.

This situation, in which a particular type of bronze was utilized by and, in a sense, became the hallmark of each of the two regions we have been discussing, changed dramatically with the formation of the Inca state. Arsenic bronze persisted in the north until the time of the Inca conquest of the Kingdom of Chimor and even somewhat later in areas remote from direct highland control (see table 9.2, for example). Scholars have long argued that tin bronze displaced arsenic bronze in the Near East because on manufacture the latter released lethal arsenic fumes, but the much clearer picture given by the Andean case weakens that argument. Northern metalworkers amassed arsenic bronze and valued it highly. They utilized it consistently for at least 500 years. Whatever toxic effects the manufacturing processes may have had, the craftsmen obviously learned to control them. Indeed, McKerrell and Tylecote have shown that danger from arsenic fumes upon smelting copper-arsenic ores is not significant and is easily managed.[136] Thus the adoption by Andean peoples throughout *Tawantinsuyu* of copper-tin bronze upon the establishment of the Inca empire had little to do with metallurgical considerations or with health hazards. In terms of their use and their properties, arsenic bronze and tin bronze appear to be quite similar.[137] Neither was superior, neither represented a metallurgical advancement over the other. But they were not interchangeable ideologically. The spread of tin bronze throughout the Inca realm was, I suspect, a political act. Tin bronze was the imperial alloy par excellence, the standard of empire. The Inca, thoroughly familiar with its maufacture and easily able to control the supply of tin, could impose tin bronze throughout the Andes just as they imposed Quechua as a language. Both were deliberate attempts to unify, standardize, and control aspects of culture that could easily be equated with membership in the state.

Comments   The Andean case is instructive because it illustrates so clearly that we must break away from the traditional and rather rigid views we have held about the way in which metallurgies develop, that is, along rather narrow courses that begin with native copper, move along stage by stage, and end with tin bronze. The inevitable, underlying assumption of this view is that the progression is dependent upon increasing technological sophistication and that the final product achieved is somehow metallurgically superior. While the great metallurgical traditions did, of course, proceed generally from the simple to the complex in their technologies, current views of that progression seem to me overly evolutionary in spirit. In an effort to build models and to trace developments over long periods of time, scholars have not entertained seriously enough the role of experiment or the realities of actual practice from region to region or culture to culture. Clair Patterson expresses the kind of reasoning and the inbuilt biases upon which it rests that plague research in this area: "Since the Moche, or their local contemporaries, were the discoverers of reduction smelting, it is hardly credible that they would have then immediately leapfrogged into oxidation smelting, a development that was evolutionary over a period of 3000 yr in southwest Asia."[138] In terms of the discussion presented here, it seems to me that a reexamination of the data of Old World metallurgy might reveal that arsenic/tin bronze use is not so easily explained and that in neither the Old World nor the New did tin replace arsenic for purely technological or technique-related reasons.

An important question to explore, however, is why tin did, finally, win out. What is it about metallic tin or about tin bronze that resulted in its adoption, to the exclusion of all contenders, by peoples in vast geographic regions in such disparate culture areas as the Andes and the Near East? In the Near East, where cassiterite is scarce, we have not yet found the major sources of the tin ore being used.[139] Some deposits may have been as distant as south central Asia in the area at Bukhara and the Fergana Valley.[140] Thus tin used in Persia or in Anatolia traveled incredibly long distances; it is not surprising that the metal was accorded special value. Why it was brought from so far when, at least in Iran, arsenic bronze had already developed and was in common use is the crucial question. In the Andes, by contrast, tin was abundant and near at hand. Considering that the Inca incorporated many cultural features of the peoples they conquered into their own repertoire—for example, we know that the finest Chimú metalsmiths were brought from the coast to Cusco to practice their art for the royal lineage, and it is certain that such northern technical inventions as depletion gilding[141] were introduced to the sierra at that time, if not earlier—it is interesting that the bronze technology of the superior craftsmen of the north was rejected outright. Whereas gold and silver were reserved for royal use, tin bronze was closer to a "people's alloy," and the impact of its dissemination throughout the empire must surely have been calculated in this sense. Whatever the mystique of tin, the answers to these issues, I am sure, lie much more in the realm of economics, politics, and ideology than they do in the realm of pure metallurgy.

REFLECTIONS

Several points have been addressed in the course of these discussions that I believe deserve reemphasizing with respect to their bearing upon Andean metallurgy.

The Andean Vertical Landscape

We have seen that, as a consequence of the topography of the Central Andean region, the normal movement of people and of the goods they exchanged was vertical, up and down the steep slopes of the Andes mountain range, on both its western and eastern sides. Life was lived vertically because one survived and prospered by controlling or having access to the resources of ecological zones that varied with altitude. Metals were one such resource. It should come as no surprise, for example, that the Kingdom of Chimor—the largest and most powerful of the coastal states that emerged in the Central Andes—when it quite clearly needed to enlarge upon its supply of copper ores, looked to the highlands immediately to its east as the natural source of such ores. Whether the Chimú actually prospected for ores in the north-north central sierra, whether they controlled the mines worked there, whether they obtained the ore by exchange with highland peoples who exploited it, or whether the state had outliers or colonists living in the highlands to work the prospects[142] we do not know. But it must have been as a result of that quest for new supplies of ore to supplement the modest amounts present and by that time probably exhausted on the north coast, that the copper sulfarsenides so typical of the north sierra were found and put into service. The north Andean arsenic bronze that resulted from the smelting of such ores may, to put it bluntly, have been nothing more than "dirty copper," smelted copper that contained residual arsenic. Even today, when these same ores are mined and processed chemically, the high levels of arsenic retained in the concentrates constitute the chief obstacle to the sale of such copper on the international market. Some Peruvian firms have begun roasting the concentrates to drive off the arsenic and purify the copper![143] Needless to say, arsenic bronze had many properties that were evidently valued by the Chimú, and there is no question that it was purposefully made and extensively used. One of these valued properties may have been the formation of silver-colored enriched arsenic coatings on the surfaces of castings made from the higher arsenic alloys.[144]

The point is simply that people use what they have, what is at hand to use. And in the Central Andes, since what is at hand usually comprises a modest range of choices because the ecological zones are so narrow, what is at hand translates into what is accessible, what can be made available. In Andean thinking and in Andean patterns of behavior, what is available to any locale includes the resources that come from those who live higher up or lower down along a vertical landscape. These are the traditional directions from and to which exchanges are made.

Thus the concurrent manufacture and use of copper-tin bronze with the copper-arsenic type are perfectly understandable in terms of the Andean scene. The tin resources of the south were and still are vast. Tin bronze was invented there and remained there until the Inca disseminated it for reasons of their own. The two bronze alloys developed as they did because specific types of ores were locally available and because the technologies had been worked out by which to process and to smelt them. Each type belonged to an economic and political sphere between which there was little if any interchange. Verticality and regionalism have always been crucial factors in Andean sociopolitical and technological development, and the particular way in which bronze became manifest in the Andes reflects these overwhelming aspects of Andean life.

The Andean Horizons

Nevertheless, there were periods during which regionalism and cultural diversity in the Central Andes gave way to communication and a much larger measure of cultural unity. What effects did these Horizon periods have upon Andean metallurgy?

Again, the situation is most clearly drawn for the Late Horizon. The Inca were not innovators in metal technology. The important advances in alloying, smelting, depletion gilding, and other processes central to Andean metalworking had been made by the end of the Middle Horizon. As in all other aspects of their civilization, the Inca exhibited their resourcefulness in metal technology primarily through their organization of that technology, at least insofar as we have evidence about their mining industry. In fact, the Late Horizon is the only period of Andean prehistory when we can refer to any aspect of metal production, and particularly to mining, as having occurred on a near-industrial scale, by comparison with the metallurgical activities of other ancient societies. The Inca were innovators in terms of the scale of their operations, the number of new mines they opened and ran, the numbers of people they were able to mobilize to work in those mines, and the distances to which they, the state, could send people to fulfill their corvée responsibilities through extraction of the state-owned and state-controlled mineral resources.

The 16th century chroniclers mention groups of miners sent from Peru to Bolivia to extract silver ores from the rich workings there. Gold and silver had become prerogatives of the state, bound up with its religion, closely related to the origin myth of the royal dynasty, and in every respect controlled by the Inca. Andean metals moved from where they were mined and smelted to Inca centers from which they were redistributed—in the case of gold and silver, primarily to Cusco; in the case of other metals, to those areas where it was politically expedient to move them. Bolivian tin, in the form of tin bronze, made its way as far north as Ecuador.

The Early Horizon was almost surely the period during which, as we have seen, "true metallurgy" began, but the invention of metallurgy seems to bear little relation to the prime vehicle through which cultural unity was achieved in the Central Andes at that time, namely the Chavín cult itself. This period remains the most confusing and difficult to interpret because of the scantiness of our data, but the discovery of alloying and the manipulation of copper ores appear to have occurred at local centers which were outside of Chavín influence. The beginning of copper metallurgy was probably a highland phenomenon and a restricted one at that. It may have been spurred by the facilitation of communication particularly along the north–south axis of the Andes in the area connected with the Chavín cult. It seems more likely, however, that it was the vertical communication between highlanders and coastal peoples, now settled and practicing irrigation agriculture, that may have stimulated interest in the new metal.

The one Horizon period that does seem to have been unequivocally related to significant changes in the development of metal technology in the Central Andes is the Middle Horizon. Yet we know embarrassingly little about the relationships between metallurgy and the events that characterize that Horizon. The Middle Horizon saw the military conquest of large portions of what is today Peru by highland peoples living in the Mantaro River basin, near the site of Huari. The empire that was established is often referred to as the Huari Empire, and the city of Huari appears to have been its capital. Planned urbanism was an important feature of Huari civilization,[145] and Willey has remarked that it may also have been during this time that "state control of the distribution of foodstuffs—on a wide territorial scale—came into being,"[146] implying that the complex organization of a system that permitted such distribution was invented by the Huari imperialists and not by the Inca. In any event, as we have already seen, by the fall of the empire and the end of this period, tin bronze was being used in the south central and southern highlands. Lumbreras reports having found objects of bronze (though he did not chemically analyze them) from the early phases of this period in his excavations at Conchopata, a site very near Huari.[147] But so few Middle Horizon sites have been excavated, particularly in the highlands, that our metal corpus from this important period is extremely small. It is fair to say, however, that associated with the Middle Horizon was an increase in the utilization of sulfide ores of copper so that by the ensuing Late Intermediate Period, both in the northern and southern parts of the Central Andes, the manufacture of bronze was well under way as a result of the manipulation of such ores. The Middle Horizon seems to have been the point of departure for the serious exploitation of sulfide ores and the generation of sulfide smelting technology in a systematic way in the Central Andean region.

Thus the Horizon periods were central to Andean metallurgical development. Metallurgy began during the first of these periods, reached the height of its sophistication as a result of the second, and became centrally organized and near-industrialized during the course of the third. On the other hand, the significant elaboration of new techniques and metallurgical processes and the developmental aspects of the technology seem to have occurred locally during the regionally oriented intermediate periods.

If Wertime is correct in his assessment of the preconditions for the emergence of iron metallurgy among early societies, that is, that iron develops when there has been wholesale invasion of the sulfide zone together with an industrial scale of metal production,[148] then the Inca achievements in metallurgy by the time of the Spanish invasion can be seen as barely sufficient to satisfy such a set of conditions. Had the empire continued to exist, the situation may have changed, but there are indications that iron would not soon have been added to the Andean repertoire of metals.

Metals and Andean Values

During the roughly 3200 years of Andean prehistory during which metals were used, there was a double focus to Andean metallurgy that certainly affected the way in which the technology itself developed. Gold—and, particularly in the later periods, silver—was the locus of a whole series of activities and attitudes that played an extremely prominent role in Andean society from the first appearance of that metal on the scene. Copper and its alloys formed the other locus that was sustained throughout the period under consideration.

As we have seen, gold was undoubtedly the most important of the metals in terms of its symbolic content, and the cultural value accorded it grew steadily from what were largely religious associations in Chavín to political and cosmological associations among the Inca. The metallic aspect of gold and silver carried such a heavy load of meaning that the earliest Andean alloy systems were developed in order to produce golden and silvery metallic surfaces on objects made from those alloys. In fact, Andean metallurgy made some of its most significant advances in its efforts to devise suitable gilding and silvering systems to transform baser metals into metals that appeared precious. The culmination of this long-standing involvement with gold and silver occurred during the Late Horizon when both metals were mined—and silver was smelted—throughout the four quarters of *Tawantinsuyu* on a grand scale that was outdone only by the activities of the Spaniards soon after their invasion and conquest of the Inca state. Goldsmithing continued to be an important, highly specialized craft, the products of which were the prerogatives of the state, used by the royal dynasty in its palaces and temples and, without question, as royal gifts to administrators, leaders of the army, and other officials of high status. Gold and silver symbolized the descent of the royal dynasty from the sun and the moon.

Gold was collected from placer deposits but was also mined from auriferous quartz veins. It was used for display, primarily in the form of ornamental or ceremonial objects. Silver was also mined in the native state, and Georg Petersen claims that, indeed, native silver was not only abundant in prehistoric times but was found in surface outcrops associated with weathered reddish-brown *pacos*, or iron oxide gossans.[149] On the other hand, there is also evidence for the smelting of silver ores or argentiferous lead ores during the Late Horizon[150] using techniques that involved reducing the silver ores in the presence of lead sulfide (galena). Such processes evidently did not necessitate the addition of iron ores as fluxes as Wertime suggests was the case in the Near East.[151] Thus, although Inca miners had certainly invaded the sulfide zone in order to extract silver-rich lead ores or galena with which to smelt their silver ores, the smelting practice they used did not produce iron as a by-product to any appreciable extent.

The gold–silver focus within Andean society was, by the Late Horizon, transformed into a state-monopolized industry and one to which the state committed substantial resources of labor and energy, especially in the extraction and processing of the metals. They remained metals of "charisma," concentrated in the hands of the few and redistributed as tokens of royal esteem.

Copper and bronze were also highly valued, as is indicated by their use in burial practice not only among the Mochica and other Early Intermediate Period north coast cultures but also by the powerful elites among the Chimú. The content of that value is difficult to assess, however. Copper was often used for ornamental display, but tools, implements, and weapons were all made of copper or of bronze. To the extent that metal ever became an important utilitarian material in the Andes—and that in and of itself is a moot point—it was through copper and copper alloys that such functions were served. During the Late Horizon, at the same time that the Inca became the royal custodians of Andean gold and silver, the state began to democratize copper metallurgy by its broad dissemination of bronze objects throughout the empire. For the first time in Andean prehistory, metal that was used for nonornamental purposes began to be a common item among peoples at many social levels who occupied many different ecological zones over a vast geographic area. Although bronze metal may have been as carefully controlled by the state as gold and silver were, one has the distinct impression that, had the Spanish invasion not occurred, bronze would have become a household item throughout *Tawantinsuyu*.

The balance between gold and silver, on the one hand, and copper and its alloys on the other was never an equal balance probably because the former always had behind them the weight of religious and political institutions. Copper was nevertheless the vehicle through which the real achievements in Andean metallurgy took place, and it was on the threshold of assuming a much more important role in Andean life when Andean civilization was cut down by Spanish invaders in search of the rich gold and silver deposits of the land.

NOTES

1. Heather Lechtman, "Style in Technology—Some Early Thoughts," in *Material Culture: Styles, Organization and Dynamics of Technology*, eds. Heather Lechtman and Robert S. Merrill (St. Paul: West Publishing, 1977), pp. 3–20; idem, "Issues in Andean Metallurgy," in *Pre-Columbian Metallurgy of South America*, ed. Elizabeth P. Benson (Washington, D.C.: Dumbarton Oaks, 1979), pp. 1–40.

2. The following studies are useful as guides to the ore geology of the Central Andean area: Federico Ahlfeld and Jorge Muñoz Reyes, *Las especies minerales de Bolivia* (Bilbao: Banco Minero de Bolivia, 1955); Federico Ahlfeld and Alejandro Schneider-Scherbina, *Los yacimientos minerales y de hidrocarburos de Bolivia*, Departamento Nacional de Geología, Boletín 5 (La Paz, 1964); Eleodoro Bellido B. and Luís de Montreuil D., *Aspectos generales de la metalogenia del Perú*, Geología Económica No. 1, Servicio de Geología y Minería (Lima, 1972); Benjamin Miller and Joseph T. Singewald, *The Mineral Deposits of South America* (New York: McGraw-Hill, 1919); Ulrich Petersen, "Regional Geology and Major Ore Deposits of Central Peru," *Economic Geology* 60 (1965): 407–76; Ulrich Petersen, "Metallogenic Provinces in South America," *Geologischen Rundschau* 59 (1970): 834–97.

3. Colin Renfrew, *Before Civilization* (New York: Knopf, 1973), specifically chap. 9, "The Beginning of European Metallurgy."

4. V. Gordon Childe, "Archaeological Ages as Technological Stages," *Journal of the Royal Anthropological Institute of Great Britain and Ireland* 74 (1944): 7–24.

5. Theodore A. Wertime, "The Beginnings of Metallurgy: A New Look," *Science* 182 (1973): 875–87 (note in particular fig. 1, the Diagrammatic Tree of Metallurgy); Renfrew, *Before Civilization*.

6. C. F. Gorman, P. Charoenwongsa, W. M. Schauffler, "Archaeological Background to the Study of Early Metallurgy in Southeast Asia" (Paper presented at the International Symposium on Archaeometry and Archaeological Prospection, Philadelphia, March 1977); Tamara Stech Wheeler and Robert Maddin, "The Techniques of the Early Thai Metalsmith," *Expedition* 18 (1976): 38–47.

7. Wertime, "Beginnings of Metallurgy," pp. 875, 876.

8. The Andean culture area is that region of western South America dominated by the Andes mountain chain and where certain overriding ecological factors characteristic of the zone fostered cultural adaptations that were similar over vast areas of the region. The entire culture area was unified politically only once, by the Inca, between 1476 and 1534, when their empire (*Tawantinsuyu*) included most of present-day Ecuador, Peru, Bolivia, and parts of Chile and Argentina. Archaeologists have divided the area into three zones: the Northern Andes (Ecuador–Colombia); the Central Andes (Peru

and north to central Bolivia); the Southern Andes (southern Bolivia, northwest Argentina, and northern Chile).

9. Erland Nordenskiöld, *The Copper and Bronze Ages in South America*, Comparative Ethnographical Studies 4 (Göteborg, 1921).

10. The following is a partial listing of the relevant works of these scholars: Eric Boman, *Antiquités de la région andine de la République Argentine et du désert d'Atacama* (Paris: Imprimerie Nationale, 1908); Juan B. Ambrosetti, *El bronce en la región Calchaquí*, Anales del Museo Nacional de Buenos Aires 11 (Buenos Aires, 1904); Ricardo E. Latcham, *Arqueología de la región Atacameña* (Santiago: Universidad de Chile, 1938); Erland Nordenskiöld, *Copper and Bronze Ages*; Paul Bergsøe, "The Gilding Process and the Metallurgy of Copper and Lead Among the Pre-Columbian Indians," *Ingeniørviden-skabelige Skrifter* A 46 (1938): 1–56; C. H. Mathewson, "A Metallographic Description of Some Ancient Peruvian Bronzes from Machu Picchu," *American Journal of Science* 40 (1915): 525–616; William C. Root, "The Metallurgy of the Southern Coast of Peru," *American Antiquity* 15 (1949): 10–37; William C. Root, "Gold–Copper Alloys in Ancient America," *Journal of Chemical Education* 28 (1951): 76–78; William C. Root, "Pre-Columbian Metalwork of Colombia and Its Neighbors," in *Essays in Pre-Columbian Art and Archaeology*, ed. Samuel K. Lothrop (Cambridge, Mass.: Harvard University Press, 1964), pp. 242–57; Earle R. Caley, "Chemical Composition of Ancient Copper Objects of South America," in *Application of Science in Examination of Works of Art*, ed. W. J. Young (Boston, 1973), pp. 53–61; Earle R. Caley and Dudley T. Easby, Jr., "The Smelting of Sulfide Ores of Copper in Preconquest Peru," *American Antiquity* 25 (1959): 59–65; Dudley T. Easby, Jr., "Los vasos retratos de metal del Perú," *Revista del Museo Nacional, Lima* 24 (1955): 137–53.

11. John V. Murra, "El 'control vertical' de un máximo de pisos ecológicos en la economía de las sociedades andinas," in Iñigo Ortiz de Zúñiga, *Visita de la Provincia de León de Huánuco (1562)*, vol. 2 (Huánuco, Peru: Universidad Nacional Hermilio Valdizan, 1972), pp. 429–76.

12. John Howland Rowe, "Cultural Unity and Diversification in Peruvian Archaeology," in *Men and Cultures*, ed. Anthony F. C. Wallace (Philadelphia: University of Pennsylvania Press, 1960), pp. 627–31. The chronology of Peruvian pre-Hispanic cultures, based on the work of John H. Rowe and Edward P. Lanning, is given in table 9.1. Except for the Late Horizon, dates are approximate and were determined by C-14 measurements based on a half-life of (5568 ± 30) years. The C-14 values are uncorrected. John H. Rowe, "Stages and Periods in Archaeological Interpretation," *Southwestern Journal of Anthropology* 18 (1962): 1–27; Edward P. Lanning, *Peru Before the Incas* (Englewood Cliffs: Prentice-Hall, 1967). More recently, Rowe has revised these dates based on the C-14 half-life of (5730 ± 40) years, which was accepted as the most probable value at the Fifth Radiocarbon Dating Conference held in Cambridge, England, in 1972. See John H. Rowe, "Kunst in Peru and Bolivien," in *Das alte Amerika*, ed. Gordon R. Willey (Berlin: Propyläen Verlag, 1974), pp. 285–97.

13. Dennis Lee Heskel, "An Examination of the Development of Pyrotechnology in Iran During the Fourth and Third Millennia" (Ph.D. diss., Harvard University).

14. Joel W. Grossman, "An Ancient Gold Worker's Tool Kit," *Archaeology* 25 (1972): 270–75.

15. Laura Marcela Ríos R., "Forma y función de los metales en el Perú prehispánico (B.A. thesis, Universidad Nacional Mayor de San Marcos, Lima, 1974).

16. Lanning, *Peru*; Luís G. Lumbreras, *The Peoples and Cultures of Ancient Peru*, trans. Betty J. Meggers (Washington, D.C.: Smithsonian Institution Press, 1974).

17. The summary presented here is not exhaustive. A good review of the metal finds from Peru in all of the periods prior to the Spanish invasion is provided by Ríos, *Forma y función*.

18. Grossman, "Ancient Tool Kit"; Joel W. Grossman, personal communication, 1980.

19. Max Uhle, "Die muschelhügel von Ancon, Peru," *International Congress of Americanists, Proceedings of 18th Session* (1912), pp. 22–45; Rebecca Carrion Cachot, "La cultura Chavín—dos nuevas colonias: Kuntur Wasi y Ancón," *Revista del Museo Nacional, Lima* 2 (1948): 99–172; Gordon R. Willey and John M. Corbett, *Early Ancón and Early Supe Culture*, Columbia Studies in Archaeology and Ethnology 3 (New York: Columbia University Press, 1954).

20. Thomas C. Patterson, personal communications, 1968 and 1979.

21. Willey and Corbett, *Early Ancón*.

22. Luís G. Lumbreras, "Informe de labores del proyecto Chavín," *Arqueológicas* 15 (1974): 37–56.

23. Richard Burger, personal communication, July 1977; Luís G. Lumbreras and Hernán Amat O., "Informe preliminar sobre las galerias interiores de Chavín," *Revista del Museo Nacional, Lima* 34 (1965–66): 143–97.

24. Seiichi Izumi and Kazuo Terada, eds., *Andes 4: Excavations at Kotosh, Peru—1963 and 1966* (Tokyo: University of Tokyo Press, 1972), pp. 272–73, 310.

25. Samuel K. Lothrop, "Gold Ornaments of Chavin Style from Chongoyape, Peru," *American Antiquity* 6 (1941): 250–62.

26. John Howland Rowe, "Form and Meaning in Chavin Art," in *Peruvian Archaeology, Selected Readings*, eds. John Howland Rowe and Dorothy Menzel (Palo Alto: Peek Publications, 1967), pp. 72–104; André Emmerich, *Sweat of the Sun and Tears of the Moon* (Seattle, 1965), fig. 1.

27. Lothrop, "Gold Ornaments."

28. Samuel K. Lothrop, "Gold Artifacts of Chavín Style," *American Antiquity* 16 (1951): 226–40. See p. 226.

29. Ibid.

30. Ibid. p. 237; Heather Lechtman, Lee A. Parsons, and William J. Young, "Seven Matched Hollow Gold Jaguars from Peru's Early Horizon," *Studies in Precolumbian Art and Archaeology* 16 (1975): 1–46, esp. p. 14.

31. Lothrop, "Gold Artifacts," p. 238.

32. Of the objects comprising the last and most sophisticated of Chavín-style gold-work, the spatulalike spoons made of preformed and soldered pieces of gold sheet may be of Early Horizon manufacture. They closely resemble spoons made of bone that are found frequently in tombs at the Peruvian north coast site of Cupisnique and other associated sites. The pottery from these sites, known as Cupisnique or "coastal Chavín," exhibits strong stylistic similarities with Chavín pottery, and Cupisnique "culture" is considered a north coast manifestation of Chavín. For a discussion of the Cupisnique

material, see Rafael Larco Hoyle, *Los Cupisniques* (Lima, 1941).

33. Thomas C. Patterson, "Chavín: An Interpretation of Its Spread and Influence," in *Dumbarton Oaks Conference on Chavín,* ed. Elizabeth P. Benson (Washington, D.C., 1971), pp. 29–48.

34. Rowe, "Form and Meaning"; Lanning, *Peru*; Richard S. MacNeish, Thomas C. Patterson, and David L. Browman, *The Central Peruvian Prehistoric Interaction Sphere,* Papers of the Robert S. Peabody Foundation for Archaeology 7 (Andover: R. S. Peabody Foundation, 1975).

35. Carlos Ponce Sanginés, *Las culturas Wankarani y Chiripa y su relación con Tiwanaku,* Academia Nacional de Ciencias de Bolivia 25 (La Paz, 1970), see p. 42 and table 2; David Browman suggests that the site of Wankarani from which the slags were removed probably dates from about 1100–500 B.C. (personal communication, May 1977).

36. David L. Browman, personal communications of May 1976 and May 1977. The earliest copper ore excavated by Browman at Chiripa dates to a 900 B.C. level. The ores were identified by Dr. Ernest G. Ehlers of the Dept. of Geology and Mineralogy, Ohio State Univ.

37. Wendell C. Bennett, *Excavations at Tiahuanaco,* Anthropological Papers of the American Museum of Natural History 34 (New York: American Museum of Natural History, 1934), p. 427.

38. Thomas C. Patterson, personal communications, 1968 and 1979; T. Patterson, "Chavín." Patterson claims there was no Initial Period occupation at Malpaso. His radiocarbon dates are quite good for Early Horizon 1–Early Horizon 3 (1050–750 B.C.) at the site. The Early Horizon 4 date is an educated guess.

39. A chemical and metallurgical analysis of the bead is given in Lechtman, "Issues."

40. Root, "Metallurgy of Southern Coast."

41. David L. Browman, "Trade Patterns in the Central Highlands of Peru," *World Archaeology* 6 (1975): 322–29.

42. David L. Browman, personal communication, May 1977.

43. Browman, "Trade Patterns"; MacNeish, Patterson, and Browman, *Peruvian Interaction Sphere.*

44. MacNeish, Patterson, and Browman, *Peruvian Interaction Sphere.*

45. Ibid., p. 45.

46. Gabriela Schwoerbel, "Máscara funeraria de Tablada de Lurín," *Boletín del Seminario de Arqueología del Instituto Riva Agüero* 1 (1969): 130–31; G. Schwoerbel, "Armas de cobre en la necrópolis de Lurín," *Boletín del Seminario de Arqueología del Instituto Riva Agüero* 3 (1969): 46; G. Schwoerbel, "Adornos grabados de metal," *Boletín del Seminario de Arqueología del Instituto Riva Agüero* 6 (1970): 48; G. Schwoerbel, "La metalurgia de Lima" (Paper presented at the Segundo Congreso Peruano del Hombre y la Cultura Andina, Trujillo, Peru, 1974).

47. Schwoerbel, "Metalurgia de Lima:" "Los ganchos de estólica son de cobre macizo martillado; ya se encuentra uno de estos ganchos asociado a los restos con el fechado de 950 ± 100 A.C."

48. Schwoerbel, "Metalurgia de Lima:" "El enchapado se observa en casi todos los objetos que han sido excavados.... El enchapado ya se encuentra en las piezas correspondientes al fechado de 950 ± 100 A.C...." In Lima in 1974, Ms. Schwoerbel

showed me several large and very thin sheets of hammered copper that were gilt. These were from her excavations at the Tablada de Lurín, and she said they were from the 950 ± 100 B.C. levels.

49. Ríos, *Forma y función*, pp. 68–71.

50. Heather Lechtman, "Ancient Methods of Gilding Silver—Examples from the Old and the New Worlds," in *Science and Archaeology*, ed. R. H. Brill (Cambridge, Mass.: MIT Press, 1971), pp. 2–30; idem, "The Gilding of Metals in Pre-Columbian Peru," in *Application of Science in Examination of Works of Art*," ed. W. J. Young (Boston: Museum of Fine Arts, 1973), pp. 38–52; idem, "Issues"; idem, "A Pre-Columbian Technique for Electrochemical Replacement Plating of Gold and Silver on Copper Objects, *Journal of Metals* 31 (1979): 154–60.

51. Georg Petersen, *Minería y metalurgia en el antiguo Perú*, Arqueológicas 12 (Lima: Museo Nacional de Arqueología y Antropología, 1970), pp. 1–140.

52. Elizabeth P. Benson, *The Mochica* (New York: Praeger, 1972); Christopher B. Donnan, *Moche Art and Iconography* (Los Angeles: UCLA Latin American Center Publications, 1976).

53. Lanning, *Peru*, p. 126.

54. Alan R. Sawyer, *Mastercraftsmen of Ancient Peru* (New York: Solomon R. Guggenheim Foundation, 1968); Hans D. Disselhoff, *Vicús* (Berlin: Gebr. Mann Verlag, 1971).

55. A. L. Kroeber, *Peruvian Archeology in 1942* (New York: Wenner-Gren Foundation, 1944); William Duncan Strong and Clifford Evans, Jr., *Cultural Stratigraphy in the Viru Valley Northern Peru* (New York: Columbia University Press, 1952).

56. Christopher B. Donnan, "A Precolumbian Smelter from Northern Peru," *Archaeology* 26 (1973): 289–97; Clair C. Patterson, "Native Copper, Silver, and Gold Accessible to Early Metallurgists," *American Antiquity* 36 (1971): 286–321; Kroeber, *Peruvian Archeology*.

57. Heather Lechtman, "A Metallurgical Site Survey in the Peruvian Andes," *Journal of Field Archaeology* 3 (1976): 1–42.

58. Rafael Larco Hoyle, "A Culture Sequence for the North Coast of Peru," in *Handbook of South American Indians*, vol. 2, ed. Julian H. Steward (New York, 1946), p. 167.

59. Lechtman, "Metallurgical Site Survey."

60. C. Patterson, "Native Copper," pp. 305, 306.

61. Kroeber, *Peruvian Archeology*.

62. C. Patterson, "Native Copper," table 11, no. 4–2610Ea.

63. Root, "Metallurgy of Southern Coast."

64. Lechtman, "Ancient Methods" and "Gilding of Metals"; P. Rivet and H. Arsandaux, *La métallurgie en Amérique précolombienne*, Travaux et Mémoires de l'Institut d'Ethnologie 39 (Paris: Université de Paris, 1946).

65. Root, "Metallurgy of Southern Coast"; Easby, "Vasos retratos."

66. Kroeber, *Peruvian Archeology*, p. 129.

67. Root, "Metallurgy of Southern Coast."

68. C. Patterson, "Native Copper"; Root, "Metallurgy of Southern Coast."

69. C. Patterson, "Native Copper," table 11, no. 4–3324.

70. Kroeber, *Peruvian Archeology*, p. 132.

71. Root, "Gold-Copper Alloys"; Lechtman, "Gilding of Metals."

72. Lechtman, "Gilding of Metals."

73. Our studies indicate that gold was dissolved in aqueous solutions of mixtures of commonly occurring salts (such as potassium nitrate, potash alum, and common salt) and was deposited from solution onto copper that was either dipped into the solution or painted with it. See Lechtman, "Electrochemical Replacement."

74. Lechtman, Parsons, and Young, "Seven Gold Jaguars." The set of hollow gold jaguars referred to was originally published by Lechtman, Parsons, and Young as belonging to the late Early Horizon. Since that publication, extensive survey work and preliminary excavations at the site of Pampa Grande, where the jaguars were found, have been conducted by a team of archaeologists under the direction of Kent C. Day of the Royal Ontario Museum, Toronto. The results of their studies indicate, without any doubt, that Pampa Grande is a Moche V site and that, therefore, the group of jaguars belongs to the early stages of the Middle Horizon, probably to Middle Horizon I. The date of construction of the *huaca* at Pampa Grande where the jaguars were found is not yet known, but it might fall anywhere between about A.D. 560 and 900. See Kent C. Day, "Midseason Report, Royal Ontario Museum Lambayeque Project," Royal Ontario Museum (Toronto, Canada, Sept. 1975).

75. Heskel, *Pyrotechnology in Iran.*

76. This section and the following section ("Cultural Meanings of Bronze") originally formed part of a longer paper entitled "Issues in Andean Metallurgy," which was presented at the Conference on South American Metallurgy held at Dumbarton Oaks, Washington, D.C., in October 1975. It appears in *Pre-Columbian Metallurgy of South America*, ed. Elizabeth P. Benson, pp. 1–40.

77. My use here of the terms "northern" and "southern Andes" is somewhat different from the way in which those terms are normally employed. I am distinguishing essentially between a N. Peruvian–S. Ecuadorian tradition and a S. Peruvian–N. Bolivian tradition of metallurgical technologies. See n. 8 for the more traditional definitions of north, central, and south Andean areas.

78. Ambrosetti, *Bronce en Calchaquí*; Boman, *Antiquités*; Latcham, *Arqueología Atacameña*; G. A. Fester, "Copper and Copper Alloys in Ancient Argentina," *Chymia* 8 (1962): 21–31; Alberto Rex González, "A Note on the Antiquity of Bronze in N.W. Argentina," *Actas del XXXIII Congreso Internacional de Americanistas*, vol. 2 (San José, Costa Rica, 1959), pp. 384–97; Alberto Rex González, "Precolumbian Metallurgy of Northwest Argentina: Historical Development and Cultural Process," in *Pre-Columbian Metallurgy of South America*, ed. Elizabeth P. Benson (Washington, D.C.: Dumbarton Oaks, 1979).

79. Raphael Pumpelly, *Explorations in Turkestan* (Washington, D.C.: Carnegie Institute, 1908); Earle R. Caley, "On the Prehistoric Use of Arsenical Copper in the Aegean Region," *Hesperia* Suppl. 8 (1949): 60–63; Robert J. Braidwood, Joseph E. Burke, and Norman H. Nachtrieb, "Ancient Syrian Coppers and Bronzes," *Journal of Chemical Education* 28 (1951): 87–96; H. H. Coghlan, "Prehistorical Working of Bronze and Arsenical Copper, "*Sibrium* 5 (1960): 145–52; I. R. Selimkhanov, "Spectral Analysis of Metal Articles from Archaeological Monuments of the Caucasus," *Proceedings of the Prehistoric Society* n.s. 28 (1962): 68–79; I. R. Selimkhanov, "Was Native Copper Used

in Transcaucasia in Eneolithic Times?" *Proceedings of the Prehistoric Society* n.s. 30 (1964):
66–74; Colin Renfrew, "Cycladic Metallurgy and the Aegean Early Bronze Age,"
American Journal of Archaeology 71 (1967): 1–20; J. A. Charles, "Early Arsenical Bronzes
—A Metallurgical View," *American Journal of Archaeology* 71 (1967): 21–26; J. A. Charles,
"Arsenic and Old Bronze," *Chemistry and Industry* 12 (1974): 470–74; P. R. S. Moorey,
"An Interim Report on Some Analyses of 'Luristan Bronzes,'" *Archaeometry* 7 (1964):
72–80; P. R. S. Moorey, *Catalogue of the Ancient Persian Bronzes in the Ashmolean Museum*
(Oxford; Clarendon Press, 1971); Hugh McKerrell and R. F. Tylecote, "The Working
of Copper-Arsenic Alloys in the Early Bronze Age and the Effect on the Determination
of Provenance," *Proceedings of the Prehistoric Society* 38 (1972): 209–18; E. R. Eaton and
Hugh McKerrell, "Near Eastern Alloying and Some Textual Evidence for the Early
Use of Arsenical Copper," *World Archaeology* 8 (1976): 169–91; Heskel, *Pyrotechnology
in Iran.*

80. Caley, "Chemical Composition"; Caley's original presentation of this material
was in a joint article by him and Lowell Shank. His 1973 paper, however, focuses primarily
on arsenical copper. See Earle R. Caley and Lowell W. Shank, "Composition of Ancient
Peruvian Copper," *Ohio Journal of Science* 71 (1971): 181–87.

81. Caley, "Chemical Composition," p. 60.

82. Arthur Baessler, *Altperuanische metallgeräte* (Berlin: Georg Reimer Verlag, 1906);
Boman, *Antiquités*; Morris Loeb and S. R. Morey, "Analysis of Some Bolivian Bronzes,"
Journal of American Chemical Society 32 (1910): 652–53; Nordenskiöld, *Copper and Bronze
Ages*; Wendell C. Bennett, "The Andean Highlands: An Introduction," in *Handbook
of South American Indians*, vol. 2, ed. Julian H. Steward (New York: Cooper Square
Publishers, 1946), pp. 1–60; Caley, "Chemical Composition"; Fester, "Copper and
Copper Alloys"; Kroeber, *Peruvian Archeology*.

83. Root in Kroeber, *Peruvian Archeology*; Morley, in A. L. Kroeber, "Quantitative
Analyses of Ancient Peruvian Metal," *American Antiquity* 20 (1954): 160–62; C. Patterson,
"Native Copper."

84. C. Patterson, "Native Copper," p. 306. The three high-arsenic ornaments were
referred to in the previous section.

85. Wendell C. Bennett, *Archaeology of the North Coast of Peru*, Anthropological
Papers of the American Museum of Natural History 37 (New York: American Museum
of Natural History, 1939).

86. The objects from the *Huaca del Sol–Huaca de la Luna* cemetery were excavated
in 1972 by Dennis Heskel and Sheila Pozorski; those from Chan Chan were excavated
in 1969 by John Topic; those from El Milagro de San José, Cerro la Virgen, and Medaños
La Joyada in 1969 and 1970 by Richard Keatinge. All the excavators have kindly consented
to the publication of these analyses.

The objects from the *Sol–Luna* cemetery were found in individual graves.

The objects from Chan Chan were found in an area occupied by small, irregular,
agglutinated rooms on the west side, but outside of the Ciudadela Laberinto at Chan
Chan. John Topic considers the two needles to be very late in the Chimú sequence,
dating to approximately A.D. 1400–1450 (John Topic, personal communication, Sept.
1975).

El Milagro de San José is a semi-isolated complex of buildings situated on the flat, elevated east bank of the Río Seco some 9 km north of Chan Chan. Keatinge considers it a major Chimú rural administrative center dating either to the end of the Early Chimú phase or the beginning of the Imperial Chimú phase. His C-14 dates from this site indicate that it was fully in use by A.D. 1200 and possibly somewhat earlier. Cerro la Virgen is located on either side of the main Chimú intervalley highway 5 km northwest of Chan Chan and ca. 2.5 km inland from the ocean. The site consists of a village of over 400 agglutinated rooms covering an area of ca. 14 hectares supported by agriculture and utilization of marine resources. Keatinge considers it as probably of Late Chimú date, ca. A.D. 1300–1450. Medaños La Joyada is situated on a stretch of beach some 15 km northwest of Chan Chan. It is characterized by a cluster of subsurface cultivation plots (*puquios*) surrounded by midden deposits. It seems to have been a semi-isolated fishing village with some crop production in the sunken fields. Keatinge dates it definitely to the Chimú–Inca phase but suggests that it might date entirely to the Colonial Period (1450–Colonial). See Richard Keatinge, personal communication, Sept. 1975; Richard Keatinge, "Chimu Rural Administrative Centers in the Moche Valley, Peru," *World Archaeology* 6 (1974): 66–82.

The two sites excavated by Wendell Bennett in the Lambayeque Valley, "Túcume One," commonly known as El Purgatorio, and "Lambayeque One" are described by him in his 1939 publication of his north coast excavations (Bennett, *Archaeology*). For a more up-to-date evaluation of the date of his sites, see n. 133.

87. Caley, "Chemical Composition," table 7.

88. G. Petersen, *Minería*, pp. 16–21.

89. I disagree with Charles here (Charles, "Arsenical Bronzes," p. 25). While it is certainly true that early miners and metalworkers relied heavily on color distinctions to identify minerals—so do all geologists today—and thereby were able "to control the use of raw materials to a substantial extent on this basis of hand sorting by colour," orpiment and realgar are not related in any way to the kinds of minerals or ores such metalworkers were normally seeking. The green alteration products of copper sulfarsenide ores, such as olivenite or chenevixite, might have caught their attention and been recognized soon as a distinct variety of mineral that imparted certain properties to the metal smelted from it. The proximity of such minerals to the parent ore, i.e., the black, lustrous enargite or tennantite, might also have led them to experiment with these. But the connection between orpiment and realgar, colored minerals normally thought of and used as pigments, and any metallurgical value they might have seems to me extremely fragile and unlikely to have occurred.

90. For example, see Heskel, *Pyrotechnology in Iran*.

91. Caley, "Chemical Composition," p. 61.

92. C. Patterson, "Native Copper," p. 306.

93. Lechtman, "Metallurgical Site Survey."

94. In independent interviews in Lima during the month of August 1974 with Ing. Eleodoro Bellido B., director of the Servicio de Geología y Minería and author of *Aspectos generales de la metalogenia del Perú* (see n. 2); with Ing. Edgardo Ponzoni S. of the Ministerio de Minas and technical editor of the Mapa Metalogenético del Perú, 1969, published by the Sociedad Nacional de Minería y Petroleo; and with Professor Ulrich Petersen of the Geology Department of Harvard University, all three maintained that

orpiment and realgar were uncommon in Peru and that domeykite was particularly rare. Ponzoni and Petersen also stated that there was virtually no arsenic on the Peruvian north coast.

95. Ahlfeld and Muñoz Reyes, *Minerales de Bolivia*; Miller and Singewald, *Mineral Deposits*. Domeykite is apparently often found in intimate association with native copper. Otto and Witter (in Selimkhanov, "Was Native Copper Used") found it in native copper deposits in Zwickau, Germany, and artifacts made from that copper contain arsenic in the 0.3 to 2.8% concentration range. Domeykite is present only in extremely small quantities in the native coppers of the Lake Superior region, however. F. Beyschlag, J. H. L. Vogt, P. Krusch, *The Deposits of the Useful Minerals and Rocks*, trans. S. J. Truscott (London: Macmillan, 1914); Waldemar Lindgren, *Mineral Deposits* (New York: McGraw-Hill, 1933).

96. Charles Palache, Harry Berman, and Clifford Frondel, *Dana's System of Mineralogy*, vol. 1 (New York: John Wiley, 1944), p. 172.

97. Palache et al., *Dana's System of Mineralogy*, vol. 2 (New York: John Wiley, 1951). p. 861.

98. G. Petersen, *Minería*, p. 8.

99. Although Locke states that "the ferric and copper arsenates are rather insoluble and their survival is not contrary to expectation," Ulrich Petersen, who is one of the leading scholars of Andean metalogenesis (see n. 2 and 94) and is thoroughly familiar with Andean ore exploitation, is of the opinion that the copper arsenates would not have survived in any quantity in the Andean highlands because of the high rainfalls there during approximately 5 months of the year (Ulrich Petersen, personal communication, 1973). This opinion was shared by Ing. Edgardo Ponzoni S. (see n. 94). He felt that copper arsenates would dissolve rapidly in the highlands. See Augustus Locke, *Leached Outcrops as Guides to Copper Ore* (Baltimore: Williams and Wilkins, 1926), p. 85.

100. C. Patterson, "Native Copper," p. 306.

101. Ponzoni, personal communication, Aug. 1974.

102. Lechtman, "Metallurgical Site Survey." During a conversation with Ulrich Petersen at Harvard University in Sept. 1975 we discussed the relative abundances in Peru of the various minerals mentioned here that might have been used in the manufacture of copper-arsenic alloys in the pre-Columbian period. Orpiment and realgar are minerals that normally form at the surface of ore deposits containing sulfarsenides. He has seen them in the upper levels of mines at Casapalca, Julcani, and Huancavelica, for example, all large mines in the central sierra. His estimate of the relative abundance of the primary sulfarsenide ores (e.g., enargite and tennantite) in comparison to that of orpiment or realgar is about 1000 : 1 or higher. Neither domeykite nor olivenite has been identified in Peru. Even at Corocoro, Petersen claims that domeykite is extremely rare. Thus far, chenevixite has been identified in Peru only at the mine at Cobriza. It forms only where there are primary sulfarsenides present and is between about 0.01 and 0.1 times as abundant as malachite, with which it may be confused on visual examination. The major ore minerals in Peruvian mines are chalcopyrite, enargite, and lesser amounts of tennantite. Of these, the first is not an arsenic-bearing mineral. Arsenopyrite, which does not contain copper, is a gangue mineral in some copper and lead-zinc ores, but it is much less abundant than either enargite or chalcopyrite. See U. Petersen, personal communication.

103. Professor Ulrich Petersen mentioned that at Yauricocha, the large highland copper mining district in the Department of Lima, Central Andes, enargite persists almost to the surface (personal communication, 1973). Thus the shallowness of the copper sulfarsenides is not an unusual feature in Peru.

104. See Lechtman, "Metallurgical Site Survey."

105. Caley, "Chemical Composition," table 7.

106. C. Patterson, "Native Copper," p. 316.

107. Caley and Easby, Jr., "Smelting of Sulfide Ores"; Caley and Shank, "Peruvian Copper"; Caley, "Chemical Composition."

108. Caley, "Chemical Composition," p. 57.

109. McKerrell and Tylecote, "Copper-Arsenic Alloys."

110. McKerrell, personal communication, May 1975.

111. McKerrell and Tylecote, "Copper-Arsenic Alloys."

112. I do not wish to suggest that sulfide smelting in the Andes had not occurred before the Middle Horizon. Indeed, I pointed out in the section on Mochica metallurgy that there are some indications that complex lead-silver sulfide ores were already being smelted in the Early Intermediate Period. What we do see in the copper-arsenic data, however, is a large-scale shift from one system to another.

113. See Lechtman, "Metallurgical Site Survey."

114. Murra, "Control vertical."

115. Fester, "Copper Alloys."

116. Alberto Rex González has pointed out to me that three of the objects analyzed by Fester (n. 78) are not Aguada but are associated with the Condorhuasi complex, which predates Aguada, in northwest Argentina. The analyses of these objects (nos. 5550, 12.526, 5571), an ornament and two bracelets, were also published by González in 1959 (González, "Antiquity of Bronze"). The dates assigned to the Condorhuasi complex run from about A.D. 300–600. See A. Rex González, personal communication, Nov. 1976, and "Precolumbian Metallurgy."

117. Boman, Antiquités. In a footnote, Boman suggests that the ore from which this object was made was probably enargite, which, he points out, is especially common at Famatina (La Rioja) and Las Capillitas Catamarca).

118. Caley, "Chemical Composition," p. 58.

119. Loeb and Morey (see n. 82) analyzed six objects in the collection of the American Museum of Natural History, all of which are described as having been collected in the region around Lake Titicaca, but no other clues as to their provenance are given. Five of these objects are copper-tin bronzes; the sixth is a copper-arsenic bronze containing 2.14% arsenic.

120. Charles W. Mead, "Prehistoric Bronze in South America," Anthropological Papers of the American Museum of Natural History 12 (1915): 15–51; Boman, Antiquités.

121. Ponce, Wankarani y Chiripa.

122. Caley, "Chemical Composition."

123. Ibid.

124. Mathewson, "Bronzes from Machu Picchu."

125. Ambrosetti, Bronce en Calchaquí.

126. Georg Petersen (see n. 51) explains that in smelting copper ores, tin is sometimes

incorporated in minor proportions in the resultant metal because of the presence in the copper ore of minerals such as stannite (Cu_2FeSnS_4), a copper sulfide containing iron and tin. Such minerals frequently accompany minerals of copper and silver and are found in copper and tin veins. He states that stannite is an important ore in Bolivia. The inclusion of such minerals with the more common minerals of copper would account for the presence of tin in artifacts from the southern Andes in concentrations of about 1.5% or less. Petersen goes on to say, however, that to produce metallic tin such as that found at Machu Picchu by Bingham, one would smelt cassiterite. See Mathewson, "Bronzes from Machu Picchu," p. 536, and Hiram Bingham, *Machu Picchu, A Citadel of the Incas* (New Haven: Yale University Press, 1930).

127. Both Caley and Mathewson are of the opinion that copper ores and cassiterite were smelted separately, producing metallic copper and metallic tin which were then melted together to form bronze. Caley also believes that on the basis of the sulfur content of the objects from Machu Picchu sulfide ores were used in manufacturing the copper of which the bronze was made. See Caley, "Chemical Composition," and Mathewson, "Bronzes from Machu Picchu."

128. See Lechtman, "Gilding of Metals."

129. Mathewson, "Bronzes from Machu Picchu."

130. I use this term as it is set forth by Maquet (Jacques Maquet, "Introduction to Aesthetic Anthropology," *Current Topics in Anthropology* 1, module 4 [1971]: 1–38).

131. Lechtman, "Metallurgical Site Survey."

132. Bennett excavated 38 graves in a cemetery located within a low mound at a site he designated as Lambayeque One (Bennett, *Archaeology*, pp. 95–106). From his description, the site is "on a sandy pampa about halfway between the small town of San José and Lambayeque" (p. 95). In describing the nonceramic contents of the graves, he points out that "almost every grave contained copper in some form. Outstanding is a group of agricultural implements. These are heavy, wedge-shaped tools with a hollow socket, slit along one side, for hafting. Below the socket the tool is rectangular in cross-section, gradually tapering to the wedge blade. . . . Another tool somewhat like the above is also probably an agricultural implement. It is a long point with a hollow hafting socket at one end" (p. 104). From the ceramic evidence alone, Bennett felt that the site belonged to a "Middle Chimú" phase. "The position of this material, disregarding for the moment the geographic position of the valley in relation to the north coast region, is post Early Chimu and pre-Inca Chimu" (p. 105).

133. Ibid., p. 116. In a recent conversation, Kent C. Day of the Royal Ontario Museum in Toronto, who is currently conducting site surveys and excavations within the Lambayeque Valley, indicated that Bennett's Lambayeque One site most probably belongs to the Imperial Chimú phase, which is dated to approximately A.D. 1150–1300. Túcume One, or El Purgatorio, is a Chimú–Inca phase site, which would place it within the A.D. 1450–1530 period. See Kent C. Day, personal communication, May 1976.

134. Another chisel-like object, similar to the one excavated by Bennett, from the site of Sipán, Lambayeque Valley, was studied at MIT, but the analytical results are not included in table 9.2 since the object was not scientifically excavated. A combination of quantitative spectrographic analysis and wet chemical analysis proved the metal to be a copper-arsenic bronze containing 91.8% copper and 4.18% arsenic.

135. Kroeber, *Peruvian Archeology.*

136. McKerrell and Tylecote, "Copper-Arsenic Alloys."

137. James Charles and I concur in our estimation of the closeness in working properties of the copper-arsenic and copper-tin alloys. Unfortunately, there have been few studies of the properties of copper-arsenic bronzes containing arsenic in the concentration range with which we are concerned here, i.e., about 2–8%, by weight. Maréchal's work suggests that the hardness of 8% copper-tin alloys and 8% copper-arsenic alloys that were reduced in thickness from between 6 and 300% is practically identical. The high arsenic coppers appear to be more ductile, however, at least up to a concentration of about 7 wt % and are as easily worked hot as they are cold. Tin bronzes, by contrast, are easily cold-worked but become brittle when worked hot. See Jean R. Maréchal, "Étude sur les propriétés mécaniques des cuivres à l'arsenic," *Métaux: Corrosion—Industries* 33 (1958): 377–83; J. A. Charles, "The Development of the Usage of Tin and Tin-Bronze: Some Problems," in *The Search for Ancient Tin,* ed. Alan Franklin, Jacquelin Olin, and Theodore Wertime (Washington, D.C.: Smithsonian Institution, 1978), pp. 25–32; idem, "From Copper to Iron—the Origin of Metallic Materials," *Journal of Metals* 31 (1979): 8–13.

138. C. Patterson, "Native Copper," p. 311.

139. The number of books and articles devoted to attempts at identifying the sources of the tin used in the manufacture of Old World bronzes, particularly bronzes of Near Eastern provenance, is legion. The intensity of scholarly concern about this issue is attested by a two-day international conference on the theme, "The Search for Ancient Tin," sponsored by the Smithsonian Institution and the National Bureau of Standards and held in Washington, D.C. in March 1977. A recent article, "Tin in the Ancient Near East: Old Questions and New Finds," *Expedition* 19 (1977): 35–47, by Robert Maddin, Tamara Stech Wheeler, and James D. Muhly explores some interesting new data on the subject.

140. V. M. Masson and V. I. Sarianidi, *Central Asia: Turkmenia Before the Achaemenians* (New York: Praeger, 1972).

141. Lechtman, "Gilding of Metals."

142. See Murra's archipelago model of verticality in his 1972 article on vertical control of ecological levels (in n. 11).

143. José Vidalón and Henry Walqui, "Desarsenización de concentrados de cobre," *Trabajos Técnicos,* XIII Convención de Ingenieros de Minas, part VII–1 (Lima, 1976), pp. 1–10.

144. McKerrell and Tylecote, "Copper-Arsenic Alloys."

145. Lanning, *Peru;* Lumbreras, *Peoples of Peru;* Gordon R. Willey, *An Introduction to American Archaeology,* vol. 2 (Englewood Cliffs; Prentice Hall, 1971).

146. Willey, *American Archaeology,* p. 164.

147. See Ríos, *Forma y función,* p. 93.

148. Wertime, "Beginnings."

149. Georg Petersen, *Minería.*

150. Lechtman, "Metallurgical Site Survey."

151. Wertime, "Beginnings."

10

Iron and Early Metallurgy in the Mediterranean

ANTHONY M. SNODGRASS

Metallurgical ingenuity has always been devoted to weapons on one hand and to items of adornment on the other.

Cyril Stanley Smith

GENERAL PRINCIPLES OF STUDY

It will be argued in this chapter that the cultures of the Mediterranean area played a vital part not so much in the pioneering of the early technology of iron as in the harnessing of it to produce a broadly based iron economy. Although a number of these cultures were literate, our knowledge of the processes of early ironworking is not founded primarily on written sources. On the contrary, it rests on archaeological and scientific evidence, which exerts a corrective force on the often misleading written sources and reduces our dependence on them. Written records are unreliable because the introduction of iron in most regions coincided with a period of severe cultural recession in which historical records are temporarily deficient. The sources—primarily Greek—which purport to treat of this vital development therefore do so at some distance of time and usually quasi-mythologically. We should not dismiss the testimony of Strabo and other geographical writers as to the location and condition of some Mediterranean metal sources in later classical times, but their value for the formative period is very indirect.

Most ancient writings on ironworking, however, and a number of modern ones also, have been bedeviled by the fact that an effective iron-based technology was in most cases achieved only after a very long period —in some areas more than a thousand years—of more or less inconse-

335

quential experimentation. Distorted ancient memories of miraculous ironworkers, if they have any historical origin, may well refer to early points
in this long process rather than to the critical developments which mark
the arrival of a true Iron Age; the assignment of these legendary figures
to various geographical areas may likewise reflect the importance of those
areas at some indefinite point in the distant past. Only by some such
explanation, indeed, can we begin to reconcile the mutually contradictory
accounts of the early development of iron. Likewise, many modern
writers on the subject have paid attention to the isolated early occurrences
of iron artifacts rather than to the advances on a broader front.

It is therefore necessary to devise a criterion or a system for evaluating
the progress of ironworking in antiquity. That criterion should single
out those steps which were of real industrial and economic significance
while avoiding the many distractions. One such distraction is the conventional terminology of local "Bronze" and "Iron" ages, which often
proves, on closer inspection, to be based on criteria other than that of
industrial metal usage. Such a terminology has other values, and in any
case it is probably too late to attempt to replace it with one that has a
sounder basis in literal terms; but we should bear this limitation in mind
throughout.

The criterion used in this chapter is that of "working iron," that is,
iron used to make the functional parts of the real cutting and piercing
implements that form the basis of early technology. The qualification
"real" is important, as will be seen. The functional parts may be defined
as those parts which come into direct contact with the material to be cut
or pierced, whether inanimate or (as in the case of weapons) animate.

Using this criterion of working iron, we can discern three broad stages
in the development of an iron technology; they are I think applicable
to every area of Eurasia and are certainly valid for the Mediterranean
region. The first of these lies outside the scope of this chapter, but it is
important nevertheless to establish its distinguishing characteristics.

In *stage 1*, iron may be employed with some frequency, but it is not
true working iron according to the definition given above. In the main,
its employment is for ornament, as is appropriate for the expensive commodity which we know it to have been in many cases. But this ornamental
use must be extended to cover objects that have the outward *form* of real
weapons and tools, yet whose circumstances reveal that they played no
practical role. Iron-bladed daggers are worth mentioning specifically

because of the time-honored use of the dagger as a prestige object, a component of "dress uniform," and the consequent tendency to choose materials for their costliness rather than their effectiveness.

In *stage 2*, working iron is present but is used less than bronze for implements of practical use.

In *stage 3*, iron predominates over bronze as the working metal, although it need not, and usually does not, completely displace bronze even in this role.

Working iron is the criterion which distinguishes stages 2 and 3 from stage 1 and excludes the use of iron as a decoration or as a means of gaining prestige. It also excludes certain other usages, which appear in the *later* stages of Iron Age technology rather than in the early and experimental phases: for example, the choice of metal for beaten vessels or defensive armor. The continued use of bronze for these and other purposes has led certain scholars to postulate a long transitional, or "chalcosideric," period between the Bronze and Iron ages, at least for the areas of Asia Minor and the Aegean.[1] By this broad measure, however, many ancient cultures *never* entered a strict "Iron Age." Paradoxically, one of the characteristics of a fully developed Iron Age economy is a rich and varied technology of bronzeworking, the quality of the bronze artifacts often being dependent on that of the iron instruments used in their production.

Simple proportion alone is used to distinguish between stages 2 and 3. It might be thought that such an abstract criterion could have had little economic or industrial significance for the period in question. Yet study of many ancient cultures shows a fairly abrupt change, at a certain point, from a predominant use of bronze to a predominant use of iron, within the strict field of working metal. The change reflects economic developments of some importance, but it did not necessarily cause them. The criterion of proportion has also a great practical value from the point of view of modern research: a reasonable quantity of excavated material can be expected to give a fair picture of the proportionate use of iron in a given area and period whereas an evaluation based on single early occurrences of iron implements is largely dependent on chance.

Another method that is useful in isolating these successive stages is metal analysis, by which we can usually detect whether carburization, quenching, and tempering have been employed in the making of an object; if they have, then it is extremely likely that the iron was intended for practical use—in other words, that the transition has been made from

stage 1 to stages 2 and 3. The presence of carburization alone, without
the subsequent hardening processes, is more problematic: the question
becomes one of degree. Even primitive wrought iron normally possesses
a certain carbon content, and the sharp fluctuations in the carbon content
of different parts of the same implement make it especially difficult to
lay down precise criteria. Generally, any object that shows a mean level
of 0.5 percent carbon, the same as that of modern medium steel, can be
assumed to have been intended for practical use; but there is at least one
example of an object, the iron-bladed ax from Ras Shamra with a gold-
damascened copper socket,[2] which has a carbon content as high as 0.41
percent in its blade but whose luxurious appurtenances and apparently
early date (said to be in the region of 1400 B.C.) argue against its having
any practical utility. But this remains an isolated instance at the date
claimed for it; it is the repeated achievement of a high carbon content
which denotes intentional steeling and, at least in the Mediterranean area,
heralds the arrival of an effective iron industry. (For the viewpoint that
an effective iron industry could exist without deliberate carburization,
see chaps. 1, 11, 12, and 14.) Since the skill of individual smiths will vary,
however, the converse condition need not necessarily apply; even in a
fully iron-based economy, there may still be iron artifacts which bear
no traces of carburization or hardening.

The cultures of the Mediterranean lands fall into three main groups
or patterns with respect to their adoption of ironworking: first, there
are the pioneer regions, which moved at a relatively early date to an iron-
based economy. Their progress is not achieved independently of one
another; plainly, the discoveries in one such region were swiftly applied
in others. Nevertheless, the pattern of progress is sufficiently varied to
allow us to distinguish between the main centers of Cyprus, the Aegean,
and the Levantine coastlands. Other Mediterranean regions may ultimately
prove to belong to this group: coastal Anatolia (excluding the West coast,
which is here grouped with the Aegean) is an inherently likely case, but
the present evidence does not yet substantiate its claims, while inland
areas such as Urartu show a surprisingly long delay in abandoning bronze.
The peculiar and even more surprising instance of Egypt will be considered
below.

The second group moved toward an iron-based economy under the
direct influence of commercial or colonizing activity from one of the
areas in the first group. Northern Africa definitely conforms to this

pattern, and Spain probably does so. Other, smaller "colonial" areas, including some of the Mediterranean islands, should probably be assigned to this group.

The third group moved, so to speak, at their own speed toward the adoption of iron. They were not directly influenced by other Mediterranean cultures, although their economic links with other non-Mediterranean centers may have been the decisive factor in determining their progress. To this pattern Italy and Sicily conform, as do Dalmatia and probably Mediterranean France, all of them cultures which were in indirect contact with a separate nucleus of metallurgical expertise, the smiths of the Central European Hallstatt era. Not all these regions were dependent on Hallstatt Europe for their iron technology; some of them apparently adopted iron before the European smiths. The uniting factor is that, unlike the areas of the second group, these did not wait for the colonizing activities of other Mediterranean peoples to introduce them to ironworking. Egypt is best accommodated in this third group, amazingly for a culture which very early experimented with iron—the metal occurs in Old Kingdom contexts, if not earlier—and which produced its share of somewhat more developed artifacts in the later Bronze Age (it is sufficient here to refer to the finds from Tutankhamun's tomb).

The distribution of iron ores in the Mediterranean lands presumably determined in part the very different rates of progress in iron technology. But there are many unknown factors here. For one thing, we are uncertain as to which deposits were worked in antiquity; for another, we are largely in the dark as to whether ancient shipping practices favored the transportation of iron in the form of ore or in already-smelted bars. The discovery that an ancient foundry on Ischia was working with hematite imported from the mines of Elba, 250 miles to the northwest, was an important landmark here.[3] Further, the delayed advent of the Iron Age in some regions that were rich in iron ores and the incidence of early iron objects in other regions without such wealth suggest that availability of supplies was altogether less important than technical knowledge. Even on such a basic question as that of the existence of iron-bearing deposits, considerable obscurity persists. One particularly significant instance arises in the case of Egyptian iron: authoritative Egyptological works often assert that Egypt has no iron ores;[4] this is certainly untrue,[5] although it is unlikely that her deposits were exploited until later antiquity.[6] This facile and inaccurate explanation for the delayed arrival of the Iron Age in Egypt should serve to warn us against accepting simplistic theories in a field where very complex factors operated.

Since we are able to reach only broad and generalized conclusions in the matter of the indebtedness of ironworking to earlier metallurgies in the Mediterranean area, we will deal with the question here. The previous chapters have thrown light on the first tentative steps in the smelting of iron. At the risk of repetition, I note that certain Mediterranean copper ores are quite rich in iron, particularly those from Cyprus and Anatolia.[7] The occurrence of copper and bronze objects with a substantial iron content might in some cases be attributed to this fact, in others to the deliberate use of iron as a flux. The latest investigations suggest that iron was not always eliminated in very early copper–bronze metallurgy, the samples in question from the Aegean extending back to the Early Bronze Age at Servia in Macedonia and including Late Bronze Age material from Nichoria in Messenia.[8] Bronze Age samples from Sardinia were also included. A further example of an iron-rich copper comes from the Cape Gelidonya shipwreck[9] and dates to about 1200 B.C. Clearly the conditions were present in several of the Mediterranean Bronze Age cultures for the possibilities of iron to be explored by metalworkers at their leisure, before the question of adopting a thoroughgoing Iron Age economy had arisen. Early experimentation would explain the confidence with which certain Mediterranean smiths tackled technical processes, such as carburization and quench-hardening, which had not been appropriate to bronzeworking, and perhaps also the sharp differentiation in the speed with which different areas of the ancient world proceeded with their iron technology.

REGIONAL STUDIES IN THE MEDITERRANEAN IRON AGE

We will consider each of the main ancient Mediterranean cultures in turn, according to the three groupings suggested in the previous section. The order of the regions *within* each section is not necessarily significant. We begin with the regions that, on present evidence, belong to the most advanced group.

Cyprus

The developments in Cyprus during the Bronze Age would hardly lead one to expect that it played a leading role in the ensuing phase of metallurgy. True, the circumstance of the high iron content in Cypriot copper ores has been noted, but no startlingly early iron artifacts are known, and the bronze industry itself remains conservative and rather uninspiring until the arrival of a strong wave of Aegean influence about 1200 B.C.[10] Yet, as recent scientific study and archaeological discoveries have combined to show, the almost immediate sequel was a phase of fairly intensive experimentation with working iron (stage 2 as defined earlier), roughly corresponding with the Late Cypriot III A period, and a transition to a full Iron Age (stage 3) no later than the end of Late Cypriot III B, that is, ca. 1050 B.C. This remarkable achievement, not precisely matched anywhere else in the ancient world, can be documented at each stage in the process, suggesting that the crucial step of committing the resources of a community to the new metal was first taken in Cyprus.

This step is most fully illustrated in the case of single-edged knives, and the evidence has increased so much in recent years that it is worth assembling here. Table 10.1 lists the finds, from Late Cypriot Bronze Age contexts only, in two separate groups: first, the iron knives with bronze rivets in the hilt, which have been recognized[11] as forming an important and chronologically restricted transitional phase; and secondly, the all-iron knives.

We can now consider this body of 23 iron knives according to the criteria set out in the previous section. First, we have the invaluable metallurgical study by E. Tholander of 2 of these knives, nos. 10 and 12 in table 10.1.[12] This yielded the most startling results, especially for no. 12, which proved to have been carburized, quench-hardened, and tempered, and which achieved a Vickers hardness measurement of 385 in its blade, well up to the standard of modern high-carbon steel. Our no. 10 had also been carburized and quench-hardened, but the use of tempering could not be established with certainty here. This evidence alone is enough to show that Cyprus in the Late Cypriot III B period had advanced into the era of working iron.

Next we may apply the factor of proportion. Of the 23 knives in table 10.1, at least 3 or 4 belong to Late Cypriot III A, while 12 to 14 are definitely datable to Late Cypriot III B and the transition at its end. For bronze usage in knives of these periods, we turn to the lists of H. W. Catling and L. Åström, where a probable total of 9 knives is assembled for the whole Late Cypriot III period;[13] of these, it seems that the preponderance lies fairly early in the period, as one might expect. On the

Table 10.1. Iron Knives in Late Cypriot Bronze Age Contexts

No., site, and context	Date	Type in L. Åström's classification (SCE IV, 1D[1972]; 473)	References
a. With bronze rivets			
1. Kourion, Bamboula, settlement, inv. B.1382	LC III A/B	(2)	J. L. Benson, *Bamboula at Kurion* (1972), 130
2. Enkomi, Ashlar building, Room 13, inv. 7	LC III B (early)	(3)	P. Dikaios, *Enkomi* (1969), 201, 302, 714, 761, pls. 135 : 76; 172 : 5
3. Kourion, Kaloriziki Tomb 19.32, inv K.1106	LC III B	(1)	J. L. Benson, *The Necropolis at Kaloriziki* (1973), 124
4. Lapithos, Tomb 501	LC III	unk.	Cyprus, *Annual Report of the Curator of Antiquities*, 1915, 8–9; SCE I (1934), 163
5. Katydhata, Tomb 89	LC III	unk.	Cyprus, *Annual Report of the Curator of Antiquities*, 1916, 11
b. All iron			
6. Kouklia, Evreti Tomb 8	LC III A	(different)	*Illustrated London News*, 2 May 1953, 711, fig. 5
7. Kourion, Bamboula, settlement, inv. B.1386	LC III A	unk.	J. L. Benson, *Bamboula*, 130
8. Enkomi, Foundry Hoard	LC III A	(3)	A. S. Murray, A. H. Smith, H. B. Walters, *Excavations in Cyprus* (1900), 15, fig. 25, 994*; C. F. A. Schaeffer, *Enkomi–Alasia I* (1952), 31, n. 3, pl. lxiv : 6
9. Enkomi, Ashlar building, court (or Room 19?), inv. 203	LC III B	(1)	P. Dikaios, *Enkomi* 296, 526, 762, pl. 172 : 17
10. Idalion, settlement, inv. 1068	LC III B	(1)	SCE II (1935), 558
11. Idalion, settlement, inv. 1132	LC III B	(2)	SCE II, 560, pl. 173 : 1132

Table 10.1. (cont'd)

No., site, and context	Date	Type in L. Åström's classification (SCE IV, 1D[1972]; 473)	References
12. Idalion, settlement, inv. 106	LC III B	(3)	SCE II, 534, pl. 173 : 106
13. Kourion, Bamboula, settlement, inv. B.1383	LC III B	unk.	J. L. Benson, Bamboula 130
14. Enkomi, Area III, inv. 1455	LC III B, late	(?3)	P. Dikaios, Enkomi 302, 767, pl. 176 : 37
15. Enkomi, Ashlar building, Room 24, inv. 5509/7	LC III B, late	(3)	P. Dikaios, Enkomi 772, pl. 147 : 38; 176 : 53
16. Kourion, Kaloriziki Tomb 40.36, inv. K.1104	LC III B, end	(3)	J. L. Benson, Kaloriziki 124
17. Kourion, Bamboula Tomb 16.20, inv. B.1385	LC III B?	unk.	J. L. Benson, Bamboula 19, 130
18. Kourion, Bamboula Tomb 32.13, inv. B.1387	LC III	unk.	J. L. Benson, Bamboula 28, 130
19. Enkomi, Old Tomb 58	LC III	(trace only)	A. S. Murray, A. H. Smith, H. B. Walters, Excavations 31, pl. II : 995; E. Gjerstad, Studies on Prehistoric Cyprus (1926), 285, n. 3
20. Enkomi, Tomb 6.13 (French excavations)	LC III	(3)	C. F. A. Schaeffer, Missions en Chypre (1936), 137, no. 13
21. Palekythro, Tomb 2	LC	unk.	L. Åström, SCE IV, 1D (1972). 473
22. Salamis, Tomb T.1, inv. 36	LC III B/C-G I A	(3)	M. Yon, Salamine de Chypre II: La tombe T.1 du XIe siecle av. J.-C. (1971), 18, pls. 15 : 36, 18 : 36
23. Salamis, Tomb T.1, inv. 37	LC III B/C-G I A	(3)	M. Yon, ibid. 18, pls. 15 : 37, 18 : 37.

*Apparently confused by Murray et al., ibid., p. 25, with the bronze knife 1482.

basis of knives, therefore, it seems a fair provisional deduction that Late Cypriot III A can be roughly equated with stage 2 as defined earlier, while Late Cypriot III B belongs to stage 3. There are signs, however, that the knives do not give a representative picture of the overall choice of metal. The Cypriot smiths seem, for whatever reason, to have moved faster to adopt the new metal for knives than for other practical implements. There is, on the published evidence, no other class of object in the Late Cypriot Bronze Age which shows anything resembling this preponderance of iron. The Enkomi excavations published by P. Dikaios, which offer a large corpus of material spanning nearly the whole of the Late Cypriot III period, include a couple of iron sickles to add to the occasional iron daggers and pins noted by L. Åström;[14] but they show bronze heavily preponderating in these classes of object and reigning almost unopposed in other classes. Against this, one can set only C. F. A. Schaeffer's general statement that in his excavations at the same site iron knives appeared in level IV (the latter part of Late Cypriot III A) and that thereafter iron came into common use, and H. W. Catling's suggestion that this unpublished material includes an iron sword or swords.[15] There is also a problematic sword from the Acropolis site at Idalion, published as belonging to a final Late Cypriot III B level; but its close resemblance to a sword later found in a Cypro-Archaic tomb at Kouklia, and the fact that the Cypro-Archaic period was strongly represented in the ensuing levels at Idalion, inevitably raise the question whether this sword may not be of much later date.[16] Even when one turns to the Cypro-Geometric period (ca. 1050–750 B.C.), when iron generally prevailed for practical implements, knives continued to be treated specially. D. H. F. Gray in 1954 published a valuable table showing a total of no fewer than 35 iron knives from Cypro-Geometric contexts against not a single bronze one, and her figures stand to be augmented by further finds from Ktima and elsewhere; the predominance of iron for arrowheads, axes, daggers, and especially spearheads is less extreme.[17]

The overall picture of the Cypriot adoption of ironworking is thus somewhat modified by this evidence. Although the whole Cypro-Geometric period clearly falls within out stage 3, it is doubtful whether this stage can be extended very far into the preceding Late Cypriot III B. But none of this detracts from the significance of the early Cypriot experimentation with iron knives: there is no evidence of comparable date from elsewhere, and it seems that the Cypriot success, so clearly attested by

Tholander's study, provided the vital breakthrough for the Iron Age in the Mediterranean area and indeed for the Old World generally. The extensive overseas contacts of Cyprus in the 12th and 11th centuries B.C. explain the diffusion of this discovery both eastward and westward. The simultaneous occurrence of this episode and the great wave of Aegean influence on the island suggests the possibility that Aegean immigrants may have initiated these experiments. Further evidence from the finds of the Levantine region supports such a view (see the section on the Levantine coastlands below). Meanwhile, we can assign our stage 2 in Cyprus to a period beginning at or soon after 1200 B.C., down to a date rather before 1050, when it appears to have given way to stage 3. The criterion of working iron, as defined earlier, does not include dress accessories such as fibulae and pins, so the continued predominance of bronze for these objects throughout the Cypro-Geometric period (see n. 17 above) and indeed for long afterward does not controvert the fact that Cyprus had entered the full Iron Age.

The Aegean

Although the pattern of the adoption of iron in the Aegean, especially in its early stages, resembles that of Cyprus and follows it closely in time, nevertheless the sequel is rather different. The clue to this difference almost certainly lies in the more varied, ambitious, and indeed militaristic bronze technology of the antecedent Aegean Bronze Age. Some faint trace of this spirit seems to have survived the fall of the Mycenaean civilization and shows itself in the different sense of priorities of the smiths of the Greek Early Iron Age, as against their Cypriot contemporaries.

In the initial phase, however, the developments in the Aegean follow those in Cyprus with a fidelity which argues a close dependence on Cypriot technological secrets and perhaps even a reliance on importing Cypriot artifacts ready-made. Could the dependence not have been in the other direction? We have raised the possibility that Aegean immigrants helped to bring about the metallurgical revolution in Cyprus. But all the evidence is against this hypothesis. The story of working iron in Greece begins, as in Cyprus, with the appearance of iron knives with bronze rivets in the handle. These are as uncommon in the Aegean as in Cyprus, but during the comparable era, the last century and a half of the Bronze Age, iron knives in general are heavily outnumbered in the Aegean by the all-bronze knives—the reverse of the Cypriot situation. The few Aegean specimens are somewhat scattered in date: one from level II of the settlement at Lefkandi in Euboea will definitely belong in the later 12th century, but another, from tomb 38 at Perati in Eastern Attica, is one of the latest finds in that cemetery and is therefore to be dated probably in the early 11th; a further example, from Gypsadhes tomb VII at Knossos, will belong somewhere toward the middle of that century, and a fourth, from chamber tomb 1 at Vrokastro in East Crete, is likely to be later still.[18] These Aegean examples are also rather heterogeneous in type: the Knossos knife alone falls readily into type 3 of Åström's Cypriot classification. But the Perati tomb 38 knife approximates in shape a bronze example for which the excavator has convincingly argued a Levantine, and ultimately Egyptian, derivation; another iron knife with bronze rivets at Perati, unfortunately from the destroyed and not precisely datable tomb 28, is of a much simpler shape, not otherwise found in this material. The Lefkandi example bears a certain resemblance to Åström's type 3, but the Vrokastro one is of unknown form.

The unusual combination of metals and the chronological coincidence must mean that the two groups of knives, from Cyprus and the Aegean, are connected; although it is at present impossible to show any chronological priority on the part of Cyprus, the incidence of all-iron knives from an equally early period on the island (see table 10.1) surely excludes the possibility that the direction of the influence was from the Aegean to Cyprus. All-iron knives are neither so common nor so early in appearance in the Aegean: they begin only in the middle years of the 11th century, a date corresponding to that of nos. 22 and 23 in table 10.1; when they do so, they form a relatively inconspicuous part of a wider range of ironwork, as we shall see. They only other class of iron object for which a similar derivation may be possible is the sickle, of which an iron specimen was found in the Tiryns hoard of the very late Bronze Age, and whose parallels at Enkomi in Cyprus are likely to be earlier.[19]

The onset of the true Iron Age in Greece around 1050 B.C., our stage 3, is marked by several signs of independence, showing that Aegean iron metallurgy has swiftly come of age. The first is the appearance of iron daggers of a type hardly known previously (nor indeed for some time afterward either) in Cyprus. Flange-hilted daggers of this type are well established in bronze, but the only precedent for its translation into iron is the new dagger of slightly different form from Kition (see n. 14 above). From the mid-century we have 2 all-iron specimens from a grave at

Tiryns, and there are 2 contemporary examples from graves in the Athenian Kerameikos which appear to be of the same form but which still retain their bone hilt-plates. One of the Athens daggers has bronze rivets, like the Kouklia one. Of unknown type, but possibly earlier than any of these, is an iron dagger from chamber tomb A at Kamini on the island of Naxos; the context might even be as early as the 12th century. The first all-iron knives in the Aegean seem to coincide with the main group of daggers in the mid–11th century, and one of them was found in the fill of the same grave (A) at the Kerameikos as one of the daggers.[20]

More important and surprising, however, is the appearance of the first Aegean iron swords at this same time. Two Athenian graves of the end of the Submycenaean period or the transition to Protogeometric have produced iron swords. In this case, as we have seen, the evidence for Cypriot antecedents is obscure; but one can say that at least one of the Athenian swords is of a particular variety of the flange-hilted type, in which the tang for the pommel is lengthened and the "ears" are reduced or eliminated; this variety is known earliest, in its bronze version, at Enkomi in Cyprus, and it continues to have a mainly Levantine distribution in both bronze and iron. Another, slightly later Athenian sword has a blade which tapers evenly from hilt to tip, and for this the only known precedent in bronze is, once again, from Cyprus.[21] All of this suggests that the pioneer work in developing the first effective iron swords may have taken place in that very inventive final period of the Cypriot Bronze Age. Nevertheless, the sequel tells a different story: there are no further Cypriot iron swords for some centuries, whereas their development in the Aegean is traceable in a full and continuous series from the 11th century until the 7th, when new types emerge. The pattern of the iron swords, and even more that of the daggers, suggests a sequence in which technical advances achieved in Late Bronze Age Cyprus were greatly extended in the Early Iron Age Aegean.

All the Greek iron finds that we have considered so far come from a few centers—Athens, Tiryns, Naxos—which appear to have been relatively advanced in the adoption of the new metal. We shall presently extend our survey more widely within the Aegean, but it can be said now that the distribution of early ironworking in the Aegean area is very uneven and shows a heavy concentration toward the east side of the Greek peninsula and the islands of the Aegean Sea. As is often true, the best-documented site is Athens. The large number of burials and relative

Table 10.2. Comparative Use of Bronze and Iron in Athens during the
Protogeometric Period

Type	No. of bronze examples	No. of iron examples
Swords	0	8
Spearheads	4	4
Daggers*	0	2
Knives*	0	4
Dress-pins	>13	>47
Fibulae	9	12
Axes, tools, and arrowheads	0	3

*I class the "dagger" in *Kerameikos* I, 192, plate 76, tomb 17 as a knife.

clarity of the chronology here make it worthwhile assembling the evidence for the first phase of ironworking in Athens. Table 10.2 shows the comparative use of bronze and iron as working metals within the lifetime of the Attic Protogeometric pottery-style in Athens, that is, approximately between 1050 and 900 B.C.[22] Pins and fibulae have been included, although their working status is doubtful. All the finds are from graves.

The overall preponderance of iron is striking. It accounts for some four-fifths of all the working metal, and this dominance is not affected by the continuing use of bronze for other purposes (shield-bosses, vessels, and the decorative globes on the iron pins) which are not included in the table. Most surprising is the high incidence of iron for pins and fibulae, which is not often encountered anywhere else, and which is specifically absent in both the preceding and the ensuing periods in Athens. Submycenaean graves here produced at least 27 dress-pins and at least 38 fibulae of bronze and none of iron;[23] in the Geometric period the predominance of bronze for these classes of objects, though not total, is once again marked. Even for spearheads and arrowheads there is a detectable swing back to bronze from about the 8th century on in Greece as a whole (see any publication of a major sanctuary site with dedications of weapons).

These facts, together with the indirect evidence of the absence of exotic materials such as gold, ivory, faïence, and amber from Greece during the later 11th and 10th centuries, have led me to argue elsewhere for the hypothesis of a bronze shortage in the Early Iron Age in Greece.[24] The shortage centered on the difficulty of obtaining tin, which was not mined anywhere within easy reach of the Aegean; it forms part of a general pattern of isolation during these years. The hypothesis could be

applied elsewhere, in proportion to the strength of similar evidence, but
I do not think that other areas show quite such a pattern of extreme dependence on iron. The pattern does not extend even over the whole Greek
world, as we shall see. But we may first consider briefly those other Aegean
centers which at least share with Athens the feature of a fairly early mastery
of practical ironworking.

The cemeteries at Lefkandi in Euboea are not yet published in full,
but Desborough, in his recent book *The Greek Dark Ages*, writes that one
early tomb there contained an iron dagger not unlike those from Tiryns
and Athens we described earlier; the date may be very little later. The
graves belonging to this general period recall their Athenian counterparts
in showing an incidence of iron among objects normally made of bronze:
rarely among the fibulae, but actually constituting a majority of the
dress-pins. Desborough shows that this habit occasionally recurs among
the later burials at Lefkandi, where he notes another practice known from
Athens, that of "killing" swords by bending them round the necks of
funerary amphorae.[25] Overall, the evidence for contact with Athenian
metallurgy is strong, and this is reflected in the signs of ceramic influence.

There are in fact several indications that a kind of early ironworking
koinē existed along the eastern coastal area of the Greek mainland. The
rather curious Athenian practice of threading a bronze decorative globe
on to the iron shaft of a pin, is found also at four sites in the Argolid (Tiryns,
Argos, Asine, and Mycenae) and much farther north at Theotokou in
Thessaly. This cannot be a coincidence. There are also resemblances in
the types of weapons and knives found over this area, although no site
as yet has an adequate body of published evidence for a detailed comparison
with Attica.[26]

The early mastery of ironworking was not, however, confined to the
relatively small area of this eastern mainland *koinē*. We find other Aegean
centers that scarcely, if at all, lagged behind in their adoption of iron but
that do not show the same close typological resemblances. The early
dagger from Naxos suggests that the Cyclades may have included such
centers, but on present evidence a much more prominent iron industry
is that of Crete. Here, in the graves around Knossos and much farther east
at the cemetery and settlement sites of Mouliana, Vrokastro, and Kavousi,
there is a remarkably rich and individual range of iron finds, beginning in
the 11th century. Here too there are links with Cyprus, but there is every
sign that they were independently established. The close correspondence

Table 10.3. Comparative Use of Bronze and Iron at Vergina during the Early Iron
Age Period of the Cemetery

Type	No. of bronze examples	No. of iron examples
Swords	1	19*
Spearheads	0	36
Daggers	0	1
Knives	0	75
Dress-pins	13	2
Fibulae	>227	3
Arrowheads	0	20

*One of these swords has a bronze hilt.

with Athenian types is not found. A further region of the Aegean where
ironworking was probably established early is that of the new settlements
of the Ionian Migration on the Aegean coast of Turkey and on the offshore
islands; but in this case the evidence is not yet so full. The most surprising
feature is the occurrence, in graves on Kos, of the iron pin with bronze
globe, the standard type of the eastern mainland; but here it does not seem to
occur before the second half of the 10th century.[27]

In Macedonia, a major ironworking region that belongs in a category
of its own, these is a cemetery site, Vergina, that excels those farther south
in the richness of its metalwork. In addition there is a number of smaller
sites. The chronology of these sites is problematic since the painted Protogeometric and Geometric pottery on which the dating of the Aegean
Early Iron Age is largely based occurs much more rarely here. In the main
site publication, M. Andronikos favors an initial date in the later 11th
century for the earliest group of burials at Vergina, which includes some
iron finds; a detailed recent study by K. Kilian argues that the first Iron
Age phase at Vergina extends back to about 1100 B.C., with the initial
date of the cemetery considerably earlier.[28] This is not the place to rehearse
detailed typological arguments, but I do not find convincing evidence for
dating the first ironworking in Macedonia earlier than that from farther
south, although it may have begun quite soon afterward, that is, by about
1000 B.C. On this assumption, the iron finds from Vergina will have a
similar initial date to those from Athens set out in table 10.3 and, although
the terminal date of the Early Iron Age period of the cemetery is very
considerably later, it is worth setting out the substantial body of evidence
from Vergina in the same way:[29]

In some respects, the use of iron within the strict definition of working metal shows a similar pattern here to that in Athens; but once we turn to the fibulae and dress-pins, there is a glaring contrast. Indeed, even within the class of weapons there is a clear discrepancy over the treatment of spearheads: in Athens, all the bronze examples are early, but it is nevertheless demonstrable, sometimes from the evidence of the same grave, that they overlap in date with iron swords, daggers, and knives; at Vergina, all the spearheads are of iron, although it is possible that none of them belongs in the earliest period of the Iron Age cemetery. But when we compare the practices with pins and fibulae, no reconciliation between the two sites is possible.

Conditions in Macedonia clearly differed from those in Athens. In my view the people of Vergina, guided only by considerations of suitability, were free to choose between bronze and iron. The quantity of other ornamental bronzes in the female graves exceeds that of the working iron in the male ones and shows that there was no difficulty in obtaining bronze. With the spearheads, where the balance between the two sites is tilted somewhat in the reverse direction, there may be a significant chronological difference, as suggested above; but the production of a socketed spearhead in iron would present a technical problem not found in the making of swords or knives, and it is possible that a solution was more readily found in Macedonia. One final, possibly relevant feature is that very rarely at Athens and almost never at Vergina are sword and spearhead found together in the same burial in the periods covered by these tables; so in this respect the patterns of the two sites are in agreement.[30]

The evidence of the regions examined so far suggests that an early and roughly contemporaneous adoption of ironworking was compatible with clear regional differences in the details of its application. But the correspondences in date and the typological resemblances, approximate though they are in most cases, suggest that the developments in these regions were not entirely independent of each other. Even the early iron industry of Macedonia, although free of some of the constraining factors which operated farther south and quite distinct in its overall pattern, shows sufficiently close resemblances in the typology of swords, knives, fibulae, and pins to make an independent origin highly unlikely.

Yet when we consider the remainder of the Greek world, in particular the western parts of central Greece and of the Peloponnese, we must conclude that transmission of new techniques in the Early Iron Age of

Fig. 10.1. Early Iron Finds in the Aegean: Iron Objects of Practical Use, ca. 1200–900 B.C.

Greece was far from automatic. In the whole of this western area there is almost no ironwork that can be shown to be earlier than about 900 B.C. Despite our lack of a substantial body of metal finds comparable to those farther east, but it is evident that iron technology spread slowly across

Fig. 10.2 Iron Ore: Major Sources in the Aegean (after "Matallogenetikòs chártis tîs 'Elládos," Institute for Geology and Subsurface Research, Athens, 1965).

Greece. Two western regions, Messenia and Epirus, present a more distinctive picture. At Malthi in Messenia, a find of iron objects in a purely Mycenaean level made some years ago included a dagger and a knife, both fragmentary. Enough of the dagger survives to show that it is of a much more primitive type than those from Tiryns and Athens (see p. 347 above). It seems credible that some precocious experimentation with iron had taken place in this thriving region of Bronze Age culture perhaps as early as the 12th century. Recent finds have added to the picture in Messenia, but they are of much later date. A tholos tomb near the Palace of Nestor contained traces of at least three pins and two knives of iron associated with a burial of the later 10th century. One of the pins proved to have a bronze globe attached to it. This surely means that Messenia was by now in touch with the centers where this unusual practice had started, as may also be inferred in the parallel case of Kos (p. 350 above) at much the same period. Further iron knives and a pin come from a tholos of similar date at Karpophora. For Epirus, the evidence of ironworking is fuller but more difficult to date. Since this region evidently lacks iron ore, the incidence of early iron weapons and knives is most easily explained by the proximity of Macedonia, with which Epirus was undoubtedly in contact during the period after the rise of the Macedonian ironworking industry.[31]

A distribution map of early iron finds in the Aegean shows a certain correspondence with the distribution of the major sources of iron ore, but not so close as completely to explain the pattern (figs. 10.1 and 10.2). Not until the 9th century had the whole Greek world passed into the full Iron Age of our stage 3, a step which its more advanced centers had taken some 200 years earlier. This is shown not only by further grave finds but also by the deposits of arms and other dedications at the great sanctuary sites of Greece. The publications of these deposits have tended to concentrate on the more attractive and better preserved bronze finds and thus to give a misleading picture of the range of metalwork. Some of the scholars publishing such material state candidly that the iron finds disintegrated.[32] Iron seems to have become universally available, while at the same time the wealth and variety of the bronze industry—paradoxically, a sign of the developed Iron Age economy—increased out of all recognition. Further technological advance was of course still possible, but in essentials the iron-based economy of the Aegean was fully shaped.

Until recently there has been no evidence at all on the development of steel in the Aegean. But in 1973 G. J. Varoufakis showed that two of the three iron spearheads dating from the 7th to 6th centuries B.C. that he examined had been carburized; the better preserved one had a carbon content of 0.65 percent. Examination of earlier objects of working iron in Greece would undoubtedly yield similar results, if not necessarily at quite such an early date as in Cyprus. Varoufakis's study raises the matter of importation of iron ore: his chemical analysis of the Greek spearheads led him to conclude that they were made of Near Eastern ore. Given the free intercommunication between Greece and the East during this period, the conclusion is reasonable, but whether the same conditions prevailed earlier, at the start of the Aegean Iron Age, is doubtful. It has been suggested that the very first examples of Aegean working iron, the iron knives with bronze rivets, may have been imported as ready-made artifacts from Cyprus. Undoubtedly the idea for this combination of metals came from Cyprus, but the absence of close typological resemblances between the Cypriot knives and most of the Aegean ones makes it doubtful that significant numbers of ready-made imports were present except at the very outset; presently, too, the knives are joined by other types, such as the flange-hilted iron daggers, for which no Cypriot (or other) ancestry is traceable. But the import of raw iron ore and of iron bars, it must be admitted, is more plausible.[33]

Because of the relative precision of their chronology, as well as their early adoption of iron, Cyprus and the Aegean repay detailed study. Since these conditions are not present in the same degree elsewhere, our examination of the other Mediterranean regions will perforce be less detailed. But there is one further area which has traditionally been given a more prominent place in early ironworking than either Cyprus or the Aegean, and indeed is usually allowed a historical priority over them in this and other matters.

The Levantine Coastlands

Within the Levantine Coastlands, Palestine has produced a fairly full body of evidence to compare with those from the Aegean and Cyprus, and farther north there is an important cemetery site at Hama in Syria. Many years ago, G. E. Wright contributed an important study of the Palestinian evidence, and more recent finds have suggested that his conclusions were substantially valid. The introduction of working iron, he showed, occurred in the latter part of the 12th century, but the information from the best-dated cemeteries, notably Beth Shemesh, suggested that bronze predominated in this field until about the middle of the 10th. On this showing, our stage 2 will begin at much the same period as in

Cyprus and the Aegean, and there is much evidence to connect its appearance in Palestine with the advent of the Philistines. But it seems that there was then rather a longer delay before the development of our stage 3 than in Cyprus or Greece. The finds from Lachish, showing iron heavily predominant throughout the period ca. 1000–700, even appearing for a few fibulae (4 out of 25) and already present in a tomb-group (521) at the very beginning of the period, favor a slight raising of Wright's chronology. For the initial stages, more recent finds have confirmed both the approximate dating and the Philistine connections. But the question has been bedeviled by arbitrary interpretation of the written sources: it has been stated that the 13th-century Papyrus Anastasi I describes the activity of ironworkers at Joppa, and that a biblical passage (1 Samuel 13: 19–21) records how at a later period the Philistines had established a monopoly of iron. In fact, neither of these two sources appears to mention iron specifically.

Jane Waldbaum has shown that throughout the 12th and 11th centuries iron objects were completely outnumbered by bronze in Palestine, as witness such sites as Tell Jemmeh. The Aegean connections, both of the Philistines in general and of the specific context in which one of the earliest iron weapons in Palestine was found, have been pointed out by Trude Dothan. This further reinforces the connection between the movements of Aegean peoples in the Eastern Mediterranean after 1200 B.C. and the first adoption of working iron, for which the developments in Cyprus present the strongest evidence.[34]

The material from the Hama cremation cemetery in Syria suggests a similar but perhaps more accelerated progress in the adoption of iron. There are, however, chronological difficulties here because, as P. J. Riis has shown in his publication, the absolute dates of the termini of the four periods of the cemetery are very approximate. Period I at Hama, which begins early in the 12th century and may end as early as ca. 1075, seems certainly to represent our stage 2: it produced another iron knife with bronze rivets and (in a later level of this period that Riis assigns to the 11th century) an iron sword, apparently of a variety similar to that of the first iron sword from the Kerameikos at Athens; also present were a bronze sword, spearhead, and miniature axes.

Here again there are connections with Cyprus and the Aegean, although it is difficult to guess in which direction influences are traveling. Period II (approximate dates 1075–925 B.C.) sees the arrival of our stage 3, though not necessarily from its very beginning. The period shows an overall predominance of iron for practical purposes, yet it still contained four bronze swords, a bronze sickle, and a preponderance of bronze among the arrowheads in a ratio of 15 to 1. Only in Period III (roughly 925 to 800 B.C.) is the balance comparable to that in Protogeometric Athens or Early Iron Age Vergina (tables 10.2 and 10.3).[35] Broadly speaking, the developments in Palestine and in Syria seem alike in that they begin at much the same time as in Cyprus and Greece, but thereafter progress with less urgency toward a completely iron-based economy. The implication is that, unlike Cyprus and Greece, the Levant suffered no strong constraint in the acquisition of copper and tin.

Asia Minor

Since the Hittites had demonstrated a notable interest in iron during the Bronze Age, scholars are naturally predisposed to assign a high initial date to the Iron Age in Asia Minor. But J. Waldbaum has shown that here too an element of modern mythology is operating. The well-known Hattušiliš letter, written to an unknown correspondent shortly before the middle of the 13th century B.C., falls far short of demonstrating the existence of a Hittite monopoly of ironworking; but the modern theory of this monopoly has been largely founded on the letter. What the document does show is the Hittite king's striking concern with iron, specifically, working iron. As such, it may betoken the advent of our stage 2 in central Anatolia, and if so, is certainly the earliest such evidence that we have anywhere. But it is an oversimplification to believe that this precocious interest in iron led to a correspondingly early entry into the full Iron Age, and in fact the evidence is heavily against such a view.

We are concerned here with the Mediterranean coastal areas of Asia Minor and the main site of Tarsus. Unfortunately, the chronological position is yet again less definite that one would wish: the excavators' dating of their Early, Middle, and Late Iron Age periods has been called into question by J. Boardman, who has proposed a lower chronology.[36] But even if one accepts the excavators' dates as approximately correct, it is clear that we are dealing with a slower progress in ironworking than was the case in the neighboring Levant and Cyprus. The "Early Iron Age" period is dated to between 1100 and 850 B.C., and the metallic finds from this period, although slight, show that this is a transitional era, comparable with our stage 2 elsewhere. Even among the knives, which throughout

Table 10.4. Comparative Use of Bronze and Iron at Tarsus During the Middle Iron
Age and Late Iron Age (Assyrian) Periods, ca. 850–600 B.C.

Type	No. of bronze examples	No. of iron examples
Swords	0	2
Spearheads	0	4
Daggers	0	1
Knives	2	22
Dress-pins	4	0
Fibulae	11	5
Axes, tools, and arrowheads	21	58

the Eastern Mediterranean are the first type to be translated into iron, there are two bronze examples as against three iron; the arrowheads, nails, pins, and chisel are all of bronze. In the excavators' "Middle Iron Age" and "Late Iron Age (Assyrian)" periods proportions resembling those of our stage 3 appear. These periods are dated, respectively, to ca. 850–700 and ca. 700–600 in the publication, but because of Boardman's well-founded doubts about the chronological dividing line between them, I think it is better to present a combined picture of the metalwork of both phases, as in table 10.4.

On this showing, perhaps the most important site in Cilicia was about 200 years behind other Eastern Mediterranean centers in adopting iron to a comparable degree. Another region of Anatolia, Urartu, shows an even longer delay in accepting the new metal, even though it lies close to the land of the Chalybes, who were among those credited by legend with the discovery of iron. The time lag is further suggested by the quantities of bronze weapons and implements—in contexts as late as the end of the 8th century—that are described in the Assyrian annals of King Sargon during his Urartian campaigns and that have been discovered in the Soviet excavations of Urartian sites, notably Karmir-Blur.[37] The picture may yet be modified when the results from such sites as Gordion are published in full, and a definite exception has to be made for the sites on the Aegean coast of Anatolia (these are briefly mentioned in the section on the Aegean), which show a distinctly earlier progression to iron.

We now move on to the second group of Mediterranean cultures: those whose adoption of ironworking is the direct result of immigration and settlement by peoples in the first group, that is, by the Phoenicians and the Greeks.

Northern Africa

The North African coast, excepting Egypt and its sphere of direct influence, provides a classic case of a colonial introduction of iron. There is no evidence, as far as I know, of the use of iron before the arrival of the Phoenician and Greek settlers. There are strong differences of opinion as to when the Phoenicians established their colonies in this area. Some believe that Phoenician commercial enterprise in the West was already well established in the Late Bronze Age, but even if true this would not be of immediate relevance to the introduction of iron. It seems to me most unlikely that any permanent Phoenician settlements in the West were established until late in the 8th century—a period, that is, when the colonists has long since adopted a full Iron Age economy.

Although it is quite impossible to use metallurgical evidence to determine the initial date of the colonies, one can say that the evidence does not contradict such a dating: early evidence is not yet forthcoming from Tripolitania, but from Tunisia to Morocco the finds from Phoenician graves dating probably from the 7th century onward give the first evidence for the common use of iron. At Carthage, some inkling of the frequency of iron objects can be gleaned from R. P. Delattre's periodical reports to the Académie des Inscriptions et Belles-Lettres. In Morocco, Phoenician cemeteries have likewise yielded quite copious evidence of iron objects. There is also the interesting possibility that, in the Berber dialects, the word for "iron" is derived from the corresponding Phoenician term. In Cyrenaica, finally, where the settlers were not Phoenician but Greek, and the date of their arrival in the later part of the 7th century, we find iron implements present in the early deposits, as expected.[38]

Spain

In Spain, too, a number of recent discoveries on the southern coast have supported a date in the late 8th century B.C. for the first arrival of Phoenician settlers; Greek objects are also present on these sites from very early on, although the establishment of Greek settlements comes later. Perhaps the very earliest iron objects of practical use in Spain are those found on these Phoenician sites, for example, the iron point found in tomb 19 of the cemetery of "Laurita" at Almuñécar, along with Proto-corinthian kotylai of the early 7th century. Soon afterward, iron knives and other objects begin to occur on other sites in the hinterland that were under Phoenician influence: for example, both in a settlement and in graves at Huelva and in burials excavated long ago in the area of Carmona. Such an attribution of the earliest iron in Spain to the Phoenicians is supported by some recent authorities, and it does seem the likeliest hypothesis on present evidence.[39] Nevertheless, Spain itself is rich in iron ores (iron is among the metals which Ezekiel lists as being traded from Tarshish [xxvii, 12]), and if the colonists in the south of the country were responsible for the first exploitation of the metal, then it was only a little later, and possibly by independent development, that the Iberians themselves began to practice ironworking farther north. The initial date of this process used to be set in the 6th century B.C., but in a detailed recent study W. Schüle has argued that the first iron weapons of the Meseta culture belong at the latest in the 7th. Whatever the precise chronology, the Iberians certainly developed a very comprehensive range of ironwork, as was shown long ago by Horace Sandars in his classic study of Iberian weapons. They remained, however, receptive to foreign influences in this sphere, as is shown by their later adoption of the *espada falcata*, presumably borrowed from the Greeks.[40]

A somewhat similar pattern of "colonical" introduction of iron can be detected on the Mediterranean islands of Sardinia, Corsica, and the Balearic Islands. But these instances also show that the arrival of foreign settlers by no means inevitably led to the adoption of iron by the natives. In Sardinia, for example, although there are iron objects which probably go back as far as the 8th century and reflect the earliest stages of Phoenician influence on the island, there was a notable reluctance for some centuries afterward to move to an iron-based economy. By contrast, the frequency of iron finds in the Ebuso necropolis on Ibiza suggests a different reaction to the appearance of iron-using Phoenicians there; while on Corsica, though at a later date and under Etruscan rather than Phoenician influence, a complete acceptance of ironworking is shown by the finds from the first period of the cemetery at Aléria, dated between ca. 500 and 340 B.C.[41]

Our final group of iron-using cultures embraces those areas which, although adopting iron distinctly later than the pioneering centers of the Eastern Mediterranean, nevertheless appear to have done so independently of them.

Italy and Sicily

To place Italy in this grouping is to accept a compromise between conflicting factors and conflicting schools of thought. Once again, chronological difficulties obtrude; but it seems true that systematic ironworking in several areas of the peninsula antedates any strictly colonial activity from the peoples of the Eastern Mediterranean. The richness of native resources, particularly in the ore deposits of Elba, must have been an influential factor; but future discoveries may yet confirm what has already been suggested, that the stimulus of foreign interest in these resources before the advent of actual colonies was also a decisive factor.[42] Even more problematic is the relation of the first Italian ironworking to that of Hallstatt Europe; chronologically, it remains a possibility that the first practical application of iron in Italy, our stage 2, developed under the influence of the parallel change in Central Europe; but as we shall see, stage 2 in Italy was of long duration, and before its end the factor of Greek involvement had undoubtedly begun to prevail.[43]

The adoption of iron in Italy was piecemeal and uneven. In certain areas, we can establish that working iron was known before the end of the 9th century B.C., but it is often found, even in adjacent centers, arriving distinctly later. The cemetery at Torre Galli in Calabria provides some of the fullest, as well as earliest, evidence. In P. Orsi's original publication, the proportions of the metals over the cemetery as a whole are given as follows: daggers and short swords, 4 bronze to 12 iron; spearheads, 71 to 11; fibulae, 88 to 14. Clearly this community combined an ability to work in iron with a general preference for bronze for most purposes; yet we find, perhaps unexpectedly, that the use of iron for fibulae, characteristic of the 10th century in Greece, was also practiced here at times. The iron at Torre Galli is by no means confined to the later stages of the cemetery: a recent study by B. d'Agostino has singled out two groups of burials, on the evidence of fibula types, as being of relatively early date, probably before 800 B.C.; among these, tombs 36, 46, 57, 58, 93, and 188 have among them produced several iron knives and fibulae and a short sword of iron. Ninth-century ironwork is also probably represented by the sword and fibula in tomb 5 of the Osta cemetery at Cumae.[44]

For central Italy, perhaps the fullest evidence is that from the cemeteries of Veii. Here, phase IIA is expressly distinguished for the sudden increase in the use of iron; its dating is approximately 800–760 B.C. On this showing, Etrùria may have moved to the adoption of iron somewhat later than parts of southern Italy but in the end more comprehensively. It is in this specific context that the stimulus of Greek interest, shown by the first imports of Greek pottery at Veii, has been posited (see n. 42). The evidence of early iron has been filled out for Etruria by the chronological ordering of tombs at Tarquinia by H. Hencken: here the strange phenomenon of a bronze sword with iron rivets, together with an iron fibula, is dated to the 9th century if not the 10th, with iron fibulae becoming frequent (and iron weapons known) well before 750 B.C. A cemetery at Cerveteri has also produced an iron dagger and fibula of the early 8th century. Farther south, we have at least one early iron knife from tomb 4 at San Martino sul Sarno, which is said to antedate phase IIA at Veii, with further knives and fibulae falling in the period contemprary with that phase. Another Campanian cemetery at Sala Consilina near Salerno has produced an early iron sword, with fairly numerous iron finds from later phases of the cemetery; the use of iron for fibulae here continues as late as the 6th century.

In Latium, the adoption of iron seems to have occurred detectably later: working iron is rare before the 7th century (period III of P. G. Gierow's chronology), and even then it only slowly displaces bronze as a practical metal. The Esquiline tombs in Rome, however, show working iron in the 8th century. In northern Italy the first iron appears at much the same period as in the centers that we have been considering, but significantly L. Barfield has stated that down to the 5th century B.C. iron was much less used than bronze.[45] Only a small selection of Italian finds has been cited here, partly because the extensive chronological revision of recent years makes it wise to depend only on the latest discoveries; but the outlines of the picture are fairly consistent. Only in the initial stages can the iron industries of Italy claim an independent origin, unaffected by developments in the Eastern Mediterranean, and even this is open to some question. What followed was a long transitional period during which, despite the oddity of occasionally employing iron for fibulae, there was only a partial dependence on iron as a working metal. In Italy, as earlier in the Eastern Mediterranean, iron was often used for knives at first, although there are some conspicuously early iron short swords.

In Sicily, the picture is not essentially different. A few significant iron finds appear to occur before outside influences can have begun to operate; they certainly antedate colonization. A small but telltale discovery was made at Motya in 1962: the remains of a burial dating from before the establishment of the Phoenician colony in the late 8th century were found to include traces of iron objects, probably weapons. But evidence from the native cemeteries of eastern Sicily had long since been found, in contexts of the Siculan Period III from just before the arrival of the Greek colonists, to show an occasional use of iron: iron finger-rings and knives, for example, from Pantalica and a fibula from Monte Dessueri.[46]

For Italy as a whole one might not wish to go so far as L. Banti's statement, arising from the use of iron for decorative additions to a bronze chariot at Populonia in Etruria, that iron was still a rare and precious metal there in the 7th century B.C.; but clearly Italy pursued an unhurried course in accepting the new metal and turning it to practical uses. The delay is surprising because from about 775 B.C. on, when the Euboean Greek colonists arrived at Pithecoussai on Ithaka, the southern part of the peninsula and Sicily were being progressively settled by immigrants who had long since entered a full Iron Age of our stage 3; and these same colonists, at least those of Ischia, were actively exploiting Italian iron ores as early as the 8th century.[47] Obviously the peoples of ancient Italy had different attitudes toward iron from those of the peoples of the Eastern Mediterranean.

The Adriatic Coastlands

The example of Italy provides a good basis for understanding the developments in the remaining areas of the Mediterranean, notably the Adriatic. One particular region, northern Epirus, which now lies within Albania, has been dealt with, if briefly, in the section on the Aegean. The proximity of Epirus to the iron industries of the Aegean and specifically to that of Macedonia, with which Epirus had evident connections, led to some sporadic occurrences of iron weapons and implements which are likely to be distinctly earlier than anything that we shall find farther north. The adoption of iron in Dalmatia and at the head of the Adriatic, by contrast, seems to owe much more to developments in Italy and in the Central European interior.

The Italian connection in particular has been described by J. Alexander and K. Kilian in recent years: coastal Dalmatia was more accessible than the interior to influences from across the Adriatic, and here the crucial stage of acceptance of iron seems to begin in the later 8th century under strong Italian influence. A corollary to this process was the adoption of more or less identical fibula types on both sides of the Adriatic; the immediate, if not always the ultimate, source of their distribution in Dalmatia was Italy. A single find of some potential importance was the cave deposit at St. Kanzian in Istria, which included an iron sword and 11 iron spearheads (one of them only partly of iron). Unfortunately the dating of the main body of finds here is disputed, although its basic homogeneity seems assured; W. Kimmig in an important paper (see n. 43) argued for a date in Hallstatt B1, perhaps the 10th century B.C.; but a more orthodox view would place the find in Hallstatt B3, and in any case the iron weapons must be seen in the context of the rest of the find, which comprised 11 bronze swords and no fewer than 220 bronze spearheads. Tentatively one can conclude that the transition to working iron may have begun rather earlier here than the Dalmatian evidence would suggest, perhaps from a date near 800 B.C. But one could not wish for a clearer illustration of our stage 2 than this deposit.[48]

France

Coastal France provides as late an instance of the acceptance of working iron as we have found anywhere in the Mediterranean. The occurrence of iron even in a 7th century context is treated as exceptional in J. J. Jully's recent study. Yet here again the date is just early enough to show that ironworking did not have to wait for the establishment of permanent colonies, which came relatively late to this coast; although, as in Italy, the possibility of overseas influence as a decisive factor is there. The context of the early iron finds is somewhat equivocal on this point: in the Grand Bassin I cemetery at Mailhac (Aude), where iron horse-bits are among the first finds, and farther east at St. Julien, Pézenas, where by the 6th century iron arms were common and iron fibulae also used, there are indeed signs of Punic influence, exercised no doubt through the medium of precolonial trade from Carthage. But at the same time there are un-doubted contacts with northern Italy and Central Europe, both areas where ironworking was by now well established. The relative lateness of the process is underlined by the finds from the Rochelonge shipwreck from near Agde, which is assigned to the 6th century but which contained quantities of bronze tools and other practical objects. Despite its late start, the Gaulish iron industry, helped by the wealth of resources, became widespread and indeed famous in the pre-Roman period.[49]

Egypt

Egyptian iron must be treated on its own, as a unique case, for Egypt witnessed some of the earliest pioneering experiments with iron in stage I, while its long-delayed progression into a full Iron Age may very well have been precipitated by the permanent settlement of Greeks in the Nile

Delta. It provides the clearest possible illustration of the differing attitudes to iron and of the absence of any historical necessity to move from an early mastery of iron technology to the application of it. The vexed question of Egyptian iron ores has been alluded to in the introductory section (see nn. 4–6); in the present state of our knowledge, we cannot use this factor as a complete explanation of the anomalies of Egyptian ironworking. Indeed, there are definite signs that problems of supply, if any, were readily overcome.

Much attention has been given to the strikingly early first occurrences of worked iron in Egypt. They extend back to Old Kingdom and even Predynastic times. The main value of these finds lies in their showing that the Egyptians were well able to handle iron-smelting without foreign instruction, a fact which has been forgotten in the context of the New Kingdom and the period of the alleged "Hittite monopoly."[50] J. Waldbaum points out that of the well-known collection of 19 iron objects in Tutankhamun's tomb all but one show every sign of being Egyptian artifacts produced by Egyptian craftsmen (see chap. 3). For a rather later period, the researches of Carpenter and Coghlan have shown that Egyptian smiths remained abreast of later technological advances in the field. Egyptian axes and other implements dating from about 900 B.C. onward were found to have been carburized, quenched, and probably tempered as well, a finding that is quite incompatible with the picture of backwardness and isolation that is sometimes painted. All these considerations, however, must be set apart from the essentially economic question of the Egyptian adoption of iron into common use: in this and in this alone can Egypt be judged backward and the operation of outside influences likely to have been significant.

During the 7th century B.C. Egypt was, first, repeatedly though always briefly occupied by Assyrian armies and later infiltrated by Greek and other Aegean elements in a military and subsequently a commercial context. It can hardly be coincidental that this same century provides the first really copious evidence for Egyptian ironworking, though there is a residual conviction, stemming perhaps from Flinders Petrie, that this evidence essentially represents the activity of foreigners. Certainly one of the earliest excavated deposits of iron tools, found by Petrie at Thebes in association with a bronze helmet of Assyrian type, has a distinctly non-Egyptian look and may well be an intrusive relic of the Assyrian armies. But the much fuller evidence from Tel Defenneh and Naucratis, beginning

toward the end of the century, is not entirely susceptible to such an explanation. The finds at both these sites included iron slag, which at least
proves that smelting was taking place on Egyptian soil; at Tel Defenneh
particularly large slag deposits were found. Further, examination of the
artifacts illustrated by Petrie shows that quite a high proportion of them
are altogether strange to Greece in their typology—the Aegean being
the source of the foreign elements at both these sites—while some were
positively recognized by Petrie himself as Egyptian types. Within the
lifetime of the same Twenty-Sixth Dynasty, iron became quite common
in purely Egyptian contexts, as for example in the Palace of Apries, and
indeed it would have been strange if such intensive metallurgical activity
could take place in Egypt without having some impact on native practices.
The old view that ironworking could have come to Egypt from the Sudan,
finally, may today be rejected as representing the opposite of the truth.[51]
But when all is said, the delay in the adoption of a fully iron-based economy
in Egypt—corresponding to our stage 3—until the 7th century B.C. is
an instance of the extreme prolongation of stage 2.

GENERAL CONCLUSIONS

A few recurrent features in the early iron industries of the Mediterranean
world are rendered all the more conspicuous by the generally variegated
background against which they appear. They may be discussed in turn
before we finally consider whether any universal inferences are justified.

Early Discovery of Steeling

As noted above, metal analyses have shown the early transformation
of wrought iron into steel in three Mediterranean areas, namely Cyprus,
the Aegean, and Egypt. In Cyprus, this is established for the strikingly
early date of the 12th century B.C.; in Greece, the objects tested were
much later (7th to 6th centuries), but as far as I know they are the only
experiments carried out on Greek ironwork, and one can argue from
the quenching metaphor in the *Odyssey* (10. 459: see n. 33) that the relevant
knowledge in Greece goes back a little further; indeed it would hardly
be surprising, in view of the Cypriot connection, to find it near the very
beginnings of Greek practical ironworking. The Egyptian evidence,
dating apparently from about 900 B.C., is particularly impressive in the
quality of its products. To these instances we can add findings from, first,

Etruria, where tests carried out under the supervision of C. Panseri have shown that carburization was already present by the 7th century; and secondly, from areas away from the Mediterranean. Here one may mention weapons from Luristan (Iran), which on more than one occasion have been found to show evidence of steeling, from a date which is likely to be as early as the 9th century; from Mesopotamia, where R. Pleiner was inclined to believe in a form of steel process by the neo-Assyrian period of the 8th to 7th centuries; and from Alpine Central Europe where the presence of carburization, if in the somewhat later era of the 7th to 4th centuries B.C., was long ago confirmed by tests.[52] It is becoming clear that the testing of early iron artifacts of practical purpose more often than not indicates traces of carburization at least, often adventitious, and sometimes of quenching and tempering too. In this, as in other respects, one hopes that the extension of modern scientific experiment will lead to a truer appreciation of the achievements of early ironworkers.

The Transport of Raw Materials

Transportation of raw materials is a much less clear-cut issue than early steeling. Only in Ischia (cited in the introductory section [see n. 3 above]) has a precise localization of the source and destination of ancient iron ore shipment been established. The distance there was 250 miles; but we have seen hints in several areas of the portability of the raw materials for ancient ironworking over lesser distances. The extensive finds of iron slag at Naucratis and Tel Defenneh in northern Egypt are a case in point: they occur at some distance from the known iron ore deposits, although it is not true that all ironworking in ancient Egypt was carried out with imported material (see nn. 4–6). Even in the Aegean, where the correlation between iron sources and early iron industries was relatively close (see the section on the Aegean and maps 1 and 2), there are cases such as those of Epirus and Messenia, which entail either the shipment of unworked iron or the import of ready-made artifacts—more probably the former. Here again, our reaction should be one of increased appreciation, this time of the degree of economic organization involved in early ironworking.

Unexpected Applications of Ironworking

To some extent it is a matter of opinion whether to regard the use of iron for such objects as dress-pins and fibulae as in any way odd. But there is a certain objective confirmation in the fact that most ancient cultures, after a period of partial experimentation with such practices, then generally reverted to using bronze for these purposes. Experimental use of iron for making fibulae was widespread. Its most intensive and earliest use was in the Aegean area during the 10th century, and here the reversion to bronze is already marked by about 900 B.C. But we also encountered the practice, although more rarely, in contemporary Cyprus (see n. 17: one instance in Gray's table), in 9th- to 7th-century Tarsus (see the section on Asia Minor and table 10.4), in 9th- to 8th-century Calabria and 8th-century Sicily (see the section on Italy and Sicily), and in 6th-century southern France (see the section on France). Outside Greece, the practice is so uncommon that it may be judged insignificant. Certainly the wide temporal span of the experimentation and the great variety of the fibula types involved rule out any explanation that relies on a theory of simple diffusion, and suggest if anything the operation of some universal factor such as the temporary shortage of bronze that was inferred in the case of Greece. The question perhaps merits further exploration.

The main general conclusion that emerges from the study of Mediterranean ironworking is that it was applied in an almost endless variety of patterns and that underlying those patterns is a great range of known or conjectured factors—technical, economic, political, commercial. To understand the spread of early ironworking one must distinguish between the essentially *technological* factors, such as those that brought about the initiation of our stage 1 and the transition to stage 2, and the essentially *economic* factors that must lie behind the change from stage 2 to stage 3. The conditions which generated the former may have been unconnected with those responsible for producing the latter. Only thus can we explain the great discrepancies in the duration of stage 2—perhaps less than a century in the Aegean, over four hundred years in Egypt—and indeed the widely differing initial dates for stage 3 in countries known from independent evidence to have been in contact with each other.

Under these conditions, universal generalizations become difficult and even undesirable. Certainly the old statements, often made in a deterministic vein—that the arrival of iron destroyed the hierarchy of Bronze Age societies, that the superiority of iron weapons explains the success of ancient conquests and migrations, that iron precipitated the decline of Egypt, and so on—seem today quite unjustified. Iron was both more important and less important than they suggest. Its introduction was far too complicated a process to have a direct influence on the known events of history; but in the longer term, it did have economic, social, and even historical effects. For all the baleful reputation of iron, it is hard to believe that some of these were not beneficial.

NOTES

The following abbreviations are used for the most frequently cited journals.

AAA	Athens Annals of Archaeology
AD	Arkhaiologikòn Deltíon
AJA	American Journal of Archaeology
AM	Mitteilungen des deutschen archäologischen Instituts, Athenische Abteilung
BCH	Bulletin de correspondance hellénique
BSA	Annual of the British School at Athens
CRAI	Comptes rendus de l'Académie des inscriptions et belles lettres
JdI	Jahrbuch des deutschen archäologischen Instituts
JEA	Journal of Egyptian Archaeology
JHS	Journal of Hellenic Studies
MonAnt	Monumenti Antichi (Reale Accademia dei Lincei)
NSc	Notizie degli Scavi di Antichità (Accademia Nazionale dei Lincei)
ProcPS	Proceedings of the Prehistoric Society
RA	Revue archéologique

1. Stefan Przeworski, *Die Metallindustrie Anatoliens* (*Internationales Archiv für Ethnographie*, suppl. 26 [Leiden, 1939]), pp. 175–87; Radomír Pleiner, *Iron Working in Ancient Greece* (Prague, 1969), pp. 11–15, 31, 33.

2. Claude F. A. Schaeffer, *Ugaritica* I (Paris, 1939), pp. 107–25, esp. 110, n. 2.

3. Giorgio Buchner, *Archaeological Reports* 17 (1970–71): 66.

4. John A. Wilson, *The Culture of Ancient Egypt* (Chicago, 1956), p. 81; William C. Hayes, *The Scepter of Egypt*, vol. 2 (New York, 1959), p. 373.

5. James D. Muhly, *Copper and Tin* (New Haven, 1973), p. 359, n. 75.

6. T. G. Harry James, *A General Introductory Guide to the Egyptian Collections* (London: British Museum, 1964), p. 19; cf. A. F. Shore, p. 203.

7. Claude F. A. Schaeffer, discussion contribution in *The Mycenaeans in the Eastern Mediterranean* (International Archaeological Symposium, Nicosia, 1973), p. 337; George J. Varoufakis, "Metallourgiki Ereuna," in George E. Mylonas, *Ho taphikos kuklos B' tōn Mukinōn* (Athens, 1973), pp. 363–75, esp. 367.

8. Strathmore R. B. Cooke and Stanley Aschenbrenner, "The Occurrence of Metallic Iron in Ancient Copper," *Journal of Field Archaeology* 2 (1975): 251–66. Note too Liliane Courtois's arguments from pottery with a high ferrous content ("Étude géologique des céramiques anciennes." *Comptes rendus de l'Académie des sciences*, série D, 276 [Paris, 1973], pp. 263–64).

9. Robert Maddin and James D. Muhly, "Some Notes on the Ancient Copper Trade in the Ancient Mid-East," *Journal of Metals* 26 (1974): 24–30.

10. Hector W. Catling, *Cypriot Bronzework in the Mycenaean World* (Oxford, 1964), pp. 199–202.

11. Vincent R. Desborough, *The Last Mycenaeans and Their Successors* (Oxford, 1964), pp. 25–26.

12. Erik Tholander, "Evidence for the Use of Carburized Steel and Quench Hardening in Late Bronze Age Cyprus," *Opuscula Atheniensia* 10 (1971): 15–22.

13. Catling, *Bronzework*, pp. 102–04; Lena Åström, *Swedish Cyprus Expedition* IV, 1D (Lund, 1972), pp. 483–84; and Robert Merrillees's contribution in *The Mycenaeans in the Eastern Mediterranean*, pp. 338–39.

14. Porphyrios Dikaios, *Enkomi* (Mainz, 1969), pp. 279, 463, 519, 701, pl. 163: 9, inv. 3458 (Late Cypriot III A), pp. 194, 296, 526, 725, pls. 135 : 77; 172 : 16, inv. 647 (IIIB); Åström, *SCE IV*, 1D, pp. 473–74, 558–59. But there is an important new dagger, iron with bronze rivets, from a LC III B level at Kition (*BCH* 102 [1978]: 916, fig. 84).

15. Claude F. A. Schaeffer, *Enkomi-Alasia* I (Paris, 1952), pp. 350, 357, 418; Catling, *Bronzework*, p. 116.

16. *Swedish Cyprus Expedition* II (Lund, 1935), p. 537, pl. 171, 208; Anthony M. Snodgrass, *Early Greek Armour and Weapons* (Edinburgh, 1964), p. 94, no. I, 1; Kouklia sword, Vassos Karageorghis, "Chronique des fouilles à Chypre en 1965," *BCH* 90 (1966): 322, fig. 59. The resemblance was noted by Andreas Dimitriou in "Cypro-Aegean Relations in the Early Iron Age" (Ph.D. diss., Edinburgh, 1973).

17. Dorothea Gray, "Metal-working in Homer," *JHS* 74 (1954): 11; add, e.g., an additional 6 iron knives and 3 spearheads in Jean Deshayes, *Le nécropole de Ktima* (Paris, 1963), tombs III b, IV, VIII.

18. Perati tomb 38, Spyridon Iakovidis, *Perati* (Athens, 1969–70), I, pp. 283–84, II, pp. 343–46, pl. 82; Lefkandi, Mervyn H. Popham and L. Hugh Sackett, *Excavations at Lefkandi in Euboea, 1964–6* (London, 1968), p. 14, fig. 22; Knossos, Sinclair Hood, George Huxley, and Nancy Sandars, "A Minoan Cemetery on Upper Gypsades," *BSA* 53–54 (1958–59): 234, 248–49, VII. 12, fig. 32, pl. 60a; Vrokastro, Edith H. Hall, *Excavations in Eastern Crete: Vrokastro* (Philadelphia, 1914), p. 139; Perati tomb 28, Iakovidis, *Perati* I, p. 18; II, p. 343, pl. 3. A further knife of different form comes from Kakavi in northern Epirus, but is to be dated after the Bronze Age: see Anthony Harding, "Illyrians, Italians and Mycenaeans," *Studia Albanica* 9, 2 (1972): 217–18; Klaus Kilian, "Trachtzubehör der Eisenzeit zwischen Ägäis und Adria," *Prähistorische Zeitschrift* 50 (1975): 42–43.

19. Tiryns, George Karo, "Schatz von Tiryns," *AM* 55 (1930): 135–36, fig. 6, top; Enkomi, Dikaios, *Enkomi*, n. 14.

20. Tiryns, Nikolaos M. Verdelis, "Neue geometrische Gräber in Tiryns," *AM* 78 (1963): 14–16, f. 8, Beil. 5, 4; Athens, Wilhelm Kraiker and Karl Kübler, *Kerameikos* I (Berlin, 1939), pp. 100–03 (grave A), 103–04 (grave B); Naxos, Anastasios K. Orlandos, *To Ergon tis Arkhaiologikis Etaireias* 1960, p. 191.

21. Athens, Karl Kübler, *Kerameikos* IV (Berlin, 1943), p. 47 (grave 2 north); *AD* 22 (1967), Chroniká, p. 93 (23/4, Kriezis St., tomb lxxix). Cypriot forerunners, Hector W. Catling, "A New Bronze Sword from Cyprus," *Antiquity* 35 (1961): 120, group IV; later Athens sword, *Kerameikos* I, p. 106, fig. 1 (grave E) and Catling, pp. 115–18, no. 30, pl. xvi, a–b.

22. The main problem is that of chronological demarcation. I have included all graves classified as "Late Submycenaean B," "Transitional," and "Protogeometric" by Carl-Gustav Styrenius, *Submycenaean Studies* (Lund, 1967), pp. 51–121; omitted those classified as "Early Geometric" by J. Nicolas Coldstream, *Greek Geometric Pottery* (London, 1968), pp. 10–15; and added a few further burials—Kerameikos grave PG 48 (*Kerameikos* IV, pp. 44–46); a grave in the Agora (Hermann Müller-Karpe, "Die Metallbeigaben der früheisenzeitlichen Kerameikos-Gräber," *JdI* 77 [1962]: 126, fig. 27, 5–6); the finds from Nea Ionia presumed to be from cremations 1 and 4 (Evelyn L. Smithson, "The Protogeometric Cemetery at Nea Ionia, 1949," *Hesperia* 30 [1961]: 173); graves in Odos Lykourgou, *AD* 18 (1963), Chroniká, p. 36; in Odos Ag. Markou, *AD* 19 (1964), Chroniká, pp. 55–56; on the Acropolis S. slope, *AD* 28 (1973): 26; and Kerameikos grave hS 92a, *AM* 81 (1966): 7.

23. Here I include the "Early Submycenaean" to "Late Submycenaean A" phases of Styrenius (see n. 22), and add the graves at Odos Erechtheiou, *AD* 23 (1968), Chroniká, p. 55.

24. Anthony M. Snodgrass, *The Dark Age of Greece* (Edinburgh, 1971), pp. 237–39.

25. Vincent R. Desborough, *The Greek Dark Ages* (London, 1972), p. 190 (dagger); pp. 68, 199 on use of iron; p. 196 on "killing" of sword.

26. Snodgrass, *The Dark Age of Greece*, pp. 233–36 with references.

27. Ibid., pp. 249–53 for Crete; pp. 236–37 for Asia Minor; p. 242 on Dodecanese.

28. Manolis Andronikos, *Vergina* I (Athens, 1969), esp. pp. 274–79; Kilian, "Trachtzubehör der Eisenzeit," pp. 63–104, esp. 65–74.

29. This table incorporates those finds published in *Vergina* I, and by Photios Petsas in "Anaskaphi arkhaiou nekrotapheiou Verginis," *AD* 17 (1961–62): 218–88 and 18 (1963), Chroniká, pp. 217–32, which appear to belong to the Early Iron Age period of the cemetery.

30. At Vergina the only apparent exception is in Petsas's tomb LXVIII Z; but over the chronology of tumulus LXVIII in general there is radical disagreement, with Andronikos ("Sarissa," *BCH* 94 [1970]: 101 and n. 13) seeming to favor a date about 400 years later than Kilian ("Trachtzubehör der Eisenzeit," pp. 65, 71–72) and myself.

31. On western areas, see Snodgrass, *The Dark Age of Greece*, pp. 239–49. Malthi, Nathan Valmin, *The Swedish Messenia Expedition* (Lund, 1939), pp. 371–73, pl. xxx, 13–14; Pylos, Carl W. Blegen, Marian Rawson, William Taylour, and William P. Donovan, *The Palace of Nestor* III (Princeton, 1973), p. 240, fig. 298 (cf. p. 226 for another early iron pin); Karpophora, A. Choremis," Tholotostaphos eis Karpophoran Messenias," *AAA* 1 (1968): 205–09. On Epirus, Snodgrass, *The Dark Age of Greece*, pp. 257–61, and Kilian, "Trachtzubehör der Eisenzeit," pp. 29–62, argue for a higher chronology.

32. E.g., Hans Weber in *Olympische Forschungen* I (Berlin, 1944), pp. 152, 166; Sylvia Benton, "Further Excavations at Aetos," *BSA* 48 (1953): 343.

33. Georgios J. Varoufakis, *Metalleiologikà Metallourgikà Chroniká* 10 (1973): 23–34; import of early knives, Desborough, *Greek Dark Ages*, p. 308. By the late 8th century, at least, the Greek poets betray some familiarity with iron technology, cf. Homer, *Odyssey* 10. 459; Hesiod, *Theogony*, 864–66.

34. G. Ernest Wright, "Iron, the date of its introduction into Palestine," *AJA* 43 (1939): 458–63. Lachish, Olga Tufnell, *Lachish* III (London, 1957), pp. 385–96, with a helpful discussion of fibulae, pp. 392–95; tomb 521, Tufnell, *Lachish* III, pp. 224, 387. On recent

finds see, e.g., Trude Dothan in *The Mycenaeans in the Eastern Mediterranean*, pp. 337–38, and Jane Waldbaum, "Hittites, Philistines and the Introduction of Iron in the Eastern Mediterranean" (forthcoming). On Pap. Anastasi I, cf. Robert J. Forbes, *Studies in Ancient Technology* 9 (Leiden, 1964), pp. 229, 234; text, James B. Pritchard, ed., *Ancient Near Eastern Texts* (Princeton, 1950), pp. 475–79, esp. p. 478.

35. Poul J. Riis, *Hama, Fouilles et Recherches 1931–8*, II, 3 (Copenhagen, 1948), pp. 116–41, 192–204.

36. Main publication in Hetty Goldman, ed., *Excavations at Gözlü Küle, Tarsus* III (Princeton, 1963), pp. 359–79; cf. John Boardman, "Tarsus, Al Mina and Greek Chronology," *JHS* 85 (1965): 5–15, 232.

37. See Boris B. Piotrovskii, *The Ancient Civilization of Urartu* (New York, 1969), pp. 113, 159.

38. Early Phoenician enterprise, George F. Bass, *Cape Gelidonya: A Bronze Age Shipwreck* (*Transactions of the American Philosophical Society* 57, 8, Philadelphia, 1967), pp. 77, 166; Tripolitania, Teresa H. Carter, "Western Phoenicians at Lepcis Magna," *AJA* 69 (1965): 123–32; Carthage, e.g., *CRAI* (ser. 4) 26 (1898): 98, 212, 555, 623; 27 (1899): 102, 319, 557; 1 (1900): 93, 503. Morocco, Michel Ponsich, *Nécropoles phéniciennes de la region de Tanger* (Paris, 1969), Ain Dalhia Kebira tombs 1, 20, 24, 25, 42, 74, 80; Djebila tombs 22, 27, 31, 79, 99. Word for iron, Stéphane Gsell, *Histoire de l'Afrique du Nord* I (Paris, 1921), pp. 212, n. 4; 368, n. 4. Cyrenaica, John Boardman and John W. Hayes, *Excavations at Tocra* I (London, 1966), p. 160; II (1973), p. 83.

39. Manuel Pellicer Catalán, *Excavaciones en la necrópolis púnica "Laurita" del Cerro de San Cristobal (Almuñécar, Granada), Excavaciones Arqueológicas en España* 17 (Madrid, 1962): 38, fig. 32, 5; cf. Hans G. Niemeyer and Hermanfrid Schubart, *Toscanos 1964 (Madrider Forschungen* 6, 1969). Juan P. Garrido Roiz, *Excavaciones en Huelva; El Cabezo de la Esperanza (EAE* 63 [1968]), p. 16; Roiz, *Excavaciones en la necrópolis de "La Joya," Huelva (EAE* 71 [1970]), tombs 5, 7, 9, 10. Carmona, George Bonsor, "Les colonies agricoles pré-Romaines," *RA* (ser. 3), 35 (1899): 254, 257, 278, fig. 101, 379–80. Hubert N. Savory, *Spain and Portugal* (London, 1968), pp. 237–38.

40. Antonio Arribas, *The Iberians* (London, 1965), p. 41; cf. Wilhelm Schüle, *Die Meseta-Kulturen der iberischen Halbinsel* (Berlin, 1969), pp. 9, 91–92, 169. Horace Sandars, "The Weapons of the Iberians," *Archaeologia* 64 (1912–13): 205–94, esp. 231–58 on the *espada falcata*.

41. Margaret Guido, *Sardinia* (London, 1963), pp. 103–04, 166, 171, 182, 198; Arturo Pérez-Cabrero, *Ibiza Arqueológica* (Barcelona, 1911), p. 11; Jean and Laurence Jehasse, *La Nécropole préromaine d'Aléria* (Gallia, suppl. 25, Paris, 1973), pp. 60–70, pls. 146–60.

42. See, most recently, David Ridgway in *Greeks, Celts and Romans: Studies in venture and resistance*, Christopher Hawkes and Sonia Hawkes, eds. (London, 1973), p. 26.

43. Wolfgang Kimmig's paper, "Seevölkerbewegung und Urnenfelderkultur," in *Studien aus Alteuropa* I, Rafael von Uslar and Karl J. Narr, eds. (Köln, 1964), is discussed by the present writer in "Barbarian Europe and Early Iron Age Greece," *ProcPS* 31 (1965): 229–40; Kimmig shows clearly that at least the Hallstatt B3 phase of the earlier 8th (and later 9th?) century B.C., lies within our stage 2, with the full European Iron Age developing in Hallstatt C.

44. Paolo Orsi, "Le necropoli preelleniche Calabresi," *MonAnt* 31 (1926): 1–211, esp.

154–76; Bruno d'Agostino, "Tombe della prima età del ferro a S. Marzano sul Sarno," *Mélanges d'Archeologie et d'Histoire* (École française de Rome) 82 (1970): 600. Cumae, Hermann Müller-Karpe, *Beiträge zur Chronologie der Urnenfelderzeit* (Berlin, 1959), pp. 37–38, pl. 18A, 7, 11; d'Agostino, p. 603.

45. Joanna Close-Brooks, "Veio," *NSc* 19 (1965): 58 on the intensification of iron-working at Veii, and "Considerazioni sulla cronologia delle facies arcaiche dell'Etruria," *Studi Etruschi* 35 (1967): 323–29 on the chronology. The latest report on the Veii cemetery is by Emanuela Fabbricotti and others in *NSc* 26 (1972): 195–384. Hugh Hencken, *Tarquinia and Etruscan Origins* (London, 1968), p. 116, pl. 50; 50, pls. 88, 89 and fig. 10b. Ingrid Pohl, *The Iron Age Necropolis of Sorbo at Cerveteri* (Stockholm, 1972), p. 100, tomb 423. San Martino sul Sarno, d'Agostino, "Prima età del ferro," pp. 584, 603 (tomb 4), 584, 592 (tombs 12, 52, 18; 53, 54, 55, 37, 52). Sala Consilina, Juliette de la Genière, "La céramique géometrique de Sala Consilina," *Mélanges d'Archeologie et d'Histoire* 73 (1961): 14, 53, pl. 5 : 13 (S. Nicola tomb 44), with other iron finds, pp. 15, 17, 51–65. Latium, Pär Göran Gierow, *The Iron Age Cultures of Latium* (Lund, 1964), esp. vol. 1, pp. 353–58 and vol. 2, p. 282; also vol. 2, pp. 126–29, 152, 163–64, 168, 187–88, 190, 354, 387–88. Lawrence Barfield, *Northern Italy* (London, 1971), p. 104.

46. Motya, Anthony M. Snodgrass, "The Metalwork," *Annual of the Leeds University Oriental Society* 4 (1962–63): 129–30 (cf. 108, 123 for context); Benedict S. J. Isserlin and Joan du Plat Taylor, *Motya* I (Leiden, 1974), p. 73. Pantalica, e.g., Paolo Orsi, "Pantalica," *MonAnt* 9 (1899): 72, 73; *MonAnt* 21 (1912): 337, 338. Monte Dessueri, Paolo Orsi, "La necropoli Sicula di M. Dessueri," *MonAnt* 21 (1912): 379, 403–04.

47. Luisa Banti, *Etruscan Cities and their Culture* (London, 1973), p. 143; Ischia, Buchner, *Archaeological Reports* 17 (1970–71): 66.

48. See, e.g., John Alexander, "Greeks, Italians and the Earliest Balkan Iron Age," *Antiquity* 36 (1962): 123–40; "The Spectacle Fibulae of Southern Europe," *AJA* 69 (1965): 7–23, esp. 8 on type II spectacle fibulae in Dalmatia. Klaus Kilian, *Actes du VIIIe Congrès Internationale des Sciences Préhistoriques* (Belgrade, 1971), pp. 219–31; "Zum Italischen und Griechischen Fibelhandwerk des 8 und 7 Jahrhunderts," *Hamburger Beiträge zur Archäologie* III, 1 (1973), pp. 1–39.

49. Jean J. Jully, "Le marché du métal en Méditerranée occidentale," *Opuscula Romana* 6 (1968): 27–62, esp. 31 on Mailhac (Odette Taffanel and Jean Taffanel, "Deux tombes de cavaliers du Premier Age du Fer à Mailhac," *Gallia* 20 [1962]: 3–32) and 35 on St. Julien. On the developed Gaulish iron industry, see, e.g., Forbes, *Studies in Ancient Technology*, pp. 239–40 with references.

50. On early Egyptian iron, see, e.g., Gerald A. Wainwright, *JEA* 18 (1932): 3–15 and *Antiquity* 10 (1936): 21–23; also Forbes, *Studies in Ancient Technology*, pp. 224–29. Waldbaum, "Hittites, Philistines and the Introduction of Iron" (in press). Sir Henry C. H. Carpenter and John M. Robertson, "The Metallurgy of Some Ancient Egyptian Implements," *Journal of the Iron and Steel Institute* 121 (1930): 417–54; Herbert H. Coghlan, *Notes on Prehistoric and Early Iron in the Old World* (Pitt–Rivers Museum, Oxford, Occasional Papers on Technology 8 [1956]), pp. 134–65.

51. Thebes, W. M. Flinders Petrie, *Seven Tombs at Thebes* (London, 1897), pp. 18–9, pl. xxi; id., *Naucratis* I (London, 1886), p. 39, esp. pl. 11 : 6; Tel Defenneh, id., *Tanis* II (London, 1888), pp. 77–79, esp. pls. 37 : 3, 7, 9–11, 17, 19, 20; 38 : 5–7, 24: id., *Palace of*

Apries (*Memphis* II, London, 1909), p. 13. On Nubia, D. Williams, "African Iron and the Classical world," in *Africa in Classical Antiquity*, Lloyd A. Thompson and John Ferguson, eds. (Ibadan, 1969), pp. 62–72, esp. 73–74.

52. Etruria, Carlo Panseri, *La tecnica di fabbricazione delle lame di acciaio presso gli antichi* (Associazione Italiana di Metallurgia, Milan, 1957), pp. 19–33. Luristan, Herbert Maryon, "Early Near Eastern Steel Swords," *AJA* 65 (1961): 173–84, and Vera Bird and Henry W. M. Hodges, "A Metallurgical Examination of Two Early Iron Swords from Luristan," *Studies in Conservation* 13 (1968): 215–23; but note also Rachel Maxwell-Hyslop and Henry W. M. Hodges, "Three Iron Swords from Luristan," *Iraq* 28 (1966): 164–76 on perhaps earlier examples. On Assyrian practice, Radomír Pleiner and Judith K. Bjorkman, "The Assyrian Iron Age," *Proceedings of the American Philosophical Society* 118 (1974): 307. Central Europe, H. Rupe and F. Müller's tests (1916), quoted by Earle R. Caley, *Analysis of Ancient Metals* (1964), p. 148, table 54.

Early Iron Metallurgy in Europe

RADOMÍR PLEINER

Europe must be considered a zone of secondary development in the spread of ironworking technology, lagging behind Southwest Asia by about a millennium. The technology based on iron, however, eventually became a major factor in European civilization. In some respects, the modern iron industry is related more closely to developments in Europe than to those in Southwest Asia. There is much evidence that in contrast to the Near East iron was introduced in Europe before strict systems of social organization were developed; iron rapidly became the most important material and its use and technology influenced the development of organized social systems. The reason for this phenomenon is not yet well understood. It may be related to the specific geographical and ecological conditions of European areas of settlement where the effectiveness of iron and steel tools played a significant role in the deforestation process, as well as in woodworking and agriculture. Indo-Europeans who settled Europe in prehistoric times were certainly not the inventors of iron technology, but they adopted and developed it in such a manner that they were able to spread highly developed ironworking technologies throughout the world.

The physical environment encouraged prehistoric Europeans to develop ironworking, since resources of iron ore in the form of gossans were and are abundant in modern centers of iron ore exploitation, and smaller deposits of iron ore were available for limited production in all settled areas. Forested Europe had no lack of fuel in antiquity. Traditions in working nonferrous metals and alloys, developing in Southwest Asia since the 5th or 4th millennium B.C., established the necessary cultural conditions for adopting the new technology.[1] Moreover, the spread of these traditions must have brought, either directly or indirectly, the first specimens of iron into Europe in the pre-Iron Age.

The study of prehistoric and early ironworking in Europe is of im-

portance also from the heuristic point of view. Although written records
are rare, there is significant and extensive archaeological evidence; hundreds and thousands of smelting sites, furnaces, and smithies have been
discovered and excavated and thousands of excavated iron artifacts have
been analyzed chemically and metallographically. Such rich sources of
information are, however, not regularly distributed in all parts of Europe
but, compared with other parts of the world, there is considerable evidence
to use in reconstructing the technical, economical, and social aspects of
early ironworking in Europe. The following discussion aims to characterize the first steps in the process.

THE FIRST IRON IN CENTRAL EUROPE AND THE BEGINNING OF THE IRON AGE

The problem of the spread of iron into European cultural provinces used
to be solved by different approaches and with different results. There are
theories presupposing a Southwest Asiatic origin of the iron industry,
while other views stress autochthonous development in Europe or even
influence toward the Near East. Scholars accepting the thesis of *ex Oriente
lux* differ in their delineations of the routes by which iron was introduced into Europe: the route via Greece–Balkans–Central Europe is put
against that of Greece–Italy–North Balkans–Central Europe. The importance of the Caucasus–South Russia–Carpathian Basin route also used
to be emphasized.[2]

The way in which iron was introduced is clearly far from being understood and much research must be done before definite conclusions can
be made. This paper tries nonetheless to reconstruct the picture as it
is reflected in published material.* First, consideration is given to the
chronology of finds, and their position in the entire cultural milieu is
then discussed.

There are several isolated iron objects in Central and even North
European contexts dating from the 2d millennium B.C. (fig. 11.1, items
4–6). They represent totally foreign elements and must be interpreted as
imports from those areas where this metal was being worked, even in
limited quantities. One area emerges as a possible site of origin; it includes

* The present paper was finished in 1975; it reflects the state of the bibliography and sources
accessible at that time.

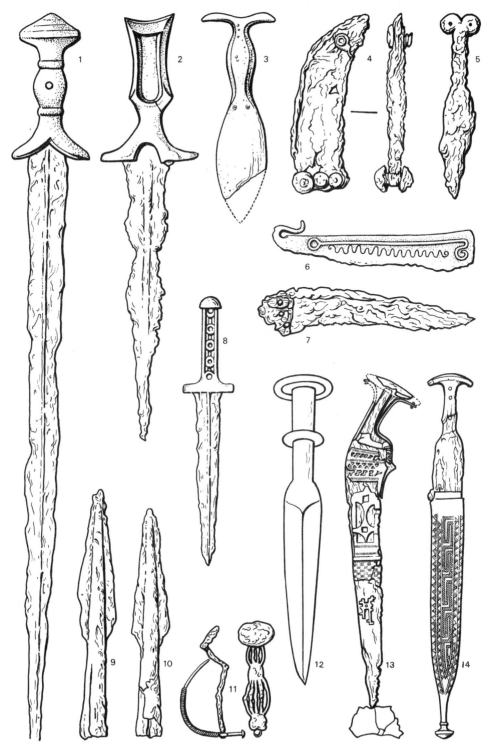

Fig. 11.1. Examples of the most ancient iron objects in Europe. 1, Forte di Rivoli; Hag, 2, Souš near Most, Bohemia; 3, Cumae, Campania (after Randall MacIver); 4, Gánovce, North Slovakia (dagger hilt); 5, Norbjär, Sweden (miniature iron sword); 6, Arnitlund, Jutland (bronze razor with inlays of iron); 7, Tarquinia-Impiccata, Etruria gr. 74; 8, Kotouč-Štramberk, Moravia; 9, 10, Hostomice, Bohemia; 11, Tarquinia-Impiccata gr. 74 (brooch with bronze pin); 12, Vetulonia-Sagrona, Etruria; 13, Servici, Picenum; and 14, Torre Galli gr. 99 (bronze sheath). Dating: 4 about 1500 B.C., 6 about 1000 B.C., the rest about 800 B.C., 1 after Barfield, 2, 9, 10 after Pleiner, 3, 12–14 after Randall MacIver, 5, 6 after Stjernquist, 7–11 after Randall MacIver, 8 after Podborský.

East Anatolia, North Syria, and Cyprus. However, European finds of early iron do not help to define the direction in which ironworking technology spread. One of the earliest known iron objects in Europe, not including the well-known iron rings from Mycenaean tombs in Greece and Crete, is a stratified iron dagger hilt from Gánovce (North Slovakia), found in a ritual well of the Otomani culture of the Early Bronze Age and dating from about the 14th century B.C. From the Middle Bronze Age (about 12th century B.C.) are an iron pin or nail embedded in a bronze cake from Suchdol (hoard found in Central Bohemia) and the famous iron blade fragment from a grave at Grödeby, Bornholm. Approximately one century later may be dated a small iron fragment from Hötting, awls from Völs, Austria, and two ornamental iron inlays on bronze razors from Denmark (Arnitslund and Kjelbymagle). There are other small iron curiosities which predate the more systematic occurrence of iron (Simris and Norbjär in Sweden, dating from MV or HB_2 periods, ca. 9th century B.C.).* It is of interest that in the Western Mediterranean there are no very early finds of iron but this may be due to lack of investigation or publication of detailed assemblages. The Pantalica Sud culture of Sicily yielded small iron rings (Mulino della Badia, ca. 10th century). Evidently no reliable conclusions are to be drawn from these intrusive iron objects and their exact origin remains unknown.[3] At least one of them is of smelted iron, since no traces of nickel could be detected in the rust of the Gánovce dagger hilt.

The situation changes in archaeological complexes in which iron objects appear—still extremely rare—but with several examples of the same type of weapons and ornaments, followed immediately by a slow but steadily increasing frequency of iron artifacts of various kinds in the next period (fig. 11.1).

The starting point is the Greco-Aegean world, extending roughly up to southern Macedonia. The people in this area presumably learned about ironworking from cultures in southeastern Asia Minor, Cyprus, or North Syria. Apart from some analyzed iron slags from Vardaroftsa (12th century B.C.) which can represent either bloomery or smithing

---

*Frequently used common abbreviations of different chronological systems appear in the text, e.g., PG = Greek Protogeometric, H = Hallstatt in the Reinecke scale with phases A–D and numbered subphases, M = Bronze Age period after Montelius, with numbered phases (e.g., V).

waste, there are finds of iron knives (Gypsades VII, Crete, Perati; 12th century), flange-hilted daggers, and swords and pins in Attica and the Peloponesos (Tiryns XXVIII, Kerameikos S 36 and 87, PG 2-N, PG B, 11th century B.C.). The chronological priority of the common use of iron in this area is not challenged by finds from other parts of Europe. Agora grave XXVII contains a set of eight iron weapons, tools, and pieces of horse harness in forms which in Central Europe occur more than two centuries later. In spite of a short stagnation which Snodgrass thinks took place around 1000 B.C., the Greek world developed a civilization based on iron relatively quickly and during the 8th century B.C. was able to influence not only neighboring but even distant countries.[4] It is difficult to define the means of this influence; physical imports of ready-made goods must not have been the most important vehicle. Diffusion of knowledge and of individuals who could work iron effectively, which appear to have moved against the direction of contemporary migrations, were probably responsible for spreading the use and the technology of the new metal. It is thus necessary that a reworking of important types, imitating and transforming them into products congenial with local tastes, must be taken into account.

At any rate, before 800 B.C. or during the 8th century there is a significant occurrence of iron weapons in the western Balkans and at the Head of Adria; iron spearheads and knives together with bracelets at Škocijan and Ruše (Maria Rast) and Sisek (period HB_1 to HB_2) were followed by swords, lanceheads, and axes of the Glasinac IVb group (HB_3). In this phase diffusion must have been relatively rapid. At almost the same time iron replicas of local bronze artifacts, objects equipped with iron blades, and iron inlays on bronze objects occur in Austria (Stillfried, Hadersdorf), Switzerland (Zürich–Alpenquai, St. Aubin, Mörigen) and Bohemia (sword from Souš near Most, lanceheads from Hostomice, and several other artifacts from the HB_3 groups). The trend reached even North Germany, where the variety of iron objects increased steadily—especially in the Neisse-Oder, Harz-Elbe, and Weser regions—although even in the succeeding HC or M VI period iron represented only 10–20 percent of the metal used. A similar picture appears in northern parts of Poland, Denmark, and South Scandinavia (knives, pins, fibulae, and so on; cf. Randbøl, Vedsted, Røgerup, Sjögestad, and so forth).[5]

Another European area where iron was used early is the Lower Danube, where several HB_2 and HB_3 iron finds are known, such as the dagger

blade from Hida, trunnion axes from Birlad, and the dolabris from
Şomartin (Rumania); this collection was recently supplemented by the
discovery of a chisel, axes, knives, and a set of iron bars found at Cernatu,
and by a bar from Babadag II (about 800, or 8th century B.C.). At Babadag,
and at Dervent, were found, moreover, pieces of ore and iron slag in an
HB context. This material has appeared only in a preliminary publication.
It is difficult to determine if early Danubian ironworking was stimulated
by contacts with the Greco-Macedonian area or with Anatolia directly.[6]

On Sicily and in southern Italy the introduction of iron followed an
irregular pattern, since in coastal regions such as Calabria this metal is
found in much greater abundance (two to four objects in one grave
complex), possibly a bit earlier, and, ornaments not withstanding, in
larger forms than inland (T-shaped swords, spears, javelins, and knives
of Torre Galli 136, 147, 99; Canale, tombs 18, 49, 56 with 8 iron spears,
mostly 8th century). In the inner Campania or Basilicata there were many
areas without iron for a long period. The Sala Consilina cemetery has a
few small iron objects such as fibulae in phase I (early 8th century) and the
first iron short swords begin to appear in the late 8th century. The source
of this iron is unknown. Many objects predate the Greek presence but
the Greek role in their distribution comes into question; shapes of T-
swords are, for instance, related to Aegean types. The Greek colonization,
started in the early 8th century, must have stimulated the process of
diffusion of iron technology. New discoveries at the Euboean Pithecoussai (Ischia) confirm this statement. In the acropolis and in the adjacent
settlement were found clear traces of ironworking. Apart from the blacksmith's workshop with its slags and tuyeres, there are some indications of
smelting operations using pure hematite of Elban origin. The activity
on the acropolis is to be put into the 8th century, in other areas into the
7th century. However, this throws a light not only on Greeks as active
bearers of metallurgical tradition and technology in Magna Graecia but
also on the exploitation of the rich ore deposits of Elba and on the role of
early Etruscans, who must have managed this mining activity in the
succeeding periods.[7]

It is extremely interesting that the west coast of central Italy, known
traditionally as an Etruscan domain, emerges as one of the most progressive iron-using parts of Italy, reflected by finds from the cemeteries of
Veii, Vetulonia, and Tarquinia. Whereas only small sporadic finds of
iron occur in the period of Tarquinia I (or Villanovan I), their number

increased during period II, simultaneously with strong influences from the Near East and Greece (Selciatello, Monterozzi, Impiccato). In addition to ornaments, knives, arrow- and spearheads, swords, bridle bits, and even iron nails were observed in the Villanovan II graves. It appears that iron usage spread from east to west. Iron, a rare metal in Umbria and Picenum in the 9th–8th centuries (Terni II, grave 160), spread in the next period as shown in the warrior graves of Novilara with their iron falcatae and other types of short swords and daggers.

On the other hand, in the south and in the north of the central Italian area iron was a belated newcomer. In Latium iron ornaments and knives, spears and tools occur as isolated finds until the 7th century B.C. (Marino, Caracupa, and Valvisciolo), and only during the 6th century did iron become the dominant metal. This is connected with a strong cultural influence from Etruria. North of the Apennines, the population (Bologna, Este, and Golasecca) became more familiar with its use more slowly and somewhat later, at the same time as did Hallstatt C in Central Europe.[8]

The preceding remarks indicate that Greek (and Etruscan) influence was the principal source supplying South Alpine Europe with materials, ideas, and knowledge of how to use and work the black metal (fig. 11.2). However, iron artifacts, reaching the central parts of the Continent very early in the HB_3, i.e., roughly during the 8th century B.C., came, in addition to the streaming from the Balkans, from the East. They are mostly iron blades of bronze-hilted daggers of the North Caucasian types (Kotouč-Štramberk in Moravia, Gamów in Silesia, Leibnitz in Styria, Komárno in South Slovakia, Panad in Siebenbürgen, and Matra in Hungary) and represent another iron-bearing tradition coming into Europe before the Scythian Iron Age. In comparison with the Greco-Italian impact it remained limited (with exceptions, e.g., Pecs-Jakabhegy), represented by a small number of individual intrusions.[9]

Western Europe obtained its first iron, as it were, secondarily (fig. 11.3). Greek and Phoenician traders were responsible for importing iron artifacts to the coastal colonies of Spain and southern France during the 8th or 7th century B.C. At Cortes de Navarra IIb–IIa and in certain other sites in the Ebro Valley, there was iron smelting in the 7th century, but in the hinterland and even in Catalonia iron remained a rare material even in the late 6th century. Due to Greek colonization of the Golfe du Lion the penetration of iron technology and the search for iron ores possibly took place, but farther to the northwest iron appeared regularly about or after

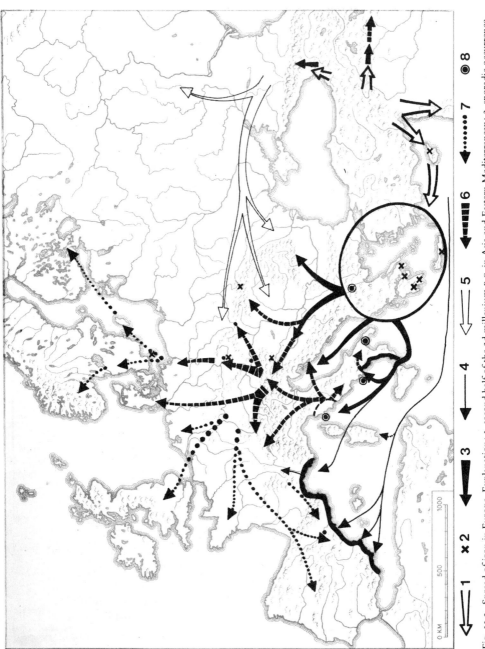

Fig. 11.2. Spread of iron in Europe. Explanation: 1, second half of the 2d millenium B.C. in Asia and Eastern Mediterranean; 2, sporadic occurrence of iron objects; 3, the area of Greece with earliest finds and with primary directions of spreading; 4, Phoenician influence; 5, Cimmerian and Scythian influence; 6, iron in Central Europe and Italy in the Late Bronze Age and beginning Iron Age; 7, spread of iron in north and west of Europe about 500 B.C.; and 8, important early metallurgical activity.

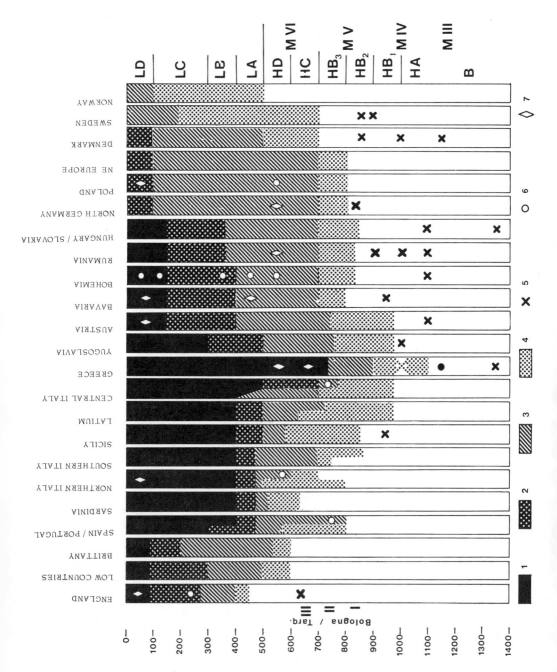

Fig. 11.3. Introduction of iron into Europe. Explanation: 1, exceptional occurrence of (imported) iron objects; 2, introduction of iron weapons and objects; 3, Early Iron Age; 4, developed Iron Age; 5, full and fledged civilization of iron; 6, important metallurgical features; and 7, occurrence of iron bars.

500 B.C. (Brittany, England). Despite some early finds, Northern Europe began to use iron in significant volume substantially later, during the second half of the last millennium B.C. or at its end.[10]

It should be stressed that the periods discussed above were not the Iron Age in the strict sense. Up to the end of the 8th century B.C. bronze was equally or more important for manufacturing weapons and tools.

Only the following period, comprising in general both the Hallstatt C-D and Early La Tène (A), can be described as the beginning of the true Iron Age. Indirect and direct evidence leads to this conclusion. Weapons and tools of bronze almost disappeared and the frequency of archaeological iron increased in the broad strip of the southern half of Europe from tens up to thousands of objects in the period 700–400 B.C. However, individual regions vary in their absolute numbers of iron objects due to the extent of archaeological research in each area. In general, iron remained an extremely valuable metal; the idea of iron as a cheap and easily obtainable and worked material is obsolete. Moreover, most iron dated to this period came from rich graves, so that its real role in everyday life is not yet fully clear. But the assortment of manufactured objects now includes, in addition to the already known categories, such specialized tools as chisels, sickles, firedogs (Hořovičky, Bohemia), and roasting spits (chieftains' graves at the Hallstatt cemetery, Austria). Iron fittings of princely chariots deserve special attention: tires and nails, nave fittings, clamps, and wheel-pegs. Among the Scythians of the earlier period (7th–6th centuries B.C.), heavy iron scale hauberks and iron bands on shields are worth mentioning because they also indicate the yields of total iron production (fig. 11.4). The consumption of iron by some groups reached not tens of grams but many kilograms of iron.

The first rare traces of the smelting process in European territory are direct evidence of the beginning of the Iron Age. Apart from the early smelting site of Coppa Nevigata, Apulia, about which relatively little is known due to the absence of documentation,[11] and from the finds at Dervent and Babadag, all known European bloomeries dating between 600 and 0 B.C. are overshadowed by Etruscan iron production at Populonia. We have already noted that the exploitation of Elba's iron ores must have started during the 8th century B.C. Many written sources confirm that the period of greatest production falls in the last five centuries B.C.[12] This site is irretrievably destroyed by the heavy exploitation of ancient slags after 1920, so that the original extent of the industrial

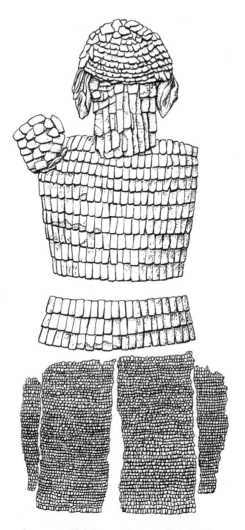

Fig. 11.4. Scythian iron scale armor with helmet, cuirasse, and trousers from a warrior grave at the Ingul River (5th century B.C.). After Šapošnikova.

area cannot be reconstructed. At the Baratti bay at Populonia an area of about 2.2 km² is covered with a 2 to 4 m thick layer of iron slag (about 2 million tons). Should we estimate about 500 years of intensive production, hundreds of tons of iron per year must have been smelted.[13] The ore of good quality (up to 89.3% Fe_2O_3 and 8.9% SiO_2, P only in traces) came mostly from Elba, where it was smelted (Porto Lagone, Porto Ferraio)

until lack of fuel caused by deforestation forced the transfer of metallurgical activities (except for roasting) to the mainland coast near the
town of Fufluna, Populonia. Local mainland ore deposits (Monte Valerio,
Monte Calvi) were of minor importance. Based on a study of numerous
slagged stones, the process was carried out without any fluxes in stone-
walled open hearths similar to the Catalan or Corsican types, lined with
refractory clay and adapted to slag tapping. Forced draft was necessary.
Recent analyses of slags give the following percentages: SiO_2, 14.5;
Fe_2O_3, 17.7; FeO, 53.5; MnO, 0.1; CaO, 0.9; MgO, 0.2; P_2O_5, 0.1; and
Al_2O_3, 0.6. The melting point was between 1290 and 1320° C. Charcoal
from pines, oaks, chestnuts, and ash trees served as fuel.[14] It seems to be
evident that this center supplied most of the Central Mediterranean in
the later 1st millennium B.C. No other smelting area in Europe including
those of the Celts has surpassed it in terms of the amount of production.

In the older archaeological bibliography of Europe one can find many
notes on Hallstatt period iron smelting sites but without chronological
verification. In fact, reliably dated evidence of iron extraction in the mid-
1st millennium B.C. is extremely rare. A pit nearly 2 m in diameter was
found at Hillesheim, West Germany (HD period) but it is not certifiably
for iron manufacture. Pieces of bloomery slag with about 50 percent
FeO do indicate smelting activity in the vicinity; the large pit may be
connected with roasting and/or reheating operations. Unfortunately
there are no other traces of iron smelting from the succeeding LA period
in this part of Europe. Therefore it is not possible to confirm theories of
causal relations between the wealth of the LA princely graves and tumuli
on the middle Rhine and the exploitation of good oolithic hematites by
those chieftains.[15]

On the other hand, definite evidence—although also rare—comes
from other parts of the Continent. In northern Moravia in 1932 a
bloomery connected with HD sherds of the Silesian culture at Králová
was discovered. In a sunken-floored hut was a circular pit in the corner
with a small open smelting hearth at the bottom. Pieces of slags and good
hematite ore, together with charcoal, were present. The most conclusive
evidence appeared recently in Austria, in the hill-site of Waschenberg
(fig. 11.5), dated from the end of HD, or about 500 B.C. In the southeast
there was a quarter with 9 open smelting hearths (diameter 30–40 cm,
approximately the same depth). They were lined with refractory clay
and slagged. Slags contained 39–55 percent iron (given as Fe), 1.6 to 4

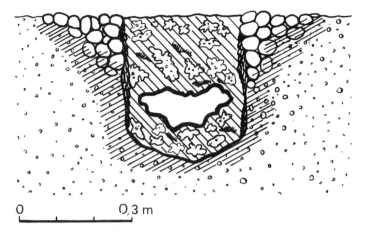

Fig. 11.5. Late Hallstatt period smelting hearth with iron bloom. Waschenberg, Austria (after Pertlwieser).

percent CaO, and 0.15 to 0.3 percent P_2O_5. A fragment of a spongy iron bloom (0.41% C, 0.08% P, 0.16% Ni) indicates the purpose of the hearths. In addition charcoal pits were used as smithies. A clay drum-bellows deserves special attention.[16]

A second category of direct evidence for the beginning of the Iron Age includes features and objects directly connected with blacksmithing activities. At the hillfort of Smolenice-Molpír, an important HC site in western Slovakia, a complex consisting of a large forging hearth, numerous blooms, and semifinished products (knives) was discovered. At Waschenberg were found flat sunken-floored huts with smith's hearths. From the mid-1st millennium B.C. we have the first blacksmith's tools (fig. 11.6). In the inventory of the curious chieftain's cave burial at Býčí skála, Moravia, there is a set of heavy sledgehammers, a block anvil, and pincette-shaped iron tongs. This last implement might have served for operations with gloaming charcoal in the forge; another specimen of about the same date is known from a Scythian kurgan at Yablonovka in the Ukraine. Isolated finds of forging tools such as hammers or chisels were found in other kurgans and fortified sites of the earlier Scythian period (Perepovka, Pekari, Gorodnoye, and Lyubotinskoye, 6th or 6th/ 5th centuries B.C.).[17]

The progress of European ironworking technology around 500 B.C. can be traced through the physical appearance of the finds. After a transitional period of copying current bronze models, there appear perfectly shaped iron lanceheads, complex bridge bits and wheel pegs for chariots, and new types of blades, e.g., short daggers of HD types.[18] Riveting and hammering iron sheet were mastered to a considerable extent, proved by the thin hollow ring from Býčí skála—once believed to be an iron casting.

However, exact data concerning the level of ironworking come from metallographic analyses. Until 1974 more than 500 weapons, tools, and ornaments were investigated dating from about 700–400 B.C. About 300 of this number are adequately published (220 objects from Poland alone).[19] Let us first discuss weapons and cutting tools. Their practical value is determined by (1) the quality of material used in their manufacture, and (2) techniques which developed their working properties. We discount 175 objects because their geographical distribution is so diverse that it is impossible to use them for comparative purposes. From Poland, Slovakia, Lusatia, and Saxony (East Hallstatt or Veneto–Illyrian area) we have 111 objects. The Ukrainian area of the Scythians has 45 analyzed objects but the ancient Celtic territories such as Bavaria, Switzerland, east France, and parts of Austria and Bohemia offer only 15 specimens.

The entire south of Europe together with Greece, Etruria, and Spain is represented by only 6 metallographic analyses of early artifacts. In general, we distinguish the following techniques:

(1) forging tools of wrought iron or of low carbon steel which were relatively soft at the edges; (2) forging tools from unhomogeneously carburized steel the carbon content of which may reach 0.5 to 0.9 percent C but in which carburization was uncontrolled, so that soft parts occur on the edges; (3) forging tools of quenchable steels with over 0.35 percent C; (4) forging tools of wrought iron and carburizing their edges; and (5) iron-to-steel welding in the form of faggoting different sheets or in intentionally applied layers.

The latter three types of iron possessed better qualities which could be improved by about 50 percent through attempts at heat treatment. Groups 4 and 5 represent a skilled blacksmith's or cutler's work. Joining wrought iron and hard steel required a considerable knowledge because both kinds of metals have substantially different Ac_3 (hot forging) temperatures.

If we examine, for instance, the 111 analyzed East Hallstatt specimens we find that 67 percent of them are made of poor quality (low carbon or unhomogeneously carburized material. From the point of view of applied

Table 11.1. Technological Schemes of Late Hallstatt and Early La Tene Iron Artifacts
in Central Europe

Objects	Total	Techniques applied (%)				
		O	A	Oa	U	M
Chisels	4	50	0	0	0	50
Trunnion axes	10	60	0	20	0	20
Socketed axes	19	42	10	26	11	11
Swords or daggers	16	44	19	25	8	6
Knives	61	67	15	10	5	3
Lance- or arrowheads	33	67	15	12	3	3
Sickles	18	83	11	6	0	0
Awls	9	33	66	0	0	0
Battle axes	3	(67)	0	(33)	0	0
Varia	2	(50)	0	(50)	0	0
Total	175	61	15	14	4	6
Advanced quality				39%		
Intentional improvement					24%	

Notes: Material quality and applied technology of early European (HC, LA, 700–400 B.C.) iron artifacts according to 175 available analyses. Symbols: O = wrought iron or unhomogeneously carburized steel; A = all-steel artifacts (0.35% C); Oa = carburized in the edge; U = iron-to-steel welding (faggoting); M = iron-to-steel welding (international system).

technology, 78 percent were worked by techniques 1 and 2 and 22 percent worked by techniques 3–5. If we divide all available 175 analyses from all areas in the same way, we obtain the ratio of 61 : 39 as to the quality of the material used, and 76 : 24 of simpler (1 and 2) versus more complex (3–5) techniques of manufacture. Clear welding occurs in only 6 percent of the 175 specimens.[20]

Table 11.1 shows that the above proportions differ slightly according to type of object, i.e., weapons as opposed to tools. Better materials and often more advanced techniques were used in the production of swords, axes, and chisels than for lanceheads, knives, or sickles. Before we comment on this we must take into account another large category of artifacts —ornaments. The quality of work is not significant in this category since necklaces, bracelets, and even garment pins need not be sharp or hard. Among the total number of 104 investigated iron ornaments of

Table 11.2. Material Used for Manufacture of Ornaments of the HC/LA Periods
According to Analyses Published from Poland

Objects	Total	O	Q	A
Bracelets	55	56	33	11
Pins	32	69	22	9
Necklaces	12	67	25	8

Notes: Symbols: O = wrought iron or mild steel under 0.35% C; Q = unhomogeneously carburized steel with spots up to 0.9% C; A = steel with over 0.35% C.

the Late Lusatian and Pomeranian cultures of Poland we distinguish 59 percent wrought iron objects, 31 percent made of unhomogeneous carbon steel, and 10 percent made of more homogeneous steel with over 0.35 percent carbon. It is striking that in the second group there occur unhomogeneous steels with spots containing up to 0.9 percent C. Together with the third group it means that 40 percent of the ornaments were manufactured of a relatively hard (and in two or three cases hardened) steel which would have been better used in cutlery or tool manufacture. This is because most metalworkers and blacksmiths in Central Europe were not able to distinguish and deliberately separate suitable steels for different purposes. Smelters were not able to control the carburization processes in their smelting hearths and so produced iron blooms with unhomogeneously distributed carbon-free and carbon-rich zones. Polished and etched sections of several Hallstatt period blooms show that carbon-rich spots are few but that the carbon content sometimes reaches 0.7 to 1.2 percent.[21] Of investigated bracelets 33 percent are made of the same unhomogeneous metal as is found in blooms (table 11.2). This means that the metal of iron blooms with strong variability in its carbon content was randomly divided for further working. In ornament manufacture, no selectivity was necessary, but to make certain kinds of weapons, such as swords and hatchets for community or tribal leaders, skilled masters who were more familiar with the secrets and properties of the new metal were hired.

In connection with the quality of iron it is necessary to mention sporadic finds of nickel-containing metal.[22] Among European finds from about 500–300 B.C. there appear objects made of iron with 12–18 percent Ni (HD bracelets from Częstochowa-Raków, Poland) and artifacts of bloomery iron with welded-in plates of nickel-containing steel (8–10% Ni: socketed axes from Wietrzno-Bóbrka and Jezierzyce in Poland, and a ceremonial lancehead from the Fanum Voltumnae sanctuary, Etruria). The question has arisen whether the metal is of meteoritic origin and was intentionally selected for manufacture of certain objects or whether it was the result of accidental smelting of nickel-containing iron ores.[23]

The data discussed above indicate that the centuries between 800/700 and 400 B.C. represent the beginning stage in the development of the blacksmith's technology in Europe. On the other hand, one has to admit that some more advanced techniques may have been derived from supposedly more developed areas.[24]

Let us draw preliminary conclusions. About the middle of the 1st millennium B.C. Central Europe lagged by about four centuries behind Greece and about a hundred years behind Etruscan Italy in the use of iron as a metal. At about that time smelting of iron ores started north of the Alps, at least up to the edge of the North German Lowland. The extent of this production is not known. On the evidence of contemporary sources (which consist mainly of objects found in graves) we can state that bronze implements disappeared and those of iron were still scarce. The principles of simple and advanced ironworking had been developed but were used variably depending on the rapidity and direction of the diffusion of knowledge. Also, some blacksmiths were more proficient than others and their products represent excellent examples of ferrous technologies.

THE AGE OF THE IRON SWORD

Further progress in European iron metallurgy took place under the Roman republic, when substantial quantitative and qualitative successes were certainly achieved. Unfortunately, the direct evidence of these achievements is almost nonexistent: no excavations of workshops (except for a smithery in Pompeii published by Overbeck), no investigations of artifacts and no analyses of museum collections of iron assemblages are available at present. Therefore we are obliged to substitute another, somewhat later model of developments in ironworking: the history of this craft among the Celts. Special attention is to be paid to Continental Celtic territories and to their neighbors.

Apart from the semiforged blooms mentioned above, the circulation of iron is attested by bi-pointed bars in prehistoric Central Europe in about 500 B.C. (HD period). Many of them are replicas of Assyrian ex-

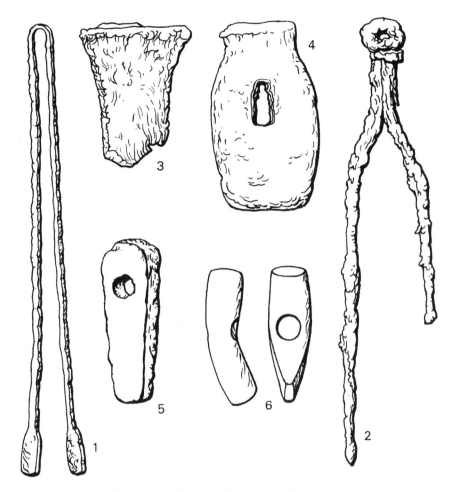

Fig. 11.6. Iron tools of blacksmiths of the late Hallstatt and Scythian periods (about 500 B.C.).
Tongs: 1, Yablonovka, Ukraine; 2, Býčí Skála, Moravia. Anvil: 3, Býčí Skála. Hammers: 4, Býčí
Skála; 5, Percepetovka, Ukraine; 6, Pekari, Ukraine. 1, 5, 6 after Šramko, 2, 3 after Pleiner.
Different scales.

amples of three centuries earlier. Slightly bent horns look like a bird's
beak; some of them have holes near one end.[25] This early type occurs
mainly in the ancient Veneto–Illyrian area of Europe (fig. 11.6). The
only hoard of bi-pointed bars which can be ascribed to the Celts of that
period consists of pieces of a different shape: short and squat, with straight
horns. This type is also represented by the find of Mont-Lassois, Seine[26]

and is similar to the short variant of bi-pointed bars, which are widespread in Europe. A striking concentration appears in Württemberg and in the Middle Rhineland, i.e., on the territory of the extremely important Celtic domain of the 6th–5th centuries B.C. (fig. 11.6). The majority of hoards with these heavy bars (more than 700 individual pieces are registered to date, with each weighing up to several kilograms) is undated.[27]

The hoard of Bechtheim consisted of 60 pieces of the long variant; one of the Sauggart hoards had 24 bars weighing 151 kg and the hoard of Rodalben had 9 pieces representing 42 kg iron. These curious bars were welded together, usually from several pieces of iron. Relatively numerous metallographic investigations show their extremely unhomogeneous carbon content (0.05 to 1.3% C in one bar).[28] This is due not only to joining different parts of bloom but also to the uncontrolled manner of carburizing during smelting. Other types of iron bars (*taleae ferreae*) were forged into shapes of swords, spits, and even narrow plough-shares. They are found, except for the latter, in hoards of southern England, Switzerland, central Germany, and occasionally in Bavaria.[29]

According to the few available analyses these bars consist of pure ferritic wrought iron, of unhomogeneous steel, or of piled structures. Because of the well-known passage in Caesar, *Bell. gall.* 5. 12 they are called currency bars.

The role of all types of premonetal means of exchange must be called into question, in the light of analogies around the world, disregarding the reason for burying them in hoards. In spite of dating problems, it may be that bi-pointed or spindle-shaped bars hint at increasing Celtic iron production immediately before and during the great expansion. Celtic raids, the outer sign of deep changes in the economic and social life of the Celts, were carried out with the aid of iron swords and lances. At that time iron became the only material for making weapons in large quantities for this Central European folk.

Celtic cemeteries of the 4th–2d B.C., from the Marne down to Hungary, have numerous burials with iron weapons: long swords, big lanceheads, shield fittings, and iron chain-belts of warriors. Celtic warriors fighting or having fought their battles in Italy were armed abundantly with swords.[30] Literary tradition indicates that the swords were of bad quality. This corresponds not only with the exterior appearance of many blades with nicks in their edges but also with the results of metallographic analyses. More than two-thirds of about 45 examined swords were made

simply from wrought iron.[31] Nevertheless, some show attempts to
harden blades by surface carburization or by the welding together of
iron and steel bands in various arrays. Thus, another tradition is revealed:
that of the Celtiberian area in the southwest. Celtic weapons were good
enough for Punic troups marching through southern Gaul and there
changing their armament.[32] All this leads to the conclusion that Celtic
ironworking underwent quantitative and qualitative growth. Swordsmiths applied techniques which created optical effects: they etched strips
and waves, covered blade surfaces with minute hammered depressions,
and sometimes experimented with twisting and welding wire of alternating carbon and phosphorus content, thus creating what may be interpreted as the initial stage of the pattern-welding technique.[33] They also
mastered riveting, sheet work, and ornamenting in the manufacture of
scabbards. The quality and structure of thin rapiers known as *Knollen-
knaufschwerter* are not known at the present time but their system of
hafting reminds us of a precise locksmith's work. The purpose of stamped
marks in the shape of symbols, discovered on certain swords, was not to
distinguish renowned workshops of masters as previously believed but
to provide apotropaic safeguards for prominent customers.[34] It is interesting that technical innovation did not lead to the improvement of weapons.
The analyzed late La Tène swords from oppida (Steinburg, Staré Hradisko,
and Stradonice) are all of low quality. In several late La Tène contexts
fragments of coats of mail have been found. Were they imported? The
progress in the Celtic ironworking technology is characterized rather by
introducing more iron equipment into everyday life and by constructing
excellent iron and steel implements. The age of the iron sword developed
into the age of iron and steel tools.

CELTIC METALLURGY OF IRON

In Celtic territories there are many sites with evidence of iron smelting.
Apart from those which represent local metallurgical activities, in some
areas there arose first mining and metallurgy centers, whose production
was disseminated beyond their immediate vicinity. We have written
sources on iron mines with galleries, operated by Aquitanian and central
Gallic tribes (Sotiati, Petrocorii, and Bituriges). Preliminary reports present new data on mining and smelting in Languedoc, south of the Massif
Central. Roman iron industries, well illustrated by the old excavations

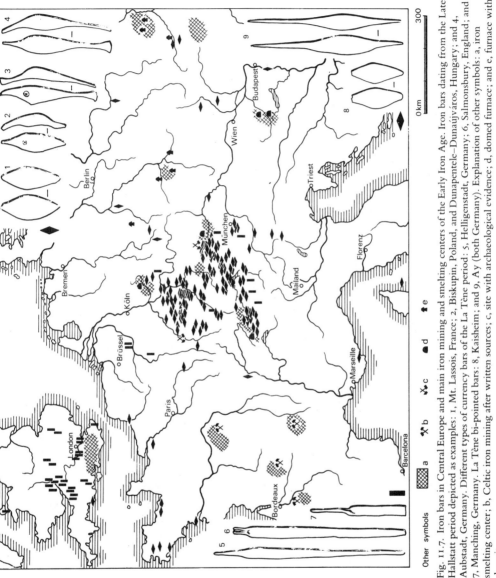

Fig. 11.7. Iron bars in Central Europe and main iron mining and smelting centers of the Early Iron Age. Iron bars dating from the Late Hallstatt period depicted as examples: 1, Mt. Lassois, France; 2, Biskupin, Poland, and Dunapentele–Dunaújváros, Hungary; and 4, Aubstadt, Germany. Different types of currency bars of the La Tène period: 5, Helligenstadt, Germany; 6, Salmonsbury, England; and 7, Manching, Germany. La Tène bi-pointed bars: 8, Kaisheim; and 9, Ay (both Germany). Explanation of other symbols: a, iron smelting center; b, Celtic iron mining after written sources; c, site with archaeological evidence; d, domed furnace; and e, furnace with slag pit.

of Quiquerez in Jura Bernois and sites examined recently in Jura Vaudois, have their roots in the La Tène period, indicated by the radiocarbon date 350 ± 80 for furnace X, Bellaires I.[35] An important center must have been in Siegerland, Germany, on the northern periphery of the Celtic domain, where good siderites and many smelting sites are found. Similarly, in the region of Donaumoos near Ingolstadt, and in that part of Kelheim where the Danube and Altmühl rivers join, there occur mining pits from which limonites were removed and bloomery sites in abundance.[36] Smelting activity of local significance flourished in west central Bohemia in the area of Mšec (end of the 2d century B.C.). Sub-Tatran bloomeries in North Slovakia must have produced on a larger scale; archaeological evidence from those regions strengthens the possibility of placing there the Celtic-speaking and iron-mining tribe of Cotini, mentioned by Tacitus. Another smelting center played a role in the Late La Tène period: the Holy Cross Mountain area, about 200 km to the north, in Little Poland. In the East, in the Carpathians, another center flourished: Mukačevo (Halic–Lovačka, Novoklinove).[37] More information, especially in regard to dating, is needed. Important La Tène period monuments of iron metallurgy have been recently discovered in Burgenland, east Austria (fig. 11.7).[38]

In the Roman world, the most renowned center was Noricum, present Carinthia, whose production was based on the excellent sideritic manganiferous ores of the Hüttenberg area. The beginning of industrial activity there must be connected with Celtic settlement of the Alpine valleys. At Magdalensberg, under the Augustan temple levels, occurs a set of hearths, possibly bloomery furnaces. The question of iron smelting within the walls of the oppidum is still debated, but ironworking is attested with certainty by smithing slags and unfinished products. Metallography reveals the working of hypereutectic steels with 0.8 to 1.3 percent C. Magdalensberg was an important trading post as well. Commercial inscriptions on walls of *tabernae* close to the temple district date from about 35 B.C.–A.D. 45 and concern the production of Noric Celts; they are notes on deliveries of ironmongery for different Mediterranean markets, including Africa.[39] Only four sorts of artifacts (ambosses, hoes, hooks, and rings) exported in sets of 100–500 pieces are mentioned and may represent different kinds of bars.

Except for Noricum, however, we have no exact idea as to the production, distribution, and social organization of early Celtic iron-making districts. Also their relation to small local production is not clear due to a shortage of dates. But we do have some information on Celtic metallurgical processes. Until 40 years ago few archaeologists collaborated with metallurgists, and it used to be widely believed that in early Europe the production of cast iron was the basic method. Nowadays, ethnographic and medieval data are acknowledged as relevant, a number of furnaces of different construction have been submitted to comparative studies, components and products have been the subjects of analytical research, and the observations on them have been verified by numerous trial smeltings. All this has enabled a look into the so-called direct process of extracting iron from its ores. The method is based on reduction of iron oxides by CO_2 and CO, developed from burning charcoal in small hearths of furnaces under relatively low temperatures below $1500°$ C. Iron absorbed carbon in the course of this reduction. Its extent was limited by the texture and composition of the ore, by thermal and chemical atmospheres in the furnace, and by the circulation of gases; these factors were related to natural conditions in individual areas and to the skill and experience of the smelters. Under favorable conditions the carburization process formed high carbon steels or even cast iron particles, but the original carbon content was diminished by streaming air into the oxidation zone of the furnace, where the final product sintered together in the form of a pasty sponge of malleable wrought iron or of unhomogeneously carburized steel, not fully separated from melted and solidified slag. Forgeable blooms were prepared by subsequent reheating and refining, which caused, of course, considerable losses of metal.[40] The first stages of the development of the bloomery process can be clearly traced in the technological remains of the Celts.

The simplest device in which this process took place was the open smelting hearth. Complete hearths come to light only rarely and it is difficult to recognize clay superstructures erected over furnace bottoms. Therefore, we do not know the extent to which this type survived into the La Tène period. Some examples are known from Britain (Kestor Rock and Chelms Combe) represented by shallow, partly slagged pits of 20 cm depth and 25–35 cm diameter, situations where bellows operation was necessary.[41]

Ancient smelting hearths had small capacities. It was difficult to separate the smelted metal from slag. A wall of stones or clay around the pit is thought to have kept together larger portions of ore and fuel. In fact,

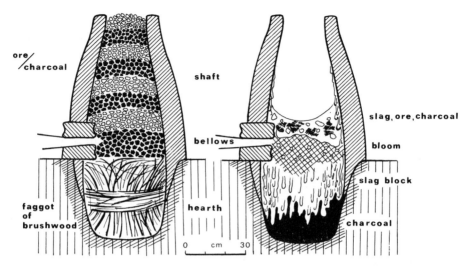

Fig. 11.8. Function of the slag pit shaft furnace. Left: before smelting; right: after smelting.

this theoretical missing link pointed to the development of a revolutionary type, the shaft furnace, and to its transitional variant, the furnace
with a slag pit. In such a furnace the process took place in a low clay shaft
above the ground level, which was also the level of air supply. The hearth
changed into a recipient of slag, blocked by straw or rubbish faggots at
the beginning of the smelt. Later, when the filling had burned out, slag
moved into the space through the pores of the reduced iron sponge,
sintering at the tuyere level. The sponge could be removed by destroying
the wall and then by striking with an ax. The slag remained in the shape
of a heavy block in the hearth. The origin of this ingenious device is
obscure.

In Europe, we meet it at the beginning of the late La Tène period in
connection with Celtic settlement. The geographical spread of this furnace type suggests that it had more ancient roots in the Veneto–Illyrian
countries of Central Europe: North Bohemia (Podbořany, the best-
preserved model of the type, Mšec, Kostomlaty), Thuringia (Riestedt),
Little Poland (Wyciąże, some Holy Cross Mountains localities) and
recently documented for the western edge of the Pannonian Lowland.
In any event, eastern Celts adopted the type and had great success in using
it (fig. 11.8). The original slag pit furnace had a shaft 60–100 cm high
and a slag pit 30–50 cm deep, the diameter at the ground level was about

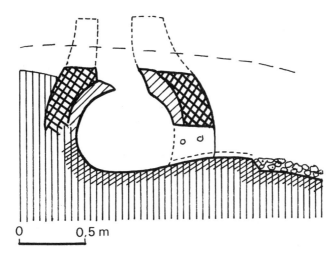

Fig. 11.9. La Tène period domed furnace. Silberquelle, Siegerland (after Gilles).

35–45 cm, and walls had a refractory lining 5–10 cm thick. It produced
3–10 kg of iron sponge, which was unhomogeneously carburized with
carbon contents ranging from 0.05 up to about 1 percent C.[42]

North of the Alps, in the central Celtic areas, iron smelting furnaces
of a more developed type occur. At Bellaires I in Switzerland, at Engsbach
and Oberdorf-Silberquelle (fig. 11.9) in Siegerland, possibly at Tauchen-
weiler in Württemberg, at Karlskron in Donaumoos, and at Kloster-
marienberg and Oberpullendorf in Burgenland large furnaces without
pits have been excavated, built in the shape of massive, domed, clay
superstructures. Slag tapping was usual, so that slag heaps were produced.
At least some of those furnaces might have been operated by induced
natural draft. The development of the shaft furnace required creating a
temperature gradient, with several zones of differing temperatures, and
enlarging the capacity of the charge volume, both techniques fully realized
here. The dome was about 1 m in diameter at the hearth level and about
20–30 cm in the throat; the estimated height was 100–200 cm. Walls
about 30–40 cm thick ensured stability.[43]

The capacity[44] of these Celtic furnaces was surpassed in antiquity only
by Romano-provincial shaft furnaces. In our opinion, these furnaces
contributed to the general increase in Celtic iron production.

Apart from the apparatus described above we occasionally find other
features related to ironworking. For instance, a curious tunnel-shaped

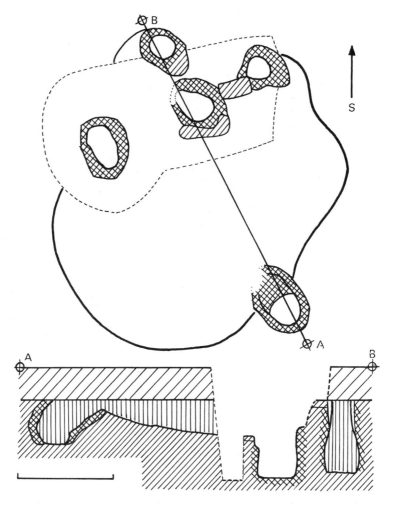

Fig. 11.10. La Tène period bloomery, Chýně, Bohemia (after Turek and Pleiner).

furnace has been discovered in the oppidum of Michelsberg, near Kelheim (length 186 cm, width 80 cm).[45]

The reheating of blooms was carried on in larger open hearths known mainly from Bohemian sites. They were of circular or elongated plan (Mšec, Kostomlaty). Special reheating furnaces with four reduction chambers appear in Chýně near Prague (fig. 11.10). Early smelters preferred good ores such as hematites or nodular limonites, wherever they were accessible. The large scale exploitation of bog ores began later, in the early Middle Ages. Ore dressing consisted of crushing to pea size and of preroasting in order to dehydrate and to create a porous texture in the ore. No fluxes were added, as far as we know. For charcoal manufacture, which took place in deep pits (Prague) or in piles (Donaumoos), wood was chosen according to local conditions; pine charcoal was often used in eastern Europe.

Celtic bloomeries consisted either of a group of features including furnaces, reheating hearths, and roasting places in the open air or they were placed in small, sunken-floored, and obviously roofed workshops.[46] The latter type was typical of local peasant production and good examples occur in central Bohemia. This type was used by Teutonic tribes in the early Roman period, a milieu in which the Celtic metallurgical tradition can be clearly traced.

The description of iron making by the Celts should be completed by a discussion of the industrial activities of their neighbors who were at similar stages of development, for instance, the Iberians in Hispania and the Dacians in the southeast. Unfortunately, relevant sources are still lacking. If we assume that the ironworking craft in those countries was not retarded, we do it on the basis of indirect evidence. Especially in the Dacian area in Rumania, there are many large hoards of iron objects: at Gradiştea Muncelului 8 hoards of sets of scythes, at Negri Bacău 314 pieces of ploughshare-shaped bars and sections of flat chains, at Oniceni 19 similar bars, and so on. Metallographic examination of some of the specimens, dating from the 2d or 1st century B.C., revealed very hard steels. A steel bloom from Piatra Craivii contained particles of white cast iron.[47]

THE FIRST FULL-FLEDGED CIVILIZATION OF IRON IN EUROPE

At the end of the 1st millennium B.C., the full-fledged Iron Age prevailed in the southern countries of the European continent. The use of iron influenced all crafts and the entire style of life. We demonstrate this by the situation in the Celtic cultural provinces. We state that iron was used not only for the production of traditional objects like weapons and basic tools of work but also for the manufacture of household utensils (chains, keys, locks, spoons, cauldrons, and forks), sometimes of substantial size (massive fire dogs), and was employed for structural purposes (nails,

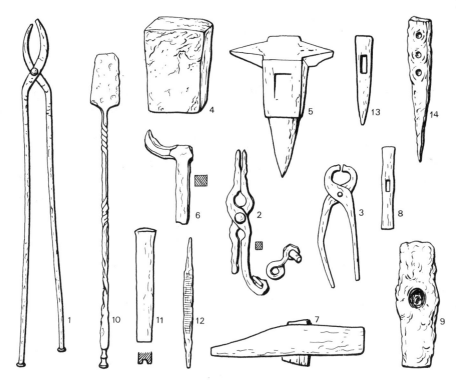

Fig. 11.11. Late La Tène metalworking implements. Tongs: 1, St. Georgen, Austria; 2, Manching, Germany; 3, Llyn Cerring Bach, Man; Anvils: 4, Plavecké Podhradie, Slovakia; 5, Szalacska, Hungary; 6, Manching. Hammers: 7, Stradonice, Bohemia; 8, St. Georgen; 9, Sanzeno, North Italy. Hearth spoon: 10, Manching. Rivet snap: 11, Stradonice. File: 12, Manching. Drift: 13, Stradonice. Nail iron: 14, Staré Hradisko, Moravia. 1, 8 are after Taus, 2, 6, 10, 12 after Jacobi, 3 is after Fox, 4 after Paulík, 5 after Hunyady and Szabó, 6, 7, 11, 13 are after Píč, and 9 is after Fogolari. Different scales are used.

clamps, and mountings). Building of ramparts of the *murrus gallicus* type consumed tons of long iron nails. British tribes did not hesitate to use a quantity of valuable iron for making ship anchors measuring 1.4 m in length (Bulbery)[48], and Caesar mentions the use of iron in naval building among Armorician Gauls (*Bell. Gall.* 3. 13). Significantly, during the La Tène period for the first time in the history of Central Europe, iron in the shape of ploughshares helped to cultivate agricultural soils. There were more than 90 kinds of artifacts made of iron. In this respect, Celtic civilization was not much behind the developed urban world of the Mediterranean.

Table 11.3. Technology of Late La Tène Artifacts (1st century B.C.)

Area/sites	Total	Techniques applied (%)				
		O	A	Oa	U	M
Carinthia (Magdalensberg oppidum, ready-made tools)	12	15	55	15	0	15
Bohemian and Moravian oppida (Stradonice 10, Závist 13, Hrazany 1, Lhotice 1, Staré Hradisko 18, Hostýn 10 tools)	52	33	23	27	7	12
Peripheral oppida (Steinsburg Thuringia, 44 cutting tools from the later phase; Liptovská Mara, North Slovakia 4)	48	54	11	33	0	2
Poland (settlements and cemeteries mostly of non-Celtic manufacture)	35	80	14	3	0	3
Total	147					

Notes: Symbols: See table 11.1. Under Oa in the case of Steinsburg are included faggots with carburized (and hardened) parts which often reach into the edge of the implement.

Another symptom of general progress is the creation of implements for individual crafts, including tools for special operations in metal, wood, bone, leather, and the like. This process may be observed also in the tools of Celtic blacksmiths: in addition to basic items, there appear special tongs, horned anvils suitable for bending of rods, many types of hammers both small and heavy, nail irons, draw plates for wire, and rivet snaps (fig. 11.11).

Sets of implements are part of the tomb equipment of blacksmiths in peripheral zones of the Celtic world (St. Georgen in Austria, Leipzig–Thekla in Central Germany, Wesolki in Poland).[49] The bulk of iron comes from rich hoards and from numerous oppida (native Celtic city agglomerations and centers of crafts). According to earlier discoveries (Mont Beuvray-Bibracte) and to recent excavations (Manching) blacksmiths inhabited special quarters.[50] Obviously, they supplied the broader environment with ironmongery. Concentration of location and other favorable conditions point to specialization within the blacksmith's craft, which is also reflected in the rich assortment of iron goods and also in the improvement of the technology of manufacture.

There is no doubt that Celtic blacksmiths achieved great skill in hot forming. The minute work observable in certain types of iron fibulae and bracelets is to be esteemed for its high artistic feeling and execution.[51]

Table 11.4. Proportions of Applied Technologies as Reflected in 47 Specimens of
Cutting Implements from Celtic Oppida in Czechoslovakia

Implements	Number	O	A	Oa	U	M	Total	Hardenable steel
		Techniques applied (%)					Hardening (%)	
Scythes	4	0	25	25	0	50	75	100
Axes	6	50	0	17	0	33	50	100
Other woodworking implements	8	25	39	12	12	12	44	60
Knives	25	36	24	24	12	4	56	88
Scissors	4	25	25	50	0	0	75	75
Total	47	32	19	27	9	13	67	77
Advanced quality		68%						
Intentional improvement				49%				

Notes: Two spades examined were of wrought iron and two files were of hard steel
and marquenched. For symbols, see table 11.1.

Nonetheless, the real technical level is better illustrated by metallographic
examination of implements and arms, including blades of all kinds. Up
to now we have investigated only a small number of tools from Celtic
oppida.[52] Table 11.3 presents the proportional relation of simple and
more complicated techniques. From this we may derive preliminary
conclusions on specific conditions of ironworking at Magdalensberg,
Noricum, based on the occurrence of high carbon steels, and, on the other
hand, on the decrease of progressive techniques on the northern periphery
of the Celtic milieu. In non-Celtic areas of Poland, achievements did not
exceed those of the Late Hallstatt period.

In general, in the central Celtic areas the number of deliberately
improved artifacts substantially increased in comparison to the Late
Hallstatt/Early La Tène periods, notably in regard to iron-to-steel welding. In all periods, skilled use of this technique indicates the practical
knowledge of the smith.

The combination of both materials gave the edges of blades sufficient
hardness and gave the whole blade resistance against bending and brittleness. However, it required great skill, since high carbon steel and low
carbon wrought material have different optimal temperatures for heating

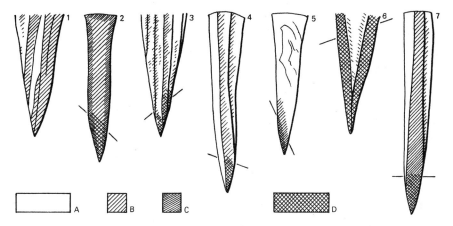

Fig. 11.12. Cutlery from Celtic oppida: construction of blades (polished and etched sections). A, wrought iron; B, mild steel; C, hard steel, and D, marquenched steel. Short lines mark the quench bath level. Provenance: 1, Steinsburg; Thuringia, 2, 4, 6, Staré Hradisko, Moravia; 3, Stradonice, Bohemia; 5, Závist, Bohemia; and 7, Hostýn, Moravia. (After Pleiner.)

and welding. Yellow or white heat (1200° C and more), suitable for welding wrought iron, could cause decarburization and therefore loss in strength of the steel. Table 11.4 shows that the more complex techniques found their major application in the manufacture of harvesting implements and woodworking tools; knives reflect only slightly the more advanced technologies.

Let us emphasize that iron-to-steel welding occurs in two main categories in terms of quality: the first group includes simple piles of iron or steel plates, or even irregularly carburized sheets, welded more or less to faggots; the second group represents intentional schemes of building blades. In addition to the skill needed to make welds, smiths were noteworthy for their ability to select appropriate and varied types of steel (fig. 11.12).

Another sign of technical progress in tool manufacture was the spread of hardening, especially marquenching, a process encouraged by the introduction of a broader range of carbon-rich materials. Smiths also sometimes tried to quench wrought iron, poor in carbon. They may have been accustomed to carry out heat treatment and mistakenly estimated the quality of the worked metal.

Instead of an epilogue, let us touch on the succeeding development of European iron extracting and working. Historical events split the Celtic world into two parts; the larger of these was incorporated into the Roman provincial system. There Celtic technology contributed to the general advance of technology and economy: iron ores were mined, extracted, and worked on a large scale with refined technical skill. A smaller part of the Celtic world was assimilated by the expanding Teutons, whose civilization stood at that time (beginning of the A.D. era) at a somewhat lower stage of development. Interestingly, Germans were able to adopt fully the metallurgy of iron which flourished in east Celtic cultures.[53] On the other hand, the blacksmith's craft, having lost its base after the fall of Celtic agglomerations of the oppidum type, underwent, even in former Celtic territories a considerable regression and decentralization. These two poles influenced European metallurgy of iron (and other branches of production as well) for a long time. Signs of recovery and stabilization were felt only in the 6th–9th centuries A.D., but the promising beginnings of European ironworking did not reach a culmination until the High Middle Ages. At that time, under different socioeconomic conditions, somewhere in eastern France—in the Rhineland, or in the Austrian Alps, territories formerly Roman and superior in their natural resources—a new phase of metallurgical progress began.

NOTES

1. Cyril S. Smith, "Material and the Development of Civilization and Science," *Science* 148 (1965): 908–17; Theodore A. Wertime, "Man's First Encounters with Metallurgy," *Science* 146 (1964): 1257–67; Theodore A. Wertime, "The Beginnings of Metallurgy," *Science* 182 (1973): 875–87.

2. A Southwest Asiatic origin was presumed by many scholars, with variations. Some of the recent contributions are quoted here: Leslie Aitchison, *A History of Metals* (New York, 1960), vol. 1; Robert J. Forbes, *Studies in Ancient Technology* (Leyden, 1964), vol. 9; A. M. Snodgrass, "Iron Age Greece and Central Europe," *American Journal of Archaeology* 66 (1962): 408–10; A. M. Snodgrass, *Dark Age Greece* (Edinburgh, 1971), pp. 217–21; V. R. d'A. Desborough, *The Last Mycenaeans and Their Successors* (Oxford 1964); Radomír Pleiner, *Iron Working in Ancient Greece* (Prague, 1969), pp. 12–13; Spiridon Iakovidis, "The Appearance of Iron in Greece," *Athens Annals of Archaeology* 3, no. 2 (1970): 280–96. Allusions of independent development in Central Europe or radiation from there can be found in, e.g., Stephen Foltiny, "Athens and the East Hallstatt Region: Cultural Interrelations at the Dawn of the Iron Age," *American Journal of Archaeology* 65 (1961): 283–98; Wolfgang Kimmig, "Seevölkerbewegung und Urnenfelderkultur," in *Studien aus Alteuropa* (Cologne and Graz, 1964), vol. 1, p. 244; Cimmerian influences are

stressed by Dumitru Berciu, "Este și o Cale Cimmeriană în Difuzionea metalurgiei fierului," *Studi și cercetari de istorie veche* 14 (1963): 395–401; Dumitru Berciu, "Pour une voie Cim-mérienne de diffusion de la métallurgie du fer," *Archeologické rozhledy* 16 (1964): 264–79. There is no attention paid to previous African theories or to views on the independent origin of iron smelting in different parts of the Old World which still occur in the litera-ture.

3. Gánovce: Emanuel Vlček and Ladislav Hájek, "A ritual well and the find of an early Bronze Age iron dagger at Gánovce near Poprad (Czechoslovakia)," in *A Pedro Bosch-Gimpera* (Mexico, 1963), pp. 427–39; Rumanian finds: A. László, "Die Anfänge der Eisenmetallurgie in Rumänien," *Studii și cercetari de istorie veche și arheologie* 26 (1975): 17–39; Scandinavian finds, summarized: Bertha Stjernquist, *Simris II, Bronze Age Prob-lems in the Light of the Simris Excavations* (Bonn and Lund, 1961), p. 79; Hötting and Völs, Austria: Karl Heinz Wagner, *Nordtiroler Urnenfelder* (Berlin, 1943), pp. 37, 115; Mulino: Juliette de la Genière, *Recherches sur l'âge du fer en Italie méridionale*, 2 vols., Sala Consilina (Naples, 1968), p. 106, n. 33 [after Bernabò Brea].

4. T. Burton Brown, *The Coming of Iron to Greece* (London, 1954); A. M. Snodgrass, *Iron Age Greece*; A. M. Snodgrass, *Early Greek Armour and Weapons from the End of the Bronze Age to 600 B.C.* (Edinburgh, 1964); *Dark Age Greece*, pp. 213–95; C. G. Styrenius, *Submycenaean Studies* (Lund, 1967); Pleiner, *Iron Working*; and Iakovidis, "Appearance of Iron."

5. John Al xander, "Greeks, Italians and the Earliest Balkan Iron Age," *Antiquity* 36 (1962): 123–30; idem, *Jugoslavia before the Roman Conquest*, (London, 1972), pp. 99, 101; Rastko Vasić, *Kulturne grupe staryjeg gvozdenog doba u Jugoslaviji* (Beograd, 1973); Radomír Pleiner, *Základy slovanského železářského hutnictví v českých zemích* (Prague, 1958), p. 73; Stjernquist, *Simris*, vol. II, pp. 77–84; Wolfgang Kimmig, "Seevölkerbewegung," p. 274; Fritz Horst, "Hallstattimporte und -einflüsse im Elb-Havelgebiet," *Zeitschrift für Archä-ologie* 5 (1971): 192–214. Chronology is based on the results of Hermann Müller-Karpe, *Beiträge zur Chronologie der Urnenfelderzeit nördlich und südlich der Alpen* (Berlin, 1959), not including the changes proposed by N. K. Sandars, "From Bronze Age to Iron Age, A Sequel to a Sequel," in *The European Communities in Later Prehistory*, Studies in honour of C. F. C. Hawkes (London, 1971), pp. 1–29.

6. K. Horedt, "Die Verwendung des Eisens in Rumänien bis in das 6. Jahrhundert v.u.Z.," *Dacia* N.S. 8 (1964): 119–32; Zoltán Székély, "Beiträge zur Kenntnis der Früh-hallstattzeit und zum Gebrauch des Eisens in Rumänien," *Dacia* N.S. 10 (1966): 209–19; Stefan Olteanu, "Cele mai vechi mărturi arheologice privino extracția și reducere a minereului de fier pa teritorul Dobrogei," *Studii și cercetari de istorie veche* 22 (1971): 295–99; Sandars, "From Bronze Age to Iron Age."

7. L. Bernabò Brea, *Sicily before the Greeks* (London, 1957); David Randall-MacIver, *Villanovans and Early Etruscans* (Oxford, 1925); David Randall-MacIver, *The Iron Age in Italy* (Oxford, 1927); de la Genière, *Sala Consilina*, pp. 105–09; Giorgio Buchner, "Mostra degli scavi di Pithecusa," *Dialoghi di Archeologia* 1–2 (1969): 85–101; D. Ridgway, "Metalworking at Pithekoussai, Ischia /NA/, Italy," *Archeologické rozhledy* 25 (1973): 456.

8. Randall-MacIver, *Iron Age*; Hermann Müller-Karpe, *Beiträge zur Chronologie*, vol. 1, pp. 64, 70; Göran Gierow, *The Iron Age Culture of Latium* I (Lund, 1966), vol. 1, pp.

353–58; Hugh Hencken, *Tarquinia, Villanovans and Early Etruscans* (Cambridge, Mass., 1968), vol. 2, pp. 570–72; Lawrence Barfield, *Northern Italy before Rome* (London, 1971), p. 104 ff.

9. Berciu, "Pour une voie…"; Vladimír Podborský, "Štramberská dýka s křížovým jílcem…," *Archeologické rozhledy* 19 (1967): 194–220. For easternmost Europe see B. A. Šramko, L. A. Solncev, and L. D. Fomin, "Technika obrabotki železa v lesostepnoj i stepnoj Skifii," *Sovetskaja Archeologija* 4 (1963): 36–57.

10. Antonio Arribas, *The Iberians* (London, 1966); H. N. Savory, *Spain* and Portugal, *The Prehistory of the Iberian Peninsula* (London, 1968), p. 257; J. Maluquer de Motes, "Late Bronze and Early Iron in the Valley of Ebro," in *The European Communities*, p. 117. Sardinia with its great nonferrous metallurgy tradition until the middle of the millennium was a backward territory in terms of the spread of iron (Margaret Guido, *Sardinia* [London, 1963], p. 171). Surveys on the situations in Brittany, England, the Low Countries, and Scandinavia may be obtained from general works by Giot, Clarke, De Laet, Stenberger, Hagen, and Gimbutas. The following items are to be specifically quoted: Brian G. Scott, "Some Notes on the Transition from Bronze to Iron in Ireland," *Irish Archaeological Research Forum* 1 (1974): 9–24; and R. B. Warner, "The Irish Bronze-Iron Transition: A Pessimistic View," *Irish Archaeological Research Forum* 1, no. 2 (1974): 45–50, for Ireland; Jørgen Jensen, "Ulbjerggraven, Begyndelsen af den aeldre jernalder i Jylland," *Kuml 1965* (1966): 23–33 for Denmark; and *Latvijas PSR arheologija* (Riga, 1974), pp. 83–84 for Lithuania.

11. A. Mosso, "Stazione preistorica di Coppa Nevigata presso Manfredonia," *Monumenti Antichi* 19 (1908): 36–386, esp. 311–20.

12. Slag deposits covered the most ancient Etruscan tombs dating from the 7th century B.C. in the S. Cerbone and Porcarecchia areas. Later the iron industry was the theme not only in historical and geographical treatises of antiquity but also in poetry. See Silius Italicus, *Punica* 7. 615–16; Diodorus Sic. 5. 13; Livy 28. 45; Pliny 3. 6; 34. 41; Virgil *Aeneis*. 10. 172–74; Varro *apud* Servium, *Ad Aeneidem* 10. 173; Strabo 5. 2, 6; and Rutilius Namatianus I. 350–53. The abandoned works at Campiglia Maritima (to the NE) are medieval (Fuciania; this information was kindly made available by O. Voss).

13. This rough estimation is based on results of recent smelting experiments made under the conditions of a primitive bloomery process; they show that 200 kg ore with about 50–60% Fe_2O_3 produces 100 kg slag and about 30 kg iron (Kazimierz Bielenin, *Starożytne górnictwo i hutnictwo żelaza w górach Świętokrzyskich* [Holy Cross Mountains] [Warsaw and Cracow, 1974], pp. 189–95; see also R. F. Tylecote et al., "The Mechanism of the Bloomery Process in Shaft Furnaces," *Journal of the Iron and Steel Institute*, 1971, pp. 342–63). One cubic meter of dumped slag in pieces represents ca. 840 kg. For a better idea of the efficiency of production it should be realized that a battle ax was made of about 0.3 kg metal, a large lancehead of 0.8 kg, a coulter of ca. 1 kg, a scythe 0.2 kg, a large knife of about 100 g, a small knife of 30 g, and a goldsmith's hammer of 60 g. The yield of one smelt in the primitive hearth, estimated at 3 kg iron, was sufficient for the manufacture of 2 or 3 larger and about 60 smaller tools. A more developed furnace with a 30 kg yield would supply the metal for the equipment of 30 or 40 warriors or 100 knives, enough for several communities. Of course, considerable loss of reduced iron (about 20%) during reheating of blooms, bars, and semiproducts must be taken into account.

14. From the bibliography on Populonia are to be cited: M. L. Simonin, "De l'exploitation des mines et de la métallurgie en Toscane pendant l'antiquité et le Moyen Age," *Annales des Mines* 5, ser. 14 (1858): 557–615; G. D'Achiardi, "L'industria mineraria e metallurgica in Toscana al tempo degli Etruschi," *Studi Etruschi* 1 (1927): 411–20; Antonio Minto, *Populonia* (Florence, 1943); Antonio Minto, "L'antica industria mineraria in Etruria ed il porto di Populonia," *Studi Etruschi* 22 (1954): 293–319. Reconnaissances made by O. Voss, Copenhagen, are in progress in the area. I am much indebted to him for valuable information. A series of slag and ore analyses has been made in the laboratory of the Archaeological Institute, Prague. These analyses will be published by O. Voss.

15. Hans-Jürgen Driehaus, "'Fürstengräber' und Eisenerze zwischen Mittelrhein, Mosel und Saar," *Germania* 43 (1965): 32–49; Richard Pittioni, "Grächwil und Vix handelsgeschäftlich gesehen," in *Helvetia Antiqua* (Zurich, 1966), pp. 113–28.

16. References to smelting sites are as follows: Hillesheim: Alfred Haffner, "Ein hallstattzeitlicher Eisenschmelzofen von Hillesheim, Kreis Daun," *Trierer Zeitschrift* 34 (1971): 21–29; Králová: Pleiner, *Základy*, pp. 81–82; Waschenberg: Manfred Pertlwieser, "Die hallstattzeitliche Höhensiedlung auf dem Waschenberg bei Bad Wimsbach/Neydharting, politischer Bezirk Wals, Oberösterreich, II. Teil: Die Objekte (Hütten, Werkstätten, Metallanalysen)," *Jahrbuch des Oberösterreichischen Musealvereines* 115, no. 1 (1970): 37–70. There are more sites with Late Hallstatt slags which are not quoted here.

17. Smolenice: Mikuláš Dušek, "Ein Burgwall der jüngeren Hallstattzeit in Smolenice," *VIIe Congrès International des Sciences Préhistoriques et Protohistoriques, Tchécoslovaquie 1966* (Nitra, 1966) [it is not out of the question that iron smelting took place in the site]; Býčí skála: Pleiner, *Základy*, pp. 86–90; Radomír Pleiner, *Staré evropské kovářství* [Alteuropäisches Schmiedehandwerk] (Prague, 1962), p. 62; Scythian finds: B. A. Šramko, "Orudiye skifskoj epochi dlja obrabotki železa," *Sovetskaja Archeologija* 3 (1969): 53–70.

18. The thin blades of these daggers suggest the use of good steel. Until now only the hilts have been studied using radiography: a hard solder was applied (Adolf Rieth, "Zur Herstellungstechnik der Eisendolche der späten Hallstattzeit," *Jahrbuch des Römisch-Germanischen Zentramuseums in Mainz* 16 1969 [1971]: 12–58).

19. This is due to the extensive analytical work of J. Piaskowski. Instead of his numerous publications in Polish, we quote his survey of 1969 (Jerzy Piaskowski, "Metallographische Untersuchungen der Eisenerzeugnisse in der Hallstattzeit im Gebiet zwischen Oder und Weichsel," in *Beiträge zur Lausitzer Kultur*, ed W. Coblenz, [Dresden and Berlin, 1969], pp. 179–210). Scythian finds: Cf. B. A. Sramko, L. A. Solncev, and L. D. Fomin, "Technika obrabotki," and B. A. Šramko, L. D. Fomin, and L. A. Solncev, "Novyje issledovanija techniki obrabotki železa v Skifii," *Sovetskaja Archeologija* no. 4 (1971): 140–53; and Jerzy Pisakowski, "Metaloznawcze badania żelaznych wyrobów pochodzenia scytijskiego," *Archeologia Polski* 4 (1959): 29–45. Individual items from various countries: Jerzy Zimny, "Metaloznawcze badania halsztackich wyrobów żelaznych z Częstochowy-Rakowa," *Rocznik Muzeum w Częstochowie* 1 (1965): 329–400; Maria Cabalska, Elżbieta Nosek, and Adam Mazur, "Wyroby żelazne ze stanowiska kultury łużyckiej w Maszkowicach...," *Przegląd Archeologiczny* 19/20 (1971): 51–76; Pleiner, *Staré evropské kovářství*, pp. 50–59; Radomír Pleiner, "Schmiedetechnik der Hallstattzeit im Lichte der Untesuchung des Hortfundes von Schlöben," *Archeologické rozhledy* 20 (1968): 33–42; Adolf Rieth, *Eisentechnik der Hallstattzeit* (Leipzig, 1940) [with analyses made by Gilles

and Lembeck]; F. Morton, "Analysen von Eisenschlacken und Eisenwerkzeugen . . . vom Grabfelde in Hallstatt," *Jahrbuch des Oberösterreichischen Musealvereines* 99 (1954): 177; Pertlwieser, "Die hallstattzeitliche Höhensiedlung," pp. 68–69; Louis Lepage, "Étude d'un fer de javelot hallstattien . . . ," *Mémoires de la Société d'agriculture, du commerce, des sciences et des arts du département de la Marne* 81 (1966): 7–11; C. Panseri, C. Carino, and M. Leoni, "Ricerche metallografiche sopra aclune lame Etrusche di acciaio," in *La tecnica di fabbricazione delle lame di acciaio* (Milan, 1957), pp. 9–40; H. H. Coghlan, *Notes on Prehistoric and Early Iron in the Old World*, 1st ed. (Oxford, 1956), pp. 139–42; 2d ed. (1977), pp. 116–18; H. H. Coghlan, "Etruscan and Spanish Swords of Iron," *Sibrium* 3 (1955/56): 167–74; George J. Varoufakis, "Untersuchungen an drei stählernen Speerspitzen aus dem 7. und 6. Jahrhundert v. Chr.," *Archiv für das Eisenhüttenwesen* 41 (1970): 1023–26; Erwin Plöckinger, "Untersuchungen an Hallstattzeitlichen Eisenwerkzeugen," in *Festschrif für Richard Pittioni* II (Vienna and Horn, 1976), pp. 142–52.

20. Among the oldest specimens in Europe is the falcata from Vetulonia, 7th century B.C. (Panseri, Carino, and Leoni, "Richerche Metallografiche," p. 19). A similar principle is observed in two Polish chisels (Chojno and Gorszewice), an ax head (Brzezina), and a lancehead (Częstochowa-Raków). The ax-head from Popielów and a knife from Maszkowice have steel edges welded on the side.

21. Investigated blooms: Waschenberg, Łagiewniki, Smolenice (3 pieces, not yet published); they represent semiforged spongy iron shaped roughly in quadrangular blocks. Several other blooms are known from Slovakia and Poland (Nižná Myšl'a, Krásná Hôrka, Przybyslaw, and so forth). They all date to the Hallstatt period.

22. A high nickel content is attested for some of the well-known earliest irons from SW Asia (3d millennium B.C.). We add to the list a spearhead (3.65% Ni) from a tomb at Bičkin-Buluk (Lower Volga region, about 1500 B.C.) (B. A. Šramko, L. D. Fomin, and L. A. Solncev, "Pervaja nachodka izdelija iz meteoritnogo železa v vostočnoj Evrope," *Sovetskaja Archeologija* 4 [1965]: 190–204). Such examples used to be interpreted as having been made of meteoritic iron. Fanum Voltumnae: C. Panseri and M. Leoni, "Research of an Iron Spearhead from the Etruscan Sanctuary of Fanum Voltumnae, Fourth to Third Centuries B.C.," in *Archaeological Chemistry*, ed. M. Levey (Philadelphia, 1967), pp. 205–29.

23. Jerzy Piaskowski, "O produkcji żelaza wysokoniklowego w starożytności," *Acta Archaeologica Carpatica* 11 (1969/70): 319–28.

24. It is worth mentioning that one of the Idalion knives (no. 106, Cypriote III, about 12th–11th centuries B.C.) was manfactured by welding-on and hardening a high carbon steel edge. This is known through a detailed examination of cementite formations in the corroded matrix (Erik Tholander, "Evidence of the Use of Carburized Steel and Quench Hardening in the Late Bronze Age Cyprus," *Opuscula Atheniensia* 10, no. 3 [1971]: 15–22).

25. Pleiner, *Základy*, pp. 91–92; Witów: Jerzy Piaskowski, "Starożytne kęsy żelazne z Witowa . . . ," *Sprawozdania Archeologiczne* 14 (1962): 320–29; Maszkowice: Cabalska, Nosek, and Mazur, 'Wyroby żelazne, p. 70; Heuneburg: Wolfgang Kimmig and Egon Gersbach, "Die Grabungen auf der Heuneburg 1966–1969," *Germania* 49 (1971): 29–91, esp. 54–56. (This is the only find of a bird-shaped bar in the Celtic territory); of the same date may be hoards from Dunapentele–Dunaújváros (Miklós Szabó, "A ket-

töspirimas alakú vasrudak kérdéséhez," *Archeologiai Értesitö* 93 [1966]: 249–53) and Aubstadt, central Germany (Otto Kleemann, "Der erste Fund vorgeschichtlicher Eisenbarren in Franken," *Mainfränkisches Jahrbuch* 18 [1966]: 3–16.

26. Albert France-Lanord, "Les lingots de fer protohistoriques," *Revue d'histoire de la sidérurgie* 4 (1963): 166–77, esp. 168–71.

27. Formerly, Otto Kleemann ("Stand der archäologischen Forschung über die eisernen Doppylpyramiden (Spitz-) barren," *Archiv für das Eisenhüttenwesen* 32 [1961]: 581–85) suggested a Roman dating. Their use as material for working iron is attested to by the oppida Steinsburg (Reinhard Spehr, "Die Rolle der Eisenverarbeitung in der Wirtschaftsstruktur des Steinsburg-Oppidums," *Archeologické rozhledy* 23 [1971]: 493–94) and Manching (Gerhard Jacobi, *Werkzeug und Gerät aus dem Oppidum von Manching* [Wiesbaden, 1974], p. 248) in the context of either Middle or Late La Tène periods. The occasional occurrence of isolated pieces in Roman times (*mithraeum* in Oberflorstadt, sanctuary in Sanzeno) is to be interpreted as secondary. Most of the hoards are not dated. The La Tène hoard from Plavecké Podhradie (Jozef Paulík, "Najstaršie hromadné nálezy železných predmetov na Slovensku," *Zborník Slovenského národného múzea* 64 [1970]: 634, pl. V below) consisted of bars of a different, elongated type.

28. Metallographically analyzed bi-pointed bars: for Late Hallstatt or Early La Tène specimens see n. 24 and 25; for further Steinsburg, see H. Hanemann, "Untersuchung eines eisernen Spitzbarrens aus der vorrömischer Zeit," *Prähistorische Zeitschrift* 21 (1930): 271–74; Kaisheim and Ay: Wilhelm Rädeker and Friedrich Karl Naumann, "Untersuchung vor-oder frühgeschichtlicher Spitzbarren," *Archiv für das Eisenhüttenwesen* 32 [1961]: 587–95; Renningen: U. Zwicker, "Untersuchungen an einem Eisenbarren aus dem Depotfund von Renningen [Kr. Leonberg]," *Fundberichte aus Schwaben* N.F. 18, no. 1 [1967]: 282–83; Strasbourg (France-Lanord, "Lingots," pp. 171–73). Varieties in the phosphorus content suggested that individual bars of the same hoard came from different regions.

29. England: recently summarized by D. Allen, "Iron Currency Bars in Britain," *Proceedings of the Prehistoric Society* new ser., 33 (1967): 307–35 (with bibliography dealing also with Continental finds of analogous types); for Germany inventories were compiled by Jacoby, *Werkzeug und Gerät*, pp. 251–53 (with new finds from Manching and Gundelfingen). For the analysis of a bar from La Tène see France-Lanord, "Lingots," pp. 175–76; for those from Bouston and Worthy Down see R. F. Tylecote, *Metallurgy in Archaeology* (London, 1962), p. 210.

30. The number of warrior graves in Celtic flat cemeteries often reaches 20–30%. These gravefields are later than the major Celtic raids, and exact chronology of individual cases must be considered, as the analysis of Münsingen-Rain shows (S. Martin-Kilcher, "Zur Tracht und Beigabensitte im keltischen Gräberfeld von Münsingen-Rain (Kt. Bern)," *Schweizerische Zeitschrift für Archäologie und Kunstgeschichte* 30 [1973]: 26–39, esp. 37), in order to assess the proportion of warrior graves correctly.

31. The anecdotes of Polybius (2. 33), and Plutarch (Camillus 41. 4) on bending Celtic swords are well known. Wrought iron swords were summarized recently by Radomír Pleiner ("K otázce jakosti keltských zbraní . . . ," *Archeologické rozhledy* 26 [1974]: 461–67, with bibliography). For reports of analyses of La Tène swords, see A. Reggiori and C. Carino, "Esame tecnologico di un gruppo di spade galliche de la Lombardia nord-occi-

dentale," *Sibrium* 2 (1955): 43–55; H. H. Coghlan, "A Note upon iron as a material for the Celtic sword," *Sibrium* 3 (1956/57): 129–42; Albert France-Lanord, "La fabrication des épées de Fer Gaulosies," *Revue d'histoire de la sidérurgie* 5 (1964): 315–27; Ernst-Hermann Schulz and Radomír Pleiner, "Untersuchungen an Klingen eiserner Latène-schwerter," *Technische Beiträge zur Archäologie* 2 (1965): 38–51; Louis Lepage and Francis Claisse, "Une épée de La Tène II trouvée à Saint-Dizier (Haute Marne)," *Revue archéologique de l'est et du Centre-Est* 18 (1967): separatum; O. Taffanel and J. Taffanel: Les épès à sphères de Cayla et Mailhac (Aude)," *Gallia* 25 (1967): 1–10; Joachim Emmerling, "Die metallographische Untersuchung der Schwertklingen aus Münsingen," *Jahrbuch des Bernischen historischen Museums in Bern* 47/48 (1967/68): 147–90; Joachim Emmerling, "Metallkundliche Untersuchungen an latènezeitlichen Schwertern und Messern," *Alt-Thüringen* 13 (1975): 205–330; J. N. McGrath, "A report on the metallurgical examination of five fragmentary Early Iron Age sword blades from Llyn Cerrig Bach, Anglesey," *Bulletin of the Board of Celtic Studies* 22, pt. 4 (1968): 418–25; Massimo Leoni, "Tradizione e realta' delle spade galliche," *Sibrium* 22 (1973/75): 105–25.

32. The excellent qualities of Celtiberian swords are celebrated by Philo (*Mechaniké syntaxis* 4. 71) and by Diodorus (5. 34). For transactions with arms on behalf of Hannibal see Polybios 3. 49.

33. René Wyss, "Belege zur keltischen Schwertschmiedekunst," in *Provincialia* (Festschrift for Rudolf Laur-Belart, Basel) Stuttgart (1968): 664–80, esp. 670. Here the passage of Diodorus containing the remark of the rusting of weak parts of buried iron is explained as an allusion to the plastic etching technique. Primitive pattern-welding has been observed on swords from Cuvio (A. Reggiori and C. Carino, "Easme Tecnologico," fig. 6); Heiligenstein (Ernst-Hermann Schulz and Pleiner, "Untersuchungen an Klingen," p. 44, pls. 11.2, 12.2); Port Nidau (René Wyss, "Belege," pls. 8, 8b) and Llyn Cerrig Bach (J. N. McGrath, "Report," fig. 3).

34. In publishing the sword from Port, Switzerland, inscribed with KORISIOS in Greek letters, René Wyss ("Das Schwert des Korisios," *Jahrbuch des Bernischen Historischen Museums in Bern* 34 [1954]: 201–22) has discussed stamping with dies. Examined swords with stamps were not of exceptional quality (Schulz and Pleiner, "Untersuchungen an Klingen").

35. Caesar, *Bell. Gall.* 3. 21; 7. 22 (iron mines in Gaul in general); Strabo 4. 2. 2 (on Bituriges Cubi and Petrocorii); archaeological evidence from Périgord published recently by Claude Barrière, "A propos de la sidérurgie gallo-romaine en Périgord," *Bonner Hefte zur Vorgeschichte Nr.* (1972/73): 3–11, is of Roman date. For galleries and slag heaps in Languedoc, south of the Massif Central, see Maurice Roumilhac and Suzanne Roumilhac, "La sidérurgie Celtique en Languedoc—fouilles du Roc de la Balme," *Archeologické rozhledy* 21 (1969): 824–25; for Jura Vaudois: Paul-Louis Pelet, *Fer, charbon, acier—une industrie méconnue dans les pays de Vaud* (Lausanne, 1973), p. 206. An unsolved problem is that of British centers. Modern researchers (Tylecote, *Metallurgy*, pp. 209, 211) are skeptical about the systematic exploitation of the Forest of Dean deposits; signs of concentration (slags, furnaces, bars) there are not entirely convincing. But Caesar writes on Celtic iron production in the coastal area (*Bell. Gall.* 5. 12).

36. Siegerland: Discoveries of Otto Krasa and Josef W. Gilles are presented in Gilles's surveys, "Die Grabungen auf vorgeschichtlichen Eisenhüttenplätzen des Siegerlandes . . . ,"

Stahl und Eisen 56 (1936): 252–63; "Neue Ofenfunde im Siegerland," *Stahl und Eisen* 78 (1958): 1200–01. A revision of the rather sketchy dating would be needed. Donaumoos: Results of J. H. Seitz are discussed by Paul Weiershausen, *Vorgeschichtliche Eisenhütten Deutschlands* (Leipzig, 1939), pp. 87–96.

36. Kelheim: Huge iron-pit fields at the oppidum of Michelsberg and elsewhere, published formerly by Paul Reinecke, are medieval. Nonetheless a small portion is of La Tène date (Klaus Schwarz, Heinz Tillmann, and Walter Treibs, "Zur spätlatènezeit-lichen und mittelalterlichen Eisenerzgewinnung auf der südlichen Frankenalb bei Kel-heim," *Jahresbericht des Bayerischen Bodendenkmalpflege* 6/7 [1965/66]: 62).

37. Tacitus on Cotini: *Germania* 43 (*quo magis pudeat et ferrum effodiunt*). The homeland of that tribe has been much discussed. Sub-Tatran smelting sites are connected with the so-called Púchov culture. For the most ancient (La Tène) sites in the Holy Cross Moun-tains, see Bielenin, *Starożytne górnictwo i hutnictwo*," pp. 56–57. For the East Carpathians, see V. I. Bidzilja, "Z istorii černoj metallurgii karpatskogo uzgirja rubežu našoj ery," *Archeologija Kyiv*, no. 24 (1970): 32–47.

38. Alois Ohrenberger and Kazimierz Bielenin, "Ur- und frühgeschichtliche Eisen-verhüttung auf dem Gebiet Burgenlands," *Burgeländische Forschungen*, Sonderheft 3 (Eisenstadt, 1969), pp. 79–93. See also the papers read at the occasion of the International Symposium "Archäologische Eisenforschung in Europa," Eisenstadt, 1975, Burgenländ-lisches Landesmuseum and Comité pour la sidérurgie ancienne de l'UISPP, in press.

39. The quality of the iron produced in Noricum is cited by Roman authors of the early Imperial period (Pliny, *Hist. nat.* 34. 41; Petronius, *Sat.* 70. 3; also in the poetry). Summary articles on Noricum are by H. Malzacher, O. Schaaber, H. Vetters, K.-H. Naumann, and H. Straube, in *Beiträge zur Geschichte des Eisens im alpenländischen Raum* (Düsseldorf, 1965); Hermann Vetters, "Ferrum Noricum," *Anzeiger der Oesterreichischen Akademie der Wissenschaften*, Phil.-hist. Klasse 103 (1967): 167–85; and Harald Straube, "Beitrag zur antiken Stahlerzeugung im Raume Kärnten," *Radex-Rundschau* 2 (1973): 479–98; for trade inscriptions see Rudolf Egger, *Die Stadt auf dem Magdalensberg, ein Grosshandelplatz* (Vienna, 1961). The exploitation of Alpine iron ore deposits increased in the period of Roman occupation, as seen from epigraphical and archaeological sources.

40. Discussion on the bloomery process can be found in Eberhard Schürmann, "Die Reduktion des Eisens im Rennfeuer," *Stahl und Eisen* 78 (1958): 1297–1308; R. F. Tylecote, N. I. Austin, and A. E. Wraithe, "The Mechanism etc."; Bernhard Osann, *Rennverfahren und Anfänge der Roheisenerzeugung* (Düsseldorf, 1971); and of the Bloomery Process in Shaft Furnaces, *Journal of the Iron and Steel Institute* (1971): 342–63. *Die Versuchschmelzen und ihre Bedeutung für die Metallurgie des Eisens und dessen Geschichte*, ed. Walter Ulrich Guyan, Radomír Pleiner, and Renata Fabešová (Schaffhausen and Prague, 1973).

41. H. R. Schubert, *History of the British Iron and Steel Industry* (London, 1957), pp. 19–20:, T. H. K. Penniman, I. M. Allen, and Anthony Wootton, "Ancient Metallurgical Furnaces in Great Britain to the End of Roman Occupation," *Sibrium* 4 (1958/59): 97–127, esp. 104, 121. In isolated contexts, the bloomery hearth survived up to A.D. 19th century in Europe. The mechanism of the process was reconstructed by a series of trial smelts (see E. J. Wynne and R. F. Tylecote, "An Experimental Investigation into Primitive Iron-smelting Technique," *Journal of the Iron and Steel Institute* [1958]: 339–48).

42. The slag pit furnace has been described by Radomír Pleiner, *Základy*, and "Die

Eisenverhüttung in der "Germania Magna" zur römischen Kaiserzeit," *45. Bericht der Römisch-Germanischen Kommission 1964* (1965): 12–86. On its geographical spread see Olfert Voss, "Jernudvinding i Danmark i forkistorisk Tid," *Kuml 1962* (1964); Kazimierz Bielenin, "Dymarski piec szybowy (typu kotlinkowego) w Europie starozytnej," *Materiały Archeologiczne Kraków* 14 (1973): 5–102; and R. F. Tylecote, "The Pit-type Iron-smelting Shaft Furnace: Its Diffusion and Parallels," *Early Medieval Studies* 6 (1973): 42–47. Recently, K. Bielenin recognized this type in Burgenland (Langenthal and so forth) as stratigraphically older than Celtic domed furnaces; the publication is being prepared. This type of furnace was adopted by Teutonic tribes of the so-called Germania Libera and was in use in Bohemia until the 6th century A.D. Late examples were observed at Gotland, in England (Aylsham and so on), and in France (Lavardin).

43. Switzerland: Pelet, *Fer*, pp. 54–55; Germany: results of Krasa, Scheuthle, and Seitz are discussed by Weiershausen, *Vorgeschichtliche Eisenhütten*, pp. 5–34, 68–70, 87–96, and Josef Wilhelm Gilles, "Neue Ofenfunde"; for Burgenland see Alois Ohrenberger and Kazimierz Bielenin, "Ur- und frühgeschichtliche Eisenverhüttung."

44. Experimental smelts in the Engsbach furnace were carried out by Josef Wilhelm Gilles, "Versuchschmelze in einem vorgeschichtlichen Rennofen," *Stahl und Eisen* 78 (1958): 1690–95; he smelted about 18 kg iron (about 22% of the content in the used ore). Trial smelts, due to a lack of experience, rarely reproduce the real yield of prehistoric smelters. Here we consider rather the volume of the furnace.

45. Heinz Behaghel, "Eine Eisenverhüttungsanlage der Latènezeit im Oppidum auf dem Michelsberg bei Kelheim, Donau," *Germaina* 24 (1940): 111–18.

46. Pleiner, *Základy*, pp. 98–123.

47. Gradiştea: Constantin Daicoviciu et al., "Santierul Gradiştea Muncelului," *Studii şi cercetari de istorie veche* 4 (1953): 153–219; Negri Bacău: Iulian Antonescu, "Depozitul de obiect de fier di comuna Negri- Bacău şi implicaţile sale istorice," *Carpica* (1968): 189–97 (examined by M. Marciu); Oniceni: Mircea Babeş, "Récentes découvertes de dépôts des lingots en fer protohistoriques faites en Roumanie," *Archeologické rozhledy* 22 (1970): 608; Piatra Craivii: Volker Wollmann, "Une loupe de fer de Piatra Craivii," *Archeologické rozhledy* 22 (1970): 353–54; Poiana: Jerzy Piaskowski, "Examenul metalografic al unor obiecte antice de fier de la Poiana şi Popeşti din epoca Latène," *Materiale şi cercetari archeologice* 10 (1973): 87–95.

48. Barry Cunliffe, "The Late Iron Age Metalwork from Bulbury, Dorset," *Antiquaries Journal* 52, no. 2 (1972): 293–308; Franz Fischer, *Der spätlatènezeitliche Depot-Fund von Kappel (Kreis Saulgau)* (Stuttgart, 1959).

49. Martha Taus, "Ein spätlatènezeitliches Schmied-Grab aus St. Georgen ...," *Archaeologia Austriaca*, no. 34 (1963): 13–16; Rudolf Moschkau, "Eisernes Gebrauchsgerät der Spät-Latènezeit als Grabfund von Leipzig-Thekla," *Ausgrabungen und Funde* 7 (1962): 83–88; I. Dąbrowshe and K. Dąbrowshi, *Cmentarzysko z okresów póznolateńskiego i wpływów rzymskich w Wesólkach, pow. Kalisz* (Warsaw, Wrocław, Cracow, 1967).

50. Blacksmithing activities at Bibracte in the valley of Come Chaudron (Joseph Déchelette, *Manuel d'archéologie préhistorique, celtique et gallo-romaine*, 2d ed. [Paris, 1927], vol. 4, p. 1049; smelting furnaces described by Bulliot and by Déchelette are not documented and so are not discussed; at Manching, two concentrations of blacksmith's tools and waste products were discovered during the campaign of 1961 (Gerhard Jacobi, *Werkzeug und Gerät*, pp. 262–68).

51. The manufacture of iron fibulae involves the fine work of winding and forming wire (Hans Drescher, "Die Herstellung von Fibelspiralen," *Germania* 33 [1955]: 340–49). Metallographical examination shows that the material was usually hot formed of soft wrought iron wire. From 16 fibulae investigated in Poland only one was made of un-homogeneously carburized steel (Jerzy Piaskowski, "Metaloznawcze badania zapinek celtyckich znalezionych na ziemiach Polski," *Archeologia Polski* 15 [1970]: 387–417). The spiral spring was eventually submitted to secondary carburization for elasticity (Radomír Pleiner, analyses of three fibulae from a Závist oppidum, not yet published). No traces of cold work remained. Presumably, ready-made fibulae were heated during the process of browning against corrosion.

52. The initial research work was done by Hans Hanemann, "Metallographische Untersuchung einiger altkeltischer Eisenfunde von der Steinsburg," *Prähistorische Zeitschrift* 13/14 (1922): 94–98, who metallographically investigated a set of implements from the Steinsburg oppidum. He detected the use of wrought iron and hard steels, and mar-quenching. Detailed commentaries on the structures are not present in his reports. Recently, a large collection from the same site was examined by Reinhard Spehr, "L'examen métallographique des objects de fer trouvés à l'oppidum de la période de La Tène à Kleiner Gleichberg [Thuringie]," *Archologické rozhledy* 20 (1968): 526; and Spehr, "Rolle." It is not yet fully published but Dr. Spehr kindly provided the necessary information for compiling table 11.4, for which I am much indebted. For implements from Stradonice, Bohemia, and the technology of those areas see Pleiner, *Staré evropské kovářství* ... , pp. 64–101, 261–65. A few analyses were published by Gabriel Chapota, *Le matériel de La Tène III trouvé sur la Colline de Sainte-Blandine—Vienne Gauloise* (Lyon, 1970), p. 90. Some objects from the northeast Celtic peripheral zone (Nowa Cerekwia, Stradów) are published by Jerzy Piaskowski ("Badania technologii przedmiotów żelaznych na Pomorzu Zachodnim ...," *Metalurgia* 17 [1971]: 131–60; "Sprawozdania z metaloznawczych badań przedmiotów żelaznych z póżnolateńskiego cmentarzyska w Stradowie etc.," *Sprawozdania Archeologiczne* 23 [1971]: 215–38; and "Metaloznawcze badania przedmiotów żelaznych z Sobociska, Nowej Cerkwi i Kościelisk," *Sprawozdania Archeologiczne* 25 [1973]: 151–72).

53. Radomír Pleiner, "Die Eisenverhüttung ... " Linguistic research confirms that many Teutonic or ancient German terms connected with the metallurgy of iron were loan words from Celtic, (Helmut Birkhan, *Germanen und Kelten bis zum Ausgang der Römerzeit* [Vienna, Graz, and Cologne, 1970]).

The Iron Age in Western Iran

VINCENT C. PIGOTT

The development of iron metallurgy is without a doubt a significant step in the technological development of civilizations. This chapter attempts to evaluate the nature of the transition to iron metallurgy in one particular region of the ancient world, western Iran. A satisfactory understanding of the transition depends upon the scope of the archaeological, metallurgical, and geological information at hand. It is only by establishing a broad data base concerning the ancient cultures involved that an adequate understanding of the significance of such a major technological innovation can be interpreted. Here the archaeological and metallurgical data are reviewed in an attempt to establish the conditions under which the change occurred and to evaluate the significance of the change within this particular region. Only when scholars from a variety of disciplines concerned with archaeometallurgy have amassed comparable bodies of data from various regions of the world can generalizations be made on the nature impact of such a technological transition.

Western Iran lends itself especially well to such an investigation. It is an area that is well defined geographically, comparatively well researched archaeologically, and important metallurgically. The Zagros Mountains as well as the great central deserts of Iran provided ancient metalworkers with a variety of ores. Western Iran's geographical position was critical to ancient trade networks linking Central and South Asia with the Caucasus, Anatolia, Mesopotamia, Syria-Palestine, and beyond. Moreover, during the past 25 years, a great deal of archaeological research has been done in Western Iran, making it particularly appropriate for an anthropological interpretation of the role of ancient metallurgy. In this area the transition from bronze to iron metallurgy occurred at the end of the 2d and beginning of the 1st millennium B.C. A number of excavations have been carried out on occupations and graves from this time span. Most important, a well-established chronological framework with which to document the sequential development of the metallurgical traditions of iron-working is now available.

Archaeologists working on the prehistory of Iran have defined a major cultural change occurring in western Iran during the second half of the 2d millennium B.C. At this time a new complex of traits appears. It is widespread throughout the region and continues with some variation into the mid-1st millennium B.C. This complex includes a characteristic gray pottery which replaces the earlier prehistoric pottery throughout the region, the gradual appearance of iron, extramural cemeteries, and the presence of fortifications (although this final point is subject to some debate).[1] The suddenness of this transition and its broad spread over what had been up to that point a variety of regional Bronze Age cultures have led to a great deal of speculation. To this day the most convincing hypothesis is one proposed by Young. He suggests that during this period tribes of Iranians migrated down into western Iran from the east.[2] Charles Burney, on the other hand, has suggested that the tribes might have come from the north.[3] It is thought that these peoples brought with them advanced skills in ceramics and metallurgy and introduced them among the native populations. Although still far from being conclusive, these arguments have prevailed in discussions of the Iron Age in western Iran.

The period in question was labeled the Iron Age and was subdivided into three periods distinguished by changes in the configuration of the complex of defining artifacts. The original definition of each of these periods was strictly cultural, based on changes witnessed within the assemblages. Each area within western Iran underwent change at different times and it soon became apparent that a strictly chronological periodization of the Iron Age was necessary. Rather than establish a new sequence, the terms *Iron I*, *Iron II*, and *Iron III* came to be used chronologically. The dates of each of these periods were taken from the dates of the actual cultural changes from which it had been defined in the archaeologically well-studied reion of western Azerbaijan. In this manner, Iron I encompasses the period from ca. 1450/1350 to 1100 B.C., Iron II from ca. 1100 to 800 B.C., and Iron III from ca. 800 to 550 B.C.[4] The change from cultural to chronological periods has caused some confusion in the literature and therefore it is still necessary to define the usage in each individual work. For ease of description and comparison of the various areas within western Iran, the terms Iron I, II, and III will be used strictly as chronological indicators.

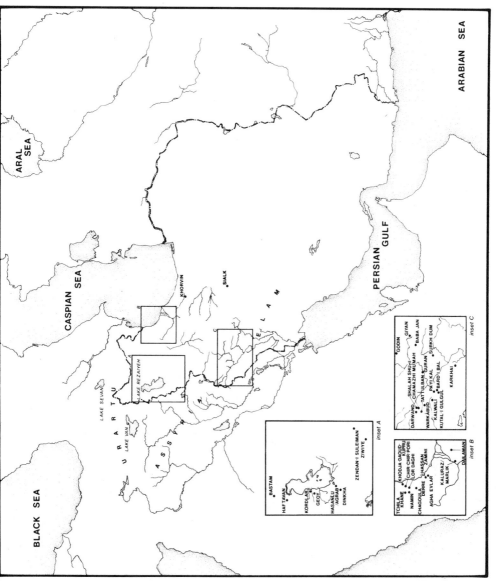

Fig. 12.1. Map of Major Excavated Iron Age Sites in Western Iran. Inset A, West Azerbaijan and Kurdistan; inset B, Talysh and Gilan; inset C, Luristan.

Nevertheless, the goal here is an understanding of the cultural changes occurring. It is believed that research into one aspect of the cultures being discussed, their metallurgical traditions, can offer insight into the nature of the changes occurring and can help to clarify the actual homogeneity of the new metallurgical innovation across the various areas as well as the abruptness with which it comes about. In this manner hypotheses as to the influx of new peoples and the skills of indigenous craftsmen can be evaluated.

First a brief outline of the evidence for the earliest iron during the Iron I period is presented.[5] Then a detailed account of the context and nature of the iron artifacts of Iron II and III provenience is presented area by area. Finally the information is summarized in an attempt to establish a coherent picture of the nature of the development of iron metallurgy in western Iran. The relevance of this transition to hypotheses concerning culture change within protohistoric Iran can then be evaluated.

THE EARLIEST IRON

The evidence for the appearance of metallic iron in the initial period of the Iron Age (Iron I, ca. 1450/1350–1100 B.C.) is so scarce as to be almost nonexistent. In western Azerbaijan, the site of Hasanlu (see fig. 12.1) has provided a single iron finger ring from a Hasanlu V (Iron I) grave.[6] Additional relevant iron of a potential Iron I date comes from another site not far from Hasanlu, Geoy Tepe. However, the dating of the levels of this site is too imprecise to permit an accurate assessment of the chronological significance of the smelting scoria excavated there.[7] Whatever its date, the Geoy evidence is metallurgically important as it has been analyzed and has been shown to consist of iron slag and partially smelted hematite ore. Exactly what sort of smelting was being done is not clear.

Some distance to the south and east of Azerbaijan in what today is known as Central, or Tehran, province lies the site of Sialk with two Iron Age necropoli, Sialk A and B. From grave 4 in the Iron I A necropolis came a single iron dagger and an iron punch.[8] This is the only grave containing iron in the 15-grave necropolis located several hundred meters from the later B necropolis. The ceramics in the grave do associate with ceramics from other A necropolis graves and thus the 2 iron artifacts in this necropolis come from a reliable Iron I context. The possibility may exist that grave 4 was among the later graves laid down in the A necropolis at Sialk.[9]

To the southwest of the central province, in the province of Luristan, Tepe Giyan level I[3] grave 23 yielded an iron dagger dated to the final quarter of the 2d millennium B.C.[10] The date of this iron artifact is also controversial. Young suggests the possibility that grave 23 might be intrusive and of later date although this cannot be demonstrated conclusively.[11]

In addition to Giyan two other sites in Luristan deserve mention. The ornamental iron artifacts from the sites of Bard-i Bal and Pa-yi Kal could be dated to ca. 1100 B.C., late Iron I, on the basis of in situ association with bronze lappet-flange daggers and spike-butted axes, which have inscribed counterparts in personal and museum collections.[12] However, this type of dating by association is not precise enough to allow certainty, as the inscribed artifacts have a longevity greater than just the 11th century B.C.

The above-mentioned Iron I sites offer scant evidence for the pre-1000 B.C. presence of iron in western Iran. Even if the dating of this iron were more secure, one could hardly consider its presence a harbinger of what was soon to come in the Iron II period.

During the Iron II period (ca. 1000–800 B.C.) iron was characteristically present in the settlements and graveyards of western Iran. Iron artifacts now occur at almost every major excavated site. In fact, amid the "development of regionalism and the disappearance of cultural uniformity which marked the Iron I period" it has been suggested that some form of common metallurgical tradition might have been in evidence among certain sites of this period.[13] The presence of gray pottery persists during this period as does the practice of extramural burial. Whether major fortifications characterize this period remains unclarified.[14]

Young has documented the above-mentioned development of regionalism during the Iron II period at sites such as Hasanlu, where gray ware pottery shapes and the "Burned Building" architecture of the citadel as well as some metal artifacts such as bimetallic spear points unique to the site appear. Assyrian and Urartian influence notable at Hasanlu is less apparent south of Azerbaijan whereas cultural traits distinctive to individual sites appear also at Sialk and Giyan. Young suggests that in Iron II "each site represents something of an entity in itself."[15]

In his theory of Iranian tribal migration into the Zagros Young hypothesizes as to why this development of regionalism might have occurred:

[As] carriers of that culture now widely distributed over Western Iran increasingly lost contact in time and space with their common cultural origin and with each other, it was only reasonable that regional variation on that common base should have developed in a natural evolutionary process even without the spur of foreign stimulus. Finally and perhaps most important of all, much of the cultural breakup which characterized Iron II times can probably be traced to indigenous influences which were at first masked by the new Iron I culture but which were undoubtedly not totally lost. In time, these native traditions would reassert themselves and have a considerable modifying effect on the new culture introduced in the Iron I period. . . . Regional variation in Iron II times can be attributed to new and renewed but less sweeping foreign contacts, to natural cultural evolution and to an indigenous cultural revival."[16]

In the midst of the regional variation, however it might have happened, came iron's floruit.

Following Iron II, during the Iron III period (ca. 800–550 B.C.), iron continued its exponential growth. Plain buff pottery, sometimes painted or incised, became the predominant ware, with the gray pottery fading out of use. But this is seen as a gradual transition rather than as a radical shift. Thus there is continuity between the Iron II and III periods. Extramural burial continues and several sites now are fortified. The settlement pattern in western Iran broadens considerably during Iron III with a widespread homogeneity in ceramics and material culture in general, similar, Young suggests, to conditions in Iron I times.[17]

The following is a review of the evidence of iron metallurgy during the Iron II and III periods in each of the various areas of western Iran. The aim is to document the appearance of early iron and evaluate the nature of the transition from bronze to iron metallurgy.

IRANIAN TALYSH

The iron from this northeastern area of Azerbaijan comes from a number of graves in scattered cemeteries excavated by Henri and Jacques de Morgan in 1901. In 1948 Claude Schaeffer assessed the Talysh material.[18] More recently Roger Moorey has suggested that Schaeffer's proposed chronology for the Talysh material should be lowered by about two centuries.

The nature of the necessary adjustments may best be stated by examining the date of the transitional phase from bronze to iron

Table 12.1. Iranian Talysh: Iron Age II Graves

Weaponry		Personal ornament		Tools/implements etc.	
Agha Evlar					
Sword	I	Ring	I	Knives	12
bimetallic	I			Ax	I
Daggers	2			Bit	I
Spearpoints	6			Chopper	I
Arrowpoint	I			Mirror	I
Macehead	I			Buckle	I
hematite					
Chagoula Derre					
Swords	#	Bracelet	I		
Swords				Knives	3+
bimetallic	2			Hook	I
Daggers				Points	#
bimetallic	3				
Spearpoints	8+				
Namin					
Blade					
Khodja-Daoud-Küprü					
Spearpoints and other iron artifacts					
Chir Chir-Pori					
Sword	I			Knife	I

Sources: Schaeffer, *Stratigraphie* (1948), *Agha Evlar:* [sword] p. 440, fig. 237, no. 16; [daggers] pp. 440, 441; [spearpoints] pp. 440, 441; [arrowpoint] p. 439, fig. 237, no. 8; [macehead] p. 440, fig. 236, no. 28; [ring] p. 440; [knives] p. 439; [ax] p. 440, fig. 237, no. 29; [chopper] p. 440; [mirror] p. 441; [buckle] p. 440. *Chagoula Derre:* [swords] p. 434, fig. 232, nos. 1, 12; [daggers] pp. 433–34, fig. 232, nos. 3, 4, 11; [spearpoints] p. 434, fig. 232, nos. 15, 16; [bracelet] p. 433; [knives] p. 434; [hook] p. 430; [points] p. 434. *Namin* p. 418. *Khodja-Daoud-Küprü* p. 419. *Chir-Chir-Pori* p. 439.

metallurgy, dated by Schaeffer [Talyche Fer I]. De Morgan had suggested from ca. 900–400 B.C., Hančar ca. 1000–900 B.C. for this phase.

Schaeffer himself points out many typological links between the artifacts of Georgia (Trialeti), Russian Armenia (Levlar) and Talish at the outset of the Iron Age. In the central Caucasus the earliest stage in the appearance of iron metallurgy is now attributed to the eleventh and the tenth centuries B.C.; .... As more evidence accumulates in the Caucasian region it seems less and less likely that full scale iron production, of tools and weapons like those reported from Talish, began much before the tenth century B.C.[19]

The iron artifacts from the Talysh graves therefore probably date to the early Iron II period. These artifacts seem to derive mostly from Late Bronze Age graves that were reutilized in Iron Age times. The Talysh iron consists primarily of weaponry such as daggers and spearpoints (see table 12.1). Bimetallic daggers are found with bronze hilts having been cast-on to iron blades among these weapons.[20] This technique of casting-on appears to be characteristic of the Iron II period in western Iran and is representative of a technology in which iron is being worked as well as bronze.[21]

In the Talysh and northern Azerbaijan only half the story of iron metallurgy is available because the evidence from Transcaucasia proper has yet to be coordinated adequately with the Iranian evidence. Because this region is in a critical location between areas for which a substantial amount of archaeological evidence is available, the Talysh evidence should be reviewed again incorporating data from Transcaucasia and western Iran. Metallurgical analyses could possibly reveal technological innovations and influences within this region, which has long been considered a cultural backwater during protohistoric times.

GILAN

Four sites in Gilan had graves with iron artifacts. Excavations from the site of Kaluraz are as yet unpublished and although iron is present nothing is known about it.[22] The other three excavated sites, Marlik, Ghalekuti, and Lasulkan, have iron artifacts which have been reported.

At the site of Marlik, among the contents of 53 excavated tombs there were at least 3 iron artifacts: a punch or rock wedge, a spearpoint, and an iron dagger with a bronze hilt.[23] (see table 12.2) The excavator, Ezat O. Neghaban, dates the complex of tombs to the late 2d and early 1st millennium B.C.[24] R. F. Tylecote, who undertook the metallographic analysis of the 3 iron artifacts, suggested a date of ca. 1000 B.C. on the basis of comparison with a punch from the Sialk A necropolis dated to about that time. [25] The presence of a bimetallic dagger suggests that this iron dates to the early 1st millennium. The production of bimetallic artifacts is seen to be an Iron II development on the basis of artifacts from

Table 12.2. Gilan

Weaponry		Personal ornament		Tools/implements etc.	
Marlik: Iron Age II graves near occupation site					
Dagger				Punch or rock wedge	
bimetallic	I				
Spearpoint	I				
Dailaman vicinity					
Ghalekuti: Iron Age II or III graves					
Daggers	5	Bead	I	Knives	3
Spearpoint	I			Tube	I
				Butt end	I
Lasulkan: Iron Age II or III graves					
Sword	I				
Spearpoint	I				

Sources: Tylecote, *JHMS* (1972), Marlik: [dagger spearpoint, punch/rock wedge] pp. 34–35; Namio Egami, Shinji Fukai, and Seiichi Masuda, *Dailaman* I (Tokyo, 1965), Ghalekuti: [daggers] p. 68, pls. LI-11–LI-13, p. 70 pls. LXXXVI-92, LXXXVI-94; [spearpoint] p. 70, pl. LXXVI-93; [bead] p. 71, pl. LXXV-85; [knives] p. 69, pls. LXVIII-37, LXVIII-38, p. 72, pl. LXVIII-10; [butt end] p. 72, pl. LXVIII-11; *Lasulkan*: [sword] p. 73, pl. Xca-5, [spearpoint] p. 73, pl. Xca-6.

dated western Iranian contexts. The scarcity of iron at Marlik, only 3 pieces, suggests that most of the graves there were earlier in date.

The analyses done by Tylecote indicated low-carbon "steel" in the dagger and spearpoint most probably not homogeneously or intentionally carburized. The punch had an inconsistently high hardness reading, which Tylecote suggested might be due to high phosphorous content in the metal.[26] If this punch were in fact a rock wedge, such hardness could have facilitated the work to which it was put.

The excavators of the iron artifacts from the 14 graves at Ghalekuti and the 3 graves at Lasulkan in Gilan believe that the artifacts are pre-Achaemenid in date and thus should placed in the first half of the 1st millennium B.C.[27] From Ghalekuti, 4 graves provided about 13 artifacts, mostly weapons. Within the grave chambers, only bronze weaponry was found whereas the immolation burials outside the chambers contained both bronze and iron weapons.[28] At Lasulkan 2 iron artifacts, a sword and spearpoint, came from the fill of stone circle IV.[29]

Gilan's relative isolation on the Caspian littoral may have impeded its

Table 12.3. West Azerbaijan:

Geoy Tepe: Iron Age I (?), II (?) and later (?): occupation site

Smelting debris		*Artifacts*	
Iron slag	Pre-Iron I	"Cast" iron sheet	Iron I or II
Hematite partially smelted	Iron I	Weapon fragment	Iron II or later
Hematite ore	Iron I		
Iron slag	Late Iron I or Early Iron II		
Iron slag and magnetite ore	Iron II or later		

Dinkha Tepe: Iron Age II graves in occupation site

Weaponry		*Personal ornament*		*Tools/implements etc.*	
Dagger	1	Pins	24	Knives	5
Spearpoints	3	Bracelets	13	Ax	1
Macehead (?)	1	Rings	23	shaft hole	1
Archer's rings	6			Bit	1
				Pin-hooks	2
				Chain	#
				Stud	1
				Needle	1
				Point	1

Agrab Tepe: Iron Age III small fortress

Spearpoint	1			Knife	1
Arrowpoints	21			Ax	1
				shaft hole	1
				Ferrule/plowshare (?)	1

Haftavan Tepe: Iron Age II graves

Pins	2
Bracelets	4
Beads	#

Table 12.3. (cont'd)

Haftavan Tepe: Iron III occupation site

Spearpoint	1
Arrowpoints	8

Hasanlu: Iron Age II occupation site and graves

Weaponry and armor

Swords	47
bimetallic	22
Dagger (B)	1
Spearpoints	408
bimetallic	11
Spear shaft fragments	64
bimetallic	
Pikes	10
Spear butts (?)	5
Points or butts	5
Blades	29
Arrowpoints	685
Quivers (B)	2
Maceheads	5
bimetallic	8
Helmet ear flaps	1
bimetallic	3
Armor scales	3
Objects	3

Personal ornaments

Pins	36
bimetallic	101
Rings	15
Bracelets	39
bimetallic	1
Belts	6
bimetallic	8
Beads	11
Torques	2
Boss/stud	1
Comb (B)	1
Object	1

Decorative ornaments

Bosses/studs	48
bimetallic	66
Plaques	3
bimetallic	21
Sheets	3
Discs	2
Disc plaques	2
Animal figurine (B)	1
Human figurine (B)	1
Object	1

Tools

Sickle blades	90
Knives	86
Celts	19
Wedges	13
Chisels	11
Tools (?)	5
Needles	2
bimetallic	3
Spatulas	4
Spoons	3
Axes	3
Punches	2
Saws	2
Tridents	2
Tweezers	2
Adze	1
Bident	1
Hammer	1
Hoe	1
Ladle	1
Sieve	1
Tongs (?)	1
Objects	2

Equipment

Rings	36
Tubes	19
Snaffle bits	17
bits	15
Nails	1
bimetallic	15
Bars	5
Horse trappings	7
bimetallic	4
Hooks	5
Ingots (?)	4
Handles	3
bimetallic	1
Spikes	3
Rollers	3
Loops	3
Jars (B)	3
Bowls (B)	2
Tripod (B)	1
Pan (B)	1
Mirror	1
Lamp	1
Horse cheekpiece	1
Cosmetic jar	1
Chain and rivet (B)	1
Bell (B)	1
Objects	13

Miscellany

Rods	16
Points	9
Blades	4
Straps	3
Sheets	2
Objects	42

(Continued overleaf)

Table 12.3. (cont'd)

Bastam: Iron Age III occupation site (finds from the ca. 590 B.C. destruction level)

Weaponry		Personal ornament		Tools/implements etc.	
Sword hilt (?)	1	Pins	2	Knives	2
Spearpoint	1			Sickle	1
Lance point	1			Chisel	1
				Pick	1
				Socket	1

Bastam: Iron Age III occupation site (general finds thought to be Urartian)

Personal ornament		Tools/implements etc.	
Bracelet	1	Handles (?)	2
Ring	1	Bladed object	1

Note: (B) denotes that the artifact type is bimetallic.

Sources: Brown, *Azerbaijan* (1951), Geoy: 201–03; Muscarella, *MMAJ* 9 (1974). *Dinkha:* [dagger] B8a, burial 1, pp. 70, 71 fig. 45; [spearpoints] B8e, burial 5, pp. 72, 73 fig. 47; B10a, burial 6, p. 65 fig. 36, p. 67; [macehead] B10a, burial 6, p. 67; [archer's rings] B10b, burial 11, p. 61; B10a, burial 6, p. 65 fig. 36, p. 67; B10a, burial 15, p. 67; B8e, burial 5, p. 72; [pins] B10a, burial 15, p. 67; B8e, burial 5, pp. 72, 74 fig. 48; B8a, burial 1, p. 71; B8a, burial 1, pp. 69–70, 71 fig. 45; B10b, burial 11, p. 61; [bracelets] B8e, burial 5, pp. 72, 74 fig. 48; B8a, burial 1, pp. 68, 70; B9a, burial 9, p. 60 fig. 26; B10a, burial 6, p. 65 fig. 36, p. 67; B10a, burial 12, pp. 67, 68 fig. 39; [rings] B9a, burial 3, p. 75; B9a, burial 9, p. 60 fig. 26; B10a, burial 6, p. 65 fig. 36, p. 67; B10a, burial 13, p. 67; B10a, burial 15, p. 67; B10b, burial 8, p. 68; B8e, burial 5, pp. 72, 74 fig. 48; B10b, burial 8, pp. 68, 69 fig. 43; [knives] B8a, burial 1, pp. 70, 71 fig. 45; B8e, burial 5, pp. 72, 74 fig. 48; B10a, burial 6, p. 65 fig. 36, p. 67; [ax, bit, point] B10a, burial 6, p. 65 fig. 36, p. 67; [pin-hooks] B10a, burial 6, p. 65 fig. 36, p. 67; B8e, burial 5, pp. 72, 74 fig. 48; [chain] B10a, burial 1, pp. 70, 71 fig. 45; [stud] B9a, burial 9, p. 60 fig. 26, p. 61; [needle] B8e, burial 5, p. 72; Muscarella, *MMAJ* 8 (1973): 67 fig. 27; *Agrab.:* [spearpoint] #14; [arrowpoints] #5–13; [knife] #19, [ax] #15; [ferrule/plowshare (?)] #21; *Haftavan:* [pins—area N1, grave 5 Burney, *Iran* 8 (1970): 168 fig. 7; [bracelets—area P1, grave 5, area P2, grave 3] Burney, *Iran* 10 (1972): 135–37 fig. 9; [beads—area P1, grave 2, area P2, graves 3, 4] ibid., pp. 134, 136; [spearpoint, arrowpoints—area/level HX4B] ibid., p. 140. *Hasanlu:* The compilation of the Hasanlu evidence was made from the excavation registry in the Near East Section, University Museum, Philadelphia, Pennsylvania; *Bastam:* Finds from the ca. 590 B.C. destruction level: Hans-Jörg Kellner, *Urartu, Ein Wiederentdeckter Rivale Assyriens* (Munich, 1976): 70–71 #36, 38, 39, 40, 43–45 (hereafter Kellner, *Urartu* 1976). *Bastam:* General finds thought to be Urartian: Wolfram Kleiss, "Ausgrabungen in der urartäische Festung Bastam (Rusaḫinili)," *Archäologische Mitteilungen aus Iran* 5 (1972): 52–53, n. 42 #3, 6–9 (hereafter Kleiss, *Bastam* 1972).

access to iron or iron technology from metalworking centers farther to the west. Only the iron from Marlik has been analyzed. Moreover, the archaeological record of the region is not properly understood, leaving this iron with uncertain dates and no contextual relationships.

WEST AZERBAIJAN

This province of western Iran has the most extensively excavated Iron Age sequence. Moreover, in this region iron is found in contexts other than graves, making it extremely important to interpretations of the function and significance of the metal during the early periods of its development. Occupations of the Iron II and III periods significant to this investigation are found at Geoy Tepe, Kordlar Tepe, Haftavan Tepe, Dinkha Tepe, Hasanlu Tepe, Agrab Tepe, and Bastam (see table 12.3).

The Geoy evidence, as stated earlier, consists mostly of scoria and remains in chronological limbo. One artifact which was analyzed, a piece of sheet metal, proved to be "cast" iron in structure.[30] This is of particular interest since cast iron is not known from elsewhere in the ancient Near East at this time. This fact, combined with Brown's uncertainty as to its exact provenience, relegates this artifact to an enigmatic position.

Excavations at Kordlar Tepe have produced occupations dated to the Iron I/II periods; however, iron artifacts have yet to be discovered in the relevant levels. Lippert, the excavator of Kordlar, sees this as indicative, in part, of Kordlar's isolation.[31]

Haftavan IV (Iron II) produced only iron jewelry, which occurred in the few burials of women. Pins, beads, and bracelets of iron were found in three burials along with bronze jewelry and silver beads. The iron beads found were in necklaces including beads of carnelian, bronze, glass, and frit. On the basis of these grave goods, Burney suggested that iron was restricted to decoration in the Iron II period at Haftavan.[32]

All iron artifacts from the occupation levels of Haftavan III (Iron III), on the other hand, were weapons. A spearpoint with the charred remains of its shaft and 7 arrowheads plus the tang of an eighth came from the destruction level of the Urartian citadel at Haftavan, which was sacked in the late 8th century B.C., Burney suspects, by perhaps Sargon II of Assyria in 714 B.C. or the Cimmerians.[33]

Since the sondage of Sir Aurel Stein at Hasanlu in 1936, ancient iron artifacts were known to come from the Solduz Valley of west Azerbaijan.[34] At Dinkha III (Iron I) located in the adjacent Ushnu Valley, 33 graves were excavated but yielded no iron artifacts, whereas about 10 graves out of 68 from Dinkha II (Iron II) contained approximately 100 iron artifacts.[35] Most of the Dinkha iron grave goods consisted of personal ornaments such as pins, bracelets, and rings but various types of weapons and tools also were found.

It was not until Robert H. Dyson, Jr. began his excavations at Hasanlu in 1957 and after nine seasons of work at that site that a large and diverse collection of iron artifacts became available for study. In approximately 800 B.C. Hasanlu had been destroyed in an attack.[36] The major portion of the 2000-plus iron artifacts from Hasanlu date to the period immediately preceding its destruction, Hasanlu IV (Iron II). What makes the collection of artifacts from Hasanlu so significant, other than its quantity and diversity, is that it provides a rare opportunity to study a full scale assemblage of metal artifacts which are not part of a collection of grave goods but rather make up the tools, weapons, and ornaments of day-to-day existence in the 9th century B.C. citadel.[37]

The balance of iron artifacts from Hasanlu leans heavily in the direction of weaponry in terms of sheer number. Arrowpoints, spearpoints, and dagger/swords are the largest overall categories, with sickle blades, knives, studs, and bosses also numerous. There is also a high incidence of personal ornaments such as pins, bracelets, and rings.

Perhaps most surprising is the diversity of types of artifacts within the Hasanlu collection that are classified as tools and implements. Within the span of the 10th and 9th centuries B.C. Iron Age smiths grasped that iron was a versatile, utilitarian metal capable of performing a variety of tasks. The technology of iron may still have been in its infancy, but its application to various tasks as seen from the Iron II evidence at Hasanlu appears to have been broadening considerably. Among the artifacts from Hasanlu there are a number of bimetallic types, which, as has been suggested, are indicative of a transitional phase in the metallurgy of iron.[38] Iron was being experimented with to see how it could perform in comparison to bronze and to see what range of versatility this new metal actually had.

To date, excavations at Hasanlu have been carried out only on the main citadel of the settlement and in the graveyard. There is some evidence of bronzeworking (most probably crucible melting and casting) in the form of stone molds, crucibles, and related scoria on the citadel mound.[39] There is as yet no certain indication that iron was being either smelted and/or forged on the citadel. Large pieces of an ore of iron, magnetite, were excavated from within the citadel,[40] but it is illogical to assume that smelting might have been going on within the citadel proper what with the heat and smoke associated with such operations. Hasanlu's outer town, which rings the base of the citadel mound, would have been a more logical place to look for metallurgical installations by utilizing methods such as a magnetometer survey to locate subsoil, fire-related, magnetic anomalies.[41]

In 1963, Reed Knox published the initial metallographic study of iron from Hasanlu.[42] Knox determined that in the heavily oxidized iron artifacts from Hasanlu there remained minute fragments of metallic iron and, most significantly, relict carbide, ghost idiomorphs of the original internal structure of the artifact. These ghost idiomorphs indicate that pearlite was present. Pearlite "has a fine lamellar structure and is found in all carbon steels that have been cooled in air from approximately 725° C. It consists of alternate parallel plates of iron and iron carbide (cementite) which are visible microscopically on a polished and etched surface."[43] Through the metallographic study of the remanent idiomorphs Knox demonstrated that one could establish some idea of the internal structure of the iron artifacts and therefore be able to say something concerning the degree of technological sophistication attained at Hasanlu in the 9th century B.C. In many instances, past and present, either heavily oxidized iron artifacts have been discarded or their analytical potential has been ignored by scholars.

In a Hasanlu iron dagger examined by Knox both remanent pearlite and pearlite idiomorphs were found to exist, thus indicating the presence of steel. Two critical questions arise. First, was the dagger steel throughout and second was steel being produced intentionally at Hasanlu?[44]

To answer these questions, metallographic examination of the Hasanlu iron artifacts was resumed by the author at the University of Pennsylvania, under the guidance of Robert Maddin and with the assistance of Reed Knox.[45] The results so far indicate that "steeling" at Hasanlu was not intentional. It seems that the importance of prolonged heating in either the charcoal-stoked smelting furnace or forge was not understood in Iron II times at Hasanlu and most probably throughout the whole

metal-producing region of western Iran. Maddin, in describing the forging of a bloom of iron taken from a smelting furnace not unlike the type
which probably produced iron for Hasanlu, says:

> The initial hammering was done at temperatures around 1050° to
> 1075° C and intermittent reheating to about 800° C was obtained.
> The initial hammering removed a large part of the slag, welded
> grains together, and reproduced a reasonably coherent metal. There
> was certainly no homogeneous product produced but most likely
> the product contained bands varying in composition from wrought
> iron to eutectoid steel. See for example, the surviving iron in a 9th
> century B.C. spearhead from Hasanlu, Iran. . . . It appears reasonable
> to suggest that the continual reheating during the hammering
> operation resulted in carburizing.[46]

In other words, to date, Hasanlu iron artifacts give no indication of having
been uniformly case-hardened and/or steeled throughout by means of
prolonged heating in a charcoal-stoked forge. What carburization is seen
to have occurred in Hasanlu artifacts appears unintentional and is seen
to occur with an inconsistent frequency of distribution.

Cyril Smith has suggested why homogeneous carburization was not
a commonplace occurrence in early iron smelting operations. With
reference to an iron dagger from Hasanlu which Reed Knox had analyzed
metallographically, Smith wrote:

> Although it is unquestionable that the dagger had been made of steel,
> I do not think that there is any evidence that it was made by what
> might be called a carburization process, as you state. Terminology
> is difficult here. What I mean is that there is not any evidence that a
> forged dagger or a semi-fabricated piece of iron was packed in a
> carbonaceous material and heated for a long time to produce deep
> surface carburization by diffusion at temperatures of 1000° C or so.
> This is not the common opinion. The literature first describing real
> cementation is 1130 A.D. (Theophilus), and even then produces only
> very superficial hardening. In *all* structures of old steel that I have
> seen the carbon gradients can most logically be explained by varia-
> tions in carbon content in an original rough spongy lump of metal
> as it came from the refining hearth or, in later pieces, by welding and
> forging together of material of different carbon contents. Before the

16th Century A.D. the carbon was, I think, introduced mostly by short time high temperature treatments in the hearth, perhaps even occasionally involving the momentary presence of small amounts of molten high-carbon cast iron running superficially over the surface and into interstices of the loose and porous sponge. Though your dagger contains about 0.8 percent carbon (or perhaps even a little more) in some places, it has much less in others, and the general distribution of these areas is attributable, I think, entirely to variability in the sponge. There may have been a number of separate irregular chunks welded together but I have the impression that the variation is no more than would result naturally from an irregular lump in the reduction hearth, without conscious separate welding.[47]

Thus evidence at 9th century B.C. Hasanlu suggests that ironworking in western Iran had not crossed the technological threshold to the intentional homogeneous carburization of iron. Only through a systematic program of analysis of well-stratified collections of iron artifacts will we be able to state with some degree of assurance at what points in time major technological transitions such as intentional "steeling" were made in the region of western Iran and for the whole of the ancient Near East.[48]

During the Iron II period, then, in the Solduz–Ushnu valleys at the southern end of Lake Rezaiyeh, iron is found in great abundance in the graves at Dinkha and in the citadel at Hasanlu. Whereas in the same period somewhat farther north along the western shore of the lake, the sites of Geoy Tepe (scoria), Kordlar (no iron as yet), and Haftavan (meager jewelry) provide almost nothing in iron by comparison. Is this scarcity of iron on the western shore simply a result of lack of preservation and/or of the selectivity of excavation? Or, is it conceivable that the western shore sites had a limited access to iron and/or its technology? If this were true, Hasanlu during Iron II might have been producing iron only for itself and its immediate hinterland (Dinkha, for example).

In the Iron III period the picture changes somewhat as most of the sites of the period, Hasanlu IIIB, Agrab, Haftavan III, and Bastam, fall under Urartian hegemony. Here the iron produced is potentially technologically sophisticated but proper analyses of the Urartian materials have not yet been carried out.

Agrab Tepe, a small fort about 3 km southwest of Hasanlu, appears to be of Urartian construction. It seems to have been built shortly after the destruction of the Hasanlu IV citadel. Iron weaponry was excavated here.[49]

The iron from Hasanlu IIIB and the site of Bastam, ancient Rusai-URU·TUR, provide the most substantial collection of Iron III period artifacts. The iron from Hasanlu IIIB has not yet been analyzed. Both these sites, as well as Haftavan III and Agrab Tepe, date to the 7th century B.C.

At Bastam, the German team under the direction of Wolfram Kleiss has excavated the Urartian site and placed its destruction (probably by the Medes) in the first quarter of the 6th century B.C., ca. 590 B.C.[50] The destruction level of the site has produced a small but interesting array of iron artifacts, and some additional iron finds are known from other parts of the site, still of Urartian date.[51]

Among the collection of iron at Bastam there are two particularly interesting pieces. The first artifact is of special symbolic significance as interpreted by Kleiss. This piece is an unusually large iron lance-point (42 cm long × 21.3 cm at its maximum breadth). It was found amid burned debris in a triangular room, possibly a guardroom, near the South Gate. Kleiss sees this lance as an insignia of rank of the gatekeeper which was dedicated to the Urartian "Reichsgott" Haldi.[52] In addition, it has been suggested that the iron portion of the spear now extant may well have served only as a core around which an outer shell of possibly another metal had been formed.[53]

This lance point is of special importance because few iron artifacts of this period can definitely be distinguished as having a ceremonial significance. This is due, for the most part, to their location in nonceremonial, non-text-bearing, protohistoric contexts in western Iran. The only other clearly ceremonial artifacts are those from the foundation deposits in the sanctuary of Surkh Dum in Luristan.

A second intriguing artifact from Bastam, this one utilitarian, is an iron pick (ca. 20 cm × 5 cm square tapering to a point) with a shaft hole.[54] Presumably this pick was used in the extensive cutting in bedrock of wall footings to support the elaborate stone masonry fortifications of Bastam. The Urartian predilection for fortifying mountain tops could well have been facilitated by their development of an iron industry capable of producing intentional steel or, at a minimum, case-hardened cutting tools such as the pick.[55] Furthermore, if such techniques for hardening cutting tools were being applied to Urartian iron weaponry it too would have been of prime quality, highly prized, and extremely effective.[56] It would be premature to suggest that Urartians had gained the knowledge of how to quench-harden the iron they were producing, but on the other hand it would be surprising if the demanding work of stonecutting were being done with wrought iron tools of an unhomogeneously carburized nature.

If the latter situation were the case, the Urartians would have found it necessary to produce substantially large numbers of iron tools and to resharpen them frequently, adding to the rapid rate of exhaustion of such tools. Conceivably in this case the archaeological record would have produced a certain number of such exhausted tools, provided, of course, that they were not being systematically recycled by the smiths. In the end, then, what is needed is a systematic program of metallographic analysis of the artifacts from Bastam, paralleling the studies done on Hasanlu, Marlik, and Luristan artifacts.

Although the Urartian annals make reference to iron in only one instance in which Sarduri II (ca. 760–30 B.C.) inscribed on an iron seal a commemoration of his victory over Qulha (Colchis),[57] the Urartian domain included "iron ore-rich regions around Mus, Bitlis and Van, as well as the mountains west Lake Urmia."[58] Urartu might have had the organizational capabilities, not available to the mosaic of petty principalities which preceded them, for developing an industry on a large scale which could have supplied its work forces and its armies.[59]

At the Urartian site of Toprakkale, ancient Rusaḫinili in eastern Anatolia, early German excavations produced 500–600 iron artifacts in the form of arrowpoints, spearpoints, flange-hilted daggers, swords, large knives, tridents, tethering rings, battle axes, hammers, plowshares, and hooks. At another Urartian site, Karmir Blur, ancient Teišebaini, at Yerevan in the Armenian SSR, archaeologists found iron artifacts comparable to those from Toprakkale and also adzes, rings with clasps for bolting doors, spades, hoes, sickles, axes, saws, equestrian gear, phalerae, candlesticks, and scale armor.[60] Only a few western Iranian sites such as Hasanlu and to a lesser extent sites such as Sialk B, Bard-i Bal, or Chamazi Mumah could come close to equaling similar amounts of iron artifacts even though these latter sites are gravefields and not occupations.

Radomír Pleiner has referred to Urartu as "the key to the early Iron Age in Iran and [the] Caucasus."[61] He suggests that Urartian influence spread to the north, east, and southeast of Urartu carrying with it iron, especially weaponry, and its technology.[62] During the Iron III period in

West Azerbaijan, in Hasanlu IIIB, Bastam, Agrab, and Haftavan III, the Urartian presence appears to have held sway not only politically but also in terms of the technology of iron production. However, the crucial specifics of the role of Urartu in West Azerbaijan are far from having been identified. This research is yet before us.

CENTRAL (TEHRAN)

The two Iron Age sites excavated from this province have provided evidence of iron artifacts from predominantly Iron II contexts. They are the necropoli of Khorvin and Sialk A and B (see table 12.4).

For the Khorvin material Dyson has proposed a potential time span of ca. 1200–700 B.C.[63] His chronology places an amorphous lump of iron from grave 9 at Khorvin later than 1000 B.C.[64] There are also two other artifacts of iron, either small maceheads or large pins, which come from Khorvin but whose exact proveniences and dates are not known.[65]

The controversy regarding the date of the two pieces of iron from Sialk A, Iron I period, has been discussed above. The Sialk B necropolis produced a large collection in graves that cover the time span of Iron II into Iron III.[66] Some 217 graves were excavated, 19 of which contained a total of 84 iron artifacts. A few tool/implements were found but they are far outnumbered by iron weaponry and decorative iron. Bimetallic artifacts exists in the collection although they are few in number.

Among the Iron II artifacts at the Sialk B necropolis several merit individual mention. Unique among the bladed weaponry is one artifact which Ghirshman described as a sword 55 cm long with its pommel still intact. This weapon is unusually long compared to the daggers found at Sialk. Interestingly, Ghirshman maintains that a warrior painted on a B necropolis potsherd carries a sword secured to his waist similar to the one found.[67] Grave 15, in which this unique sword was found, is notable for the quantity of iron found within it, 17 pieces in all.

Among the other iron artifacts found at Sialk B were 4 iron bidents and 1 iron trident. These artifacts also occur frequently in bronze and seem randomly distributed in graves of males and females, rich and poor alike. Ghirshman interprets them as skewers for the grilling of meat rather than as "armes d'apparat" or as indicators of status. He reports that some of the bidents had bones of birds adhering to them, suggesting that they were used in a funerary meal prior to the burial.[68] Such bidents in iron are also known from Hasanlu.

Table 12.4. Central (Tehran):

Weaponry		Personal ornament		Tools/implements etc.	
Khorvin: Iron Age II graves near occupation site					
		Pins	2		
Sialk A: Iron Age I graves near occupation site					
Dagger	1			Punch	1
Sialk B: Iron Age II graves near occupation site					
Sword	1				
Daggers	13	Pins	23	Knives	4
bimetallic	3	Bracelet/anklets	6	bimetallic	1
Sheaths	3	Torques	2	Bidents	4
Arrowpoints	12			Trident	1
Quiver	1			Sickles	2
				Bits	3
				Punches	2
				Bell clapper	1

Sources: Vanden Berghe, *Khurvin* (1964): p. 27–28, 32 pl. XLIII, nos. 311, 312. Also found was an amorphous lump of iron in grave 9, ibid., p. 5; Ghirshman, *Sialk II* (1939), *Sialk A:* [dagger, punch] grave 4, p. 210, pls. V, XXXIX; *Sialk B:* [sword] p. 218, pls. XXVI, LVII; [daggers] grave 74, p. 243, pl. LXXV; grave 15, pp. 218, 233, pls. XXVI, LVII; grave 52, p. 239, pl. LXVIII; grave 62, p. 241, pl. LXXI; grave 76, p. 248, pl. XCII; [daggers, bimetallic] grave 67, p. 218, pl, XXVI; grave 3, pp. 48, 218, pls. XXVI, L; [sheaths] grave 52, p. 239, pl. LXVIII; grave 15, p. 233, pl. LVII; [arrowpoints] grave 3, p. 229, pl. L; grave 15, p. 233, pl. LVII; [quiver] grave 15, p. 233, pl. LVII; [pins] grave 21, p. 234, pl. LIX; grave 84, p. 219, pls. XXVIII, XCIII; grave 53, p. 240, pl. LXIX; grave 31, p. 237, pl. LXIII; grave 61, p. 241, pl. LXX; grave 7, p. 229, pls. LI, LII; grave 123, p. 246, pl. LXXIX; grave 149 (?), p. 249, pl. XCII; grave 52, 239 pl. LXVIII; [bracelet/anklets] grave 78, p. 245, pl. LXXVII; grave 66, p. 243, pl. LXXIII; grave 94, p. 245, pl. LXXVIII; [torques] grave 184, p. 249, pl. XCIII; [knives] grave 21, p. 234, pl. LIX; grave 52, p. 239, pl. LXVIII; grave 15, p. 233, pl. LVII; [knife, bimetallic] grave 74, p. 243, pl. LXXV; [bidents] grave 52, p. 239, pl. LXVIII; grave 15, p. 234, pl. LVII; [trident] grave 15, p. 234, pl. LVII; [sickles] grave 52, p. 239, pl. LXVIII; [bits] grave 52, p. 239, pl. LXVIII; grave 15, p. 232, pl. LVI; [punches] grave 74, p. 243, pl. LXXV; [bell clapper] grave 15, p. 233, pls. LVI, XXV.

From the Central Province, then, Khorvin is significant only inasmuch as it appears to have a small quantity of iron from Iron Age graves at a point significantly farther to the east than the other western Iranian sites, save Sialk. Sialk stands as an Iron Age outpost in the east with its large and diverse collection of iron. It is possible that at least a portion of the iron in the Sialk II graves could be a product of a well-established trade relationship with a production center or centers to the west.[69]

LURISTAN

As with western Azerbaijan, Luristan is a region from which we have
an extensive amount of excavated information relating to the Iron Age.
Excavations at Tepe Giyan, Tepe Guran, and Baba Jan Tepe plus a
number of gravefields recently dug have provided much information
pertaining to the development of iron metallurgy in western Iran (see
table 12.5).

The internal chronology of the site of Giyan, first set down by its
excavators, Contenau and Ghirshman, was later reassessed by Young.[70]
Young has subdivided period I at Giyan into the periods Giyan I⁴–I¹.
Periods I⁴ and I³ fall within the Iron I period in western Iran. Giyan I⁴,
the earliest of these levels, includes graves 59–29 but they contained no
iron.[71] Basing his opinion on ceramic comparisons, Young feels that
"Hasanlu V probably began a little before Giyan I⁴."[72]

Giyan I³ includes graves 28–20. As has been mentioned in the discussion
of the Iron I period, a single tanged iron dagger came from grave 23
dated to the final quarter of the 2d millennium B.C.[73] Giyan I² graves
19–6 are, in Young's assessment, later than Hasanlu V but not so late as
the 8th century B.C., hence of early Iron II date.[74] From this period a single
iron finger ring was found in grave 12. Thus it is not until Iron III, Giyan
I¹ times, that iron is common in Giyan graves.

Giyan I¹ graves 5–1 are believed to date to the 8th century B.C. or later.
Giyan I¹ may well have ended ca. 750–700 B.C. although Young states
that there is the "possibility of a hiatus between the end of Giyan I² and
I¹."[75] It is probable that Giyan I¹ graves 5, 3, and 1 fall into the Iron III
period. Grave 5 yielded 1 broken, tanged iron dagger blade.[76] Grave 3
contained 1 tanged iron dagger blade, 8 laurel leaf-shaped iron arrowpoints, and 2 iron punches.[77] Grave 1 held but a single iron bracelet.

In Young's estimation a significant change has occurred within the
cultural assemblage of the Giyan I¹ period:

> On the whole, the four sub-periods of Giyan I are quite alike in their
> material remains. Two internal developments of importance, how-
> ever, stand out against this background of similarity. First, the
> pedestal-base goblet, popular early in Giyan I, became less common
> and eventually disappeared. This shape accounts for thirty-five per cent
> of the Giyan I⁴ complex, eight per cent of the Giyan I³ complex, and
> sixteen per cent of the Giyan I². It is not found at all in Giyan I¹.

Table 12.5. Luristan:

Weaponry		Personal ornament		Tools/implements etc.	
Tepe Giyan: Iron Age I graves in occupation site					
Dagger	1				
Tepe Giyan: Iron Age II graves in occupation site					
Daggers	2	Ring	1	Punches	2
Arrowpoints	8	Bracelet	1		
Pa-yi Kal–Late Iron Age I (?)/Iron Age II graves					
		Pin	1		
		Rings	7		
		Bracelets	3		
Bard-i Bal: Late Iron Age I (?)/Iron Age II graves					
		Pins	10		
		Rings	10		
		Bracelets	3		
		Rein rings	#		
Bard-i Bal: Iron Age I to Iron Age III graves					
Daggers	2	Pins	6	Knives	3
bimetallic	1	bimetallic	2		
		Rings	31		
		Bracelets	2		
		bimetallic	3		
		Fibula	1		
Bard-i Bal: Iron Age III graves					
Dagger	1	Pins	2	Knife	1
Spearpoint	1	Ring	1	Ax	1
		Fibulae	2		
Kutal-i Gulgul: Iron Age II graves					
Dagger	1	Ring	1	Knife	1
Arrowpoint	1				
Darwand (Sector B): Iron Age II graves					
Arrowpoints	#	Rings	#	Wire	#
		Bracelets	#		
		Anklets	#		
Chamazhi Mumah: Iron Age III graves					
Swords					
bimetallic	14			Figurine	1
Daggers	6				
bimetallic	31				
Arrowpoints	67				
Axes	2				

(Continued overleaf)

Table 12.5. (cont'd)

Weaponry		Personal ornament		Tools/implements etc.	
War Kabud: Iron Age III graves					
Swords				Axes	4
bimetallic	23			Bits	2
Dagger-knives	40			Rings (equestrian)	3
Arrowpoints	135			Indeterminate objects	2
Spearpoints	6				
Shalah Shuri: Iron Age III graves					
Dagger	1			Ax/Adze	1
Arrowpoints	3				
Tepe Kalwali: Iron Age III graves					
Dagger	1	Anklets	2	Knife	1
Arrowpoints	2				
Tepe Tattulban (Chinan): Iron Age III graves					
Swords	2				
Arrowpoints	7				
Baba Jan: Iron Age II/III occupation site					
Arrowpoint	1			Sickle	1
				Nail	1
Baba Jan: Iron Age III occupation site					
Daggers	2				
bimetallic	1			Sickle	1
Spearpoint	1			Knives	3
Arrowpoints	2			Wedge	1
				Chisel	1
				Spatula	1
				bimetallic	
				Hoe	1
				Spade	1
				Bit	1
				Fragment	1
Tepe Guran: Iron III graves in occupation site					
Sword	1	Bracelet	1		
Spearpoint	1				

Surkh Dum: Iron Age II/III sanctuary
10th Century B.C. levels: 5 artifacts
9th Century B.C. levels: 20 artifacts
8th Century B.C. levels: 20 artifacts
7th Century B.C. levels: 97 artifacts

Table 12.5. (cont'd)

Sources: Contenau and Ghirshman, *Giyan* (1935), *Giyan I³:* [dagger] grave 23, p. 22, pl. 12; *Giyan I²:* [ring] grave 12, p. 20, pl. 10; *Giyan I¹:* [daggers] grave 5, p. 19, pl. 9; grave 3, p. 18, pl. 8; [arrowpoints] grave 3, p. 18, pl. 8; [bracelets] grave 1, p. 18, pl. 8; [punches] grave 3, p. 18, pl. 8; Vanden Berghe, *Bard-i Bal* (1973): p. 61, table 6 *Pa-yi Kal:* [pin] grave 1969/5; [rings] graves 1969/2; 1969/5; 1970/2; 1970/6; [bracelets] graves 1970/1; 1970/2; 1970/3; Vanden Berghe, *Bard-i Bal* (1973), *Bard-i Bal (Iron I–II):* [pins] graves 17; 62, p. 49 fig. 11 nos. 64–72, pl. XXIV no. 2; [rings] grave 17, p. 49 fig. 11 no. 76; grave 68, p. 49; [bracelets] grave 17, p. 49 fig. 11 no. 73; [rein rings] grave 17, p. 49; *Bard-i Bal (Iron I–III):* p. 49: [pins] graves 10; 26; [pins, bimetallic] grave 29; [rings] graves 10; 11; 23; [bracelets] graves 59; 44; 29; *Bard-i Bal (Iron III):* p. 49: [dagger] grave 19, p. 49; [spearpoint] grave 54, p. 27 fig. 13 no. 6; [pins] graves 51; 38; [ring] grave 19; [fibulae] grave 57; [knife] grave 54, p. 27 fig. 13 no. 5; [ax] grave 54, p. 27 fig. 13 no. 4; Vanden Berghe, *Kutal-i Gulgul* (1973) *Kutal-i Gulgul:* p. 21 [dagger, arrowpoint], grave A2; [ring, knife] grave A10; Vanden Berghe, *Bard-i Bal* (1973) *Darwand:* p. 69 [arrowpoints] grave 5; [rings, bracelets, anklets] grave 3; [wire] grave 8; Vanden Berghe, *Chamazhi-Mumah* (to be published) [swords, bimetallic] graves 16, 17, 18, 21, 27, 34, 37, 39, 47, 53, 54, 56, 64, 75; [daggers] graves 13, 16, 17, 24, 33, 73; [daggers, bimetallic] graves 2, 3, 7, 10, 15, 21, 22, 24, 26, 30–32, 35, 38, 39, 46, 48, 49, 53–55, 63, 70; [arrowpoints] 2, 17, 18, 21, 26, 31, 32, 35, 37, 39, 46, 48, 49, 53, 54, 56, 63, 64, 70, 73; [axes] graves 39, 73; [figurine] grave 53; Vanden Berghe, *War Kabud* (1968), *War Kabud:* [daggers] grave, p. 167 pl. 27a; [dagger, bimetallic] grave 10, p. 109 fig. 21 no. 7, p. 167 pl. 27b; grave 116, p. 113 fig. 25 no. 7, pp. 119, 167 pl. 27b; grave, p. 167 pl. 27c; [arrowpoints] grave 10, p. 109 fig. 21 no. 8, pl. 27a; grave 116, p. 113 fig. 25 no. 7; grave 106, p. 111 fig. 23 no. 5; [spearpoint] grave, p. 167 pl. 27a; [knife] grave 106, p. 111 fig. 23 no. 6; [ax] grave 106, p. 111 fig. 23 no. 7; Van Loon, *War Kabud* (1972), *War Kabud:* [bit] pp. 67–68; Vanden Berghe, *Bard-i Bal* (1973), *Shalah Shuri:* [dagger, arrowpoints, ax/adze] grave 1, pp. 71, 72 fig. 27, pl. XXXI no. 2; Vanden Berghe, *War Kabud* (1968) *Kalwali:* [dagger] grave, p. 168 pl. 8c; [arrowpoints] grave 12, p. 163; [anklets] grave 12, p. 163, pl. 7c; [knife] grave 12, pp. 163, 105 fig. 19 no. 7; Vanden Berghe, *Phoenix* (1968), *Tattulban (Chinan):* [sword, arrowpoint] grave 4, p. 126–27; Vanden Berghe, *Archaeology* (1971), *Tattulban (Chinan):* [sword] grave 4, p. 265–67; Goff Meade, *Iran 6* (1968), *Baba Jan:* See nn. 83, 86; Thrane, *Archaeology* (1970), *Guran:* [sword, spearpoints] grave 7, pp. 32, 33; [bracelet] grave, p. 32; Van Loon, *Dark Ages* (1967) *Surkh Dum*, p. 24.

Second, except for a single iron spearhead in grave 23 in Giyan I³, no iron objects were found in Giyan I⁴ to I². On the other hand, in Giyan I¹ twenty-nine per cent of all metal objects were made of iron. This marked increase in the use of iron in period I¹, taken with the complete disappearance of the pedestal-base goblet in the same period, indicates that though Giyan I⁴–I² remain difficult to distinguish on internal grounds alone, Giyan I[1] definitely represents a period of significant cultural change.[78]

At Tepe Guran 4 graves were excavated but their chronological relationships are not clear. One grave contained a bronze dagger, 2 bronze vessels (one having a long beaked spout), an iron bracelet, and an iron finger ring on almost every finger of the skeleton in the grave.[79] The spouted vessel suggests an earlier date for the grave, in accordance with Thrane's chronology. "The spouted jug, related to similarly shaped jugs of Sialk level B, should probably be dated to 800–750 B.C."[80] Young would give Sialk IV, which is associated in time with the B necropolis, a range from ca. 1000/900 to 750/700 B.C.[81] This grave would then be of late Iron II date.

A second grave at Guran, grave 7, is judged by Thrane on stratigraphic grounds to be later than the one just mentioned. This grave contained an iron short sword, an iron spearpoint and a pottery beaker. Grave 7 was of a different construction from the previous one. Moreover, Thrane feels that the presence of iron weaponry confirms a later date.[82]

In Luristan the site of Baba Jan yielded 20 artifacts of iron from occupational contexts of the Iron II/III and Iron III periods.[83] Most of these iron artifacts stem from an Iron III squatter's occupation within the ruins of earlier Iron Age buildings on the East Mound. Of special interest among the artifacts from this occupation is a set of probable wood working tools from the carpenter's shop. The wedge, knife, and chisel which make up this tool set demonstrate that by Iron III times iron was supplanting bronze for utilitarian purposes. Furthermore, well-preserved iron tools are rare; this set particularly invites metallographic studies to ascertain which, if any, methods of heat treatment had been applied to the metal by the blacksmith.

Other tools from Iron III Baba Jan include a hoe found with the tool set, paralled at 7th century B.C. Nimrud. A large spade found is comparable to a spade fragment known from Persepolis. The iron sickle blades found are similar to those from Sialk and Hasanlu. Vanden Berghe has excavated from Iron II contexts in the Pusht-i Kuh region of Luristan iron tools wrapped in bronze sheet in a style similar to the Baba Jan spatula.[84] What impact the use of more iron and fewer bronze tools may have had during the Iron III period is a question which remains open at this time.

Iron III weaponry from Baba Jan includes 2 fragmentary daggers with ornamental, parallel midribs running down the centers of their blades. A similar design on iron daggers is known from Hasanlu in the Iron II period. Arrowpoints similar to those from Baba Jan (midribbed) are found at Sialk, in Pusht-i Kuh cemeteries, and at Nimrud.[85]

The manor house yielded but one iron artifact, a snaffle bit from an intrusive (Iron III) horse burial cut into the building at its front entrance. Goff describes the bit thus:

> Although too corroded to allow us to see the details of its construction, it appears to have a twisted, jointed snaffle, circular rein rings, and separate cheek pieces. Whether these were pierced like the rather similar examples from Sialk, Necropolis B, or had small loops attached to the side corresponding to the blobs of corrosion remains uncertain.[86]

Similar bits are known also from Hasanlu.

From the late Iron I period (ca. 1100 B.C.) down into the early Iron III period (ca. 750 B.C.) persons were interred with grave goods of iron in the cemetery of Bard-i Bal in Luristan.[87] Through careful excavation Louis Vanden Berghe has been able to refine the chronological associations of a number of specific graves at this site. A total of 79 artifacts of iron and 10 bimetallic artifacts were found in 17 of the 70 tombs at Bard-i Bal.[88] The 3 graves which Vanden Berghe assigns to the period late Iron I/early Iron II, which were discussed earlier, contain only iron of an ornamental type such as pins, rings, bracelets, and rein rings. The next 9 graves are either of the Iron II or Iron III period. Iron weaponry (daggers) along with knives and ornamental iron are found in these tombs.[89] Five tombs with iron are clearly Iron III in date (ca. 800–750 B.C.). These 5 tombs also have a mixture of weaponry and ornamental iron.[90] Five of the tombs of all the periods contained bimetallic artifacts such as a dagger with its hilt sheathed in bronze, bracelets sheathed in bronze, and iron-shanked pins with bronze heads.[91]

At the gravefield of Pa-yi Kal, 12 graves dated by Vanden Berghe to the end of Iron I and the beginning of Iron II (ca. 1100–900 B.C.) produced about 11 artifacts of ornamental iron. The only weapon recovered from the gravefield was a single bronze dagger, which was associated with ornamental bronze.[92]

Vanden Berghe has recently proposed that iron was unknown in western Luristan during the Iron I period and perhaps most significantly that "new immigrants" were probably responsible for the introduction of iron into Luristan in the Iron II period.[93] Vanden Berghe has been able to show that in reused graves at Kutal-i Gulgul, the Iron II inhumations near the entrance to the graves differ in ceramics and metal artifacts from those inhumations deeper inside the graves. Certain ceramic types do survive from Iron I down into Iron II at Kutal-i Gulgul. With the Iron II inhumations new ceramic types appear and along with these there appears some iron in the form of rings, bracelets, daggers, knives, and arrow-points.[94] It is these new immigrants at approximately the start of Iron II whom Vanden Berghe would see as the bearers of the new ceramics and the iron objects found among the inhumations at the entrances to the tombs at Kutal-i Gulgul. Comparable evidence is said to come also from Bard-i Bal.[95]

Before turning to sites with strictly Iron III materials, we must mention one additional site of Iron II date. Ten tombs were found intact at the Darwand gravefield (sector B). Three of the tombs contained iron objects, rings, open bracelets, anklets, arrowpoints, and a piece of iron wire used as a clasp on a bracelet. Vanden Berghe dates the tombs to the Iron II period (ca. 1000–800/750 B.C.).[96] Perhaps the most interesting artifact here is the piece of iron wire. The production of wire requires specific techniques and thereby specific understanding of materials and their behavior. Iron wire is a decidedly rare occurrence, which may suggest the difficulty involved with its production.

Evidence for iron in the Iron III period from Vanden Berghe's excavations comes from the gravefields at Karkhai, War Kabud, Tepe Kalwali, Shalah Shuri, Tattulban (Chinan), and Chamazhi Mumah.

In the Karkhai gravefield, a simple pit-grave of a woman yielded abundant funerary furnishings: a vase and cup in bronze with hammered decoration, a necklace with 243 beads, hairspirals, silver rings, iron pins with silver-covered heads, an iron button, iron bracelets, and anklets. Also in the tomb was found a glazed pyrix of the late Elamite style like those found at Susa which aided Vanden Berghe in dating this burial to the 8th century B.C.[97]

The gravefield of War Kabud consisted of 200 graves.[98] Of these 200 graves, 66 were found to contain a total of 215 iron artifacts.[99] These iron artifacts included bimetallic swords, dagger-knives, spearpoints, arrowpoints, axes, and equestrian trappings.[100] Van Loon mentions one burial at War Kabud in which "the dead was accompanied by his horse, equipped with iron bit and bronze rein rings."[101] [He goes on to describe other iron found]: "At both sites [Kalwali and War Kabud] iron daggers had crescent-shaped (i.e. widely splayed) hilts. At War Kabud they were occasionally sword sized (ca. 60 cm) and had bronze-mounted hilts. Similarly anklets, while made of iron at Kalwali, occur only in bronze at War Kabud (up to 7 pairs were found on one woman)."[102]

From Tepe Kalwali, 1 dagger, 2 knives, 2 arrowpoints, and 2 anklets all of iron were excavated from 22 graves in this Iron III (ca. 650–600 B.C.) gravefield.[103] Interestingly there were no bronze artifacts in any of these graves.

Two tombs of the Iron III period were found intact by Vanden Berghe at Shalah Shuri. Grave 1 held 1 iron dagger, 3 arrowpoints, and what Vanden Berghe describes as a "hache-herminette" or an ax/adze.[104] This ax/adze, however, resembles more a hammer/adze.

Yet another gravefield, Tepe Tattulban (Chinan), excavated by Vanden Berghe produced 4 Iron III graves dating to ca. 750–700 B.C. Grave 4 contained an iron dagger with bronze on the hilt and 7 iron laurel leaf-shaped arrowpoints.[105] Grave 1 had another iron dagger of similar type to that in grave 4.[106] Similar daggers and arrowpoints come from War Kabud graves.

Chamazhi Mumah, another gravefield excavated by Vanden Berghe, provided some of the largest Luristan collections of carefully excavated iron. Seventy-nine graves yielded a total of 121 iron artifacts.[107] These were overwhelmingly in the weaponry class with 14 swords, 37 daggers, 67 arrowpoints, 2 axes, and 1 figurine (rare in itself). With the exception of the iron figurine, ornamental iron was not found among the graves at this site.

Finally, the last Luristan site to be discussed, Surkh Dum, is not a gravefield but rather a sanctuary site excavated by Erich Schmidt in 1938.[108] Much of the metal found at Surkh Dum appears to have come from hoards or foundation deposits situated within the walls of the sanctuary rooms. Maurits Van Loon has described the occurrence of iron at Surkh Dum:

Iron occurs in all levels at Surkh Dum, increasing from 5 pieces in the tenth century to 20 pieces each in the ninth and eighth centuries to

97 pieces in the seventh century B.C. level. The fact that no iron objects were actually lying on the earlier floor of the sanctuary (all were part of foundation deposits) may indicate that iron was still a valued metal in the ninth century B.C.[109]

Although further details on the types of iron artifacts found and on how such exact sequencing of artifacts was established await publication, the Surkh Dum material is of special importance because it represents a new contextual category. The sequential increase of iron over time in the Surkh Dum deposit could reflect the increasing importance of iron as a metal, presumably as its production became more frequent and efficient. But one suspects that as iron became more common any particular reverence attached to the metal would diminish.

Based on his analysis of the revised Luristan sequence, Vanden Berghe has presented a sequence for the utilization of bronze and iron in the Iron Age Pusht-i Kuh region of western Luristan. In the Iron I period bronze was virtually the only utilitarian metal used for weapons, tools, and ornamental artifacts. By the Iron II period, bronze was still in demand for weapons and tools while iron appeared in ornamental items such as bracelets, rings, pins, anklets, and rein-rings and at times as ceremonial weaponry. Bimetallic artifacts occurred in the form of iron pinheads, bracelets, and daggers covered in a thin sheet of bronze. The shapes of the iron artifacts in the Iron II period are much the same as those in bronze.[110] Then, during Iron III, one significant development was that iron was made into weapons and tools which, by necessity, had to have been strong and tough. Artifacts like daggers, spearpoints, arrowpoints, axes, and knives require the strength that comes of sound forging, which would, of course, be dependent on the ironworking techniques applied to the iron by the smiths forging these items. On the other hand, during Iron III bronze had become an ornamental material. Artifacts such as jewelry and artifacts for display or luxury items were now of bronze. Bronze was used as a means by which to decorate iron artifacts such as daggers that would have bronze rivets in the hilts or a bronze button adorning the pommel of the dagger or even have the complete hilt sheathed in bronze.[111]

The main characteristics of the transition from dependence on bronze to dependence on iron which are noted in Luristan have been distinguished by Przeworski in his pioneer study of the early metal industries of Anatolia.[112] These have been summarized below by Moorey:

> the imitations of Late Bronze Age forms in iron, the simultaneous appearance of weapons and tools of the same type and purpose in bronze and iron, the inlay of bronze with iron, the combination of iron working and bronze ornamental parts in the same object, the use of bronze rivets on iron tools and weapons, and the repair of bronze objects with iron parts. Most of these characteristics may be found in the Luristan metalworker's repertory of the earlier first millennium B.C.[113]

An overriding question in discussions of archaeological evidence from Luristan concerns the identity of the people or peoples interred with goods of bronze and iron and the location(s) of their settlements. Vanden Berghe would see these artifacts from the gravefields as the "everyday objects of a nomadic people"[114] who migrated in and out of Luristan with seasonal regularity much as can be seen occurring there today. Their metalworking could then be a seasonal occupation conducted in the regions of the summer encampment or in Luristan proper during winter encampment. A systematic survey of potential and actual routes of nomadic migration could perhaps reveal the scoria of production of metals.[115] Slag heaps and multiple furnace installations should still persist in concentrated zones, perhaps near the ore bodies which were being exploited in Iron Age times. Ancient mines, of course, might yet be found in the mountainous region of Luristan although geological investigation has yet to confirm the availability of ore.[116] The idiosyncratic nature of both the bronze and iron artifacts known to come from Luristan makes it unlikely that they were obtained by trade from other metal-producing groups.[117]

Since the 1930s, when Luristan bronzes began to appear on the art market, a number of iron artifacts have also come to light, frequently daggers and halberds, which most certainly were associated with the bronzes in clandestinely looted gravefields. A considerable number of these artifacts have been subjected to metallographic analysis.[118] The most well-known type of iron dagger from Luristan, with anthropomorphic and zoomorphic motifs affixed to the hilts, are made totally of iron and do not occur in bimetallic form. These could date to Iron III.[119]

In their composition and structure, these iron artifacts vary from wrought iron to mild steels, with little evidence that there was an awareness of the benefits of prolonged heating in the forge. There are some indications that many of these iron artifacts, the daggers, for example, could have been the products of a single workshop.[120]

Cyril Smith in his important article "The Techniques of the Luristan Smith" has described the technology involved.

> Iranian smiths in the period 800 ($\pm$200) B.C. were highly skilled, although they were unacquainted with some of the basic methods of iron working. Their forging, which involved the use of special swages, is magnificent, but there is not much evidence of welding, and the smith assembled shapes as complicated as those of bronze castings by using elaborately fitted mechanical joints, locked by peening or crimping.[121]

Smith feels that the iron of this transitional period between bronze and iron metallurgy had "decorative design that is more appropriate to the mold of the foundryman and the chaser's chisel than to the hammer of the smith."[122] The difficulty involved in attempting to work iron as bronze was worked explains, in part, the gradual rather than sudden transition from bronze to iron. "It seems that the economic advantage that lies in the greater abundance of the ores of iron compared with those of copper and tin was offset to a considerable extent by the greater labor involved in the forging operation and by the apparent inability to use scrap."[123] Time was needed to develop the technological skills needed to master the working of iron. Only then would iron become widespread.

KURDISTAN

The province of Kurdistan has not yet yielded much in the way of ancient iron artifacts, despite several Iron Age excavations. The site of the Zendan-i Suleiman, western Iran's second excavated sanctuary site, dates to the end of Iron II or the beginning of Iron III.[124] This shrine or sanctuary was constructed to encircle the unusual cone-shaped peak there. Only 2 iron artifacts are known to have come from this occupation at the Zendan, namely, an iron knife and a bronze nail with an iron core.[125]

At another mountain top site in Kurdistan, the fortress at Ziwiye, to the southwest of the Zendan, iron artifacts from the Iron III period have

Table 12.6. Kurdistan:

Weaponry	Personal ornament	Tools/implements etc.	
Zendan-i Suleiman: Late Iron Age II or Early Iron Age III sanctuary			
		Knife	1
		Nail	
		bimetallic	1
Ziwiye: Iron Age III occupation site			
Iron artifacts present			
Godin Tepe: Iron III (Median) occupation site			
Points 2		Sickle	1

See nn. 125, 126, and 128 for references.

been found.[126] Information on them has not been published yet. It is hoped that the recently resumed excavations there will provide more iron artifacts in significant contexts.

Farther south along the southern edge of Kurdistan, Young's excavations at the Median fortified manor house at Godin Tepe produced 2 iron points and an iron sickle blade.[127] This iron should date to the period ca. 750–550 B.C. (see table 12.6).[128]

CONCLUSIONS

In western Iran large quantities of iron artifacts do appear between 1000 and 800 B.C. Moreover, the iron is widespread throughout the region. With the exception of one artifact from Hasanlu and two from Sialk, the few artifacts which have been excavated and assigned earlier dates have not been found in chronologically reliable contexts.

Most interesting is the fact that the widespread appearance of iron does not appear to coincide with any major cultural change except in the area of Luristan. To the north and east of Luristan major changes were witnessed earlier, between ca. 1450 and 1200 B.C. It is at this time that the various regional Bronze Age cultures are replaced by an extensive, relatively homogeneous new set of cultural traits. There is continuity between this earlier period, Iron I, and the following Iron II period with only minor modifications in the geographical spread of the sites and in their cultural inventories.

In Luristan, however, the pattern is different. Giyan is the single site which undergoes a change earlier. Around 1200 B.C., the Giyan I[4] occupation is radically different from the preceding painted pottery culture. Monochrome gray, buff, and red pottery are introduced. It is not until Giyan I[1] that iron appears with modifications in the pottery shapes represented. Farther east in Luristan, however, the Bronze Age cultures continue basically unchanged until about the 9th century B.C., when iron appears with other major changes in the cultural inventory.

If the gray pottery cultural complex coincides with the arrival of Iranian tribes, they did not bring iron with them, at least not in the major portion of the region under discussion. The Iron I period, with its projected dates of ca. 1450/1350 to 1100 B.C., provides a significant amount of time for iron to make its appearance, if it were available. Moreover, there is no sloping horizon of the sequential appearance of iron. Iron appears in the archaeological record in Azerbaijan, Gilan, the Central province, and Luristan at approximately the same time.

The paucity of actual occupation sites that have been excavated for this period is particularly apparent. Most of the iron excavated comes from isolated gravefields. The majority of the nongrave sites date to the late Iron II or Iron III period. These include manor houses, citadel/fortresses, and sanctuaries. For the Iron II period only the Hasanlu citadel and the Kordlar occupation site are known. There is a lack, in all periods, of actual village sites which could possibly reveal metalworking areas nearby them. There is no positive evidence for the working of iron other than isolated scoria at a few sites.

As most of the iron excavated comes from graveyards the context is skewed and the associations of the iron artifacts are not functionally significant. The sample of iron artifact types is also skewed. Tools and implements do not generally occur in graves as do weapons and ornaments. We are therefore left dependent, on the large collection of tools excavated on the citadel of Hasanlu and those from Baba Jan for an idea of the range and variety of tools available. This information is critical to an interpretation of the functional uses of iron during the early stages of its development.

Among the excavated collections of iron artifacts from western Iran, those from Geoy Tepe, Marlik, Hasanlu, and Luristan have been subjected to metallographic examination. This provides us with a reasonable amount of information on the nature of the early iron artifacts. These studies indicate that ironworking technology was not yet fully developed. Western Iran is clearly still in a transitional phase.

The iron analyzed indicates that steeling was not accomplished by intentional, homogeneous carburization but probably by a sequence of forging and reheating. The Luristan iron was forged but not welded, although great skill is evidenced in the work. Moreover, in Luristan it is apparent that the metalworkers were imitating the decorative designs as well as the shapes of the bronze artifacts.

None of the Iron III iron artifacts of western Azerbaijan has yet been subjected to metallographic studies. The area had come under Urartian influence during this period and the nature of Urartian sites and weapons suggests that they must have had extremely effective tools. It is possible that they had mastered the technique of homogeneous carburization, but only actual analysis can confirm this.

A trait characteristic of this transitional phase in all areas of western Iran is the presence of bimetallic artifacts. All the gravefields of this period which contain iron also contain bronze artifacts, the single exception being the graves at Kalwali. For Luristan, where the chronology of the graves is quite precise, the sequence of artifact types has been pinpointed. It seems that the earliest iron was used strictly for ornaments. Slowly, weapons also began to be made of iron. Finally only tools and weapons were of iron, all ornaments being made of bronze.

This same pattern might have occurred in the other areas as well. However, a tight chronology for Iron II-excavated materials does not exist for certain portions north and east of Luristan. In the Talysh, Marlik, Dinkha II, Sialk B, and Hasanlu IV sites both weapons and ornaments occurred by the end of the Iron II period. This is slightly earlier than in Luristan, where the full range of artifacts did not occur until ca. 750 B.C. By the Iron III period Godin, the Zendan, Agrab, and Haftavan III have mostly weapons and few ornaments in iron. At Bastam a few ornaments do occur although iron is used primarily for weapons. It appears, therefore, that the Luristan area is again slightly more conservative than the rest of western Iran.

Assuming that Iranian tribes were responsible for the major cultural changes witnessed during the Iron I period (and the Iron II period in Luristan), it has been postulated that without introducing iron technology themselves, the Iranians could have played a very important role in the development of iron. One can posit that the establishment of contact between the new arrivals and the indigenous populations may have set in motion the process of development of industrialized iron metallurgy.

The relationship which is proposed is one of Iranians as patrons to indigenous metalsmiths among whom the knowledge of ironworking was present.[129]

It is not too much to suppose that the indigenous populations were already familiar with iron, for it is becoming increasingly apparent that Bronze Age metalsmiths throughout the ancient world had experience with iron. The recent work of Cooke and Aschenbrenner has clearly demonstrated that the presence of iron in pre-Iron Age copper–bronze artifacts is due, in part, to the use of iron ores (often hematites and/or magnetites) as fluxing agents in the smelting process.[130] Under such circumstances, the potential for a smelting operation to smelt out iron instead of copper–bronze is substantially increased. We must assume that this could have happened with increasing regularity to Bronze Age metalsmiths, to the point that the knowledge of how to extract iron was available but only rarely exercised.

Such a hypothetical reconstruction of events with incoming Iranians acting as stimuli to the development of iron production could provide an explanation for the paucity of iron from the region of Kurdistan proper. Young has shown that the Assyrian Annals record that there were no early Iranians in the heartland of the Mannean kingdom or in the kingdom of Ellipi.[131] Levine has suggested that Mannea could well have existed in northwestern Kurdistan south of Lake Rezaiyeh (Lake Urmia) and that Ellipi might have lain west of Kermanshah.[132] If in fact these regions were occupied by indigenous populations who resisted the intrusions of incoming Iranian tribes it is possible that kingdoms such as Mannea and Ellipi perisisted as refuge areas of Late Bronze Age traditions. Without the postulated stimulus from contact with Iranian tribes in these refuge areas, iron metallurgy might not have gained a foothold until late, when indigenous populations were at last assimilated into larger kingdoms such as that of the Medes.

As may be seen, significant amounts of data concerning iron metallurgy do exist for the region of western Iran. Only further intensive research on a multidisciplinary level will permit understanding of the origin and development of this type of ancient metallurgy from both a technological and a cultural standpoint. Once it is grasped on a regional basis we may be in a postion to understand the evolution of iron metallurgy in the ancient Near East as a whole.

ACKNOWLEDGMENTS

I would like to express my gratitude to Robert H. Dyson, Jr., for presenting me with the opportunity to participate in the excavations at Hasanlu and to study the iron artifacts revealed there. My appreciation also must be extended to several other scholars from whom, at various intervals, I have gained important insights into the study of archaeometallurgy: Cyril Stanley Smith, Robert Maddin, James D. Muhly, Theodore A. Wertime, Reed Knox, P. R. S. Moorey, R. F. Tylecote, Radomír Pleiner, and Albert France-Lanord. Finally, my thanks to Susan M. Howard for her numerous helpful criticisms and suggestions. I alone remain responsible for the content of this manuscript.

NOTES

The following abbreviations are used for the most frequently cited publications.

AA   *Archäolgischer Anzeiger.* Beiblatt zum Jahrbuch des Deutschen Archäologischen
        Instituts
CAH   *Cambridge Ancient History*
JFA   *Journal of Field Archaeology*
JNES   *Journal of Near Eastern Studies*
JHMS   *Journal of the Historical Metallurgy Society*
MMJ   *Metropolitan Museum Journal*

1. T. Cuyler Young, Jr., "The Iranian Migration into the Zagros," *Iran* 5 (1967): 22.
2. Ibid., p. 24.
3. Charles Burney and David M. Lang, *The Peoples of the Hills* (New York: Praeger, 1972), p. 117 (hereafter Burney and Lang, *Peoples* 1972). For cautionary notes regarding the question of population movements and western Iran in the Iron Age cf. Robert H. Dyson, Jr., "Architecture of the Iron I Period at Hasanlu in Western Iran and Its Implications for Theories of Migration on the Iranian Plateau," in *Le Plateau Iranien et L'Asie Centrale des Origines à la Conquête Islamique,* Colloques Internationaux du Centre National de la Recherche Scientifique no. 567, pp. 155–69 (hereafter Dyson, *Architecture* 1977); idem, "The Archaeological Evidence of the Second Millennium B.C. on the Persian Plateau," in *The Cambridge Ancient History,* vol. 2, pt. 2 (Cambridge: Cambridge University Press, 1973), p. 714 (hereafter Dyson, *CAH* 1973).
4. For discussions of Iron Age chronology in western Iran cf. Dyson, *Architecture* (1977); Dyson, *CAH* (1973); idem, "The Problems of Protohistoric Western Iran as Seen from Hasanlu," *JNES* 24, no. 3 (1965): 193–217 (hereafter Dyson, *JNES* 24 1965); T. Cuyler Young, Jr., "A Comparative Ceramic Chronology for Western Iran, 1500–500 B.C.," *Iran* 3 (1965): 53–85 (hereafter Young, *Iran* 3 1965); idem, "The Iranian Migration into the Zagros," *Iran* 5 (1967): 11–34 (hereafter Young, *Iran* 5 1967).

5. For a more detailed explication of the appearance of iron during the Iron I period, see Vincent Pigott, "The Question of the Occurrence of Iron in the Iron I Period in Western Iran," in Louis D. Levine and T. Cuyler Young, Jr., eds., *Mountains and Lowlands: Essays in the Archaeology of Greater Mesopotamia*, Bibliotheca Mesopotamica 7 (Malibu: Undena Publications, 1977), pp. 209–34.

6. Robert H. Dyson, Jr., "Notes on Weapons and Chronology in Northern Iran around 1000 B.C.," in Machteld Mellink, ed., *Dark Ages and Nomads c. 1000 B.C.* (Leiden: Nederlands Historisch-Archaeologisch Institutuut in het Nabije Oosten, 1964), p. 39; Dyson, *JNES* 24 (1965): 196; idem., "Early Cultures of Solduz, Azerbaijan," *Survey of Persian Art* 14 (1967): 2957; Oscar White Muscarella, "The Iron Age at Dinkha Tepe, Iran," *MMJ* 9 (1974): 49 (hereafter Muscarella, *MMJ* 9 1974).

7. T. Burton Brown, *Excavations in Azerbaijan, 1948* (London: John Murray, 1951) (hereafter Brown, *Azerbaijan* 1951); Dyson, *CAH* (1973): 700; C. Hamlin, "The Habur Ware Ceramic Assemblage of Northern Mesopotamia: An Analysis of its Distribution (Ph.D. diss., University of Pennsylvania, 1971), p. 40.

8. Roman Ghirshman, *Fouilles de Sialk près de Kashan 1933, 1934, 1937* II (Paris: Geuthner, 1939), p. 9 (hereafter Ghirshman, *Sialk* II 1939).

9. For a contrary opinion concerning the date of the iron in the Sialk A necropolis, cf. P. R. S. Moorey, "Towards a Chronology for the 'Luristan Bronzes,'" *Iran* 9 (1971): 128 (hereafter Moorey, "Chronology" 1971); P. R. S. Moorey, *A Catalogue of Persian Bronzes in the Ashmolean Museum* (Oxford: Oxford University Press, 1971), p. 316 (hereafter Moorey, *Catalogue* 1971).

10. George Contenau and Roman Ghirshman, *Fouilles du Tépé-Giyan près de Nehavend 1931 et 1932* (Paris: Geuthner, 1935), p. 22 (hereafter Contenau and Ghirshman, *Giyan* 1935); Young, *Iran* 3 (1965): 66, 68, 79.

11. Young, *Iran* 3 (1965): 68 n. 19.

12. Louis Vanden Berghe, "Recherches archéologiques dans le Luristan. Sixième campagne: 1970, Fouilles à Bard-i Bal et à Pa-yi Kal. Prospections dans le district d'Avian (rapport preliminaire)," *Iranica Antiqua* 10 (1973): 53, table 4 (hereafter Vanden Berghe, *Bard-i Bal* 1973); Louis Vanden Berghe, "Prospections archéologiques dans la région de Badr," *Archeologia* 36 (1970): 14, 15, fig. 8; Louis Vanden Berghe and Rene Joffrey, *Bronzes-Iran-Luristan-Caucasus* (Belgium: René Loiseau, 1973), Evocations Métallurgiques XIII.

13. Young, *Iran* 5 (1967): 25 n. 78.

14. It is now less certain that major fortifications characterize the Iron II period since it was demonstrated recently by Dyson that the major fortification wall at Hasanlu, thought to be period IV, is probably period IIIB and of Urartian construction. See Robert H. Dyson, Jr. and Vincent C. Pigott, "Survey of Excavations in Iran 1973–4: Hasanlu," *Iran* 13 (1975): 185 (hereafter Dyson and Pigott, *Iran* 13 1975); cf. also Young, *Iran* 5 (1967): 25 n. 79.

15. Young, *Iran* 5 (1967): 25.

16. Ibid., pp. 26–27.

17. Ibid., pp. 27–29.

18. Claude F. A. Schaeffer, *Stratigraphie Comparée et Chronologie de l'Asie Occidentale*

(London: Oxford University Press, 1948), pp. 404–43, 496–533 (hereafter Schaeffer, *Stratigraphie* 1948).

19. Ibid., p. 443 (Talyche Fer 1); Jacques de Morgan, *Mission scientifique au Caucase* (Paris, 1889), pp. 190 ff.; Franz Hančar, "Kaukasus-Luristan," *Eurasia Septentrionalis Antiqua* 9 (1934): 81; A. Krupnov, "A propos de la chronologie de l' Age du Fer en Caucase nord," in *Report of the VI Congress of Pre- and Protohistoric Sciences,* Moscow (1962); Schaeffer, *Stratigraphie* (1948), figs. 232, 237; and A. A. Martirosian, *Armenia in the Bronze and Early Iron Age* (1964) (in Russian), all footnoted in Moorey, *Catalogue* (1971): 24.

20. Schaeffer, *Stratigraphie* (1948): fig. 232, nos. 1, 3, 4, 11, 12.

21. Moorey, *Catalogue* (1971): 315 (as quoted on p. 447).

22. Ali Hakemi, "Kaluraz and the Civilization of the Mardes," *Archeologia Viva* 1, no. 1 (1968): 63–66.

23. R. F. Tylecote, "A Metallurgical Examination of Some Objects from Marlik, Iran," *JHMS* 6 (1972): 34–35 (hereafter Tylecote, *JHMS* 1972).

24. Ezat O. Negahban, "The Seals of Marlik Tepe," *JNES* 36 (1977): 81–102.

25. Tylecote, *JHMS* (1972): 34.

26. Ibid., p. 35.

27. Namio Egami, Shinji Fukai, and Seiichi Masuda, *Dailaman I* (Tokyo: Yamakawa, 1965), pp. 27–28.

28. Ibid., p. 11.

29. Ibid., p. 73.

30. Brown, *Azerbaijan* (1951): 72, 199. Metallographically this piece of iron sheet, perhaps part of a stand (6.7 in. long × 3.7 in. wide × 1 in. thick) has been shown to be cast iron. Its high carbon content (3.5%), characteristic of cast iron would make the metal virtually unhammerable. Therefore this object had to have been produced by casting. As stated, from the Iron Age Near East there are no documented examples of cast iron. However, the possibility that cast iron structures were being produced accidentally in blooms from Iron Age iron smelting operations supposed to produce wrought iron cannot be discounted, as Cyril Smith has indicated. Cf. n. 47 and C. S. Smith, "On the Nature of Iron," in *Made of Iron* (Houston: University of St. Thomas, 1966), p. 32; C. S. Smith, "The Techniques of the Luristan Smith," in Robert H. Brill ed., *Science and Archaeology* (Cambridge, Mass.: MIT Press 1971), p. 52 (hereafter Smith, "Techniques" 1971).

31. J. Dorner, K. Kromer, and A. Lippert, "Die Zweite Kampagne der österreichischen Ausgrabungen am Kordlar-Tepe, Aserbaidschan," *Mitteilungen der Anthropologischen Gesellschaft in Wein* 104 (1976): 111–36; K. Kromer and A. Lippert, "Die österreichischen Ausgrabungen am Kordlar-Tepe in Aserbaidschan," and A. Lippert, "Vorbericht der österreichischen Ausgrabungen am Kordlar-Tepe in Persisch-Aserbaidschan: Kampagne 1974," *Mitteilungen der Anthropologischen Gesellschaft in Wien* 106 (1976): 65–112.

32. Charles Burney, "Excavations at Haftavan Tepe 1968: First Preliminary Report," *Iran* 8 (1970): 168, fig. 7 (hereafter Burney *Iran* 8 1970); idem, "Excavations at Haftavan Tepe 1969: Second Preliminary Report, "*Iran* 10 (1972): 135–37 (hereafter Burney *Iran* 10 1972); idem, "Excavations at Haftavan Tepe 1971: Third Preliminary Report, *Iran* 11 (1973): 155.

33. Burney, *Iran* 10 (1972): 140, 142.

34. Sir. M. Aurel Stein, *Old Routes in Western Iran* (London: Macmillan & Co., 1940), pp. 390–404, pl. XXVI (hereafter Stein, *Old Routes* 1940).

35. Muscarella, *MMJ* 9 (1974): 36, 38, 58, 59 n. 14. In this footnote Muscarella mentions that the exact number of metal artifacts at Dinkha was not calculable. He estimates that at Dinkha there were "about 172 pieces of bronze jewelry and 81 of iron, and among the weapons there were 16 of iron and 3 of bronze" (ibid., p. 59).

36. Dyson, *JNES* 24 (1965): 202–03; The substantial evidence for the Urartian occupation at Hasanlu in the IIIB (Iron III) period could point toward their participation in the destruction of the site ca. 800 B.C. (Dyson and Pigott, *Iran* 13 [1975]: 185).

37. A detailed investigation of the iron artifacts from Hasanlu will be presented in my Ph.D. dissertation for the Department of Anthropology, University of Pennsylvania. Cf. Clifford C. Lamberg-Karlovsky, "The Development of a Metallurgical Technology, Documented Early Finds of Metal in the Near East and the Evidence from Hasanlu, Iran" (Ph.D. diss., University of Pennsylvania, 1965), for an initial, partial catalogue of Hasanlu iron artifacts.

38. Cf. Rachel K. Maxwell-Hyslop, "A Note on the Significance of the Technique of 'Casting-On' as applied to a Group of Daggers from North-West Persia," *Iraq* 26 (1964): 50–53. This discussion also has relevance for typological considerations of dagger types found throughout western Iran during the Iron Age. Cf. also H. Drescher, *Der Überfaugguss* (Mainz, 1958), which is the definitive technical volume concerning "casting-on."

39. One important find at Hasanlu, possibly an indicator of where additional metal-working installations might be found, is the "Artisan's House" in the Outer Town at the base of the citadel. This mudbrick structure had in its courtyard a two-chambered hearth and a crucible possibly for the melting of copper–bronze (Percy Knauth, *The Metalsmiths* [New York: Time-Life Books, 1975], p. 93). In addition, I have seen scoria of copper–bronze working excavated from within the confines of the citadel itself. Cf. also Stein, *Old Routes* (1940): pl. XXVI.

40. Three samples of "iron ore" were selected for analysis from finds made during the 1974 season at Hasanlu. Dr. Khadem, Director of the Geological Survey of Iran, kindly permitted the analyses to be done at the Geological Survey's laboratories in Tehran with the following results:

Geological Survey Of Iran Chemical Laboratories Report # 53–173 Sample Description:
Sa-1456 (Has74/4)—Sample taken from large black, heavy, magnetic boulder which was part of a wall foundation of a room attached to the west side of Burned Building II in the citadel.
Sa-1457 (Has74/5)—Sample consisted of fist-sized, black, heavy, magnetic nodule which appears to have been used as some type of burnisher. It was excavated from the ruins of Burned Building IVE in the Citadel.
Sa-1458 (Has74/6)—Sample found as a black, heavy, irregular shaped chunk of ore which had been used as a part of floor paving in the floor of Burned Building IVE. This piece appears to have been shattered from a larger matrix, presumably the ore body, as its edges were rather sharp and jagged.

Sample Analysis:

Lab no.	Field no.	$SiO_2(\%)$	$Fe_2O_3(\%)$	$TiO_2(\%)$	$CaO(\%)$	$P_2O_5(\%)$	$S(\%)$
sa-1456	HAS74 = 4	9.05	36.77	2.71	5.93	0.11	n.d.
7	HAS74 = 5	5.04	94.06	0.02	n.d.	0.21	n.d.
8	HAS74 = 6	7.96	39.13	4.05	n.d.	0.15	n.d.

n.d. = not detected.

41. Cf., e.g., the successful application of a magnetometer survey to the location of iron smelting installations at a modern industrial archaeological site (Bruce Bevan, "A Magnetic Survey at Les Forges du Saint-Maurice," *Museum Applied Science Center for Archaeology Newsletter* 2, no. 2 [Dec. 1975]: 1).

42. R. Knox, "Detection of Iron Carbide Structures in the Oxide Remains of Ancient Steel," *Archaeometry* 6 (1963): 44–45 (hereafter Knox, *Archaeometry* 1963). Cf. also Robert H. Dyson, Jr., "Sciences Meet in Ancient Hasanlu," *Natural History* 83, no. 8 (1964): 25 (hereafter Dyson, *Natural History* 83 1964).

43. Knox, *Archaeometry* (1963): 44.

44. Vincent C. Pigott, "A Consideration of Evidence Relating to the Introduction of Iron Metallurgy in Western Iran c. 1350–800 B.C." (unpublished manuscript, Department of Anthropology, University of Pennsylvania, 1969); Dyson, *Natural History* 83 (1964): 25.

45. Preliminary data from this program of analysis have been presented in Vincent C. Pigott and Robert Maddin, "What You Can Learn from a Fossil: A Preliminary Report on the Metallurgy of Hasanlu Iron," paper read at the Conference on Archaeometry and Archaeological Prospection (Mar. 19–22, 1975), Oxford; Robert Maddin, "Early Iron Metallurgy in the Near East," *Transactions of the Iron and Steel Institute of Japan* 15 (1975): 67–68 (hereafter Maddin, *Transactions* 15 1975).

46. Maddin, *Transactions* 15 (1975): 67–68.

47. Cyril Smith kindly granted me permission to quote this paragraph from his letter of June 25, 1963, to Reed Knox which is now part of the Hasanlu Project files in the Near East Section of the University Museum, Philadelphia, Pennsylvania.

48. Recent work on early iron from Palestine by Robert Maddin, Tamara S. Wheeler, and James D. Muhly at the University of Pennsylvania is suggesting "that iron came into common use with the discovery that iron objects could be made harder by allowing the iron to remain in the charcoal hearth for long periods of time; i.e., case-carburization. This discovery is crucial to understanding the beginning of the true Iron Age in Palestine." "The Case for the Steeling Process in Ancient Palestine," in *Abstracts of the International Symposium on Archaeometry and Archaeological Prospection* (Mar. 16–19, 1977), Philadelphia; see also "From Bronze to Steel," *Scientific American* 236, no. 5 (May 1977): 61.

49. Oscar White W. Muscarella, "Excavations at Agrab Tepe, Iran," *MMJ* 8 (1973): 69, also 71–75 (hereafter Muscarella, *MMJ* 8 1973).

50. Kellner, *Urartu* (1976): 33.

51. Ibid., pp. 70–71; Kleiss, *Bastam* (1972): 52–53.

52. Kleiss, *Bastam* (1972): 51.

53. Ibid.

54. Kellner, *Urartu* (1976): 29, figs. 2 and 4.

55. "What must, however, have given a great stimulus to the development of iron industry in Urartu was the need to hew irrigation channels through living rock in many places. In turn, the availability of stone-hewing tools made possible the extraordinary proliferation of rock-cut tombs and fortresses built of well-dressed stone on foundations excavated from bed rock" (Maurits Van Loon, *Urartian Art* [Leiden: Nederlands Historisch-Archaeologisch Instituut in het Nabije Oosten, 1966], p. 84) (hereafter Van Loon, *Urartian Art* 1966).

56. There is some indication that Urartian weaponry might have been intentionally carburized. Robert Maddin and Tamara S. Wheeler at the University of Pennsylvania have analyzed the tip of an iron spearpoint from Toprakkale courtesy of the British Museum (#1931–4–11), which appears to have been heavily carburized. I would like to thank Dr. Maddin and Dr. Wheeler for allowing me to use the report of their analysis.

57. G. Melikishvili, *Urartskije Klinoobraznyje Nadpisi* (Moscow, 1960): #155, line 11; Van Loon, *Urartian Art* (1966): 81; cf. Radomir Pleiner's comments on this particular seal in *The Beginnings of the Iron Age in Ancient Persia*, Annals of the Náprstek Museum 6 (Prague, 1969): 16 (hereafter Pleiner, *Persia* 1969).

58. Van Loon, *Urartian Art* (1966): 80 cites H. Quiring, "Die Erzgrundlagen der ältesten Eisenerzeugung," *Zeitschrift für praktische Geologie* 41 (1933): 128 ff. The whole question of potential sources of iron ores used during the Iron Age in the ancient Near East is sorely in need of updating. Cf. Rachel K. Maxwell-Hyslop, "Assyrian Sources of Iron," *Iraq* 36, pts. 1, 2 (1974): 139–54.

59. For a comprehensive treatment of the probable disposition of petty principalities distributed throughout western Iran in the early 1st millennium B.C. see Louis D. Levine, "Geographical Studies in the Neo-Assyrian Zagros," *Iran* 11 (1973): 1–28; idem, "Geographical Studies in the Neo-Assyrian Zagros II," *Iran* 12 (1974): 99–124 (hereafter Levine, *Iran* 12 1974).

60. Van Loon, *Urartian Art* (1966): 83; Pleiner, *Persia* (1969): 17–18, fig. 2.

61. Pleiner, *Persia* (1969): 16–22.

62. Ibid. p. 18.

63. Dyson, *JNES* 24 (1965): 195, 206.

64. Louis Vanden Berghe, *La Nécropole de Khūrvīn* (Leiden: Nederlands Historisch-Archaeologisch Instituut in het Nabije Oosten 1964), p. 35.

65. Ibid., pl. XLIII, nos. 311, 312.

66. Ghirshman, *Sialk II* (1939). For discussions of Sialk and its Iron Age chronology cf. Young, *Iran* 3 (1965); idem, 5 (1967); Dyson, *JNES* 24 (1965); Muscarella, *MMJ* 8 (1973); idem, 9 (1974); Rainer M. Boehmer, "Zur Datierung der Nekropole B von Tepe Sialk," *AA* 80, no. 4 (1966): 802–22.

67. Ghirshman, *Sialk II* (1939): 49 and frontispiece 1.

68. Ibid. pp. 53–54.

69. Young, *Iran* 5 (1967): 24–25 n. 78, points outs what he feels could be "a common metallurgical tradition in Iron II times" between Hasanlu IV and the Sialk VI/B necropolis.

70. Contenau and Ghirshman, *Giyan* (1935); Young, *Iran* 3 (1965): 62–68.

71. Young, *Iran* 3 (1965): 66.

72. Ibid.

73. Ibid., pp. 66, 79; Contenau and Ghirshman, *Giyan* (1935): 22.

74. Young, *Iran* 3 (1965): 79.

75. Ibid., p. 83.

76. Contenau and Ghirshman, *Giyan* (1935): pl. 9.

77. Ibid., pl. 8.

78. Contenau and Ghirshman, *Giyan* (1935): 68.

79. Henrik Thrane, "Tepe Guran and the Luristan Bronzes," *Archaeology* 23, no. 1 (1970): 32 (hereafter Thrane, "Guran" 1970).

80. Ibid.

81. Young, *Iran* 3 (1965): 79.

82. Thrane, "Guran" (1970): 33.

83. Clare Goff, "Excavations at Baba Jan: The Pottery and Metal from Levels III and II," *Iran* 16 (1978): 39, fig. 14, p. 56; fig. 15, p. 57 (hereafter Goff, *Baba Jan* 1978).

84. Goff, *Baba Jan* (1978): 39.

Hoe: David Stronach, "Metal Objects from the 1957 Excavations at Nimrud," *Iraq* 20 (1958): p. 32, no. 15.

Spade: Erich F. Schmidt, *Persepolis II: Contents of the Treasury and Other Discoveries* (Chicago; Oriental Institute Publication 69, 1957), pl. 73, no. 4.

Sickles: Ghirshman, *Sialk II* (1939): pl. 71, no. S.891d; pl. 78, no. S.973c.

85. Goff, *Baba Jan* (1978): 39.

Arrowpoints: Ghirshman, *Sialk II* (1939): pl. 78, no. S.973a; pl. 71, no. S.892e.

86. Clare Goff Meade, "Excavations at Baba Jan, 1967: Second Preliminary Report," *Iran* 7 (1969): 126.

Bit: Ghirshman, *Sialk II* (1939): pl. 56, nos. S.835, S.841, S.588.

87. Vanden Berghe, *Bard-i Bal* (1973): 52–54.

88. Ibid., p. 36, table 2; p. 49, table 5.

89. Ibid., p. 53.

90. Ibid., p. 54.

91. Ibid., p. 36, table 2; p. 49, table 5.

92. Ibid., p. 61, table 6.

93. Louis Vanden Berghe, "Le Luristan à l'age du fer. La nécropole de Kutal-i Gulgul. VII (1971) et VIII (1972) campagnes," *Archeologia* 65 (1973): 25 (hereafter Vanden Berghe, *Kutal-i Gulgul* 1973).

94. Ibid. The same ware, light brown, persists at Kutal-i Gulgul from the end of the Iron I period into Iron II but the new vessel shapes appear in the Iron II inhumations. The quantity of iron from Kutal-i Gulgul was not stated exactly.

95. Ibid. p. 22.

96. Vanden Berghe, *Bard-i Bal* (1973): 67–69.

97. Vanden Berghe, *Kutal-i Gulgul* (1973): 25, 29.

98. Cf. Maurits Van Loon review of L. Vanden Berghe, *Het Archeologisch Onderzoek Naar de Bronscultuur van Luristan. Opgravingen in Pushi-i Kuh I Kalwali en War Kabud (1965 en 1966)* (Brussels: Koninklijke Vlaamse Academie voor Wetenschappen, Letteren en Schone Kunsten van België, 1968) hereafter Vanden Berghe, *War Kabud* 1968). Reviewed in *Bibliotheca Orientalis* 29, nos. 1, 2 (1972): 67 (hereafter Van Loon, *War Kabud* 1972).

99. My thanks to Dr. Vanden Berghe for making unpublished War Kabud data available to me.

100. Vanden Berghe, *War Kabud* (1968): 167.

101. Van Loon, *War Kabud* (1972): 67.

102. Ibid., p. 68.

103. Vanden Berghe, *War Kabud* (1968): 163; Van Loon, *War Kabud* (1972): 68. Van Loon proposes that Kalwali could be earlier in time than War Kabud. Based on the evidence that at Kalwali there are only artifacts in iron and none in bronze, I suspect that such a gravefield would more likely be later than the gravefield (War Kabud) with the combination of bronze and iron artifacts.

104. Vanden Berghe, *Bard-i Bal* (1973): 70–73.

105. Louis Vanden Berghe, "Belgische opgravingen en navorsingen in de Pusht-i Kuh, Luristan, 3ᵉ campagne," *Phoenix* 14, no. 1 (1968): 126–27.

106. Louis Vanden Berghe, "Excavations in Pusht-i Kuh (Iran)," *Archaeology* 24, no. 3 (1971): 265–66.

107. Dr. Vanden Berghe kindly allowed me the use of his unpublished tables of data from the Chamazhi Mumah excavations. See also Louis Vanden Berghe, "Mission Archéologique dans le Pošt-e Kũh Lorestãn. La Nécropole de Čamahzĩ-Mumah 1974," in Firouz Bagherzadeh, ed., *Proceedings of the IVth Annual Symposium on Archaeological Research in Iran* (Tehran, 1976): 337–67, and idem, "La Nécropole de Chamzhi-Mumah X (1974) et XI (1975) Campagnes," *Archeologia* 108 (1977): 52–63.

108. E. Schmidt, "The Second Holmes Expedition to Luristan," *Bulletin of the American Institute for Iranian Art and Archaeology* 5, no. 3 (1938): 205, 209.

109. Maurits Van Loon review of: Machteld Mellink, ed., *Dark Ages and Nomads c. 1000 B.C.* (Istanbul, 1964) in *Bibliotheca Orientalis* 24, nos. 1, 2 (1967): 24 (hereafter Van Loon, *Dark Ages* 1967).

110. Louis Vanden Berghe, "La chronologie de la civilisation des Bronzes du Pusht-i Kuh, Luristan," in Firouz Bagherzadeh, ed., *Proceedings of the 1st Annual Symposium on Archaeological Research in Iran* (1973) Tehran, p. 5.

111. Ibid.

112. Stefan Przeworski, *Die Metallindustrie Anatoliens in der Zeit von 1500 bis 700 vor Chr*, Internationales Archiv für Ethnographie XXXVI (Leiden, 1939).

113. Moorey *Catalogue* (1971): 315.

114. Louis Vanden Berghe, "The Bronzes of the Shepherds and Horsemen of Luristan," *Archaeologia Viva* 1, no. 1 (1968): 105.

115. The benefits which can accrue from archaeometallurgically oriented field surveys are obvious in Theodore A. Wertime, "A Metallurgical Expedition through the Persian Desert," *Science* 159, no. 3818 (1968): 927–35, and Heather Lechtman, "A Metallurgical Site Survey in the Peruvian Andes," *JFA* 3, no. 1 (1976): 1–42.

116. An important investigation of ancient copper mining in Iran has recently been initiated (T. Berthoud, R. Besenval, F. Cesbron, S. Cleuziou, J. Francaix, and J. Liszak-Hours "*Les anciennes mines de cuivre en Iran: deuxieme rapport préliminaire*, Recherche Cooperative sur Programme N° 442, Commissariat a L'Energie Atomique. Laboratoire de Recherche des Musées de France, Unité de Recherche Archéologique N° 7 [Paris, 1977]).

117. Cf. P. R. S. Moorey, "Prehistoric Copper and Bronze Metallurgy in Western Iran (with special reference to Luristan)," *Iran* 7: 131–48 (hereafter Moorey, "Metallurgy" 1969); Moorey, "Chronology" (1971); Moorey, *Catalogue* (1971).

118. The number of analytical reports dealing with Luristan iron are too numerous to detail here in full, so only a few significant references other than those referred to in the text are listed. Cf. Jane C. Waldbaum (with C. S. Smith), "A Bronze and Iron Iranian Axe in the Fogg Art Museum," in D. G. Mitten, J. G. Pedley, and J. A. Scott, *Studies Presented to George M.A. Hanfmann* (Mainz: Phillip von Zabern, 1971), pp. 195–210; Albert France-Lanord, "Le fer en Iran au premier millénaire avant Jésus-Christ," *Revue d'histoire des mines et de la metallurgie* 1 (1969): 75–126; Vera Bird and Henry Hodges, "A Metallurgical Examination of Two Early Iron Swords from Luristan," *Studies in Conservation* 13 (1968): 215–223; Radomír Pleiner, "Untersuchung eines Kurzschwertes des Luristanischen Typus," *AA* 1 (1969): 41–47; F. K. Naumann, "Die Untersuchung alter eiserner Fundstücke und die dazu verwendeten Verfahren," in M. Levey, ed., *Archaeological Chemistry* (Philadelphia: University of Pennsylvania Press, 1967), pp. 181–204. Joseph Ternbach, "Technical Aspects of the Herzfeld Bent Iron Dagger of Luristan," in Machteld Mellink, *Dark Ages and Nomads c. 1000 B.C.* (Istanbul, 1964), pp. 107–23; R. Damien et al., "Sur des épées en fer provenant du Louristan," *Revue Archéologique* 2 (1962): 17–41.

119. Moorey, "Chronology" (1971): 128.

120. Herbert Maryon, "Early Near Eastern Steel Swords," *American Journal of Archaeology* 65 (1961): 183.

121. Smith, *Techniques* (1971): 51.

122. Ibid.

123. Ibid.

124. Dyson, *JNES* 24 (1965): 201, 211.

125. H. Oehler and S. Zachrisson, "Die Ausgrabungen auf dem Zindan-i-Suleiman," *Tehraner Forschungen* 1 (1961): 77, 78, table 43.

126. Iron artifacts from Ziwiye are in the Iran collection of the University Museum, Philadelphia, Pennsylvania.

127. T. Cuyler Young, Jr. and Louis D. Levine, *Excavations of the Godin Project: Second Progress Report*, Occasional Paper 26 Royal Ontario Museum Art and Archaeology (Toronto, 1974), p. 36, fig. 50.

128. T Cuyler Young, Jr. and Harvey Weiss, "Survey of Excavations in Iran During 1972-3, The Godin Project: Godin Tepe," *Iran* 12 (1974): 209.

129. Cf. Burney and Lang *Peoples* (1972): 117; Moorey "Metallurgy" (1969): 137, 148.

130. Strathmore R. B. Cooke and Stanley Aschenbrenner, "The Occurrence of Metallic Iron in Copper," *JEA* 2, no. 3 (1975): 251–66.

131. Young *Iran* 5 (1967): 29.

132. Levine *Iran* 12 (1974): 104–06, fig. 2, 113–16.

13

The Advent of Iron in Africa

NIKOLAAS J. VAN DER MERWE

In much of Africa the coming of iron is of more importance in the historical record than in most other parts of the world. In Africa south of about 16°N the appearance of iron cannot be thought of as a logical step upward from bronze, because there was no bronze to precede it. From the available evidence on the African Iron Age it emerges that iron was the first and foremost metal to be produced. Copper did not achieve great technological significance; its introduction accompanied that of iron and may well have followed it in many places. Gold and tin achieved importance in a few areas in a subsidiary capacity. It is not unreasonable, therefore, that some Africanist archaeologists considered adoption of the term *Metal Age* for Africa as late as 1950, to underline the unique character of the local Iron Age.

In a discussion of metallurgical history, Africa must be divided into two parts. The area south of the Sahara and south of the Ethiopian highlands forms the part to which the foregoing remarks apply. The countries of the Mediterranean basin, the Nile Valley, and the Red Sea coast form another. In the latter case, some regions were participants in the rise of Bronze Age civilization, most notably Egypt. Nubia (the Sudan) was strongly influenced by Egypt and rose to prominence when the power of the Egyptian New Kingdom declined. Ethiopia was colonized by Semitic speakers from Arabia in the 1st millennium B.C., while Arab and possibly Indian trade influence extended along the coast of the Horn of Africa. In the Mediterranean, Phoenician colonists served the same function along the coast of North Africa. As a result of indigenous developments and foreign influences, therefore, these regions participated in at least some of the developments of a true Bronze Age. Iron did not have the revolutionary impact there that the introduction of bronze had. An early "copper age" is also being documented on the southern fringes of the Sahara, especially in Mauretania and Niger, but requires further confirmation.

In the southern half of Africa the story is considerably different. Here the coming of iron was a catalyst which woke half a continent from the slumber of the Stone Age. The food-producing revolution of the Near East, which set the stage for the ensuing Bronze Age, had penetrated only as far as North Africa, the Nile Valley, and the Red Sea coast. The principal crops of the Mediterranean, wheat and barley, could not be grown successfully in the African savanna or tropics. While Bronze Age civilizations rose in the Eastern Mediterranean, the southern half of Africa became isolated by barriers of desert and culture. Several thousand years were required for the idea of food production to bear fruit in the form of locally domesticated African plants: sorghum, millet, and rootcrops. By 1000 B.C., when parts of Sub-Saharan Africa had joined the foodproducing age, iron was already being diffused around the Mediterranean.

It is not clear how iron entered the lower half of Africa. The most obvious routes of transmission are from the Phoenician settlements in North Africa overland to West Africa or from Meroe in the Sudan to the Lakes region. There may, in fact, have been several such routes. We do know that iron was being manufactured in Nigeria and in northern Tanzania in the late 1st millennium B.C., but the archaeological evidence is still pretty thin. Nor is it clear what technological and social processes were set in motion by the combination of food and metal production. The consequences are well known, however. A large-scale movement of people from West Africa, primarily of Bantu speakers, resulted in the Iron Age occupation of most of the southern subcontinent by ca. 300 A.D. These Iron Age peoples were village farmers and pastoralists, with the social organization of small-scale societies. In the Later Iron Age, after ca. 1000 A.D., larger political entities emerged in West Africa and Zimbabwe. The process of state formation was still underway at the time of European colonization, notably in the case of the Zulu kingdom of South Africa, while large areas of Africa remained at the level of village organization.

As a result of metallurgical experimentation in many small communities, African iron technology achieved a number of important breakthroughs in the areas of high carbon steel production, the invention of the natural draft furnace, and such processes as the preheating of air. These advances are described in some detail, while the coming of iron to Africa is treated area by area.

EGYPT

"Egypt was the last country of the Near East to enter the Iron Age." Wainwright's phrase sums up two essential points for this discussion: Egypt's conservative resistance to the incorporation of the new technology, and its cultural links with the Near East, rather than Africa.[1] The Nile Valley served as a potential pipeline of ideas and materials from the Near East into the heart of Africa. As far as iron technology is concerned, however, it appears that its influence did not extend much farther than the sluggish waters of the Lower Nile itself, feeding only the narrow strip of floodplain on its banks in Egypt and Nubia.

During the period 4000–1500 B.C. the Egyptians developed an excellent technology of bronze casting and also made the all-important breakthrough from glazes (for faience) to the production of the first glassware. While they also evinced sporadic interest in the use of iron as a rather pricey curiosity, the material was not seriously produced in Egypt until the 7th–6th centuries B.C. (see also chap. 10 by Snodgrass). Some evidence for the consumption of iron exists in the New Kingdom (ca. 1570–1080 B.C.), but it is barely enough to indicate local manufacture.

A list of Egyptian iron objects dating from earlier than the New Kingdom stretches back to ca. 4000 B.C., with two finds of tubular beads at El Gerzah.[2] They were strung with semiprecious stones and gold beads, which gives a fair indication of their perceived value at the time. With a nickel content of 7.5 percent, they are clearly of meteoritic origin. The use of meteoritic iron for amulets persists in the archaeological record; one small iron amulet with a silver head of the Eleventh Dynasty (ca. 2130–1900 B.C.), found at Deir el Bahri, has been shown to have a 10 percent nickel content.[3] The best early evidence for iron objects of apparently nonmeteoric origin are the traces of iron oxide found in the Valley Temple of Menkaure at Giza (IV Dynasty, ca. 2550 B.C.).[4] These were probably the remains of small ritual objects. A similar find was made by Petrie at Abydos, where a group of copper adzes of the Sixth Dynasty (ca. 2350–2150 B.C.) were found cemented together by a wedge-shaped mass of iron rust.[5] Other iron finds dating to the period before the New Kingdom can be found in many compilations but have by now been discredited.[6] These include a list compiled by Maspero,[7] an iron tool from a crack in the facing stones of the Great

Pyramid at Giza (IV Dynasty), and a Twelfth Dynasty (ca. 1990–1780 B.C.) socketed spearhead from a tomb at Buhen in Nubia.[8]

These enigmatic finds of iron in Egypt, from a time when the metal appears to be better known in other countries of the Mediterranean, led Sir Flinders Petrie to coin the term *Sporadic Iron Age*. The objects are small, primarily of a ritual nature, and most of them are of meteoric origin. A lack of iron ore and wood in Egypt has been advanced by some authors by way of explanation, but this argument is unconvincing in the light of later iron production in the country. The lack of early experimentation with iron can best be explained through the general conservatism of Pharaonic Egypt.[9] The country was at all times somewhat isolated, solidly agrarian, and less subject to foreign influences. Egyptian axes and adzes of copper, for example, remained unsocketed for nearly 2000 years after socketed haftings had become accepted elsewhere in the Near East. The sporadic finds of early iron in Egypt could perhaps be the accidental by-product of copper smelting with iron oxide as a flux.[10] This procedure can be documented in African Iron Age cultures with considerably less technological sophistication in copper production than that possessed by the Egyptian Old Kingdom; the process was also known in the Bronze Age of the Near East. Furthermore, hematite is frequently present in copper ores as a result of the oxidation of chalcopyrites. In either case the presence of iron oxide in copper smelting would result in the growth of solid iron crystals at the copper–slag interface. The iron would be hot-short, due to its copper content, and difficult to forge into anything but small objects.[11]

After the rise of the New Kingdom in Egypt (starting ca. 1570 B.C.), more iron appears in the archaeological record and the material is mentioned in some of the texts. Amenhotep III (who reigned ca. 1400–1370 B.C.) received a royal gift of iron from King Tushratta of Mitanni in northern Syria. As related in the Tell Amarna letters, the gift included some iron jewelry and a dagger with a particularly fine handle; the latter was presumably made of gold.[12] The middle palace of Amenhotep III at Thebes has yielded an elongated, tanged projectile point which seems Egpytian in design.[13] From Akhenaten's capital at El Amarna (ca. 1370–50 B.C.) come a small block of oxidized iron attached to the head of a bronze ax, and a pair of iron bracelets decorated with dogs' heads.[14] The most impressive iron objects of the Eighteenth Dynasty are known from the tomb of Tutankhamun (ca. 1350–40 B.C.), where they occupied a position of special honor. Lying on the wrappings of the mummy was a miniature iron headrest of Egyptian design which exhibited a poorly executed weld. Its companion was a dagger with an excellent blade and elaborately decorated sheath and handle of gold. The tang of the blade is somewhat too long to fit properly into the handle recess. Wainwright speculates that Tutankhamun had imported a replacement blade from Syria for the handle of his father's dagger, but the original matching sheath seems to be a good fit. In the annex to the burial chamber 16 miniature chisels of iron were accompanied by similar miniatures in copper. Both sets are of traditional Egyptian design; miniature tools were standard burial goods at the time.

The finds from the Eighteenth Dynasty suggest that small iron items of ritual importance were being made in Egypt but that local metalworkers were not able to forge something like a dagger blade, which requires carburization of a large area. Although Ramses III (ca. 1180–50 B.C.) of the Twentieth Dynasty recorded the making of an iron statuette of a god during his reign, very few iron objects dating to this dynasty have been found. Few everyday implements of iron can, in fact, be attributed to the period before the Assyrian invasion of the 7th century B.C.

Egyptian archaeology has traditionally been concerned with the decipherment of inscriptions and with a study of the artistic and architectural manifestations surrounding the ruling elite. The result of this preoccupation is a lack of knowledge of peasant and village crafts and an emphasis on objects rather than technology. It is not surprising, therefore, that the objects listed so far have received no close scientific scrutiny, except for nickel content determinations on unexpectedly early finds. Carpenter and Robertson achieved a notable breakthrough in this respect in 1930 with a metallographic examination of a series of Egyptian iron implements.[15] The items were selected by Sir Flinders Petrie from his collection at University College, London, and were carefully mapped over sizable surface areas for microstructure and hardness. The investigators agreed to the nondestructive but extremely laborious procedure of polishing representative flat areas of the implements by means of emery paper and polishing cloth fastened to a small steel rule. The whole specimens were then leveled and carefully balanced on the microscope stage by suspending one edge from a thin wire. Even so, Petrie must not have been too sanguine about the idea of letting out really good specimens for this purpose, since no provenience is supplied and ages are described in only the vaguest terms ("believed to date from," "supposed to date from," and so on). Of the nine specimens examined, five deserve special mention.

1. Two small knife-blades, assigned to about 1200 B.C., were found to have been welded along the midline from two strips. Made from bloomery iron carburized to about 0.6 to 0.8 percent carbon, the final product was reheated to the critical range of 700–900° C and rapidly air cooled, producing fanlike structures of pearlite. One blade had a Brinell hardness of about 250 overall.

2. An ax-head of ca. 900 B.C., which had never been used or sharpened, proved to consist primarily of ferrite, carburized to about 0.9 percent carbon for a distance of 25 mm behind the cutting edge. The edge had then been heated to the critical range and quenched, producing a Brinell hardness of 444 at the tip, which decreases to 62 near the blunt end. This specimen apparently still ranks as the earliest quench structure known to metal historians.

3. A chisel of ca. 700 B.C. had been similarly carburized on the cutting edge, reheated, and quenched, yielding Brinell hardnesses between 229 and 137.

4. A sickle, believed to date to the Roman period (ca. 2d or 3d century A.D.), had been carburized on the cutting edge to 0.35 to 0.5 percent carbon, quenched, and then tempered. The tempering had been carried out at too high a temperature—experimentally determined as about 600° C—thus destroying most of the hardness achieved through quenching. The edge showed a Brinell hardness of only 116, compared to a value of 96 for the uncarburized back.

The fact that the objects described were reheated after carburization implies that the carburization process was carried out in a manner which prevented rapid cooling; an enclosed space like a crucible suggests itself. To impart a carbon content above 0.5 percent to ferrite requires prolonged heating in reducing conditions. It is clear that the process could be applied to a small area only, e.g., the cutting edge of an ax or chisel, or a thin strip which can be folded and welded. The sequential use of carburization, reheating, and cooling at 1200 B.C., quenching at 900 B.C., and the addition of tempering in the Roman period are consistent with available knowledge of the blacksmith's art in the Mediterranean basin. The lack of accurate information about the origin and age of the specimens, however, makes firm conclusions difficult. The two knives, for example, do not appear on other lists of Eighteenth Dynasty finds, while the possibility that the pre-Roman objects were imported from elsewhere in the Near East must be kept in mind.

Incredibly, further technical reports on Egyptian iron did not appear for nearly 50 years. A well-known cache of implements, found at Thebes and collected by Petrie in 1895, has recently been investigated by Williams and Maxwell-Hyslop.[16] The collection is now in the Manchester Museum and consists of 23 tools (an adze, file, rasp, saw, sickle, punch, chisels, drill cranks, center bits, and so on) associated with a copper bowl and pointed helmet. The latter was attributed by Petrie to the Assyrian invasion of Thebes (see fig. 13.1) in 663 B.C., but Maxwell-Hyslop suggests dates between the 7th and 4th centuries B.C. Williams's analysis of the implements shows them to consist primarily of ferrite. Some examples were carburized on the most important working surfaces to low carbon steels of 0.1 to 0.2 percent carbon and were then rapidly quenched. A certain amount of self-tempering from the hot core of the implement is evident, but no intentional tempering. One chisel consists uniformly of 0.2 percent carbon steel, with no obvious welds. Most of the specimens were found to have hardnesses below Rockwell C-20, with the exception of some of the carburized and quenched areas, which have Vickers pyramid hardnesses from 300 to 464.[17]

Pharaonic Egypt, which held political sway and exerted considerable cultural influence in the Nile Valley as far as Nubia during the New Kingdom, went into decline at the end of the Twentieth Dynasty (ca. 1080 B.C.). By 950 B.C. the country had been overrun by Libyans, whose leaders were to reign over different sections of Egypt for two centuries. The disintegration of Egyptian political unity allowed a new power to arise on the Nile: the Kingdom of Kush in Nubia. This kingdom started at Napata in the 9th century B.C.; by 722 B.C. it had become sufficiently powerful for its ruler Piye (Piankhy) to strike at the Libyans and claim control of all Egypt. No mention is made of iron weapons on either side during this campaign, and not many iron objects have been attributed to the Twenty-fifth Dynasty, the period of Nubian rule in Egypt (722–664 B.C.). From 667 B.C. onward, the Assyrians were beginning to exert their influence in the Nile Delta, driving back the Nubians. The Assyrian presence culminated in the sack of Thebes by

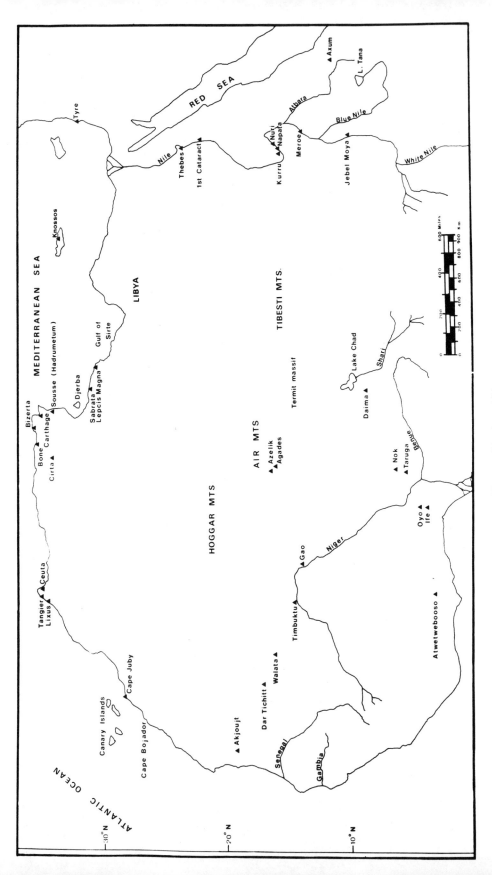

Fig. 13.1. Northern Africa.

Ashurbanipal in 663 B.C., at which point the Nubians lost control of Egypt; the Assyrians departed soon afterward. At the time of its Egyptian campaign, the Assyrian army was well equipped with iron weapons, according to some of the supply lists.[18] Their short-lived presence in the country probably contributed to making iron a more common material in Egypt. It was in the subsequent Saite period (663–525 B.C.), however, that iron became common in Egypt.[19] This development is attributed to the Greek, Ionian, and Carian mercenaries in the Delta. Iron was as common as bronze in their settlements, and evidence of iron smelting has been found. By the 5th century B.C., Herodotus notes that iron was in general use among the Egyptians.

It is evident from this overview that the Egyptians were slow in accepting iron and that it made relatively little impact on their every-day lives. By the time iron finally came into general use, Egyptian influence on neighboring regions had waned and the Iron Age had already started south of the Sahara. It is necessary, therefore, to look at other parts of the continent as possible source areas for the spread of iron working knowledge.

The Kingdom of Kush

The rise of the kingdom of Kush in Nubia provides a continuation of the history of iron in the Nile Valley; its Meroitic capital has commonly been mentioned as the source from which knowledge of the metal was diffused to Sub-Saharan Africa. Ruled successively from Napata (9th century to early 6th century B.C.) and Meroe (6th century B.C.–ca. 320 A.D.), the kingdom became a world power during part of its existence.[20] It was the impressive slag heaps of Meroe, of course, which led Sayce.[21] to christen the ancient city the "Birmingham of Africa" in a moment of Victorian ethnocentrism, and which have caused the widespread belief in its influence on African metallurgy.

Our knowledge of the kingdom of Kush is based primarily on the excavation of its royal tombs by Reisner, as published by Dunham.[22] Since the tombs had escaped the sort of plundering visited on their counterparts in Egypt, a fairly complete sequence is available which divides the history of Kush into 73 well-dated reigns. The royal cemeteries at Kurri and Nuri, near Napata, cover a period from the 9th century to ca. 337 B.C. (reigns 1–26), while those at Begrawiyeh, near

Meroe, were used thereafter (with a few exceptions) until the collapse
of the Meriotic state in ca. 320 A.D. The graves of a series of lesser nobility stretching from the 8th century to ca. 275 B.C. also occur at
Begrawiyeh South. The metal finds from these tombs have been summarized by Trigger,[23] who deals critically with the idea of Meroitic
influence on the African Iron Age, concluding that the iron industry
at Meroe developed too late to have contributed to early iron production in West Africa. It is noted, of course, that royal grave goods do not
necessarily reflect local industry, especially at the village level. The discussion which follows is based primarily on Trigger's summary.

The earliest iron in Nubia does not occur in the well-dated royal
graves but rather in those of the nobility, for which dating is somewhat
less secure. The first occurrence probably derives from the reign of
Piankhy (ca. 747–716 B.C.), i.e., around the time of the conquest of
Egypt. A list of objects from graves of the nobility during the Twenty-
fifth Dynasty (ca. 780–664 B.C.) includes an iron bangle, tweezers, an
arrowhead, a hook, a triangular blade, an ax-head, plus a socketed knife
and adze. The first royal grave with iron goods, at Nuri, dates from the
end of reign 4 (ca. 689 B.C.); the items are an unsocketed adze and a
possible spearhead. The number of iron objects from the period of
Nubian rule over Egypt are few, and it is difficult to determine their
origin. The socketed forms, however, are not traditionally Egyptian,
and they do not survive in Nubia into Meroitic times. Socketed haftings were common in the Near East and Greece at the time, which
suggests importation from more distant sources by way of Egypt. The
last occurrence of a socketed spearhead in Nubia dates from reign 29
(ca. 297–284 B.C.).

It should be observed that imported goods from Egypt are present
in royal Nubian graves before the reign of Piankhy. These items include
alabaster bowls, faience, and gold jewelry. The Napatan rulers, therefore,
were able to obtain luxury goods from Egypt before the time of the
conquest. Because iron objects occur in Nubian graves well before the
Egyptian campaign of Ashurbanipal, it also follows that the Assyrian
invasion did not play a critical role in the introduction of iron to the
Nile Valley. The picture which emerges is that of sporadic importation
of iron objects from Near Eastern sources, penetrating Nubia by way
of Egypt. Once again, the selective nature of grave goods must be kept
in mind. Most of the early Nubian burial items are of bronze, but they

are the kinds of objects (e.g., cups) which must necessarily be cast. Arrowheads do occur, however, and in the early graves they are made almost exclusively of carefully flaked stone.

The first clear evidence of local iron manufacture to come from a grave was found at Nuri and dates to reign 18 (471–466 B.C.). The item is a tanged spearhead, a style which continues into Meroitic times. Confirmation of iron smelting at this time comes from Shinnie's excavations at Meroe, where three radiocarbon dates of ca. 500, 300 and 280 B.C. are associated with iron and slag.[24] Epigraphy and radiocarbon dating are not entirely compatible dating methods, of course, but the designation of ca. 500 B.C. for the beginning of iron production in Nubia seems acceptable. From the reign of Harsiyotef (reign 23, ca. 416–398 B.C.) onward, sufficient evidence accumulates from among the grave goods to show local manufacture. Tanged forms now occur frequently and continue to do so for centuries thereafter. Few iron objects have been found for the period from ca. 322 to 99 B.C. (reigns 28–40), but this may be due to a lack of well-dated graves. After reign 40 iron became common, bearing witness to the rise of the undoubtedly massive iron industry at Meroe.

The skyline at Meroe is dominated by low hills of slag on the north and east sides, while six mounds occur inside the city itself. The ruins of a temple can be seen on one of the mounds; Wainright dated its construction to the 1st century B.C.[25] These impressive slag heaps and Wainright's conclusions have given rise to the widely held assumption that iron smelting knowledge in Sub-Saharan Africa diffused from Meroe—an assumption which deserves close scrutiny. One of the slag mounds was cut into and found to consist of a 1 m slag capping on top of a natural hill; in a second case the entire mound, 12 m high, consisted of slag. The temple on top of a slag mound, however, is now known to have been built around 250 A.D. Shinnie's recent excavations at Meroe have gone far toward illuminating this confused situation, while Tylecote's study of the furnaces and slag provides useful new information.[26] Two distinctly different stages of smelting technology can be identified, the earliest of which may coincide with the first occupation of the ancient city, i.e., at or even before 500 B.C. The evidence consists of small, hemispherical furnace bottoms (slag casts of furnace interiors) and some pieces of iron with adhering slag. The slag contains ca. 63 percent iron oxides, 21 percent silica, and only 3 percent alkalis, suggesting an inef-

ficient process in which no attempt was made to raise the iron yield with
the addition of flux. The furnace bottoms show that the slag collected
in the furnace and was not tapped. The second phase at Meroe coincides
with the Roman period, i.e., the first two centuries A.D. Free-standing
furnaces of mud brick, 1 m high and 50 cm in internal diameter, were
in use; provision was made for tapping the slag, thus raising furnace
productivity tremendously. Meroe's hills of slag date from this period.
Additional conclusions about Meroitic iron production before the Christian era can be drawn from the nature of the objects themselves. Meroitic cemeteries centain more items of bronze than of iron. The latter
are small objects, including both everyday implements and small weapons (arrowheads, spearheads, knives). Nothing the size of a sword-
blade of iron has been found, although bronze swords are common
enough. The conclusion reached about early iron metallurgy in Egypt
seems to hold true for Nubia as well: small items could be manufactured,
but the carburization of larger pieces was not attempted.

The theory that a number of cultural traits found in West Africa—
ironworking, brick architecture, and divine kingship—diffused across the
Sudan grasslands from Meroe was first conceived by Arkell and has
gained a fair amount of acceptance. There is no solid archaeological
evidence to support this view. Artifacts of Meroitic age have been
found west of the Nile in the Bayuda Desert and Kordofan, but both
sites are near the river.[27,28] In any case, it appears that iron smelting
started in West Africa at the same time as in Meroe and probably from
dissimilar sources. The possibility still remains that ironworking diffused
southward from Meroe into East Africa, since the swamp region of the
southern Sudan does not constitute much of a barrier to the movement
of people. The presence of cattle-herding peoples in East Africa by 1000
B.C., and the modern distribution of Eastern Sudanic speakers from the
Sudan to East Africa, form only some of the evidence for long-term
penetration from the Sudan southward. Of particular interest in this
connection are the smelting furnaces found in Tanzania and Rwanda,
to the west and southwest of Lake Victoria.[29] Some of these furnaces
were built of clay bricks and date to the first two centuries A.D. It is
natural to relate them to the Roman-influenced furnaces of Meroe,
although no provision was made for slag tapping in the Tanzanian case.
Schmidt's excavations at Buhaya in Tanzania also yielded a series of
radiocarbon dates between 500 and 400 B.C. in association with iron

slag and Urewe pottery in pits. There seems to be some doubt about the association between the charcoal and pit fill in this part of the site, however, and it may be necessary to consider the closing centuries B.C. as more appropriate ages for the earliest ironworking at Buhaya. In any case there is a good chance that the early iron smelters of this area followed a technique distinctly different from that of Meroe; this problem is discussed later.

ETHIOPIA AND ARABIA

The collapse of the Meroitic kingdom at the beginning of the 4th century A.D. resulted, to a major extent, from the rise of the kingdom of Axum in Ethiopia. The Axumites encroached on the economic preserves of the Meroitic kingdom over a long period and finally sacked Meroe in ca. 320 A.D.

The history of this Ethiopian kingdom is still virtually a closed book, although the excavations of recent years will help to alleviate the problem.[30] Axum was the capital of an area in northern Ethiopia which had been sporadically settled by Semitic speakers from southern Arabia from about 1000 B.C. on. Close cultural contact was maintained between the two areas. Consequently, evidence for the local manufacture of iron at Hajar Bin Humeid in southern Arabia in the 10th–9th centuries B.C. probably implies that the metal was known in Ethiopia at the same time.[31] The word for iron in the Kushitic languages spoken by many Ethiopians—languages brought to the country by peoples from the Sudan well before 1000 B.C.—is accordingly a Semitic one.[32] Excavations at Matara and Yeha have yielded Bronze Age artifacts of the 5th–4th centuries B.C., while evidence for ironworking occurs at Yeha at the same time.[33] Useful information about the economics and metallurgy of Axum comes from such records as the *Periplus of the Erythraean Sea*, a navigator's handbook of the 2d century A.D. It describes Adulis, the Red Sea port of Axum, through which flowed imports of cloth from Egypt and India, glass from Thebes, sheets of brass and copper for local reworking, and Indian iron and steel for the mak- of spears. Swords and axes were also imported. Axum is described as the center of a flourishing ivory export trade, with control of ivory resources over an area stretching as far as Khartoum.

Little is known about the influence of Axum on highland Ethiopia and areas to the south. At the sites of Natchabiet and Lalibela caves near Lake Tana, excavated by Dombrowski, iron does not appear until after A.D. 1000. This "seem[s] to lessen the possibility that iron may have entered Sub-Saharan Africa via the highland plateau of Ethiopia."[34] Chemical analysis of iron objects from the two sites shows variations from mild to very high carbon steels, the carbon contents varying from about 0.2 to 1.6 percent.[35]

During the 1st century B.C., Greek traders—and possibly also Arabs and Indians—were bartering iron objects to the inhabitants of the East African coast.[36] This trade may well have started much earlier, but it is not documented; neither is the early penetration of East Africa by Indonesians and Chinese.[37] The possibility that African metallurgists may have been influenced by technologies developed in the East should be kept in mind at all times.

NORTH AFRICA AND THE PHOENICIANS

The history of Phoenician settlement on the North African coast is of crucial importance to an understanding of the start of the Iron Age south of the Sahara. By 1000 B.C., Negro Africans had developed a settled Neolithic way of life in some parts of the savannah belt south of the desert and in the West African forest. Village life, which was by no means universal for the whole region, was based on food production: cattle and small stock, and the cultivation of millets or rootcrops, depending on the location.[38] The Sahara and the North African coast was populated by Berbers—some of them settled agriculturalists in the Tunisian plain, the majority nomadic pastoralists following their flocks and the seasons between the coast and the desert edge. These were the Libyans of classical literature, and they provided the link between the areas north and south of the desert.

By the end of the 2d millennium, the Phoenicians of the Levantine coast were gaining independence in their small homeland; for the next 1000 years they were to play a prominent role in the diffusion of goods and ideas in the Mediterranean and Red Sea basins. With the decline of the Minoan and Mycenaean states, the way was left open for them to expand their maritime trade aggressively into the western Mediterranean. Their first trading settlement was at Gades (Cádiz) on the coast of Spain, traditionally dated to the 12th century B.C., and it was soon followed by Utica on the North Africa coast.[39] Carthage was founded in ca. 814 B.C., and the Moroccan cities of Mogador, Tangier, and Tamuda in the 7th–6th centuries B.C. By 500 B.C. Phoenician colonies existed at Sabrata and Lepcis Magna on the Tripolitanian coast; at Carthage (modern Tunis), Djerba, Hadrumetum (Sousse), and Bizerta in Tunisia; at Bône and Cirta in Algeria; and at Ceuta, Tangier, Lixus, Tamuda, and Mogador in Morocco (see fig. 13.1). From Carthage and Gades maritime exploration extended down part of the West African coast.[40]

The Phoenicians, with their square-rigged ships and steering oars, could not navigate farther south than Cape Juby, on the latitude of the Canary Isles. The prevailing wind on this coast blows strongly from the north-east year-round. It is essential to be able to tack against it to accomplish a return voyage from south of Cape Juby.[41] If any Phoenician captains attempted a voyage farther down the West African coast, they never returned to tell the tale.

The Phoenician colonies were essentially independent, but Carthage became sufficiently rich and powerful to control western Phoenicia (i.e., the Spanish and North African coast) economically and, in part, politically. While the Phoenician colonists concentrated on agriculture with great success, especially in the Tunisian plain, they were also renowned craftsmen in wood, stone, copper, bronze, and the production of cloth dyed by means of *Murex* shells.[42] Copper was obtained from Cyprus, silver and gold were derived from Ethiopia. They must obviously have had iron and the knowledge to produce steel, since their roots in the Eastern Mediterranean were practically in the heartland of ironworking of the time. No direct evidence for metalworking has been found in Phoenician sites on the North African coast, but many references to iron and copper smelters occur on the stelae. Metal production probably took place elsewhere in the interior, the coastal towns having been sited for reasons other than a metal industry. Ironworking in this region is likely to have been of a utilitarian nature, with emphasis on the tools of war.

The Phoenicians traded extensively with the Berbers, who in turn bartered with the Neolithic peoples south of the desert. To the existing Saharan trade of salt for West African gold and slaves the Berbers probably added Phoenician goods, including iron.[43] Considerable evidence for ancient trade routes across the Sahara exists, both in rock paintings and in the later writings of Herodotus.[44] Two major routes can be traced, one from the Gulf of Syrtis to the bend of the Niger at Gao, with a branch into the Tibesti, the other from Morocco along the Tichitt–Walata escarpment of Mauretania to Timbuktu.

Trading objects of iron, of course, is not the same as trading the technology of their production. The Neolithic villagers of West Africa, however, were culturally ripe for the introduction of a metal technology at ca. 500 B.C. That they acquired it through the Sahara trade is merely a hypothesis at the moment, but the available evidence points in this direction. The coming of iron to West Africa was soon to spark developments on the same order of importance as the Bronze Age did in the Neolithic Near East.

WEST AFRICA AND THE SPREAD OF BANTU SPEAKERS

For lack of data the transmission of metalworking knowledge to West Africa and its subsequent spread to areas east and south of the tropical forest form weak links in this discussion. A few Early Iron Age sites have been excavated in West Africa (mostly in Nigeria), but the connection of Iron Age West Africa with the southern subcontinent can be treated only through linguistic evidence. The outlines of the problem can be stated briefly. Around 500 B.C., or shortly thereafter, iron production existed in West Africa among peoples who had achieved a food-producing economy during the preceding 1000 years. A similar pattern of events was unfolding in the area west and south of Lake Victoria, as described in a previous section. It is not clear whether these early developments in the two areas were related or independent.

During the closing centuries B.C. and the early centuries A.D., Iron Age peoples spread rapidly over the southern subcontinent; by A.D. 300 their villages were scattered from Kenya to Natal Province in South Africa. These migrations are commonly associated with speakers of Bantu languages, who form a clear majority of the inhabitants of the southern subcontinent today—an area covering about one-third of the continent. Bantu languages, in contrast to their wide distribution, are closely related. They form a single sub-sub-family of the Niger–Congo language family, exhibit a time depth of linguistic separation estimated at about 2500 years, and have their ancestral roots in the Cameroon–Nigerian border area.[45] A secondary center for the dispersal of Bantu languages is postulated for the area southeast of the Congo forest.[46] From the archaeological evidence of eastern and southern Africa, especially the pottery styles, it is also possible to relate most of the Early Iron Age migrants of the region to the Urewe tradition which developed around Lake Victoria during the last centuries B.C.[47] It is inevitable, therefore, that we should find connecting links between West and East Africa during the Early Iron Age in future archaeological excavations.

The evidence for early iron production in West Africa comes from the Jos plateau in Nigeria, north of the Niger–Benue confluence. The archaeological material belongs to the Nok culture, which is primarily known for pottery sculptures uncovered in the course of modern tin mining. The site of Taruga, excavated by Fagg,[48] yielded pottery sculptures, slag, and no fewer than thirteen furnaces (located by proton magnetometer) with associated radiocarbon dates of 440, 300, and 280 B.C. The furnaces, which have been investigated by Tylecote, varied in internal diameter from 30 to 100 cm and had thin-walled mud shafts built over pits cut in the decomposed granite of the site.[49] The smaller ones were probably about 1 m high from floor to rim and the larger ones about 2 m high. There was no provision for slag tapping. Slag occurred in the furnaces primarily as small pieces (nothing over 5 kg); a chemical analysis gives the composition as about 57 percent iron oxides, 26 percent silica, 9 percent aluminum oxide, 2 percent alkalis, plus minor constituents. The smelting procedure at Taruga, in other words, did not include the addition of any flux.

The only other well-dated evidence of early iron smelting in West Africa comes from Ghana at the site of Atwetwebooso, which has been dated to the 1st–2d centuries A.D.[50] An example of the cultural changes wrought in a Stone Age food-producing economy by the introduction of iron comes from the Nigerian site of Daima, near Lake Chad,[51] but the appearance of iron at this site is not securely dated.

The pottery from early sites like Taruga does not resemble Early Iron Age pottery from Lake Victoria or other parts of eastern and southern Africa. Soper finds a possible resemblance in the Early Iron Age pottery of Chad, where the introduction of iron remains undated but is guessed at about 2000 years ago.[52] This suggests an introduction of an Early Iron Age ceramic tradition to eastern and southern Africa from the savanna belt of the southern Sahara and Sudan. The situation is undoubtedly complex, covering several centuries and thousands of miles and

involving large-scale cultural changes. At the moment it is more instructive to view the changes which must have taken place in West
Africa and the savanna region adjoining it from a remove of many miles
and a few centuries, at the time when Early Iron Age peoples were
settling in eastern and southern Africa.

EASTERN AND SOUTHERN AFRICA

Before the advent of the Iron Age, eastern and southern Africa was
populated by sparsely distributed bands of Stone Age hunter-gatherers.
Modern surviving remnants of these peoples can be found among the
Bushmen of Botswana and the Kalahari desert. Exceptions to the rule
existed in East Africa and the Horn by ca. 1000 B.C., where Stone Age
pastoralists arrived from the Sudan. They were probably Cushitic
speakers[53] who made pottery, herded cattle, and may have cultivated
cereal foods. At the end of the 1st millennium B.C., Stone Age hunters
with small flocks of sheep also appeared on the southernmost coast of
Africa; their origins are entirely obscure and their physical type is indis-
tinguishable from those of the earlier hunter-gatherers of the region. In
contrast to these early stirrings of a "Neolithic" way of life, food production (both animal and vegetable), pottery making, metalworking,
and village life arrived in the rest of eastern and southern Africa as a
package, carried by Iron Age peoples who were presumably Bantu
speakers. Archaeological evidence for this movement of people consists
primarily of pottery, radiocarbon dates, and modern language distribu-
tions but is quite convincing. Early Iron Age pottery is sufficiently
similar throughout the whole region to indicate a relatively short period
of evolution from a common source;[54] it can be related to the Urewe
wares from Lake Victoria of ca. 300–0 B.C. By ca. 300 A.D., the presence
of Iron Age peoples can be documented at sites in the Kivu Province
of Zaire (fig. 13.2); in Rwands, Burundi, southern Uganda, and northern Tanzania; near the coast and inland from Mombasa in Kenya; in
Malawi, southern Zambia, Zimbabwe, Transvaal, and Natal. Early
Iron Age pottery from Transkei has been dated to A.D. 700.[45] Undated
finds of Early Iron Age pottery have been reported from many other
sites, indicating that the information gaps will be filled in due course.
This means that Early Iron Age migrants settled essentially all those
areas of the subcontinent that were suitable for sorghum agriculture

Fig. 13.2. Early Iron Age Sites in Southern Africa.

and that they did so in a period of time which cannot be easily subdivided by radiocarbon dates. The only obvious parallel to a movement of people on this scale is the settling of North America by Europeans, or Europe by Neolithic farmers.

The culture of the earliest Iron Age peoples cannot be described with much confidence at the moment. By compiling the evidence from all the areas mentioned and by extrapolating from later finds of the Early Iron Age—which lasted until ca. A.D. 1000—some attempt can, however, be made. Early Iron Age peoples were organized in village communities and were already living in the clay-walled huts which are such a commonplace of the African countryside. Their food sources consisted of small stock and some cattle, as well as cultivated cereals, supplemented to a great extent by the teeming game population and wild plant foods. They were able to smelt iron for the making of most of their implements, as well as copper for smaller items of decoration.

A catalogue of metal artifacts from the earliest Iron Age is rather brief. Sites of the Gokomere and Ziwa facies (ca. A.D. 250–550) in Zimbabwe are best known; they have yielded iron spear-or arrowheads with flat-faced blades, and bracelets made of copper wire wrapped around a fibre core. Iron and copper slag occur in several places. In southern Zambia, the mounds at Kalundu and Gundu, dating to the same period, have yielded flat-bladed arrowheads, a razor, a finger ring, and strips of iron which may be thumb-piano keys.

During the second half of the 1st millennium A.D. and during the Later Iron Age which follows, Iron Age populations increased progressively in the southern subcontinent. The area involved is vast and there was little competition against these metal-equipped farmers and pastoralists. The Stone Age inhabitants were absorbed through client relationships and marriage, or compressed toward the southwestern tip of Africa. Remnant Stone Age groups eventually came to occupy those areas of the Cape Province that are unsuitable for cattle and sorghum agriculture (i.e., the Karoo and the winter rainfall belt along the coast) or else retreated into mountains and deserts. Their influence on the Iron Age populations can be seen today in both the physical characteristics of South African Negroes and the Khoisan elements in Southern Bantu languages. In addition to these influences from local inhabitants, a constant movement and dispersal of Iron Age peoples served to give rise to the great number of closely related languages and dialects of the Bantu subfamily.

Around A.D. 1000 a "second wave" of Iron Age immigrants arrived in Rhodesia and parts of Zambia, probably from the Congo basin. In Zimbabwe these Later Iron Age people are associated with modern

Shona speakers; in the archaeological record they are identified with the so-called Ruins Tradition of Great Zimbabwe.

They engaged in trade with the Arabs on the East Coast, at first perhaps only in ivory but later certainly in gold. A large number of mineshafts in the granite regions of Zimbabwe attest to a period of intensive mining, while the remains of stone buildings on many hilltops give an indication of the extent of the trading organization which developed as a result. The center of this system was at Great Zimbabwe, where a series of well-known dry stone buildings arose between A.D. 1250 and 1450.[56] In addition to the interest in gold there is evidence for the making of bronze in this period.[57] Iron production was probably a localized phenomenon, but Zimbabwe, Zambia, and Katanga shared a common copper ingot type at this time, in the shape of an X-shaped cross. After the demise of Great Zimbabwe, this tradition was continued at other centers such as Khami and Dhlo-Dhlo.

During the 2d millennium A.D. a strong tradition of iron and copper smelting also developed among the Sotho-speaking peoples of the Transvaal. From Phalaborwa and the Lowveld region around it, metalworkers traded their wares for agricultural products, among other things, because they lived in a rather infertile region. The author has worked extensively in this area, which accounts for the emphasis that follows.[58]

Copper was extensively mined in the Lowveld, with the miners concentrating on secondary mineralizations of malachite. Their smelting techniques (fig. 13.3) did not include the art of roasting sulfide ores of copper, but they got a good yield from the scarce malachite outcrops by using iron oxide as a flux. Copper was used almost exlusively as a decorative item in the form of wire or bangles. Bronze and brass were also being produced, but the few cases of chemical analysis indicate that alloying was somewhat haphazard. Extensive tin-mining was being carried out at Rooiberg, on the Transvaal Highveld, but very little is known about the circumstances surrounding it[59] as the evidence was largely destroyed by industrial mining.

The iron smelters (fig. 13.4) of Phalaborwa used fairly pure magnetite pebbles as an ore source, adding quartz sand to the charge to produce a slag. The blacksmiths rendered their product into chisels, axes, adzes, spears, arrows, and agricultural hoes. The ubiquitous iron hoe, still in use today, was probably the most common implement of the African Iron Age. It consists of a large tanged blade, which is hafted at right

Fig. 13.3. Nineteenth century copper smelting furnace at Molotho, near Phalaborwa, Transvaal. Photographed by C. E. More (1960).

Fig. 13.4. Nineteenth century iron smelting furnace of Phalaborwa type in Dahvane's chiefdom, Venda area, Transvaal. Diameter approximately 1 m.

angles through a wooden handle and is used in a chopping motion like a pick. The shape of the blade varies from one area to the next: diamond-shaped in the Transvaal, heart- or leaf-shaped in Zimbabwe, shovel-shaped in Zambia. Iron hoes were often used as a medium of exchange, especially in the payment of brideprice.

In the early 19th century the militaristic kingdom of the Zulu developed in Natal Province of South Africa. The repercussions of the campaigns launched by Shaka and Dingane were felt as far as the Kenya coast. Large areas of the Highveld plateau in South Africa and Zimbabwe were virtually depopulated. Into this vacuum moved European settlers, bringing industrial iron production into the interior of Africa.

Today, traditional Iron Age culture still survives in many rural areas of Africa. Blacksmithing is still common, but industrially produced iron forms the raw material. Indigenous iron smelting can be reconstructed only with difficulty in eastern and southern Africa, using octogenarian informants, and the art is dying out rapidly in West Africa as well. Enough ethnographic recording has been done, however, to lead to some fairly startling conclusions.

IRON SMELTING: ARCHAEOLOGY AND ETHNOGRAPHY

The tremendous impact of the introduction of iron technology on Africa south of the Sahara is now readily recognized, while the spread of Iron Age peoples over the southern subcontinent is known at least in outline. The technology of metal production, however, is poorly known. This is doubly unfortunate, for Africa provides a unique laboratory for the understanding of preindustrial iron metallurgy, in both its ethnography and archaeology. Iron smelting continued in most parts of Africa until this century and is still practiced in a few areas today. Recent revivals of interest in metal technology have also led to the reproduction of smelting techniques by old craftsmen who can still remember the process as used in their youth. Ethnographic observations, therefore, provide a record of iron smelting procedures for the African continent which cannot be equaled anywhere else. Historical inferences can be made from the distribution of some of these techniques, while archaeological evidence can be employed to put them in time perspective. The latter, however, is still rather scanty and patchily distributed.

At first glance, the available ethnographic information is remarkable for its bewildering variety. Every conceivable method of iron production seems to have been employed in Africa, some of it quite unbelievable. To some extent this is due to the lack of metallurgical knowledge on the part of the observers—travelers, missionaries, and anthropologists alike. A major contributing factor to the current lack of understanding of African metallurgy, however, arises from the fact that a number of its procedures do not fit comfortably into the traditional categories of metallurgical wisdom. African iron smelting is generally seen as a 2000-year elaboration of the Early Iron Age techniques of the Mediterranean, but this is a limited view. It resulted from an external infusion of ideas, to be sure, but new inventions were added locally. Its evolution followed ideas which were highly observational and inventive, producing a wide variety of approaches, furnace designs, and smelting products. In several recorded cases, African iron smelting cannot be described in terms of either the direct or indirect process, because its primary product is neither wrought iron nor cast iron. Instead, a bloom of *high carbon steel* was produced directly from the smelting furnace and subsequently *decarburized* in the forge.

This fusion of the direct process with incipient cast iron production is an African invention, though it may have been anticipated by the famous natural steel of Noricum. It requires furnace temperatures which are intermediate between those of the bloomery hearth and the blast furnace, and reduction of a metal-rich slag by an excess of carbon. It is not surprising to find, therefore, that two other inventions can be credited to African metallurgists. These are the induced draft furnace with its tall shaft (2–7 m), on the one hand, and a measure of preheating of bellows-driven air on the other. Ironically, the arts of the blacksmith received rather short shrift. The laborious procedures of carburization, quenching, and tempering, which form such essential components of the European and Near Eastern traditions, were rarely applied in Africa in a systematic way. They should probably be seen as necessary elaborations of a process which yields low carbon iron as the primary product and was consequently rendered unnecessary by the African shortcut to high carbon steel.

A detailed catalogue of 19th and early 20th century observations on African metallurgy is provided by Cline;[60] this is still the major work on the subject. A recent revival of interest in metal technology has produced a number of new publications[61] and several more can be expected in due course. A very short outline of the literature, with emphasis on the distribution of certain critical items, is provided here.

Ore, Fuel, and Flux

In contrast to more elaborate mining methods for gold and copper ores, the gathering of iron ore in Africa was a very simple process. Surface deposits of high-grade iron ore, which are fairly common, could be exploited by picking up the material or by the simplest form of open-stope mining. At two Iron Age smelting areas investigated by the author (Phalaborwa in the eastern Transvaal, South Africa, and Buhwa in southwest Zimbabwe) pebbles of magnetite and hematite, respectively, with iron oxide contents in excess of 90 percent, occurred in quantity on the surface.[62] One of the largest known deposits of magnetite occurs in the Murchison Range of the eastern Transvaal and was extensively utilized by early smelters. The ore includes as much as 20 percent titanium oxide and cannot be used in industrial blast furnaces; at the relatively modest temperatures of traditional smelting furnaces, however, the titanium was not reduced and the ore was therefore perfectly suitable for iron production.

Preindustrial iron smelters require ore with at least 70 percent iron oxide content to achieve success if a flux is not used. Below this value smelting becomes self-defeating because two parts iron oxide are required to form a slag with one part of the unwanted silicious material. Where iron ore of this purity was not available, washing and panning methods were used to concentrate iron oxides from lower grade ores. These procedures are well documented in Africa.[63] Bellamy and Harbord describe a roasting, washing, and panning process, used by the Yoruba of Nigeria, which converts an ore of 43 percent silica, 49 percent Fe_2O_3 and 3 percent Fe_3O_4 to a concentrate of 85 Fe_2O_3 plus silica.[64] The author has observed the apparent use of ferricrete (about 40% Fe_2O_3) for smelting at sites near Livingstone, Zambia; some method of concentrating the oxide would have been necessary. The panning of ilmenite from river sand by the Mbeere of Kenya is described by Brown; while similar observations have also been made in West Africa.[65] The latter examples illustrate the grade end of the iron ore spectrum.

The use of a concentrated iron oxide charge in smelting implies that no flux was used to replace iron oxide in the slag. Tylecote notes one exception to this rule for preindustrial iron smelting: the use of small quantities of sea shells in Malabar, India.[66] At least one other example has subsequently been documented in Africa, among the Mbeere of the Kiritiri area in Kenya. They use a simple, unplastered hole in the ground to smelt iron but add as a flux some ground shells of the giant *Achatina* land snail.[67] Cline mentions other ethnographic accounts of the use of shell and bone as a flux, among the Fipa (Northern Zambia) and Venda (Northern Transvaal), for example, but these are not convincing.[68] A copper slag from the Venda area has been shown to have a calcium oxide content of 21 percent;[69] the copper ore deposits of this region are said not to be high in calcium, implying the use of a flux in this case. It should be noted, however, that calcium oxide is effective as a flux only in concentrations of about 10–15 percent. At increased concentrations it rapidly raises the slag melting point above the capabilities of the furnaces under discussion.

The use of magnetite as a flux in copper smelting has been documented at Phalaborwa.[70] Because copper ores like malachite are frequently associated with iron oxides, natural fluxing presumably also occurred on many occasions. The resultant slags are iron rich and have led investigators to mistake copper smelting sites for examples of iron smelting. It is possible that slag misidentifications have contributed to the apparent lack of information about copper production in Africa, especially in the Early Iron Age.

Fluxing may have taken place in many cases of iron smelting as a result of the type of fuel used. Iron smelters usually choose dense, hot-burning woods to make charcoal. At least one example of such a wood which is widespread in the savanna of southern Africa (*Combretum imberbe*, leadwood) yields ash with an alkali content of 90 percent, which has a folk use as whitewash. The same may be true of many other species of dense African woods. In the Phalaborwa case the ore used was nearly pure magnetite (above 95% Fe_3O_4), but the slag produced from it contained about 50 percent iron oxides, 10 percent alkalis, 20 percent silica, 5 percent alumina, plus other constituents. This means that aluminosilicates (probably quartz sand) were added to the charge to produce a fluid slag in which reduced iron particles could move toward one another to form a bloom; the iron yield was improved by the high alkali content of the fuel.

Furnaces and Bellows

In the variety of its furnace designs Africa occupies a clear first place in the history of iron metallurgy. This may be due, in part, to the late survival of many traditional smelting methods and their consequent recording in ethnographic accounts, but the variety of local inventions plays a principal role as well. The furnaces can be divided into four types. These are (1) simple bowl furnaces of the most rudimentary sort; (2) low shaft furnaces, with no provision for slag tapping during smelting; (3) low shaft furnaces, with an entry hole for removal of the bloom and the tapping of slag; and (4) tall shaft furnaces which produce a natural draft. The bellows associated with the first three types are usually of the double drum or pot variety, although bag bellows are also known in defined areas. The distribution of these items are significant and may provide some insight into the evolution of African smelting techniques.

Simple bowl furnaces, with one or more tuyeres directing an air blast into a shallow hole in the ground or into a simple hearth made of a few blocks of clay, occur primarily in the Lakes region and East Africa. Intermittent cases are also recorded for the Congo basin and Angola. These furnaces are usually associated with the use of drum or pot bellows, i.e., a pair of solid air chambers of wood or ceramic, covered with movable diaphragms of skin. Valves are not used; the air nozzles are therefore only loosely connected to the trumpet-shaped inlets of the ceramic tuyeres in order to prevent hot air from being sucked back into the bellows. This arrangement also creates a venturi effect in the tuyere inlet, thus aspirating air into the furnace. Cline sees the combination of bowl furnaces and drum or pot bellows as a survival of the earliest form of African smelting, which suggests a movement through the Congo basin toward East Africa and Angola. Bellows of this type are illustrated in tomb paintings of ca. 1450 B.C. in Egypt in connection with copper smelting. It should be remarked that bag bellows are also associated with bowl furnaces in a few cases, as indeed they are with all three types of the bellows-driven furnaces mentioned. These pliable leather bags can be opened and closed by hand during pumping, thus providing a rudimentary valve effect. Bag bellows occur in the Upper Niger and Senegal, along the East African coast, and in southern Africa. This distribution is correlated with "leather-working, pastoral tribes, or in areas most open to influence from the Horn of Africa, Berber lands or the Indian Ocean trade."[71] Tuyeres in Africa are almost exclusively made of baked clay with heavy quartz temper. The only known exception to this rule is stone tuyeres found in the southern half of Southwest Africa.[72]

Later developments in African smelting have all but obliterated the use of bowl furnaces. Low shaft furnaces built of clay are distributed intermittently all over Sub-Saharan Africa. They are virtually the only type to be found south of the Zambezi and in most of southern Zambia. These furnaces have an internal height of 1 m or less and may be partially sunk into the ground. They are, in fact, a logical elaboration of the bowl furnace and make no provision for slag tapping during smelting. The bloom is removed through the top upon completion of the smelt. Bellows supply the air blast through inlets which may vary from two to five. The air inlets are placed well above the furnace floor to allow for the accumulation of the bloom and slag in the bottom. In the Transvaal the air inlets are narrow slits starting near the rim of the furnace and continuing to ground level; this design may well have a wider distribution.

A later development of the bellows-driven, low shaft furnace makes provision for slag tapping and removal of the bloom through an entrance in the wall. During smelting, the doorway functions as an air inlet but is plastered shut around the tuyeres directed through it. Furnaces of this type are widely distributed throughout Sub-Saharan Africa but do not occur farther south than Zimbabwe. In the latter case they are associated with the Later Iron Age, i.e., with arrivals postdating A.D. 1000.

The distribution of bowl furnaces probably represents an early, exploratory phase of the earliest Iron Age migrants. In the case of low shaft furnaces the distribution is easier to interpret. Most of the Bantu speakers of South Africa are now regarded as descendants of Early Iron Age peoples who entered the country between ca. A.D. 300 and 1000. The occurrence of these furnaces in southern Africa and their sporadic presence in the rest of Sub-Saharan Africa can thus be seen as a survival of Early Iron Age technology. The low shaft furnace with side entrance, associated with the Shona of Zimbabwe and groups farther north, is presumably an elaboration of the Later Iron Age and dates after A.D. 1000.

The distribution of tall shaft furnaces are of particular interest. They are tall enough (2–7 m) to produce a natural draft, requiring no bellows. They can be found in Ghana, Nigeria, the Cameroons, parts of the Congo basin, Northern Zambia, Malawi, and among people like the Galla in the Horn of Africa. In Zambia they are associated with peoples who entered the country from Katanga after ca. A.D. 1500. Two possible examples have been excavated in Zimbabwe[73] in an undated context, but no other cases occur this far south. Their limited distribution suggests African invention in Later Iron Age times, providing a specialized adaptation to the process of making high carbon steel at relatively high temperatures. The only other occurrence of contemporary natural draft furnaces in the world seems to be in Upper Burma.[74]

HIGH CARBON STEEL PRODUCTION

The African smelting process by which high carbon steel is produced directly from the furnace has been sporadically reported during the 20th century without making much impression on metal historians. It has been documented in both archaeological and ethnographic contexts for several widely separated parts of the continent and now deserves serious consideration. Much of the work on this subject is still unpublished and cannot be described in detail in this chapter.

Nigeria

Bellamy and Harbord provide a classic description of the high carbon steel process as practiced in Nigeria.[75] Bellamy observed iron production in the village of Ola Igbi, about 25 km north of Oyo; the whole village population of 120 people was almost exclusively involved in mining and smelting. The inhabitants of Ola Igbi excavated 1.5 to 2.5 kg chunks of siliceous hematite (about 40% SiO_2) and roasted them overnight on a fire of green timbers. The roasting process would presumably cause multiple fissures in the ore and impregnate it with carbon deposits. The ore was then pulverized in a mortar and concentrated by washing and panning. The final result was an ore concentrate of 85 percent Fe_2O_3 and less than 15 percent SiO_2. In the course of smelting, a "flux" of iron slag (38% SiO_2, 10% Fe_2O_3, 38% Fe_3O_4) from a previous smelt was added to the furnace. The furnace was of the natural draft variety, egg-shaped inside, with a maximum interior diameter of 0.75 m, a height of 1.8 m, and a circular opening of 0.23 m diameter in the top. The walls were pierced by six vertical apertures, 0.5 m high and 0.15 m wide on the interior surface, plus a doorway which occupied about one-quarter of the interior diameter at floor level. During smelting, a pair of tuyeres was inserted through each of the six apertures and three pairs of tuyeres were inserted through the doorway; the spaces around them were closed with clay. In the middle of the furnace floor an aperture of 0.1 m diameter communicated with a tunnel underneath the furnace. The aperture was plugged from below with wet sand but was frequently pierced during smelting to tap off slag. With tuyeres in place and all apertures closed, the total cross-sectional area of air inlets relative to the outlet at the top of the furnace was in the ratio 3 : 7, inducing a strong draft.

In the smelting operation the furnace was charged through the top twelve times at 2-hour intervals, with slag being tapped at the same time. The first two charges involved about 2.25 kg slag from the previous smelt plus "2 bushels of charcoal" each; the third charge consisted of 2.25 kg each of slag and ore, plus charcoal. Only ore and charcoal were added thereafter, with the amount of ore being gradually increased to a maximum of about 11–13 kg for the last three charges. The slag tapped from the last three charges was saved for further use. The total amount of ore used was in excess of 75 kg, producing a bloom of about 35 kg. Harbord considered the smelted metal to be "pig iron which had been partially decarburized by the oxidizing flux; it is really a puddled steel, low in sulphur and phosphorus." The carbon content averaged 1.6 percent but was subsequently reduced in a blacksmith's forge (in another village) to 1 percent. Depending on the type of implement to be made, decarburization could be carried further. It comes as no surprise that the smith considered the locally smelted metal vastly superior to imported European hoop iron, which was available for forging and cost 80 percent less.

In 1976 the author visited an Ibo village near Nsukka, in the eastern region of Nigeria. Most of the men in the village are blacksmiths who produce iron objects of traditional design from imported metal. Their forges consist of a simple depression in the ground, one tuyere, and a pair of wooden drum bellows pumped with sticks. Previously, iron had been smelted in natural draft furnaces in a neighboring village, but it is no longer produced. One blacksmith exhibited a small anvil which had been forged from locally smelted iron and likewise claimed that it was "much stronger" than the imported metal currently available. Analytical corroboration is unfortunately not available but I assume that it is high carbon steel.

Ghana

Iron smelting was practiced until about 1920 by peoples of the Upper Region of Ghana. In the early 1970s the techniques were reproduced for study purposes (sometimes unsuccessfully) in several villages and were recorded by Pole.[76] The furnaces were of a relatively tall shaft variety (1.3 m) and were activated by pot bellows which were rapidly pumped for 8 hours. The ore used appears to have been rather low grade lateritic hematite (about 50% Fe_2O_3 or less), requiring frequent slag tapping and resulting in only 3–8 kg of bloom (of which half may be slag and charcoal). The bloom is broken up on an anvil to remove the worst impurities; the remaining nodules are packed together in a ball of clay, heated in a forge, and hammered together. The consolidated bloom is then immediately forged into an implement. The blacksmith, therefore, knows what he is going to make before he starts consolidating a piece of bloom.

From the configuration of the furnaces described by Pole it seems that the active zone is directly above a puddle of slag and that the resulting bloom is raked from this same area. The smelting procedures observed were not always successful, as the blacksmiths involved were working from rather hazy memory and seem not to have concentrated the ore properly. Metallographic analyses of blooms produced earlier in the century in the same area, however, show a product which cannot be explained through solid reduction.

A specimen from Lambussie proved to be a two-phase metal consisting of pearlite and ferrite, with an average carbon content of about 0.5 percent.[77] Due to heating in the 1300–1400°C range, the ferrite exhibits a Widmanstätten structure. The structure is not what one expects in a solid, sintered bloom but exhibits crystals which grew slowly in a liquid wüstite slag.[78]

Another sample was taken from a bloom kept as a curiosity in the compound of Sowle Wakyesu at Lawra. The bloom was a saucer-shaped specimen of about 4 kg, with a fairly smooth surface covered with oxide. One assumes that it had already been reheated and hammered together since the sponge-coral surface normally associated with a bloom is absent.

In an attempt to cut a sample from this bloom in Accra, seemingly no impression could be made on it with an alloyed rotary diamond blade. A nodule which was not thoroughly attached to the main body of the specimen was broken off and proved to have a most unusual structure (figs. 13.5 and 13.6). It varies from a partly oxidized cast iron containing free graphite flakes (carbon content about 3.5%) on one side to a Widmanstätten structure of ferrite and pearlite on the other. Zones of pearlite and of carbide needles in a pearlite matrix can be observed between the two extremes. This sample appears to be an oxidized cast iron; it could also have resulted from a reaction between cast iron and a piece of ore. The average carbon content is that of a high carbon steel, above 1 percent.

Examples of implements forged from known bloom specimens could not be obtained. Sections of hoe blades from the same area show low carbon materials (0.02 to 0.15% carbon) with signs of excessive hot and cold working. One example exhibits laminations achieved through multiple lap welds. The forging techniques employed were clearly not of the same sophistication as the smelting process; they decarburized the high carbon smelting products.

Other Ethnographic Examples

High carbon products of smelting furnaces have been observed in two other cases. Shona smelters from Zimbabwe recreated the process at the 1930 Agricultural Show in Johannesburg. An analysis of the forged bloom by Stanley showed areas of high carbon steel, interspersed with low carbon regions.[79] Stanley attributed this phenomenon to carburization of the bloom during prolonged contact with excess charcoal in the furnace.

During a recent reconstruction of iron smelting by elders of Buhaya in northern Tanzania, who had smelted iron as young men, similar high carbon steels were produced. The process was observed by Avery and Schmidt, who measured temperatures above 1500°C in the furnace.[80] These were achieved by means of wooden drum bellows pumped very rapidly and attached only loosely to the tuyeres. The tuyeres extended 0.4 m into the furnace; part of the blast passed back along the outside of the tuyeres, producing a high level of preheat and air blast temperatures of 500–800°C at the tips. During the first stages of the smelt a highly fluid slag, including a substantial amount of metallic iron, was produced and absorbed in a bed of grass in the bottom of the hearth.

Fig. 13.5. Microstructure of iron bloom from compound of Sowle Wakyesu at Lawra, Upper Region, Ghana. Magnification of 40× on 35 mm negative.

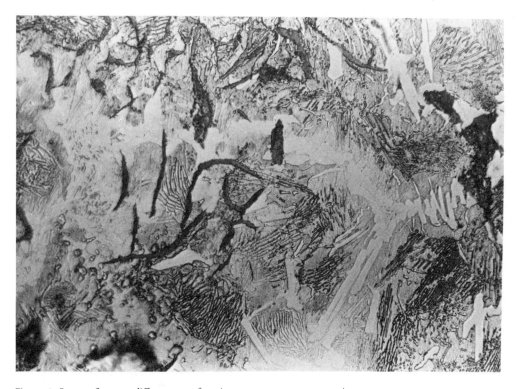

Fig. 13.6. Same as fig. 13.5; different area of specimen, 157× on 35 mm negative.

Capillary action by the charcoal skeletons of the grass stems served to produce thin alternating surfaces of slag and carbon. Further reduction of the slag produced the same sort of high carbon material as observed in the Ghanaian case. In the subsequent forging of implements the bloom was progressively decarburized to yield objects of mild steel. It is important to note, however, that the familiar sandwich structure of low carbon iron carburized on the surface is absent here.

Avery explains iron bloom production in terms of two quite distinct technologies. In the traditional sponge iron or bloomery iron process a relatively cold air blast causes reduction in the furnace shaft. This is a gas–iron oxide reaction which produces a fine dispersion of solid, metallic iron particles. The atmosphere must be highly reducing, with a CO/CO_2 ratio above $2:1$ below $1000°C$ and increasing to $4:1$ at $1500°C$. As soon as the ore melts, further reduction of the glassy slag stops for all practical purposes. The bloom consists of a solid, metal-filled slag at this stage. As the slag dissolves more impurities and fluxes and becomes more homogeneous, its melting point drops and it drains away from the solid iron, which coalesces into a bloom. In this case slag removal through tapping or draining into the furnace bottom is very important. The slag is fluid and has a low melting point.

The Haya process involves the formation of a fluid wüstite–fayalite slag and its infiltration into a bed of solid carbon, in this case grass char. The fluid slag then reacts with the solid carbon, releasing CO bubbles and allowing iron crystals to nucleate. As oxygen is removed from the slag, the iron crystals grow and the slag becomes increasingly iron-lean and more refractory. The final product is a low iron, porous slag with very high melting point and a conglomerate of large, relatively perfect iron crystals. Where carbon is entrained in the growing crystals they become carburized, yielding a highly variable microstructure and a high average carbon content. It is clear that Avery's analysis, with variations, also explains the other high carbon blooms described in this section.

Examples from Archaeology

Africanist archaeologists have been remiss as far as the analysis of iron specimens is concerned. A few examples can be found in the literature, however, and some of these serve to put African metallurgy in time perspective.

Stanley's metallographic examination of specimens from Great Zimbabwe illustrates the state of the art in 14th century Zimbabwe; it resembles the smelting and forging process described in the previous section.[81] The specimens include a small piece of iron excavated by Caton-Thompson from underneath the Conical Tower, consisting of low carbon and medium steel separated by a line of slag inclusions.[82] A spear blade from beneath the floor of the Maund Ruins shows medium carbon steel in the center with low carbon material surrounding it. This is, of course, the exact opposite of a carburized structure; it is medium carbon steel decarburized on the surface during forging.

Iron specimens excavated by Dombrowski[83] from caves near Lake Tana in Ethiopia and dated to the 13th–14th centuries yielded carbon determinations of 0.62, 0.79, and 1.62 percent. No metallographic examinations were done, but a value of 1.62 is much higher than is likely to result from carburization in a forge. It sounds much like the material described by Bellamy in Nigeria.

Several specimens from archaeological sites near Phalaborwa, Transvaal (excavated by the author), and from the Orange Free State[84] exhibit structures of uniform medium steel.[85] These specimens date from the last 500 years and their production is associated with simple low-shaft furnaces, local survivals of a technology which arrived with Early Iron Age peoples.

The question remains whether the African method of making high carbon steel blooms is a logical elaboration of the direct process of the Early Iron Age in the Mediterranean, the result of influences from India and China, or a local invention. This question must perforce be left unanswered.

Nonferrous Metals

Africa is unusual in metallurgical history in that the major part of it skipped the Bronze Age entirely, its technology changing directly from stone to iron as the common material for the making of implements. Other metals were also known, however, and their relationships with iron require attention. It will suffice here to deal with gold, copper, and tin.

Gold was probably known in several parts of Africa before the coming of iron. Egypt obtained some of its gold supply from the Upper Nile as early as the Sixth Dynasty (ca. 2300 B.C.) and also imported this prized metal by sea from the Land of Pwene (Punt), presumed to be the Horn of Africa. The Carthaginians are known to have bartered for gold with Africans on the coast of South Morocco.[88] The gold trade from West Africa became highly lucrative for Arab traders in medieval times, who were also obtaining it from the East African coast during the heyday of Great Zimbabwe. In spite of this trade, gold was never considered particularly important for internal consumption, being readily traded for salt or manufactured goods. Its production was not necessarily tied to the spread of ironworking.

When looking at the history of copper in Africa, the picture is confusing. It is generally assumed that copper production spread alongside iron in areas south of the Sahara, but this has by no means been demonstrated. North Africa, by contrast, can be shown to have shared in the Bronze Age of the Middle East. In Egypt, copper was known in the 5th millennium B.C. By the 3d millennium, bronze had been discovered in the Middle East and was diffusing around the Mediterranean basin. In Nubia, copper first occurs at Khor Bahan in the 4th millennium B.C.[87] and was being mined by Egyptians at Abu Seyal by ca. 1950 B.C. After the decline of the Egyptian Middle Kingdom, Nubians produced it extensively at Kerma (ca. 1750 B.C.). Copper and bronze were introduced into Ethiopia from Arabia during the 1st millennium B.C.

A list of booty, plundered in Libya by Egyptians during the 13th century B.C., includes bronze objects. The Phoenicians in Northwest Africa had bronze and were presumably trading it into the Sahara. Evidence for a "Copper Age" which precedes the arrival of iron is accumulating for sites as far south as 16° N.[88] Archaeological investigations by Mauny in Western Mauretania, followed by excavations of Lambert,[89] have uncovered early copper artifacts, evidence of local copper production, and mines dating to the 5th century B.C. at Guelb Moghrein near Akjoujt. Two copper arrowheads of a tanged. leaf-shaped type have recently been found near Agades in Niger; evidence for early copper mining also exists. P. L. Gouletquer, who is working south of the Air Mountains, reports copper furnaces near Azelik with two radiocarbon dates of ca. 90 and ca. 1360 B.C.; further documentation of these interesting finds is awaited.[90]

South of the Sahara, finds of copper are rather enigmatic. The metal is not mentioned in Ghana before ca. A.D. 900; its earliest known occurrence in Nigerin is at Daima, where it dates to ca. A.D. 800.[91] In Katanga, copper cross ingots have been found in graves at Sanga in association with Kisalian pottery, dated to ca. A.D. 700–900. Other objects from the graves include tubular beads, pieces of sheet copper, and well-made necklaces of interwoven wire.[92]

In Zambia and Zimbabwe, by contrast, small finds of copper (mostly core-wrapped wire bracelets) occur in Early Iron Age contexts before ca. 500 A.D. A copper mine at Phalaborwa in the Transvaal has been dated to A.D. 750 and earlier evidence of copper in the area is likely. On the basis of these early dates for copper at the southern end of the continent it is assumed that copper smelting was known to the earliest Iron Age migrants and that the apparent absence of early copper in some areas to the north is a result of incomplete archaeological investigation.

During the 2d millennium A.D. copper achieved considerable importance in several regions of Africa. The lost wax "bronze" castings of West Africa, especially the elaborate objects from Igbo Ukwu and the human heads from Ife and Benin, have become widely known.[93] These castings belong to a tradition of craftsmanship that spans most of the 2d millennium and probably has its roots in the Arab trade from North Africa. The materials used were leaded bronze and brass for casting and nearly pure copper for objects produced by smithing and chasing.[94] The raw materials were imported across the Sahara, as testified by Arab records from the 11th century onward.

In Shaba (Katanga) a flourishing export trade in copper was based on rich malachite deposits, and "Katanga cross" ingots became widely dispersed toward the East Coast. The ingot shape was copied with variations in size as far south as the Limpopo. In Zimbabwe, copper was intensively mined from surface mineralizations (i.e., malachite). At Great Zimbabwe bronze became of sufficient interest to be made into objects like spears.[95] Ancient tin mines are not known in Zimbabwe; the alloying material was probably imported in smelted form from the tin mines of the Rooiberg area of the Transvaal.[96] Copper was also intensively mined from surface mineralizations in the Transvaal Lowveld, Messina, and Waterberg areas, with bronze being made in some cases.[97] Brass was also produced, but the origin of the zinc in the alloy is unknown and has been ascribed to the East Coast trade.[98]

By the time of European colonization of the Cape of Good Hope, copper trinkets were observed among the Stone Age peoples of the area, while iron tools were still extremely scarce among them. This reemphasizes the role of copper in this part of the world as an item of trade and personal adornment, while iron served as the technological base of agricultural peoples.

CONCLUSIONS

An attempt is made in this chapter to describe the metallurgical history of Africa in the Iron Age. This is a frustrating task, for the quality of information available varies widely from area to area. Some glaring gaps exist in the record of archaeological research, while metallurgical information is scarcer still. It has been necessary, therefore, to bridge the gaps with ethnographic information and with inferences drawn from the areas where archaeological data are more plentiful. The areas of Africa which are best known historically and archaeologically— specifically Egypt, Nubia, and Carthage—are comparatively less exciting to the student of metallurgy when viewed in the broad sweep of the technological history of iron. Sub-Saharan Africa, which holds potential information about a new departure in the history of iron metallurgy, is not well known at all.

Two central points emerge with respect to iron in Sub-Saharan Africa. The first is that the coming of iron to the region sparked a major social revolution, leading to large-scale population movements and the settling of the southern subcontinent by Negro peoples. The Bronze Age is missing from the culture history of this area; instead, the introduction of iron fulfilled the role which copper and bronze did in other parts of the Old World. Knowledge about this period is rapidly increasing, but the archaeological coverage is spotty. The areas through which the introduction must have taken place, i.e., West Africa and the Sahel, are particularly poorly known.

The second important item is the nature of African iron metallurgy itself. A number of independent inventions were made, notably the induced draft furnace and the preheating of bellows-driven air. More significant still, African smelters devised a smelting technology which is apparently unique, producing high carbon steel directly from the furnace. The evolution and distribution of this method are little known in the archaeological record and can only be documented with any success from ethnographic observations. Between the early 1930s and the 1960s virtually no significant work was done on African metallurgy; the result is a nearly complete lack of time depth to the description of its technology.

A large proportion of the current generation of Africanist archaeologists have turned their attention to a study of the Iron Age. This is due to a realization that archaeology holds the key to a historical description of the present destribution of African peoples and the not inconsiderable political implications of such a history. At the moment, the focus of interest is still on the construction of ceramic sequences and documentation of the movements of peoples during the past 2000 years. Beyond such a culture history, however, lies the problem of explanation of the observed events. A study of Africa's iron technology forms an important part of the explanation and it is already under way. It is an exciting new chapter in archaeology and the history of pyrotechnology.

ACKNOWLEDGMENTS

I thank Donald H. Avery, Thomas N. Huffman, Raymond Mauny, Irving Rouse, and Thurstan Shaw for valuable comments on an earlier draft of this chapter. Avery, a former student of Cyril S. Smith, also generously provided unpublished information for inclusion in this Festschrift.

NOTES

1. Gerald A. Wainwright, "The Coming of Iron," *Antiquity* 10 (1936): 5–24.

2. Ibid.; for lists of iron objects see also J. Leclant, "Le fer à travers les âges," *Annales de l'est* (Nancy), 16 (1965): 83–91, and Alfred Lucas and James R. Harris, *Ancient Egyptian Materials and Industries* (London, 1962).

3. Cecil H. Desch, "Report on the Metallurgical Examination of Specimens for the Sumerian Committee of the British Association," *Reports of the British Association for the Advancement of Science*, 1936, 308–10.

4. Dows Dunham and W. J. Young, "An Occurrence of Iron in the Fourth Dynasty," *Journal of Egyptian Archaeology* 28 (1942): 57–58.

5. Herbert Garland and Charles O. Bannister, *Ancient Egyptian Metallurgy* (London, 1927).

6. Bruce G. Trigger, "Meroe and the African Iron Age," *African Historical Studies* 2 (1969): 23–50.

7. Hermann Olshausen, "Die Erfinder der Eisentechnik—Diskussion," *Zeitschrift für Ethnologie* 39 (1907): 373.

8. David Rańdall-MacIver and C. Leonard Woolley, *Buhen* (Philadelphia, 1909).

9. Trigger, "Meroe and the African Iron Age."

10. Theodore A. Wertime, "The Beginning of Metallurgy: A New Look," *Science* 182 (1973): 875–87.

11. Donald H. Avery, personal communication, 1977.

12. Wainwright, "The Coming of Iron."

13. Alfred Lucas and James R. Harris, *Ancient Egyptian Materials and Industries*, 4th ed. (London, 1962), pp. 238–39.

14. Leclant, "Le fer à travers les âges," p. 85.

15. Henry C. H. Carpenter and John M. Robertson, "The Metallography of Some Ancient Egyptian Implements," *Journal of the Iron and Steel Institute* 121 (1930): 417–54.

16. Alan R. Williams and K.R. Maxwell-Hyslop, "Ancient Steel from Egypt," *Journal of Archaeological Science* 3 (1976): 383–85; Arthur Harden, "The Composition of Some Ancient Iron Implements and a Bronze Found at Thebes," *Memoirs of the Manchester Literary and Philosophical Society* 41, no.14 (1897), provides a chemical analysis of the two specimens.

17. Rockwell C-20 approximately equals 200–240 VPH (Vickers pyramid hardness). A modern steel of 0.2% carbon might have a VPH of 100–120; fully quenched it has VPH of perhaps 150 or a Brinell hardness of about 145. Vickers and Brinell hardness values are about equal below 300. Other equivalents: VPH 460 = Brinell 433, VPH 300 = Brinell 295. The hardness values given by Williams do not square with his observed carbon contents; the values given by Carpenter and Robertson do. It is possible that the dissimilar metallographic techniques (polished cross sections of the Theban materials versus polished surfaces for the others) may account for some of the apparent differences in carbon contents reported.

18. Radomír Pleiner and Judith K. Bjorkman, "The Assyrian Iron Age: The History of Iron in the Assyrian Civilization," *Proceedings of the American Philosophical Society* 118 (1974): 283–311.

19. Trigger, "Meroe and the African Iron Age."

20. Peter L. Shinnie, *Meroe, a Civilisation in the Sudan* (London, 1967).

21. Henry A. Sayce, "Second Interim Report on the Excavations at Meroe: the Historical Results," *Liverpool Annals of Archaeology and Anthropology* 4 (1912): 53–65.

22. Dows Dunham, *The royal Cemeteries of Kush*, 5 vols. (Boston Museum of Fine Arts, 1950–63).

23. Trigger, "Meroe and the African Iron Age."

24. Peter L. Shinnie, "The Sudan," in *The African Iron Age*, ed. Peter L. Shinnie (Oxford, 1971) and H. S. Green, "Sudanese Radiocarbon Chronology: a Provisional List," *Nyame Akuma* 6 (1975): 10–24.

25. Gerald A. Wainwright, "Iron in the Napatan and Meroitic Ages," *Sudan Notes and Records* 26 (1945): 5–36.

26. Ronald F. Tylecote, "The Origin of Iron Smelting in Africa," *West African Journal of Archaeology* 5 (1975): 1–3.

27. Anthony J. Arkell, *A History of the Sudan to 1821* 2d ed. (London, 1961), pp. 174, 176–77.

28. Anthony J. Arkell, "A Roman Coin of the Emperor Diocletian at El Obeid," *Sudan Notes and Records* 16 (1933): 187.

29. Jean Hierneaux and M. Maquet, "Cultures prehistorique de l'âge de metaux au Rwanda-Urundi et au Kivu, Congo Belge, II," *Memoires de l'Academie royale de Sciences d'Outer-Mer* 10 (1960): 5–88; Brian M. Fagan, "Radiocarbon Dates for Sub-Saharan Africa V," *Journal of African History* 8 (1969): 513–27; Peter R. Schmidt, Historical Archaeology: A Structural Approach in an African Culture (Westport, Ct., 1978).

30. François Anfray, "Aspects de l'archeologie Ethiopienne," *Journal of African History* 9 (1968): 345–66, and Neville Chittick, "Excavations at Aksum 1973–4: A Preliminary Report," *Azania* 9 (1974): 159–205.

31. Gus W. van Beek, *Hajar bin Humeid* (Baltimore, 1969), pp. 285, 361.

32. Leclant, "Le fer à travers les âges."

33. Anfray, "Une campagne de fouilles à Yehà"; Anfray "Matara," *Annales d'Ethiopie* 7 (1967): 33–88, Merrick Posnansky, "Bantu Genesis—Archaeological Reflections," *Journal of African History* 9 (1968): 1–11.

34. Joanne Dombrowski, "Preliminary Report on Excavations in Lalibela and Natchabiet Caves, Begemeder Province," *Annales d'Ethiopie* 8 (1970): 29.

35. Joanne Dombrowski, "Excavations in Ethiopia: Lalibela and Natchabiet Caves, Begemeder Province" (Ph.D. diss., Boston University, 1971), pp. 141–42, 222.

36. Posnansky, "Bantu Genesis."

37. George P. Murdock, *Africa, Its Peoples and Their Culture History* (New York, 1959), pp. 212–70; Jan J. Duyvendak, *China's Discovery of Africa* (London, 1949).

38. Roland Oliver and Brian M. Fagan, *Africa in the Iron Age* (Cambridge, 1975), pp. 1–21.

39. Donald B. Harden, *The Phoenicians* (London, 1963), pp. 52–68.

40. Oliver and Fagan, *Africa in the Iron Age*, p. 9.

41. Raymond Mauny, "The Western Sudan," in *The African Iron Age*, ed. Shinnie (Oxford, 1971), pp. 66–88.

42. Harden, *The Phoenicians*, pp. 127–47.

43. Oliver and Fagan, *Africa in the Iron Age*.

44. Mauny (1977, personal communication) notes that more than 500 rock paintings and engravings of chariots occur along the two routes.

45. Joseph H. Greenberg, *The Languages of Africa*, 3d ed. (Bloomington, 1970).

46. Malcolm Guthrie, *Comparative Bantu*, 4 vols. (Farnborough, 1968–71).

47. David W. Phillipson, *The Later Prehistory of Eastern and Southern Africa* (London, 1977).

48. Bernard Fagg, "Recent Work in West Africa: New Light on the Nok Culture," *World Archaeology* 1 (1969): 41–50.

49. Ronald F. Tylecote, "Iron Smelting at Taruga, Nigeria," *Journal of the Historical Metallurgical Society* 9 (1975): 49–56, and "The Origin of Iron Smelting in Africa," *West African Journal of Archaeology* 5 (1975): 1–3.

50. Merrick Posnansky, "Iron Furnace Excavations at Srede and Dapaa (Debidi)," *Nyame Akuma* 7 (1975): 21–22.

51. Graham Connah, "The Daima Sequence and the Prehistoric Chronology of the Lake Chad Region," *Journal of African History* 17 (1976): 321–52.

52. Robert Soper, "A General Review of the Early Iron Age of the Southern Half of Africa," *Azania* 6 (1971): 5–37.

53. John E. G. Sutton, "The Archaeology and Early Peoples of the Highlands of Kenya and Northern Tanzania," *Azania* 1 (1966): 37–57.

54. Thomas N. Huffman, "The Early Iron Age and the Spread of the Bantu," *South African Archaeological Bulletin* 25 (1971): 3–21; Soper, "General Review of the Early Iron Age"; Phillipson, *The Later Prehistory of Eastern and Southern Africa.*

55. Michael Cronin, "Early Iron Age Pottery from the Ciskei and the Transkei," *Eastern Cape Naturalist* 60 (1977): 20–21.

56. Roger Summers, *Zimbabwe, a Rhodesian Mystery* (Johannesburg, 1963); Thomas N. Huffman, "The Rise and Fall of Zimbabwe," *Journal of African History* 13 (1972): 353–66; Peter S. Garlake, *Great Zimbabwe* (London, 1973).

57. G. H. Stanley, "The Composition of Some Prehistoric South African Bronzes with Notes on the Methods of Analysis," *South African Journal of Science* 26 (1929): 44–91, and "Primitive Metallurgy in South Africa: Some Products and Their Significance," *South African Journal of Science* 26 (1929): 732–48.

58. Nikolaas J. van der Merwe and Robert T. K. Scully, "The Phalaborwa Story: Archaeological and Ethnographic Investigation of a South African Iron Age Group," *World Archaeology* 3 (1971): 178–96.

59. M. Baumann, "Ancient Tin Mines of the Transvaal," *Journal of the Chemical, Metallurgical and Mining Society of South Africa* 19 (1918): 120–32; C. J. Gray, "Ancient Tin Mines of the Transvaal," ibid., pp. 211–14; Tudor G. Trevor, "Some Observations on Ancient Tin Mines in the Transvaal," ibid., 12 (1912): 267–75; 13: 48–49; "Ancient Tin Mines of the Transvaal," ibid., 19 (1919): 282–88.

60. Walter Cline, *Mining and Metallurgy in Negro Africa* (Wisconsin, 1937).

61. Ronald F. Tylecote, "Iron Smelting in Pre-industrial Communities," *Journal of the Iron and Steel Institute* 203 (1965): 340–48; "Iron Smelting at Taruga, Nigeria;" and "The Origin of Iron Smelting in Africa;" various authors in the *Journal of the South African Institute of Mining and Metallurgy* 74 (1974): 211–72; Peter R. Schmidt and Donald H. Avery, "Complex Iron Smelting and Prehistoric Culture in Tanzania," *Science* 201 (1978): 1085–89; and Nikolaas J. van der Merwe, "Production of High Carbon Steel in the African Iron Age: The Direct Steel Process," *Proceedings of the VIIIth Pan-African Congress of Prehistory and Quaternary Studies*, in press.

62. Van der Merwe, *The Carbon-14 Dating of Iron* (Chicago, 1969), and "Field Methodology and Iron Age Metallurgy at Buhwa, Rhodesia," *Occasional Papers of the National Museums and Monuments of Rhodesia*, ser. A, 4 (1978): 101–05; van der Merwe and David J. Killick, "Square: An Iron Smelting Site near Phalaborwa," in *Iron Age Studies in Southern Africa*, ed. van der Merwe and Thomas N. Huffman (South African Archaeological Society, Goodwin ser. 3, 1979), pp. 86–93.

63. Cline, *Mining and Metallurgy in Negro Africa*, pp. 26–27.

64. Charles V. Bellamy and F. W. Harbord, "A West African Smelting House," *Journal of the Iron and Steel Institute* 56 (1904): 99–127.

65. Jean Brown, "Ironworking in Southern Mbeere," *Mila* 2 (1971): 37–50, University of Nairobi Institute of African Studies; Rene Gardi, "Sickles from the Sand," *100Al* (Bulletin published by Lloyd's Register of Ships) no. 4, (1959): 32–35; Hamo Sassoon, "Iron-smelting in the Hill Village of Sukur, North-eastern Nigeria," *Man* 64 (1964): 175–78.

66. Tylecote, "Iron Smelting in Pre-industrial Communities."

67. Brown, "Ironworking in Southern Mbeere."

68. Cline, *Mining and Metallurgy in Negro Africa*, pp. 74–75.

69. Stanley, "Primitive Metallurgy in South Africa."

70. Van der Merwe and Killick, "Square: An Iron Smelting Site near Phalaborwa," and Willem J. Verwoerd, "Sekere produkte van primitiewe koper-, yster-, en bronssmeltery in Oos-Transvaal met besondere verwysing na Phalaborwa," *Tegnikon* 9 (1956): 91–104.

71. Cline, *Mining and Metallurgy in Negro Africa*, p. 102.

72. Beatrice H. Sandelowsky and Wayde C. Pendleton, "Stone Tuyeres from Southwest Africa," *South African Archaeological Bulletin* 24 (1969): 14–20.

73. Michael D. Prendergast, "A New Furnace Type from the Darwendale Dam Basin," *Rhodesian Prehistory* 7, no. 14 (1975): 16–20.

74. Tylecote, "Iron Smelting in Pre-industrial Communities."

75. Bellamy and Harbord, "A West African Smelting House."

76. Leonard M. Pole, "Iron Smelting in Northern Ghana," *National Museum of Ghana Occasional Paper* 6 (1974); "Account of an Iron Smelting Operation at Lawra, Upper Region," *Ghana Journal of Science* 14 (1974): 127–36; "Iron-working Apparatus and Techniques: Upper Region of Ghana," *West African Journal of Archaeology* 5 (1975): 11–39; "Iron Smelting Procedures in the Upper Region of Ghana," *Bulletin of the Historical Metallurgical Group* 8 (1975): 21–31.

77. Ghana National Museum no. 54–346.

78. N. J. van der Merwe, J. A. Berger, and D. H. Avery, unpublished.

79. G. H. Stanley, "Some Products of Native Iron Smelting," *South African Journal of Science* 28 (1931): 131–34.

80. Donald H. Avery, unpublished field notes, and Schmidt and Avery, "Complex Iron Smelting and Prehistoric Culture in Tanzania."

81. Stanley, "Some Products of Native Iron Smelting."

82. Gertrude Caton-Thompson, *The Zimbabwe Culture* (Oxford, 1931).

83. Dombrowski, *Excavations in Ethiopia*, p. 222.

84. Timothy M. O'C. Maggs, *Iron Age Communities in the Southern Highveld*, Occasional Publications of the Natal Museum 2 (1976).

85. Van der Merwe, unpublished.

86. Mauny, "The Western Sudan."

87. Bruce G. Trigger, *Nubia under the Pharoahs* (London, 1976).

88. Mauny, personal communication, 1977, and "The Western Sudan."

89. Nicole Lambert, "Les industries sur cuivre dans l'ouest Saharien," *West African Journal of Archaeology* 1 (1971): 9–21.

90. Mauny, personal communication, 1977.

91. Connah, "Daima Sequence."

92. Jacques Nenquin, "The Congo, Rwanda and Burundi," in *The African Iron Age*, ed. Shinnie (Oxford, 1971), pp. 183–214.

93. Thurstan Shaw, *Nigeria: Its Archaeology and Early History* (London, 1978).

94. Frank Willett, "Spectrographic Analysis of Nigerian Bronzes," *Archaeometry* 7 (1964): 81–83; Thurstan Shaw, articles in *Archaeometry* 8, 9, 11 (1965, 1966, 1969), and

"The Analysis of West African Bronzes: A Summary of the Evidence," *Ibadan* 28 (1970): 80–89.

95. Stanley, Composition of Some Prehistoric South African Bronzes," and "Primitive Metallurgy in South Africa."

96. Trevor, "Some Observations on Ancient Tin Mines of the Transvaal"; "Ancient Tin Mines of the Transvaal"; Bauman, "Ancient Tin Mines of the Transvaal"; Gray, "Ancient Tin Mines of the Transvaal"; Cline, *Mining and Metallurgy in Negro Africa.*

97. G. H. Stanley, "Notes on Ancient Copper Workings and Smeltings in the Northern Transvaal," *Proceedings of the University of Durham Philosophical Society* 3 (1910); "Some Observations on Ancient Mine Workings in the Transvaal," *Journal of the Chemical, Metallurgical and Mining Society of South Africa* 12 (1912): 370–72; Percy A. Wagner and Hugh S. Gordon, "Further Notes on Ancient Bronze Smelters in the Waterberg District, Transvaal," *South African Journal of Science* 26 (1929): 563–74; Percy A. Wagner, "Bronze from an Early Smelter in the Waterberg District," *South African Journal of Science* 23 (1926): 899–900.

98. Cline, *Mining and Metallurgy in Negro Africa.*

14

The Evolution of Iron
and Steel Technology
in East and Southeast Asia

JOSEPH NEEDHAM

INTRODUCTION

The fundamental feature of the development of siderurgy in East Asia, differing in this from all other culture areas, is that iron could be melted and cast there almost as soon as the metal was known.[1] Elsewhere in the Old World nearly three millennia elapsed between the first ironworking and the first casting of iron, while the New World never knew the metal independently at all.

To appreciate the significance of this accomplishment, one must recall a few basic facts about iron, a metal whose properties depend not only on the small quantities of metallic or nonmetallic substances mixed with it but also upon its history, that is, on the succession of treatments to which it has been subjected. In the first place, iron ore is treated in a blast furnace at a temperature of not less than $1130°$ C; here the ore loses oxygen, gains carbon, and is converted to liquid metal which, when cooled, is known as cast iron. It is hard and very brittle, neither weldable nor malleable; and suitable only for objects unlikely to suffer shock or impact. Its carbon content lies between 1.5 and 4.5 percent, the carbon being either free in the form of graphite or combined as iron carbide (Fe_3C). It is this compound, known as cementite that confers the hardness and brittleness.

To rid cast iron of its carbon content, it must be treated under exidizing conditions. In modern times, in the West, this has been achieved in a reverberatory, or "puddling," furnace, in which the fuel and the cast iron to be refined are kept separate, the cast iron being heated by a flame blown over it. In such a furnace the carbon, silicon, sulfur, and phosphorus present are oxidized and pass away as slag or vapor. Pure, or "wrought," iron is thus produced. The melting point of wrought iron (1535° C) is much higher than that of cast iron, but in a reverberatory furnace it never becomes molten; it only reaches a pasty state from which it can be forged into slabs, balls, or blooms. In ancient and medieval China, as in the West, before the invention of the reverberatory furnace, refining by repeated forging, hammering, and heating in a blast of air was employed to achieve similar results. Wrought iron has qualities entirely different from those of cast: it is tough, fibrous, malleable, and useful for wire and nails, chain links, horseshoes, and agricultural implements. Its carbon content will usually be not more than 0.06 percent, or some 80 times less than that of cast iron. In medieval and later times cast iron was always known in China as "raw iron" (shêng thieh) and wrought iron as "ripe iron" (shu thieh).

The basic fact about steel is that its carbon content is intermediate between that of cast iron and wrought iron. In low carbon steels it ranges from 0.1 to 0.9 percent, and in high carbon steels rises to as much as 1.8 percent. Broadly speaking, the higher the carbon content the harder the steel. For all cutting edges a hard steel is required, but the rest of the blade should ideally be ductile and have a certain elasticity. From early times ironworkers appreciated that these associated properties depended not only on the steel but also on the durations and successions of heating and cooling. Hardening by plunging hot steel into a cold liquid, that is, "quenching," was a very early discovery. Annealing, or slow cooling, makes the metal more ductile, while tempering (raising to a moderate heat after quenching and then cooling slowly) allows the smith to obtain almost any desired combination of hardness and ductility.

The passage from one form of iron to another has been achieved in practice in a number of different ways. In the West, the withdrawal of carbon from cast iron was carried out in the fining, or puddling, process. The introduction of more carbon into wrought iron was accomplished in ancient times by the process known as cementation, where soft bars were packed with charcoal and heated for a considerable time at about 1100° C. Under these conditions carbon entered the iron and produced what is known as "blister steel"—steel with a hardened outer layer—and this was certainly the oldest steel-making process in the West. In modern times, after it became possible to generate enough heat to melt the steel

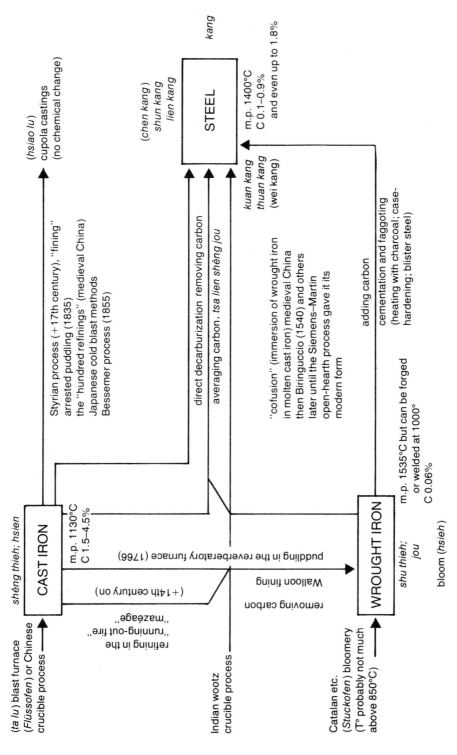

Fig. 14.1. Three processes for making steel: Chinese crucible (using cast iron), Indian wootz crucible, and Catalan bloomery (using wrought iron).

in crucibles, it became more logical to add a specific amount of carbon. Equally simple, once the carbon content of different kinds of iron had become known and sufficiently strong furnaces were available, the technique of melting either cast iron and wrought iron or cast iron and ore together in suitable proportions became possible. This was the Siemens-Martin, or open hearth, process; as we shall see (p. 527), the principle was known and used in China before A.D. 500. Since about 1860 direct transition from cast iron to steel has been carried out in the West by the Bessemer process in a converter, in which a blast of air is blown through the white-hot metal to oxidize the carbon in it. This process again had Chinese antecedents far earlier (p. 534).

Throughout antiquity and the Middle Ages down to the 14th century, the extraction of iron was carried on in small-scale furnaces filled with alternate layers of iron ore and charcoal. In these nothing melted but the slag, which could be tapped off, the iron remaining as a pasty "bloom" that needed long hammering on an anvil to free it from the pieces of slag still embedded in it. In Roman times cast iron seems to have been made only unintentionally, probably as the accidental product of the overheating of these "bloomery" furnaces. The wrought iron from the ancient and medieval bloomeries was variable in carbon content, probably in general very low, but steel could be obtained from it by cementation. Of course the primitive smith, both in the East and West, added or removed carbon, as well as other elements, without understanding the chemistry of what he was doing, but he knew the properties that he wanted to obtain and had his own rough tests as well as a skilled and experienced eye. There is some evidence that iron was occasionally liquefied in Roman and Carolingian times in Europe, but again this would have been the exception, not the rule, and not repeatable at will. Not until the 14th century were true blast furnaces built in Europe.

There is as yet no precise date for the appearance of blast furnaces in the West. Manuscript evidence points to A.D. 1380, but the locality is uncertain—perhaps the Rhineland, perhaps the region of Liège. The first illustrations of blast furnaces are of a much later date, probably from the early 16th century. They were only 6 m high or less; indeed, some were no more than about 2 m. These small sizes should be borne in mind when we come to consider the Chinese furnaces of similar and much earlier date. (The foregoing facts are summarized in fig. 14.1.)

The Earliest Chinese Developments

Like other civilizations, the Chinese used copper and bronze for weapons, for agriculture, for cult vessels, and for domestic purposes from the middle of the 2d millennium B.C. onward. By this time cast bronze objects already had existed in the Middle East for a millennium and a half (back to 3000 B.C.), and casting as such, for the precious metals, had begun at least a millennium earlier (4000 B.C.). Shang copper and bronze can be dated to 2000 B.C. at the earliest. As a background to the Chinese techniques for handling iron and preparing steel one has to consider the knowledge available in the Bronze Age. Here it must be borne in mind that in the occidental world the true Iron Age did not begin until about 1100 B.C.

Let us start by taking as a focal point the reference in the *Lü Shih Chhun Chhiu* (Master Lü's Spring and Summer Annals) of 239 B.C. to straight double-edged bronze swords. Probably a standard weapon in the middle of the 1st millennium B.C., they are the subject of a discussion between a sophist and a swordsmith.

> A swordsmith said, "White metal [tin] makes the sword hard, yellow metal (copper) makes it elastic. When yellow and white are mixed together, the sword is both hard and elastic, and these are the best ones." Somebody argued with him, saying, "The white is the reason why the sword is not elastic, the yellow is the reason why the sword is not hard. If you mix yellow and white together the sword cannot be hard and elastic. Besides, if it were soft it would easily bend, and if it were hard it would easily break. A sword which easily bends and breaks—how could it be called a sharp one?" Now a sword does not change its nature, yet some may call it good and some bad; that is only a matter of opinion. If you know how to distinguish between good and bad arguments, nonsense will cease. If you do not, then there is no difference between Yao and Chieh.

Three points are evident here. First, Bronze Age swordmakers could vary little the properties of their weapons, and only by changing the proportions of the metals used. Secondly, the sophist is arguing in terms that lacked linguistic precision, confusing hardness with brittleness and elasticity with malleability. The third point, which enshrines the whole essence of ancient siderurgy, is the value of empiricism: the knowledge that comes from practical experience compared with that derived from theoretical reasoning only. Nothing less than the making and manipulation of welded steel would solve the swordsmith's problem, but it was to be a long time before this could be achieved.

Moreover there are grounds for thinking that as long as wrought iron and cast iron alone, the one so malleable and the other so brittle, were available, bronze necessarily retained some of its preeminence, at least for weapons. The significant transition was not so much from bronze to iron as from bronze to steel.

Yet there is evidence that for some centuries there was a transition period while iron was replacing bronze. Examples have long been known of axes with iron cutting edges attached to bronze heads, long-hafted dagger-axes which have an iron core covered with bronze, as well as arrowheads with bronze points and iron stems. Such items as these indicate ironworking, though not a true iron technology, as far back as the very beginning of the Chou period (1030 B.C.). The iron in these weapons seems to have been meteoritic. More recently another bimetallic ax has been found, this time at a late Shang site, Thai-hsi Tshun, and in this case the iron part is definitely smelted. That takes us back to about 1300 or 1200 B.C., comparable with the time of the Hittites, though this ironworking was presumably not systematic as theirs was.

DEVELOPMENT OF IRON AND STEEL TECHNOLOGY IN SOUTHEAST ASIA

Spearheads with cast-on bronze sockets and blades of smelted iron have been discovered in tombs at Ban Chiang in northeastern Thailand. Their discoverers have dated them to a period between 1600 and 1200 B.C., that is, contemporary with the Hittite smiths or indeed rather earlier, but doubt persists about the validity of their estimate. Excavations in recent years at this site and at another, Non-Nok-Tha, also in northeastern Thailand, have revealed a wealth of bronze objects from levels which, it is claimed, indicate datings as far back as 3500 B.C., a time when the alloy was not yet known in China and was rather rare even in the Middle East. The 3d millennium B.C. was the apogee of bronze technology in the Middle East and in Europe, while in China it was the 2d, as already noted, the great age of the Shang bronze founders. These Thai bronzes, some of which have a very high tin content, differ little in technical style from both China and the West. Other objects of iron alone found in the burials are also claimed to go back to 1600 B.C. or slightly later.

The difficulty of dating the Thai finds lies in the stratigraphy of the sites. Both Ban Chiang and Non-Nok-Tha are large, low mounds which have been used for untold centuries as burial places. In the words of one of the chief excavators, there has been "extensive disturbance at the site during its long history as a cemetery, and later as a source of cinerary urns, compounded by the very difficult soil conditions, with contamination of the samples ... possibly from rootlet penetration after deposition but before excavation." This means that the layering has for millennia been disturbed by the digging of intrusive burial pits to widely varying depths, and they were never sealed off by brick walls from the surrounding soil. Yet there has been a tendency to assume that radiocarbon datings from fragments of wood in the vicinity will give the age of the burials themselves and the objects buried with them. Evidently this is a dangerous supposition. All the burials were inhumations, not cremations. Logically less questionable would be the estimates of the age of potsherds from the actual burials, but it is doubtful that the thermoluminescence method is applicable to the type of pottery in question, which contains little or no feldspar or quartz. Best of all would be the radiocarbon datings from the collagen remaining in the skeletons, and these agree on a period from about 750 to 50 B.C., entirely in keeping with Chinese figures for the developed Bronze and Early Iron ages. Thus a high antiquity for Thai iron and bronze objects has not yet been proved.

At the same time it may turn out that Thai bronze metallurgy antedated that of China, if only because the great tin deposits of Malaya, so well known, were close at hand. For iron, however, there would be no reason for expecting such a lead. In neighboring Vietnam there was perhaps an earlier start than in China, as the Gò-Bông period (Early Bronze Age) is placed at 2000 to 1500 B.C., the Dông-Dâu period (Middle Bronze Age) at 1500 to 1000 B.C., the Gò-Mun period (Late Bronze Age) at 1000 to 500 B.C., and the Dôngso'n period, with its famous bronze drums, at 500 to 258 B.C. The 5th century B.C. was the time when Vietnam's Iron Age also began. These dates are based on radiocarbon measurements. Compared with Thailand, Vietnam is relatively rich in Bronze Age sites. In Burma there is no known bronze before iron, but at Thaungthaman thermoluminescence results give dates ranging from 700 to 400 B.C. for early iron, which again is not inconsistent with what we know for China.

The recent controversies about radiocarbon dates and the beginnings of metallurgy in Southeast Asia have all been part of a broad reassessment of the prehistoric relations between the Austronesian and Chinese cultures. The arguments include much very speculative material, some of it concerned with linguistics, into which we cannot go here. But it is not contested that influences from the south played an important role in the development of classical Chinese culture; sinologists have recognized this in the *Lokalkulturen* concept for many years past.

Very little study has been made so far of the later development of iron and steel technology in Southeast Asia, but insofar as iron casting took the most prominent place there rather than iron forging, the outspread of Chinese siderurgy would be the most probable explanation. Steeling would therefore have been done by decarburization rather than by cementation. Whether the cofusion method also reached Southeast Asia in due course remains another open question. Evidence for a Chinese export trade in iron comes from the Tabon caves in the Philippines, where iron tools datable at 180 B.C. have been found in association with trade beads.

DEVELOPMENT OF IRON AND STEEL TECHNOLOGY IN CHINA

The central questions now are, when did iron metallurgy arise in Chinese civilization and when did iron weapons come into general use there? Our investigation will center on Chinese smelting. Let us examine some of the relevant Chinese technical terms since they provide important clues.

There are two technical terms in Chinese for smelting, *chu* and *yeh*. *Chu* combines the "metal" radical with "longevity," *shou* as the phonetic. *Shou* is itself composed of a graph of ploughed fields and a shortened form of the word *lao*, meaning old, a picture of an old man with a stick. By a transference of meaning, the strokes for a ploughed field may have come to signify ore, some kinds of which were indeed obtained by ploughing, that is, by a primitive type of open-cast mining. But the pictograph of *chu* includes a new element, a pair of hands above a kind of hopper or opening at the top of the furnace, and a vessel (the finished casting or perhaps a mold) below it. As the character Chu was also the name of an ancient principality in the northern part of the northeastern state of Chhi, one cannot help wondering whether it derived from a location of one of the earliest iron foundries there.

The other word, *yeh*, derives from an ancient personal pronoun as phonetic and the "ice" radical to indicate the subject of discourse. Curiously, it foreshadows our modern sophisticated way of talking of a metal's freezing point.

Particularly important is that both these words have the primary meaning of smelting ore in such a way as to produce liquid molten metal, and do not merely refer to melting metal already produced. There are other words for the latter, *shuo* and *lien*, for example. Moreover, *chu* and *yeh* are to be sharply distinguished from *tuan*, which means to forge by hammering, and indeed, reveals in its pictographic form what seems to be a hand holding a hammer beside two bars of iron on an anvil. All these words are significant, and with them in mind one can look at the earliest mentions of iron in Chinese records.

First, there is a poem ascribed to Duke Hsiang of the state of Chhin, who reigned from 776 to 764 B.C. The poem speaks of four dark gray horses, *ssu thieh*. The phonetic of *thieh* seems originally to have meant gray-colored, but the earliest commentary on the poem claims that the word meant "iron-colored." If so, this would be one of the most ancient literary references to iron. Secondly, we find in Chou texts the word *tuan*, meaning forging, and since bronze is not commonly forged, this could refer to ironworking. However, if we accept this meaning at that date (900 to 700 B.C.), it might imply that an iron shortage or perhaps a bronze abundance later followed.

We are on firmer ground when we come to the 5th century B.C. or a little earlier. The *Yüeh Ling* (Monthly Ordinances of the Chou Dynasty), one of the ancient calendars, speaks of "metal and iron" as if the latter were something different from ordinary metals like gold, silver, copper, and tin. Again, the *Tso Chuan* (Master Tsochhiu's Enlargement of the Spring and Autumn Annals), a work of the 3d century B.C., refers to iron cauldrons being cast in the state of Chin in 512 B.C. A new legal code was engraved or cast on these vessels.

This century is also the time ascribed to the famous makers of iron weapons, and in this connection a passage of much interest occurs in the *Wu Yüeh Chhun Chhiu* (Spring and Autumn Annals of the States of Wu and Yüeh). This is a history of those regions (later known as Chekiang, Chiangsu Chiangsi, and Fukien) written in the 2d century A.D. by Chao Yeh. It certainly embodies many local traditions.

Ho Lu [king of Wu, reigned 514 to 496 B.C.] invited Kan Chiang to cast (*chu*) [metal] and make two swords which should be famous. Now Kan Chiang was a man of Wu. He had had the same teacher as Ou Yeh, and both were good swordsmiths. Formerly the Yüeh country had presented three swords, and Ho Lu treasured them very much; this was why he asked his smith to make two more. One was to be named after Kan Chiang himself; the other after his wife Mo Yeh. To make these swords, Kan Chiang collected refined iron [*thieh ching*] from the five mountains, the best metal in the world [*chin ying*]. [But although] he chose the right time and place, with the Yin and the Yang in bright harmony, and the hundred spirits assembled to watch, while the *chhi* of the heavens descended; yet the essence of the iron would not melt and flow [*pu hsiao lun liu*]. Kan Chiang did not know the reason.

[Then came] Mo Yeh and said: "By your skill as a swordsmith you have become known to the king. Yet you have been about making these swords three months without any success: why is this?" Kan Chiang said, "Alas, I do not know the principle [*li*] of it." To which she replied, "The changes of these mysterious things depend on the person concerned. Perhaps you could succeed in this task if you had the right person." Kan Chiang said, "I remember once when my teacher could not bring the iron to fusion [*pu hsiao*], he and his wife threw themselves into the furnace, and afterwards the work was completed. [Therefore] nowadays when on the mountainside men smelt, they wear sashes of hempen cloth and clothes of retted fibre; only then do they dare to liquefy the metal. Now I am trying to get metal for the swords, and yet it will not undergo its change [*pu pien hua*]—could it be because of this?" She replied, "Your teacher knew when to give his body to the flames in order to accomplish the work; I would not hesitate to do the same." So cutting off her hair and paring her nails, she threw them into the furnace. Then the three hundred young men and women [metalworkers] were ordered to ply the bellows and pile on more charcoal, and so [in due course] the iron knives were quenched [*ju*] and the swords successfully made.

There is much more to this quotation than meets the eye. First, human sacrifice to furnaces to make the metal flow is a legendary idea common to many civilizations; the West knows it in bell-founding. This does not mean there is any need to regard Kan Chiang and Ou Yeh as wholly legendary. We know that there were certainly swordsmiths at the time they were supposed to have lived. Secondly, there is nothing remarkable in their wearing ritual garments: Japanese swordsmiths have continued this practice down to the present time. But third, and more important, is the strong evidence the text affords for iron casting on a considerable scale in the Warring States period (5th to 3d centuries B.C.). Most interesting, however, is the statement that Mo Yeh threw something into the furnace to make the metal melt more easily; to this we shall return later.

In the 4th century B.C. we find a number of authentic texts which mention iron. Perhaps the Yü Kung (Tribute of Yü) chapter of the *Shu Ching* (History Classic), with its reference to iron and steel, ought to be placed here, though most of it goes back more likely to the 8th century B.C. Elsewhere there are several references to the abundance of iron ore in Szechuan. Then, about 310 B.C., comes the passage in *Mêng Tzu* (Book of Master Mêng) where the philosopher Mencius (Mêng Kho) refers to Hsü Hsing cooking in pans of metal and pottery and ploughing with iron. Interestingly, Hsü Hsing came from Chhu state in the south, a pointer to the origin of an iron industry there. And just about the same time (assuming that the *Kuan Tzu* book was written between 318 and 290 B.C.) there is the famous passage on the iron tax which says that every woman needs a needle and a knife, every farmer his hoe and ploughshare, and every cartwright his ax, saw, awl, and chisel.

Also dating from the 4th century are the cast iron agricultural tools excavated from tombs at Hui-hsien in Honan and other places. They are exhibited in the Palace Museum at Peking and in many other Chinese museums. The metallographic structures of the tools are very much varied, ranging from pearlitic-ferritic gray iron with flakes of free graphite to a remarkably low-carbon iron with graphite rosettes or nodules in a ferrite matrix. Again, still more recently, iron molds used for making castings have been discovered at Hsing-lung in Jehol.

From the Hui-hsien material Sun Thing-Lieh concludes that the tools were made by swage molding—that is, by pressing the pasty masses of bloomery iron into molds rather than by pouring liquid cast iron. No ancient Chinese texts clearly refer to bloomery furnaces, however, though there is, it is true, a term of uncertain significance, *hsieh* which may have meant pasty bloom iron. If swage molding was indeed the technique used at Hui-hsien, then it must have been a very ancient one still being carried on at the same time as fully developed iron casting, evinced by the Hsing-lung tools and molds from the state of Yen. Certainly these molds could have been used for casting bronze, but they would have been quite serviceable for casting iron too; similar molds are in wide use today for this purpose, having the advantage of producing a chill casting with increased hardness and resistance to wear. The use of such molds must be regarded as an astonishingly high development of technology for the 4th century B.C.

The next reference to steel brings us back to weapons. About 250 B.C., the philosopher Hsün Chhing, arguing that military techniques are useless if morale is low, said:

> The people of Chhu [State] use shark-skin and rhinoceros hide for armour, as hard as metal or stone, and spear-heads of steel from Wan sharp as a bee's sting [*Wan chü thieh shê, tshen jo fêng chhai*]. They are quick and active, as fast as the whirlwind. Yet the army [of Chhu] was almost destroyed at Chhui-sha, and Thang Mieh was killed.

All commentators, from Hsü Kuang in the 4th century A.D. to Jen Kuang in the 12th, have supposed that *chü thieh*, "great iron," here means hard iron (*kang thieh*), or, in other words, steel (*kang*). Yet not only spearheads but swords also of iron or steel were becoming common in the 3d century B.C., as museum examples show. One of the results of the spreading use of iron or steel for swords was that sword blades became longer, the 80 cm bronze sword being replaced by swords of 95 or even 120 cm in length.

Among other evidence for a developed steel industry in Chhin times is the engraving of an inscription on a meteorite of 211 B.C., which would have necessitated the use of a steel implement. In addition, shaving the hair or beard, probably with a steel knife or razor, was now generally practiced; formerly it had been a form of punishment. The working of jade might also have required a hard metal. Although we cannot describe here in full the iron and steel industry of the Chhin and Han, it must be remembered that the last half of the 3d century B.C. was remarkable for the existence of a whole group of primitive industrialists who succeeded in amassing great wealth by developing production almost on a factory scale. Among them were some who reached a position of real importance in the national life by their control of the iron industry; one founded an iron works in Szechuan that employed nearly 1,000 young men. And it was during the Han, about 130 B.C., that metallurgical deserters from the retinue of a Chinese embassy were spreading the technique of iron casting to the people of Ferghana and Parthia.

For the years 91 and 27 B.C. we have circumstantial accounts of cupola explosions or furnace breakouts. A century later, in A.D. 84, Wang Chhung, in discussing the natural origin of thunder, describes the effects of throwing a bucket of water into a furnace of molten iron.

> Thunder is (only) the explosion (*chi*) of the *chhi* of the solar Yang principle. . . . How can we test this? Throw a bucket of water into a smelting-furnace. The *chhi* will be stirred and will explode like thunder; those who are near may well be burned. . . . When founders melt iron (*tang yeh kung chih hsiao thieh*) they make molds of earth and when they are dry the metal (is allowed to) run down into them. If they are not, it will skip up, overflow and spurt about. If it hits a man's body it burns his skin.

One could hardly ask for a more graphic description.

Han reliefs that show the work going on exist; there are scenes of forging and of molten iron pouring from a furnace complete with tuyere pipes to convey the blast. Han dictionaries have preserved some of the terms used. And from the end of the Han there comes the oldest known complex iron casting, a funerary cooking stove, while from the beginning of the same dynasty onward for many centuries statues and statuettes of cast iron have come down to us. Texts of unusual or abnormal events also frequently contain references to iron casting in Han times.

Remains of Han blast furnaces are yet another source of evidence. One of the most interesting is that near Lu-shan (a city in Honan 112 km south of Loyang), which was discovered by Ho Kuei-Chieh. The site was quite active until comparatively late, as there are references to it in 13th-century sources. The identification of the foundations of the five furnaces as Han was assured by the presence of Han tiles and pottery, as well as scoria and slag. With mouths 1.4 m in diameter, the furnaces were built of large refractory bricks of different shapes from 46 to 90 cm across. Tuyeres of refractory clay with very thick walls were found; originally they were white but were burned to a purple-black color outside and yellow inside. They measured 1.4 m long and from 28 cm in diameter at the nozzle to 61 cm at the far end. Flat bars of cast iron 6 cm by 60 cm were found buried beside the furnaces. There was no evidence of any fuel except charcoal, or of animal- or water-power applied to the bellows; these were probably worked by government slaves. Heaps of iron-sand were seen.

Lu-shan derived its ore from two localities, one yielding red hematite (ferric oxide) and the other magnetite sand (ferrosoferric oxide). They seem to have been mixed in use. Lumps of unreduced or partly reduced ore and iron were still present at the bottom of some of the furnaces.

Chinese Crucible Processes

In China, crucible processes were also prominent. In some provinces, such as Shansi, the iron ore was reduced in batteries of elongated tubelike crucibles (*khan kuo*) packed in a mass of coal. The use of coal in China for smelting was an extremely important factor, going back to the 4th century A.D. at least. The crucible method produced true cast iron, but also sometimes a mixture of cast iron lumps and masses of bloom iron which were separated by hand after cooling. This was a localized process and evidence of it comes mainly through the accounts of modern observers. We do not know exactly how far back such crucible reductions go, though further research may be expected to uncover texts which will help dating.

In Shansi, a small amount of "black earth" (*hei thu*) was habitually added to the ore to promote full fusion of the metal and its perfect running in the molds. This substance has turned out to contain abundant crystals of vivianite (iron phosphate) and was associated with the coal used, which also contained phosphate. Since amounts of phosphate up to 6 percent in the iron reduce its melting point from 1130 to about 950° C, this may have been the reason—although not a conscious one—for some of the early successes in iron casting. Here then might be the reality behind the symbol of the black hair which Mo Yeh threw into Kan Chiang's furnace.

Chinese Blast Furnaces

It is rather hard to believe that in other places, and presumably at earlier dates, there were never any bloomeries similar to those of the West. But in East Asia evidence for them is wholly lacking, whether archaeological or textual, and in China the small blast furnace was the most characteristic iron producer. Its classical illustration is that given by Sung Ying-Hsing in his *Thien Kung Khai Wu* (Exploitation of the Works of Nature) of A.D. 1637. Entitled "The Blast Furnace and the refining platform," the illustration shows a furnace about 3 m high receiving a blast from a double-acting piston bellows. The liquid cast iron is shown flowing forth after being tapped and making its way to the fining hearth, or puddling basin. Decarburization took place here by stirring and the addition of silica.

This celebrated picture is neither the oldest nor the most beautiful. A collection compiled in 1334 by Chhen Chhun, who was salt commissioner at Hsia-sha-chhang, includes a picture that shows a similar scene and may even have been the model for the drawing by Sung Ying-Hsing who also gave a description worth quoting:

Iron [he wrote] may be of two kinds, raw iron [*shêng thieh*, that is, cast iron] and ripe iron [*shu thieh*, that is, wrought iron]. The former is that which comes out of the [blast] furnace but is not yet roasted [chhao], while the latter is that which has been roasted. A mixture of the raw and the ripe iron heated together becomes steel.

The [blast] furnace is made of "salt" [probably gypsum] mixed with clay and built into walls; often it is placed beside a mountain cave. Some use a framework of great logs as an encircling support for the clay and "salt" walls. A month is not too much for the building of it [and it must be allowed to dry as thoroughly as possible]; this is something which cannot be hastened. For if any fissures develop during the operations all the labour will be wasted.

A furnace can take more than two thousand catties of ore. [As for the fuel] sometimes hard wood is used, sometimes coal, and sometimes charcoal—whatever is convenient in the locality.... The piston-bellows of the [blast] furnace need four or six men working in unison. When the ore has been converted into molten iron, it is allowed to flow out from a hole at the side of the furnace which has previously been closed with clay. Every day at the sixth and first [double] hours the furnace is tapped, and after the iron has flowed out the hole is closed again. Then the blast is urged [*ku*] once more for a further melting [*jung*]. The pig iron thus prepared for [later] casting [*yeh chu*] [into vessels and objects] flows out into a mold and takes the shape of a long round strip, after which it is removed for use.

As to the wrought [ripe] iron, the cast iron is made to flow into a square basin [*fang thang*, i.e. fining hearth] with low walls placed a few feet away from the tapping hole and at a level several inches lower. When the cast iron has collected in the basin some of the workmen scatter over it dirty estuarine mud which has been dried, pounded and sifted until it is as fine as flour; meanwhile others, standing on the walls, keep stirring the metal and the dust energetically together, with poles of willow wood. After a time the roasting converts the iron to wrought [ripe] iron. The willow poles get burnt away several inches, but they use them again as long as they can. When the roasted iron has cooled it is either cut into square pieces on the fining hearth, or else it is taken out and hammered into round cakes to be sold.

From what has already been said, it is clear that the regular industrial production of cast iron in China must have existed from about the 4th century B.C. And among all the inventions and discoveries that contributed to this extraordinary development none can have been more important than the construction of bellows to give a powerful and continuous blast. Perhaps the key invention was the double-acting piston bellows shown in all the metallurgical illustrations of the *Thien Kung Khai Wu*.

CHINA AS AN IRON CULTURE AND THE PROBLEM OF ITS WESTWARD TRANSMISSION

In modern times the world has seen China as a culture of bamboo and wood, in contrast with Europe and America, which are dominant in their wealth of iron and steel. If we look beyond the last three centuries, however, we find that, paradoxically, the opposite was true. Between the 5th and 17th centuries A.D. it was the Chinese, not the Europeans, who could make as much cast iron as they wanted and who, as we shall see, were accustomed to make steel by advanced methods that were unknown to the Western world until a much later date.

The comparative wealth of cast iron in medieval China can be seen, for example, in its use by Buddhist architects in their designs of pagodas. For instance, the pagoda of the Yü-chhüan Ssu temple at Tang-yang in Hopei, which dates from A.D. 1061 and is 21 m high, is reckoned to contain 53 tons of iron in its thirteen storys, the walls being made from cast iron plaques fixed to a skeleton framework. Another, probably of similar date, is at the Kan-lu Ssu temple near Chen-chiang in Chiangsu province; only two of its storys now remain. Yet another, near Chi-ning in Shantung, has eleven storys. Cast iron was also used for the tiles of temple roofs.

Other evidence for the relative richness of the use of iron in medieval

China is to be found in the presence of suspension bridges with iron chains. The region surrounding the Tibetan massif is the Old World home of the suspension bridge, and in ancient times plaited bamboo was used for the cables. In southwest China, however, there were many suspension bridges also, and because of the constant need of renewal, the original bamboo cables were replaced with cast iron chains or linked rods from the 6th century onward. Twelve centuries passed before the first cast iron suspension bridge was built in Europe.

Cast iron also became a favorite medium for Chinese artists, and extant statues and statuettes date from late Han times onward. The largest iron casting ever made was set up by an emperor of the Later Chou dynasty in 954, and cast iron was frequently used for making large bells. Casting iron columns was also carried out in the same century; twelve pillars for the Chhien-ho Hall, each over 2.25 m in circumference and over 3.5 m high, were not an untypical example. But among the most extraordinary of all the iron projects were those initiated by the great Thang empress Wu Tsê Thien, who ruled the empire alone for more than 20 years before her death in 705. First there was a cosmological temple, completed in 688. This was a broad pagoda of three storys, almost 90 m in height, with the uppermost story resting on nine enormous cast-iron dragons, and a crowning canopy surmounted by a gilded phoenix of cast iron, 3 m high. Yet even this structure was outdone metallurgically by the "Celestial Axis commemorating the Virtue of the Great Chou Dynasty with its Myriad Regions," a grandiose monument on an artificial cast-iron hill. With some bronze dragons as well as its extensive iron structure, the whole monument used 1359 tons of metal.

Meanwhile, through all the centuries, the small ironworks scattered throughout the length and breadth of China continued to produce plough-shares and agricultural implements just as they had done since the beginning of the unified empire in the 3d century B.C. Great skill was developed in the manufacture of large cast-iron pans (kua) with extremely thin walls and therefore very economical of fuel. These were used in the chemical industries as well as domestically. Cupola furnaces of special type, some-times tipping, were utilized for making them. The ironworks also provided a considerable quantity of iron for shipbuilding, as well as iron for the minor domestic industries such as wire drawing and needle making. Iron was of course supplied too for military purposes.

Throughout antiquity and the Middle Ages, so far as we are aware, the blast furnace giving its liquid iron was known nowhere in the world outside China. There were small blast furnaces in northern Iran using paired bellows worked by horizontal waterwheels in the Chinese manner, but these probably derived from China, and may, if they were in use before A.D. 1400, have been instrumental in bringing about the beginning of cast iron production in medieval Europe. Another zone intermediate between China and Europe is the Turkish culture area, and an application of André Haudricourt's philological methods has been valuable in investigating this. He has pointed out that Western languages have no special word for cast iron but that many Central Asian languages do. More than twenty such words adduced by him from some fourteen languages seem to be related to East Turki; they include similar sounding words in Russian and Bulgarian, Karaïte Turkish, Osmanli Turkish, and Uzbek. This, he believes, indicates the presence of an original loanword (something like *chujun*[2]) in the Central Asian languages taken from Chinese, a word which accompanied the spread of cast iron products and techniques westward.

STEEL MAKING AND HARDENING

The most important thing about steel making in the Chinese culture area was the abundance of cast iron. Since the Chinese thus had iron with a very high carbon content, wrought iron or a hammered bloom was not the only starting point for steel, and the cementation process not the only way to it. Cementation may possibly have been known and used in ancient China, but it seems clear that from an early date much more steel was being made by the tricky process of direct decarburization of cast iron under a cold blast. Then, perhaps in the 4th century A.D., some metallurgist of genius conceived the idea of heating wrought iron and cast iron together, thus averaging the carbon content of the two forms rather than reducing (or increasing) the carbon content of one alone. For want of a better name we call this process "cofusion." Considering that the men of that time knew absolutely nothing about the chemistry of ironworking, this invention must be regarded as quite extraordinary. And it seems likely that it was this process that broke through the limitations of iron and steel production which still prevailed in medieval Europe. Perhaps even the prosperity of cities like Hangchow, which so profoundly impressed Marco Polo, was not wholly unconnected with a siderurgical industry much greater in scale than any other part of the world had at that time. Some quotations may underline these points.

First, a link with legend is provided by the story of the first Han emperor's sword, recorded here by Wang Chia about A.D. 370 but relating to events of about 230 B.C.

> When [Thai Shang Huang] was travelling in the mountains near Fêng and Phei he stayed in remote upland valleys, where he met with a metal smelter of Ou Yeh's [tradition]. Shang Huang stopped and asked him what was the vessel for which he was melting [metal]. The smith laughed and said, "I am melting it to make a sword for an emperor, but I must ask you not to disclose my secret." Shang Huang took it as a joke, suspecting nothing. Then the smith said: "Now I have melted the iron, but getting the steel and grinding and forging are difficult. If you would give me the weapon that hangs at your belt I would melt it and mix it into a sword so marvellous that it will subdue the whole world. . . ." [Shang Huang was very reluctant, telling the smith that it was a *pi shou* dagger of matchless sharpness, able to kill men and spirits without damage to its edge. But the smith peristed, saying,] "Without this dagger to mix and melt, even Ou Yeh and the metalworkers of Yüeh would be able to produce only an inferior weapon." So Shang Huang took it off and threw it into the furnace, and after a short while smoke and flame rushed towards the sky, darkening the day so that it seemed night.

The reality behind this ancient account is presumably the attempts of metalworkers to get the carbon content right for a fine steel, and already the complete fusion of the metal is assumed. Again, a century before Wang Chia's time, a particularly famous metalworker named Juan Shih was said to have got his art from a spiritual visitant (a Metal Spirit) who taught him methods of quenching, the nature of alloys, and the "harmony of the hard and the soft." This phrase must have meant either the combination of cast iron with wrought iron under prolonged heating to produce steel, or alternatively (and at that date more probably) the combination of hard and soft steels in pattern-welded swords.

The production of a desirable metallographic structure in steel can be effected by rapidly cooling, that is, quenching, red- or white-hot metal. The ancients found empirically that an oil bath gave less drastic cooling; they also paid particular attention to the kinds of water which they used.

Although some superstition may have played a part, it seems possible that the amount of dissolved salts or suspended matter might make a slight difference to the rate of heat dissipation. Thus the *Phu Yuan Pieh Chuan*, the biography of Phu Yuan (fl. 200 to 240 A.D.), says:

> Phu Yuan was a man of great natural genius . . . . Suddenly he undertook at Hsieh-ku to smelt [the iron to make] three thousand sabers for Chuko Liang. His method of melting the metal [*jung chin*] was markedly different from that generally used. After the sabers were all finished [up to a certain point] he reported that the water of the Han river was pure and weak, unsuitable for quenching [*tshui*], while the rivers of Szechuan being swift and fierce, their water was called "the original essence of the great metal." Heaven [itself] had made these [geographical] differences. So [Phu Yuan] sent men to Chhêngtu to get water from there. Upon [testing the water] which the first man brought back, by quenching a saber in it, he said that it had been mixed with water from the Fou Chiang [river] and could not be used. The man protested strongly, saying that it was pure, but Phu Yuan, indicating a portion of the water with his saber, insisted that eight shêng [of the Fou Chiang water] had been added to it. He would take no denial. So [in the end] the man bowed deeply and admitted that some had been upset when crossing the Fou Chiang ferry, and that he, being afraid, had then added some Fou Chiang water. After that time everyone was astonished at the mysterious skill of Phu Yuan, and admired him.

So went the work in the arsenals of Shu. There are other, much earlier references to quenching with special waters. Lung-chhüan on the Fukien border was famous in the time of the Warring States (ca. 4th century B.C.) for the suitability of its water; indeed, it was the traditional location of the ironworks of Ou Yeh.

COFUSION STEEL

The following text from the *Pei Chhi Shu* (History of the Northern Chhi Dynasty) brings us to the heart of the matter and gives us a transition to the more fundamental processes of steel making. Although it mentions oily material for mild steel quenching and introduces us to the welding of blades from steels of diverse qualities, its importance lies in the fact that it is one of the earliest statements we have of the cofusion steel making process.

> [Chhiwu Huai-Wên] also made sabers of "overnight iron" [*su thieh tao*, that is, iron heated continuously for several days and nights in succession]. The method was to bake [*shao*] the purest cast iron [literally, the essence of raw iron] piling it up with the soft ingots [*jou thing*] [of wrought iron], until after several [days and] nights, it was all turned to steel.
>
> To make the backbone of the saber he used soft iron [*jou thieh*]. For quenching [*yü*], the urine of the five animals was used, and for [another kind of] quenching [*tshui*], the fat of the five animals. Such swords could cut through thirty layers of armor plate.
>
> [Chhiwu] Huai-Wên used to say that the city of Nan-kan-tzu in Kuang-phing province was the place where Kan Chiang smelted [the iron for his famous] swords, and that the earth there was good for polishing them.

Here then, early in the 6th century A.D., was what seems clearly to have been an ancestor of the Siemens–Martin open-hearth process. Evidence we will discuss below indicates strongly that the cast iron did actually melt, but the lumps of wrought iron which it bathed certainly remained no more than pasty.

Given Chinese cast iron, the idea of a cofusion process could have arisen from attempts to combine the properties of cast and wrought iron to reduce the brittleness of the one and to increase the hardness of the other, just as the swordsmith of the *Lü Shih Chhun Chhiu* had long before sought to combine the advantages of copper and tin. One would like to think that Chhiwu Huai-Wên was the actual inventor of the cofusion process, but it was not he, for there are references to it before his time. A clear statement has come down to us from about A.D. 500, some 50 years earlier than Chhiwu's work, writtern by the great alchemist and physician Thao Hung-Ching:

> Thao Hung-Ching says: "Cast iron [*shêng thieh*] is [for] things like lock-bolts [*hsü*], tripod cauldrons [*chhêng*] and boiling-pans [*fu*], such as are not [easily] broken [*pu pho*] [in the fire]. Steel [*kang thieh*] is [made when] the raw [cast iron] and the soft [wrought iron] are mixed and heated together [*tsa lien shêng jou*]. It is for making sabers and sickles [*tao lien*]."

The authenticity of this passage is confirmed by its appearance in the first official pharmacopoeia (659) and then in a Japanese one of 918.

But the *locus classicus* for the cofusion process may be found in the *Pên Tshao Thu Ching* (Illustrated Pharmacopoeia), compiled in 1070 under the leadership of the famous astronomer, engineer, and horologist Su Sung. There we find:

> Iron from all the different districts and provinces is not separately recorded, for it is as if the same place produced it all. South of the River, or in Western Szechuan—wherever there are blast furnaces [*lu yeh*], they all have it. . . . The first refining process [in ironmaking] is the removing of the gangue [*kung*] [i.e., smelting]. That which is used for melting and running into molds [*chu hsieh*] to make objects and vessels is called raw iron [*shêng thieh*, cast iron]. Repeatedly softened [literally, melted] and beaten [*tsai san hsiao pho*], it can be made into a bloom [*hsieh*]; this is soft iron [*jou thieh*], and it is also called ripe iron [*shu thieh*, wrought iron]. By mixing and uniting the raw and the soft [*i shêng jou hsiang tsa ho*] [a metal is obtained] for making the edges and points of sabers and swords; this is called steel [*kang thieh*].

Nothing could be clearer, but in 1637 Sung Ying-Hsing added certain rather important details.

> The method of making steel is as follows. The wrought iron is beaten into thin plates or scales as wide as a finger and rather over an inch and a half long. These are packed [literally, wrapped] within [wrought] iron sheets, and all tightly pressed down by cast iron pieces piled on top. The whole [furnace] is then covered over with mud [or clay] matted with worn-out straw sandals. The bottom of the pile is daubed with mud [or clay] as well. Large furnace piston-bellows are then set to work, and when the fire has risen to a sufficient heat, the cast iron comes to its transformation [i.e., melts] first [*hsien hua*], and dripping and soaking [*shen lin*], penetrates into the wrought iron. When the two are united with each other, they are taken out and forged; afterwards they are again heated and again hammered. This is many times repeated. The product is usually called "lump steel" [*thuan kang*] or "irrigated steel" [*kuan kang*].

Thus, in the fully developed form of the process, the aim of getting more perfect union of the two metals led to the use of quite small pieces in the nonliquefying phase. Possibly the idea of these little leaves or scales was derived from scale armor. And the quotations suggest that the carbon-rich phase really did liquefy; indeed the typical technical term of the Sung, *kuan kang*, "suffused," "interfused," literally "irrigated" steel, is written with the "water" radical and implies unambiguous fluidity. The fact that Chhiwu Huai-Wên had to heat his furnace or his crucibles for "several days and nights" may be an indication that his temperature did not quite reach $1130°$ C; if his cast iron had fully liquefied, a shorter time would surely have been enough. Yet fluid cast iron had been produced commercially in China long before his time. In any case, if the cofusion cast iron was not quite liquid in his furnaces, it must soon have become so as the practice continued during the centuries between his time and the Sung and Ming.

In the ultimate refinement of the cofusion technique, tools were first forged in wrought iron and their cutting edges then exposed to molten cast iron. Known as the *su kang* method since it was developed chiefly in Chiangsu province, the technique was still in use a few years ago.

In 1954 and 1955 an experimental investigation was made in England of the Chinese cofusion process. A pile of wrought-iron strips was heated in a furnace chamber on a refractory layer to about $975°$ C, then withdrawn and forged with a hand hammer. As the chamber was lined with graphite. the atmosphere was kept well reducing (chiefly due to carbon monoxide). The results of the introduction of varying proportions of powdered white cast iron between the layers were then examined with a metallographic microscope, and it was found that as the proportion increased, a carbon distribution increasingly uniform throughout the welded mass was obtained. There was an increased carbon content at the welding planes, with a considerable amount of unabsorbed white cast iron at the junction of each weld. Furthermore, after allowing carbon migration to occur by continuing heating for 8 hours at $900°$ C, just as Chhiwu Huai-Wên did with his "overnight iron," a uniform steel of eutectoid composition was obtained. Such specimens responded to hardening treatments like good tool steel, and sometimes showed a damascene quality. This was a most interesting repetition of its earliest form, namely, that in which cast iron was present incompletely fused.

Direct Decarburization Steel

Chhiwu's family name sounds barbarian, but it was not; yet he certainly served a barbarian dynasty (the Thopa Wei). It is important not to underestimate the metallurgical skill of the barbarian peoples on the fringes of the Chinese culture area. When the whole story of metallurgy there becomes known, they will be found to have made noteworthy contributions to it. The following text speaks not only of the art of such people but also reveals in passing a metallurgical fact of great significance. It comes from the *Tu Hsing Tsa Chih* (Miscellaneous Records of the Lone Watcher), written about A.D. 1176 by Tsêng Min-Hsing.

> When I was living in Hsiang [Hunan] I used to see the Yao tribesmen coming to the temples to worship the gods, and every man carrying a sword. These were made of yellow steel, and only the barbarian tribesmen could make them. They also had a [curious] custom that whenever a son was born, all the relatives who came to see the baby would bring along with them a bar of iron and throw it into [a tub of] water. Then, when the boy had grown up, and there was to be a feast to celebrate his wedding, his friends would take out the iron and refine it over and over again a hundred times [*pai lien*] to obtain the essential steel [*i chhü ching kang*]. When the sword was completed, there was not a grain of extra weight left [*pu shih yu chu liang chih hsien*]. Thus he who started out with plenty of iron eventually has a sword so splendidly sharp that with one swing it will cut right through the body of an ox. Even swords second-rate in comparison cannot be made by the Han [Chinese] people. The tribesmen wear their swords throughout their lives, and any Han person wishing to obtain one must first kill the wearer.
>
> Smiths in neighboring districts have often tried to imitate these swords. Old metalworkers have told me that they call such imitation steel "up-to-a-certain-point" steel [*tao kang*] for the refining has been carried on only to a certain degree.

In this account we have to deal with two processes which were probably entirely different. What the tribesmen did constitutes simply a Chinese version of a practice quite widespread among ancient peoples, namely, submitting a bloom of mixed pure iron and steely iron to conditions of corrosion such that the former will rust away preferentially, leaving a steel which can be forged into weapons and tools. But what the Chinese smiths were doing, in imitation of the Hsi-jung, was something quite different, for the starting point was not a bloom containing steely lumps but bars of cast iron. One way of making steel from this was the cofusion method, the other was that of the "hundred refinings" (*pai lien*). This could have been the cementation of wrought or bloom iron, though that is unlikely because nothing is ever said of heating it while packed in charcoal. On the other hand, there is ground for believing that the Chinese process was nothing else than direct decarburization of the blast furnace product, a particularly difficult technique when partial rather than total removal was aimed at so as to give steel, not wrought iron. Indeed, this process was carried out by later Chinese ironworkers through the centuries.

To contrast here the steels made by cofusion with those made by direct decarburization, it will be best to begin by considering a Sung quotation from the *Pên Tshao Yen I* (General Ideas of the Pharmaceutical Natural Histories), presented to the throne by Khou Tsung-Shih in A.D. 1116.

> The first smelting [*lien*] of the iron ore as it comes from the mine gives what is called raw (cast) iron [*shêng thieh*]. . . . Soft iron [*jou thieh*] is iron which has been roasted; it is ripe iron [*shu thieh*]. Steel [*kang thieh*] is a refined iron from which the dross [*tzu*] has been purged away. . . . Since the cast iron is that which comes out from the ore in the fire of the [blast] furnace, people call it raw iron.
>
> Now for [making] steel, they take [bars of] soft iron [*jou thieh*] and fold them up in coils, inserting pieces of cast iron between the layers. Then they seal up [the furnace] with clay, and heat it. Afterwards the masses are forged so that they interpenetrate one another, and the product is called "lump steel" [*thuan kang*]. It is also called "interfused steel" [literally, irrigated, or poured-over, steel] [*kuan kang*]. This is a rough [literally, rustic, or makeshift, low quality, steel] [*tshao chhuang*]—indeed, it can hardly avoid being [considered] false. For raw iron, although hard, after several refinings, becomes ripe, that is to say, soft iron [*jou thieh*]. Yet hardly anyone realizes that it [the lump steel] is false.
>
> But at the ironworks at Tzhu-chow they recognize what is true steel. Iron has steel [within it] like flour has gluten, that which re-

mains when the flour has been thoroughly washed and rubbed. The refining of steel is just like this. If one starts [for example] with more than a hundred catties of pure [cast] iron [*ching thieh*], and it is weighed after each forging [before being returned to the hearth for further aeration] its weight will be found to decline, until eventually it loses no more. Then it is pure steel. This is because the essence of the iron is pure and through a hundred refinings is not lost. Its color is pure and gleaming, and when polished it becomes intensely blue-black. Some kinds of iron there are which after extreme refining give no steel; the quality of pureness or roughness all depends on where the iron comes from.

From this interesting passage we see that, unlike Su Sung in 1070, the writer had a distinct prejudice against steel made by the cofusion method, though he described it well. And he was not alone in this. Like others at the time he failed to appreciate the rationale of the cofusion process because he could not see how a soft thing could be made hard by a hard thing which, under appropriate conditions, itself became soft. Though among the best scientific minds of his day, Khou Tsung-Shih was still rather in the position of the sophist who argued with the Bronze Age swordsmith; this is yet another example of how far practical technique can reach beyond theory in some periods.

The reference here, and others elsewhere, to repeated weighings and the eventual approach to a constant weight are rather difficult to explain. The balances available at the time could almost certainly not have detected the losses of carbon and other elements, but they might have measured loss as oxide in red scale; yet in that case constant weight would never have been reached. Indeed, the admission that some kinds of iron never did so goes some way to suggest that the constant weight was an illusion. At all events these indications of the use of the balance in metallurgy in China in the 11th century are precious enough in themselves.

Our next text is from the Ming mathematician and poet Thang Shun-Chih, writing in 1550, quoted in the *San Tshai Thu Hui* encyclopaedia (1609) of Wang Chhi, whose account of the direct decarburization process was the best down to this time.

Steel. The *Wu Pien* says that there are two kinds of steel, "cast-iron steel" [*shêng kang*] and "wrought-iron steel" [*shu kang*]. The former is made at Chhuchow; its nature is brittle [*tshui*], and unskillful workers find it difficult to make [literally, refine, *lien*]. For when it [the cast iron] comes forth from the smelting furnace [*yeh lu*] it is mixed with much dross [slag] and charcoal ash [*fên than hui*] and the lumps are rough and big. So only a skillful workman [*chhiao kung*] is able to beat and hammer it exactly to the right point, neither hastening nor delaying but attending to the correct "fire times" [*huo hou*]. If the heating is too prolonged, [the steeliness] will all flow away with the dross; if the heating is not enough, then the intrinsic substance [*pên thi*] [of the metal] will not be [well] fashioned and mixed [literally, molded, *jung*], and [therefore] not made uniform [literally, mutually united together, *hsiang ho*].

There is no question of cementation here, since cast iron was the raw material. The fining hearth must therefore have been something similar to those of the Styrian processes which were to come into use a little later, and equally surely must have been derived from the 11th-century craftsmanship spoken of by Shen Kua.

Two more quotations are relevant here, one late and one early. The first is from the *Kuangtung Hsin Yü* (New Description of Kuangtung province) of about 1690:

As for the roasting [*chhao*] of the iron, the cast iron [*shêng thieh*] is made into a lump [*thuan*] and put into the furnace, where it is baked [*shao*, i.e., in minimal contact with the fuel] until red-hot through and through. Then it is withdrawn and placed upon the anvil [*chên*]. One man holds it steady with tongs while two or three others forge it with hammers. During this more than ten youths direct a cold blast on it [literally, fan it, *shan chih*] from one side; they must sing chanties [and work] without stopping for a moment. Thus the iron is [eventually] transformed into the ripe metal [*shu*] [i.e., wrought iron] and becomes a bloom [*hsieh*], [or into steel]. There are several tens of these iron-roasting [i.e., fining or refining and steel making] workshops, and there are several thousands of workmen, for each shop has several tens of anvils and each anvil needs more than ten men. These [works] are classed as "small furnaces."

Clearly it was possible by means of a cold blast skillfully applied to obtain steel by manual operations, using cast iron as a raw material.

That this may have been going on for eighteen centuries in China is suggested by the following brief statement in the *Huai Nan Tzu* (Book of the Prince of Huai-Nan) of about 120 B.C.

> One may have the furnace, the bellows, the tuyere and the molds, but without clever smelters one will not be able to melt the metal. They it is who violently work the bellows and send the blast through the tuyeres in order to melt the bronze and the iron. Then [the metal] abundantly spreads and flows [*mi liu*], and [later] is forged until it becomes hard [*chien tuan*]. They work at this and do not weary all the day long.

If we accept the "hundred refinings" as a technical term referring specifically to this method, we can trace it through a number of centuries between the *Huai Nan Tzu* and the Sung.

From all the above it is clear that in ancient and medieval China steel was made by processes quite different from those used by Wayland Smith and the Gallo-Roman guilds, and from the faggoting (cementation) of their prehistoric forefathers. This can only have been a consequence of the abundance of cast iron which the Chinese had at their disposal from the 4th century B.C. onward. They probably first found a way of obtaining steel directly from cast iron by the discreet use of an oxidizing blast, and they then discovered that by combining cast and wrought iron together in the cofusion method, still more steel could be made. The former technique seems to have been used at least as early as the 2d century B.C., and the latter cannot have come into use later than the 5th century A.D. In Europe the dates are very different. Fining to wrought iron must clearly have followed the first blast furnaces of the late 14th century or early 15th century A.D., and direct decarburization to steel apparently arose in the 16th century, just about the same time as the first European references to the cofusion process. There seems to be something rather suspicious about the appearance of all these correlated techniques within such a short period, but no direct evidence of transmission of Chinese know-how to the West at that time has yet appeared.

However, Otto Johannsen has envisaged a diffusion of at least a stimulus from East Asia in the invention of the blast furnace. Noting that these furnaces first appeared in the Rhine Valley, he has pointed out that this is the same European region which first implemented the inventions of gunpowder and printing. Although this was not of course their original home, the juxtaposition of the three technique complexes may be highly significant. The truth is that mastery of cast iron takes its place among a number of other European adoptions of East Asian techniques in what has been called the "Fourteenth-Century Cluster."

While on this subject of the transmission of techniques from East Asia to the West, we should consider certain further facts which point to a curious connection. In 1639 a Dutch merchant named J. A. von Mandelslo traveled in Japan and later wrote in his memoirs,

> They [the Japanese] have, among others, a particular invention for the melting of iron, without the using of fire, casting it into a tun done about on the inside with about half a foot of earth, where they keep it [melting] with continual blowing, and take it out by ladles full, to give it what form they please, much better and more artificially than the inhabitants of Liége are able to do.

For 200 years nobody noticed this statement, which is significant not least for the fact that in the Bessemer-type processes no fuel is required to maintain the temperature of the metal. Not until the 1860s was this point appreciated, and the obvious conclusion drawn that the Japanese probably derived their method from that home of ironworking, China. Two other facts are also significant. The first is that in Britain and Ireland it was long the practice of nail makers to increase the temperature of red-hot iron by a blast of cold air, thus making a metal very close to steel. The second is that when Chinese experts were imported in 1845 into the United States to carry on smelting in West Kentucky, they are said to have brought with them some "pneumatic principle" of steel making. We come here very close to the Bessemer process, and it would be indeed an extraordinary dénouement if it should turn out that the Chinese and Japanese methods of cold-blast direct decarburization were just as much ancestral to the Bessemer process as the old cofusion method was to the Siemens–Martin open-hearth furnace.

Welding of Hard and Soft Steels

In the last ages of medieval Japan, the art of making sabers by welding together various pieces of different kinds of iron and steel reached the height of perfection. In essence a plate of soft steel acted as a foundation on which a number of pieces of hard, quenched steel were welded, and the whole was folded over and over to form a laminated structure of sixteen or more layers. This then became the cover material for an inner core of soft steel and a strip of extremely hard steel for the edge. The laminated steel was used primarily for weapons, its use was not confined to them.

As in the case of several other arts that were brought to great perfection in Japan, the foundation for this kind of sword making was laid in China. In the 17th century Japanese swords were considered by the Chinese to be superior to their own, and although the exact process of Japanese swordmaking was not clear, the general principles were no mystery, as Sung Ying-Hsing was well aware. In the *Thien Kung Khai Wu* of 1637 he wrote:

> The best of all sabers and swords have a hundred times refined steel for the outer layers, but inside as their "bones" [*ku*] they have iron which has not been made into steel. If they were not made with steel outside and iron inside they would break when struck violently against anything. Precious swords can even cut through iron nails. But after several thousand sharpenings on the grindstone, the steel may wear away and the iron appear. Japanese swords are no wider at the back than two tenths of an inch or a little more, yet they will stand up when balanced on the fingers of the hand; ... The strengthening of sabers and axes [pikes or halberds] is brought about by the smooth insertion of steel [*chhien kang*] or the even wrapping of it [around softer metal] [*pao kang*], and then plunging in water for quenching [*ju shui tshui*].

Retracing our steps in time we find other passages. One from the 12th century shows an evident understanding of the welding together of steels of different hardness. But more useful is the discourse of about 1083 by Shen Kua on ancient Chinese swords. In his *Mêng Chhi Pi Than* (Dream Pool Essays) he wrote:

> Ancient swords have the so-called *shen-lu* and *yü-chhang* effects. Now the word *shen* should be pronounced here *chan*, that is to say, "dark-colored." Ancient people used *chi kang* ["combined steel"] for the edge, and a soft iron [*jou thieh*] for the back, otherwise it would often break. Too strong a weapon will cut and destroy its own edge; this is why it is inadvisable to use nothing but "combined

steel." As for the *yü-chhang* [fish intestines] [effect] it is what is now called the "snake-coiling" steel sword [*phan kang chien*] or alternatively the "pine-tree design" [*sung wên*].

Here again it is clear that a combination of steels was used, a practice attributed to the work of previous centuries. Also, by this time sophisticated polishing techniques were used to make the patterns clearly visible.

So far we have nothing decisive between China and Japan as to antiquity. According to Japanese tradition, however, the making of welded steel swords and sabers began when "some naturalised smiths taught it at Oshinumi" around A.D. 607. In those days Chinese artisans of every kind were flocking to Japan, by way of Korea, from the capitals of the Liang and Wei kingdoms. Among Chinese sources details of the art can be found in the *Tung Hsiang Ssu Ming Ching* (Divination Manual of the East Country), of which long passages are preserved in encyclopaedias; this book is almost certainly pre-Thang, the text dating quite likely from about the time of Chhiwu Huai-Wên (fl. A.D. 545) himself. Then earlier still the 3d-century swordsmith Juan Shih was said, as we saw, to be skilled at "combining in harmony the hard and the soft," and this is most probably a reference to the multiple-welded blade. There can be little doubt then, in view of all the circumstances, that the basic process grew up in a purely Chinese milieu.

The problem of determining the origin of this technique would be comparatively simple if East Asia were its only home, but in fact it spread in a vast zone all across the northern part of the Old World. It was not characteristic of the peoples of the Roman Empire but rather of the Celts, Germans, Scandinavians, and Slavs, and by the 11th century the technique was well known to the Arabs. If its original home was not in China or with the Celts, who practiced the art from the 1st to the 9th centuries A.D., then a focus will have to be found among such peoples as the Sarmatians, Huns, or ancient Turks.

DAMASCENING AND WOOTZ IN CHINA

In the quotation above, Shen Kua referred to "fish-gut" effects, "coiling-snake," and "pine-tree" designs in swords. What he was describing was the effect known as "damascening," the appearance of innumerable veins in the metal, circling or meandering, like moiré or shot silk. This is to be found both in the welded blades, of which we have just been speaking, and in homogeneous blades fashioned either from Chinese cofusion steel or from the wootz steel of India. Wootz steel was made either from bloom iron, or even directly from magnetite ore, by packing it in refractory clay crucibles together with a mass of chips of the wood and leaves of special plants, to give it just the right amount of carbon. In brief, hypereutectoid steel must be present. All through the Middle Ages the high-quality crucible wootz produced in Hyderabad and exported from India was the principal source from which the Damascus blades of the Muslims were made. But did the swordsmiths of China and Japan use wootz steel at all in their welding techniques?

The Japanese have a term, *namban tetsu*, "iron from the southern barbarians," for this kind of steel, so it would seem likely that there was some export eastward. And in 1590 Li Shih-Chen enumerated three kinds of steel, among them that "which comes from the mountain islands in the midst of the southwestern sea, and which is in appearance like *tzu shih ying* (i.e., amethyst, purple quartz, or green flourspar veined with purple)." More interesting still, Li Shih-Chen quotes from the *Pao Tsang Lun* (Discourse on the Contents of the Precious Treasury of the Earth):

> Of iron there are five kinds. Iron of the Ching district comes from Tang-yang [in Hupei], its color is purple and it is hard and sharp. Another [sort] is the iron of Shang-jao [in Chiangsi]. Steely iron [*pin thieh*] comes from Po-Ssu, hard and sharp, it can cut gold and jade. Thai-yuan [Shansi] and Szechuan mountain iron is stubborn and hard to work [*wan chih*] [cast iron?]. Hard iron [*kang thieh*] comes from the rocks of the mountains among the aguish southwestern seas, and in appearance it is like [veined] purple quartz. Water and fire cannot hurt it; it will cleave pearls and cut through jade.

The *Pao Tsang Lun* is lost, but we know its date of finalization is A.D. 918. Some of the earliest material in it may be of the 3d or 4th century, so it points to the import of wootz steel from India in pre-Thang times (i.e., 6th century A.D. and before). Later references are more explicit. Thus the *Ko Ku Yao Lun* (Handbook of Archaeology) of 1387 says that *pin thieh* is produced by the Western barbarians and that its surface exhibits patterns like those of a conch-shell or those on sesame seeds or else like snowflakes. The term *pin* is suspected to be a loanword from one of the Turkic or Iranian languages transliterated into Chinese, and it would not be going too far to accept it as a technical term for wootz steel. But it is highly unlikely that any significant quantity of wootz steel was ever produced in China.

We should, however, not look on pattern-welding and wootz-damascening as archaic processes of purely historical interest. They are techniques which have descendants in the most modern products of the iron and steel industry. When Juan Shih made his 3d century harmonies of "the hard and the soft" he was starting more than he knew.

SUMMARY

In China metallic iron, first meteoritic, then smelted, seems to have been known and used from about the 12th century B.C. onward, though systematic iron technology started only from about the 7th century B.C. If the first products of smelting were blooms of carbon-free iron, as in the Western part of the Old World, they have left hardly any traces, archaeological or textual.

Cast iron appears from the 4th century B.C. onward at the latest, used both for agricultural implements, molds for tools and implements, and weapons of war. The factors connected with this early appearance of the fully liquid metal, some seventeen centuries before it could be obtained at will in the West, probably include the following: the use of ores exceptionally rich in phosphorus or the addition of phosphorus-rich minerals to the blast furnace charge; the availability of good refractory clays, which allowed adequate though small blast furnaces to be built as well as crucibles in some parts of the country; the application of reciprocating motion to double-cylinder piston-bellows for metallurgical work as early as the 4th century B.C.; the invention, probably in the 2d century B.C., of the double-acting single-cylinder piston-bellows, which allowed a continuous blast; iron tuyeres were provided at least as soon as the beginning of the 3d century A.D.; the application of water power to these bellows and perhaps even to larger hinged types in the 1st century A.D. or a little before; the use of coal, at least from the 4th century A.D., and perhaps long before, which permitted the building of a very hot pile around crucibles, the contents of which were protected from sulfur by luting. The consequent abundance of cast iron in ancient and medieval China constituted a radical difference from the siderurgical industry in the rest of the Old World.

If steel was produced by cementation of wrought iron in the Chou and Chhin periods, there is little or no trace of it, archaeological or textual. The characteristic Chinese process of steel making was decarburization direct from cast iron, known for centuries as the "hundred refinings." It depended on the direct employment of an oxidizing blast of cold air. Developing alongside the more drastic process of fining cast iron to wrought iron, it was fully in use, it seems, from the 2d century B.C. onward. By the 17th century A.D. the oxidizing technique had led in China and Japan to procedures whereby something like cast steel was produced. Direct migration of Chinese workmen skilled in the technique immediately preceded the inventions associated with the name of Bessemer. From the 5th century A.D. onward a great deal of Chinese steel was made by the "cofusion" process. Although in the 11th and 12th centuries cofusion steel was sometimes considered of less quality than decarburization steel, under suitable conditions it could match it. It is theoretically ancestral to the Siemens–Martin open-hearth and similar processes.

The welding of hard and soft steels for weapon blades was practiced in China at least as early as the 3d century A.D., and in the 7th century the art was transmitted to the Japanese. Since the process was also practiced among some Western European peoples from the 1st to the 9th centuries, the original focus may have been in Central Asia, whence it would have spread both east and west from about the 2d century. The damascene pattern in the Chinese culture area derived not from welding processes only, but also, though less extensively, from the importation of hypereutectoid wootz steel from India by about the 6th century A.D. Once cast iron became available in Europe from about A.D. 1380 onward, all these ways of using it appear within about two centuries. If they and the blast furnaces had been, as has usually been supposed, independent inventions, one would perhaps have expected a slower evolution.

ACKNOWLEDGMENTS

Although this paper bears my name alone, none of the work would have been possible without the Chinese collaborators in our group, notably Professor Wang Ching-Ning (Wang Ling) and Dr. Lu Gwei-Djen. To all of them I acknowledge most grateful thanks.

NOTES

1. Many of the documentary references and Chinese characters will be found in "The Development of Iron and Steel Technology in China," by J. Needham (Newcomen Society, London, 1958, repr. Heffer, Cambridge, 1964, now available from Cambridge University Press, 1975). All of them will be made available in vol. 5 of *Science and Civilisation in China* (Cambridge University Press, forthcoming).

2. The system of romanization for Chinese used is that of Wade–Giles, with the substitution of an *h* for the aspirate apostrophe.

Index

Abri Blanchard, France: ocher at, 136
Abri Castanet, France, 130–31
Abri Labatut, France: ocher at, 132–33
Abu Matur, Israel: crucible furnaces, 197–98, 201
Abydos, Egypt: iron finds, 121
Adir, Mount, Israel: iron finds, 121
Aegean region: development of iron technology, 51; ironworking center, 338; iron knives, 345–46; distribution of ironworking, 347; steel in, 353–54; iron fibulae in, 368. *See also* Crete; Cyclades; Cyprus; Greece
Aeschylus, 7, 18
Africa: geographical division, 463–64; survival of Iron Age culture, 485; contemporary blacksmithing, 485; contemporary iron smelting, 485; invention of decarburization, 486; panning of iron ore, 487; no Bronze Age in, 497; copper production, 498. *See also* East Africa; North Africa; southern Africa; West Africa
Agades, Nigeria: copper finds, 498
Agrab, Iran: iron finds, 433–34; Urartian influence on, 433, 435–36
Ain Mallaha, Jordan: ocher at, 140
Alaca Hüyük, Turkey, 17; iron finds, 21, 34, 70–71, 73, 76–77; meteoritic iron, 73
Alalakh: iron in texts from, 50; iron use, 75; iron finds, 76
algodonite: in arsenic bronze, 259
Ali Kosh, Iran, 141–42
Alishar Hüyük, Turkey: iron finds, 74
Al Mina, Turkey: deliberate quenching at, 124
Almuñécar, Spain: iron finds, 359
Altamira, Spain, 134, 135, 136; iron finds, 120
aluminosilicates: as slag, 488
aluminum, 151, 157
Amarna letters, 41–42, 50
amūtum, 20; as bloom iron, 7, 35; price, 35, 36; refined, 35; interchanged with aši'um, 36; as expensive commodity, 36

Anarak, Iran: copper ingots at, 15; source of copper arsenides, 233; as polymetallic deposit site, 258–59. *See also* Talmessi–Messkani region
Anatolia, 17; early metallurgy in, 18; arsenic bronze in, 25; tin bronze in, 25; ironworking center, 338; iron ore in, 340
Anau, Iran: archaeological study of, 231
Ancon, Peru: copper finds, 276; silver smelting, 289
Andes region: metallurgy and culture, 271; topography of, 271, 273, 317, 323n8; central highlands pastoralists, 282; mining in, 282; copper ores in, 296; iron not used, 320; geographical division of, 323–24n8. *See also* Bolivia; Mochica culture; Peru
Angles sur l'Anglin, France, 135–36
annealing: of copper, 102–03, 161; of steel, 508
annealing twins, 103
antimony, 208; in copper ores, 291–92
antimony sulfide: in lead smelting, 207–08
antlerite, 280
Apliki, Cyprus: Bronze Age metalworking in, 190
Arcy-sur-Cure, France: ocher at, 128, 129, 130
Argentina: analysis of metal finds, 305–10 passim
argentojarosites, 207
Aristotle, 5
Armant, Egypt: iron finds, 69–70
Arnitslund, Denmark: iron finds, 378
arsenic: in copper smelting, 28, 176, 303; properties of, 106, 185; as deoxidant in copper smelting, 170–71; effect on health, 177–78, 259–60, 315; in North Andean bronze, 317
arsenic bronze. *See* bronze
arsenides: discovery, 169; natural, 233
arsenopyrite, 168–69, 303; as gangue in lead ore, 334n137
Asameia, Turkey: bowl furnace at, 211–12
ash: in copper smelting, 204–05